POINT
-to-
POINTING

IN OUR TIME

POINT
-to-
POINTING

IN OUR TIME

MICHAEL WILLIAMS

Foreword by Captain Tim Forster

Quiller Press

Dedication

I am dedicating this book to my long-suffering wife, Mary, to two of my grandchildren, Giles and Jessica Hardman, for their invaluable assistance behind the scenes; and to all the others who have made its publication possible. Those of them who are still alive will know who they are without my having to name them; and I would like to include in this dedication the compilers of the various formbooks that are essential equipment for the racing man.

Michael Williams

 The publishers and author would like to thank Greig Middleton & Co Ltd for their contribution towards this book.

Greig Middleton are soon to embark on their third season as National Sponsors of the Ladies Open Championship. A series of 26 qualifying races will be held throughout the UK – each race supported by one of their national network of offices.

Mark Kemp-Gee, chairman, commented: *"We have supported point-to-point meetings in the past, but this is a major sponsorship commitment for us as a company. The series has increased our involvement in the sport significantly, provided tremendous entertainments for our clients and professional contacts and, not least, supported the lady jockeys who continue to go from strength to strength."*

Greig Middleton are proud to support point-to-point racing through the sponsorship of this national series and wish to thank everyone involved for making it such a success.

The author and publishers draw to readers' attention the fact that pages 1-42 are reprinted from the author's previous book The Continuing Story of Point-to-Point Racing *(Pelham Books 1972)*

CONTENTS

FOREWORD

By Captain Tim Forster

I was tidying up my desk the other day, when I found a letter from Michael Williams, which he had written to me on the 2nd January 1959. He was asking me to give him my observations on the Cumberland Point-to-Point Open Race.

At that time I was a soldier at Carlisle and to be asked by Michael to do something for him was about the greatest honour that it was possible for me to have.

From then on I was hooked and have since read every word that he has ever written. To me and to so many others, Michael has for so long been Mister Point-to-Pointing and I have always felt that when he gives up, the sport may well cease!

He has done so much for racing between the flags and, as a self confessed adict, I am thrilled that he has written *Point-to-Pointing In Our Time*.

This labour of love will, I know, become a treasured possession for so many and we are indeed fortunate that Michael has produced this wonderful History book and proved once again what a great stayer he is.

This book will rekindle so many memories for those whose life starts each year in January and ends early in June.

The work, research and dedication which has gone into this book is mind boggling and for that alone our grateful thanks.

I am sure that many people are going to find a place for this epic on their bookshelves. It certainly deserves one.

Tim Forster

THE EARLY POINT-TO-POINTS & THE FIRST LADIES' RACES

I t is virtually impossible to pin-point the first point-to-point meeting. Col. Lyon put the date of it 'about 1885 or a little later'. But it is certain that there was some kind of hunt racing even before that. According to one source I have consulted, that invaluable Point-to-Point Calendar edited by the late Arthur Coaten in the thirties, Mr W. E. Oakeley, Master of the Atherstone in the early 1870's, 'used to claim that he was one of the first Masters of Hounds to have an annual Hunt point-to-point meeting pure and simple', with the races run over natural country, and hunt members paying all the expenses out of their own pockets. The same source reveals that, in 1883, Philip Muntz won the hunt race at the Pytchley on Sir Robert carrying 16 st. 9 lb. and giving away 65 lb. to most of his competitors.

The most authentic claim I have come across, however, is contained in a history of the Worcestershire Hunt which was compiled from original sources by Thomas Read Quarrell (Hon. Sec. of the Hunt from 1917-1922) and printed and published in 1929 by Phillips & Probert at the Caxton Press, Worcester. This book gives the date of the first Worcestershire Hunt meeting as March 2nd, 1836, 'over a course on the west bank of the Severn from a point at Frieze Wood by the Old Hills on the Madresfield Estate of Earl Beauchamp, to the centre of the Lower Powick Ham, where Capt. Lamb's Vivian ridden by Capt. Becher won'.

The next meeting of this hunt was at Crowle on March 28th, 1841, when it appears that there were two races, won by Cotton Ball and Fairy. The first meeting to have more than two races was on April 30th, 1851. There were sundry other meetings up to Easter Monday, 1864, and then nothing until the memorable meeting in 1883 which is very often taken to be the first of the Worcestershire point-to-points, and of which Quarrell writes:

> The Meeting was attended by an enormous crowd of people mounted, who rode alongside of and behind the competitors, with the result that much confusion occurred, and Mr. E. Woodhouse, the Judge, had great difficulty

in deciding the winner of the Red Coat Race and ultimately the result was given as a dead heat between Messrs. F. Lort Phillips and R. V. Berkeley.

One of those who rode at this meeting was Tom Andrews, father of Mrs Nina Guilding and grandfather of point-to-point riders Roger and Diana Guilding; and in his book, *Fox Hunting Reminiscences*, written under the pseudonym of 'Gin and Beer' and published by Phillips & Probert in 1930, this stalwart of the Croome Hunt has left us a vivid description:

> Johnnie Widger sent me a good powerful hunter, going in his wind, and bred by Sir Robert Paul, Waterford. This horse I rode in the first point-to-point in Worcestershire in 1883, arranged by Mr. F. Lort Phillips and Mr. Arthur James. They selected a course at Hill Croome, and a real course it was, very different from the course of today. We jumped Jack's Paddock brook in two places, and it is now thirty six years since I saw it cleared by "Bruiser" Woodward. There were also five big bullfinches to go through, and two stiles with footboards, also three roads to cross. Nine started in the Farmers' and Tradesmen's Race and the horse I was riding was the only one that kept on its legs, but I must admit that I was whispering in his ear on two occasions, and was leading at one time by a quarter of a mile, then only to get third, with three to finish!

Mrs Guilding told me that her father weighed 16 st. and stood 6 ft. 1 in. when she was born in 1907 and that he often rode barebacked, so that on one occasion when he was riding in this manner in the farmers' race at the Croome he heard someone shouting 'Look at that fool, he's lost his saddle'. Before he rode in that race in 1883 (when he did have a saddle, as he was only eighteen years old at the time) he got a friend from Cheltenham to try his horse out over some fences and, on asking for the verdict, received the reply: 'A very big jumper. I could light a cigar while he was in the air and smoke it out before he got to the next fence.'

It was in 1888 that the Midland Sportsmen's Races were started at Kineton, Warwickshire, by the then Lord Willoughby de Broke. These races were so styled because they were confined to five hunts in the area, the Warwickshire, North Warwickshire, Pytchley, Bicester and Heythrop, and they were run over a four-mile course with 'fences of fair and proper hunting type'. It was at this meeting that the House of Commons point-to-point used to be held. Sir Elliott Lees, M.P., won the House of Commons race three years running, between 1888 and 1890, on his big bay gelding Damon. But this race was never run after 1892, the year that Capt. 'Bay' Middleton and the Rt. Hon. James Tomkinson, Liberal M.P. for the Crewe division of Cheshire, were killed. The latter was seventy years old and had hunted with the Cheshire for half a century.

The Stock Exchange point-to-point races, which alas are held no longer, date back to 1892; and the Pegasus Club (Bar) races, which were last held at Little Horwood in 1996, to 1895, when the Pegasus Club was founded with the object of encouraging riding and hunting among members of the legal profession.

The first Bar point-to-point was held at Coombe, near Malden, over a three-mile course; and in his book *Bench and Bar in the Saddle*, which had been kindly lent to me by Edward Cazalet, who had his first ride in a point-to-point when he was still at Eton, C. P. Hawkes says that there were two races, one for heavyweights and one for lightweights, both confined to hunters 'belonging to H.M. Judges, practising Barristers or Students of one of the Inns of Court reading in the Chambers of any practising Barristers. No horse that had won a steeplechase under N.H. Rules was considered eligible, and winners of open races at point-to-points had to carry 14 lb. penalties. The lightweight race was won by Mr A. Gee on his seven-year-old Defiance (a horse reputed to have been trained on turnips), and the heavyweight race, in which one horse broke her back and another his neck, by the Hon. Alfred Lyttelton (later Colonial Secretary in H.M. Government).' Lyttelton, however, declined to receive the cup on the grounds that the runner-up, Mr J. G. Butcher, Q.C., M.P. (afterwards Lord Danesfort, K.C.), 'was worthier of it as he had entered and ridden his own horse'.

The most famous of the Bar riders in those days was H. G. Farrant, who subsequently became His Honour, Judge Farrant. Farrant rode his last winner at the age of fifty-nine, in 1923, the year he was elected President of the Pegasus Club. He was then, writes Hawkes, a 'County Court Judge on a Circuit which included the metropolis of racing and all the best hunting country in Bedfordshire and Cambridgeshire'.

The Cambridge University races must also have a fairly long history, since there is in existence a painting of Mr J. G. O. Thomson winning the Farewell Cup for the university heavyweight race on his grey Ballymore II in 1904. But that was well before these races were run on the permanent course of the Cambridgeshire Harriers at Cottenham, where the first fixture took place in the 1930's.

Sir Alfred Pease, who was Liberal M.P. for York from 1885 to 1892, and died in 1939 at the age of eighty-one, rode in many point-to-point races during his term of office, and in the article he wrote for *The Field* in April, 1933 this is what he said about the courses of his youth:

> Those who selected the course guarded their secret jealously; the only indication the entrants had as to the district was the announcement shortly before the race of the "rendezvous". Competitors, restricted to members of the Hunt, were mustered near the winning flag, the only flag in those days. They were then escorted by roads to a point four, five or six miles away and dispatched on the journey. I cannot remember one of those early races in which one could see the winning flag, until at least half the journey had been accomplished; but that did not matter, as the line was a bee-line, provided you could ride it.
>
> ...The rules were simple; the chief thing to remember was that to open a gate or to ride more than 100 yards up or down a road was to be disqualified. Every good hunter had a chance, and many a clever horse deficient in pace scored a victory.

There was little or no attempt to cater for the public (it was the necessity for this in later years that played a large part in changing the character of point-to-point racing), and the racing was so hazardous, and took such a toll in casualties, that some hunts (including the Hurworth and the Cleveland in the North) abandoned their meetings for several years. Sir Alfred records that 'you saw men arrive home after a succession of bullfinches and other rough obstacles with clothes and faces in rags'.

Although there were rules and regulations of a kind before the turn of the century, it was not until 1913 that point-to-point racing got its own charter. This was when the Masters of Hounds Point-to-Point Association was formed and a committee set up to regularise the position of point-to-point racing and frame a new set of rules.

These rules were not, however, so tight that they precluded ladies from riding against the men, and in the early 1920's quite a number of them did so, notably in East Anglia, where Miss Wentworth-Reeve was the pioneer and Miss Joan Parry and Mrs Cooper Bland were also well to the fore.

Whether or not any of these ladies rode side-saddle, I do not know; but one who certainly did was Mrs Mabel Aitken, who was over seventy when she rode her horse Ware Wire into third place in the members' and subscribers' race at the Old Berkshire meeting at Faringdon. In order to ride at 12 st. 7 lb. Mrs Aitken had to carry 5.5 st. of lead; and I am told, by someone whose memory is rather longer than mine, that she presented a splendid picture in a green habit and silk hat.

Another lady who rode side-saddle against the men in those days was Miss V. Selby-Lowndes, who subsequently married Col. H. N. H. Wild. Riding her mare Pandora, Miss Selby-Lowndes won the lightweight race at the West Street Harriers in March, 1929 on the same day that her brother, Brig. (as he later became) M. W. W. Selby-Lowndes, won the members' race there; while Mrs A. Heald won the open nomination race on her noted Shepherd's Pie, and soon afterwards won a similar race on the same horse at the Ashford Valley.

The Kent ladies, in fact, were almost as strong as the East Anglians, and another lady to win races there against the men was Miss J. M. Magee. Miss Jean Sanday was similarly successful in Cheshire, as were Miss Melvill and Miss Sylvia Spooner in the West Country. Miss Spooner, the leading lady rider in England in the early thirties, was probably the last lady to win against the men for nearly forty years. A week after she had won on her pony Mohun at the East Cornwall banking fixture on April 24th, 1929, the Masters of Hounds Association passed a new rule rendering ladies ineligible to ride except in races confined to their own sex, and it was not until 1967 that this rule was relaxed. In Ireland, however, the ladies have been riding against the men in point-to-points since time immemorial. But that is another story.

The first ladies' race seems to have been at the South & West Wilts at Motcombe, near Shaftesbury, in 1921; and someone who trusts his memory writes: 'I recall that the favourite was Slauntha, who was saddled up by Geoffrey Phipps-Hornby. In this race Lord Stalbridge, the Master of the South & West Wilts, rode behind the competitors in case any of them should need assistance. To the best of my recollection, he was left far behind!' The race was won, in a field of twelve, by Lady Jean Douglas-Hamilton (the aunt of Anneli Drummond-Hay), who rode her horse Cavalier II side-saddle and went like the wind. The next ladies' race – one that I have seen in several reference books named as the first – was at the Berks & Bucks Staghounds fixture at Sonning in 1925, when Mrs Weatherby won on Reggie. But it was only after the ladies were forbidden to ride against the men that these races gathered momentum.

SOME SOLDIERS
AND A PRINCE

For a number of years the point-to-points were supplemented by the *bona fide* hunt meetings, which were introduced in 1912, and the *bona fide* military meetings which came on the scene in 1927. These were, in fact, little more than glorified point-to-points, although in the case of the military fixtures the courses were often semi-permanent ones.

The rules in both cases were very similar, and the ceiling of prize money was always 20 sovereigns. The main difference between a *bona fide* hunt meeting and a point-to-point was that, whereas there was no charge for admission to the latter, apart from the car-park fees, hunts holding *bona fide* fixtures were empowered by the N.H. Committee to hold their fixtures over an enclosed course and charge a modest fee to each member of the public. The horses that ran at these meetings were more or less the same ones that were to be found contesting point-to-points; and by comparison with the number of point-to-points held in a season, *bona fide* hunt meetings were few and far between. Thus, in 1937, when 163 point-to-point fixtures were held, only the following hunts were holding *bona fide* meetings: the Badsworth and the Rockwood Harriers in the North, the Eridge, Southdown, East Sussex and Old Surrey & Burstow, in the South; the Brocklesby in Lincolnshire and the Tedworth and Royal Artillery Harriers in the South West.

The *bona fide* military meetings were meetings for hunters held under National Hunt Rules by units of the Regular Services and all horses running in these races were required to be 'the property of serving Officers of the Regular Army, Navy or Air Force, except that Regimental Races confined to one Regiment may be open to Officers serving or who have held permanent Commissions in the Regiment'. And, as in the case of the *bona fide* hunt meetings, the courses had to be officially approved by the National Hunt Committee's inspectors.

When point-to-point racing acquired 'a new look' after the war, and a great deal more attention was given to the courses and to the needs of the public, there was no longer any necessity for the *bona fide* hunt meetings, which became submerged in the point-to-point scene. But I am sure I am not alone in regretting the passing of the military fixtures, which disappeared at the same time, along with those delightful courses at Windmillhill and Hawthorn Hill. Tweseldown, where there was National Hunt racing up till 1932, has, however, survived, and is now the setting for a number of point-to-points; and for this we must be thankful. I never set foot on this permanent course near Aldershot without having my imagination stirred by memories of the past; and some of these memories were vividly brought back to me not so long ago when an official there pointed to one of the obstacles and declared with obvious pride: 'This is the fence where H.R.H. usually came to grief.' He was, of course, referring to the later Duke of Windsor, who, as Prince of Wales, was more enthusiastic than skilful as a point-to-point rider, though he rode thirteen winners.

In the spring of 1928, the Prince had a momentous afternoon at the Harkaway Club races at Chaddesley Corbett, and a particularly delightful account of it appeared in the *Birmingham Post*, which I now propose to quote from:

> The news that the Prince of Wales was a competitor attracted, of course, a gathering that was unusually large for this annual event. Thousands of people splashed and struggled about on the precarious footing offered by the muddy hillside, which, in places, soon became a quagmire. It was essentially a day for topboots, and luckless, indeed, were those numerous members of the fair sex who were not so equipped. Their thin and elegant shoes of suede, and lizard and alligator, and whatnot quickly became shapeless repositories for liberal coatings of Worcestershire soil. As for the men, one saw here and there some of the type which one naturally associates with a point-to-point meeting: the jackbooted, heavily overcoated, hardbitten and rubicund sort, somewhat terse of speech, who suggest, by their very appearance, that a good sample of horse-flesh may be accounted the most important figure on their horizon. But there were others to whom a gathering such as this was a new experience, who looked for, and expected – in vain – the comforts and conveniences of an up-to-date racecourse. They had obviously come there to see, not the racing, but the Prince of Wales.

But if they hoped to see H.R.H. ride a winner, they were doomed to disappointment. In the first race, he rode a brown mare, Lady Doon, who had been hunted with the Quorn, and about this animal odds of 2-1 against were offered. 'The Prince of Wales led to the fifth fence, when his mount refused, and shot him off. He remounted and jumped it, but fell. He went on very strongly for another three-quarters' circuit of the course, when he pulled up.' The winner was Possible, ridden by Sir John Grey, so at least spectators had a titled victor to console themselves with. The fence where Lady Doon refused was a rather notorious one, somewhat euphemistically known as the Open Ditch. Its reputation for causing disaster was apparently well known, and around it were crammed a group of expectant onlookers. The writer in the *Birmingham Post* goes on:

> 'He's leading,' said a man with a pair of field glasses; and, of course, there

was no need to ask who he meant. So the horses came to the fence, and then it seemed – although one could not swear to it – as though something shot over it; but it was not a horse. 'His mare has refused,' said the man with the field glasses. Another man – one who looked as though he might be knowledgeable about horses – started in surprise. 'Are you sure?' he asked. 'Quite sure,' said the first one. The knowledgeable man stood with the pained expression of one who has been dealt a buffet in the face by a friend. 'Well, I've known Lady Doon for years,' he said. 'I've seen her hunting all over the Quorn country, and never before have I known her to refuse. Never!' He kept repeating the assertion at intervals in a dazed kind of a way.

'When the Prince rode into the paddock,' adds the writer, 'he was covered with mud from head to foot, and it was difficult even to distinguish his features through the caking. He retired and changed, and about half-an-hour later walked into the paddock spick and span as ever.'

But this was not the end of the Prince's adventures at the Harkaway Club races. He rode another mare from the Quorn, Degomme II, in the open nomination race; and once again he was leading until he got to the Open Ditch, only to be decanted when Degomme pecked in the treacherous going as she landed and rolled over on her side in the mud. Nothing daunted, H.R.H. eventually resumed his partnership with the mare, some way behind the field, and did well to survive another mistake before finishing fourth. But how many runners there were, and who received the challenge cup that was presented by Lord and Lady Ednam is not revealed. The article ends with a splendid peroration, however: 'Here was the Prince of Wales, one reflected, a tremendous asset to the Empire, risking life and limb not once but several times at a country point-to-point, going down before a lot of flying hoofs, any one of which might have dealt a fatal blow.'

The military meetings of the twenties and thirties brought out many fine riders and horses, the like of which will never again be seen in soldiers' races, which today are but a pale reflection of the past. The names roll off the tongue like poetry, and some of them have their echoes in the present: Major-General Sir Richard McCreery, Capt. Sir Peter Grant-Lawson, Peter Payne-Gallwey, Geoff Phipps-Hornby, Ronnie Holman, Dickie Courage, Peter Herbert, Harry Misa, 'Babe' Moseley, 'Roscoe' Harvey, Frank Cundell, Capt. G. H. Smith-Dorrien; Herbert Lumsden with More Magic and Silver Gill, Sir John Pigott-Brown with The Stroller, Capt. A. G. Martyr with Ablington, Capt. the Hon. C. B. Bernard with that beautiful little mare Brownly, a grand-daughter on her dam's side of the 1910 Derby winner Lemberg; W. Scott-Plummer, with the two full brothers March Brown IV and Canfly, both bred by his father in Scotland; Capt. Mark Roddick with the trio that won him three Grand Military Gold Cups at Sandown, Buck Willow, Kilstar and Fillip; Capt M.P. (later Sir Michael) Ansell, and the post-war Olympic horsemen Harry Llewellyn and Henry Nicoll.

Enough is enough. But I must mention two more names: Capt. Neville Crump, the former Middleham trainer, who won the 4th Queen's Own Hussars' Challenge Cup on John de Moraville's King's Cross II at the Aldershot Military Meeting in

1936; and Guy Cunard, who had his first winning ride at the military meeting on Salisbury Plain in 1932 on Golden Light, a horse who cost him only 28 guineas and won thirteen races for him.

And here's a remarkable thing. At the Garth point-to-point at Arborfield in 1930, Fulke Walwyn, the former Lambourn trainer, won the Royal Military Academy (Sandhurst) lightweight race; Frank Furlong, who was killed while serving with the Fleet Air Arm during the War, won the lightweight race; and Bobbie Petre, then still a schoolboy, won the hunt heavyweight race. Three riders who all went on to win the Grand National, Frank Furlong on Reynoldstown in 1935, Fulke Walwyn on the same horse the following year, and Bobbie Petre on Lovely Cottage in 1946.

ADMINISTRATION
IN THE THIRTIES

As a result of the growing difference of opinion between the Masters of Hounds Point-to-Point Committee and the National Hunt Committee as to how to administer point-to-point racing, at the Annual General Meeting of the M.F.H. Association in May, 1934, Lord Lonsdale proposed the following resolution:

> That a Select Committee be appointed with a view to having a conference with the National Hunt Committee to consider the whole question with the Point-to-Point Committee of the Masters of Foxhounds Association.

Lord Lonsdale was not the sort of man to keep his thoughts to himself and he expressed some strong, if somewhat incoherent, views at this Meeting. Here are some of them:

> A point-to-point in 1919 was to be a point from one point to another, and beyond the safety of the fences, there were to be no marks or signals. One may go to a great number of point-to-points now, and one really finds them nothing more than miniature steeplechase courses, and in some cases they are absolutely ridiculous. Also the condition of the horses that run. The point-to-points were made originally not so much for the best horses, but for the best man. Gradually they worked out into an amalgamation of the two, but there are some point-to-points which are perfectly ridiculous. I was at a point-to-point not very long ago where one gentleman complained that the fences were too big, and there was a ditch on the take-off side. That is only one instance. There are many other instances of things that happen at point-to-points which are very far from being in the best interests either of the owners or racing. You get people who keep horses solely for point-to-point races, and there have been many difficulties raised as to point-to-

point meetings and a great deal of discussion as to what is and what is not proper.

Clearly, something was not only about to be done, but about to be seen to be done, and when the National Hunt Committee met in July, 1934 they approved the formation of a Joint Advisory Committee comprising three Members of the National Hunt Committee and three representatives selected by the Masters of Foxhounds Association. The three representatives selected by the M.F.H. Association to act on their behalf were Col. J. G. Lowther (Master of the Pytchley), Capt. T. Wickham-Boynton (Master of the Middleton East) and Col. R. Thompson (Master of the Rufford). And as from the July lst, 1934, in time for the 1935 point-to-point season, point-to-point racing came directly under the jurisdiction of the National Hunt Committee, Appendix C of the National Hunt Rules being created for this purpose.

The new rules did not differ much in essentials from the old ones. The most important changes were the appointment of accredited N.H. inspectors to approve the courses and the introduction of a rule banning horses who had won three open nomination races from competing in any more such events (other than at *bona fide* hunt meetings) during the same season. There was also a stipulation that 'No horse which, since January lst of the current hunting season has been trained by a licensed trainer, unless the horse be his own property, or by an unlicensed person (other than his owner, groom, or the proprietor of the stable from whence the horse has been hunted), shall be eligible to be entered for a point-to-point steeplechase.'

And there was a clear definition from the National Hunt Committee as to what constituted a professional rider: 'Professional Hunt servants, grooms, apprentices, stable lads, and persons who are or have been employed as paid servants in any capacity in private, hunting, racing, livery, or horse-dealers' stables, also persons who have ever received payment, directly or indirectly, for riding in a race, are regarded as having ridden for hire, and are professional riders and are not eligible to ride...'

The reactions to the new administration were, on the whole, fairly favourable, although one complainant went so far as to observe, 'The National Hunt Committee have, in my opinion, been very stupid in interfering with point-to-point racing. It is pure jealousy...' But mostly it was a case of congratulations all round, and there was surprising support for the new rule restricting the number of open nomination races that a horse could win in a single season. But there was one cogent criticism from a well-known rider who suggested that it would be more sensible to confine horses who had won three nomination races to these events, instead of driving them into the adjacent hunts' races. The same rider (clearly one based in the Midlands) suggested with some feeling that one of the worst side-effects of this rule was that it reduced the status of championship races, such as the Lady Dudley Cup at the Worcestershire, the Lady Bullough Cup at the Ledbury and the Osmaston Cup at the Meynell.

There were, of course, recurring complaints throughout the thirties that point-to-points were becoming too much like steeplechases and that the average hunter had little chance in them. The correspondence columns of *Horse & Hound* of the period are a marvellous barometer of reflected opinion, with the indicator going up and down like a yo yo. Thus one correspondent wrote (in 1939):

> Point-to-point races were designed for hunters carrying hunting weights and ridden by hunting men. Unfortunately they have changed considerably. A large number of ex-racehorses are now competing, and point-to-points have progressed a long way towards becoming merely bad race meetings.

And another replied:

> Where are the large number of ex-racehorses? I attend many point-to-point races, but I do not see such horses. Many winners of point-to-points can win steeplechases, but the discarded racehorse has not 'an earthly' in a present day point-to-point race.

Some of the letters published by that journal were so absurd that they achieved a kind of poetry:

> I have had a good deal of experience in the point-to-point races, and have often seen these races won by very bad hunters, pulling brutes and refusers with hounds. I suggest the best way out of the difficulty of not having good hunters winning these races would be to have courses for them with some very sharp turns, so sharp that the competitors had to nearly pull their mounts up. Say, two such turns.

There were various other suggestions made throughout the thirties. In fact, the Editor of the *Point-to-Point Calendar* went out of his way to solicit them, and was seldom disappointed. Among these suggestions were several about the weights carried. The Hon. Sec. of a northern meeting wanted the minimum weight in men's races to be raised from 12 st. 7 lb. to 13 st., maintaining that the extra 7 lb. would 'help to stop these thoroughbreds as compared with the genuine hunter'.

Some people, however, thought that the weight was already too much, and a 7 lb. allowance for maidens was a not infrequent suggestion. 'I am convinced that 50 per cent of the young men out hunting could not ride 12 st. racing,' said a correspondent to *Horse & Hound*, an observation which inspired the reply, 'If a man who has got himself fit cannot do 11 st. 7 lb. he should not ride in point-to-points at the pace they go nowadays, as he is too big, and will get himself hurt.'

'Reduce the scale to 11 st. 7 lb.' wrote another correspondent disgustedly, 'and it will not be long before Lady Dudley's Cup is won by a well-bred discard from Northolt Park,' which at that time was a centre of professional pony racing.

Among other suggestions made during the period were a 2s. 6d. admission charge to the paddock, the introduction of handicapping (repeated by Gregory Blaxland in *Horse & Hound* in 1970) and, from a Gloucestershire Hon. Sec. who didn't think 'that any horse winning an open nomination race in February could possibly have been "regularly and fairly hunted",' no point-to-point racing before March lst. A Yorkshire official described the inspection of courses as 'a farce and a waste of time'; and a Gloucestershire one remarked piously that, whilst his own hunt scrupulously observed the 'rule' about not levying a charge on bookmakers for the use of pitches, others did not. In fact, it is simply a question of how one interprets this rule. Bookmakers have always been expected to make a donation to hunt funds, and most hunts have the sense to leave the collection of the cash to the leading bookmaker.

Despite the constant complaints that point-to-points were becoming more and more like miniature steeplechases, and the often repeated plea for 'more natural' fences, the old-style type of point-to-point course had by no means died out in the thirties, and some were even to linger on after the War. The Equitation School at Weedon used to have a different course each year and contestants were told nothing about it until the day of the race, when they were told where to meet and shown where they had to finish. This is how the *Point-to-Point Calendar* describes the course for the 1935 event:

> The race was held over a very stiff line in the Bicester country, starting in Mr. Tew's field half a mile due west of Boddington Fields Farm, near Priors Hardwicke. The course ran for two miles to Blackdown, at which there was a red and white flag which could easily be seen from the start. From Blackdown Hill a white directing flag could be seen a mile and a half away at an angle of about 75 degrees. The finish itself was in a field near the Charwelton-Byfield road, about half a mile north of Byfield. The total distance by the shortest way was 3.75 miles. The heavy-weights and light-weights were run together, the former in black coats and the latter in red.

The Puckeridge Hunt course at Brent Pelham, which was in use throughout the thirties, included posts and rails, ditches and combination obstacles; and in 1936, the High Peak meeting at Flagg Moor (where these races are still held today) ran a combined light-weight and heavy-weight members' race over a four-mile course with walls (thirty-six of them) instead of the birch fences used for the other races.

In 1937, three years after the point-to-points had come under the direct control of the National Hunt Committee, the old Masters of Hounds Point-to-point Committee was dissolved. The motion proposing dissolution was put before the Annual General Meeting of the Masters of Foxhounds Association on May 31st that year by Col. C. Spence-Colby, the chairman, in these terms:

> This Committee is of the opinion that it is not practicable or necessary to have two bodies dealing with point-to-point racing, and as the Advisory Committee, appointed jointly by the National Hunt Committee and the Masters of Foxhounds Association is now doing the work in a satisfactory manner, and also in view of the fact that the National Hunt Committee have expressed a desire to deal with only one authority, they recommend that the Masters Point-to-Point Committee be dissolved, with a very hearty vote of thanks for their extremely valuable services in the past.

The motion was seconded by Major Gordon Foster and carried unanimously. And, needless to say, it received the approval of the National Hunt Committee, on whose behalf Lord Stalbridge made the following statement:

I have been authorised by the Stewards to say this, that although they cannot bind themselves or their successors in any way as to the future, still at the moment they foresee no difficulties ahead, and if difficulties did arise they think the Advisory Committee is the best possible means of thrashing out all sides of any question, and they sincerely hope that point-to-point matters will go on as smoothly and happily in the future as they have done in the past three years.

There were to be no more startling innovations until after the war.

THE DUDLEY CUP

I n all sports there is usually one event which takes precedence over all others, and this event in point-to-point racing is the Lady Dudley Cup at the Worcestershire, which is the point-to-point equivalent of the Cheltenham Gold Cup. When one considers that the system of prize money in point-to-points is a uniform one, and that even today the ceiling for an open nomination race is comparatively low, it is remarkable that the Dudley Cup has acquired such a reputation, especially as the Worcestershire has never been exactly a fashionable hunt. How has this come about? This is a question to which there is no simple answer, and the best explanation I can think of is that the race has a very long history and has been won over the years by some outstanding horses. But it has also been suggested to me that the excellence, and testing nature, of the original course at Crowle, near Worcester, has a lot to do with it. Mr Jervis Foulds, who, I think it is safe to say, knew more about the history of the Worcestershire point-to-point than anyone else, described this course to me as the best he had ever seen. The distance, he said, 'measured from the centre of each fence, was 4 miles 100 yards. No fence was jumped twice. I have been told that at one time there was no fence under 5 ft. and that the tops could be walked on!' And it goes without saying that the best horse always won. Which I think was also true of the later course at Upton-on-Severn.

The Earl of Dudley was Master of the Worcestershire from 1896 to 1902; and in 1897 the Countess of Dudley presented a £50 cup for the open event, which was then known as 'The Ladies' Plate'. This was won by Mr R. Cave-Brown-Cave's Triton. But it was not until 1898 that Lady Dudley presented the first challenge cup (valued at £105), with the proviso that if it were won by the same owner 'twice in succession or three times in all' it became his own property. Capt. H. R. M. Porter, who won the 1898 race on his horse Rajah, also won again on the same horse in 1901 and 1902. He is now dead, but the original challenge trophy is still in the possession of his grandson at Birlingham, the Porters' family home.

15

'Of all wild, mad riders,' wrote our old friend 'Gin and Beer' in his book, 'Harry Porter took the biscuit, and was never satisfied unless he fell five times a day over the most impossible leaps.' But in later years, 'he crossed the Croome and the Worcestershire country with judgement and was hard to beat.'

Lady Dudley gave a second challenge cup, which was won in 1903 and 1904 by H. G. (Judge) Farrant on Red Hall, a horse who was never beaten in point-to-points, and after his career in these races ran third in the National Hunt Chase at Cheltenham in 1904 and was sixth to Rubio in the Grand National of 1908.

'Red Hall,' says C. P. Hawkes in *Bench and Bar in the Saddle*, 'was said to be a son of Winkfield and thus an inheritor of Barcaldine blood. He was hunted by Farrant from a five-year-old, mostly with the Ledbury and the Croome, and was probably as genuine a hunter as ever ran in a race. A chestnut, with magnificent shoulders, back and quarters, and with exceptional bone, he was a perfect performer. Fast for a hunter, he represented a combination of qualities not easy to find in an individual horse.'

And 'Gin and Beer' wrote of Red Hall's owner-rider:

He was gifted with the best of hands, seat and brains, whether riding a race or to hounds, never losing his head, and doing damage to either fences or crops. I once saw him jump into an allotment (or to be correct, he fell into it) and he looked at me as much as to say, 'I have no right here'. There Mr. Farrant sat and as I thought expounding the law and the prophets, until on drawing a little nearer I found he was only expatiating on the merits of the finish of his chestnut horse Red Hall in the Grand National. Many good judges of horses think today that his horse Red Hall was the best hunter that ever won Lady Dudley's Cup.

In 1905 Lady Dudley gave a third challenge cup, which is the one that is competed for today. The first winner of this was Mr W. V. Beatty on his Rufus. Ned Holland, who won the Dudley Cups of 1907 and 1909 on Potheen II, and was an uncle of Edward ('Ruby') and Thurstan Holland-Martin, is another to find a place in 'Gin and Beer's' book:

...Ned Holland, a gentleman who never knew how to spell fear. Had he hunted twenty years previously, he would have met Mr. Harry Porter, and then it would have been Greek meeting Greek. The bigger the country the better they liked it. I can see them now in my dreams two fields in front of hounds riding against each other. I once remarked to Mr. Holland (near to the Vernon Arms, Hanbury) 'It's no use, Sir, it can't be done.' Away he went at it, with the result that he broke his horse's back. Charles West, then first whip, went to Mr. Wilson, a farmer, who fetched a gun and shot him. Mr. Holland, never thinking, sold the horse for 10/- to a knacker man instead of letting the hounds eat him.

The first horse to win the Dudley Challenge Cup after the First World War was the 1920 winner, Liffey Bank, owned by Capt. M. W. Muir and ridden by Mr G. S.

Campbell. Conjuror II, who won the following year, went on to win the National Hunt Chase at Cheltenham and finish second in the Cheltenham Gold Cup and third in the Grand National. Seti the First, the 1925 winner, won the Liverpool Foxhunters'. Minstrel Boy and Herode Bridge, the winners in 1931 and 1933, both won the Cheltenham Foxhunters'.

O'DELL AND HIS CONTEMPORARIES

Although there may have been better racehorses running in point-to-points during the thirties, the greatest point-to-pointer of this period – and indeed one of the greatest of all time – was O'Dell, owned by Major Harold Rushton, the Master of the Worcestershire. This famous grey thoroughbred (by Book out of Scapegoat II, by Morganatic out of Madame Dreyfus, by Bird of Freedom), who got his name from his breeder in Ireland, was hunted regularly by Major Rushton riding at 15 st. O'Dell won forty races, including the Liverpool Foxhunters' two years running in the years when this race was run over the full Grand National distance. At Liverpool, O'Dell was ridden by Major Otho Prior-Palmer of the 9th Lancers, but in most of his other races Major Rushton himself had the mount.

What is it that makes a great horse? Probably it is something that cannot be analysed. But one thing I do know is that it cannot be measured in terms of the number of races won. I prefer to think of it as something that is determined in the mind by a combination of experience and instinct, and felt in the blood. Sometimes, as in the case of The Dikler, in 1969, it is recognized immediately, and sometimes it takes time. As I never myself had the privilege of seeing O'Dell, I do not know what I would have thought about him on a course. But his name is hallowed by the memory of his feats, and instinct tells me that he was a great horse; and that two other well-known horses owned and ridden by Major Rushton during the same period, Ebon Knight and Signet Ring, were simply good ones.

I did, however, see the Ledbury mare Pucka Belle, the horse I think of next to O'Dell. One of a long line of point-to-pointers who have gone on to distinguish themselves in races under N.H. Rules, this beautiful daughter of Pucka Sahib, bred, like O'Dell, in Ireland, and ridden invariably by her owner, Mr E. W. W. Bailey, had won sixteen point-to-points by the end of the 1936 season, when she reached the peak of her career as a hunter with a win in the National Hunt Chase. The following season she was third to Royal Mail and Cooleen in the Grand National.

Can it be mere coincidence that two other outstanding point-to-pointers of the thirties, Hopeful Hero and Duty Paid, were also bred in Ireland? I have particular occasion to remember the grey Hopeful Hero, because it was through him that I had my first experience of being welshed, when I was still a schoolboy. On the day this prolific point-to-point winner won the National Hunt Chase, in April, 1937, I had half-a-crown of my pocket money on him at 12-1 with a bookmaker at the Crawley & Horsham point-to-point, which in those days was held at Littleworth, Partridge Green. No doubt some bigger bets than this were struck with the same bookmaker, thus causing him to chalk up St George II as the winner. It wasn't until I saw the evening papers some time afterwards that I discovered that Hopeful Hero, in the capable hands of Mr W. L. ('Slotty') Dawes, had beaten St George II by a length. It was a lesson well learned. But perhaps that bookmaker, whose name I haven't forgotten, although prudence tells me that this isn't the place to reveal it, should be given some credit for showing prophetic insight, since it was St George II who won the National Hunt Chase the following year, when he was ridden by Bobbie Petre.

The West Kent mare, Duty Paid, who was brought over to England after being shown in hunter classes at the Dublin Horse Show of 1935 and was ridden in all her races by Harry Freeman-Jackson, appeared first on a racecourse in 1936, when she won all three of her races. But her best season was 1938, when she won five open nomination races, an adjacent hunts' race and the Skeynes Plate over three miles at the United Hunts' Meeting at Lingfield, where Capt. Freeman-Jackson had to ride on the girth after her saddle had slipped four fences from home. In four seasons, the last of them cut short by the war, Duty Paid ran in nineteen races, won fourteen of them and was third in the Cheltenham Foxhunters'; and had it not been for the cut hocks she sustained during the 1937 season and a stumble at the last fence when she was beaten by a short head in her first race of 1938, she would probably have been unbeaten in point-to-points.

In 1949 Harry Freeman-Jackson went to live permanently in Ireland, where he was Master of the Duhallow Hounds in County Cork from 1950 to 1968, and during that period he represented his new country in the three-day event at four Olympiads. It gives me particular pleasure to write these words about Duty Paid, because when I reminded him about the mare after he had won the Burghley Horse Trials for Ireland in 1963 on St Finbarr, his reply was: 'Good Lord, I didn't think anybody would remember Duty Paid, let alone the day that I won the Skeynes Plate at Lingfield on her.' Well, some of us do, and I have since been delighted to hear that the mare produced six foals after being put to stud and that Capt. Freeman-Jackson had a five-year-old grand-daughter of hers who was very much like her.

The outstanding rider in the South during the thirties was Ryan Price, who was to make such a name for himself as a trainer after the war. I thought then, and still think so in retrospect, that this fine horseman, who hunted mainly with Lord Leconfield's hounds in Surrey, would have been capable of winning on a cart-horse. And he had a personality to match his ability, presenting a handsome, debonair figure as he rode round the paddock before each race smoking the inevitable cigarette. He denies this now and says he never smoked in those days, but I have the picture so firmly imprinted on my mind that it will take more than this to erase it.

Ryan Price, who had his first winner in his early 'teens, rode many horses for many owners, and on one occasion he had five winners in an afternoon. Many of his wins were in farmers' races, on such horses as Arun Lad, Swan River, Hardham Gate, Harkaway II and Mrs E. A. S. Murray's Rufus III, a horse who would have looked quite at home in front of a cart. But the two best horses he rode were probably Sir John Leigh's pair, Goldfish III and Thistle Blue. Neither of these horses had the build of weight carriers, but both were thoroughly genuine performers. Little is known of the background of Goldfish, except that he was purchased in Ireland in 1931 and was twelve years old when Ryan Price won three open nominations on him in 1936; this was the year Capt. Price won the amateur riders' hurdle race at the West Norfolk Hunt Steeplechases at Fakenham on Tom Grantham's Jap. Thistle Blue, a rather temperamental little mare, was more difficult to ride than Goldfish and frequently took her fences by the roots, but she was the better of the two. In 1937 when Ryan Price won three open nomination races on her, she put up a great performance in the Gone Away Open Hunters' Chase at Lingfield, where Bobbie Petre was riding her, giving 5 lb. to March Brown IV and St George II and beating them both.

Among other good winners in the South during those years were two horses hunted with the Crawley & Horsham, Capt. G. Hornung's Gaickster and Eric Covell's Cavalcade II. Another was Philip Kindersley's Michael, from the Whaddon Chase. Michael, whose owner later became Joint-Master with his son, Gay, of the Mid-Surrey Farmers' Draghounds, was a really splendid animal. In a career stretching from 1932 to 1939, this big bay gelding by St David won twenty-two races, including the lightweight race at the Whaddon Chase three years running. He completed the course in the Liverpool Foxhunters' of 1936 and 1937 and was fourth in this race in 1935; and in 1934, when Mr Kindersley took him over to Ireland, he was second in the Ward Union Cup at Fairyhouse.

Castle Gris, a tubed horse from the Old Surrey and Burstow, won twenty-seven races for Kenneth Urquhart, who became a Master of Harriers in Ireland after the war; and another horse to win over twenty races was Mr Snip, who stood only 15.3 hands high and was bred by his owner, Mr G. T. Nixon, in North Devon, from his Royal Sovereign mare, Queenie, whose mother T'Ould Kitty, twice won the Hunt Cup at the Stevenstone. This was a race Mr Nixon won with three generations of the same breed. Mr Snip, the outstanding banking horse at the West Country meetings, was ridden in all his races by Mr F. W. B. Smyth, whose nine winners in 1933 were only surpassed by Major Rushton's thirteen.

For many years, the point-to-point meetings of Devon and Cornwall were distinguished from those in other areas by providing opportunities for horses to run over banks and/or fly fences, and some of the West Country horses were equally proficient over both types of obstacle. One such was Duhallow Queen, owned by Mr Reginald Paltridge, a former Master of the East Cornwall. This grand-daughter of the famous Craganour (the disqualified Derby winner of 1919) came over to England from Ireland in 1934 as a four-year-old and won five races over banks in her first two seasons. In her next, 1936, she won four races over banks and the open nomination race at Mr Spooner's Harriers over fly fences. The following year she again won the nomination race at Mr Spooner's, beat that good horse Charlie Chaplin II in the ladies' race at the South Devon & Haldon Harriers; and won two races over banks in Cornwall; and in 1938 she won four more races over banks.

One of the most consistent performers in Essex, in both men's and ladies' races, Lt. Col. J. Dalton-White's Charlie Chaplin II was sixteen years old when he finally retired after recording his twentieth win, in the adjacent hunts' ladies' race at the Essex Farmers' in April 1938, when he was ridden by Col. Dalton-White's daughter Valerie. A brown gelding by Darigal out of a mare by Simon the Jester, Charlie Chaplin II was acquired as a six-year-old for £27 10s.

A bargain buy? I should say so. But Sawfish was an even bigger one. The son of a Derby winner (Spion Kop), Sawfish was bought for a fiver by Mr A. G. Anderson, a Herefordshire farmer, at an auction near Hereford in the autumn of 1937; and it appears that his new owner thought so little of him that he tried to sell him for a 10s. profit, without success, and was then given 10s. for luck by the horse's former owner. After being hunted during the winter with the South Herefordshire & Ross Harriers, Sawfish ran in the farmers' race at his local meeting ridden by Geoffrey Scudamore (the father of Michael, who became a professional jockey and later trained at Hoar Whithy, near Hereford). Sawfish won that race easily, and also his next two. He was then sold to Mr W. R. Tate, whose son Martin, himself a distinguished point-to-point rider, now trains at Chaddesley Corbett, where the Dudley Cup is run today. Mr Scudamore having broken his collarbone, Sawfish was ridden in his last two races of 1938 by Geoffrey Hutsby, who saw to it that this six-year-old reject from a professional racing stable finished the season unbeaten. Before being put down the first year after the war, when he went lame behind, Sawfish won eight hunter chases, three of them in a week.

If one excludes Harry and Frank Atherton Brown, who virtually confined themselves to N.H. racing, I suppose the two most famous brothers riding in point-to-points during the thirties were Thurstan and 'Ruby' Holland-Martin. Ruby, the younger of the two, I recall, as a particularly elegant horseman who used to ride in a monocle; and when he gave up steeplechasing, he turned his attention to international show jumping with equal success. In 1935, when Ruby had ten wins with three horses, Grasshopper II, Cutty and Cheerful Marcus, the first two being bred by him from the same mare, Nancy Joycey (by Duke of Westminster), he was third on Grasshopper in the Liverpool Foxhunters' and the three hunter chases he won on the lop-eared Cheerful Marcus included the United Hunts' Cup at Cheltenham. The same year, both brothers were winners at the New College & Magdalen point-to-point and Thurstan was runner-up in the National Hunt Chase on Evasio Mon and second to his brother in a hunter chase at Newbury.

Alas, Harry and Frank Atherton Brown have now both passed on. Thurstan Holland-Martin died of a heart attack whilst out shooting in 1968; and Ruby was crippled in the hunting field in 1952. But at least the story of the Holland-Martin family continued in the person of Thurstan and Ruby's nephew Tim, one of the leading point-to-point riders in later years.

In Yorkshire, of course, Major Cunard, who had his first ride in a race when he was a schoolboy at Eton in 1928, and whose great grand-father on his mother's side was a Joint-Master of the York & Ainsty, was already going strong, although it wasn't until after the war that this long lean greyhound of the North had his best years. Other highly successful riders in this area during the thirties were Bobby Renton (the Ripon trainer), W. Carr (a wellknown flat-race trainer), the formidable W. H. ('Gunner') Wellburn, Adrian Scrope, P. C. Oldfield, Capt. R. M. Fanshawe, H. Megginson and Lord Grimthorpe.

And it was Ralph Grimthorpe, a man beloved by the local farmers, and whom I remember after the war standing on the hill at Whitwell surveying the Middleton course like an eagle, who gave his name to the race which is now acknowledged as the point-to-point Grand National.

The first Middleton point-to-point was held near Howsham in 1922, and it was not until 1929 that it moved to its present site at Whitwell-on-the-Hill, near Malton. Three years later, Lord Grimthorpe gave his cup for the open event, which was then run over three and a half miles (today's distance is four miles); and the first person to win it was Lord Grimthorpe on First Venture, a horse with a fairytale history. I am now going to let Harold Charlton, who rode in the farmers' race at the first Middleton point-to-point, take up the story:

> I went with my friend Eric Parke to Malton Horse Sales, which were held monthly in those days, he taking a pony to sell which made 12 guineas. In the sale was a four-year-old owned by his father's next-door neighbour, Philip Burnett, who had bred him by his own stallion, Sir Harry. This horse was First Venture, an animal with shocking bad hocks who had been fired on one of them. Eric bought him for 17 guineas, and although he had already been broken he turned out to be a rare handful (could he buck!). So I took him and hunted him that season, and the next season Eric rode him in the farmers' race, his first ride, and finished third. After that, First Venture won seven races, including five open events, without being beaten. He was then sold to Lord Grimthorpe, for whom he won numerous point-to-points and hunter chases before breaking down badly on his final gallop for the Liverpool Foxhunters'. Sir Harry was also the sire of Macmoffat, runner-up in the last two pre-war Grand Nationals. First Venture and More Honour were the two best horses I have seen win the Grimthorpe Cup.

Another fine winner of the Grimthorpe Cup in the thirties was Little Tommy Tucker, the last horse that Adrian Scrope won on before a crashing fall in the Heart Of All England at Hexham ended his racing career. Although this horse used to chance his fences, he had so gentle a temperament that he was regularly hunted, in his pre-Grimthorpe Cup days, by two young teenagers, the children of his original owner, Dr H. Wynne-Davies, of Thirsk, for whom he won a number of point-to-points, including one in which he was ridden by his owner's fifteen-year-old son, a Rugby schoolboy who was having his first ride in a race. That was in 1935, the year before Little Tommy Tucker passed into the hands of Mr J. Stephenson, of Bridlington. It was whilst he was in Mr Stephenson's ownership that he won the Grimthorpe Cup, in 1936.

Further North the outstanding riders were Major Ian Straker (whose two sons, John and Clive, were to continue the good work after the war); John Eustace Smith, who became a first-class amateur under N.H. Rules after the war and was tragically killed in a bad fall at Catterick Bridge in 1951; Ted Green, an extremely tough rider who came from an old Northumbrian farming family, the Greens of Lucker; Eustace Renwick; Reg. Tweedie, who became the owner of that great horse Freddie in the post-war years; and John Marshall, who had what was perhaps the best point-to-pointer in the Border Country in those days. This was Speckled Spear, a horse who was not considered fast enough for N.H. racing but won the William Bell Gold Cup at the Tynedale twice in three years (he was second on the other occasion) and many other good point-to-point races.

And there was also Calverly Bewicke, who was to become one of the leading N.H. trainers in the post-war years and saddle a winner of the Cheltenham Gold Cup. Major Bewicke had his first ride in a race during his last Easter Holidays from Eton; and between 1933 and 1938 he rode twenty-four point-to-point winners and won the Territorial Army Cup at the Grand Military Meeting at Sandown on Noble Artist. His best point-to-pointer was Jugged Hare, a horse on whom his father won four races before him. Calverly Bewicke's ten wins on Jugged Hare embraced two Tynedale Gold Cups, and if he had been a little older he would probably have won hunter chases on him as well. As it was, Jugged Hare's appearances were restricted to point-to-points.

Two noted performers in the Eastern Counties were Mrs J. A. Keith's home-bred Hill Call, by London Cry out of a mare by Manxman; and Mr Walter Wales's King High, by Kingsborough out of a mare by Highlander. Hill Call was hunted with the West Norfolk, a pack which has produced a prodigious number of winners over the years, and King High with the Henham Harriers.

Walter Wales, whose familiar fawn and white checks have been inherited by his elder son David and are now carried by his grandson William, won twenty-six races on King High, who made twenty-eight winning appearances in thirty-three starts. Hill Call's record was not quite so spectacular, but then her career was short-er, as she didn't start it until two years before the war. She won five races in six appearances in her first season and fourteen altogether. Many years later the Keiths were to own one just as good – if not even better – in Mr Shanks; and Walter Wales was to go close to winning the Cheltenham Foxhunters' on his grand mare Salvage when past the age of fifty.

I would like to end this chapter with two stories told me by that colourful character Len Coville, who won many races on his good horse Al Capone in the thirties. The first concerns his old friend and rival, Stanley White, doyen of the Hertfordshire Hunt. Stanley was very anxious to win the open race at his local meeting on a good horse of his called Sailor Boy. Len Coville was riding a useful young horse for Sidney Banks, and this horse was going so well that after about a mile, said Mr Coville, 'I was offered the Cup, after two miles the stake, and at two and a half miles I could name my present.' At three miles, however, Basil Comerford, came up from behind and did them both.

The second story is set at Cottenham, where, on a very wet day, Len Coville was riding a young horse that he couldn't hold one side of, owing to the slippery reins. So, needing something to go in front of him, he turned to Jack Nichols, who was just behind him, and shouted to him to come on, for God's sake. Jack, being an habitual stutterer, it took him most of the race to say that his horse was incapable of coming on; although, come on, in the end it did, to such an extent that it won the race.

LADIES' RACES
IN THE THIRTIES

I n the late twenties and early thirties, Miss Sylvia Spooner, the leading lady
rider in England, won over thirty races, some of them against the men before
the rule was altered. And if anyone tells me that this is nothing in comparison
with the total of over 100 successes achieved in Ireland over roughly the same
period by Mrs Masters, the Master of the Tipperary, I will agree. But Ireland has
always been a law unto itself, because there are virtually no restrictions put upon
women riders in that country and it is quite possible for them to have as many as
three or four rides at a single meeting.

Ladies' races in England before the war were largely open races and, since most
women could not hope to get more than half a dozen rides in a season, to ride
anything over four winners was a fairly considerable achievement.

Two of the most famous lady riders in England were, in fact, Irishwomen, Mrs
Evadne Bell and her daughter Diana, who hunted with the South & West Wilts
and the Blackmore Vale. Mrs Bell was the wife of Isaac Bell, who hunted the
Kilkenny hounds from 1908 to 1921 and was later Master of the South & West
Wilts for nine seasons. The Bells' most prolific winner was Rattles, who was
acquired from his breeder in Ireland as a five-year-old and had twenty wins, seven
seconds and a third to his credit in thirty-two appearances before he retired after
breaking down at the Cotswold in 1935. Mrs Bell won many races on Rattles riding side-saddle; and Diana, who was the leading lady rider of the season on three
occasions between 1933 and 1939, and never rode fewer than four winners in a
season during that period, had five of her six successes in 1933 on this horse, who,
with Peter Payne-Gallwey in the saddle, was the first winner of the Prince of Wales
Cup at the South & West Wilts.

Other notable performers owned by the Bells were Fils de Herod, who was also
bought from his breeder in Ireland, and two horses bred by Mrs Bell herself, Iliad
II and that charming mare Margery Daw III, by Jackdaw of Rheims. Margery Daw
made her début in the year that Rattles retired. She had her first success in the

ladies' open race at the Royal Air Force, Middlesex Yeomanry and 7th Hussars point-to-point at Kimble that season, and won four races in 1936, three in 1937 and four of the five races she started in in 1938.

Another rider with a fine record was the Hon. Mrs Edward Greenall (the former Joyce Laycock), who later became Lady Daresbury and died in 1966. Mrs Greenall was leading lady rider in 1934 and again in 1938; and in 1935 she was the joint leading lady with Diana Bell, Miss B. de Winton and Joyce Seaton (later Mrs Newland). Of the last-named, Len Coville said: 'I always thought her the best lady rider I ever saw. She rode all sorts well. I called her the Gerry Wilson of the ladies, and of course the two came from the same village.'

Mrs Greenall won many races on Silicon and Mimosa II, two of the horses she hunted in Leicestershire with the Belvoir. The late Lord Daresbury, who was Master and Huntsman of the Limerick Foxhounds from 1947 to 1977, described Silicon to me as 'a great stayer but not too good a jumper' (this horse gave his former owner, Lady Harrington, a very nasty fall at the last fence in a race at the Blankney); but of Mimosa II, a mare bought for £400 from a dealer in Leamington, he wrote: 'She was the best of jumpers and learned the art from leading three-year-olds over hurdles.' But she was apt to turn doggy when headed and could never be touched with the whip, or even shown it. The best horse the Greenalls had was the one who taught Joyce Greenall to ride, Torchlight Tattoo, 'a mean, tall horse by Spion Kop, bought from Gerald Balding before he became an international polo player and set up as a public trainer.' A great hunter, Torchlight Tattoo broke his neck, and his rider's pelvis, when James Seely, of Green Carnation fame, was hunting him with the South Notts to qualify him for ladies' races.

One of the best ladies' horses of the period was Miss de Winton's Just Jane, who was hunted by her owner with the Cotswold in Gloucestershire. Before she went to stud, after the 1938 season, this little mare by Furore won twenty-one races, fourteen of them in succession; and at one time or another she beat most of the best ladies' horses in her area.

Among Just Jane's victims was Miss M. J. Parham's Another Result, from the South & West Wilts. This horse, who didn't appear on a course until he was six, once cleared an 8 ft. bullfinch which had a 6 ft. drop into a tarmac lane on the landing side. That was before Miss Parham acquired him, when he was being schooled as a five-year-old by his former owner, Mr A. G. Cowley, who used to have a number of good horses in Surrey. After Miss Parham bought him, Another Result won three races for her in 1936, beating Margery Daw III and Iliad II in two of them, and four in each of the next three seasons. Miss Parham was the leading lady rider in 1939, with seven wins, her other three being on a new horse, Fair Clune, who was still running in point-to-points after the war.

Seven wins in ladies' races in one season was mighty good going. In fact, I believe it was a record in those days. But, if so, it was shared with Miss A. M. Everitt, who was later to become Mrs Sidney Parker. In 1937, Miss Everitt won four races on her Mr Cinders III and three on Tellnell, who were hunted, respectively, with the North Warwickshire and the South Atherstone.

On Mr Cinders, a horse bred in Shropshire and obtained from Mr W. R. B. Dodgson, the Secretary of the North Warwickshire, Miss Everitt had a particularly frightening experience. It occurred in 1936, just after she had recovered from a broken jaw sustained in the Grafton Hunter Trials. Mr Cinders, a free-running horse who liked nothing better than to lead from start to finish, was favourite for the ladies' race at the South Staffordshire when the bridle broke as he rounded the first bend. With the bit out of his mouth, and his rider a helpless passenger, he went tearing on until he came to the last bend four fences out. Here there was a very sharp turn and Miss Everitt was quite unable to steer him round it. Fortunately, she managed to pull him up before any damage was done. In his other two races that season, Mr Cinders made all the running and won easily.

Few horses were kept busier in ladies' races during the thirties than Great Hope, the rather plain-looking chestnut gelding by Bachelor's Hope owned by Miss R. J. Crossman, of Bishop's Stortford, and hunted with the Essex hounds. Plain, Great Hope may have been, but he was a horse of no mean ability; and he would doubt-less have won many more races if Miss Crossman had not broken her leg during the 1935 season and had a crashing fall at a ditch on the old New Forest course at Christchurch the following season. During those two seasons, when he was ridden by some half a dozen different riders, Great Hope ran in twenty races and won seven of them, with Miss Crossman up on four occasions.

One of Great Hope's chief rivals in Essex was Charlie Chaplin II, against whom he came up three times in 1936, being beaten by him at the Enfield Chace, revers-ing the placings at the Essex & Suffolk, and again finishing in front of him at the East Essex, where the two ran in the open nomination race and Great Hope was third to Mr W. H. Chaplin's Successful Penalty, one of the best farmers' horses in the area. In 1937, when she rode five winners and was equal second with Diana Bell to Miss Everitt in the leading lady riders' stakes, Valerie Dalton-White won three races on Charlie Chaplin II and two on his stable companion Laureate, a horse who had won several races for Miss Evelyn Bothway in East Anglia in previ-ous seasons.

To get some idea of how difficult it was to accumulate winning rides in ladies' races in Britain during the thirties, we need look no further than the 1933 season, when the redoubtable Mrs Masters rode ten winners in Ireland. The nearest to this in England was Diana Bell, with six winners; and only three riders, Mrs W. L. Dawes in Kent, Miss B. W. Barrett in Berkshire and Wiltshire, and Mrs F. Broome with the Hampshire-hunted Volplane, rode as many as three winners. In the North, there was even less chance, because very few ladies' races were held there. The most successful riders in that area were Miss Annette Ussher, Miss Malise Wilson, Miss E. K. Hesketh and Miss E. M. Paterson; but between 1933 and 1938, only the last-named managed to ride three winners in a single season, and these were in Derbyshire and Cheshire.

I think Mrs Dawes undoubtedly deserves the accolade south of the Thames, though a word must be put in for Mrs Dorothy Merckel, who married Derek Evatt in December 1946 and had her last ride in a race when she was over fifty. This was in April 1959, when she was second on Jack O'Donoghue's Duo in the adjacent hunts' ladies' race at the Chiddingfold & Leconfield. Mrs Evatt, who won the ladies' race at the Surrey Union five times and the corresponding event at the Old Surrey & Burstow three times, rode about twenty-five winners, post-war and pre-war. She was seldom unplaced and had several bad falls; and on one occasion I recall her being carried off on a stretcher at a meeting where her husband was giving the running commentary.

Another rider who was going strong pre-war and post-war was Miss Kit Tatham-Warter, who might be described as a late starter, since it was not until she was twenty-two that she had her first ride in a race, in Jersey, over banks. That was in 1932, when the Jersey Drag Hunt held their first point-to-point fixture and Miss Tatham-Warter rode in four races, riding two winners, a second and a third. Her mother then bought her a horse called Camrose Pride, who had been hunted in Co. Cork and placed at Punchestown. Kit Tatham-Warter was later a successful trainer of Event horses, and she said of Camrose Pride that he taught her all she knew about the art of remaining in the plate, and that when he didn't get rid of his jockey he was always placed. At that time she was living in Dorset and therefore constantly coming up against Diana Bell, of whom she wrote: 'Although very young, she was by far the best jockey of our sex and an excellent judge of pace; the best I could do was to follow her home day after day. But, whilst doing so, I was able to acquire a great deal of knowledge about pace and judgement in race-riding.' And she adds that she won on Camrose Pride on the only two occasions when Diana Bell was absent from the field.

In 1934 Kit Tatham-Warter went to ride the horses of Sir Warden Chilcott in Hampshire. One of the horses she won on for him was Wavelet, who took such a firm hold on the gallops that he was guaranteed to get anyone fit. But he was a sweet ride in a race for a rider who knew his ways, and at the Hambledon in 1935 he won two races in an afternoon. Kit Tatham-Warter's best season was 1939, when she acquired a useful horse of her own in Glen Alder II. That season she won more races than Diana Bell and her total of five winners was exceeded only by Miss Parham. There are some riders – although not all that many – who will get up on anything they are offered, and Kit Tatham-Warter was of this select number. Not even a fractured skull could keep this courageous rider out of the saddle for long.

Some ladies showed considerable enterprise. One such was the Hon. Ulrica Thynne, later the wife of Lt. Col. G. A. Murray Smith, Joint Master of the Fernie. In 1934 this lady stepped out of an aeroplane on the old Chiddingfold course at Knowle, Cranleigh, just in time to ride a horse called Greenwell's Glory in the ladies' race. I remember the incident most vividly, because at that time I was living in Cranleigh and knew every blade of grass on the course. It was one of those old-fashioned courses where the horses soon disappeared into the distance and one waited interminably for them to reappear over the last few fences. It was a great moment when Greenwell's Glory hove into sight on the horizon, and a greater one still for the schoolboy who had his pocket money on him when he came home at odds of 8-1.

THE LAST YEARS
BEFORE THE WAR

In the early thirties, Major Rushton and Mr E. W. W. Bailey all but monopolised the leading riders' positions; but this monopoly was broken in 1935, although Major Rushton's Signet Ring and Mr Bailey's Pucka Belle were still the leading horses of that season, along with Miss de Winton's Just Jane, who also had six wins. The leading rider, for the first time, was Gersham Wood, whose total of thirteen winners included three wins in hunter chases and a treble at the Cotswold, where he finished second in the members' race on his only other mount. Mr Bailey was his nearest rival, with twelve winners, including two hunter-chase wins on his Little Briton and a win on Pucka Belle in the open nomination race at a bona fide military meeting at Windmillhill; and then came Kenneth Urquhart, who pulled off doubles in three different counties and whose eleven successes included three on Rufus, a chestnut gelding by Capt. Ross who won every race he ran in (four) that season. This horse was owned by Tom Gifford, the father of Josh and Macer. 'Ruby' Holland-Martin had ten winners, the same as Capt. W. G. Carr, who achieved the feat of riding four of the five winners at the Henham Harriers; and there were nine winners that season for Guy Cunard.

Little Tommy Tucker won the open nomination race at the York & Ainsty for the third year running. Major Rushton won the Heygate Gold Cup at the North Hereford on O'Dell. Pucka Belle won her second Jim Morgan Cup at the South Herefordshire & Ross Harriers and beat O'Dell by half a length in the Dudley Cup. And one of the best ladies' races of the season was at the Wilton, where there were eight starters from amongst fifteen entries, including several top-class performers. But there was some atrocious luck for two of them. Diana Bell lost a leather at the half-way stage on Margery Daw III but carried on until the mare fell two out; and Mrs Greenall was concussed when Silicon came down. The winner was Miss de Winton on Just Jane, who beat Joyce Seaton on Ballenvulla.

Mr E. W. W. Bailey and Ruby Holland-Martin shared the chief riding honours of 1936, with eleven winners apiece, two more than 'Slotty' Dawes, Thurstan

Holland-Martin, Mr W. Carr in the North, and Capt. H. C. Phillips, of the 17th Field Brigade, who won two races in two days on Bright Gem at the February military meeting at Tweseldown, two more on Herbert Lumsden's More Magic there and a fifth on the same owner's Silver Gill, on whom he also won a hunter chase at Wincanton. Five of Capt. Phillips's successes were on his own horses, Bright Gem accounting for four of them and Gold Cup winning the R.A. steeplechase at the Old Surrey & Burstow bona fide meeting for him.

But the most prolific winners of that season were Hopeful Hero, who won seven races, and Surgeon Major, on whom Tom Brake (who was to distinguish himself after the war in the showjumping field) won the open nomination races at the Cattistock, the West Somerset & Quantock and the Taunton Vale, and the farmers' races at the Blackmore Vale, the Mendip Farmers and the South & West Wilts.

Down in Cornwall, the Four Burrow had a new course over fifteen banks, all of them reputed to be over 5 ft. high; and it was a West Country horse, Mr R. Glanville's Ballykeating, ridden by Capt. J. P. A. Graham, who dead-heated with the great O'Dell in the Dudley Cup. This was O'Dell's thirty-eighth win and Ballykeating was unbeaten that season.

A record crowd of 20,000 (Can this really be true? If so it must make some present-day Clerks of the Course turn green with envy) was reported at the Barlow meeting, near Chesterfield; the Greenjacket Club had ninety-one runners for the five races at their Hampshire fixture; and the point-to-point correspondent of *The Field* was writing: 'I do not think the average point-to-point committee have any conception of the very real interest the general public are taking in these meetings today...' But here's what the same writer had to say of what was presumably an un-average meeting, that of the South Oxfordshire, which in those days was held at Little Milton:

> I can say unhesitatingly that I like this meeting. It is not a fashionable one, neither are the committee blest with a perfect course. But a thoroughly sporting atmosphere prevails, and I have a genuine admiration for the manner in which those responsible make the very most of what they have... Quite a few point-to-point programmes show a map of the course, but the South Oxfordshire went one better and gave a brief description of the conformation of each fence as well.

In Dorset, the Portman went so far as to print on their racecard a warning to the effect that no one who used 'foreign' oats and hay would be welcome to hunt with the Portman hounds, and all hunting folk were urged to 'feed their horses on oats and hay grown within the Hunt, and to bed their horses on straw grown by their own farmers'. If they did this today, no doubt they would be prosecuted by the Race Relations Board!

After Dick Hunt had won the open nomination race at the Mendip Farmers on Red Knight II, the tote paid out £20 to a 2s. stake. Two years later, Red Knight II was to finish second in the National Hunt Handicap Chase at Cheltenham and run sixth behind Battleship in the Grand National. The runner-up to Red Knight at the Mendip Farmers, and no doubt the favourite, was Diana Bell's Iliad II with Tom Brake up.

In the holding going at the South Herefordshire & Ross Harriers, where there were a record number of fallers, Mr E. W. W. Bailey won the Jim Morgan Cup for the third year running, this time on Vizmah, a brown gelding by The Vizier with a grey mane and tail. A certain Frank Weldon, who was to achieve post-war fame as a member of our winning three-day event team in the Olympic Games at Stockholm when he took the individual bronze medal on Kilbarry, won three races on his Golden Norris. And at the West Norfolk there was a treble for Major Eldred Wilson, who won both the lightweight race and the open race on Lt. Col. Oliver Birkbeck's Golden Sprig and then finished alone on his own Hardy Annual in the military race.

At the Pegasus Club (Bar) point-to-point at Kimble there were two dead-heats, the first in the open nomination race, between Mr R. J. Norbury's Red Hot and Mr J. S. R. Edmunds's Chatty, both ridden by their owners; and the second in the farmers' race, where two of the most consistent winners in the area, Mr P. Franklin's Cushendun and Mr C. B. Harper's Stolen Prince, each carrying 14 lb. extra, could not be separated.

Edward Paget, a most distinguished amateur who had finished second in the Grand National of 1932 on Egremont, won the lightweight race for the Jack Russell Cup at the Stock Exchange point-to-point at Billericay on Silver Lizzie; and Mr G. H. Sheppard, later the Clerk of the Course at Stratford, finished third in this race and second in the heavyweight race.

Alec Marsh, later a Starter under N.H. Rules, brought off a notable double, winning the Cheltenham Foxhunters' on Herode Bridge (the Dudley Cup winner of 1933) and the Liverpool Foxhunters' on Don Bradman. The latter was probably the best hunter chaser of that period, though I don't think this one-time show hunter, who dead-heated with Delaneige in the Grand Sefton of 1937 and finished sixth in the Grand National after falling and being remounted, ever ran in point-to-points.

Objections galore followed the Hon. Lavinia Strutt's win on Little Tommy Tucker in the ladies' open race at the Sinnington & Derwent. But the Stewards had their own idea of how to deal with them. They disqualified the runner-up for failing to draw the correct weight and over-ruled the others. Which reminds me of a dialogue I heard outside the weighing tent at a meeting after the war.

Ist Steward: 'I say, that beastly fellow Cunard has objected.'

2nd Steward: 'Has he, by God! Then we'll over-rule it.'

Gersham Wood was again the leading rider in 1937, with seven winners, but this time he had to share the title with Capt. J. P. A. Graham, of the Oxford & Bucks Light Infantry, five of whose seven wins were on his own horses; and Miss Everitt, of course, had as many winners in ladies' races, a remarkable achievement with her fewer opportunities. Mr E. W. W. Bailey, Mr E. Hocking in the West Country, Ruby Holland-Martin, Mr E. G. Langford, Capt. A. G. Martyr and Major J. A. L Schreiber all rode six winners.

This was the year that Hopeful Hero won the National Hunt Chase and O'Dell had his first win in the Liverpool Foxhunters'. It was not O'Dell, however, but

Ragman II who was Major Rushton's most prolific winner in 1937. With this horse, who was bred by a tenant farmer in Worcestershire from a half-bred mare mated with the premium stallion Commodore, Major Rushton won five races, in four of which Ragman was ridden by Jack Fowler, a Worcestershire farmer who was to have two post-war successes in the Dudley Cup. The only other horses to win five races that season were Hill Call (on whom Mrs Donald Steward won four ladies' races in East Anglia), Just Jane (on whom Gersham Wood won one race and Miss de Winton four), and Mr L. Whiteman's well-bred Titterstone from the Ludlow. This eight-year-old chestnut gelding, who didn't have a saddle on his back until he was six years old and won two races as a seven-year-old in his first season, traced back to Sceptre on his sire's side and was a grandson of Challacombe, the 1905 Leger winner, on his dam's side.

The outstanding military combination were W. Scott-Plummer and his March Brown IV, whose four successes included the United Hunts' Cup at Cheltenham, and two races at Sandown, the Grand Military Hunters' Chase and the R.A. Gold Cup. It seems likely that if Mr Scott-Plummer had run March Brown IV in the Grand Military Gold Cup instead of waiting for the Grand Military Hunters' Chase the next day, he would have prevented Major Roddick from recording his first success in the race on Buck Willow.

Capt. A. G. Martyr, of the Royal Scots Greys, had a highly successful season on his eight-year-old Ablington, a horse bred by Capt. Wickham-Boynton, M.F.H., and purchased from 'Gunner' Wellburn in Yorkshire. Ablington's four successes in 1937 included a hunters' race at Tweseldown and the Old Etonian Association Race, which at that time was held at the V.W.H. (Earl Bathurst's) at Siddington.

Ballykeating continued his winning vein, taking the open nomination races at the V.W.H., the Berkeley and the Mendip Farmers; and one horse who won all three of the races he started in (two open nomination races and a military hunters' chase at Windmillhill) was Mr F. H. G. Higgins's Camrose, a bay gelding by Transcendent who was bought as a replacement for another good point-to-pointer, Hiram Borlace. At Tidworth, Camrose started at odds of 20-1 and saw off such accomplished performers as More Magic and Ablington.

Mr and Mrs Dawes had a good season in Kent with Me Too, who was then in his first season of point-to-point racing and won three races with Mrs Dawes up and the Lloyd's Race at the Stock Exchange meeting with 'Slotty' Dawes in the saddle. Tom Brake won four more races with Surgeon Major in the West; and in the same area, Mr T. Pickard's Main Doctor, from the Tetcott, opened his winning account at the Fowey Harriers on Bodmin Racecourse and won four races within a fortnight.

Ryan Price, who rode five winners, had a double at the Hampshire, winning the open nomination race on Thistle Blue and the farmers' race on Mr R. Pitt's Arun Lad, a dour stayer who took a lot of beating in the mud; but his most spectacular ride, and one that says much for his horsemanship, was on Thistle Blue at the Vine. After Sir John Leigh's little mare had fallen in the open nomination race, and been remounted, she was the best part of a mile behind the field. But even a 10 lb. penalty didn't stop her making up the lost ground so fast that she passed one horse after another and was only beaten four lengths by a good horse from the Worcestershire, Mr W. R. Tate's Vestige.

Which brings me to the Dudley Cup of 1937. This was won, in a close finish, by Mrs Geoffrey Freer's Christopher Bean, thirty years before Mrs Freer won her second Dudley Cup with Tailorman. The rider of Christopher Bean was Geoffrey Shakerley, a highly promising young amateur who won several races under Rules riding against the top professionals and makes an intriguing first appearance in Frank Atherton Brown's book as a 'determined young character, in rather a loud check coat and very smart jodhpurs'.

In 1938, O'Dell won the Liverpool Foxhunters' again, Mark Roddick won the Grand Military Gold Cup at Sandown on Kilstar, Mr E. W. W. Bailey won the Cheltenham Foxhunters' on Winter Knight, and a new regulation crept into the point-to-point rules. It read: 'No horse shall be eligible to be entered or run in a point-to-point steeplechase, which since November 1st of the current hunting season has run in any race under National Hunt Rules except the National Hunt Steeplechase and steeplechases confined to horses certified by a Master of Hounds to have been hunted.' This regulation was later expanded to include horses which have won any non-hunter race during the current season, including the National Hunt Chase, which although frequently contested by hunters is not a race confined to them.

The leading rider of 1938 was Harry Freeman-Jackson, who rode twelve winners and finished one up on Guy Cunard. Capt. Freeman-Jackson had seven wins on Duty Paid and the rest on five other horses, none of them his own. Guy Cunard, still only a subaltern in the 4/7th Dragoon Guards, but already getting about the country a bit, won as far North as Cornhill-on-Tweed and as far South as Tweseldown, with four successes on his own horses (including two in two days on his More Cash at the Tweseldown military meeting) and seven on other people's. His most consistent winner was Mr A. W. Greenwood's Lady Billing, on whom he won the maiden race at the Badsworth, the members' race at the Rockwood Harriers and the open nomination races at the Bramham Moor and the Craven Harriers; and on Lt. Col. H. E. Joicey's Venturesome Knight, which I believe he considered the best horse he had ever ridden, he had a single success in the members' heavy-weight race at the Border Hunts'. This horse finished fifth in the Grand National two seasons later with a broken blood vessel, but that time it was not Guy Cunard who was riding him.

Stolen Prince, with seven wins (he was also second four times), was the joint-leading horse of 1938 with Duty Paid. Philip Kindersley's Michael won six races; and so did Jack of the Vale, who was hunted by his owner, Mr I. K. ('Kim') Muir with the Belvoir and the Cottesmore. This chestnut gelding by Prester John had formerly been in training with Reg. Hobbs and was bought for £60 after dead-heating in a selling hurdle at Buckfastleigh, but he was no good steeplechasing because he wouldn't jump ditches. Hunting soon cured him of that, however. Kim Muir, then a subaltern in the 10th Hussars, was killed in the war and his name is now commemorated in the title of a famous amateur riders' race at Cheltenham.

Mr and Mrs Dawes had another good season south of the Thames with Me Too, Irish Silver and Youngtown and are entitled to be regarded as the leading owners of 1938 with their eleven successes, which included the United Hunts' Plate over two miles at Lingfield won by Youngtown with Slotty Dawes up. And one race I particularly remember, for a curious reason, was the 4th Queen's Own Hussars' race at Tweseldown in April, won by Major J. L. Powell on Mr (later Lt. Col.) George Kennard's Notice Board. The runner-up was the same owner's Bayleaf III, who had started a hot favourite and was beaten a distance with his owner up. When the unfortunate Mr Kennard came in he was greeted with a storm of boos. It was the first time that I had heard booing at a military meeting.

The most consistently successful performer in military races that season was Brownly, who trotted up in four regimental races with her owner aboard each time.

The Middleton was a casualty of the weather, so there was no Grimthorpe Cup in 1938. But the Dudley Cup was won by a horse from the Cottesmore, Away, the only horse running in the colours of Mr James Hanbury, of the Equitation School at Weedon. In seven appearances during the season, Away's sole defeat was in the open nomination race at the Cambridgeshire Harriers' meeting at Cottenham, where he was beaten half a length after Mr Hanbury had lost his whip as the result of a bad mistake at the final obstacle. Away's last race before the Dudley Cup was the open nomination race at the Old Berkeley, where he convincingly beat Stolen Prince. Later the same season he won two steeplechases under Rules, beating that famous horse Victor Norman over two miles at Sandown at level weights, and he was second in a three-mile handicap chase at Cheltenham carrying 12 st. 6 lb. Away was one of the vintage Dudley Cup winners.

The *Point-to-Point Calendar* for 1938 was stuffed with suggestions for the improvement of point-to-point racing, and they came from all areas. There were, of course, the customary outcries about horses not being hunted properly, and a Sussex owner went so far as to suggest that 'M.F.H.'s continue to give certificates to the most glaring cases of horses which have never been properly hunted in any sense of the word'.

A Devonshire farmer wanted to 'Stop all horses that have won a race for more than a £20 prize' (which in fact was the maximum prize money allowable for winning a point-to-point race); and a Dorset one decided that he was not going to run any horse at a point-to-point where the entry fee was more than £1.

From Hertfordshire came the cry that 'A charge should be allowed for bookmakers' stands, because by this means undesirable ones could be kept away'. I wonder what made him imagine that only undesirable bookmakers would be unable to afford paying money for pitches.

There was a suggestion from Northumberland that, except in ladies' races, all horses should carry at least 13 st.; and a Yorkshire owner-rider wanted 'the regulation distance of three and a half miles more strictly adhered to'. Nowadays, of course, the minimum allowable distance for a point-to-point race is 2 1/2 miles.

Best of all there was the observation that came from a Sussex owner, who remarked touchingly that 'Point-to-points get harder to win every year'. A cry from the heart, indeed, and one that is as true now as it was then.

The last season of point-to-point racing before the war was to put a stop to it for six years was the 1939 one. Point-to-point racing was then riding so high on the crest of the wave that some people considered it a serious threat to the senior sport, and a Kelso reader of *Horse and Hound* delivered himself as follows:

> One of the chief causes of the poor attendance at racing under the National
> Hunt Rules is that large numbers of people get quite a number of days rac-
> ing at point-to-point meetings practically for nothing, and, therefore, will
> not pay to go to a regular steeplechase meeting. As point-to-point racing
> increases in popularity, regular meetings under National Hunt Rules are
> declining in popularity, and one meeting after another is abandoned. Is it
> coincidence, or cause and effect?

Needless to say, no one felt disposed to answer. But it is not difficult to see in
the rigorous limitations (such as the absurdly low ceiling of prize money) that
have been imposed upon point-to-point racing over the years by the National
Hunt Committee, and which are now being perpetuated by the Jockey Club, a
rather suspicious attitude to the sport between the flags, and a clear desire to
ensure that it doesn't get too big for its boots. But what the authorities don't seem
to have been able to limit, though they have made various abortive attempts to
do so – the restriction on horses that had won three open races was one such – is
the quality of the sport, which has increased almost yearly, so that today it is not
unusual to find an ex-point-to-pointer starting favourite for the Grand National or
being seriously backed for the Cheltenham Gold Cup.

In 1939, there was a new leading rider, Mr L. G. Scott, whose fifteen winners
in the West Country included a treble at the Tiverton. Main Doctor and Mr F. W.
B. Smyth were making hay over the banking courses; and in the South West, the
farming family of Dufosee, a great name in point-to-point racing over the years,
were making their presence felt again, this time with Drin Royal, who was purchased from Lord Stalbridge at a time when Harry Dufosee was managing two
farms for him and Drin Royal was turned out on one of them. On Drin Royal,
Harry Dufosee's son Tony won the open nomination race at the Blackmore Vale
on the same day that his brother Peter won the adjacent hunts' race on Demand,
who was bought off the same farm for £25. Other races won by Drin Royal in 1939
were the open nomination race at the South Dorset, the farmers' race at the
Sparkford Vale and the adjacent hunts' race at the Portman. But he was beaten in
the Prince of Wales Cup at the South & West Wilts by Ballykeating.

And it was Ballykeating who won the Dudley Cup, three years after his dead-
heat in that race with O'Dell. This time, with Harold Payne as his pilot, he beat
Mr Hugh Sumner's Shannon Boy, who was being ridden by that polished horse-
master Jack Gittins.

The Grimthorpe Cup that year was fought out by two local combinations,
Major R. F. (Bob) Wormald with his good horse Putty and Guy Cunard on
Coxwold Countess; and it was Putty, a horse bought for £50, who had the better
of it. This horse was third in the Dudley Cup after the war, when Bob Wormald
held the position of Clerk of the Course at the Middleton for twenty-two years.

Among other good open-race winners of the 1939 season were Sirocco II and
No Side, who were owned by two Old Etonians, the Hon. P. M. Samuel and the
Hon. M. R. Samuel. I am not quite sure which of the brothers, as I presume they

were, owned which horse; but M.R. seemed to have the most mounts, and it was he who won the open nomination race at the V.W.H. (Earl Bathurst's) on No Side and the Old Etonian Association race on Sirocco II. The latter also won the old boys' race the previous year, and on that occasion I believe P.M. was riding.

Several future N.H. trainers were also amongst the winners, including Calverly Bewicke again. Arthur Stephenson won the maiden race at the Zetland on Tyros. Ken Oliver won the open nomination race at the Lauderdale on Evadne. Bobby Renton was being described in *Horse and Hound* as 'a bit of a veteran these days...'; and Ryan Price had been made to turn professional.

And some people still appreciated the correct gear, as the *Horse and Hound* point-to-point correspondent made it sternly clear in his report of the Essex Union meeting:

> In the Members' Heavy-weight event the Hon. Secretary, Major V. S. Laurie, was, as usual, the only rider correctly dressed in 'hunting' costume, his top hat, however, being a bit of a liability in the high wind.

In the circumstances, it seemed a pity that the Major failed to gain a place in the field of four.

Mark Roddick won the Grand Military Gold Cup at Sandown for the third and last time. On his eight-year-old Fillip, a horse that had won on the Flat and been acquired for 620 guineas in February 1937, he beat James Hanbury on Away by six lengths. At this point, it is interesting to note that Kilstar, Major Roddick's Grand Military winner of the previous season, had since been purchased by Miss Dorothy Paget, for whom he won the National Trial Steeplechase at Gatwick and finished third to Workman (an Irish hunter) and Macmoffat (a Scottish one) in the Grand National, for which he started favourite.

Harry Llewellyn won the United Hunts' Cup at Cheltenham on his brother's Tapinette, a French-bred seven-year-old out of a winner of the French Guineas who later won the Lincoln. Duty Paid was third to the 20-1 Kilshannig in the Cheltenham Foxhunters', for which Venturesome Knight started favourite but unshipped his jockey at the fence after the water; and the Liverpool Foxhunters' was won by Capt. Peter Herbert on Mrs G. M. Lees's 11-year-old Nushirawan, a classically-bred horse for whom the Aga Khan paid 4,500 guineas as a yearling and disposed of for fifty-five after he had failed to win a race.

Six lengths behind Nushirawan and four in front of Venturesome Knight (who again started favourite) came the gallant O'Dell, aged seventeen years. It was O'Dell's last race and the end of an era.

THE FIRST YEARS
AFTER THE WAR

O nly 91 point-to-point meetings were held in 1946, the first season after the war. But this was more because of the difficulty of starting up again, owing to petrol rationing, than through any lack of enthusiasm; and when the first post-war fixture took place, at Cottenham in February, the Cambridgeshire Harriers had so many runners for their open nomination race that they had to run it in two divisions, sixteen horses going to the post for the first, won by Capt. T. Hanbury on Mrs Harry Llewellyn's five-year-old Bay Marble, and eighteen for the second, in which Mr E. J. Delfosse's Irish Bachelor beat Maltese Wanderer, the horse that was to give Major Dermot Daly his second successive win in the National Hunt Chase at Cheltenham the following season.

Bay Marble was one of four horses to win their quota of three open nomination races in 1946, the others being Main Doctor and Missed the Bus (the latter in the Ballykeating colours) in the West, and Marques in the West Midlands.

Only the West Country mare, Diana II, who won six races over banking courses and on two occasions scored twice in an afternoon, won more races than Marques that season. Many good judges considered Marques to be the best point-to-pointer of the first post-war decade. Owned by Mr Edward Turner and hunted with the North Shropshire, Marques was purchased as a foal at Newmarket December Sales in 1940. A six-year-old by Sandyman out of Blue Beauty, by Blue Ensign, he won all five of his point-to-points, ridden each time by his owner's son, R. V. (Dick) Turner, who farmed at Aston, where Marques was trained.

At the end of the 1946 season, Marques was sold to Lord Bicester and went into training with Reg Hobbs. But after easily winning a novice hurdle, something went wrong with him and he never ran again. Dick Turner, later Hon. Secretary of the North Shropshire Hunt Point-to-Point, wrote: 'Marques was a horse with a wonderful temperament, never upset and always sleepy in the paddock but like a machine to ride – wonderful long stride and a beautiful jumper.'

For some reason, Marques did not run in the Dudley Cup of 1946, possibly because by that time the old course at Crowle had ceased to exist. That year, and for the next four, the race was run at Chaddesley Corbett, the setting to which it reverted in 1970 after nineteen years at Upton-on-Severn. The 1946 Dudley Cup was won, in a very small field, by Thurstan Holland-Martin riding his brother's Hefty, who also won the members' race at the Harkaway Club (over the same course), the open nomination race at the Beaufort and the adjacent hunts' race at the Cotswold, though he was beaten by Bay Marble at the Berkeley and by Fred Hutsby's Playbill at the North Warwickshire. On his last appearance that season, Hefty was a faller in the Clifton-on-Teme open race, won by Missed the Bus from Merry Knight, the Dudley Cup runner-up.

Excluding wins in hunter chases, the leading riders of the 1946 season, with six winners apiece, were Dick Turner, Henry May and Tommy Southern (who confined themselves mainly to Kent) and Tony Grantham, who later became a top-class professional, and of whom it was once said: 'the boy's riding so short you can hardly tell his head from his arse'.

The leading lady riders, each with four winners, were Kit Tatham-Warter and Ida Croxon. The latter, one of the seven daughters of the late Fred Croxon, who used to have the Seven Sisters Riding School at Northolt and lived to the age of ninety-five, was soon to become famous for her duels with Pat Rushton, the present Mrs John Tollit.

My point-to-point going in those days was largely restricted to the area south of the Thames, where one horse I particularly remember, perhaps because his owner-rider seemed to me to personify the very spirit of point-to-point racing, was Tangerine II. This white-legged horse with a parrot mouth was one of a number brought back from Ireland by Tom Grantham, the father of Tony; and such was the reputation of this noted horsedealer that people in Surrey and Sussex were said to queue up at the station to acquire these Irish horses, much in the same way that Kent owners did in later years in the case of E. J. ('Joss') Masters, the wizard of Tenterden, who later took up permanent residence in Kildare.

Tangerine was purchased for 120 guineas by Mr H. L. Ireland, a neat little figure of a man who invariably rode in hunting costume. Mr Ireland was an accomplished horseman but not exactly an expert jockey, though he rode quite a few winners. In 1946 he won four races on Tangerine and would probably have made it five but for the well-laid plans of Tony Grantham and Brian Thompson before the adjacent hunts' farmers' race at the Crawley & Horsham. In this race Grantham was riding Eric Covell's Old Iron III and Thompson (who later managed the horses of Bill Shand Kydd with such expertise) was up on Wilfred How's Highland Chieftain, and they had decided beforehand that the only way to beat Tangerine was to take him on at his own game and go out in front with him from flagfall. The plan worked almost too well, with the three horses setting off at a speed more appropriate for a two-mile hurdle; and when they came to the sixth, a drop fence, where Tangerine was between the other two but fractionally behind them, Mr Ireland found himself squeezed for room and horse and rider ended up on the floor, leaving the two conspirators to reduce their pace to a nice schooling gallop and chat to each other all the way to the last fence, at which point Highland Chieftain produced the better turn of foot and went away to win by six lengths.

This wasn't quite the end of the story, because the Stewards called Grantham and Thompson up before them and required to be satisfied that they hadn't reached a gentleman's agreement regarding which of their horses should pass the post first. The next time Tony Grantham and Brian Thompson rode against each other a spectator bawled out, 'Have you got it sorted out this time, then?'

During the 1947 season (and thereafter) no horse that had run under N.H. Rules in a race other than one confined to hunters between the dates of November 1st and March lst was eligible to run in point-to-points. And, for the first time, the regulations made mention of the prize money for places: 'The value of the prizes for second and third horses shall not exceed ten sovereigns and five sovereigns respectively.' No fourth prize was permissible, an anachronism which persisted into the seventies.

The leading point-to-point rider of 1947 was Wilfred How, a 41-year-old farmer who hunted with the Crawley & Horsham in Sussex and won fourteen races with three good horses, Toiview, Ashurst Lad and Old Venture, the last-named coming to him via Tom Grantham, as did Highland Chieftain the previous season. Toiview and Old Venture later went into training with Ryan Price, but the former smashed a leg out at grass and the latter broke down; and the only one of the three who did any good after Mr How had sold them was Ashurst Lad, who went on to win a number of ladies' races in Kent and lived to the age of twenty-five.

No such things as lists of winning riders were published in those days, so I am not going to vouch for the strict accuracy of what is coming next; but by my calculations, after Wilfred How (who has given me his figures himself), with 11 winners, came Bertie Hill, that great West Country horseman, who was a member of our winning three-day event team at the Stockholm Olympics in 1956 and trained our gold medallists for the 1968 Olympic Games in Mexico. Guy Cunard rode nine winners that season, Arthur Stephenson, the Bishop Auckland trainer, rode eight and shared fourth place with F. W. Ward, the Shropshire owner-rider who had six of his successes on the unbeaten Poker III. And Jack Nichols, riding Sidney Banks's nine-year-old Lucky Purchase, became the first post-war rider to win both the Liverpool Foxhunters' and the Cheltenham Foxhunters'.

At that time, very few hunts held ladies' open nomination races, because to do so meant that they had to forfeit their men's open. Consequently, these races enjoyed a status which they do not have nowadays. The ones which seemed to take most winning, and therefore had some claim to be regarded as championships, were the Warwick Vase at the Essex and the race at the Ludlow which later became known as the Corvedale Cup. The latter event, in particular, invariably attracted the cream of the ladies' horses and was usually run in two divisions. Such was the case in 1947 when Jack Cann's Wise Lad (Miss Marigold Coke) came from the West Country to win Div. 1, and Div. 2 was won by an outstanding horse from the Whaddon Chase, the late Frank Gee's Signet Ring, on whom Mrs A. G. Delahooke had previously won the Warwick Vase in a field of seventeen. This was not, of course, the same Signet Ring that Major Rushton had before the war.

With two wins on Wise Lad and three on Jack Cann's other horse, Robber, Miss Coke was joint leading lady rider of the season with a fifteen-year-old girl in

Sussex, Angela Covell (now Mrs Derek Ellis), one of the three daughters of Eric Covell, who then farmed at West Grinstead and later had the Southdown Stud at Shipley, where such horses as Bleep-Bleep, River Chanter and Best Song were bred.

Angela Covell's five wins of 1947 were all on her father's Schedule, a good-looking bay with plenty of quality in the blood. His sire, Trigo, was a Derby winner; and his dam, Facette, bred Seneca, who won the Champion Hurdle at Cheltenham in 1941. Who would have thought that 15 seasons after Angela Covell had proved so conclusively that young girls of tender age could sometimes teach their elders a thing or two, the Stewards of the National Hunt Committee would be bringing in legislation forbidding girls under eighteen from riding in point-to-points?

Schedule was also one of the stars of the 1948 season, when Eric Covell, who won four races with this horse and three with Texas Dan, was the leading point-to-point owner. In addition to winning two ladies' races with Angela Covell up, and successfully shouldering thirteen stone in the two races he won with Guy Lerwill riding, Schedule was the winner of a hunter chase at Wye, where his rider was George Hobbs, who subsequently became a professional jockey and then achieved fame as a showjumping rider.

For Signet Ring it was also another good season. He started by winning in an enormous field at Cottenham, with Ronnie Holman riding; and then, with Mrs Delahooke up again, won his second Warwick Vase and the adjacent hunts' ladies' race at his home meeting; and after a walk-over at the Oakley, he won the hunt race at the Grafton. What matter if, in between, he came to grief in the Liverpool Foxhunters' and was unplaced in the National Hunt Chase? These two races were both won by Guy Cunard, then reaching the height of his powers, the former on San Michele, the Grimthorpe Cup winner of the past two seasons, and the latter on Bruno II.

Another rider to bring off a notable double that season was Harry Llewellyn, who won the United Hunts' Cup at Cheltenham on Bay Marble and, two days later, the four-mile Foxhunters' Cup on State Control, a horse who broke his back in the Liverpool Foxhunters'.

But it was a serving soldier stationed at Larkhill, Major Peter Rawlins, who had the distinction of riding the most point-to-point winners. Four of Major Rawlins's eleven wins were gained on Mr T. F. Denning's Billdare, the best horse he rode. On this eight-year-old gelding from the Mendip Farmers, Major Rawlins won the maiden race at the South & West Wilts and the open nomination races at the Sparkford Vale, Blackmore Vale and the Cotswold.

I doubt, though, if Billdare was the equal of Doughcake, whose owner, Geoffrey White, had produced an exceptional horse in the twenties called Streak, who won twenty-nine races for him. Doughcake was cast in the same mould; and this Wiltshire mare, who stood 17 hands high and was descended from two St Leger winners, was one of only three horses to win four races in 1948 and remain unbeaten. Another was the Meynell nine-year-old, Aquilo, owned and ridden by Brig. C. B. (Roscoe) Harvey, who was not permitted to run his horses under N.H. rules by virtue of his being an official of the Jockey Club (which he still is). I see that I have a letter on my files in which Roscoe Harvey says, 'I do not think there is a horse in the Midlands who would beat Aquilo this year.' But I would have liked to have seen Aquilo come up against Signet Ring.

And I would have liked to have seen both these horses opposed in a race by Rolling River, the third horse unbeaten in four races. An eleven-year-old bay gelding by Roidore, Rolling River was the best point-to-pointer seen out in Yorkshire, where his crowning achievement was his success in the Grimthorpe Cup.

Further north, in the Vale of Lune country, there was a very good point-to-pointer in Mrs E. M. Cousins's Five Letters. Ridden each time by his owner's son, this six-year-old by Dastur won four point-to-points, a hunter chase at Hexham and a steeplechase at Kelso; and he finished his season dead-heating for the Rothbury Cup.

In the Puckeridge country, Frank Harvey, over whose land at Bishop's Stortford the Puckeridge Hunt races were run for so long after the war, was winning races on his wife's Corbawn Lad, a horse bred by the Hon. Peter Beatty and so poor when the Harveys got him that he could hardly walk. This was another well-bred animal, by Sind (by Solario) out of Tetranella, a mare by The Tetrarch who produced six other winners.

But I mustn't give the impression that all the horses winning point-to-points in 1948 were bred in the pink. One of the most consistent winners in the West Midlands, an area where it has never been easy to win races, was a real commoner, Mr A. G. Hartland's Nut Gold. But this didn't prevent him from winning as many races as Signet Ring and sharing the top honours that season.

The best horse confining himself to ladies' races was probably Blue Heaven, running in the colours which were to figure so prominently in more recent years on Snowdra Queen, the McAlpine tartan of Mrs 'Jackie' Brutton. Mrs Brutton won four races on Blue Heaven, who might well have remained unbeaten but for being struck into when finishing third on three legs in his division of the ladies' open nomination race at the Ludlow. And from her stable in the Cotswolds, Mrs Brutton also produced Compton Abdale, an outstanding novice who was to make his mark at Cheltenham the following season when Mrs Brutton became the first lady to train a winner of the United Hunts' Cup there.

I now come to the achievement of Monica Birtwistle, who started race-riding at the age of twenty-three in 1947, when she had three winners in four rides. In 1948 at the Holcombe, Miss Birtwistle was riding a mare called Hill Vixen, who possessed considerable ability but usually managed to make at least one bad mistake in every race. This time she made it three fences from home when three lengths in the lead. She didn't come right down but she went clean through the fence and Miss Birtwistle came off but had the presence of mind to hold on to the reins as the whole field passed her by. The temptation to give up must have been very strong. But Hill Vixen was an odds on favourite and Monica's fiancé had had £25 on her, which was a lot more than he could afford. So she yelled to a policeman to give her a leg up and set off in hot pursuit. She rode the next fence as if it didn't exist, caught all but one of the leaders before the final obstacle and the remaining one almost on the post to win by a neck. Later that season Monica Birtwistle became Mrs Tony Dickinson, and between them they produced their famous son Michael.

The year Monica Birtwistle won on Hill Vixen at the Holcombe was also the year Pat Rushton won at the Cheshire Forest on her father's old chaser Merry Knight. It was her first winner and she was sixteen years old.

1946 TO 1970

*In which an anti-hunting bill is defeated, the distance of the
Grimthorpe Cup is increased, a five-year-old wins the Dudley Cup,
The Dikler makes his presence felt, and point-to-point racing
comes under the jurisdiction of the Jockey Club.*

I have now come under instructions from my publisher, the sainted Jeremy
Greenwood, to compress into the nearest I can get to 5,000 words the happenings of the first 2.5 decades of post-war point-to-point racing, as a lead-up
to where my earlier book left off at the end of the 1970 season. It is a formidable
task, and I feel that I must begin it with an expression of regret for what,
inevitably, I shall be compelled to omit, most of which, however, has already
secured a safe place in the earlier book. Not that this makes it any less painful.

Let us start then with a few vital statistics concerning some point-to-pointers
within this period who went on to distinguish themselves in the Cheltenham
Gold Cup and the Grand National. The first I remember is Halloween, who made
an indelible impression on me when I saw him winning a memorable open nomination race in Cowdray Park on a day in 1950, and wrote afterwards, "I think
most of us who saw this five-year-old beat Here's Edward and Johnny Pedlar II in
Cowdray Park on Easter Monday, when the rain swept across the course in tor-
rents, knew that we were seeing something out of the ordinary." For me, it was
akin to the feeling I got some years later when watching The Dikler win for the
first time.

Owned and ridden by Capt. Dicky Smalley of the Royal Marines, and hunted
by him with the Hambledon in Hampshire, Halloween was unbeaten the following season, when he finished his five wins in hunter chases with a most impressive display in the four-mile Cheltenham Foxhunters'; and while he never quite
managed to win the Gold Cup at Cheltenham when he went into a professional
yard afterwards, between 1953 and 1956 he was a runner-up in it twice and third
twice.

Two of those who did go on to win the Cheltenham Gold Cup after losing their
maiden certificates in point-to-points were the 1954 Gold Cup winner Four Ten,
and Limber Hill, who won it in 1956; and both these home-bred horses did so in
the same season, 1952, the 17 h.h. Four Ten as a six-year-old for Alan Strange in

Dorset at the New Forest fixture, then held at Wellhouse Farm, Salisbury, and Limber Hill for Lincolnshire's Jim Davey as a five-year-old making his first appearance on a course at the Brocklesby. The really remarkable thing about Limber Hill was that when he graduated to N.H. racing in the winter of 1953 his first four wins under Rules were all over hurdles. A reversal of the normal procedure.

The record of former point-to-pointers in the Grand National is even more impressive. Five of them from within this period went on to win it. Russian Hero, the 1949 winner, was the most surprising of them. On his two appearances in point-to-points three years earlier he couldn't even win his hunt race at Sir W.W. Wynn's. Ridley Lamb's Teal, hunted in Yorkshire with the Hurworth, was undoubtedly one of the best point-to-pointers to win the Grand National after losing his maiden certificate between the flags at the Cleveland in 1950 two years before he won at Aintree. Another was Scotland's Merryman II, who,became the first Scottish-bred horse to win the Grand National when he scored at Aintree in 1960, the year after he won the Liverpool Foxhunters' and the Scottish Grand National; and he was the runner-up to Nicolaus Silver in the 1961 Grand National.

Merryman, who first began to make his mark in ladies' races with his owner up in 1958 as a seven-year-old, was hunted with the Buccleuch; and so was Reg Tweedie's top-class hunter-chaser Freddie, the runner-up to Jay Trump in the 1965 Grand National and to Anglo in the 1966 race.

The two other Grand National winners of this period who lost their maiden certificates in point-to-points were Oxo in 1959 and Highland Wedding in 1969, and both had changed hands by this time. Geoffrey Mason's Oxo, a six-year-old from the West Norfolk, had his first win in a maiden race in 1957 at Cottenham with his rider, Peter Mason, putting up a few pounds in excess of 12-7; and the seven-year-old Highland Wedding, owned and ridden by the Wiltshire veterinary surgeon Peter Calver, lost his maiden certificate at the Portman in 1963.

One must, however, bear in mind that this was a period that produced some of the best hunter chasers who ever set foot on a course; and the three who come immediately to mind are The Callant, Colledge Master and Baulking Green. It is anybody's guess which was the best of them; but it is perhaps worth recalling that the great Australian Olympic rider who owned and rode Colledge Master, Lawrence Morgan, once remarked of his horse's charismatic rival, that if The Callant had run in the Cheltenham Gold Cup of 1957 (the year it was won by another former point-to-pointer, David Brown's Linwell) he would have won it. That was the year The Callant, ridden by his regular pilot, Jimmy Scott-Aiton, beat Colledge Master in the Cheltenham Foxhunters'. It was also the year that Colledge Master had the first of his two successes in the Liverpool Foxhunters'.

The Callant and Colledge Master were evenly matched. The Callant was a dual winner of the Cheltenham Foxhunters' in 1956 and 1957. Colledge Master was a dual winner of this race in 1961 and 1962; and in 1961 Lawrence Morgan and Colledge Master became the first partnership to complete the hunters' double at Cheltenham and Liverpool since Jack Nichols and Lucky Purchase did so in 1947.

Baulking Green, one of the favoured few who has had a book written about him, must surely be the best hunter chaser Tim Forster has ever trained. His feats speak for themselves. Numerous successes in point-to-points for Jim Reade, the

Berkshire farmer who bred him, were followed by a career in hunter chases which saw him winning the United Hunts' Cup at Cheltenham four times and the *Horse and Hound* Cup at Stratford three times.

No more than 91 point-to-points were held in 1946, the first year of point-to-point racing after the War, when petrol rationing was still in force; and no rider managed to win more than six point-to-points. But in 1947, when 140 meetings took place, the leading rider of the season, Wilfred How, a 41-year-old Sussex farmer who hunted with the Crawley & Horsham, was one of two riders to get into double figures. "I see from the *Raceform* point-to-point results book," he wrote in a private letter, "that I rode 12 winners. It ought to have been 14," he added cryptically. But whether it was 12 or 14 it was still more than the 11 winners ridden by the great Olympic horseman Bertie Hill; and How's wins were achieved on three of his own horses, Toiview, Ashurst Lad and the unbeaten Old Venture.

Lady riders had fewer opportunities to shine in those days, and it wasn't until 1955 that one of them reached double figures. This was Jennifer Renfree (later to become Mrs. David Barons), ten of whose 13 successes were achieved on that phenomenal West Country pony Lonesome Boy, who was unbeaten in his 11 appearances, bringing his grand total of wins at this stage up to 33, with Jennifer Renfree up on him on 17 occasions.

Not a great many hunts were in the habit of putting on ladies' open races in those days because to do so meant having to dispense with a men's open. The prestige ladies' races were the Corvedale Cup at the Ludlow (so often a target for Pat Rushton), the Warwick Vase at the Essex Hunt fixture, and, when they were christened in 1954 and 1955, the Gibbon Bowl at Larkhill's Royal Artllery fixture and the Blankney Vase in Lincolnshire. The Corvedale Cup and the Warwick Vase are still being competed for today; but the Larkhill race has been replaced with a four-mile mixed open, and the Blankney Vase by the Oh! Mavis Cup in memory of one of the area's outstanding performers in ladies' races.

By 1949 the *bona-fide* hunt meeting had disappeared from the scene, and point-to-point racing had started at Tweseldown, the scene before the War of those attractive military fixtures and, in 1948, of the Three-Day Event at the Olympic Games. So there were permanent buildings there.

1949 was also the year – and it is as well to be reminded of the fact, since a Labour Government was in office at the time – that a bill to ban hunting was defeated in the House of Commons, thanks in no small part to the speech made against its adoption by the Minister of Agriculture, the late Tom Williams.

Guy Cunard, with his 20 point-to-point winners in 1949, became the first rider to break Wilfred How's record score, only to be rewarded in his native Yorkshire the following season when he was about the only person in the county affected by the decision to impose a 71b. penalty on any rider there who had ridden 15 winners under N.H. Rules. He still rode 17 point-to-point winners in 1950, however, even though losing the men's title to Bertie Hill, who was on a score of 19; and in 1951, when the imposition was dropped, the Major was back at the head of affairs, starting a run which was to give him the title three years in succession.

Meanwhile, Worcestershire's Pat Rushton, the leading lady rider of 1951 and, as Mrs. Pat Tollit, five more times in subsequent years, was continuing her duels with Warwickshire's Ida Croxon (a sharer with Kit Tatham-Warter of the first post-war ladies' title in 1946 and the runner-up for it in 1951). All nine of Pat Rushton's wins in 1951 were on her own horse Lucky Dip, five of Ida Croxon's eight were on Mrs. Cecily Gaskell's spectacular grey, almost white Don Isle; and at the North Ledbury in March these two great protagonists of the art of race-riding dead-heated with each other on the same two horses.

In 1952 the distance of the Middleton Hunt's famed Grimthorpe Cup race at Whitwell-on-the-Hill in Yorkshire was extended to four miles; and such was the success of this venture that several hunts followed suit in 1953. The most enduring of these new four-milers has proved to be the men's open for Lord Ashton of Hyde's Cup at the Heythrop; and in its first running at Fox Farm, Stow-on-the-Wold, where 18 went to the post for it, there was a winner worthy of the occasion in Len Coville's locally-hunted Dark Stranger, who had lost his maiden certificate at the Bicester & Warden Hill over the stayers' course at Kirtlington that season under Ivor Kerwood and went on in 1954 to win the Liverpool Foxhunters' under John Bosley.

In the year 1953 there was cause for celebration on a wide scale. This was the year that saw the coronation of our present Queen, and the occasion was suitably celebrated on the point-to-point scene, notably when H.M. The Queen was present at the United Services fixture at Larkhill to see the inaugural Coronation Cup open race run in two divisions, the first won by Peter Dufosee on his Lucrative and the second by the youthful Ted Edgar on Paul Pry, the horse he had recently acquired from Archie Thomlinson in Yorkshire.

200 point-to-points took place in 1954, the highest number so far; and at Larkhill, the Royal Artillery, with their race for the Gibbon Bowl (run in two divisions), were staging the first ladies' open race to be run on Salisbury Plain.

It was also an historic year at Whitwell-on-the-Hill, where the Middleton, combining with the Middleton East, increased the distance of their Grimthorpe Cup race to 4.5 miles, making it a true Point-to-Point Grand National; and in a high-class field of 15, including some of the best stayers in northern parts, the winner was a horse who had come all the way up from the Vine country in Hampshire for the occasion, Mrs. Joan Makin's ten-year-old mare Kitty Brook, who had already won open races in three different counties, including the new four-miler at the East Essex; and now, with Charlie Smith up again, cruised into the lead at the last roadside bend and was still on the bridle as she passed the post ahead of May King and Mazawattee.

But it was the 1955 Grimthorpe Cup that attracted the biggest field for the race since the War, with 23 going to the post for a race that was won for the third time in six years by Arthur Stephenson, riding three different horses. This time he was up on a horse he had bought ten days beforehand, the 17 h.h. Mr. Gay, who finished full of running in a time that was a good deal faster than Kitty Brook's. Not surprisingly, Mr. Gay, who had started the season a maiden, went on to make his mark in handicap chases.

In 1956, the first year of the second post-war decade, there were outstanding winners of all three point-to-point classics; and one horse was successful in two of them. Cash Account, owned by a Worcestershire farmer, Joe Ballard, and ridden by Bill Foulkes, trotted up in the four-mile men's open for Lord Ashton of Hyde's Cup at the Heythrop and finished his season winning a division of the Lady Dudley Cup at the Worcestershire for the second year running, his first win in that race having been with Martin Tate up. It is true his bid to win the 1956 Grimthorpe Cup failed but the horse that won this gold-cup race, Sidney Webster's owner-ridden More Honour, a nine-year-old from the Derwent, was unbeaten in his five races; and he was also unbeaten in his four races three seasons later when he won his second Grimthorpe Cup. Not only was More Honour the best Grimthorpe Cup winner of the decade, and the fastest on record over the 4.5-mile trip with his time of 8 mins. 43.5 secs. in 1956, he was one of the best ever.

The same applies to Cash Account in the case of the Dudley Cup; and when he won this race for the third time in 1957 with a new rider up in Billy Wynn, a 47-year-old Shropshire farmer, he was also successful in the Grimthorpe Cup. He is therefore the only horse so far to have won three post-war Dudley Cups and all three classic point-to-points.

1956 was also the occasion for the re-forming of the Melton Hunt Club under the inspired guidance of Lance and Urky Newton, and the first staging of the prestigious Melton Hunt Club point-to-point at Garthorpe, the course that was already used by the Belvoir and was later to be the setting for the Cottesmore and the Quorn, as well as the brief home of the ill-fated National Point-to-Point Festival.

The following season girls employed in a professional capacity with horses were permitted to ride in point-to-points, with a consequent improvement in the general level of riding in ladies' races; and in the same season the first ladies' race to be run over four miles was inaugurated by the North Warwickshire at Alcester Heath, with a cup presented for it by Lady Leigh, the wife of the Joint Master. So many entries were received for it that it had to be run in two divisions, both of them won by exceptionally good horses in the Dartmoor mare Coo, ridden by her owner, Mrs. Gillian Chamberlain, and the unbeaten Joyess from the Meynell with Pat Wint up.

And, never mind the three Grand National winners he has trained, I feel sure that 1957 must be a year that is engraved on the mind of Capt. Tim Forster and his fellow officers in the 11th Hussars who had not long returned from Malaya. From their base at Carlisle they brought six horses down to the V.W.H. (Earl Bathurst's) at Siddington in an elephant truck and won both divisions of the open race, Tim Forster winning the second division on his own horse Struell Well.

I remember 1958, in particular, because it marked the first (and, one imagines, the last) occasion on which the Dudley Cup was run in three divisions. The three winning riders were Colin Davies (later the trainer of that great hurdler Persian War), the Kent rider John French (husband of the indomitable Sheilagh); and, the only one of them not riding one of his own horses, John Thorne.

1959 was the last year in action of the record-breaking Lonesome Boy; and he went out with a blazing final success at the age of 14 in the adjacent hunts' ladies' race at the Bolventor Harriers, extending his unbroken sequence of wins over his last six seasons to 53 and his grand total of wins to 65. In his last season he was ridden in all seven of his races by the leading lady rider of the season, Mrs. Diana Coaker, who was also the title-holder in 1950 as Diana Brooke. But the rider who won most races of all on Lonesome Boy, no fewer than 41, was Jennifer Renfree, who won the ladies' title five years running between 1954 and 1958, three times outright and sharing it twice.

As one diminutive hero went out a larger one came in. 1959 was the year that George Barber's Hard Frost started to strike fear into the heart of his opponents in the Eastern Counties. In his first season in point-to-points at the age of nine this former two-mile chaser was a winner of five races, including the four-mile men's open at the East Essex; and by the end of a point-to-point career which lasted for six seasons Hard Frost had won 38 of his 51 races, which included 32 open races and a hunter chase at Market Rasen, all of them with Mick Barber up. For his final appearance, at the Enfield Chace in 1964, he was presented with a walk-over in the open event. So they were still frightened of him in his retirement year!

In 1960 there was a landmark of a different sort when Geoffrey Sale's Annual of *Hunter Chasers and Point-to-Pointers*, dropping on the point-to-point fraternity like manna from Heaven, made its first appearance in paperback form; and with it the sage of Newmarket's individual merit ratings based on the 1959 form. These had the northern hunter chaser Whinstone Hill heading the list at 12-7. Lonesome Boy was rated at 11-1, 1lb. above the unbeaten More Honour.

It was in 1961 that we had the first increase in point-to-point prize money since the year dot (as it seemed) when the National Hunt Committee raised it from £20 to £40 for the winner of an open event and up to £30 for the winner of any other race, with the prize money for second and third places remaining at £10 and £5, and a nasty sting in the tail stipulating that "No further prize from any source whatsoever may be given." So, at the stroke of a pen, it was goodbye to those cocktail cabinets and paintings of winners that some meetings had been handing out.

This restriction was not well received; and neither, on the distaff side, was the one that came in 1962 forbidding girls from riding in point-to-points until they reached the age of 18. Especially when it was recalled that both Pat Rushton and Sue Aston had ridden winners before they reached that age.

But at least in 1963 there was a relaxation of the regulation that any hunt holding a ladies' open would not be able to have a men's open on the card; and in Yorkshire the Middleton were quick to seize the opportunity of putting a ladies' four-mile open race on the same card as their Grimthorpe Cup race. The new race, named after its sponsors, the Malton brewers Charles Rose & Co, attracted a field of 14 and was won in a memorable battle for supremacy, with the lead changing twice on the run-in, by Scotland's Lucky Willie, with 21-year-old Margaret Usher getting the 11-year-old home by a head from the experienced Mrs. Bobby Brewis on Devon Flame. For the winner's owner, Willy Hamilton, it was sweet compensation for the unlucky defeat in the 1960 Grimthorpe Cup of his good horse Earlshaugh, who had failed to secure the verdict that most observers considered should, by right, have been his.

There was more repressive legislation in 1964 when horses that had won four open point-to-points during the season were barred from running in any more of them, as was already happening in Ireland. It was thought, in the Eastern Counties, that the chief reason for this was to halt the domination of the scene there by Hard Frost. In fact, though, it was to encourage more of the top point-to-pointers to go hunter-chasing; but if this was the case it can hardly be said to have been a success, as only two of the horses who won their quota of four open races, Straight Lady (the winner of two of the three point-to-point classics, the Heythrop four-miler and the Dudley Cup) and Burnished Gold, actually won hunter chases.

Guy Cunard broke his own record, riding 22 winners this season; and in the West Country it was the last season for the banking courses. The ones that had survived this long were those at the North Cornwall, Cury Harriers, Four Burrow, the Tetcott and the Western.

Before the start of the 1965 season, the last of the second post-war decade, there was a body-blow for women when a new regulation decreed that all owner-trainers of hunter chases must have a full permit to train; and since women were not eligible for such permits they were ruled out. It was a major step backwards, as both Mrs. Jackie Brutton in the Cotswolds and Miss Lucy Jones in Somerset had saddled winners of the United Hunts Cup at Cheltenham in the past; and Mrs. Brutton had another horse ready-made for the occasion in her brilliant mare Snowdra Queen, whose five successes in 1965 included the 4-mile race for Lord Ashton of Hyde's Cup at the Heythrop and the Lady Dudley Cup at the Worcestershire. Fortunately, she didn't have to wait too long. In 1966, when the regulation was rescinded, Snowdra Queen, with Henry Oliver up again, emulated the feat of Mrs. Brutton's Compton Abdale in 1949 by winning the Cheltenham race. What is more, after being beaten by Baulking Green in the 1967 race, the mare got her revenge on him in the 1968 race with Derek Edmunds up this time.

The regulation restricting the number of open races that could be won was wisely consigned to the scrapheap in 1966, the year that David Tatlow won his second men's title and beat Guy Cunard's previous record by riding 25 winners.

In 1967, the year the *Daily Telegraph* and *Sporting Life* Cups for the leading point-to-point riders of the season were first presented, there was some good news for the so-called weaker sex when they were graciously permitted to ride against the men in hunt members' races. They were still precluded from riding against them in any other races. But at least it was a start.

Another major change in the rules was that hunts were now granted the option of running their open races off the 12st. mark if they so desired; provided that a penalty of not less than 71b. was imposed on previous winners of an open point-to-point or a race under N.H. Rules within the current season and/or the two previous ones. Among the meetings not taking advantage of this concession were those staging the three point-to-point classics, the Worcestershire, the Heythrop and the Middleton.

Although 1968 was a season much afflicted by Foot and Mouth, particularly in Cheshire, where there was no point-to-point racing at all, and also to quite a large extent in Shropshire, it was also a season for innovations. The minimum height of point-to-point fences was raised from 4ft. to 4ft. 3in; and, thanks to the sponsorship of the Nottingham tobacco manufacturers John Player & Sons, we had the first-ever men's point-to-point championship, with qualifying races at point-to-points and a final on the professional racecourse at Newbury, with £1,304 going to the winner. The Players Gold Leaf Trophy race produced a stirring finish between two of the best point-to-pointers in the country, with John Daniell getting Lucy Jones' Bartlemy Boy home by a short head from Richard Shepherd on his Poulakerry in a field of 17.

David Tatlow, with 18 winners, was the champion male rider of the 1968 season for the fourth year running; and the 25-year-old Sue Aston, who was establishing herself as the natural successor to Mrs. Pat Tollit (née Rushton), won the first of her four *Sporting Life* Cups for the leading lady rider with 15 winners, equalling Mrs. Tollit's record score for a woman rider in 1965.

Westcountryman Frank Ryall rode his 200th winner in point-to-points when scoring on Peter Wakeham's Mamma's Boy in the maiden race at the Bolventor Harriers. Guy Cunard, at the age of 56 in the year of his retirement, rode his 268th point-to-point winner when scoring on Vindicated in the hunt race at the Derwent before having the fall on Johnstone that ended his race-riding career four races later; and at the national point-to-point dinner in October 'the Galloping Major', as they called him in Yorkshire, was presented with the dinner committee's inscribed salver for his outstanding services to the sport.

At Garthorpe this season there was an appropriate result to the first running of the Marie Curie Foundation novice championship (for horses who started the season as maidens) at the Melton Hunt Club fixture when it was won, in the capable hands of Tommy Philby, by Lance Newton's six-year-old Roving Lad; and up in Yorkshire at the Middleton a certain Michael Dickinson, riding his mother's 14-year-old Shandover, won the Grimthorpe Cup that his father, Tony, had won 15 years earlier on Turkish Prince.

It was in 1969 that point-to-point racing came under the jurisdiction of the Jockey Club, heralded with a stern statement from Portman Square that all riders would henceforth be required to exhibit to the clerk of the course a certificate of eligibility signed by their Hunt Secretary. In the words of the new masters, this was "to ensure that point-to-point riders are all regular hunting people and have paid their minimum hunt subscriptions before the start of the season."

On the racing front, 1969 stands out in my mind as the year The Dikler flashed across the point-to-point scene like a comet. I was completely bowled over when watching this majestic battleship of a horse losing his maiden certificate as a six-year-old in an open race at the Oxford University meeting at Crowell and almost pulling Capt. Brian Fanshawe's arms out of their sockets in the process. I was also privileged to be standing by the last fence at Cheltenham when The Dikler beat Pendil in the 1973 Gold Cup. They are two experiences I shall never forget.

The contests for the *Daily Telegraph* and *Sporting Life* Cups were both hard fought, and it were not resolved until the last day of the season in the case of the latter when, at the Tiverton Staghounds fixture in Devon, Josephine Turner, with a short-head win on her father's East Anglian invader Convoys, bidding for his eighth win of the season (and his sixth in point-to-points), got the one winner she needed to draw ahead of Sue Aston (who was without a ride at the meeting) with her 14th win.

The *Daily Telegraph* Cup was a match between Michael Bloom and Bill Shand Kydd. The turning point came at the Melton Hunt Club fixture in late May when Bloom's win on the seven-year-old Skygazer in the Marie Curie novice championship gave him his 19th win of a season which had seen him riding four of the six winners at the North Norfolk Harriers in March. Shand Kydd, who was two winners behind Bloom after Melton, got to within one of his rival's score two days later when Musk Orchid, the most prolific point-to-point winner of the season with nine wins, gave him his 18th success in the open race at the Mid-Surrey Farmers Club fixture at Limpsfield; but it wasn't quite enough to share the spoils.

The lowlight of the 1969 season was an economy drive by the Horserace Totalisator Board which saw them reducing their facilities at point-to-points quite drastically.

The death, two months before the start of the 1970 season, of that inspiring administrator Lance Newton was a grievous blow to the entire point-to-point fraternity. It was the greatest loss of its kind since that of the Worcestershire Hunt's Major Harold Rushton; and it was felt with particular sorrow at Garthorpe on the day of the Melton Hunt Club point-to-point, the meeting Lance had been largely responsible for putting on the map.

This meeting, however, continued to live up to expectations, producing high-class winners of the two divisions of the club ladies' race for the Lord Astor Cup in Tenor and Pensham, ridden, respectively, by Sue Aston and Pat Tollit; and another one in Highworth, a winner of the men's open for the Dorset owner-rider Richard Woodhouse, who had won the Cheltenham Foxhunters' on him two months earlier, repeating his 1965 win in that race on Woodside Terrace.

Major Rushton, too, would have been pleased had he been alive to see his beloved Dudley Cup race won by a five-year-old for the first time since Dust Cap in 1912; and a classy one at that in Mrs. Katie Gaze's Ledbury mare Frozen Dawn, a winner of five open races during the season with Henry Oliver up.

David Turner won his first *Daily Telegraph* Cup with 19 winners. Sue Aston won her second *Sporting Life* Cup with 14. Mrs. Jackie Brutton saddled the winner of the Players Gold Leaf Trophy (returning to Newbury after a year at Haydock) when her own horse Lord Fortune, whose three wins in open events under George Hyatt had included the Heythrop four-miler, got up to beat Michael Bloom's mount Skygazer by a head.

And there was a brand new trophy to compete for in 1970 when Marnier-Lapostolle, the makers of the famous liqueur cognac, put up, for annual presentation at the national point-to-point dinner, their Grand Marnier Trophy for the horse winning the most point-to-points during the season. The first recipient of this trophy was Alexander Gordon-Watson, whose 12-year-old Barty, a horse hunted with the Wilton, was unbeaten in his ten races, with the rides equally shared by Alexander and his sister, Mary Gordon-Watson, the international Three-Day Event rider and European champion of 1969.

1971

*In which Sue Aston wins her third ladies' title, the Tote falls
mostly by the wayside, Jeffrey Bernard is unwell again,
and a famous tipster is saluted.*

I n 1971, long before the days when Totemobiles started to appear on point-to-point courses and some hunts ran their own Totes, 57 fixtures found themselves without the services of the Horserace Totalisator Board. They were all meetings at which the average sum taken on the machine over the last three seasons was less than £1,250. The worst sufferer was the Devon & Cornwall Area, with 17 of its fixtures deprived of the facilities, though Wales and Scotland were also hard done by.

So it was not exactly an encouraging start to the season, which also saw the whisky firm of John Dewar & Sons (the sponsors, incidentally, of the launching party given by the publishers of my book *The Continuing Story of Point-to-Point Racing* in 1970), withdrawing from their sponsorship of the regional point-to-point championships in the South of England, the South Midlands and East Anglia.

Even so, this kind of sponsorship, which was pioneered in 1969 by the champagne house of Laurent Perrier in the South East, continued to flourish. Laurent Perrier extended their sponsorship to the West Midlands; and another champagne house, Veuve Clicquot-Ponsardin, came on the scene in the Midlands Area, where the spoils were distributed at Garthorpe on the day of the Melton Hunt Club's prestigious fixture.

And it was good to see amongst the three new courses springing up that two were to become long established ones and are still in use today, the late Col. Arthur Clerke-Brown's course at Kingston Blount in the South Midlands at the foot of the Chilterns and Joe Turner's at Ampton in Suffolk.

The Wiltshire-born Sue Aston, one of the select band of lady riders to ride over 100 point-to-point winners during her distinguished career, won her third *Sporting Life* Cup with 14 winners. That doesn't sound a lot these days, but, besides being at a time when lady riders had far fewer opportunities to shine than they have today, the feat was accomplished despite her being out of action for three weeks (her doctor said it should have been a month) as a result of breaking a bone in her leg (and having to have 14 stitches inserted in the deep cut above the break afterwards), in the course of finishing third on Tenor in the ladies' open race at the North Hereford in February.

The incident occurred after the first fence on the second circuit when she ripped her boot to pieces on the butt end of a gate when turning through a gap where a post and rails had been removed. Most riders would have made no attempt to continue, but the courageous Sue, who had broken two bones in her arm whilst exercising a horse shortly before the start of the season, was made of sterner stuff.

Back on the same horse at the V.W.H. three weeks later, and looking very lame, with her leg strapped up, the 14 stitches still in, and wearing an outsize riding boot loaned to her by David Tatlow (a quadruple winner of the men's title), she had the first of her 14 wins in the ladies' open, allowing the four opponents bold enough to take her on to do most of the work in the heavy ground before coming through to assume complete command in the closing stages.

The previous season, Sue Aston had won nine consecutive races on Tenor, a horse owned and trained by Kenneth Dale, a hunting farmer in the Heythrop country who had discovered this discard from a flat-racing yard in a field by the railway line at Moreton-in-Marsh, where the horse belonged to a local milkman who had acquired him for his son to ride in gymkhanas.

Sue won another six races on Tenor in 1971, and they included the two major races she had won on him in 1970, the 3.5-mile ladies' open for the Lyon Trophy at the Heythrop and the 4-mile ladies' open for the Lady Leigh Cup at the North Warwickshire.

On two occasions she was a winner at two meetings on the same day. After winning on Kiwi II at the Avon Vale she was helicoptered to the Ledbury and won there on Tenor; and this performance was repeated by the same method of travel later in the season when she won at the Berkeley on Kiwi II and at the Warwickshire on Tenor.

The one-eyed Kiwi, owned by Mrs. Hilary Trigg and trained by her in the Hambledon country in Hampshire, was an even more prolific winner than Tenor in 1971. Sue won seven races on this ten-year-old by Joy Boy; and it was only by the proverbial whisker that Kiwi, a winner of eight races on the trot, with Mary O'Shaughnessy up on him in one, lost the Grand Marnier Trophy to the season's other winner of eight point-to-points, the East Cornwall ten-year-old Golden Batman, who won seven races with his trainer Tony Hartnoll up and his eighth with Walter Dennis riding him. The horse's owner, Mr. Magin Hancock, a Truro solicitor, was enabled to collect the trophy at the national point-to-point dinner (which was in its fifth year at the Kensington Close Hotel in London) by virtue of Golden Batman having also secured two second places to Kiwi's one.

Pat Tollit and Sue Aston were two of the greatest lady riders ever seen on a course, the counterparts of today's Polly Curling and Alison Dare; and the duelling for the title that went on between the 29-year-old Sue Aston and the 39-year-old Mrs. Tollit before it was resolved in favour of the former with her 14 winners to her rival's 11, was something to savour, with honours about even, as on the two notable occasions when, in a division of the ladies' open at the Melton Hunt Club fixture, Pat Tollit got Articulation up on the run-in to beat Tenor by a length; and, on the final day of the season, Tenor replied by streaking away from Pat Tollit's mount Pensham in the North Warwickshire four-miler.

Pat Tollit, the first woman to ride more than 100 winners, had all of her 1971 wins on two horses, six of them on her mother's (Mrs. Harold Rushton) Pensham, who also won a maiden hunter chase at Leicester with Tim Holland-Martin up and was a half-sister to two of the best mares ever to run in point-to-points, Sally Furlong and Ladybank. Pat Tollit's other five wins were on her own horse Articulation.

A very bright newcomer to the scene in ladies' races was the eight-year-old Royal Charity, a winning novice chaser bought cheaply at Doncaster for 1,000 guineas in 1970. Owned and ridden by Mrs. "Fizz" Chown, who had enjoyed many successes in the past on Glen Weather and Icy Steel, Royal Charity, qualified with the newly-formed Vale of Aylesbury Hunt, won six of his eight races and broke what was to be the first of a number of course records for him when, defying a 71b. penalty, he won the adjacent hunts' ladies' race at the Oxford University meeting at Kingston Blount in a time of 6 mins. 27 secs.

Mrs. Ann Blaker and Mrs. Sheilagh French were the top lady riders in the South East; and the former, with her eight wins, was third to Sue Aston and Pat Tollit in the table of leading lady riders. Five of Mrs. Blaker's wins were on Wendy Cobden's veteran campaigner Jock Minor (who started his successful point-to-point career as a five-year-old in 1965 when he was in Joe Turner's East Anglian yard), and her other three were on the six-year-old Noble Charger VI, who had the distinction of dead-heating with Pensham in the faster division of the ladies' open for the Lord Astor Cup at the Melton Hunt Club fixture. Jock Minor also had a notable scalp to his credit. He beat Kiwi II in a race at Twelseldown.

Five of Mrs. Blaker's wins were obtained outside her area, as were four of Mrs. French's six on the family horses.

Octroi, who won five races with Celia Conley up and went under by a short head to Kiwi II out of her country at Andoversford in her last race of the season, was the star of the ladies' races in Wales. The Somerset mare Jayem won five ladies' races in the West with Heather Chard up before being beaten a head by Kiwi at Holnicote in her last race of the season.

And in Scotland, Mrs. Mabel Forrest's Maeve, a mare bought for 200 guineas as a three-year-old in 1967 at Ascot Sales, added four more wins with her owner up to the four she had won for her as a seven-year-old in 1970. The last of Maeve's four wins on the trot in 1971 was in Yorkshire, where the mare from the Lauderdale broke the course record for the trip when winning the 4-mile ladies' open at the Middleton in a time of 8 mins. 3 secs.

But what would have happened if Maeve had been taken on by the cream of the local talent, Mrs. Marie Tinkler's Bedale-hunted Flexodus, who was unbeaten in his five races with his owner up, is perhaps anybody's guess. Well, maybe not quite everybody. Geoffrey Sale and Iain Mackenzie in their *Hunter Chasers and Point-to-Pointers* annual bible had Flexodus rated at 10-11 and Maeve at 10-6 on their appearances during the season.

However, although Flexodus was rated highest of all the horses confining their appearances to ladies' races, 11-4 was the rating awarded by the sages to the hunter-chaser Humorous, a nine-year-old from the Golden Valley on whom Diana Bishop won two of the four ladies' races he contested in his seven appearances. In the first of these races, at the North Hereford, Humorous had both Octroi and Tenor behind him, despite Diana Bishop having to ride over the last five fences without any irons after her horse had made a bad mistake at the last open ditch.

Like the *Sporting Life* Cup, the *Daily Telegraph* Cup for the leading male point-to-point rider of the season, was in its fifth year of presentation at the national point-to-point dinner in London (where the Grand Marnier Trophy was in its second), and this was won by a 34-year-old farmer from Herefordshire, Bob Davies (no relation to the professional jockey of the same name who also made his début in point-to-points and was the champion jockey under N.H. Rules in the 1969-70 and 1971-72 seasons after sharing the title with Terry Biddlecombe in the 1968-69 season).

Bob Davies rode 29 winners, a post-war record at the time. All but two of his wins were on horses trained by Bill Bryan in his flourishing yard at Eardisley. At the Radnor & West Hereford he rode four of the six winners; and at the South Hereford, where all the horses he rode were winners, he had another four-timer. Not surprisingly, he was way out ahead of his nearest rival, Capt. Mike Villiers, who rode 18 winners in the South West, one more than David Turner in East Anglia.

The best horse that Bob Davies rode was Abbot's Brook, rated 10-13 by Sale & Mackenzie. On this seven-year-old by Game Rights, who put up a particularly fine performance when beating Lord Fortune and Mighty Red in a men's open at Andoversford, he won six races; and on two others, Partial and Kadamel (who started the season as a maiden), he won five apiece, all open events in the case of Mrs. Pam Morris's ten-year-old South Herefordshire mare Partial.

It was a good season for the three point-to-point classics, the 4-mile men's open for Lord Ashton of Hyde's Cup at the Heythrop, the Lady Dudley Cup men's open at the Worcestershire, and the 4.5-mile men's open for the Ralph Grimthorpe Gold Cup at the Middleton.

The Heythrop four-miler, with its traditional Tuesday date, is the first of the acknowledged point-to-point classics; and in those days it had what most of its devotees still regard as the ideal setting for it at Fox Farm, Stow-on-the-Wold.

There were 16 starters for the 1971 race, which was mostly lacking in class with the absence of such horses as Hope Again, Lord Fortune and Doctor Zhivago from amongst the 31 entries. Not, though, in the case of the winner, the Worcestershire seven-year-old Creme Brule.

Ridden by Robin Knipe, Creme Brule was sent smoothly up to join Stolen Hero five fences from home when the pair were well clear of the others; and Creme Brule, who was only cantering, drew away to win by 25 lengths, with Stolen Hero, having been overtaken by the unconsidered Gildon, toiling in third. The winner's time of 8 mins. 45 secs. on the good ground was the fastest since 1962 when David Tatlow won it on Everything's Rosy in a field of 19. The next race for Creme Brule was a hunter chase at Cheltenham in April, and he won that as well.

Bred in Cheshire by Mrs. Peter Brocklehurst, Creme Brule was by the 1961 Champion Hurdle winner Eborneezer out of a Swedish thoroughbred, Pepy, registered in the General Stud Book, who had competed in the Badminton Horse Trials and won a Three-Day Event at Harewood. His owner, Mr. J.S. Townsend, who farmed at Droitwich, bought him from his breeder as a three-year-old and hunted him with the Worcestershire and was up on him when he lost his maiden certificate at the Croome in 1970.

Somewhat surprisingly, since he is a horse reputed to have acted on any kind of going, Creme Brule was not in the field for the second of the classics, the Dudley Cup, run on good to firm ground over the extended course at Chaddesley Corbett for the second year; but although there were only five runners, it was certainly a class field. In one way or another, all five had distinguished themselves in their previous performances. None more so than the horse who started favourite and finished as a runner-up, Mrs. Dolly Nixon's Sunarise, a winner of 38 points and three hunter chases since the 12-year-old started his point-to-point career in Cornwall in 1966, when he was unbeaten in his eight races, with the Cornish farmer Walter Dennis riding him in seven of them before he was bought for 2,000 guineas at Ascot by Charlie Nixon, for whom he won his eighth race of that season with Scarlett Knipe up on him at Andoversford.

A runner-up in the 1970 Dudley Cup to the five-year-old Frozen Dawn, one of the best horses ever to run in the race, Sunarise had won seven of his eight previous races in 1971, including a hunter chase at Worcester, before he arrived at Chaddesley Corbett for this year's race. But this time he was beaten by one of the horses he had accounted for earlier in the season over the shorter trip on the same course, Dudley Surman's Real Rascal with George Hyatt up.

Although he was a fairly comfortable winner in the end, I would not say that the well-named Real Rascal, who had been a very difficult horse to break in, had an easy time of it. George Hyatt was having to niggle at him to come up with the very fast pace set by Robert Chugg on Sunarise and Bob Davies on Kadamel. The latter, a maiden at the start of the season, had won five races on the trot before being beaten by Lord Fortune at Andoversford; but he started to fade quite rapidly when he reached the open ditch for the last time, and fell at the next, by which time Real Rascal was in hot pursuit of Sunarise, who was in no condition to pull out anything extra when Real Rascal went by him before the second last.

Lord Fortune, whose five wins in 1970 had included the men's championship for the Player's Gold Leaf Trophy at Newbury, passed the five-year-old No Scotch on the run-in to finish a well-beaten third.

The winner's time of 6 mins. and 41.2 secs. was over four seconds slower than the time taken by Frozen Dawn to win in 1970. Trained by his rider on the farm at Stanton, near Broadway, that he runs with his father, Real Rascal, a horse bred by his owner, was the first foal of Venetian Bride, a mare bought for 300 guineas at the Dublin Sales in November 1960 on the same day that Mr. Surman acquired Mystery Gold II, who won 37 races for him when he was trained by David Tatlow, who rode him in all but one of these races and whose 100th point-to-point winner he was when he won on him at the Cotswold evening fixture in 1968 in the course of becoming the leading point-to-point rider for the fourth successive year.

Despite the firm going at Whitwell-on-the-Hill, there were 12 runners for the Grimthorpe Cup, which had become known as the point-to-point Grand National ever since it was first run over 4.5 miles in 1954. The most favoured in the market were two of the Scottish contenders, Sweet Sunday II, a mare owned by the man who used to ride that great hunter-chaser The Callant in the 'fifties, Jimmy Scott-Aiton; and the Dumfriesshire mare Waterford Crystal, who had won two open point-to-points and finished third to Sweet Sunday in another. But neither of these two was to figure prominently; and the winner was a horse from Leicestershire who had done 27 days' hunting with the Cottesmore.

Owned by Capt. Richard Micklethwait, a former Grenadier Guards officer, and ridden with a splendid sense of timing by Andrew Berry, a 21-year-old Lincolnshire farmer, the 11-year-old Kangaroo Jim hit the front shortly before the last and ran on stoutly to win by a length and a half from another Scottish contender, 12-year-old Mischief II, who was adding yet another second place to his score.

By the premium stallion Parting Shot out of a mare by Flag Of Truce, Kangaroo Jim was bred by Miss Helen Hall in Leicestershire, and Capt. Micklethwait bought him from her as a maiden six-year-old, winning two races with him in 1970, riding him in one of them himself, and five in 1971 with Andrew Berry up. The Grimthorpe Cup was the horse's third win in an open event.

I think, however, it would be fair to say that none of the three classic winners could be regarded as the best horse seen out in point-to-points during the season; and I am inclined to agree with Sale & Mackenzie that the title should go to Mr. E.W. Bomford's North Cotswold eight-year-old Sally Furlong, rated by them at 11-13, second only to a horse who confined his appearance to hunter chases. It is true Sally Furlong was beaten a short head by the very useful Bright Willow in her only point-to-point, the open event at the Clifton-on-Teme; but before that she won all three of her hunter chases with Tim Holland-Martin up and easily accounted for Bright Willow in the United Hunts' Cup at Cheltenham. Moreover, a bout of coughing had kept her off the course for five weeks before she met Bright Willow again.

I confess, though, to being mystified at how the Old Berkshire seven-year-old Grey Sombrero came to be top-rated at 12-1 by the famous duo on the strength of winning two fairly moderate hunter chases, since he was unplaced in four others.

To my way of thinking, there were several with better claims to this honour; and one of them was another hunter chaser, Chris Collins' seven-year-old Credit Call, who, following in the footsteps of the same owner-rider's illustrious Titus Oates, who had had a defeat of The Dikler to his credit, was going from strength to strength. A winner the previous season of six of his eight races, when he was in his first season of hunter chases from Arthur Stephenson's Bishop Auckland yard, Credit Call won five of his nine in 1971, culminating in a triumph in the *Horse and Hound* Cup at Stratford with Graham Macmillan proving an able deputy for his owner.

The only horses to beat Credit Call in 1971 when he stood up were Rome Express on his first appearance of the season at Nottingham, Hope Again and Poulakerry in the Cheltenham Foxhunters'.

Rome Express, also a winner at Wincanton, was one of the horses owned and ridden by Bill Shand Kydd and trained for him in his own yard at Leighton

Buzzard by the skilful Brian Thompson. Two others this season were Black Baize, a highly promising six-year-old mare on whom Shand Kydd won a hunter chase at Newton Abbot, and the ten-year-old Robber Baron, a winner of both his open point-to-points, beating Real Rascal by a neck in one of them.

Another in the Shand Kydd yard, though not still owned by him, was Musk Orchid. This nine-year-old by No Orchids was a winner over hurdles and fences when trained by Ryan Price before Shand Kydd bought him for 625 guineas at Ascot in 1968. He then won nine open point-to-points for Shand Kydd in 1969 before breaking down in a handicap chase and being sold to Lt. Col. James Hanbury for his 19-year-old son "Jos" to ride in point-to-points. After making a winning début on him in a men's open at Cottenham in February 1971, young Jos went on to win another open race on him at the West Norfolk fixture on the now defunct course at Moulton. Col. Hanbury, who had defied a serious illness to see him do so, died less than a week afterwards.

Master of the Belvoir for 15 years and later the Hunt's Chairman, James Hanbury was a great point-to-point rider in his day; and one of his major successes was on his own horse Away, a vintage winner of the 1938 Dudley Cup when he was at the Equitation School at Weedon. Away, later a good winner for him under Rules, won six of his seven races that season.

Denis Windel's Hope Again, a nine-year-old by Romany Air, was a horse who needed strong driving; and he certainly got it from the 22-year-old Richard Smith, who won three races in a row on him, two of them hunter chases, and also three on him the previous season, including a hunter chase at Newton Abbot. Richard Shepherd's owner-ridden Poulakerry, a ten-year-old by Mustang out of a mare by Columcille, also won three races in a row, all of them hunter chases. Both these horses were rated quite highly by Sale & Mackenzie, Poulakerry on the same mark as Black Baize at 11-10, and Hope Again at 11-5, 21b. below Real Rascal and Bright Willow.

And where, you might ask, did the winners of the Liverpool Foxhunters' and the final of the Players Gold Leaf men's point-to-point championship at Haydock Park, Bright Willow and Mighty Red, both of them owned by Alan Cure, the Chairman of the West Warwickshire Farmers' Hunt, figure in the ratings? The answer in the case of Bright Willow is equal ninth on the same mark as Real Rascal at 11-7, and in Mighty Red's case equal 21st at 11-2 on the same mark as Robber Baron along with six others, including Doctor Zhivago, the winner of five open point-to-points and a hunter chase at Hereford with the powerful David Horton up.

Ten-year-old Bright Willow, the Dudley Cup winner of 1968 when it was in its last year at Upton-on-Severn and originally a show jumper when owned by Walter Biddlecombe (the father of Terry and Tony), was a horse with many successes behind him; and in 1971, besides winning at Liverpool and beating Sally Furlong in a point-to-point, he was a runner-up in his four other hunter chases with Robert Chugg up to, among other good horses, Bullocks Horn, the horse he beat later in the Liverpool Foxhunters'.

Mighty Red, Bright Willow's seven-year-old stable companion, started the 1971 season as a maiden; but he wasn't to remain one for long, even though confined to open point-to-points and hunter chases. With Robert Chugg's brother John riding him, he had won two open races and a hunter chase at Warwick before contesting the Players Gold Leaf Trophy race, in which he came up against his stablemate Bright Willow, who started favourite but found the concession of 71b. too much for him and went under by 2.5 lengths. This was the second time during the season that the Chugg brothers had opposed each other; and on the first, in the men's open at the Croome, Robert on Sunarise beat John on Mighty Red. So it was honours even between the two.

Court Gardens, the ten-year-old from the Portman who finished a well-beaten third in the Players race, was the best open-race point-to-pointer in the South West. Trained for his wife by Percy Tory on the point-to-point course at Badbury Rings and ridden in all his races by Richard "The Jolly" Miller, he won five open races and a hunter chase at Cheltenham during the season and enjoyed his finest moment when decisively beating Bartlemy Boy (the winner of the first Players Gold Leaf Trophy race at Newbury in 1968) in the open race at his home meeting.

The Jolly Miller was also up on the best novice point-to-pointer in the area, Debonair Boy, a big green six-year-old by Romany Air owned by his rider's uncle, Richard Draper, and bred in Wiltshire by the late Geoffrey White from his mare Sweet Nap, by No Orchids.

In Yorkshire, Alan Smith produced two brilliant five-year-olds in Northern Guide and Colonial Queen. Both were unbeaten save for a single fall apiece. Colonial Queen, a mare by Sir Winston Churchill's old horse Colonist II, won a maiden race with David Smith up and three ladies' open with Carolyn Park riding her. Northern Guide, who was by Cock of the North out of a mare by Guide, won two adjacent hunts' races and an open race under David Smith, easily accounting for the quadruple winner Kirkless Lad in the latter.

Another promising young horse by Colonist II, and one who was to go on to win novice chases, was Mrs. Jack Bloom's six-year-old Non Such Hill in East Anglia, where he beat the Turner horse Culford Cottage in his maiden race with Nigel Bloom riding him and then won an open race over the stayers' course at Marks Tey.

Joe Turner, who was in his last season as Master of the Suffolk Hunt, had every reason to be pleased with the prowess of his six-year-old Culford Cottage, who was unbeaten following his defeat by Non Such Hill, winning his next six races, including a hunter chase at Fakenham, ridden in all of them by David Turner. The leading point-to-point rider of 1970, David Turner was also particularly well mounted on his father's Billy Larkin, a winner of six of his seven races, also including a hunter chase at Fakenham.

A seven-year-old by Hard Sauce out of a mare by Jock Scot, Billy Larkin was a winner of two races on the Flat in his younger days, but he was unsuccessful as a hurdler and Joe Turner bought him at Ascot for 500 guineas, starting him in point-to-points as a five-year-old in 1969, when he won a hunter chase at Fakenham with David up and three ladies' opens with David's sister Josie riding him. By the end of the 1971 season, Billy Larkin had won 14 point-to-points and two hunter chases.

Another seven-year-old to impress was a horse from the Bramham Moor, Lord Sing, who also won a couple of races on the Flat, as well as a two-mile chase over 2m 1f before he started hunt racing in 1971 and quickly made a mark for himself with Richard Whitaker winning three open point-to-points and a hunter chase at Sedgefield on him. He broke the course record at Charm Park when winning at the Derwent and put up a particularly fine performance when beating the triple winner Blue Cascade out of his country at the Grove & Rufford. Sale and Mackenzie rated him on the same mark as Debonair Boy in their annual, at 10-12, 31b. below Sally Furlong's sister Ladybank, who would almost certainly have been unbeaten but for unseating Tim Holland-Martin on the first of her three appearances on a course as a six-year-old.

Since 1959, when the race was won by the one and only Guy Cunard on Archie Thomlinson's spectacular flying machine Croizet, the Melton Hunt Club had been staging a novice championship at Garthorpe for horses who started the season as maidens; and in 1971, when it was entering its fourth year of sponsorship by the Marie Curie Memorial Foundation for the relief of cancer, it was won in a field of 16 by a rank outsider who was having his first-ever success on his eighth appearance of the season, Mrs. Peter Marshall's home-bred Aspirator, a seven-year-old from the Cottesmore by the same sire, Articulate, as Pat Tollit's Articulation.

Owing a large part of his success to the opportunist tactics of his rider, Andrew Graham, Aspirator got home by threequarters of a length from the favourite, Non Such Hill, who can be accounted extremely unlucky in more ways than one, as he had been off the course for two months and spread a plate in the course of the race. Otherwise he would no doubt have provided David Wales with his 100th winner in point-to-points. It seemed a pity, too, that such horses as Debonair Boy, Ladybank and the Yorkshire five-year-olds Colonial Queen and Northern Guide did not figure among the runners, though the latter pair had both been entered for the race, as had Culford Cottage.

It was not a good season for injuries to riders. On the same day in February, that Sue Aston had her accident at the North Hereford, Mary Gordon-Watson broke her collar-bone in a fall on Barty (the Grand Marnier winner of 1970 when she and her brother, Alexander, who owned him, both won five races on him) at the Sparkford Vale; and Hunter Rowe sustained a similar injury riding a maiden at the West Norfolk.

The following week, David Wales cracked three ribs when deputising for Hunter Rowe on Duke Of Cinchon at Cottenham, an injury that was to cost him the mount on Slave Knocker in the Cheltenham Foxhunters'. Dick Saunders dislocated his shoulder riding a young horse at the Cottesmore; and Michael Bloom fractured his collar-bone and bruised his ribs badly in a fall on a maiden at the Essex & Suffolk.

But the worst injuries were sustained by 19-year-old Bart Hellyer, who was still in a wheel-chair four months after the close of the season after a fall at the Belvoir in April on Blue Ivory, a former long-distance hurdler who had given him three wins in open events at Cottenham.

On a more cheerful note, 1971 marked the formation of the Point-to-Point Secretaries Association, with the wheel-chair-bound Christopher Glyn (the present Lord Wolverton) appointed as its first Secretary; the publication by Joe Allen of The Horseman's Bookshop in London of Ron Liddiard's exhilarating book about Baulking Green, one of the greatest of the post-war hunter chasers; and the making of the first colour film of the point-to-point scene by two German journalists, Dr. Claus Baukhage, a radio broadcaster for Deutschland-funk, Cologne, and Fritz Heimplatzer, the London correspondent of *Westdeutsche Allgemeine Zeitung*.

Shot at meetings ranging from Surrey to Yorkshire, an unedited version of the film would have run for four hours, so it can readily be imagined how much had to be cut from it. But the edited version was consistently fascinating, with bags of atmosphere. I can vouch for this because I was one of the few people to have the pleasure of seeing it at a private showing in London. The English commentary was delivered by Tim Brinton in his impeccable style; and the stars of the film, entitled "Some Like It Fast," were Gillian Kelleway (wife of the professional jockey Paul Kelleway, who got his licence as a trainer six years later), the Holland sisters from Kent, the Mahony sisters from Bucks, and the dazzling Sue Aston, who rode as short as a flat-race jockey.

Unfortunately, the film never had a public showing in this country, though it was seen on Hamburg television. It would be nice to know what has become of it, If you ever read this, Claus, perhaps you can tell us?

It was also the year when we were deprived of the colourful presence on a course of the white-robed "Gully Gully", a man who outshone all his rivals in the days when racing tipsters were seen on point-to-point courses. His knowledge of the sport was extensive; and he had a magic way of imparting it, well suited to someone who, in his palmier days, had been a conjouror on the Music Halls, and, he claimed, had attended "the best public school in the country bar none". Actually, it was 'the other' Wellington, in Shropshire, where he was known under his real name of Joe Berman. But he suffered from a rare blood disease which necessitated frequent visits to the Middlesex Hospital in London, and it felled him in the end.

Joe's funeral took place at Putney Vale Crematorium in June, and I had the very great pleasure of attending it. Pleasure yes, because his friends, who had been shifting uneasily in their seats during the solemn service, had some hilarious stories to tell about him when they were released into the crematorium gardens. Joe was never a man to mince his words. "Madam," he said to a lady on a day at the Heythrop who had been complaining bitterly at his remarks about her husband's riding ability, "I can only speak as I find, and I regret to have to inform you, since you do not seem to be aware of it yourself, that your husband couldn't ride in a bus without falling out of it."

My final recollection is of that larger-than-life character Jeffrey Bernard falling into the Kensington Close Hotel and frightening the life out of Sue Aston, to whom he was supposed to be presenting the *Sporting Life* Cup. In fact, of course, he got left at the post, or, to be more precise, on a sofa sleeping it off, leaving the paper's Managing Director, the late Norman Bardsley (who seemed to be well prepared for the job), to do the honours.

It was not long after this that Bernard, whose scurrilous weekly column in the paper had been delighting its readers for some time, received his marching orders for bringing the paper into disrepute. The incident was subsequently seized upon by Keith Waterhouse for use in his entertaining play *Jeffrey Bernard is Unwell.*

1972

In which the ladies get their first championship race, Royal Charity breaks more records, Pat Tollit rides her 150th winner, and Credit Call goes to the top of the Handicap.

The 1972 season brought with it one bad new regulation and two good ones. The bad one was that no horse that had run under Rules on and since July lst of the current N.H. season would be eligible to run in point-to-points, Previously it had been November lst. so the altered conditions reduced opportunities by four months. The good ones wore that the number of permissible adjacent hunts was increased from six to eight; and there was now an opportunity for an extra 'open' race to be added to the card. Quite a number of hunts were quick to make use of this.

One such was the Vale of Aylesbury. which had been formed in May 1970 as an amalgamation of the Hertfordshire, the Old Berkeley and the South Oxfordshire. For this meeting at Kimble on Easter Saturday the occasion was celebrated with the introduction of a restricted open in memory of a great local horse, John Robarts's Glen Weather, who lies buried on the course.

In these days the Vale of Aylesbury was the only hunt to have the distinction of holding two fixtures. The second one was on Col. Arthur Clerke-Brown's course at Kingston Blount; and here too a new race was added to the card in the shape of an open moderate race for horses who hadn't won three or more races or scored either in an open point-to-point or in any race under Rules.

The concession also proved a bonus for racing in the North, where the Sunderland-based Vaux Breweries seized the opportunity to sponsor a series of open novice races culminating in a final at Sedgefield.

At a time when more and more hunts were being compelled to amalgamate, for geographical or financial reasons, and several traditional courses wore lost for ever – and I am now quoting from what I wrote in *The Horseman's Year* – it was encouraging to see springing up some of the courses that are still in use at the present time.

One of them was on the land of John Webber and his neighbour, Harry Jeffries, at Mollington, near Banbury, where the Warwickshire held the first fixture and the

Bicester & Warden Hill the second. Another. thanks largely to some invaluable spadework done by Hunter Rowe, was at Horseheath (not far from Newmarket), where the Cambridgeshire Foxhounds (who had lost their course at Hemingford Abbots) and the Puckeridge & Thurlow held their meetings, Both courses were pronounced excellent, as was the new Bramham Moor course on Wetherby Racecourse.

Although by this time the Jockey Club had conceded the right of women to ride in a limited number of races on the Flat, they were still being denied their own hunter chase or the right to ride in any point-to-point race against the men other than a hunt race. So it was a big step forward to see them being given the equivalent of the men's championship for the Player's Gold Leaf Trophy, even though they still hadn't reached the stage of having a championship race on a professional racecourse.

But thanks to the enterprise of Chris Collins, then the far-seeing Managing Director of Goya perfumery, they now had the next best thing in a Goya ladies' championship on the well-equipped course at Garthorpe on the day of the Melton Hunt Club fixture; and for this there were qualifying races at 35 point-to-points up and down the country.

The race produced a high-class field; and the first winner of it was a horse from the Cleveland country in Yorkshire, Lady Ann Bowlby's owner-ridden Piraeus, who got up on the line to beat Sue Aston's mount Kiwi II by a neck, with the Scottish combination of Mrs. Mabel Forrest and Maeve three lengths away in third, followed home by another contender from Scotland, Young Laird, who, with Jean Thomson up, was a winner of five races during the season, finishing ahead of Maeve on five occasions and behind the mare twice.

The nine-year-old Piraeus, a former inmate of Neville Crump's stable, was given to Lady Ann by Sir Ralph Lawson after he had broken down in a hurdle race at Leicester five years ago as a four-year-old. This was his first season of point-to-point racing, during which he was a winner of four ladies' opens in his eight appearances with Lady Ann up, and a runner-up in three others.

It was a pity, though, that Royal Charity was not in the field for the Goya final. In 1972, in process of winning eight of his nine races (he unseated Fizz Chown in the other), he smashed no fewer than five more course records and equalled another.

On two of these occasions, he broke the course record at Tweseldown, beginning with a time of 6 mins. 16 secs. when getting up on the line to beat the combination of Wendy Cobden and Jock Minor by a short head in the ladies' open at the Army fixture. He then bettered this with the astonishing time of 6 mins. 2.6 secs. (although some watches made it 6 mins. 3.2 secs.) with a pillar to post success in the ladies' open at the Isle of Wight fixture scoring unchallenged in a field that included Jock Minor.

And before winning at the Isle of Wight he had smashed the course records at Lockinge when beating Tenor in a time of 5 mins. 52 secs., at Horseheath with a time of 6 mins. 19 secs., and at the Pegasus Club (Bar) fixture on his home course at Kimble when scoring by a distance in 6 mins. 20 secs.

Two Saturdays later, in the ladies' open at the South & West Wilts, he equalled the Larkhill course record of 6 mins. 5 secs. that had been recorded twice before in the 1967 men's opens, first by Court Gardens at the Royal Artillery fixture and then by the flying Bronze Miller at the Tedworth.

It was not Royal Charity, however, who took the Grand Marnier Trophy. This went to another performer in ladies' races, Mrs. Harold Rushton's Worcestershire mare Pensham. On this half-sister to Sally Furlong and Ladybank, Pat Tollit won ten races and Robert Chugg made it 11 with a win in an adjacent hunts' race. The only horse who came anywhere near Pensham's total was the octogenarian Jack Spurrier's Meynell nine-year-old Hilton Gravelle, a winner of nine races, eight of then open events, ridden each time by John Docker, joint runner-up with David Turner to Richard Miller for the men's title with 14 winners.

But Royal Charity was the top-rated ladies' horse in Sale & Mackenzie at 11-3; and after him at 10-12 came the West Country mare Jayem, who won three of her four ladies' races with Heather Chard up and would have been unbeaten but for slipping up and falling in another. Piraeus and Kiwi II were rated at 10-11, Octroi at 10-10, the same mark as Pensham, Young Laird at 10-9, Tenor at 10-8, and Maeve, who managed only a single win this season but was placed on six other occasions, at 10-7.

Several riders rode their 100th point-to-point winner during the season. David Wales, son of the inimitable Walter of Salvage and King High fame, did so on Slave Knocker, one of the first horses to qualify for the Players Gold Leaf Trophy final at the Waveney Harriers in February. West Countryman Grant Cann sent his century up on Even View at the Dulverton East, the Yorkshire veteran Tommy Wilkin had his 100th at the age of 55 when scoring on his own mare Tinker's Tower at the Middleton; and Dorset's Richard Miller, who was to wind up his season winning the men's title for the *Daily Telegraph* Cup with his 21 winners, rode his 100th winner when scoring on Major Dangerfield's All A Myth on his home course at Badbury Rings.

These achievements, however, were made to look rather pale in comparison with the feat of Pat Tollit, who became the first lady to ride 150 winners when scoring on Pensham out of her country at the Oakley.

For much of the season it began to look as if Mrs. Tollit was going to be an outright winner of her sixth ladies' title (she had her first winner as Pat Rushton in 1951 at the Cheshire Forest on her father's old chaser Merry Knight at the age of 16); and no doubt she would have succeeded in this but for cracking a rib when Tenor, in a clear lead at the time, slipped up with her ascending the hill for the last time in the ladies' four-miler at the North Warwickshire. This put her in hospital for a time.

This incident left the way open for Sue Aston to score on the Welsh mare Miss Hanago, giving her her 14th winner of the season and putting her within one of Pat Tollit's total. There were no more rides for Pat Tollit after that; and when Sue Aston had another win on Kiwi II in the ladies' open at the Exmoor on the last day of the season, beating deputy rider Fizz Chown on Pensham by a neck, she drew level with Pat Tollit on a score of 15 and the title, Sue's fourth, was shared by the two of them. Once again it was Kiwi II and Tenor who provided Sue Aston with most of her wins. She won seven races on Kiwi and five on Tenor.

The first of the season's classics, the four-mile men's open for Lord Ashton of Hyde's cup at the Heythrop, attracted a field of 17, and there was an all-the-way winner of it in Michael Ings's owner-ridden Atherstone mare Dunsbrook Lass, who relished the soft ground at Fox Farm and saw the 29-year-old Ings sitting with a double handful all the way round, easily able to withstand the storming finish put in by Nicky Bush on his father's Innisfoil.

It is possible, though by no means certain, that Dunsbrook Lass would have had more to do if the favourite, John's Joy, hadn't swerved under pressure before the fourth last and shot John Thorne out of the saddle. At the Pytchley just over a fortnight earlier John's Joy, a winner of five races during the season, had beaten Dunsbrook Lass a short head over an easier trip.

An eight-year-old mare by Daybrook Lad, Dunsbrook Lass, was bred by her rider's father from a mare he had also bred, Dunsmore Lass, and comes from a long line of winners. Michael Ings (who was to become Master of the Radnor & West Herefordshire in later years) won four races on Dunsmore Lass and before the season was out he had won four on her daughter, the first of them in 1971.

The Lady Dudley Cup at the Worcestershire was also run on soft ground. Eleven went to the post for it, and there was a thoroughly worthy local winner in Alan Cure's eight-year-old Mighty Red. Sent on by John Chugg four fences from home, he got home in a fighting finish by half a length from Cottager (the leader at the last open ditch), with John's Joy a head away in third. Considering that he had been suffering from the corns and was short of work, this was an even better performance by Mighty Red than it looked. Cottager, though, was the unlucky horse of the race. He broke down before it was over.

The Grimthorpe Cup was also run on soft ground, though it was not quite soft enough for Dunsbrook Lass. The Atherstone mare was running on strongly at the end of the 4.5-mile trip, but so was the winner, Old Man Trouble, and she failed to reach him by 2.5 lengths. The 1971 winner, Kangaroo Jim, finished eight lengths further away in third.

Owned and ridden by Joe Walton, a 23-year-old farmer in the Haydon country on Tyneside, the 11-year-old Old Man Trouble, bought for 280 guineas at Doncaster in the summer of 1968, had now won a single race in each of his four seasons as a point-to-pointer, with his owner up in all of them.

None of the three classic winners, however, were in the field for the Players Gold Leaf final at Newbury; and this was won by in a field of ten (37 had qualified for the race) by an established hunter chaser, Doctor Zhivago, who had made a solitary appearance in the men's open at the South Shropshire in order to qualify for it.

A winner of five open point-to-points and a hunter chase at Hereford with the powerful David Horton up in 1971, the eight-year-old Doctor Zhivago, with John Docker up this time, got home by a length and a half from the fast-finishing Lord Fortune, with the Cheshire hunter-chaser Bear's Slipper 12 lengths away in third. It was Doctor Zhivago's 4th hunter-chase win of the season.

Others in the field included Richard Shepherd's owner-ridden Sir Kay, a winner of six open point-to-point during the season but brought down at the sixth at Newbury; and Double Gold (a faller at the sixth), a winner of four hunter chases and his qualifier at the Radnor & West Hereford under Robin Knipe and another hunter chase at Hereford with George Hyatt up after the Player's race.

There was now growing concern, however, at the way established hunter chasers were dominating what was, after all, supposed to be a point-to-point championship; and in later years this situation was to be resolved with a stiffer penalty system.

The first running of the Vaux final at Sedgefield produced a field of 16 and was a triumph for its sponsors in more ways than one. Not only was the winner, Moyleen, an eight-year-old from the Zetland, owned by Douglas Nicholson, the Chairman of Vaux, and ridden by his son Andrew, but so was the horse who finished third with David Brown up, the seven-year-old Tar And Cement.

At Larkhill, the Tedworth Hunt introduced a 4-mile men's open with a gold cup at stake. There were 17 runners and the first winner of it was a pony-sized mare from the Mid Devon, Janet Peet's eight-year-old Delia's Diadem, who was never in any danger from four fences out under Charles Micklem. It was the mare's third win of the season, during which the only horse to beat her was the Tiverton seven-year-old Westerly Winds, a winner of six races on the trot with Grant Cann up.

Undoubtedly the top hunter chaser of the season. However, was Chris Collins', Credit Call. Trained to perfection by Arthur Stephenson and ridden as usual by his owner, Credit Call captured the Cheltenham Foxhunters', the Liverpool Foxhunters' and the *Horse and Hound* Cup at Stratford; and he was unbeaten in his seven races. Among those he disposed of on the way were Lord Fortune, Creme Brule, Bear's Slipper and Doctor Zhivago; and he was giving away weight on most of these occasions. His closest call came when, after beating Bear's Slipper by 11 lengths at Warwick and giving him 111b., he had to survive an objection for crossing.

As to the best horses running in point-to-points during the season, I think I would stick by my original choice of Sir Kay and Debonair Boy. Ridden again by the Dorset maestro (the one before Mike Felton!), Richard Miller, Debonair Boy was unbeaten in seven open races and unextended in most of them. Coincidentally, Sir Kay and Debonair Boy wore both winners early on in the season at Tweseldown, where they won the two divisions of the men's open at the Army fixture, Debonair Boy in the faster time.

The best novice point-to-pointer of the season is perhaps a little more difficult to single out; but a prize candidate for this title would be a horse from the bargain basement, the eight-year-old Demarval, who was bought for 95 guineas at the Ascot Sales in May 1971 by the Cheshire veterinary surgeon Ted Greenway, who sold him half-way through the 1972 season to James White but continued to train him. Ridden each time by Ted's son Robin, Demarval, a maiden over fences at the start of the season, had won five point-to-points and a hunter chase at Folkestone before he wound up his season, most appropriately, winning the Marie Curie novice championship at the Melton Hunt Club fixture which Robin's father had won on Saucarin in 1960.

Another strong claimant for the novice title was Capt. Bryan Parry's Desert Tyrant. This seven-year-old, who was trained by his owner and hunted with the

Cottesmore, won five races on the trot with Malcolm Arthers up after being bought for 480 guineas at Ascot in June 1971.

Throughout the long history of point-to-point racing, point-to-pointing families have played a big role in the development of the sport, notably the Hutsby family in Warwickshire, the Brookshaws in Shropshire and the Turners in East Anglia; and in 1972 it was the turn of another Warwickshire family to excel themselves, the one with the unforgettable John Thorne at the head of it.

At the Oxford University & Bullingdon Club fixture at Kingston Blount in February, John Thorne won the farmers' race on Rough House and completed a double on the horse he won five races on during the season, Basil Thwaites's John's Joy, whilst his twin daughters, Diana and Jane, finished first and third on two of their father's horses, Dubaythorn and the five-year-old Bright Daisy, in the ladies' open, with Sue Aston in between them on Kenneth Dale's Captain Cook; and the following week on the baptismal course at Mollington, where John Thorne brought off a treble, Jane had her first winning ride when scoring in a 13-horse hunt race on the five-year-old Indian Diva from her father on Ben Ruler, another of the family's five-year-olds.

Milton Bradley's mare Octroi, one of the most prolific point-to-point winners in Wales, with 22 wins in her six seasons of point-to-point racing, six of them in 1972, and ridden in all of them by Celia Conley, came to the end of her racing career when breaking a bone in her fetlock in the ladies' open at the Monmouthshire; but it was not the finish of her career, as she went to stud afterwards. Celia Conley went on to ride in the first flat race for lady riders at Kempton Park the same year.

Several well-known personalities were lost to the sport in 1972, one of them tragically at the age of 38. The Welsh rider Lloyd Jones, who is well remembered for his successes on his brother Howard's Chingley Golden Heart, a horse bought for £35, was killed in a fall on one of his own horses at the Llangeinor.

That colourful character Len Coville of Hill House fame (those with long enough memories will remember the controversy surrounding Hill House's success in the Schweppes Gold Trophy Hurdle at Newbury in 1967) died in February. An accomplished point-to-point rider in his day, especially with his good horse Al Capone in the 'thirties, Coville had his proudest moment in hunt racing when he saddled his own horse Dark Stranger to win the Liverpool Foxhunters' of 1954 with John Bosley up.

Another very colourful character, H.M. Astley ("Ding-Dong") Bell, sometimes also known an "Mr. Beaujolais", died in May. Well known as a farmer and as a breeder of pedigree cattle, Ding-Dong owned one of the great post-war point-to-pointers in Plummers Plain who was rarely beaten in ladies' races with his step-daughter Gillian Pearce up, causing Ding-Dong's face to shine with joy, not unmixed with anticipation, since Ding-Dong was an inveterate gambler whenever the combination appeared on a course. Ding-Dong epitomised the true spirit of point-to-point racing; and he may be said to have written his own epitaph in the following words:

"I have played all games with moderate success within a certain class. I have lost to inferior people and beaten players much better than myself. It is those who take their beating with a good spirit that are good sportsmen."

Ding-Dong, a good companion, was one of them.

Another loss to the scene was George Maundrell, who produced two outstanding young winners of the Dudley Cup in consecutive years, Right Again in 1952 and Cottage Lace in 1953, both of them going on to win under Rules. Right Again was a winner of a hunter chase at Cheltenham the same season; and Cottage Lace, a winner of three hunter chases on the trot the following season went on to win six handicap chases, a novice hurdle and the Grand Military Gold Cup at Sandown. Many of the horses who won point-to-points and scored under Rules for George Maundrell were sired by Game Rights and Romany Air, two of the stallions who stood at his Blacklands Stud at Calne in Wiltshire.

And in November Albert Dimes died. There will be those who recall Albert in the days when he was a leading Soho gangster who figured in a razor fight with the notorious Jack "Spot" Comer. But most will remember him in his later years as a totally reformed character who became a highly respected point-to-point bookmaker in the South Midlands, where his great charm and sense of humour were allied to the kind of generosity that is all too rarely seen nowadays amongst the bookmaking fraternity. Albert was a fearless layer who stood by the prices he chalked up on his board while his colleagues; were waiting for him to show them the way they didn't always follow. Woe betide any bookmaker who attempted to welsh on a course where Albert was operating. At Kingston Blount Albert once laid a horse at 1,000-1. I know because I was there to see it. His funeral, which I regret to say I was not able to attend, was by all accounts a memorable occasion.

I would like to end this chapter with a quotation from a distinguished horseman, the late Sir Andrew Horsbrugh-Porter, concerning two of the greatest lady riders ever seen in the hunting field or on a course:

"I have seldom seen two better women riding difficult young horses in front out hunting than Pat Tollit and Sue Aston. Sue lets down her leathers and imparts her fearlessness to any green horse – but Pat Tollit is still supreme hunting."

1973

In which the Sporting Life Cup goes to Scotland for the first time, Joe Turner wins his first Grand Marnier Trophy, the Heythrop celebrates its 21st anniversary of racing at Stow-on-the-Wold, Tenor runs his last race, and a new hunter-chase meeting is introduced at Leicester.

There were changes this season in the conditions for the two major championship races. A new penalty system for the Players Gold Leaf men's final at Newbury did much to ensure that the 1973 race would be won by a horse making more than a token appearance in a point-to-point in order to qualify; and this proved a distinct bonus, even making up, to some extent, for the fact that the race was still the only jumping race on an otherwise all-Flat card.

And in the case of the Goya ladies' championship on the point-to-point course at Garthorpe, the first three horses past the post in the qualifying races were now eligible for the final, as against the first two in its inaugural year.

Tweseldown and Larkhill were still the most-used venues. At Tweseldown, where course builder George Dudley had rebuilt four of the fences entirely and repacked others, there were six fixtures; and at Larkhill on Salisbury Plain, where the feature race, the men's open for the Coronation Cup at the United Services meeting was run in two divisions, there were five.

Although the season was well treated by the weather, with only one of the 185 fixtures, the Percy, West Percy & Milvain abandoned, and a single postponement, the East Sussex & Romney Marsh, it was a bad season for injuries to horses and riders. The Essex rider John Mayes died in hospital from the injuries he received in a fall at Ampton in February and there were crippling accidents in April for Ann Philby after a fall on Jameson at the East Devon and for Alec Bond, who was taken to Stoke Mandeville after a fall on Land Rover at the Heythrop.

Fizz Chown's brilliant horse Royal Charity, after breaking his own course record with a time of 5 mins. 59.5 secs. in the ladies' open at Tweseldown's Army fixture, broke down badly on his next appearance there. It wasn't however, the end of his racing career. After missing the 1974 season, he broke another course record on his single appearance in 1975.

The Atherstone mare Dunsbrook Lass broke her cannon bone when attempting to win the Heythrop four-miler for the second year in succession. Paul

Rackham's Kalology, a promising new recruit to the sport after nine successes over hurdles, had to be put down following a fall in the ladies' open at the Southdown after winning two ladies' opens with Sheilagh French up, beating the Grand Marnier winner in one of them.

And on April 4 at the Taunton Vale, Richard Woodhouse's great horse Highworth, on whom his owner had won the Cheltenham Foxhunters' of 1970, collapsed and died after finishing fifth in the men's open on his only appearance of the season. The 14-year-old son of Romany Air was a winner of eight hunter chases and 15 point-to-points since he started hunt-racing for Woodhouse, a Joint-Master of the Portman, in 1966; and a worthy successor to the same owner's Woodside Terrace, the winner of the Cheltenham Foxhunters' in 1965 with his owner up.

A particularly welcome feature of the season was the appearance of the first weekly point-to-point and hunter-chase formbook since the demise of *Hunterform*, which had lasted for just a few seasons, perishing after the 1970 one.

The new publication, *Hunterguide,* was produced and edited by Ray Gould, a well-known point-to-point correspondent in the West Midlands who had been covering point-to-points for the old *Sporting Chronicle*. Sadly, however, owing to the financial problems it encountered, it was to have an even shorter life than its predecessor, lasting for no more than two seasons, much to the chagrin of its generous backer, Joe Yeomans. All of which makes one wonder how on earth Iain Mackenzie & Terry Selby's magnificently produced present-day annual of *Hunter Chasers & Point-to-Pointers* manages to survive today's financial climate, not to mention their weekly loose-leaf formbook.

For the first time in six years there was an entirely new winner of the *Sporting Life* Cup for the leading lady rider of the season in the shape of Scotland's Mrs. Mabel Forrest, who farmed 600 acres in the Lauderdale country with her husband, Archie, and nursed an ambition to go out to one of the North Sea oil rigs.

Mrs. Forrest, so far the only Scotswoman to win the title, and also one of the first women to win a race against the men since they were permitted to ride against them in hunt members' races, rode 17 winners riding two of her own horses, Maeve and Dersnip. She won 11 races on Maeve, whose only defeat was on her first appearance of the season at the Eglinton; and six on the home-bred Dersnip, who was unbeaten in 1973 and also won six races for her in 1972, when he lost his maiden certificate as a six-year-old.

Considering that the Northern Area season (which embraces Scotland) didn't begin until the third week of the season and ended almost a month earlier than the last meeting of the season in the West Country, Mrs. Forrest's feat in riding five more winners than the runner-up for the title, East Anglia's Josie Bothway (née Turner and now Sheppard), was all the more remarkable. Behind Josie Bothway, each with ten winners, came Mrs. Pat Tollit and the West Country's Pip Fisher. All ten of Pat Tollit's wins were gained on her mother's mare Pensham.

One of Maeve's successes was in the 4-mile ladies' open at the Middleton which she was winning for the second time in three years when beating two other Scottish contenders, Bonnie Dundee and Young Laird. But her greatest triumph came in her last race of the season, the Goya ladies' championship at the Melton

Hunt club fixture. In a high-class field of 13, which included amongst the also-rans such horses as Kiwi II, Marshalsland (a winner of five ladies' opens in the South West with Fay Geddes up), Bonnie Dundee and John Thorne's pair Indamelia and Bright Daisy, Maeve took over the lead on the run-in from the Belvoir mare Elsea Wood (a winner of five ladies' opens with Didi Morris up) and beat her by two lengths, with the Welsh wonder horse Mandryka six lengths back in third, followed by Indamelia (who had started joint favourite with Maeve and Elsea Wood), Bonnie Dundee and Bright Daisy.

Remarkably, the horse Mrs. Forrest had intended to ride in the Goya championship was Dersnip; but she was prevented from doing so when the seven-year-old went slightly lame shortly beforehand. It is interesting to note that Sale & Mackenzie rated Dersnip at 11-3 in their annual and Maeve at 11-0.

Although Maeve won as many races as Joe Turner's Vulgan nine-year-old Master Vesuvius, who won all 11 of his races with Josie Bothway up, it was Master Vesuvius (whose 11th win was recorded in the ladies' open at the Exmoor on the last day of the season at Bratton Down) who took the Grand Marnier Trophy for his owner on account of his three second places to Maeve's single third placing. Joe Turner was also the leading owner of the season with 33 winners in point-to-points, two in the hunter chases with Even Harmony and Culford Cottage on the same day at Fakenham with David Turner up; and one in a handicap hurdle at Nottingham with his five-year-old Troopship, who was to prove highly successful in point-to-points the following season. Even Harmony won eight races for the stable in 1973 and Culford Cottage seven.

The leading male rider of the season and collector of the *Daily Telegraph* Cup for the second year running was the rider known in his native Dorset as 'The Jolly Miller'. Richard Miller surpassed his 1972 total by two, riding 23 winners, as against the 20 ridden by his nearest rival, David Turner; and in third place was the Cheshire rider Robin Greenway with 15.

Three of the best horses ridden by The Jolly Miller were Mrs. Percy Tory's Court Gardens, a winner of six open races, four of them with Miller up; Max Churches' Rich Rose, on whom he won three adjacent hunts races and four open events, including the Tedworth's four-mile men's open for the Lord Savernake Gold Cup; and Major Dangerfield's All A Myth, the winner of the four-mile men's open for Lord Ashton of Hyde's Cup at the Heythrop.

The Heythrop was celebrating its 21st anniversary of racing at Stow-on-the-Wold; and making a bit of history in the process by featuring the first Tote double and Tote treble to take place at a point-to-point, an occurrence that was to be repeated 25 days later at the West Kent fixture at Ightham. The Heythrop was also fortunate in securing the champagne house of Veuve Clicquot-Ponsardin as sponsors of the entire meeting.

There were no fewer than 27 starters for the classic, among them last year's winner Dunsbrook Lass, who got no further than the open ditch, for which she hardly took off and unseated her rider. The early pace was set by a horse who had yet to lose his maiden certificate, Peter Thelwall's East Anglian eight-year-old River Boy, who was still showing them the way at the sixteenth.

At the last open ditch, three fences out, Richard Shepherd's Sir Kay took off in front, only to lose the lead to River Boy in the air. Sir Kay regained the lead after the next. Once All A Myth took up the running before the second last, however, the issue was never in doubt and the ten-year-old son of Coup De Myth ran on stoutly to finish ten lengths ahead of Sir Kay, with River Boy a similar distance away in third.

Richard Miller said afterwards that he had a wonderful ride on the winner after nearly being brought down at the second; but he also rode a wonderful race on him, keeping him to the inside all the way and producing him at exactly the right moment. Major Dangerfield was with his regiment in Germany and All A Myth was stabled with Peter Kempe in his livery yard near Dorchester. All A Myth's time of 8 mins. 34 secs. on the good to firm ground was the fastest for eight years.

The meeting was also notable for two other fine performances, the first by Tim Holland-Martin and his six-year-old Merchant Banker, who took the Old Etonian & Old Harrovian race by the scruff of the neck, giving Holland-Martin his sixth win in the race, two of them in the six years when it was confined to Old Etonians, and the other four since Old Harrovians were admitted to it in 1965. Merchant Banker, a maiden at the start of the season, was unbeaten in his three races.

A horse used for whipping-in with the North Cotswold, Merchant Banker, said Holland-Martin, after he had won on him for the first time at the Warwickshire, was "bought as a hunter for my retirement". But that day wasn't to come yet.

The other performance I am thinking of is that of Sue Aston and Tenor in the 3.5-mile ladies' open for the Lyon Trophy, which they were winning for the fourth year in succession, in the fastest time for at least eight years, 7 mins. 32 secs. Fencing superbly, and with maximum assistance from his rider, Tenor got home from Diana Thorne's mount Dragonspen (to whom he was giving 31b.) by a head. Jane Thorne would not have been far behind on her Indian Diva but for coming down at the last.

Firm ground at Chaddesley Corbett kept the Dudley Cup down to ten runners. All the same, there were some high-class horses in the field; one of them was Convoys, a star point-to-pointer in East Anglia before being sold by Joe Turner into the Garth & South Berks country and giving his new owner-rider Philip Scouller 11 wins, most of them in open events, and six of them on the trot in 1973. Convoys, however, hit the third last hard when still in with a chance and unseated his rider, who had broken his finger the previous day.

In its later stages, the race developed into a match between John Thorne's mare Indamelia and Alan Cure's Mighty Red, ridden this time by Bob Woolley. Indamelia was slightly in front approaching the last, but Mighty Red produced the better finish to score by a length and a half and win for the second year running, with last year's winning rider, John Chugg, three lengths further behind on Rave Notice.

The Dudley Cup form was to be well franked afterwards, with Mighty Red winning the men's open at the Albrighton Woodland at Chaddesley Corbett over the shorter trip; and Indamelia going on to break the course record at Kingston Blount when beating Master Vesuvius in a ladies' open there, and then winning the Nigel Thorne Memorial hunter chase at Stratford with John Thorne up and scoring in a handicap chase at Stratford with Chris King riding her.

For the 4.5-mile Grimthorpe Cup at Whitwell-on-the-Hill, where the going was also firm, there were 16 runners; and here there was another triumph for the Nicholson family when Moyleen, who had won the Vaux final at Sedgefield for them the previous season, and was being ridden again by the 27-year-old Andrew Nicholson, asserted his superiority at the third last (which he hit hard) and stayed on well to score by two lengths from Charlie Macmillan's mount Moss Kennels. On the same day, Andrew's father, Douglas, was finishing third in the European Driving Championships at the Royal Windsor Horse Show.

This was the nine-year-old Moyleen's last appearance of the season, in which his only previous success was in the William Bell Memorial Gold Cup open race at the Tynedale; but he was a runner-up on three occasions and finished third on another.

Tenor, now aged 13, had a successful swan song in the four-mile ladies' open for the Lady Leigh Cup at the North Warwickshire, a race he was winning for the third time in four years with Sue Aston up.

During his long and distinguished career in point-to-points, which began for his owner-trainer Kenneth Dale in 1967 as a maiden seven-year-old, this son of Macherio, an Italian Derby winner, ran in 59 races, won 30 of them (including a dead-heat), and was placed in 15 others. Sue Aston, who began to ride him in 1969, won 27 races on him. The only other riders to win on him were Capt. Brian Fanshawe, who was up on him when he lost his maiden certificate at the Heythrop in 1968, and won an open race at the Ludlow on him the same season; and Fizz Chown, who won the ladies' open at the Oxford University meeting at Crowell on him in 1969.

In his two and three-year-old days, when he was trained by David Nicholson's father, Frenchie, Tenor ran unsuccessfully on the Flat; and 'The Duke' has an amusing story to tell about him in his autobiography. Frenchie's young apprentice rider at that time was Paul Cook; and Tenor, writes David, was bought by his father to encourage his young apprentice "to use his legs more skilfully" on him. "My mother," continues The Duke, "offered the young apprentice two shillings and sixpence for each horse that finished behind him in a race at Warwick. It was a lucrative lesson. That day he earned five shillings."

Despite the firm ground at Newbury, the Players Gold Leaf Trophy final attracted a field of 12; and the result of it was a very satisfying one for the point-to-point fraternity, with the finish fought out by two genuine point-to-pointers, Mr. H.J. Jewell's Taunton Vale nine-year-old Gravel Pits, with Barry Venn up, beating Mrs. Jackie Brutton's ten-year-old Lord Fortune, from the Cotswold, by a neck.

Gravel Pits, in his nine appearances during the season won three open point-to-points and four hunter chases, ridden in all but one of them by his Newbury rider Barry Venn; while Lord Fortune, in his 11 appearances, all with Derek Edmunds up, won three open point-to-points and had two wins in hunter chases, including one in the United Hunts Cup at Cheltenham.

Although three horses, Hilbirio, Matchboard and Kasim Baba, were all rated above him by Sale & Mackenzie, I would still regard Credit Call as the top hunter chaser of the season, since his five wins in hunter chases, with his owner up in all but one of them, culminated in his third successive win in the *Horse and Hound*

Cup at Stratford, where he was giving Lord Fortune 41b. and beat him by a short head. Thirty lengths behind the runner-up came Creme Brule, who was followed past the post by Doctor Zhivago. Credit Call did, however, have two lapses in his seven appearances. He failed to give the weight away to Corrievrechan 11 and Jedheads in a five-horse hunter chase at Newcastle and finished fourth to Bullock's Horn in the Liverpool Foxhunters' at level weights with him.

Bullock's Horn, no mean performer, was the second leg of a notable double for Lord Oaksey, who also won the four-mile Cheltenham Foxhunters' on him. Bear's Slipper, with Billy Foulkes up, passed the post first by a head but was relegated to second place by the stewards on the grounds of interference.

Hilbirio, like Credit Call, was owned by Chris Collins and trained by Arthur Stephenson at Bishop Auckland; and it was on this horse that Collins won the Swedish Grand National in 1972. His three wins in hunter chases in 1973 were moderate by comparison; and it would be interesting to know which of Credit Call and Hilbirio Collins considers to have been the better.

Mr. S.T. Hill's Silverton seven-year-old Kasim Baba is certainly entitled to be considered the best novice performer of the season. Making hie first appearance in point-to-points in the adjacent hunts' race at the Dart Vale & Haldon & South Pool Harriers fixture at Buckfastleigh, this son of Chou Chin Chow was unbeaten with Grant Cann up on him in three adjacent hunts' races and his two hunter chases, at Taunton and Newton Abbot.

As for Bill Shand Kydd's wonderfully consistent Straight Deal mare Matchboard, who started in hunt racing as a five-year-old in 1968, when she lost her maiden certificate at Kimble making her first appearance on a course with her owner up and won three of her four races, she was unbeaten in hunt racing in 1973, giving Shand Kydd four winning rides on her in hunter chases, beating Bullock's Horn comfortably in one of them; and she finished fourth in the Kim Muir amateur riders handicap chase at Cheltenham.

The remarkable thing about this mare, bought for 1,300 guineas at Doncaster, is that she was not even in the stud book then and was only promoted to it in the middle of her racing career. And when she went to stud herself she became the granddam of two Champion Hurdle winners and of One Man.

The new hunter-chase meeting put on by Nick Lees at Leicester, joining those which were already in existence at Folkestone and on an evening at Cheltenham in May, proved a great success, both with the public and the participants; and there ware 56 runners for the five hunter chases plus 68 for the three amateur riders' hurdle races that were also on the card.

The going was heavy, and the fastest of the three 3-mile hunter chases was the first race on the card, a race for maidens won in 6 mins. 46 secs. by John Thorne on Basil Thwaites's nine-year-old John's Joy, a winner of three open races during the season, two of them after the Leicester race, in the second of which he beat the consistent Lord Fortune by half a length. Another of the Leicester winners was Matchboard, who beat Bullock's Horn in her race two races later in a time of 6 mins. 49.9 secs.

Bob Hacking rode his 100th point-to-point winner when scoring on Brough, a horse he won four races on during the season, in the adjacent hunts' race at the

Mid-Surrey Farmers. Tim Rooney, a nephew of the legendary Willie Rooney (a Welshman who made Ireland his spiritual home), and at that time a 16-year-old trainee blacksmith, rode his first winner when scoring on his father's seven-year-old Roughan Again in the maiden race at the Curre.

Nicky Bush rode four of the winners on his home course at the Beaufort; and with one of them, his father's nine-year-old Innisfoil, he was responsible for Sir Kay's first defeat in a point-to-point for two years, though admittedly the placings would probably have been reversed if Sir Kay hadn't been very nearly brought down at the last open ditch and lost almost 15 lengths in the process. Sir Kay's only other defeat in a point-to-point this season was in the Heythrop four-miler.

At the Pytchley, Dunsbrook Lass had her fourth open-race success of the season with her owner up. The Atherstone mare's only defeat in her five appearances was when she failed to complete the course in the Heythrop four-miler.

Royal Charity and John Thorne's home-bred mare Indamelia (bred from a mare he won a novice chase on, Barton's Sister) were not the only horses to break records this season. Another, Mr. C.R. Rendell's Marshalsland, a nine-year-old from the Blackmore & Sparkford Vale, broke two. Carrying a 71b. penalty in the ladies' open at the Mendip Farmers, he smashed the course record at Nedge (a course now defunct) with a time of 5 mins. 59 secs; and later, in a similar race at the Tedworth, he broke the Larkhill course record with a time of 6 mins. dead.

As the best novice seen out this season after Kasim Baba, I don't think I would be far wrong in nominating another of the horses ridden by Grant Cann, Oliver Carter's five-year-old Otter Way, who lost his maiden certificate in style at the South Devon and won his only other race, the adjacent hunts' moderate at the Exmoor on the last day of the season just as convincingly. Otter Way was a name that was to ring many bells in later years.

Having said this, I feel I must also say that two other unbeaten novices, Merchant Banker and Home Cured, were rated higher than Otter Way by Sale & Mackenzie and that Mr. J.T. Emerson's Home Cured, a six-year-old from the Belvoir, had a sequence of five wins with Andrew Berry up.

It is not all that often that race commentators at point-to-points come in for praise. So let me quote what a bookmaker, Desmond Gleeson, wrote about the Oxfordshire farmer Henry Franklin's commentary on a 22-strong maiden race at the Warwickshire fixture at Mollington in a letter to the *Sporting Life*. "It was," he said, "positively the finest piece of commentating I have heard in 25 years – and that includes BBC and ITV."

The death in 1973, at the age of 84, in Warwickshire, of Mrs. Dorothy Freer, the widow of the Jockey Club's senior handicapper, Geoffrey Freer, brings back memories of her numerous successes as an owner of point-to-pointers. Her best-known horse was the French-bred Tailorman, who broke the course record at Upton-on-Severn with a time of 6 mins. 35 seconds when Peter Hobbs won the 1967 Dudley Cup on him. A horse more often than not in the frame, Tailorman won 11 point-to-points with Peter Hobbs up, all but one of them open events. Nor was he Mrs. Freer's only Dudley Cup winner. She also won the 1937 Dudley Cup with her Christopher Bean when the race was run at Crowle, with Geoffrey Shakerley riding him.

As a *tailpiece*, I feel I must choose Ivor Herbert's advice to riders when making the presentation of the *Sporting Life* and *Daily Telegraph* Cups at the national point-to-point dinner in London: "Get up, go straight, and don't fart about." But it wasn't advice he was always able to follow himself. After approaching the last obstacle in a race at Cottenham almost a fence in front of his nearest pursuer, he fell off, and heard an anguished voice shouting. "Stop looking for the bloody horse and win. You're 4-1 on."

1974

In which the ladies get a slight concession, random dope tests are introduced, the Turners scoop the trophy pool, Jenny Pitman makes her début as a trainer of point-to-pointers, and the bookmakers attract comment.

This was the season when lady riders, hitherto restricted in the post-war years to riding against the men only in hunt members' races, were permitted to take them on in adjacent hunts' races other than those confined to maidens.

But although it was a small step in the right direction, and naturally very popular with the public, not everyone favoured the idea. Understandably, I suppose, in the case of some of the more intransigent male riders; but the Lady Jockeys Association was also against it. However, as this Association was largely composed of the Flat-racing brigade, perhaps, after all, this wasn't so surprising.

Another administrative change was that the grant from the Levy Board, which in the past had been based upon the average of the Tote turnover – and which meant that the more successful meetings got most of the money for the maintenance of their courses – would now be paid "solely in respect of utilisation and maintenance".

It sounded fine but, since the meetings were not required to provide any figures, and payment was to be made regardless of expenditure (within an overall maximum of £35,000), clearly those who spent less on their courses would gain more than those who spent most. And this, to use an analogy from the professional front, was akin to putting Bangor and Cartmel on a par with Cheltenham and Ascot.

For a course that was used only once a year there was a grant of £225; while for those used more often it was £225 for the first meeting, £150 for the second, £125 for the third, £100 for the fourth and £50 for the fifth and sixth. Tweseldown and Larkhill, with six and five fixtures respectively, were therefore the major beneficiaries; and as on former occasions, the grants were still paid in the event of a fixture having to be cancelled on account of the weather.

There in not much to say about the random dope tests that made their first appearance on point-to-point courses; and to the best of my knowledge all of them proved negative in this first year of them.

The levels of prize money remained the same, with a maximum of £40 for the winner of an open event, £30 for the winner of any other races and £15 and £10 for horses finishing second and third.

The Players Gold Leaf men's final underwent a move from Newbury to Hereford. The Goya ladies' final continued to be held at Garthorpe during the Melton Hunt Club fixture. The Vaux final, which was a casualty of the weather last season, went ahead at Sedgefield; and Ladbrokes came on the scene with their sponsorship of an £800 final of a Mid-England championship race at Stratford for which there were qualifying races at 14 selected point-to-points in the Midlands.

Meanwhile, the area awards presentations were proliferating and had now extended to Devon & Cornwall. Larkhill was introducing its course championships. And most welcome of all, one-day instructional teach-ins (or seminars, as they are called today) were being introduced under the supervision of the Jockey Club's senior course inspector, Major Val Gorton, and his two deputies, Major Ronnie Hedley-Dent and Mr. Neil Wyatt.

David Turner was the leading male rider of the season and winner of the *Daily Telegraph* Cup for the second time in five years, this time with 26 winners, 12 more than Richard Miller. His sister, Josie Bothway, was the leading lady rider of the season and winner of the *Sporting Life* Cup, also for the second time in five years; and with a score, 20, that was the highest ever achieved by a lady rider in a single season outside Ireland. Two of her 20 wins were in adjacent hunts' races against the men, both at Horseheath. The only other lady rider to reach double figures in 1974 was Herefordshire's Diana Bishop, who rode 16 winners.

And it was David and Josie's father, Joe Turner, a former Master of the Suffolk, who collected the Grand Marnier Trophy at the national point-to-point dinner for the second year running, on this occasion with the 12 wins recorded by his seven-year-old Boy Bumble, a former show jumper who started the season as a maiden and remained unbeaten, setting the seal on his season when David won the Marie Curie novice championship at Garthorpe on him.

All David and Josie's wins were achieved on horses owned and trained by their father, who was again the leading owner of the season, with 46 winners in point-to-points and two in hunter chases. And what about this for statistics? On no fewer than eight occasions, including two in the West Country, at the Stevenstone and the Axe Vale Harriers, brother and sister were both in the winner's enclosures. Their most prolific winners were Boy Bumble, on whom David won seven races and Josie five; and Troopship, on whom Josie won six races and David's four wins included the novice chase at Fakenham which bears his father's name.

But the Turners' was not the only East Anglian stable with stars that shone bright. Another was that of Paul Rackham, then Master of the Suffolk, whose yard near Bury St. Edmunds housed Lake District and Watch Night, two horses trained for him there by Lionel Ensten after being qualified with the Dunston Harriers. With Michael Bloom up on them, Lake District won the Dudley Cup and Watch Night won the Grimthorpe Cup. A truly remarkable double for owner, trainer and rider.

Although there were only five runners for the Dudley Cup on the good to firm ground at Chaddesley Corbett, one of those Lake District had to beat was the dual Dudley Cup winner Mighty Red, who started joint favourite with him at 11-10 after a rush of late money for Alan Cure's local horse had seen Lake District drifting out from 6-4 on.

None of the five runners seemed anxious to make the running and the early pace set by John Chugg on Rave Notice was a slow one. It was taken up later by John de Lisle Wells on Near Way, but neither of these two was to retain a position in the first three; and once Lake District hit the front three fences out the race was as good as over. Bob Woolley made strenuous efforts to get Mighty Red on terms, but Lake District was still on the bit when he passed the post three lengths ahead of his market rival and became the first horse from East Anglia to win this historic race since its inception in 1897.

A nine-year-old by Neron out of the Vulgan mare French Moth, Lake District was a winner of an amateur riders' flat race and two novice hurdles before Paul Rackham bought him for 750 guineas at the Ascot Sales in August 1971 as a six-year-old. His first season in point-to-points was 1973, when he won four races with Michael Bloom up; and in 1974 he had five wins in open events, three of them with David Wales up when Bloom was on the injury list.

Watch Night's win in the 4.5-mile Grimthorpe Cup was accomplished with equal facility. His chief rival in the field of 12 was False Note, the winner of the Heythrop four-miler, who started favourite at 5-4. Watch Night, who could have been backed at 11-4, at a shade better odds than Napoleon Brandy II, the winner of the 4-mile men's open for the Duchess of Northumberland's Cup at the Percy & West Percy, was tracking False Note from the last open ditch; and although hitting the front earlier than Michael Bloom had intended, before the fifth from home, the seven-year-old galloped on resolutely to score by a comfortable three lengths. It is worth remarking, I feel, that both the winner and runner-up had travelled more than 200 miles to get to the meeting.

Brimming with confidence before the race, Lionel Ensten had said of Watch Night, "This horse will win"; and Michael Bloom said afterwards, "The further he went, the stronger he got."

A seven-year-old by Star Moss out of Santa Maria (by Tropique), Watch Night, bought for 975 guineas at Ascot in 1971, had won five times over hurdles for Rackham when he was trained in Norfolk by Rex Carter; but 1974 was the horse's first season in point-to-points, and it gave him three wins, one in an open event at Cottenham before his success in the Grimthorpe Cup, and one afterwards in a hunter chase at Fakenham, where, with Michael Bloom up again, he accounted for Even Harmony,

Paul Rackham is the first owner to win the Dudley Cup and the Grimthorpe Cup with two different horses, though Archie Thomlinson did so with one horse, Paul Pry In 1951, and Joe Ballard followed suit with Cash Account in 1957.

The Heythrop classic attracted the biggest field that has ever gone to the post for it in the 22 years that it had been run, with 29 horses facing the starter on the good to firm ground at Stow-on-the-Wold, and Ladybank, a winner of her two previous open events in big fields at Larkhill and the Beaufort, starting favourite for it with Tim Holland-Martin up.

But they were all put in their place by the Beaufort eight-year-old False Note and his owner-rider, Alastair Cowen, a student at the Royal Agricultural College at Cirencester who, through a combination of dieting and Turkish baths, had shed two and a half stone in order to get down to the riding weight of 12-7.

The finish, however, was quite a dramatic one. Rounding the bend before the last, False Note was being hotly pursued by John Dufosee on Attacker and John de Lisle Wells on his Whaddon Hero, but he showed no signs of weakening and held on to win by half a length and a short head. Ladybank, running a long way below form, finished fifth.

Bought privately from Arthur Stephenson, False Note was winning his sixth race for Cowen, three of them in 1974, when he finished third in the Heart Of All England at Hexham and fourth in the Players Gold Leaf final.

In its single season at Hereford the Players final was the first leg of a notable double for Henry Counsell's eight-year-old Stanhope Street, trained by Ann Harden in her small yard in the Cattistock country and ridden by his regular rider Barry Venn, a Taunton riding instructor.

The going at Hereford was hard, which suited Stanhope Street down to the ground. He took up the running three fences out and easily beat Lord Fortune (from whom he was receiving 8lb.) and Culford Cottage (receiving 2lb. from him).

Three weeks later Stanhope Street was in the field for the *Horse and Hound* Cup at Stratford, where he started favourite and duly obliged. Receiving 7lb. from the Bedale-hunted Weathervane, a winner of three hunter chases during the season, and of four point-to-points the previous season, he got to him on the run-in and beat him by 1.5 lengths.

A winner of four point-to-points and three hunter chases in 1974, by this time Stanhope Street had won 18 races in 29 starts since he first started in point-to-points as a five-year-old, 16 of his wins being for Henry Counsell. The only horse to beat him in 1974 was Max Churches' Rich Rose, who did so twice on the sort of going he disliked. In their list of leading horses of 1974 Sale & Mackenzie had Stanhope Street rated on the same mark as Lord Fortune at 11-11, 31b. below their top-rated horse, Chris Collins's Hilbirio, who made a single appearance when winning a hunter chase at Stratford in early February. Rich Rose, who won six point-to-points on the trot with Richard Miller up, was rated at 11-3!

For the Goya ladies' final at Garthorpe there were runners from as far afield as Scotland (Bonnie Dundee), Lancashire (Ferriby) and Herefordshire (Lucky Myth and the well-supported Velvet Coat, a winner of seven races with Diana Bishop up). Culford Cottage started favourite, marginally ahead of Headsprite, the horse Fizz Chown was riding for her uncle, Eric Robarts.

The going was good, thanks to a highly efficient watering system and some recent rain. Approaching the downhill fence three from home it was a three-horse race. Culford Cottage was leading from Headsprite, with Jane Thorne now getting a great run out of Indian Diva just behind them; but whilst she got the mare past Culford Cottage, she could not reach Headsprite, who was being eased as he passed the post a length ahead of Indian Diva, with Culford Cottage six lengths behind in third.

The winner's time of 6 mins. 10 secs. equalled the course record set up by Richard Woodhouse when winning the men's open on his Highworth in 1970. So it seemed that in the eight-year-old Headsprite, a horse bought for 5,600 guineas at Ascot from Tony Dickinson, for whom he won three times over hurdles and twice over fences, Mrs. Chown had the ideal successor-in-waiting to Royal Charity. Especially as Headsprite was unbeaten in the six races she rode him in, his only defeat being in a hunter chase at Ascot, where, with Dick Saunders up on him, he had finished third behind Forest Rock and Matchboard.

The outstanding ladies' horse in northern parts was Sir Guy Cunard's Middleton-hunted Glasserton. A winner six times over hurdles, this nine-year-old, bought at Doncaster for 720 guineas, was in the winner's enclosure on seven occasions, ridden each time by Sir Guy's head 'lad' Anne Sturdy. His single defeat in his last race of the season was when he ran out five fences from home at the Bramham Moor after he had established a commanding lead. He finished very sore after this race, but it wasn't to prevent him from continuing the good work the following season. Glasserton was rated on the same mark as Headsprite by Sale & Mackenzie, at 11-3.

But the distinction of being the first lady to win an adjacent hunts' race against the men belonged to Diana Bishop, whose seven-times winner, the Golden Valley 11-year-old Velvet Coat, scored for her in the adjacent hunts' race at the Brecon on March 9 in a field of 17.

Another prolific winner of ladies' races was the West Country seven-year-old Galloway Fabulous, who started the season as a maiden and won seven of them on the trot with the West Country ladies' champion Katie Halswell riding him.

Debonair Boy was unbeaten in his five open races with Richard Miller up, and in one of them he accounted for Miller's former ride, All A Myth; and in another for Chatham.

And a very big impact was made by a very little horse, Kevin Bishop's owner-ridden Cass, a nine-year-old hunted with the West Somerset Vale who had been bought for 200 guineas at Bridgwater Fair and stood 15.3 h.h.

Cass won eight of his 13 races, one of them a hunter chase at Newton Abbot, and was a runner-up on three occasions, twice to Troopship, at the Axe Vale Harriers and the Silverton, and once to False Note in a Players Gold Leaf qualifier at the Mendip Farmers; and when he won the open race at the Exmoor on the last day of the season he was one of only two horses to record a time under six minutes. The other was Marshalsland, recording his sixth win of the season with Fay Geddes in a time of 5 mins. 48 secs., which must surely have been a record for the Bratton Down course.

But the one who came closest to reaching Boy Bumble's score of 12 wins, apart from Troopship, was a soldier's horse, the 11-year-old Bob's Birthday, formerly an unsuccessful hurdler and now owned by Major Downs of the Royal Horse Artillery. In his 13 appearances, ridden by three different riders, Bob's Birthday also won ten races, eight of them with Sgt. Doug Robson of the School of Artillery at Larkhill riding him. His other successes were in the Grand Military hunters' chase at Sandown, where Capt. Price rode him, and, on his first appearance in an Army Saddle Club race at Tweseldown, where he was ridden by the Olympic Three-Day

Event rider Major James Templér.

Jenny Pitman made her début an a trainer, in the year before she took out a licence as one, at the Staff College & R.M.A.S. point-to-point at Tweseldown on February 9, and saddled a winner with her first runner. The horse she did it with was Lord Cadogan's Road Race, an animal who, as she has said in her autobiography, *Glorious Uncertainty*, "had lost all interest in racing," but "became one of my most loyal servants, the foundation stone upon which my professional training career was built." She also had this to say about him: "He was everything I would not want in a racehorse: long, spindly legs, a club foot, a lanky great body, and the ugliest old face you ever set eyes on."

At Tweseldown, however, in a division of the men's open, in which he was ridden by the 17-year-old Bryan Smart (who was later to become a trainer himself and saddle the winner of the French Oaks 22 years further on), he ran the race of his life, with his young rider riding a similar one on him, when getting him up near the line to beat Sir Kay by a neck, with the useful John's Joy three lengths away in third in the field of 15.

This was not Road Race's only success for Jenny. Although he was beaten on his next visit to Tweseldown, he was unbeaten thereafter, winning four more races and putting up particularly fine performances when scoring by a short head with Nicky Henderson up on him in the Old Etonian & Old Harrovian race at the Heythrop; and winding up his season winning the 4-mile Lord Savernake Gold Cup race at the Tedworth with Bryan Smart up on him again.

Another of Jenny's point-to-point winners, the second leg of a double for her at the Heythrop with Dick Saunders up, was High Tide, a former racehorse with leg problems who came to her as a gift. This nine-year-old was also a winner for her at the Army fixture at Tweseldown with Stephen Stanhope up. He didn't actually pass the post first there in his division of the open event but was promoted when it was found that the horse who did, Chatham, the 1970 Mackeson Gold Cup winner, had shed his weight cloth.

Corrie Burn, an eight-year-old mare from the Tynedale, surprised quite a lot of people when he concluded an otherwise somewhat indifferent season of hunt racing winning the Cheltenham Foxhunters' at the expense of Credit Call and Bear's Slipper. His starting price was 20-1. He did, in fact, run in one other race afterwards, the Scottish Grand National at Ayr won by Red Rum; and in this, with a former champion amateur up in the shape of Michael Dickinson, he was tenth of the 13 finishers.

The late George Maundrell's stallion Romany Air sired his 100th point-to-point winner when Mervyn Fear's April Gypsy, a mare bred by her owner from April Queen, the mare he won the Liverpool Foxhunters' with in 1970, scored in the adjacent hunts' maiden race at the Beaufort. Romany Air then promptly made it 101 when another of his progeny, Dancing Air, won the next race, division 3 of the men's open. Hope Again, who finished third to Dancing Air, was also by Romany Air, as was Horoscope, the mare who finished second to Marshalsland in the ladies' open at the Beaufort and was twice in the winner's enclosure during the season. By this time Romany Air had reached the age of 23 and was standing at the Lanhill Stud at Chippenham.

April Gypsy went on to win two more races with 20-year-old Robert Fear up and won twice again when Sue Aston, having broken her arm in two places in a fall at the Beaufort, returned to the fray two months later on her. Dancing Air won a hunter chase at Stratford with Nicky Bush up after her Beaufort success.

James Delahooke's good old Whaddon Chase horse Halfacrown, a winner of six races during the season, recorded his 20th win in point-to-points at the age of 13 when winning at the Oakley; and by the end of the season he had amassed a grand total of 24 wins, all but one of them with his owner up.

The Welsh rider Mike Williams rode his 100th winner at the Brecon (where there were 140 runners for the nine races!) two days before celebrating his 31st birthday; and David Naylor-Leyland, who was to make quite a name for himself in later years when Henrietta Knight was training his horses, rode his first winner at the age of 18 when winning the hunt race at the V.W.H. on Hidden Glance by a short head. And I mustn't omit to mention, because it was a rare feat in those days, that Joe Turner saddled four of the winners at the Dunston Harriers on their new course at the Royal Norfolk Showground at Costessey, with David winning on Boy Bumble, Culford Cottage and Cannycrack, and Josie taking the ladies' open on Hazy Dream, all of them owned by their father.

At the Warwickshire fixture at Mollington, where the first random dope tests took place on March 16 (with predictable results), there was a bonanza for a distinguished family. Diana Thorne won the hunt race on her Bright Daisy, Jane won the Goya qualifier on her Indian Diva, and their father won a division of the maiden race on his home-bred five-year-old General Diva, a half-brother, by Spartan General, to Indian Diva. John Thorne was a very brave man when it came to riding untried maidens, and it was to prove his undoing in the end.

1 have to say, though, that the most impressive winner at Mollington was the North Cotswold mare Ladybank, who made light of the testing going in the Players Gold Leaf qualifier and scored in the fastest time of the day, 6 mins. 40 secs. The nearest approach to this was Indian Diva's time of 6 mins. 46 secs. Ladybank, who was recording her fourth successive win, one of them in the previous season, was, as usual, beautifully turned out by her regular rider, Tim Holland-Martin, who had her in his yard at Overbury, near Tewkesbury.

There was another family bonanza at the North Shropshire, this time featuring the Brookshaws. Steven Brookshaw completed a double on two of the horses bred by his mother, Gwen Brookshaw, Mickley Belle in a division of the restricted open and Mickley Love Story in the maiden race; and Steven's older brother Peter won the other division of the restricted open on Mickley Seabright, a half-brother to Mickley Belle. So it was a family treble of home-breds. The other side of the story was that both Peter Jnr. and Peter Snr. found themselves on the floor in the hunt race.

Bill Shand Kydd had mixed fortunes with his splendid mare Matchboard. After winning two-hunter chasers on her, at Wolverhampton and Kempton, he found himself on a sequence of runners-up. The mare was beaten a short head trying to give Lord Fortune 51b. in a hunter chase at Leicester. At her second attempt to win the Kim Muir at Cheltenham she was beaten a neck by the Irish invader Castleruddery, to whom she was conceeding 191b.; and in her last race of the season she went under by half a length trying to give Forest Rock 51b. in a hunter chase at Ascot, where she had Headsprite behind her. She earned this epitaph in Sale & Mackenzie: "One of the great hunter chasers, who would have been really brilliant but for being troubled by splints in the past."

The Vaux Breweries final at Sedgefield saw Fezeyot, a five-year-old from the Eglinton, setting the seal on a season in which he won four of his five races, including another hunter chase at Kelso. Jolly's Clump, an eight-year-old from the Quorn with six wins in hunter chases behind him in 1973, including the John Corbet Cup at Stratford, made it seven with John Docker up when winning the first running of the Ladbroke Mid-England championship at Stratford by 20 lengths; and Chris Collins's six-year-old Cornwallis, another of the horses trained for him by Arthur Stephenson, finished his promising season winning the Adam Scott Memorial hunter chase at Hexham and the John Corbet Cup at Stratford with his owner up.

Around this time bookmakers at point-to-points were getting quite a lot of stick in letters written to the *Sporting Life*, although they did have their defendants, and one of them Michael Rolfe, a well-known contributor to the paper, went so far as to describe them as "a gentlemanly crowd of fellows," which drew the following comment from a certain Paul Mathieu: "Either the English language is becoming devalued or Mr. Rolfe is stone deaf."

However, another correspondent was writing, "There are good and bad in every profession," and he went on to nominate as a credit to the fraternity: Charlie Ball (now unhappily deceased) of Reading, R.F. Hill of Leominster, Gordon Power of Cardiff, John Richards of Worcester and Jack Lynn of Devon. He might perhaps have added the names of Gary Wiltshire and Desmond Gleeson to this lot; and there were, of course, others.

In November, ace photographer Jim Meads received a well-deserved ovation when he was presented at the national point-to-point dinner in London with the dinner committee's inscribed salver for outstanding service to the sport. And in December, Sue Aston married the Beaufort rider David Horton, much to everyone's delight.

> *Tailpiece* from David Turner after he had won the Marie Curie Foundation novice championship at the Melton Hunt Club fixture on Boy Bumble, the most prolific winner of the season: "Pity he hasn't got more speed, otherwise he would be a good animal."
> Reply from his father: "What the Hell, then, were you doing waiting at the back of the field for so long?"

1975

*In which BMW appears on the scene, the Turners do it again, Royal
Charity breaks another record, the Jockey Club is castigated, and
tribute is paid to a great West Countryman.*

The 1975 season saw a welcome reversion from the repressive rule barring
from point-to-points horses that had run under Rules since July 1st of the
previous year. The date was now extended to the old November 1st one; and
possibly this had something to do with the fact that there was a distinct increase
in the number of horses running in point-to-points.

There was also some good news from the Levy Board with the raising of the
ceiling of its grant for point-to-points to £45,000; and whilst prize money
remained at the same modest level, there was a slight increase in the permitted
value of mememtoes, from £25 to the value of the winner's prize money.

But there was to be more bad news from the Horserace Totalisator Board with
the announcement that the number of meetings without an official Tote would be
increased to 100.

An increasing number of meetings were, however, running their own Totes.
One of them was the Heythrop, where the following note appeared on the racecard: "The Tote offers you today both Win Betting and a Tote Double and Tote
Treble," followed by the observation that "The Tote has been forced to withdraw
the provision of facilities at one-third of all point-to-points because of the very low
turnover at some meetings and heavy demand on their staff on Saturdays and
Bank Holidays." Needless to say, voluntary labour was called upon by those meetings running their own Totes.

The sponsorship situation was somewhat mixed, with Ladbrokes opting out of
their Mid-England Championship, and Players giving way to BMW
Concessionaires in the case of the men's championship race, for which there were
qualifying races at 24 point-to-points and a £3,500 final on a new venue at
Chepstow. One of the qualifying meetings for this was in Northern Ireland at the
East Antrim Harriers fixture.

Chris Collins's Goya ladies' championship at Garthorpe was still going strong
in its fourth year, as were the *Daily Telegraph* and *Sporting Life* Cups for the leading

riders' contests, now in their ninth year. The Grand Marnier contest for the most prolific winner of the season was now in its sixth year; and there was some extension of the regional championships which had been pioneered in the South East by the champagne house of Laurent Perrier, who, whilst continuing with their sponsorship in the South East, were extending their activities to the West Midlands and the Midlands, and combining with grain merchants Pauls & Whites of Ipswich to sponsor small owners' and novice riders' championships in East Anglia.

In the Northern Area, the Kelso saddler A.C.M. Porter was sponsoring a championship for male riders, and the Berwickshire farm-building consultants Peter K. Dale Ltd. were doing likewise with one for lady riders; while as well at the Vaux at Sedgefield we were now to have a John Player Special point-to-point championship at Catterick for which there were also qualifying races at point-to-points.

Not only was Joe Turner once again the leading owner of the season, but his domination of the major trophies continued, with David, on a score of 24, taking the *Daily Telegraph* Cup for the third time, ten winners ahead of the joint runners-up, Grant Cann and Robin Greenway; Josie, the only lady rider to get into double figures, winning the *Sporting Life* Cup with 17 winners, eight ahead of joint runners-up Mary Crouch (the former Mary O'Shaughnessy) and Guy Cunard's head 'lad' Anne Sturdy; and Joe again securing the Grand Marnier Trophy with the 11 wins recorded in point-to-points by Even Harmony, who also won a hunter chase at Fakenham with David up.

When collecting his trophy at the national point-to-point dinner Joe Turner revealed that the three horses he had won the Grand Marnier with had all been bought for less than £1,500. Master Vesuvius, his 1973 winner, cost him £375, Boy Bumble, his 1974 winner, £600; and Even Harmony £400; and he went on to say that the ceiling of prize money permitted by the Jockey Club for point-to-points was so low that he might have to turn himself into a blacksmith. It is fair to say, though, that not everyone felt the same way. The Dorset rider Richard Miller had always maintained that the prize money on offer was just about right. But he, of course, was not speaking as an owner.

The Turner yard sustained one great loss during the season. After winning an early ladies' race at Higham, the eight-year-old Boy Bumble broke his neck when he was brought down in a men's open at Cottenham. A winner of 13 races for him, Boy Bumble was bought by Joe Turner after he had seen him win in the ring in Dublin as a yearling; the horse's first season in-point-to-points, in 1972 as a five-year-old, was an inauspicious one, and in 1973 he was showjumping. But in 1974 he carried all before him with his 12 wins.

Another big winner for the Turner yard was Culford Cottage, who lost his maiden certificate in 1971 in the fastest time of the day as a six-year-old at the Suffolk fixture at Ampton. In 1975 the ten-year-old won four races with David up and four with Josie up; and by the end of the season he had accumulated a grand total of 31 wins in point-to-points and four wins in hunter chases at Fakenham.

But the most prolific point-to-point winner of the season after Even Harmony was Sir Guy Cunard's horse from the bargain basement, Glasserton, a 720 guineas purchase at Doncaster. After being beaten by Owenogue at the South Durham on his first appearance, this ten-year-old won his nine other races under Anne Sturdy virtually unchallenged. There were few, if any, better horses seen out in ladies' races during the season than this chesnut son of Sea Wolf out of a mare by Lord of Verona, and certainly none that were better turned out.

Another to establish himself as one of the top ladies' horses was Tim Frost's Seavington seven-year-old Prince Rock, who started the season as a maiden and was unbeaten in his seven races under Gillian Fortescue-Thomas, who trained him on his owner's farm at Beaminster. Mrs. Fortescue-Thomas had already made a name for herself as a member of British Leyland's motor-racing team, and she was making another on Prince Rock, whose victims during the season included such distinguished performers as Galloway Fabulous and Horoscope, the former a winner of six races and the latter of five.

It was a great pity that Prince Rock wasn't seen in the Goya ladies' final at Melton, though he had of course qualified for it; and the same applies to Glasserton. Horoscope, however, was in the field, and the Romany Air mare from the Beaufort ran a fine race under Rosemary White, though outpaced in the closing stages by Diana Thorne's mount Ben Ruler and beaten a length. A further length away in third was the 1972 winner Piraeus, who also ran a good race.

A winner of six of his 12 previous races during the season, two with Diana Thorne up and the other four with her twin sister Jane riding, the well-bred Ben Ruler, by Indian Ruler, was bred by John Thorne at his Chesterton Stud in Warwickshire from a mare, Lady Macbeth, Thorne had won a maiden point-to-point on. So, with Indian Ruler being by Sayajirao and Lady Macbeth by Scottish Union, Ben Ruler had a St. Leger winner on both sides of his pedigree.

Another classy-looking winner at Melton was Rod Millington's Sidney, the six-year-old son of Indian Ruler who completed his hat-trick in the Marie Curie novice championship in the hands of his 43-year-old owner-rider, who had hunted him with the Fernie since acquiring him unraced out of James Delahooke's yard.

Hitting the front four fences out, the long-striding Sidney proved more than a match for his only serious challenger, Joey Newton's mount Nelson IV, who was meeting with his only defeat of the season after winning five races.

Sidney, bought for Millington at the Doncaster Sales in January for 1,500 guineas by the Northumberland-based Portman Bloodstock Agency, which had been founded a year earlier by Ivor Herbert, David Smyly, Aynsley Ridley and Arthur Moore, was a horse with an interesting background. He was bred by Mrs. Donald North at her Aynho Stud near Banbury and was the first foal of Jeannie Cook, an unraced mare by Flush Royal; and he was named after, the late great Sidney MacGregor, the breeder, among others, of Indian Ruler, the 1932 Derby winner April The Fifth (owned by the actor Tom Walls), the 1958 Ascot Gold Cup winner Gladness, and many of the first Lord Bicester's best jumpers. Mrs. North, who had the greatest admiration for Sidney MacGregor, told him that if ever she bred "a really good-looking one" she would name him after him.

At six years old, Sidney was a year younger than the best horse in the West Country, Oliver Carter's Otter Way, who was unbeaten in his six point-to-points with Grant Cann up and wound up his season winning the John Corbet Cup at

Stratford with the same rider in the saddle.

Grant Cann was also associated with another very useful horse of Carter's, the nine-year-old Lucky Rock, who, like Otter Way (a son of Salmonway Spirit), was also sired by a premium stallion, in his case Spiritus, both of them out of an unknown dam.

Lucky Rock, a winner of four open races in his eight appearances, which included some in hunter chases and some in ladies' races, was actually rated 4lb. higher, at 11-7, than Otter Way by Sale & Mackenzie in their annual, which by this time had come under the umbrella of *Horse and Hound* and was being published by IPC Magazines Ltd. Prince Rock, incidentally, had a rating of 11-1 and Sidney of 11-0.

The Portman ten-year-old Debonair Boy, who hadn't been beaten since losing his maiden certificate in 1971 and was rated at 11-3 by Sale & Mackenzie, had his 15th win in a division of the Coronation Cup open race at Larkhill's United Services fixture in February; and although he broke down in his next race there, he was in the winner's enclosure again two years later.

In the Grafton country, owner-trainer Graham Pidgeon's eight-year-old mare Last Look was beginning to fulfil the promise she had revealed when losing her maiden certificate at the Atherstone two years beforehand in no uncertain manner. Ridden each time by the Leicestershire rider Didi Morris, Last Look won seven ladies' races in six different counties; and the only time she was beaten was on her first appearance of the season when she unseated her rider at Cottenham.

For the first time in its long history at Fox Farm, Stow-on-the-Wold, the four-mile men's open for Lord Ashton of Hyde's Cup at the Heythrop, where the meeting was now in its second year of sponsorship by Veuve Clicquot, had to be run in two divisions. Out of an original entry of 74, there were 11 runners for the first division and nine for the second.

The races were run on soft ground; but the comparative sparsity of the fields was almost certainly due to the fact that the meeting had been postponed for a week on account of the weather. The second division was the better of the two, and it was run in three seconds faster time. Richard Miller won it very easily on Max Churches' ten-year-old Rich Rose, who drew clear four fences out and finished with 25 lengths in hand of the 1974 winner, False Note.

Take Cover, an eight-year-old from the Portman who was being ridden by his owner, James Brown, was a somewhat fortunate winner of the other division. The Warwickshire eight-year-old Poker, a gelding by the premium stallion Game Rights, was several lengths clear when George Hyatt asked him for a big one at the last and he came down. In their subsequent ratings, Sale & Mackenzie had Rich Rose at 11-0, Poker at 10-11 and Take Cover at 10-8.

Rich Rose's attempt to land the second of the season's classics just failed. In the race for the Lady Dudley Cup at the Worcestershire he was beaten a short head by the Brookshaws' home-bred Mickley Seabright, who, splendidly ridden by Peter Brookshaw Jnr., got up on the line after being headed half-way up the run-in by Rich Rose and coming again. Both riders, it should be said, were seen at their best. Sea Moss, the sire of Mickley Seabright, was also the sire of Reg Hindley's Prospero, on whom Peter Brookshaw Snr. had won a division of the 1957 Dudley Cup.

There was one more race for the 1975 Dudley Cup winner and runner-up, and it showed how much the two horses had taken out of themselves with their exertions. Mickley Seabright was pulled up before the third last in the BMW men's final at Chepstow; and Rich Rose broke down in the course of finishing a length and a half behind a horse he was trying to give 7 1b. to in the four-mile race at the Tedworth.

Twenty went to the post for the BMW final, and there was a 20-1 winner when William Barker's Zetland mare Jaunty Jane went on from two fences out under John Ormston after the two pacemakers, Even Harmony and Alexangle, joint third in the betting behind Tartan Slave and Otter Way, had all but cut each other's throats. Jaunty Jane scored by a length and a half from Otter Way, with Alexangle two lengths back in third under his owner-rider, Dr. David Chesney. Even Harmony, with David Turner up, finished sixth, just in front of Tartan Slave, a winner of two open point-to-points and a 3.5-mile hunter chase at Warwick.

In her previous appearances during the season the seven-year-old Jaunty Jane had won the men's open races at the Zetland and the combined Badsworth & Rockwood Harriers and been placed in her other three open events. She had one other race after the BMW when she turned out for the new John Player Special final at Catterick, where she was leading three out but had dropped back to third when she fell at the last.

The Players race was comfortably won by the nine-year-old Colonian Queen, who was recording her fifth successive win of the season, and her 17th for her Cheshire owner, Mr. A.J. Lilley, who bought her for 4,500 guineas out of Alan Smith's Yorkshire yard when she came up for sale at Ascot prior to the 1971 point-to-point season, when she was one of the outstanding novices. At Catterick Dick Saunders had the ride on her, but her pilot in most of her other races for Mr. Lilley was Robin Greenway, who was up on her when she was one of his five winners at the Cheshire Hunt fixture – a feat for which he was presented with the inscribed salver for special services to the sport at the national point-to-point dinner in September.

The Grimthorpe Cup at the Middleton attracted a field of 17 out of an original entry of 30. It was not, however, a vintage Grimthorpe. Escamist, the best horse entered for it, a winner of six races on the trot under his Southwold owner James Walker, declined the engagement, as did Mr. Toby, the winner of the four-mile race at the Percy.

The favourite was a horse hunted in Yorkshire with the Badsworth, Highlands Imp, a winner of a hunter chase at Market Rasen. But the victor was a horse from Scotland, Falling Leaves, owned by Mrs. John Gilmour and ridden by her husband, a Joint Master of the Fife. The 11-year-old mare, comprehensively outstaying the South Durham ten-year-old Mell Cloud (who was preferred to her in the betting) and Highlands Imp, was getting a nice reward for her consistency. Although this was her one and only win of the season, she had been placed in all seven of her previous races with John Gilmour up.

The four-mile ladies' open at the Middleton was won by a horse who had lost his maiden certificate in his previous race, the locally-hunted six-year-old Waggoners Walk, a first winner for his rider, 19-year-old Caroline Mason. Making steady progress through the field, Waggoners Walk came from behind to lead at the last and beat Amanda Jemmeson's mount Tseraen by 1.5 lengths. By the premium stallion Kadir Cup, Waggoners Walk was bred by his owner, George Mason, from his mare Mystery Walk, by the local stallion Top Walker. Eight years earlier, Caroline's elder sister, Patricia, had won the same race on her own mare Woodland Maiden.

Mary Crouch was well mounted on two of the star performers in the South East, Eric Covell's Crawley & Horsham pair Newcastle and Scar. The four races she won on the 12-year-old Newcastle included one in an adjacent hunts' race against the men at the Chiddingfold, Leconfield & Cowdray fixture which in those days was held in Cowdray Park at Midhurst; and Newcastle had a fifth success in a similar race with David Evatt up. Seven-year-old Scar was a winner of four ladies' opens in his eight appearances.

Making his retirement appearance at the age of 12, Fizz Chown's Royal Charity broke his eighth course record when, in his only race this season, he put up a time of 6 mins. 27 secs. in making the running from pillar to post in the ladies' open at the Oakley over the stayers' course at Newton Bromswold unchallenged from the very useful Ben Ruler. Royal Charity finished his career for Fizz with 17 wins in 22 appearances.

There was also a notable retirement on the riders' front when Frank Ryall, the doyen of West Country racing, bowed out at the age of 53 soon after riding his 218th point-to-point winner when winning the adjacent hunts' maiden race at the Bolventor Harriers on commentator Peter Wakeham's In Again, an eight-year-old half-brother to the 1986 Grand National winner West Tip.

A shock was in store for Jenny Pitman, paying another visit to Tweseldown in the year she was later to take out her licence as a professional trainer. Young Tam, her runner in the adjacent hunts' race at the Staff College & R.M.A. Draghounds fixture on the opening day of the season with Bryan Smart up, looked to most observers on the line to have done enough to get the verdict over Orientalist, and certainly Jenny thought so herself. The judge, however, thought otherwise and gave the verdict to Orientalist, by a head. When Young Tam returned to the unsaddling enclosure Orientalist was already occupying the runner-up's stall. So some weight was given to the general feeling that the judge had got it wrong in depriving Young Tam's owner, Basingstoke farmer Ted Knight, of what would have been his first winner.

After this incident there appeared in the *Sporting Life* a letter from Edward Dingle (well known in later years as a commentator at point-to-points and as Editor of the national point-to-point video) reading as follows: "I, and no doubt 99.9% of the other racegoers anywhere near the winning post, would agree that Young Tam beat Orientalist and were astounded when the race was 'given' to the latter"; and he went on to remark, "Point-to-point committees could do themselves, and the paying public would support them, a lot of good by moving the judge's box off the rails about 15 yards, but obviously still in line with the winning post." Which is more or less what the Tweseldown authorities did afterwards. Jenny Pitman's comment on losing the race was: "I don't mind being beaten, but it is a bit much when you've won by a neck, going away."

For one point-to-point personality there was near-tragedy. The West Midlands rider Colin Jackson fractured his spine in a fall at the Cotswold Vale Farmers at Andoversford in mid-May and, after a spell in Stoke Mandeville and later in Cheltenham General, was confined to a wheel-chair. A fund was started for him by Alan Cure, Tim Holland-Martin and Jack Baylis; and a substantial sum was raised for it at, among other places, the national point-to-point dinner in September.

It was at this dinner, which was then still being held in London, that the Labour peer Lord Paget (the same Reggie Paget who was an impassioned foxhunter and had still been riding in point-to-points at the age of 64) delivered his attack on the Jockey Club for its excessively tight control of point-to-point racing and refusal to permit an increase in prize money.

Point-to-point racing, he maintained, was well able to look after itself and didn't need the Jockey Club to tell them what to do about it. But these views were, in part, contradicted by Chris Glyn (the subsequent Lord Wolverton), who was in the Chair as usual and revealed that it was the fault of the M.F.H. Association, and not the Jockey Club, that the prize money for point-to-points remained as low as it was.

Although he had now changed hands, whilst still being trained by Arthur Stephenson, and passed into the ownership of the Hon. Mrs. R.L. Newton (the famous "Urky") in the Belvoir country, Credit Call continued to excel in the hunter-chase field with Mrs. Newton's son Joey up; and once again the 11-year-old brought off a notable double in winning the Liverpool Foxhunters' and the *Horse and Hound* Cup at Stratford, where he was scoring for the fourth time.

The joint favourites for the Liverpool race were Lord Fortune and Moor Lad (an eight-year-old from the Fife), both with a single previous win on their first appearance of the season. Credit Call, also with one previous win on his first appearance of the season, started at 6-1. Taking up the running two fences from home, he ran on strongly to beat Lord Fortune (giving him 21b.) by 21 lengths. Moor Lad, the leader four fences out, had been headed by Credit Call when he fell at the second last.

This was the 18-year-old Joey Newton's second winner under Rules in a season which saw him ending up as the leading rider in hunter chases with ten winners to his credit.

A month after winning at Liverpool, Credit Call was in the winner's enclosure at Newcastle; and his triumph at Stratford, where he got up on the run-in to beat Lucky Rock by three parts of a length was his fourth hunter-chase success of the season. He did, however, have some luck there. The Embiricos runner French Colonist (a son of Colonist II) was looking all over a winner when he came down in the lead at the last.

A winner of two of his five hunter chases during the season, and a runner-up to Forest Rock in another, French Colonist had won six chases and a hurdle race before he started in hunt racing. The ten-year-old was rated at 11-10 by Sale & Mackenzie on his 1975 form and had only one horse placed above him, Forest Rock, at 11-12.

Forest Rock, a ten-year-old son of Master Owen, was unquestionably the major star in the South East Area, where he had been hunted with the Chiddingfold, Leconfield & Cowdray. Owned and ridden by Paul Wates, and trained by Paul's brother Andrew at Beare Green in Surrey, Forest Rock was unbeaten in his four hunter chases in 1975; and he also finished second, beaten a neck with the same rider up, in a handicap chase at Ludlow trying to give the winner over a stone. A winner over fences and hurdles in Ireland, he started in hunt racing for the Wates in 1974, when he won two hunter chases with Paul up and one with Andrew riding him.

The death during the season of East Anglia's Walter Wales at the age of 80 removed not only a colourful character from the scene but a highly successful producer and rider of point-to-pointers who had his first win with a horse he bought for a fiver. Those with long enough memories will certainly remember the names of King High and Salvage, those two marvellous horses owned, trained and ridden by Walter. In pre-war days, King High was a winner of 28 races in 33 starts, with Walter winning 26 of them on him; and in the days after the war, Salvage was also a name to conjure with. More often than not in the winner's enclosure, this Irish mare gave Walter a wonderful ride at the age of 57 in the Cheltenham Foxhunters' of 1951.

After making most of the running, Salvage finished third to Halloween. But there was some irony about this result because, as a result of flooding in March, the race had been postponed until late April with the entries re-opened, and neither Halloween nor the runner-up, Ramright, had been among the original entries. Happily, the familiar fawn and check colours carried so successfully by Walter are still seen today on the horses owned by his son David and ridden by his grandson William.

> *Tailpiece* from Ian Balding after presenting the Grand Marnier Trophy to Joe Turner at the national point-to-point dinner: "I was just a little sad not to be making the presentation to the runner-up, Sir Guy Cunard, because I had passed on the advice Guy gave to his apprentices – 'If you can't get through, just push them through the rails'."

1976

*In which lady riders get a major concession, the Jockey Club lays
down a minimum age for all riders, a rank outsider wins the Grimthorpe
Cup, and the Turners go marching on.*

1976 was quite a year for concessions. The Beaufort opened its hunt race to
lady riders for the first time; and the Jockey Club made a two-fold concession
in allowing ladies to ride in all races at point-to-points save those open events
which were confined by the local conditions to male riders, whilst also permitting
the ladies to ride under N.H. Rules.

The first woman to ride against the men in an open point-to-point was Sue
Horton (née Aston), who put up over three stone of dead weight in order to ride
the Taunton Vale nine-year-old Earl Mouse in Div. 2 of the Coronation Cup mixed
open at Larkhill's United Services fixture and rode one of the best races of her
career to win it.

Seizing the inside berth after her horse had jumped the second last in third
place, she hurled him into the last like a true professional and got him home in a
driving finish by a length and a neck from Robert Waley-Cohen on Connello and
Geoff White on Time Out. Admittedly the time was six seconds slower than that
taken by Derek Edmunds to win the earlier division on Lord Fortune, and 11 seconds slower than Godfrey Maundrell's on Lafitte in Div. 3. But then Earl Mouse
was a horse of lesser pretensions than either of these two; and it was the way the
race was won that was so impressive.

Sue Horton also became the first lady rider to win the hunt race at the Beaufort
when she won it on her father-in-law's mare Straight Lane, seeing off Nicky Bush
on Innisfoil and Tony Harris on Gusserane. Asked what he felt about this result,
the Duke of Beaufort said, "All right."

The first woman to ride against the men over fences under Rules since the regulations were changed was Diana Thorne. Riding her father's Ben Ruler in a hunter
chase at Stratford in early February, she scored by a neck from her father on another of his horses, the Spartan General seven-year-old Air General.

The new rule stipulating that all riders must have reached the age of 16 before
being eligible to ride in point-to-points was a step forward for female riders but a

step backwards for male riders when one considers that the Bob Davies who was later to become a leading professional was no more than 14 when he had his first winning ride in a point-to-point on Green Turban in the hunt race at the South Shropshire in 1961; and while it is true that the Sussex rider Angela Covell was only 15 when she shared the ladies' point-to-point title with the West Country's Marigold Coke in 1947, in 1962 the minimum age for lady riders in point-to-points had been set at 18.

Another significant change in the regulations was the introduction of a safety factor regarding the number of runners in each race, and this was supposed to be stated on the racecard. Thus, on the Heythrop card it was 35 for the open races, 25 for the maiden race and 30 for the other races. But it did, of course, vary according to the characteristics of the course and the views of the clerks of the course and course inspectors; and it is interesting to see that for the Lady Dudley Cup at the Worcestershire at that time it was 25, the same as for the ladies' open there. I have looked in vain to see what it was for the Lord Grimthorpe Cup at the Middleton and the other races there.

One could say, I suppose, that the Turners' continuing monopoly of the major point-to-point trophies was getting to be a bit too much of a good thing. But it was certainly well deserved; and another fact in its favour was that it was achieved with their own horses; on one occasion they had a win as far afield as Yorkshire when Josie Bothway rode a brilliant race on Hardcastle, carrying a 101b. penalty, to beat Potentate in the ladies' open at the Badsworth & Rockwood Harriers at Wetherby.

Josie took the *Sporting Life* Cup for the fourth time, with a score of 17 on five different horses. Her most prolific winner was Hardcastle, on whom she won eight times; and at the Essex Farmers fixture at Beeleigh she brought off a treble, winning the adjacent hunts' race on Pennyman (a horse on whom she had five successes during the season), the ladies' open on Hardcastle and the adjacent hunts' maiden on the six-year-old Star Buck.

Besides all this, she distinguished herself in another field of activity, winning the Waterford Crystal Jockeys' Show Jumping Championship on the opening night of the Horse of the Year Show at Wembley's Empire Pool. Riding her father's Stratheden (on whom her brother David had won this championship twice), she was one of only two riders to have a clear round in a field of 24. The other was Philip Blacker, who did so in slower time.

The runner-up to Josie Bothway for the ladies' title, and the only other lady rider to reach double figures, was Mrs. Mary Crouch, who had another brilliant season on Eric Covell's Crawley & Horsham pair, winning eight races on Scar and six on Newcastle; and making it 15 wins with a success in the four-mile ladies' open for the Lady Leigh Cup at the North Warwickshire on a horse she was riding for the first time, Mrs. Rita Watkins's six-year-old Monmouthshire mare Tennessee II, who started the season as a maiden and was completing a hat-trick of wins with a third different rider up, the other two being men.

Sadly, Scar's sequence of nine wins in a row (the first of them in his last race of 1975) came to an end when he broke his leg in a fall at the second last in a two-horse ladies' open at the Surrey Union on April 24 and had to be put down. A winner four times over hurdles, this half-brother to the Irish 2,000 Guinea Winner Sharp Edge won 12 ladies' opens in 17 appearances for Eric Covell since he bought him for 2,050 guineas at the Ascot Sales in July 1974.

David Turner won his fourth men's title with 22 winners, achieved with eight of his father's horses, three of them five-year-olds in their first season of point-to-pointing. Remarkably, his most prolific winner, the eight-year-old Fashion Man, on whom he won five races in 11 appearances, started the season as a maiden. It was on Fashion Man that David had what must surely have been his most satisfying win, in the Marie Curie novice championship at the Melton Hunt Club, where the 14 starters included horses from Yorkshire, Herefordshire and Kent.

Starting joint favourite at 5-2 with Little Fleur from Bill Bryan's flourishing Herefordshire yard, Fashion Man joined his co-favourite going up the hill for the last time and drew steadily clear to score by ten lengths from Joey Newton's mount Chief Witness. But there is no doubt that Little Fleur, who finished a length away in third, would have been the runner-up but for being prematurely eased by the 16-year-old John Bryan.

Fashion Man was a horse with an interesting background. He was bred by Mrs. Lulu Donohoe in Ireland at Goresbridge, Co. Kilkenny, and had been placed in six novice chases after coming over to England. And, on his dam's side he traced back to an Irish Cesarewitch winner, Height Of Fashion, a prolific winner over fences and hurdles who would have won the Irish Grand National at Fairyhouse in 1963 but for falling at the last fence. Later on, Height of Fashion twice finished second to the mighty Arkle.

Joe Turner's fourth Grand Marnier Trophy came by courtesy of the nine-year-old Hardcastle's nine wins in his 12 appearances. But it would have been an even closer contest than it was but for Scar's fatal fall in the third week of April; and it might even have gone the other way; though Hardcastle also had a fall in a race he would otherwise surely have won at Cottenham.

Richard Miller, who rode 11 winners during the season, had his 150th winner when scoring on his uncle's Joe Swallow (a horse he had christened 'Joe Slow' on account of his being so easy to cut down) in an open event at Tweseldown in mid-February.

But for two other well-known riders there were bad falls. Sue Horton broke her pelvis in a fall at the Avon Vale which reduced her to riding only two winners during the season. David Wales broke his back when his mother's Salvage Man, a son of Salvage, was brought down in a melee at the first open ditch in a division of the men's open at the Cambridge University United Hunts' Club fixture at Cottenham. Mercifully, his spinal chord wasn't severed.

It had been a different story in the case of the unfortunate Colin Jackson the previous season when his fall at Andoversford had resulted in his being confined to a wheel-chair. It was on account of this, and the spinal injuries sustained by John Lowe at Cottenham, that a number of hunts were taking steps to ensure blanket insurance coverage for riders in the event of permanent disablement or death. Some riders had still to pay their own premiums; but it was a step in the right direction.

Eric Covell's Scar was not the only outstanding performer lost to the scene in

1976. Another was Real Rascal, who collapsed and died when being exercised by George Hyatt, who had the 13-year-old in his livery yard near Broadway. After starting in point-to-points as a five-year-old in 1968 carrying the colours of his breeder, Dudley Surman, Real Rascal won nine point-to-points and 11 hunter chases; and his successes included the Lady Dudley Cup of 1971 and two major hunter chases at Cheltenham.

There also occurred in 1976 the death of that marvellous star of the past Calypso Mio, who gave Guy Cunard so many winning rides and has some claim to be considered the best horse he ever had in his Malton yard. In a career lasting from 1955 to 1966, Calypso Mio ran in over 70 races, winning 18 point-to-points, ten hunter chases and two steeplechases, the vast majority of them with 'The Galloping Major' on board. Calypso Mio was put down at the age of 27.

For the first of the classic point-to-points, the four-mile men's open at the Heythrop, where the meeting was in its third year of sponsorship by Veuve Clicquot, there was a change in the conditions following the embarrassment of having had to run the 1975 race in two divisions. Entry for the race was now restricted to horses which had finished first, second or third in an open race (including ladies' opens and restricted opens) or a hunter chase since January lst 1974. It had the desired effect and there was a manageable field of 10 out of an entry of 26.

Although reputed to be no more than half-fit, having been off work for three weeks after injuring his leg at the Beaufort, Lord Fortune was a very convincing winner, and his time of 8 mins. 30 secs. on the firm ground was a record for this endurance test, which he was winning for the second time in eight years, ridden on the first occasion by George Hyatt and this time by Derek Edmunds. It was a remarkable performance for a 13-year-old; and although he won only one other race during the season, in a field of 25 at Larkhill, he was a runner-up to Credit Call in a hunter chase at Cheltenham.

The meeting was also notable in two other respects, for a high-clase ladies' open over the 3.5-mile trip in which Stanhope Street, with Gillian Fortescue-Thomas up, beat the Warwickshire mare Zanetta in record time; and for Colin Gee's feat on his Crystal Gazer (a former inmate of David Nicholson's yard) in becoming the first since Roger Roberts in 1970 to win the Old Etonian & Old Harrovian for Harrow. Gee had been the first Old Harrovian past the post in this race for the last three years. Stanhope Street, ridden each time by Gillian Fortescue-Thomas, won all three of his point-to-points and three of his six hunter chases, finishing a runner-up in the other three, and he was the only horse to beat Zanetta, who won four ladies' opens on the trot, ridden in the first of them by Mrs. Sally Gill at Kingston Blount, where she broke Royal Charity's 1971 course record by two seconds with a time of 6 mins. 25 secs; and in her other three races by the owner's daughter, Finetta Welton.

The Dudley Cup was also run on firm ground, with six going to the post in what was hardly a vintage race. But at least the winner, Mrs. Pam Morris's nine-year-old Jim Lad, put up the fastest time, 6 mins. 32 secs., since the race was transferred from Upton-on-Severn to Chaddesley Corbett in 1970.

A winner of five of his six previous races during the season, and his rider's first winner last season when he was only 15, Jim Lad started third favourite at 4-1 to the odds-on Sparkling Lad, a winner of five open events, three of them with Robert Alner up and two with his owner, Richard Woodhouse, aboard. Sparkling Lad, however, ran way below form and was never nearer than fourth; while Jim Lad, although running his race in fits and starts, was in command under the 16-year-old John Bryan (who was still at school in Hereford) from three fences out. He scored by two lengths from Hardiroyale, who was always prominent and had won the men's open at the Clifton-on-Teme. Jim Lad was trained for Mrs. Morris by Bill Bryan, who sent out 22 winners from his Herefordshire yard during the season, 14 of them ridden by his son John, who had a remarkable second season of race-riding in finishing runner-up to David Turner for the men's title.

Of Sparkling Lad's performance, Richard Woodhouse said, "He has always dictated matters before, and this time he couldn't. They went too fast for him and he never got into his gear properly."

17 runners from 15 different hunts lined up for the gruelling Grimthorpe Cup on good ground at Whitwell-on-the-Hill; and the winner this time was a home-bred mare from the York & Ainsty, Lawrence Barker's Villa Court, who had lost her maiden certificate at this meeting the previous season. But her only previous successes this season were in a restricted open and her own hunt race, and she was easy to back at 33-1. Her success in the Grimthorpe was well earned. She held off another home-bred mare, Arthur Johnson's Saucy Polly, by a neck. Her performance was referred to in Sale & Mackenzie's annual as "a major fluke", although the two mares were both rated by them at 10-10. Villa Court, however, was four years younger than Saucy Polly; and she did manage to win three more races in later years with a lady on top. Her success in the third of the season's classics was a breeding triumph for the Barker family. They bred both Villa Court and her dam, Miss Villa, by Haris II.

Another course record was shattered at Garthorpe when Laurie Kirkby's Potentate, an 11-year-old from the Brocklesby, won the ladies' championship, the sponsorship of which had now been taken over from Goya by Nitram, the agricultural division of I.C.I. Potentate's winning time, with 18-year-old Barbara Kirkby up, was 6 mins. 8 secs.; which was two seconds faster than the previous record for the course set up by Richard Woodhouse's Highworth in the men's open of 1970 and equalled by Headsprite in the Goya ladies' championship of 1974.

Ridden by a rider who was in her first season of race-riding, Potentate, a 2,500 guineas purchase at Ascot, overhauled the 5-2 on favourite, Even Harmony, on the run-in and scored by a length from Sidewinder, on whom Pat Caney had finished fast to take second place off Josie Bothway's mount by 1.5 lengths. This was Potentate's third win of the season for his young rider, who had finished second on him twice. Laurie Kirkby, Barbara's father, was the Master of the Brocklesby.

Max Churches' Panmure, a six-year-old from the Mendip Farmers, was an outstanding winner of the BMW men's final at Chepstow, at that time the richest hunter chase of the season, with £4,464 in prize money, followed by the Cathcart Champion Hunter Chase at Cheltenham with £3,438, the *Horse and Hound* Cup at Stratford with £2,886, the Cheltenham Foxhunters' with £2,488 and the Liverpool Foxhunters' with £1,689.

With the Somerset rider Ron Treloggen up, Panmure dominated a field which included horses from Yorkshire, Devon and Worcestershire. Never putting a foot wrong, apart from standing a bit too far back at the open ditch, Panmure was followed respectfully home by the West Country horse Devon Spirit and the Zetland mare Jaunty Jane, who was nearest at the finish but was beaten by the weight she carried (12-12 as against Panmure's 11-4 and Devon Spirit's 12-0).

Bred in Ireland by Mrs. J.J. Prendergast, Panmure changed hands as a yearling for 21,000 guineas at Ballsbridge before being bought for point-to-pointing as an entire (and cut soon afterwards) at the bargain price of 600 guineas at Ascot; and prior to his appearance in the BMW, he had won six of his seven point-to-points, after winning once on the Flat and running unsuccessfully over hurdles. He was ridden in two of his point-to-points by Heather Chard and in his other races by Treloggen.

Thanks to the generosity of the sponsors, a helicopter was laid on to ferry a few favoured members of the Press from the North Warwickshire point-to-point at Lowsonford to Chepstow for the BMW and take them back to the point-to-point afterwards. I was one of them; and, as I recall, the others were the *Daily Telegraph's* Desmond Hill and *Horse and Hound's* Hugh Condry. It was a somewhat frightening experience – Desmond and I were both very big men, and I seem to remember the plane's door flying open at one stage of the journey – but exhilarating as well; and the race was well worth the visit. Those were the days!

In the year that the distance of the race was further reduced to 2 miles 6 furlongs, Joey Newton and Credit Call took the Liverpool Foxhunters' for the second successive occasion; and it was, of course, Credit Call's third win in the race in a season which netted him six wins in hunter chases, one of them gained on a promotion after the horse that had finished in front of him at Doncaster, the Yorkshire mare Lady Annapurna, had been disqualified in Portman Square following a positive dope test.

One of the few hunter chases that Credit Call failed to win was the Cheltenham Foxhunters', in which a revitalised False Note completed a hat-trick of hunter-chase wins with Bryan Smart up, meeting Credit Call at level weights and beating him by four lengths.

False Note went on to win his next three races, ridden in the last of them by a deputy rider in Richard Stuart-Hunt (the leading rider in hunter chases with 8 wins in them), before undergoing his only defeat of the season in the *Horse and Hound* Cup at Stratford when reunited with Smart, who was in his last season as an amateur.

At Stratford False Note came up against those two noted performers Otter Way and Stanhope Street, and they proved a bit too much of a handful for him, Otter Way running on well under Grant Cann to score by five lengths from Stanhope Street, with False Note, who made a mistake three fences out, 21 lengths away in third.

This was Otter Way's sixth win in a season during which he had four different riders up, including two professionals, and had his only defeat when Oliver Carter had the temerity to run him in the Cheltenham Gold Cup. Even with Graham Thorner up, that task proved too much for him and, after holding every chance at the nineteenth, he weakened from two fences out and finished seventh to Royal Frolic.

But the eight-year-old's successes had included two races in which he was enjoying the services of Jeff King, the Betterton Chase at Newbury, where he beat Mickley Seabright by a head; and, most significant of all, the Whitbread Gold Cup at Sandown, where he was driven out to win by a length from Collingwood, to whom he was giving over a stone. The also rans in this race included The Dikler, who finished fourth, and Red Rum, who started favourite and finished just behind The Dikler.

Not surprisingly, Otter Way's performances during the season earned him top place, on a mark of 12-8, in Sale & Mackenzie's handicap afterwards, 5lb. ahead of Mickley Seabright, whose three wins in his four appearances under Rules from Fred Rimell's yard came in a hunter chase at Wolverhampton, a handicap chase at Ludlow and the Cathcart Champion Hunter Chase at Cheltenham in which he easily accounted for Stanhope Street and Tartan Slave. After Mickley Seabright in the S. & M. ratings came Stanhope Street at 11-13, Credit Call at 11-12, False Note at 11-11 and Panmure at 11-9.

It was good to see Sir Guy Cunard's eight-year-old Greystoke Pillar, a winner over hurdles and fences that he had bought for 2,900 guineas (quite a large sum for him to shell out) at Ascot Sales, finishing a successful season under Rules with veterinary surgeon Chris Cundall up in the John Player Special hunter chase at Catterick.

The Vaux final at Sedgefield went to a horse who started the season as a maiden point-to-pointer and would probably have been unbeaten in all eight of his point-to-points but for a fall in one of them, Penrith owner Bertram Johnston's Castlebeg, a home-bred eight-year-old from the Cumberland Farmers.

Ridden by the Northern Area champion, John Shadwick, in all his races, Castlebeg got up on the run-in at Sedgefield to beat the Bedale mare Bally Jewel by a length in his final race of the season.

Another very good winner ridden by John Shadwick was the Dumfriesshire mare Lady Lochans. Regarded by many (including my correspondent in the area) as the best point-to-pointer in the Northern Area, this nine-year-old was a winner of her last five men's opens. A mare who never did more than she had to, I don't think she was ever touched with the whip. She was beaten only twice in point-to-points, and that was in her first two races of the season.

The most prolific winner in the West Midlands was Mrs. Maureen Jackson's hobdayed ten-year-old Top Three, a winner of six point-to-points and a hunter chase at Cheltenham with Joe Jackson up and of a ladies' open with his owner riding. Mrs. Jackson was also up on him when he passed the post first in a ladies' open at the Golden Valley only to be disqualified later for carrying 3lb. less than the 10lb. penalty he had earned.

The West Country mare Lady Christine won seven ladies' opens with Doreen Hutchings up. Derrick Llewellin won seven races in Wales, six of them open events, on his nine-year-old South-Pembrokeshire mare Ronaheath. Reg Rendell's Blackmore & Sparkford Vale 12-year-old Marshalsland won seven more ladies' opens with Fay Geddes up to reach a grand total of 27 wins.

But the highest grand total of all was reached by the horse my Welsh correspondent Brian Lee had christened 'the Welsh Wonder', Tom Morgan's 12-year-old Mandryka, whose seven wins in ladies' opens with Shan Morgan up bumped his grand total of wins up to 33 wins in point-to-points plus one in a hunter chase.

In winning the men's open at Cottenham's Fitzwilliam fixture in a time of 5 mins. 58 secs. by a length from Even Harmony, the seven-year-old Water Sport, a horse bought at Ascot for 875 guineas and owned by Miss Janet Harris, the Master of the Oakley, was recording the fastest time there since the late Frank Harvey won an open nomination race at Cottenham on his wife's Corbawn Lad in a time of 5 mins. 56 secs. in 1948. Any time under six minutes is exceptionally fast for Cottenham.

Water Sport was a very useful open-class point-to-pointer in the more than capable hands of John Sharp. Unbeaten in his three point-to-points in 1976, when he also won a hunter chase at Worcester, he had won four of his seven point-to-points with John Sharp up in 1975, his first season in them.

Undoubtedly, the most improved horse of the season was John Stephenson's owner-ridden Lord Doolittle, the 13-year-old he had been hunting with the Pytchley, and the only point-to-pointer he had in his yard at Holdenby. This old horse last won a race when, in different ownership, he lost his maiden certificate in 1972. A transformed character in 1976, he won his last six races on the trot; and they included the R.L. Newton Memorial men's open at the classy Melton Hunt Club fixture, where he produced a devastating turn of foot between the last two fences to cut down David Turner's mount Antonius.

One disturbing aspect of the season was the appearance on point-to-point courses of the anti-hunting hit brigade, who had clearly come round to recognizing the close links between point-to-point racing and hunting. They were in action in the cause of vandalism on the eve of the Albrighton Woodland point-to-point at Chaddesley Corbett. They did not, however, manage to prevent racing from going ahead the next day.

Sadly, this was also the year that Ray Gould and Joe Yeomans' brave *Hunterguide* venture died.

> *Tailpiece* from the speech delivered by Capt. Ronnie Wallace at the M.F.H. Association's annual lunch at the Cavalry Club: "I have had more than one Joint Mistress."

1977

In which the ladies have their first championship on a professional racecourse, the Heythrop has cause for a celebration, Peter Scudamore rides his first winner, and the PPOA is founded.

Surprise! Surprise! The 1977 season saw the first increase in prize money for point-to-points since 1961. But it was only a slight one. The cash for the winner of an open event went up from £40 to £50; but for all other races the first-prize ceiling remained at £30, with the prize money for the second and third prizes unaltered at £15 and £10, and still no prize money for fourth place, even though the horse who finished fourth was required to weigh in.

There was, however, better news in the cast of the Levy Board Grant for courses. This went up to an overall sum of £62,500.

In an interesting course-inspectors' post-mortem on the 1976 season a number of criticisms were made, some of them even acted upon afterwards; especially the one about medical attention being "a bit slow." Of the Badsworth & Rockwood Harriers fixture in Yorkshire it was said, "Ambulance men could have been more alert."

The Enfield Chace was criticised for having no tent available for stewards to conduct an enquiry; and the Old Surrey & Burstow people were informed that, with a single exception, all their fences would need rebuilding. This, though, hardly presented a problem, as there was a new course for their meeting at Chiddingstone Heath.

At the Pembrokeshire, the stewards' stand was said to be "crowded with unauthorized persons," and at Tweseldown's Staff College & RMAS fixture, which had been the scene of a hotly-disputed result, it was reported that there were "too many people in the Judge's box." Even that classic mid-week fixture the Heythrop did not come off scot-free. "Fences need stiffening," it was said, "and the take-off boards need to be sunk into the ground a couple of inches."

In 1977, thanks to the sponsorship of BMW, we had the first ladies' championship on a professional racecourse, to supplement the men's championship at the same meeting at Chepstow, where they were the only jump races on an otherwise all-Flat card. For the ladies' championship there there was £1,500 added to the stakes, with qualifying races at 15 point-to-points. The BMW men's final still had £4,000 added to the stakes.

And, in addition to the Nitram ladies' championship at the Melton Hunt Club point-to-point, there was now a ladies' championship for the Yorkshire Area, arranged, somewhat unwisely, on the same day at Wetherby. Laurent Perrier, who were to have sponsored this, prudently dropped out when they discovered the clash of dates with the BMW finals, and their place was taken by the *Sporting Chronicle*. The race attracted no more than four runners – which must have left the champagne house congratulating themselves. They had, however, sponsored two of the qualifying races, the ladies' opens at the Bramham Moor and the Middleton.

At the Heythrop, where the National Westminster Bank had taken over the sponsorship of the meeting from Veuve Clicquot, though there was a magnum of champagne for the winners, and bookmakers Joe Coral were coming up with the mementoes, they were celebrating Capt. Ronnie Wallace's 25 years as Master and Huntsman of the Hunt; and doing it with a spectacular display of hounds, those of the Heythrop being joined by eight other packs of hounds attended by the hunt staffs in full livery.

In the words of another great Master, Dorian Williams, "Never before have so many famous hunts been represented mounted in one area." It was a memorable reminder of how much point-to-point racing owes to hunting. And I am proud of being able to say that I have hanging in my house a painting to recall the occasion. Not the original, it is true, but a numbered print.

Although by no means fully fit, as he had been off work for three week after injuring his leg at the Beaufort, and had not been galloped until the morning of the race, Mrs. Jackie Brutton's 14-year-old Lord Fortune, carrying the familiar McAlpine tartan, and ridden by his regular pilot Derek Edmunds, was a thoroughly convincing winner of the four-mile men's open for Lord Ashton of Hyde's Cup, which he had already won twice before.

After moving smoothly past The Trout and Debonair Boy in the field of 13 as he approached the third last, Lord Fortune soon put the issue beyond doubt, although The Trout had not given up hope when he fell at the last open ditch and gave his rider, James Evetts, a dislocated collar-bone. Debonair Boy was a weakening fourth and it was left to the unconsidered Paridel's Surprise to follow the winner home. This was Lord Fortune's second open-race win of the season, and he was to win another afterwards.

Two other outstanding winners at this meeting were Zanetta, who romped home under Mrs. Finetta Belcher (née Welton) from the Monmouthshire mare Tennessee II in the 3.5-mile ladies' open, and Edward Cazalet's owner-ridden Quilteven, who beat Crystal Gazer in the Old Etonian & Old Harrovian race.

Zanetta was unbeaten in all seven of her races during the season and never looked like going under in any of them. Quilteven, a seven-year-old by Even Money out of a Vulgan mare, was one of the best novices seen out during the season.

With his long stride and charismatic personality, Quilteven, who was bought in Scotland out of Ken Oliver's yard and hunted with the Heythrop, put me powerfully in mind of The Dikler. He was that kind of horse. A winner of five of his seven races, four of them with his owner up, he had at least one other notable scalp to his credit besides Crystal Gazer's when he beat Little Fleur (the mare who had won this year's Dudley Cup) very convincingly in a men's open at Kingston Blount. And he had the unique distinction of being owned by a barrister who was later to become a High Court Judge, and of being ridden by another one, Michael Connell, who was to be similarly elevated, when he lost his maiden certificate on his first appearance of the season at Mollington.

Another novice seven-year-old to impress was Richard Perkins's Entertaiment, from the Meynell & South Staffs. Ridden in all his races by John Docker, this son of Highland Melody out of a mare by Cacador took some time to lose his maiden certificate; but once he did so, on his fifth appearance of the season at the Atherstone, he went on to win three more races, two of them open events; and in the farmers' race at the Melton Hunt Club he beat the Grand Marnier winner Hardcastle by a neck. In his last race of the season he was the runner-up to Timmie's Battle in the John Corbet Cup at Stratford.

Entertainment was also the runner-up to the horse who gave the 18-year-old Peter Scudamore his first winning ride in a race. This was in the men's open at his home meeting, where Scudamore, who was later to become a champion professional under N.H. Rules, was riding an 11-year-old, Monty's Reward, who had won six chases. But this was the only point-to-point Monty's Reward ever won. Not so, Scudamore. The following season, his last as an amateur, he rode four more point-to-point winners.

In a season that was especially notable for the emergence of highly promising novices, three other names that come immediately to mind are Mountolive, Spartan Missile and Spartan Lace.

Richard Shepherd's owner-ridden Mountolive achieved the most in 1977. This seven-year-old from the Cotswold country, bred by Richard's father from Straight Lady, the mare that had won him the Cheltenham Foxhunters' of 1966 with his son up, began his season winning the maiden race at the Beaufort and ended it winning the BMW men's final at Chepstow. He was beaten only once in his eight races when, paying the penalty for some indifferent fencing after hitting the first fence hard, he went under by a neck to Hunting Eve (a winner of three of her four races during the season) in his second race, the adjacent hunts' race at the V.W.H.

After being pulled up in his two point-to-points, John Thorne's home-bred five-year-old Spartan Missile, who was by Spartan General out of Polaris Missile, the mare on whom Thorne had won the four-mile National Hunt Chase at Cheltenham in 1966, lost his maiden certificate with his owner putting up 7lb. over-weight on him in a hunter chase at Sandown's Grand Military fixture. He then won a hunter chase at Sandown with Jane Thorne up and one at Towcester with Nicky Henderson riding him. It was the shape of things to come.

It was also the shape of things to come, in a smaller way, for G.B. ("Bunny") Tarry's home-bred seven-year-old mare Spartan Lace, like Spartan Missile by Spartan General, but out of one of the mares Tarry had bought for breeding purposes from Miss Lucy Jones in Somerset, French Lace, by Vulgan.

Spartan Lace, who was to contribute her share of lustre to the powerful Tarry string in the South Midlands, was the runner-up to Quilteven in her maiden race; and after that she won two of her remaining three point-to-points with James Tarry up and was a runner-up to Water Sport in the men's open at the Woodland Pytchley.

Quilteven was the only one of the aforementioned novices who was in the field of 15 for the Marie Curie novice championship at Melton, and he started a red-hot favourite for it; but it was not his day. He didn't exactly do anything wrong, but he was clearly not at home on the firm ground and was off the bit throughout the last mile, beaten a distance in the end by the largely unconsidered Heath Hill, a six-year-old mare from the Albrighton with only one previous win behind her in her seven appearances. One bookmaker, J.C, of Northampton, had laid her at 66-1; and another, John O'Neill of Coventry, said he had no takers at 33-1. The Tote paid out £13.87 to a 10p stake. But there was no fluke about the result. Heath Hill made every yard of the running under Richard Aston, who was riding his only winner of the season.

It is interesting to see how the novices I have singled out were rated on their performances by Iain Mackenzie and his new partner David Phillips (who had taken over from Geoffrey Sale). Mountolive and Spartan Missile, equal seventh in their handicap behind the usual crop of hunter chasers, were on a mark of 11-4, Quilteven and Entertainment were both on 11-1, Heath Hill was on 10-11 and Spartan Lace on 10-9.

To set the cat among the pigeons, however, it is worth recalling that another of the 1977 novices was a six-year-old called Diamond Edge, who, four seasons later, after he had joined Fulke Walwyn's yard, won both the Whitbread Gold Cup at Sandown and the Hennessy Gold Cup at Newbury. In 1977, Diamond Edge, ridden by the West Country's Michael Williams, lost his maiden certificate at the Dartmoor & Modbury Harriers on his only winning appearance during the season. He was rated at 10-7 by Mackenzie & Phillips. Well, they were not clairvoyants; and neither was I.

The top-rated ladies' horses were Edward Turner's Ludlow seven-year-old Sutton Surprise and Vince Welton's Warwickshire mare Zanetta, both on the 11-2 mark. Sutton Surprise, who had an excellent pilot in the veteran Pat Kerby, was kept mainly to hunter chases, winning two of them. On his only appearance in a point-to-point he won the ladies' open at the Ledbury.

Zanetta, whom I would nominate as the ladies' horse of the season, was prevented by injury from contesting either the Nitram ladies' championship at Melton or the inaugural BMW ladies' championship at Chepstow, otherwise she might well have won both of them, since they were far enough apart for her to do so.

The hard ground at Chepstow saw only seven lining up for the BMW ladies' final, for which the favourite at 11-8 was Barbara Kirkby's mount Potentate, whose five successes during the season had included a second win in the Nitram. This time, however, his fencing was far from fluent and he finished a well-beaten third to the Beaufort mare Horoscope, who was driven out by Rosemary White to score by half a length from the Zetland mare Willow Walk, the winner of the ladies' opens at the Derwent, the Zetland and the Badsworth.

It was the 12-year-old Horoscope's fourth win of the season, and her third in a hunter chase; and in her single win in a point-to-point she beat Marshalsland by a neck in a fast-run ladies' open (her BMW qualifier) at the Beaufort; and she was a runner-up to Spartan Missile in a hunter chase at Towcester and third to Long Lane and Jim Lad in the United Hunts' Cup at Cheltenham.

Little Fleur's win in the Dudley Cup, the second one running for her trainer, Bill Bryan, and his rider-son John, was a hard-earned one. Jim Mahon's horse His Last was looking all over a winner when he fell at the last and his rider, John Weston, broke his arm; and John Bryan had to use all his strength to get the mare home by a neck from Steven Brookshaw's mount Mickley Love Story.

This was the home-bred Little Fleur's sixth win of the season, five of them on the trot; and she was to frank the form with another one when she beat Peter Scudamore's mount Monty's Reward half a length in the men's open at the Melton Hunt Club fixture, although not without having to survive an objection for taking the runner-up's ground on the run-in. There was a nice bonus at the end of this race for Little Fleur's owner, Shropshire beef farmer Robert Wynn, who collected the £500 bonanza that the *Sporting Chronicle,* somehow finding a loophole in the regulations, had managed to put up for a points championship which was concluded at this meeting. And for the mare's young rider, with a 25th win, which put him within one of David Turner, there was the prospect of his first *Daily Telegraph* Cup. He was to be frustrated in the end, but not by much.

For the 4 miles 856 yards Grimthorpe Cup at the Middleton there was a field of 20, the biggest since 1955, when there were 23. The race was won by the 7-4 favourite, Escamist, an 11-year-old from the Brocklesby who, at one stage, could have been backed at 4-1. It was a fitting climax for him in a season which gave him four open-race wins in his six appearances.

Ridden with exemplary patience by James Barton, Escamist moved smoothly past Guides Choice as he approached the second last and ran on strongly to hold off the fast-finishing Scottish contender Sea Petrel by 2.5 lengths, with Guides Choice a further two lengths away in third.

This was a remarkable performance by Escamist, who had had a somewhat chequered career since he lost his maiden certificate in 1972 in a maiden race at the Beaufort. Put into training with Michael Scudamore, he failed to win under Rules and was bought three years ago by James Walker, a Grimsby farmer who won six races in a row on him in 1975 before he broke down in the John Corbet Cup at Stratford; and this was his first season since then. James Barton said of his owner, "He has trained him from being a cripple back into stardom." Which just about sums it up.

The Turner family's clean sweep of the major trophies presented at the national point-to-point dinner continued for the fourth successive year. But it wasn't until the last day of the season at the Torrington Farmers fixture in the West Country that the contest for the *Daily Telegraph* Cup was resolved. Before this meeting commenced, David Turner had ridden 27 winners and John Bryan 26. Each of them had three rides at Umberleigh; but whereas the 17-year-old Bryan had to be content with one runner-up and a third place, David Turner completed a double and took his score up to 29.

Bryan's runner-up, Robert Wynn's Eastern Bounty in the restricted open, had been placed in four of her five earlier races, but proved no match for Turner's ride in this race, his father's seven-year-old Flaming Double, who beat her by 20 lengths. Puckham, the horse Bryan was riding in the men's open, was a winner of the hunt races at the Ross Harriers and the Golden Valley; but this time he was taking on Even Harmony and the result was a foregone conclusion. He ran a good race but was deprived of second place on the run-in.

Josie Bothway, who won the *Sporting Life* Cup for the fifth time with her 17 winners and was to become Mrs. Gurney Sheppard by the time she received the trophy at the national point-to-point dinner in September, had a wonderful season on Even Harmony and Hardcastle, the two horses on whom she shared the rides with her brother, winning seven ladies' opens on Even Harmony and four ladies' opens and an adjacent hunts' race on Hardcastle.

The runner-up for *The Life* Cup (for the third year running!) was Mrs. Mary Crouch, with 14 wins, seven of them in ladies' opens on Eric Covell's 14-year-old Newcastle, who lost another one on a disqualification and whose only other defeat in a point-to-point was in the ladies' open at the Tickham, where he was beaten a length by Sheilagh French's mount Arctic Sky.

Joe Turner, the leading owner of the season with 47 winners in point-to points and three in hunter chases, could have won the Grand Marnier Trophy with either Hardcastle or Even Harmony, both of whom won 11 point-to-points during the season, David Turner winning six of them on Hardcastle and four on Even Harmony, plus a hunter chase at Fakenham on both of them. Hardcastle however, had one second place and one third place as against Even Harmony's single second place in point-to-points. So Hardcastle was the chosen medium for the fifth Turner Grand Marnier. His owner, however, was absent from the ceremony as a protest at not being permitted to retain permanently the trophy he had won so often,

There was also a new Grand Marnier award for the leading novice rider of the season, and this went to 18-year-old Cathie Houlbrook from Cheshire, the rider of six winners. The presentation was made by Dick Francis, who revealed that one of his earliest wins was on Copper Kettle, a mare owned by Cathie's father, Bill Houlbrook.

The collector of the point-to-point dinner committee's award for special services to point-to-point racing was East Anglia's Geoffrey Sale, the producer in 1960 of the first *Annual of Hunter Chasers and Point-to-Pointers*, for which he was solely responsible until being joined by Iain Mackenzie in 1971.

This dinner was also notable as the chosen launching pad for the formation of the Point-to-Point Owners' Association, the main purpose of which was to establish a body with representation and voice at policy-making level of the sport, and liaise with bodies already involved with its administration.

The first Chairman of the Association that has been thriving ever since was the instigator of the project, that genial Irishman Jim Mahon, a man full of the right ideas. He was the unanimous choice of a steering committee of well-known point-to-point personalities right across the country; and his influence over the sport in later years was incalculable. One of his ideas was the 71b. allowance for five-year-olds that we have today, and for which he was already engaged in enlisting support.

Turning now to the hunter-chase scene, I see that Iain Mackenzie and his new partner had Long Lane and Remigio at the head of their list on a mark of 11-8, 11b. ahead of Panmure.

Richard Shepherd's home-bred Long Lane, a nine-year-old half-brother to Mountolive, started his season winning two open point-to-points and then proceeded to win five of his six hunter chases, his three at Cheltenham including the four-mile Cheltenham Foxhunters', in which he was giving Lord Fortune 21bs and beat him by 2.5 lengths, and the 3.25-mile United Hunts' Cup which he won comfortably from Jim Lad and Horoscope, giving both of them 41b. He was beaten only once when, three weeks after winning the Cheltenham Foxhunters' in heavy going, he went under to Remigio and Rough House in a 3-mile hunter chase on good to soft ground at Ascot. It must have been a great feeling for Richard Shepherd to own and ride two such good horses as Long Lane and Mountolive, and be training them in his yard at Cirencester.

By way of contrast, Mrs. Georgina Paterson's Remigio, a nine-year-old son of Even Money hunted with the Old Surrey & Burstow, was a product of professional training. A winner over fences and hurdles when trained for her by Jack O'Donoghue at Reigate, he was then sent into training with Fred Winter at Lambourn and won four handicap chases and a novice hurdle before appearing in hunter chases in 1977 and winning five of them with Winter's assistant trainer Nicky Henderson aboard.

Remigio's only defeat was in his last race of the season, the *Horse and Hound* Cup at Stratford, where he was ridden by Dick Saunders. It proved one race too many for him and he finished fourth to a 50-1 outsider, Devil's Walk. But he was not beaten by much. The margins between the first four were threequarters of a length, a short head and a head.

In the very capable hands of farrier Tim Rooney, Devil's Walk, a nine-year-old from the Gelligaer Farmers, got up on the run-in to score from Chris Collins's hunter-chaser Byzantium (ridden by Joey Newton), who just held off the Blackmore & Sparkford Vale eight-year-old Precious Jem for second place.

Owned by Mike Bishop, a wholesale fruit merchant from Caerphilly, and trained by him on the side of a mountain, Devil's Walk was the first horse from Wales to win this race since it was won in 1958, in the days before it was sponsored by *Horse and Hound*, by Bill Jones on Dark Island, a horse hunted in South Wales with the Glamorgan. The only other Welsh winner of it was a horse ridden by Tim Rooney's uncle, Barney Rooney, who won it in 1954 on Phil's Castle, from the Llangeinor.

When Mike Bishop was asked by some incredulous pressmen about the background of his horse, he replied dazedly, "Well, he was a winner at Ludlow, you know." Very true, but that was Devil's Walk's only previous success during the season, and on that day he also started at 50-1.

Fred Winter also saddled the winner of the Liverpool Foxhunters' in the ten-year-old Happy Warrior, who, like Remigio, was confined strictly to hunter chases. But Happy Warrior's win at Liverpool, with his owner-rider Nicky Henderson, was his only success in his four appearances during the season.

Although Peter Greenall's Timmie's Battle had finished behind Happy Warrior at Aintree, this six-year-old that Arthur Stephenson was training for him had a much more impressive record, winning six of his eight hunter chases with his owner up and winding up his season giving Entertainment 31b. in the John Corbet Cup at Stratford and beating him by a length. At the end of the season Timmie's Battle changed hands for 24,000 guineas at Ascot but remained in Stephenson's yard to win more races.

Arthur Johnson's Middleton mare Lady Annapurna, a prolific scorer in the past, was a good all-the-way winner of the John Player Championship on the hard ground at Catterick, even if she had only two opponents to master and it was her only success of the season. The two that followed her home, Willow Walk and Ellerby Lord, both had some useful form behind them.

With Otter Way confined to two appearances in handicap chases (neither of which he managed to win), Oliver Carter's other star Lucky Rock had strong claims to be considered the best point-to-pointer in the West. After a fall in a hunter chase at Sandown on his first appearance of the season, the 11-year-old son of the H.I.S. premium stallion Spiritus won all seven of his open point-to-points with Grant Cann up, earning a rating of 11-1 in Mackenzie & Phillips' annual; and when he attempted to win the Whitbread Gold Cup at Sandown for the second year running he held every chance until he made a bad mistake at the seventeenth.

The 13-year-old Mandryka, a winner of eight ladies' opens in Wales with Shan Morgan aboard, recorded the 41st win of his career when scoring at the Llangeinor in May. Fourteen-year-old Lord Fortune was running in his 66th race when he won a division of the Coronation Cup open race at the United Services fixture at Larkhill for the third successive year; and by the end of the season he had a grand total of 27 wins.

But for another good old stager, Max Churches' 12-year-old Rich Rose, it was curtains. He broke down badly when winning a division of the men's open at the Beaufort. It was the same leg he had broken down on once before and he had to be put down. He was a winner of 18 point-to-points.

That accomplished Flat-race jockey Brooke Sanders rode her first winner over fences when scoring on the penalised Some Jest in the hunt race at the North Hereford.

Sheilagh French and two of her daughters, Sarah and Scarlett, all rode winners over the Easter week-end. Sheilagh and Sarah completed a family double at the Ashford Valley on the Saturday, Sheilagh winning the ladies' open on her Royal And Ancient, and Sarah the hunt race on another horse of her mother's, Hadleigh Mill; and on Monday at the Eridge, Scarlett won the ladies' open on Prince Tacitus.

The hunt saboteurs were at it again at the Warwickshire meeting at Mollington, destroying two of the fences and flattening the tents after slashing them with knives. But although this prevented the fixture from taking place on the scheduled date, it was held ten days later.

At the Berkeley there was an overnight guard at every fence to stop the same thing happening. This Gloucestershire meeting is one with a great country atmosphere; and the commentator there, Jeremy Branfoot (who is still going strong today), was perched perilously up a tree in a howling wind and had to descend from it by ladder after every race. It is rather different these days, though the vandals are still around.

Tailpiece:
"It's been a busy day," said the ambulance lady at the Easton Harriers, the first point-to-point of the season at Higham. "We have had three broken collar-bones, a dislocated shoulder and a hand jammed in a car door."

1978

*In which Spartan Missile is King, the mares excel themselves,
the Turners lose their monopoly, a Cheltenham Gold Cup winner
appears on the point-to-point scene, a Yorkshire horse wins the
Dudley Cup, and a 'ringer' is uncovered.*

I would be tempted to describe 1978 as the year of Spartan Missile were it not
for the fact that John Thorne's home-bred six-year-old was to distinguish himself further in later years. In 1978, ridden each time by his owner-breeder,
Spartan Missile won five hunter chases on the trot. The climax was reached in the
Liverpool Foxhunters', in which he broke a leather at Becher's and Thorne finished minus his stirrups, leaving Peter Greenall's mount Timmie's Battle (subsequently disqualified after failing a dope test) and Nicky Henderson's mount Happy
Warrior in his wake; and when Jane Thorne rode him later in the Whitbread Gold
Cup at Sandown he was the runner-up to Strombolus, beaten no more than a
length after leading to the penultimate fence.

Not surprisingly, Spartan Missile was subsequently the top-rated horse with
Mackenzie & Phillips at 12-0, 31b. above Mountolive and 71b. ahead of Timmie's
Battle and the professionally-trained Rolls Rambler, whose six wins in a row (five
of them with Nicky Henderson up) culminated in a neck win over Devil's Walk in
the *Horse and Hound* Cup at Stratford, where Henderson rode him.

In his new ownership, but still ridden by Peter Greenall, the champion amateur of 1977, Timmie's Battle was a winner of four hunter chases. One of them was
the Cheltenham Foxhunters', in which he passed the post half a length ahead of
Mountolive, only to lose the race following the discovery of a prohibited substance in his urine. This race has now been reduced from four miles to 3 miles 2 f

Richard Shepherd's home-bred Mountolive continued on the upgrade, and not
only at Cheltenham, where he had Mickley Seabright behind him in the
Foxhunters'. His six wins on the trot with his owner up included two more at
Cheltenham; but in his last race of the season at Warwick, where Rolls Rambler
was the winner, he was in fourth place when he unseated his rider two fences out.
This race at Warwick was a race-riding swan song for Rolls Rambler's rider, Nicky
Henderson, who was now on his way to making his mark as a public trainer.

The mare of the season in point-to-points was Robert Wynn's Radnor & West

110

Hereford seven-year-old Little Fleur, trained by Bill Bryan in Herefordshire. A winner of 12 of her 13 point-to-points, ridden in 11 of them by 18-year-old John Bryan, and in one by his 16-year-old sister Karen, Little Fleur was the 1978 Grand Marnier winner.

Although possibly a bit over the top by the time she went to Chepstow to contest the BMW men's championship (at this time still the richest hunter chase, with the prize money increased to £5.000), Little Fleur would probably have added this race to her score but for collecting a nail in her foot. As it was, she was beaten 21 lengths by Mastership, an eight-year-old mare from the New Forest, who, with Barry Stevens up on her, was losing her maiden certificate on her seventh appearance of the season.

Not all that far behind Little Fleur (and rated above her by Mackenzie & Phillips) was Vincent Welton's nine-year-old Warwickshire mare Zanetta. The flying Zanetta was a winner of eight of her nine races, and a faller on the only occasion she was beaten. Finetta Welton crowned a wonderful season on her in the BMW ladies' championship at Chepstow, where the mare was out on her own from the nineteenth; and before that she was an equally impressive winner of the Nitram ladies' championship at Garthorpe's Melton Hunt Club fixture, where she recorded a record time of 6 mins. 4 secs. This was four seconds faster than Potentate's record time in the same race in 1976.

But the horse who came nearest of all to reaching Little Fleur's 12 wins was Miss Janet Harris's Oakley nine-year-old Water Sport, a winner of nine open point-to-points and a hunter chase at Worcester, all with John Sharp up; and among the victims of this 875 guineas purchase at Ascot in various parts of the country were Tartan Slave, Hardcastle and Richard Woodhouse's Dance Again, a winner during the season of five open events with Kevin Bishop up.

Another prolific winner was Little Fleur's stable companion, Mrs. Pam Morris's Sparkford. This seven-year-old son of Spartan General won nine point-to-points with John Bryan up, all but one of them open events; and his successes included the first of the season's classics, the four-mile men's open for Lord Ashton of Hyde's Cup at the Heythrop, where he was in no danger from four fences out and had the additional distinction of beating Quilteven by a distance. It has to be said, though, that, despite winning three times on the trot and being a runner-up in his other three races, Quilteven ran well below form in 1978 and was to be off the course throughout 1979.

With his 32 wins in point-to-points, the vast majority of them on horses trained by his father, the youthful John Bryan broke the previous record of 29 set up by the Shropshire rider Bob Davies in 1971 and equalled by David Turner in 1977; and it goes without saying that he was the winner of the *Daily Telegraph* Cup for the leading point-to-point rider of the season. Second and third to him, with 19 and 15 winners respectively, were David Turner and John Sharp.

Sparkford, however, was unable to land the odds laid on him for the second of the classics, the Lady Dudley Cup at the Worcestershire. In this he had to play second fiddle to Miss Joyce Hey's Sporting Luck, the first horse from Yorkshire to win this race since Archie Thomlinson's Paul Pry in 1951.

Sporting Luck was never headed after jumping the first fence in front under his confident rider, 29-year-old Tim Smith. Sparkford was nearer last than first in the early stages and, despite having moved up to fourth in the field of nine at the half-way mark, he was still some 25 lengths behind the leader. Bryan put in a great effort to get Sparkford on terms in the closing stages; but a spectacular jump by Sporting Luck at the last settled the issue, and he held off Sparkford's late flourish by threequarters of a length. Tennessee II, the third horse home, and a winner of two ladies' opens afterwards, finished 15 lengths behind Sparkford.

The 11-year-old Sporting Luck, who had never seen a course before he was seven, must, I feel, be rated a vintage Dudley Cup winner. He won all three of his point-to-points in his first season when he was in training with Peter Beaumont in 1974, and he was still with the same trainer when he won five of his six in 1978, having broken down in the second of his two races in 1975, been off the course throughout 1976 and made only a single appearance in 1977, when he developed a splint.

In the Grimthorpe Cup it was the turn of the mares again. The first and third home in a tight-run race, Sea Petrel and Hawlings Dale, were both mares. In test-ing ground, the eight-year-old Sea Petrel, from the Lauderdale Hunt in Scotland, got to Bonjedward (another of the Scottish contestants) on the run-in and beat him a neck, with Hawlings Dale, a mare from the Bicester, close up in third.

Owned and trained by Jimmy Scott-Aiton (the rider in former days of that great horse The Callant) and ridden by his 28-year-old son Ian, Sea Petrel, a mare bred in South Wales and bought for 1,500 guineas at Ascot Sales as a six-year-old in 1976, was recording her sixth success of the season; and, by a curious coincidence, the narrow runner-up was owned by the man who used to own The Callant, Charlie Scott.

The four-mile ladies' open at this Yorkshire fixture was well won by Villa Court, the mare who had won the 1976 Grimthorpe Cup. Ridden this time by the 23-year-old Heather Clarke, Villa Court drew right away from her opponents in the closing stages; and the horse who finished third to her was the horse who had won the race in 1975, Waggoners Walk. Trained by her owner, Lawrence Barker, near York, Villa Court was bred by his father, who also bred her dam, Miss Villa.

Another mare, Bonham Hill, a nine-year-old from the South & West Wilts, won the four-mile men's open for the Savernake Gold Cup at Larkhill's Tedworth fix-ture in a field of 21 and beat a doughty opponent in the process, as well as scor-ing in record time for the race, 8 mins. 3 secs. Coming late on the scene, this rank outsider, who was without a win in her last 17 races, produced too much finish-ing speed for the penalised Stanhope Street and beat him by 15 lengths. But, at the age of 12, Stanhope Street had seen his best days.

Bonham Hill wasn't the only horse to break a record at this fixture. It would be nice to say that the other record-breaker was also a mare. In fact, however, it was that very speedy customer Marshalsland, now 14 years old. Reg Rendell's old campaigner was breaking his own record with a blistering time of 5 mins. 55 secs. when he won the ladies' open with a new pilot aboard, Mrs. Elsie Mitchell (wife of the well-known amateur rider Richard Mitchell, who later became a profes-sional trainer). Mrs. Mitchell was riding her first winner.

Also certainly deserving of mention for her performances this season is Paul

Tylor's, West Country mare Hargan, on whom Pip Fisher won six ladies' opens and two hunter chases, at Devon & Exeter and Newton Abbot.

Neither must I forget that the winner of the Marie Curie novice championship at Garthorpe was also a mare, David Hockenhull's nine-year-old Gillie from Sir W.W. Wynn's. Ridden by Richard Aston, who won the 1977 race on Heath Hill, Gillie was always holding the favourite, John Bryan's mount Tartan Prince.

It was Gillie's fourth win of the season, the last three of them in a row. Bred by her owner at his Shade Oak Stud, near Ellesmere in Shropshire, Gillie was by Manicou out of a mare by Straight Deal; and she came to point-to-point racing when she missed out as a brood mare. Hockenhull named her after an Oswestry veterinary surgeon called Gilchrist who had saved her from death as a foal; and, like Heath Hill, she was trained by Richard Aston.

Ten Up, the winner of the Cheltenham Gold Cup in 1975, unlike all those former point-to-pointers who went on to win this race or the Grand National, was a clear case of a horse going backwards rather than forwards. Not that he didn't have his successes in his later years. In fact, his first appearance in a point-to-point was a winning one. He started the 1978 season winning a two-horse services race at the Army point-to-point at Tweseldown ridden by his new owner, Capt. James Hodges of the Royal Horse Artillery who had hunted the 11-year-old with the Quorn. That was his only point-to-point appearance; but, still ridden by Capt. Hodges, he was the runner-up to Spartan Missile in a hunter chase at Towcester, the winner of the Royal Artllery Gold Cup at Sandown and the runner-up to Mountolive in a hunter chase at Cheltenham. The following season one of the three races he won with his owner up was the Grand Military Gold Cup at Sandown.

A new star arose in the South East in the shape of Eric Covell's eight-year-old Flintstone, a horse who had run an undistinguished race in the Derby as a three-year-old and won two novice hurdles when trained by David Barons. Covell bought him for 2,600 guineas at the Ascot Sales in October 1977, and had his first win with him the first time he ran in a point-to-point at Tweseldown's Army meeting, where he provided his rider, David Evatt, with the first leg of an open-race double, winning the earlier division by a distance. Evatt won five more open races on Flintstone and a hunter chase at Fontwell; and this classically-bred son of Mossborough out of a mare by Rockefella was also successful in a ladies' open with Mary Crouch up. Flintstone was rather unlucky not to go through the season unbeaten. As will be apparent later, however, he was a horse with two ways of running and a distinct mind of his own.

Even more impressive than Flintstone, though, was one of the Northern stars, Graham Macmillan's Dumfriesshire six-year-old Queensberry Lad, who lost his maiden certificate on his second appearance of the season at the Cumberland Farmers. Macmillan won four point-to-points in a row on this son of New Brig who was also successful for him in a hunter chase at Kelso. Mackenzie & Phillips, who had Queensberry Lad on a mark of 11-2 in their handicap, with only eight horses above him, went right over the top in their remarks, putting him on a par with such horses as Wyndburgh, Freddie, Merryman II and The Callant.

So far as the ladies' horses in the North were concerned, the one I remember best is the massive Cool Thrust, a nine-year-old from the Buccleuch who stood over 17 hands high. Ridden in all his races by Gillian Minto, Cool Thrust, a winner of seven races for her in 1977, including a novice hunter chase at Ayr, won four ladies' opens in 1978, was never out of the first three in all seven of his races, and was a runner-up to Carndonagh, beaten half a length, in a hunter chase at Ayr.

But the lady who rode the most winners during the season, and won the *Sporting Life* Cup for the first time, was the Beaufort rider Mrs. Rosemary White, the only lady to reach double figures in point-to-points with 11 winners, two more than Yorkshire's Amanda Jemmeson and three more than Lucy King in East Anglia.

Rosemarys and Amanda Jemmeson also rode winners in hunter chases. Rosemary White's two wins in hunter chases were both achieved on Horoscope's half-brother, the seven-year-old Bright Chance, who gave her five of her wins in point-to-points and, like Horoscope, was owned by her father-in-law, Douglas White; and the two horses were bred by the man who taught Rosemary most about the art of race-riding, John Daniell, a distinguished amateur rider in his day with 175 point-to-point winners behind him and the rider of the first-ever winner of what is now the Land Rover men's championship, the Players Gold Leaf Trophy at Newbury in 1968, on Lucy Jones' Bartlemy Boy. The White horses were trained on John and Rosemary's farm at Wroughton, near Swindon.

Amanda Jemmeson's single win in a hunter chase was also on one of her point-to-point winners, Hello Louis, an eight-year-old from the Cleveland on whom she won four ladies' opens. This was in the *Sporting Chronicle* ladies' championship at Newcastle, where she got Hello Louis home by two lengths from Valerie Alder's mount Lothian Brig, but was to lose the race later in Portman Square when Hello Louis was disqualified following a positive dope test.

The winner of the Grand Marnier novice rider's award was 18-year-old Paul Hamer from Wales with his ten point-to-point winners; and the runner-up to him with eight was the East Anglian Area ladies' champion Lucy King. Lucy also had five wins in hunter chases on three of the horses trained by Libby Lees (the subsequent Libby Heath) in her yard at Bury St. Edmunds, winning three on Clonmellon, one on The Coalman and one on the horse that was to become the brightest star in the yard, Mrs. Clare Villar's five-year-old Mr. Mellors, who had lost his maiden certificate at Higham.

The leading riders in hunter chases, each with seven winners, were Peter Greenall and Jim Wilson.

Several riders who were to distinguish themselves in later years rode their first winners in 1978. Sixteen-year-old William Wales (the son of David and grandson of Walter of King High and Salvage fame) rode his with his first ride in a race on the opening day of the season at Higham when he was up on his father's West Norfolk mare Black Outlook in the adjacent hunts' race at the Waveney Harriers on the course where his father had landed his 100th winner. "Fantastic," he said afterwards, "I had just hoped to get round." His father's comment was: "And to think that I was rounding cattle up on the mare in the morning, and we had two punctures on the way to the course."

Another to land a winner with his first ride in a race was the 17-year-old Yorkshire rider Nigel Tutty, who did so in the hunt race at the Cleveland on the six-year-old Whiggie Geo, whose owner, Albert Sanderson, had lost the use of his legs in a riding accident at the York & Ainsty in 1973; but not his enthusiasm for the sport he loved.

The Essex rider Tim Moore, aged 18, was on his first winner when scoring on his father's mare Sweet Aria in the maiden race at the West Norfolk, where he did particularly well to beat the favourite, David Turner's mount French Morn, by a head.

There was, too, a first riding success for Caroline Saunders, who was to make a big name for herself as a trainer of point-to-pointers and hunter chasers in future years. Caroline, the 18-year-old daughter of Dick and Pam, was riding a mare, Teeton Lass, owned by her mother and bred by her father, when she won a division of the maiden race at the Oakley on this eight-year-old daughter of Quality Fair out of a mare by Parting Shot.

John Docker was riding his 100th point-to-point winner when scoring on his own horse Lone Soldier in a division of the restricted open at the Woodland Pytchley over the same course at Dingley where he had recorded his first win on Lone Soldier's dam, that splendid mare All Alone II. The West Country rider Ron Edwards, following in the footsteps of Frank Ryall as the doyen of West Country amateurs, rode his 100th winner when getting Col. Spencer's Quintus Fabius home by half a length from Stories Roma (the mount of Jimmy Frost) in the adjacent hunts' restricted at the East Cornwall. He was given a rousing reception.

But for one noted rider, the incomparable Sue Horton, one of the few lady riders to ride over 100 winners, it was the end of her race-riding career. She announced her retirement shortly after breaking her arm and two of her ribs in a crashing fall in the hunt race at the Beaufort in early March; and after the season was over she was the well-deserved recipient of the inscribed salver presented at the national point-to-point dinner for special services to the sport.

The Brookshaws' home-bred Mickley Seabright, now in Fred Rimell's Kinnersley yard, made a gallant attempt to win the 1978 Grand National with Peter Brookshaw Jnr. up. He didn't succeed, but he ran an excellent race, holding every chance three fences out and eventually finishing fifth to Lucius in the field of 37. A month later he won a hunter chase at Haydock.

Three of the winners at the North Cotswold were sired by Spartan General, two of them home-bred ones for the Thorne family, Jane Thorne winning the ladies' open on Madge Spartan (out of Barton's Sister) and her father winning the maiden race on the five-year-old Spalet (out of Dainty). The other Spartan General winner here was Spartan Scot, on whom Nigel Oliver won the restricted open.

The 'Welsh wonder horse' Mandryka went on winning at the age of 14. Ridden again by Shan Morgan, he won three more ladies' opens, bringing his grand total of wins up to 44.

But for Sir Guy Cunard's famous old horse of former days, Puddle Jumper, the Grimthorpe Cup winner of 1967, it was the end of the line. The 23-year-old broke a leg in his stable in February and had to be put down. "Dear Old Puddle," as Guy frequently referred to him, had carried the Major's colours in 66 races and given him 25 wins in point-to-points and three in hunter chases; in the vast majority of them with the Major in the saddle.

At the Whaddon Chase there was an unusual dispute between certain members of the bookmaking fraternity at Great Horwood and the hunt committee, with some bookmakers being refused permission to bet there and the favoured ones diplomatically refraining from setting up their pitches in protest. So there were no bookmakers operating there, and record takings of £18,000 on the Tote.

Fortunately for punters, this meeting was not one of the Easter fixtures, otherwise there would have been no betting facilities at all, with the Horserace Totalisator Board having reduced its facilities still further by having no official Tote in operation at any of the Easter fixtures, a few of which were running their own hunt totes. The Whaddon Chase situation was amicably resolved afterwards at an informal assembly held by the Jockey Club in Portman Square.

At two meetings, the Banwen Miners and the Exmoor, there was confusion amounting to near-farce; and the proceedings at the Banwen Miners bore more relation to a comic opera than a point-to-point. This meeting at Skewen in Glamorgan was held on top of a mountain, very appropriately on April Fools Day. Scheduled to start at 1.0 p.m., it didn't begin until two hours later. Not as a result of the weather which had turned it into a postponed meeting and made it necessary, owing to the lapse of time, for owners to enter their horses again, but in order to accommodate a sale of farming implements which was taking place in a lower field.

A bad beginning. But there was worse to come. Some owners of the original entries had not been informed that they would be required to re-enter their horses, presumably because the Hon. Sec. was on holiday; and when they were told they couldn't run them they were very far from pleased. One owner even complained that he had paid his entry fee twice.

Nor was there much joy for the public at Skewen; and they were not slow to voice their displeasure at being asked to pay £3 for the only car park and 50 pence for a racecard with four extra pages inserted in the centre of it. In addition to this, the tents were so far away from the paddock and the bookmakers that spectators found themselves involved in a lengthy trek; and although there were only two runners in the adjacent hunts' race, the number board operators had managed to get their names wrong. Moreover, when the right ones eventually appeared on the board it was with the names of their owners instead of their riders. It was, I imagine, a meeting that most of those present would prefer to forget. Fortunately, this sort of thing doesn't occur very often at point-to-points; and there was, after all, the consolation of seeing Mandryka win like a champion.

The confusion at the Exmoor's Bratton Down fixture occurred with the first running of a four-mile men's open that they had gone to a great deal of trouble to stage, and which involved the construction of a new fence that had to be jumped twice. Four horses were pulled up when it became apparent to their riders that they had taken the wrong course; and the horse who passed the post first by a clear margin, Kingrullah, with Paddy Doran up, was disqualified for missing out the wrong fence over a course which had a third circuit following a different line from the other two. Kingrullah's disqualification presented the race to Bahuddin, a ten-year-old from the Hambledon ridden by Barry Stevens.

The experienced Grant Cann had this to say after the race: "I don't blame Fred Rawle (the rider of Eagle Moonday, who started favourite) for taking the wrong course, I blame myself for following him. But it was extremely difficult to know where to go, and at the place we went wrong there were a lot of people around shouting directions."

But whilst the organizers clearly had to shoulder most of the responsibility for the confusion in this case, the riders themselves cannot be entirely absolved. Had they listened more carefully to the instructions they were given beforehand, it might have been a different story.

There was much excitement at the Tickham fixture at Stockbury when one of the horses due to run in the restricted open, Red Keidi, was suspected of being a 'ringer' called My Virginian, the winner of a novice chase at Carlisle in 1975. Owned by Mr. R.R. Butcher and qualified with the Staff College Draghounds based at Sandhurst, Red Keidi was no stranger to point-to-points. He had run four times in 1977 and won the hunt race at his home meeting at Tweseldown ridden by his owner. The local stewards at the Tickham were quick to act on their suspicions that the horse purporting to be Red Keidi was not what he seemed to be, ordering him to be withdrawn and reporting the matter to the Jockey Club, who confirmed their suspicions that the horse was indeed My Virginian; and at the disciplinary committee meeting in Portman Square Mr. Butcher was fined £500; while a more serious view was taken of the breaches committed by a Mr. E. Cordery, who was warned off for seven years as well as being fined £500.

According to the Jockey Club, this is the only known case of a ringer at a point-to-point.

Tailpiece:
It can't be often that a bookmaker rides a winner at a point-to-point, or anywhere else for that matter. But there was one who did so at the Albrighton Woodland meeting at Chaddesley Corbett. Tony Evans, from Ombersley, who betted under the name of Hugh Corbett, was riding his first winner when scoring on the nine-year-old Whatyournameis in the restricted open. After he had done so, he returned to his pitch to continue business.

1979

*In which five-year-olds get an allowance, prize money increases,
the PPOA launches its young horse awards, a new star emerges in
East Anglia, a Scottish contender wins the BMW men's final, and
a bookmaker springs to the defence of hunting.*

At long last, Jim Mahon, the Chairman of the Point-to-Point Owners'
Association, found his cherished dream of a 71b. allowance for five-year-
olds coming true, the Jockey Club having responded to his persistent campaigning for it. Not everyone, however, was happy about it. Dorian Williams, the
Master of the Whaddon Chase, speaking at the national point-to-point dinner in
September, was vehemently against it. "If a five-year-old cannot carry 12st. 71b.,"
he said, "then it is never likely to develop into the hunter chaser which, in my
opinion, is what point-to-point racing is all about."

The new regulation had, however, come to stay; and whilst it may not have
made an appreciable difference to the number of five-year-olds winning point-to-
points in its first year (18 of them, mostly in maiden races), included amongst the
winning five-year-olds was a former novice hurdler, Mr. Bunny, now trained by
Fred Rimell after being hunted with the Ledbury, who won three of his five hunter
chases, and was the runner-up to Spartan Missile in another at Warwick.

The best five-year-old running in point-to-points was Grant Cann's owner-ridden Village Mark (a son of Romany Air), who was unbeaten in his three point-to-
points and never properly extended in any of them. There were those who opined
that Village Mark, bred from Stewart Pike's winning point-to-point mare
Watermark II, was the best novice seen out in the West since Diamond Edge.

In a year which saw the Grant from the Levy Board for the maintenance of
point-to-point courses going up to £83,500, the prize money rose from £75 to
£100 for an open event (including ladies' opens and restricted opens), and from
£55 to £75 for all other races. The winner's share of this was usually £60 in open
events and £40 or £50 in other races, with proportionate place money; but
although a fourth prize would now have been allowable, there was little or no evidence of this happening.

As regards the prize money on offer for hunter chases, it was even stevens for
the two richest of the season, at £6,000, the Cheltenham Foxhunters', now spon-

sored by Christies, the fine arts auctioneers, and the BMW men's championship at Chepstow, where the winner had the option of a BMW car in preference to the cash.

Thanks to sponsorship from the Irish bookmaking firm of Sean Graham, the Point-to-Point Owners' Association were able to launch their young horse awards for the leading five, six and seven-year-olds in the 14 point-to-point areas with cash prizes of £100 for each of the winning owners, plus a £100 trophy for their retention. These awards were conducted on a points basis, as they are today.

The Horserace Totalisator Board was also disposed to be generous, with the announcement that it would be giving 50% of its net profits on pools betting to all the point-to-points that were taking advantage of its services; and in the case of those meetings running their own totes under licence from the H.T.B., instead of having to pay 15% of their profits to the Tote, there would now be a flat annual rate of £10 and an initial consultancy fee of £15.

What else, I am wondering, is there left to say in praise of Spartan Missile, of John Thorne, the man who bred him and rode him in most of his races, and of the stallion who begat this great horse, Spartan General, the leading sire of N.H. winners in 1979 and of point-to-pointers and hunter chasers three years running since succeeding Even Money in that role in 1977?

At least I can pay tribute to Spartan Missile's achievements in 1979 when retaining his crown. A winner of ten of his 11 hunter chases, all of them with his 52-year-old owner up, he brought off a tremendous treble in winning the Cheltenham Foxhunters', the Liverpool Foxhunters' and the *Horse and Hound* Cup at Stratford. Only one other horse had ever achieved such a feat, Credit Call in 1972. Spartan Missile's single defeat was in a hunter chase at Towcester, where he was beaten a length by Ten Up (whose three wins during the season included the Grand Military Gold Cup at Sandown) trying to give him 71b.

It is worth mentioning, I feel, that the rating of 13-0 accorded Spartan Missile in the 1980 (covering the 1979 season) edition of the famous annual was the highest since Geoffrey Sale, going it alone in the 1962 and 1963 annuals, awarded 12-10 to the Atherstone hunter Pride Of Ivanhoe; and that was at a time when Colledge Master was still running in hunter chases, and Baulking Green had appeared on the scene.

Next to Spartan Missile in their handicap Mackenzie & Phillips had Queensberry Lad, the horse he beat so convincingly in the Cheltenham Foxhunters', over a stone below him at 11-10. But although overshadowed by Spartan Missile, Queensberry Lad was the star of the North. A winner of three of his five races with Graham Macmillan up, including hunter chases at Kelso and Hexham, he began his season beating Carndonagh 20 lengths in the men's open at the Lanarkshire & Renfrewshire at Bogside; and it was the nine-year-old Carndonagh who became the first horse from Scotland to win the men's final, which was now in its last year of sponsorship by BMW at Chepstow.

At one stage it looked as if Carndonagh was going to run right away with the Chepstow race despite the 12-7 that he was carrying. In the end, however, Michael Dun had to apply vigorous pressure to hold off Guy Staight on his father's The Wrestler by half a length; but this massive nine-year-old from the North Cotswold was receiving a stone and 3lb. from the winner.

Considering his diminutive size, Carndonagh was a marvellous weight carrier; and in his ten appearances during the season he was in the winner's enclosure six times (the last five in a row) and a runner-up on his other four appearances. In all but one of these races he was ridden by Michael Dun. The exception was the four-mile men's open at the Percy where he was a first winner for Michael's brother, 17-year-old Gordon Dun, who was sitting on him in public for the first time. These two Duns are cousins of the Geordie Dun who was the leading amateur of the 1978-1979 season under N.H. Rules.

Rated 41b. above Carndonagh, however, on a mark of 11-5, was the 11-year-old Remigio from the Old Surrey & Burstow. Trained to perfection by Fred Winter, this son of Even Money was unbeaten in his six hunter chases, ridden each time by Jim Wilson, the runner-up to Geordie Dun for the amateur rider's title.

Although she ran only three times in 1979 owing to a foot infection, Zanetta was still the top-rated horse in ladies' races at 11-2. Beaten a short head in a ladies' open at Kingston Blount by Sarah French's mount Prince Tacitus, the Warwickshire mare was an easy winner of her other two races.

Just 21b. behind Zanetta in the handicap was Mrs. Clare Villar's Suffolk six-year-old Mr. Mellors, on whom Lucy King was having such a good season, winning two ladies' opens at Cottenham, beating a useful horse in Florida King on both occasions, and scoring in hunter chases at Leicester, Huntingdon and Fakenham.

Neither Mr. Mellors nor Zanetta ran in the final of the BMW ladies' championship at Chepstow, though both had qualified for it. But the veteran Pat Kerby deserved a special bouquet for winning this championship at the age of 52. Happy Returns, the Clifton-on-Teme mare she won it on, was the daughter of a Champion Hurdle winner, Saucy Kit, and a granddaughter, on her dam's side, of a Cheltenham Gold Cup winner, Fortina. She was an easy winner, but receiving a lot of weight from the two who followed her home, Tennessee II and Wiener Chic. The BMW race was the climax to a highly successful season for Happy Returns and Pat Kerby. The partnership also won four point-to-points in a row and had Little Fleur behind them on two occasions.

The German-bred Wiener Chic, a seven-year-old from the Dartmoor, who had won on the Flat and over hurdles before being bought for 750 guineas, won two ladies' opens for his owner-rider, Mrs. Sue Reynard, in 1978, beating Hargan in one of them and Lady Christine in the other; and in 1979 this son of a German and Austrian Derby winner won five ladies' opens and two West Country hunter chases for her.

Another very fine combination were Pip Fisher and Paul Tylor's Hargan, who scarcely looked back after going under to Sue Reynard and Wiener Chic at the Bolventor Harriers. They won ten of their 12 ladies' opens in the West, enabling the 29-year-old Pip Fisher, from Kingsbridge, Devon, to win the *Sporting Life* Cup for the first time with her ten winners, one ahead of the joint runners-up, Josie Sheppard and Katie Halswell. And it was also a first-time win for Hargan's owner in the case of the Grand Marnier Tophy. Paul Tylor was the first West Country owner to win this trophy since the Truro solicitor Magin Hancock won it with his

Golden Batman in 1971; and Pip Fisher was the first West Country rider to win the ladies' title since Mrs. Diana Coaker did so 20 years earlier in the days before the *Sporting Life* Cup came on the scene. Hargan, I feel I must add, was bred not in the West Country but in Lisburn, Northern Ireland.

David Turner, again well mounted on his father's horses, took the *Daily Telegraph* Cup for the sixth time, with 17 winners, two more than managed by John Bryan, who had beaten him for the men's title the previous season and prevented him from winning the title for the fifth year in succession.

But although John Bryan missed out on the *Daily Telegraph* Cup, he was still young enough to be presented with the Wilkinson Sword for the leading rider under the age of 21 at the PPOA dinner at the Hilton International in Stratford, where there was also £500 to come for Mrs. Pam Morris, whose eight-year-old, Sparkford, a winner, on the trot, of seven open point-to-points and two hunter chases, all with John Bryan up, was the winner of the *Sporting Chronicle* points championship.

And it was Sparkford who gave John Bryan and his trainer-father their third win in the Dudley Cup. The field for this point-to-point classic was a disappointingly small one, with no more than seven of the 29 entries going to the post on the good to soft ground at Chaddesley Corbett. But Sparkford could hardly have won it more convincingly; and one of the horses he had to beat was Headmaster, the winner of the Heythrop four-miler.

But it was really a case of Sparkford first and the rest nowhere. The son of Spartan General was never headed after jumping the second. The race was for second place, with the runner-up, Night School, ten lengths behind the winner, holding off Headmaster by a head for second place and Crystal Gazer, having been passed by Headmaster on the run-in, finishing a close fourth.

One of the other races won by Sparkford, and very easily, was the Sean Graham Golden Harvest hunter chase run over four miles at Cheltenham in early May. So it is reasonable to assume that, had Sparkford gone for Lord Ashton of Hyde's Cup at the Heythrop over a similar distance, he would also have won this classic.

There were 14 runners for the Heythrop race on good to soft ground at Stow-on-the-Wold; and Headmaster, who had failed to win any of his four previous races during the season but had won nine hurdle races and two chases from David Barons' yard in his younger days, could have been backed at 50-1. The joint favourites were Robert Alner's mount Dance Again, a winner of his three previous events, all of them open races, and Border Charm, a mare on whom John Sharp had won a restricted open at Horseheath. But they just weren't good enough for Headmaster, a horse trained by a farrier, ridden by a farrier and owned by a Herefordshire farmer, Mr. E.J. Bufton.

The 20-year-old Andrew James always had Headmaster lying handy and from quite a long way out it was simply a question of how much the horse was going to win by. In the end, it was a distance, from Border Charm, who ran very much better than Dance Again, a toiling fourth. Headmaster won two more races afterwards, the men's opens at the South Shropshire and the Clifton-on-Teme. He was a credit to his trainer, Richard Lee, who, in later years, was to make another name for himself and his Presteigne stable on the border of Wales in a professional capacity.

Headmaster's bid to become the first horse to win the Heythrop four-miler and the 4.5-mile race for the Grimthorpe Cup at the Middleton in the same season was, however, unsuccessful. He finished a well-beaten fifth in this race to the Yorkshire-hunted Rakamar, an eight-year-old from the Zetland recording his only win of the season and doing it in style under Tim Smith, winning by a distance in a field of 12; and even though the going at Whitwell-on-the-Hill was holding, Rakamar's time of 9 mins. 34 secs. was three seconds faster than that taken by Sea Petrel to win last year's race. Not bad for a horse out of an unregistered mare who was bought by his owner, Mark Wilson, as a five-year-old to hunt on.

Waggoners Walk, the locally-hunted ten-year-old on whom Caroline Mason won the 4-mile ladies' open at this meeting for the second time in five years and finished third in the 1977 and 1978 races, later gave Caroline her first successes as a public trainer when the races he won under Rules included the 4-mile National Hunt Chase at Cheltenham in 1980 and the Kim Muir amateur riders' chase there in 1981.

David Turner's successful visits to the West Country in the closing weeks of the season saw him completing a double at the Exmoor in June when he won the British Field Sports Society race on the stable's nine-year-old Kara-Pops, a horse bought for 2,000 guineas that he had won two races on the previous season, and the four-mile men's open on a rather more expensive purchase at 5,700 guineas, the seven-year-old Hill Point, a grandson, on his dam's side, of the 1953 Derby winner Pinza. At this point of the season Turner was one winner ahead of John Bryan for the men's title, and he made it two on the last day of the season when scoring on Hill Point in the men's open at the Torrington Farmers.

A new star emerged in East Anglia to take over the mantle there of the great Hard Frost when George Cooper's General Confusion, another son of Spartan General, started to show them what he could do in open events. This eight-year-old, a horse acquired for 3,000 guineas at the Ascot Sales in June 1976 after losing his maiden certificate at the Woodland Pytchley for his previous owner, won five open races and two hunter chases with Cooper up on him; and his victims on the way included Water Sport, four of the Turner horses, Hill Point among them, and a future Grand National winner in Grittar, who finished fourth to him in the men's open at the Fitzwilliam.

The outstanding novice of the season, both in looks and ability, was Dick Saunders' Artfull Leigh, a winner in the show-ring. This seven-year-old from the Pytchley won seven of his eight point-to-points, with his owner riding him in one of them and his 19-year-old daughter Caroline winning six on him. There is not much doubt that this brilliant young horse would have gone through the season unbeaten but for a fall at the fifteenth when in process of trotting up (with a substitute rider aboard) in the restricted open at the Fitzwilliam.

It was entirely fitting, therefore, that Artfull Leigh should wind up his season winning the Marie Curie Memorial novice championship at the Melton Hunt Club, where a field of 18 went to the post. Splendidly ridden by Caroline Saunders, who waited in front on him all the way, Artfull Leigh never put a foot wrong and won with plenty in hand from the favourite, Joey Newton's mount the five-year-

Harry Dufosee on his Royal Wilts at the South & West Wilts in 1926.

The adjacent hunts' ladies' race at the Wylye Valley in 1928 –
Miss Helen Cross on Gossiping George leads Lady Jean Douglas-Hamilton
riding side-saddle on Cavalier.

Major Harold Rushton on his famous O'Dell at the Warwickshire in 1935, when this fixture was held at Chesterton, near Leamington.

The record-breaking Lonesome Boy, a winner of 65 point-to-points, jumping over a bank in the West Country with Jennifer Renfree up.
Photo: George Ellis.

Cash Account, with Billy Wynn up, winning his third Dudley Cup at the Worcestershire in 1957. *Photo: Jim Meads.*

The Callant and his owner, Mr C.D. (Charlie) Scott, taking part in the Parade of Horse Personalities at the Horse of the Year Show at Harringay Arena in 1958.

Above: Hard Frost and Mick Barber, as usual on their own, winning at Friars Wash in 1962. *Photo: Jim Meads.*

Another of the point-to-pointers who made a great impact on the N.H. scene – Merryman II, ridden by Charlie Scott, going down to the post for the *Horse and Hound* Cup at Stratford in 1959. *Photo: Jim Meads..*

That Much, one of the few horses who managed to beat Hard Frost, achieving this feat in an open race with Ian Loftus up in 1960.

Above: The cavalry charge at the first fence in Div. 2 of the open race at Cambridgeshire Harriers Point-to-Point in 1965. The winner, Bouffon II (Mr David Tatlow), is already in the lead with Robert Case (second) on Cardinal Wolsey, just behind. *Photo: Jim Meads.*

David Wales (nearest camera) winning on Pearly Glint 1962.

Guy Cunard winning the hunt race at the
Middleton on Puddle Jumper in 1962.
Photo: Jim Meads.

Bill Shand Kydd winning on his famed No Reward at his home meeting, the Whaddon Chase
Great Horwood, in 1963, the year No Reward was the champion point-to-pointer with his eig
wins and Shand Kydd was the runner-up to Guy Cunard for the men's title. *Photo: Jim Meads*

Over a bank at one of the last 'banking' point-to-points to be held – Tetcott Hunt in North Devon. Left to right: Kipling Tors, Mr W. Brooks – winner; Taramac, Mr R. Edwards – 2nd; Discus II, Mr T. le Grice. *Photo: Jim Meads.*

Left to right: David Tatlow, Sue Aston and Guy Cunard, three of the award winners at the National Point-to-Point Dinner in London in 1968. *Photo: Jim Meads.*

The Dikler on his majestic way to the start for his
men's open at Kimble in 1969 with Brian Fanshawe up.
Photo: Jim Meads.

Two of a kind. Pat Tollit (right) with her natural successor, Sue Aston, in 1970. *Photo: Jim Meads.*

John Thorne and his twin daughters on their way to the post for the hunt race at the Warwickshire in 1972. Jane (centre) had her first winning ride in this race on Indian Diva. John, who brought off a treble on three other horses, was the runner-up to her on Ben Ruler. Diana (right) finished 5th of 13 on Bright Daisy. *Photo: Jim Meads.*

Pat Tollit recording her 150th win in point-to-points riding her mother's
Pensham in the ladies' open at the Oakley in 1972. *Photo: Jim Meads.*

'Fizz' Chown (née Robarts) and Royal Charity in 1972
with their season's trophies. *Photo: Jim Meads.*

Anthony's Cottage and Celia Conley go their separate ways at the open ditch. Photograph taken during the running of the final of the 1973 Goya Ladies' Championship at the Melton Hunt Club fixture in Leicestershire. *Photo: Jim Meads.*

Tenor's successful swan song with Sue Aston up in the four-mile ladies' open for the Lady Leigh Cup at the North Warwickshire in 1973. He is being followed by Blantyre Lad, with Didi Morris up. *Photo: Jim Meads.*

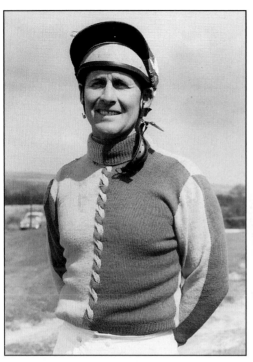

Richard ('The Jolly') Miller, a dual champion in 1972 and 1973. *Photo: Jim Meads.*

Mrs Mabel Forrest, Scotland's champion in 1973. *Photo: Jim Meads.*

21 years of point-to-point racing at Fox Farm, Stow-on-the-Wold, is being celebrated here by the Heythrop, where Alastair Cowen is seen winning the hunt race on his False Note in 1973, a year before he won the 4-mile race for Lord Ashton of Hyde's Cup on the same horse.
Photo: Jim Meads.

Top: Michael Bloom on the way to winning the Dudley Cup of 1974 on Lake District in the same year that he won the Grimthorpe Cup on Watch Night (in the picture below) at the Middleton. Jumping the fence (left) is His Last, on whom Robert Chugg finished third. The horse in the background is Rave Notice, who was last of the five starters. *Both photos: Jim Meads.*

Left: Jenny Pitman greets Road Race, who gave her the first win of her training career at Tweseldown in 1974. *Photo: Jim Meads.*

1975 Bolventor Maiden.
West Country Champion Frank Ryall bows out at the age of 53 with a hard-fought win on Peter Wakeham's In Again at the expense of Norman Lethridge (top) on Moorland Venture.

David Turner and his father in the winner's enclosure with Flaming Double after their win in the restricted open at the Torrington Farmers in 1977. *Photo: John Corsan.*

Right and below: Dual winners at Tweseldown in 1977, David Turner winning the men's open on Galway Knight and his sister Josie Bothway (as she then was) taking the ladies' open on Hardcastle. *Photos: John Grant.*

Below: Peter Brookshaw (bottom) flanked by his sons Peter and (right) Steven, who was later to train a Grand National winner. They are all winners of the Dudley Cup. *Photo: Jim Meads.*

Sporting Luck, owned by Miss Joyce Hey and ridden by 29-year-old Tim Smith, came from Yorkshire to win the 1978 Lady Dudley Cup at the Worcestershire in smooth style.
Photo: Jim Meads.

Peter Greenall (left) and Joey Newton, two
of the winning riders at the Fernie in 1980.
Photo: Jim Meads.

old Brave Charlie, who had lost his maiden certificate at the South Wold, run in those days at The Carholme, the former setting for the Lincolnshire Handicap. Brave Charlie had also scored in the restricted open at the Quorn over the Garthorpe course.

Artfull Leigh's time of 6 mins. 17 secs. at Garthorpe was a second faster than the time taken by Water Sport to beat Hill Point and Jim Lad in the men's open; and only two seconds slower than the time taken by Deep Mystery to win the Nitram ladies' championship.

Jenny Hembrow had made a 200-mile journey from the West Country to take the place of the injured Cathie Houlbrook on Deep Mystery, a seven-year-old Deep Run gelding from the Flint & Denbigh formerly owned by Cathie's father, Bill Houlbrook, who had given the horse to her for Christmas on the condition that he continued to carry his colours until Melton, where Deep Mystery, a horse bought for 825 guineas at the Ascot Sales in February 1976 after he had won three races on the Flat as a three-year-old, was recording his fourth win of the season. He had, however, won ten hurdle races for Bill Houlbrook between April 1976 and May 1978 when in training with Edward Owen Jnr. at Denbigh.

Asked what instructions she had given Jenny Hembrow before the Nitram, the gleeful Cathie Houlbrook said, "I told her I don't care where you finish as long as you bring him back in one piece."

A few words now about the last foal of Double Sail, the mare who produced Sally Furlong, Ladybank and Pensham. The horse I am thinking of was their half-brother, Tim Holland-Martin's seven-year-old Wisbech Lad, bred, like the others, by Bill and Patsy Bomford in the North Cotswold country, and bought by Holland-Martin from Bill Bomford as a three-year-old.

A faller two fences out in the Marie Curie novice championship in 1978 when he was making his first appearance on a course and held every chance, his next appearance was in a restricted open at Mollington in 1979. He won it very comfortably with his owner up. He then beat Ten Up 25 lengths in the R.A. Gold Cup hunter chase at Sandown; but on his only other appearance this season disconcerted his admirers (to put it mildly) by slipping up on landing over the third in a men's open at Larkhill. Sadly, he failed to train on after being pin-fired. All the same, this brilliant novice of the 1979 season was a horse not easily forgotten.

Neither was Cheekio Ora, the six-year-old son of Romany Air out of a mare by the St. Leger winner Chamossaire so brilliantly produced in the Cottesmore country by Capt. Bryan Parry, who bought him for 600 guineas at the Ascot Sales in December 1977 and saw him win twice as a five-year-old in 1978, his first season on a course. In 1979, on his graduation to open races, Cheekio Ora was unbeaten in his three races, ridden in one of them by Andrew Berry, his rider in his first season, and in the other two by Peter Greenall, who was to partner him so successfully in later years.

The dubious distinction of being the leading rogues of the season must surely belong to Leveramoss and Flintstone. Their unwillingness amounted almost to poetry. Levaramoss, a winner six times over hurdles, made seven appearances in point-to-points in 1979 after being hunted with the Cattistock. In his first race, the men's open at the Bolventor Harriers, he consented to start after the others had jumped two fences, but declined to jump the second fence and put his rider on the floor. Bravely remounted by Alan Walter, who had travelled from Gloucestershire for the privilege of riding him, he refused again after a further quarter mile. His next race was the men's open at the Tiverton Foxhounds, and here he was also an early refuser. Well, one can't blame him too much for that. The going was extremely holding in parts and he was carrying the welter-weight of 14st. 11lb. in a field of 20.

It was a similar story at the Quantock Staghounds a week later. He was then tried in a ladies' open at the Lamerton, where he refused at the first and again at the third. On his next appearance, in the hunt race at the Cattistock, he fell at the second; but in his last two races he did rather better, getting as far as the four-teenth before falling in a men's open at Larkhill; and then winding his point-to-point season up by completing a course for the first time in a men's open at the Seavington, where he was fourth of the five finishers.

Was he now a reformed character? What do you think? The next time he was heard of in a point-to-point, three years later, he was running in the hunt race at the Silverton under the name of Max, having changed hands at Ascot Sales for 975 guineas; and this time, after eventually getting under way, he refused at the first. His new owner was later fined £100.

Flintstone, mixing unwillingness with brilliance, began the season winning two open races at Tweseldown under David Evatt, beating The Wrestler very convincingly in the second of them. After that, however, it was downhill most of the way, causing Mackenzie & Phillips to refer to him as "an obnoxious lout now." But, after failing to complete the course in four of his six remaining races, pulling himself up in three of them and attempting to do so in another before going on to finish a remote third in a field of four, he rehabilitated himself to some extent in his last race of the season, the men's open at the Old Surrey & Burstow.

In this race, still being ridden by David Evatt, who deserved a medal for bravery and persistence, he put up a truly remarkable performance. After declining to jump the fourteenth he stopped altogether, only commencing to re-start when the others were a fence ahead. But he was travelling so strongly under Evatt in the closing stages that he managed to run the winner, Lord Of The Rings (who was recording his seventh win of the season under Bob Hacking), to a couple of lengths.

In the hunt race at the Essex Union at Marks Tey there was a first winner for the third generation of a well-known East Anglian point-to-pointing family when 16-year-old Nicola Barber, the youngest daughter of Mick and the granddaughter of George, scored on her grandfather's New Penny II, thus reviving memories of George Barber's great point-to-pointer Hard Frost, who dominated the East Anglian scene for so long.

And at the Portman meeting at Badbury Rings, Mike Felton, a future men's champion, had his first winning ride when scoring in the maiden race on Michael Tory's home-bred mare Morning Heather, the last in a line going back to Reverent Mother, on whom Michael and his sister Bridget had so many winning rides.

A new Grand Marnier award for presentation at the national point-to-point dinner was one for the leading lady novice rider of the season; and this was shared by 22-year-old Sally Piggott (a distant relative of Lester's) from Herefordshire and the 18-year-old Amanda Parker from East Anglia, each of them having ridden four point-to-point winners. Geoff Woodruff, a 22-year-old farm worker from Kent, took the male novice rider's award (which was now a separate one) with his five winners for Peter Skinner's Romney Marsh stable.

With John Marriage, Q.C. remarking at the Point-to-Point Owners' Association annual dinner, "We are at a very dangerous moment because, with a non-Labour Government for the next five years, there is a risk of everyone going to sleep," and advising his listeners to "carry the cause of field sports into the highways and byways," it was encouraging to see some support for hunting coming from a bookmaker. Keith Wright of Cambridge, a member of the Bookmakers' Protection Association, had this to say to his fellow members:

"If hunting was abolished there would be no intake of hunters for steeplechasing, which already has difficulty in filling three-mile chases. There would be no point-to-point or coursing meetings, which are part of the British way of life."

And he went on to advise members of the B.P.A. to support the British Field Sports Society in fighting the threat to hunting, and even suggested they should write to the Prime Minister reminding him of the £100 million pounds that bookmakers collect in betting duty each year.

The death shortly before the start of the season of Major Bob Wormald, for 22 years the clerk of the course at the Middleton, removed one of the most efficient administrators that the sport has ever seen. It was largely down to Bob that the Ralph Grimthorpe Gold Cup at the Middleton became known as the Point-to-Point Grand National, when he finally managed to get the distance of the race increased to 4.5 miles in 1954; and throughout his long reign he always ensured that the course at Whitwell-on-the-Hill was kept in impeccable condition. No mean rider himself in his younger days, he was himself a winner of the race in 1939 on his own horse Putty, after a prolonged duel with Guy Cunard on Coxwold Countess; and in post-war days, Bob was third on Putty, a horse he had bought for £50, in the Lady Dudley Cup of 1946 at the Worcestershire.

In June, Andy Frank died at the early age of 45. The son of Harry Frank, the breeder of the 1960 Cheltenham Gold Cup winner Pas Seul, Andy was one of the leading amateurs of his day. He rode two winners of the United Hunts' Cup at Cheltenham, Mrs W.J.A. Shepherd's Chaos in 1961 and Jim Reade's great horse Baulking Green in 1964; and he was up on Baulking Green when the horse won the *Horse and Hound* Cup at Stratford in 1963. Sadly, a bad riding accident put paid to his career as a race-rider and left him partially paralysed. He was married to Bertie Hill's sister, Ivy.

In December, soon after celebrating his 77th birthday, Jervis Foulds died. Born and bred in Worcestershire, Jervis was a dedicated point-to-point enthusiast if ever there was one; and he was the author of a book on the Dudley Cup which was published in 1978 and traced the history of the race from its beginning in 1897 up to 1977. This book was a real labour of love and no one was better qualified to write it than Jervis.

Tailpiece:

A bizarre touch was added to the proceedings at the Vale of Clettwr when Gwynfor Evans, the Welsh Nationalist M.P. for Carmarthen and leader of Plaid Cymru, insisted on delivering an election address in Welsh. Not many understood what he was saying, and punters listened in vain for any useful tips it might have contained. Come the General Election, Gwynfor Evans lost his Carmarthen seat.

1980

In which Jim Mahon has reason to smile, professionally-trained horses win more than their fair share, Lucy King wins her first major title, and a famous rogue undergoes partial reformation.

This was the year the Point-to-Point Owners' Club held their first point-to-point, and the site chosen for it was Col. Arthur Clerke-Brown's course at Kingston Blount, where, thanks to the spadework put in by the indefatigable Jim Mahon, the entire meeting was sponsored by Leyland Tractors, with the one and only Peter O'Sullevan as the race commentator, Richard Pitman as the starter and Dick Francis judging the best turn-outs.

More than that, Mahon had managed to get round the Jockey Club's inflexible decision to keep the prize money for individual races unchanged by arranging for Leyland Tractors to sponsor a farmers' points championship embracing 28 point-to-points with prize money amounting to £700 at the end of it, the winner's share being £550. This in addition to the normal prize money on offer for the concluding race in the series, the Leyland Tractors farmers' race at this meeting.

And it so happened that the winner of this race, Geoff Kittow's Star Express, a seven-year-old mare by Pony Express that he had bred on his farm at Cullompton in Devon from an unraced mare by Lancewood, was also the winner of the points championship.

Ridden at Kingston Blount by his owner's nephew, Stuart Kittow, Star Express won a good race by a length and a half from Jim Mahon's His Last, with another of the season's prolific winners, Richard Woodhouse's Dance Again, a winner of six open events with three different riders up, taking third place; and it was the 12-year-old Dance Again, who was the runner-up in the points championship with 16 points as against the 20 amassed by Star Express, who was recording his seventh win of the season, ridden in three of them by Stuart Kittow, in two by Katie Halswell and in two by Grant Cann.

Much of the credit for Star Express's successes belonged to Katie Halswell. Not just for the two races she won on him but for continuing to train him after she broke her pelvis and three of her ribs in a fall on him in a hunter chase at Devon & Exeter in March. It was very sad to learn after the season was over that Star

Express had collapsed and died on the gallops shortly after joining Fulke Walwyn's yard.

The profits from the PPOA's inaugural fixture, amounting to around £4,000, were divided between the Injured Jockeys' Fund and the Hunt Servants' Benefit Society.

There were not many new regulations introduced in 1980; but a significant one was a rule to the effect that an objection could now be lodged for an incident occurring "after the penultimate fence," whereas before it had been "after the last fence." This was in line with racing under Rules.

This was also the year that the first weekly point-to-point index became available to subscribers. Linked with the results published weekly in the *Sporting Life*, this valuable service was provided by Brian Beel, who had been issuing his hunter-chase ratings for the last 15 years. In later years this service was carried on by Jonathan Neesom.

It was sad to see BMW withdrawing from their sponsorship of the men's and ladies' championships at Chepstow after a spell of five years in the case of the former and three with the latter. But Jeep (U.K.) Ltd. and Christies were quick to step into the breach with joint sponsorship and comparable prize money, £6,000 for the men's final and £2,000 for the ladies' final.

For the third successive year Spartan Missile remained at the head of Mackenzie & Phillips' handicap, and at 13-0 for the last two. But since Spartan Missile made only three appearances in 1980, with a single win on his final appearance in a moderate field for the 2.5-mile Air Wedding hunter chase at Warwick, clearly something was not quite right with him; and one has to say that his exceptionally high rating this time owed more to his reputation than to his current form. In his other two races, he was the runner-up to King Kong II (a horse he would normally have had no problems beating, even at a difference of 7lb.) in a hunter chase at Sandown and fifth of six finishers in the Grand Steeple-Chase de Paris at Auteuil.

It was a different story, though, in the case of Rolls Rambler, the horse rated second to Spartan Missile at 11-9. This nine-year-old from the Bicester, owned by Barry Brazier and professionally trained by Fred Winter, won five hunter chases in a row under Oliver Sherwood and brought off the big treble, winning the Cheltenham Foxhunters', the Liverpool Foxhunters' and the *Horse and Hound* Cup at Stratford, the first horse to do so since Credit Call in 1972.

Another horse owned by Barry Brazier and trained for him by Fred Winter was the eight-year-old Shannon Bridge, who was unbeaten in his four hunter chases and also had Oliver Sherwood up. But for the same trainer's Remigio, now 12 years old, it was not quite such a good season. He started off his five appearances in hunter chases being beaten by King Kong II at Newbury, and ended them finishing fourth to Royal Air at Ascot. In between, however, he was a winner at Kempton and Leicester.

Not only was Oliver Sherwood the leading rider in hunter chases with his ten winners in this field of activity; but with his overall total of 29 winners under N.H. Rules, he was the Bollinger amateur riders' champion.

Whilst there was growing dismay amongst the point-to-point fraternity at the way hunter chases continued to be filled by horses from professional yards, with 28 of them won by such horses, netting over £30,000 in prize money, it was not entirely a case of one-way traffic. Graham Macmillan's Queensberry Lad, home-trained at Lockerbie, was still going strong, and the Libby Lees-trained Mr. Mellors and Capt. Bryan Parry's owner-trained Cheekio Ora were advancing their reputations.

In a season when his appearances were reduced by leg problems, Queensberry Lad completed a hat-trick in hunter chases before an attempt to make all the running for the *Horse and Hound* Cup in the soft ground at Stratford resulted in his being pulled up two fences out when his chance had gone.

Meanwhile, Mr. Mellors, the runner-up to Rolls Rambler in this race, was coming on by leaps and bounds under Lucy King. In his 11 appearances during the season, the seven-year-old son of Precipice Wood won two ladies' opens and five hunter chases; and on the three other occasions, all in hunter chases, in two of which he was giving away lumps of weight, he was a runner-up.

Despite having so many rides in hunter chases, Lucy King still managed to ride a sufficient number of point-to-point winners, 14 in all, to win her first *Sporting Life* Cup. The most prolific winner in points-to-points for the 22-year-old Newmarket-born rider, who also rode four winners in handicap chases in addition to her seven in hunter chases, was Tom Hunnable's Florida King, an eight-year-old from the Suffolk on whom she won six races; and it was this horse, who won two more races with David Turner up, that secured the Grand Marnier Trophy for his Essex owner.

Florida King was yet another of the horses trained by the brilliant Libby Lees, all seven of whose runners were winners, with 25 successes between them, 18 of them in point-to-points and the other seven in hunter chases.

But the leading owner was still Joe Turner, with his 24 winners in point-to-points, plus one under Rules, Hill Point, who won his own hunter chase at Fakenham with his son David up.

The runner-up to Lucy King for *The Life* Cup was the West Country's Pip Fisher with 11 winners. She was particularly well mounted on Jack Reddaway's Galloway Fabulous, whose usual pilot, Katie Halswell, was unable to take the rides in 1980 owing to injury. Pip Fisher won six ladies' opens and was a runner-up in three others on this 13-year-old from the Mid Devon whose dam, Galloway Gorse, was a half-sister to that spectacular chaser Galloway Braes, the King George VI Chase winner of 1953, and extremely unlucky not to win the race in 1955, when Fred Winter dropped his hands on him too soon and he got beaten a neck by Limber Hill, a former point-to-pointer who went on to win the Cheltenham Gold Cup.

For the first time in its history the *Daily Telegraph* Cup was shared, David Turner and Ian McKie each riding 20 winners. But it wasn't until the last day of the season that the East Anglian rider drew level with his South Midlands rival. Both of them had rides in the men's open at the Torrington Farmers, with Turner up on the evens favourite, Libby Lees's horse Keep, who was bidding for a hat-trick, and McKie riding the second favourite, Jim Mahon's His Last, who had been running consistently well but without scoring.

From the last open ditch, Keep and His Last were engaged in a ding-dong battle, with the 15-year-old Devon Spirit close on their heels. Keep jumped the last a length ahead of Devon Spirit but landed flat-footed. David Turner kept him going long enough, however, to hold off Devon Spirit by half a length, with His Last a similar distance away in third.

The Grand Marnier leading novice riders of the season were two of the northern riders, Yorkshire's 19-year-old Nigel Tutty with his eight winners and 18-year-old Pat Robson from Northumberland with five, the same number as Mrs. Jennifer Irish in the Berkeley country but with more second places.

Tutty, a metallurgist with the British Steel Corporation, was also the winner of the Wilkinson Sword. The best horse he rode was Whiggie Geo, who was unbeaten in his seven races and ended up winning the Jeep-Christies' men's final at Chepstow unchallenged and giving Tutty his first win under Rules.

Rosemary White had an equally smooth passage on Star Nello in the Jeep-Christies' ladies' final, despite the fact that this nine-year-old mare from the Monmouthshire was jumping to the right at nearly every fence. Sally Williamson, riding the runner-up, Jason Bach, had the misfortune to break a stirrup leather at the third, and she had to ride over the 19 remaining fences with only one iron. Although it probably didn't make any difference to the result, she might otherwise have gone closer on this ten-year-old, who had Hargan behind her.

Star Nello, a winner of three of her seven races during the season, was bought as an unbroken four-year-old at Ascot Sales for 210 guineas by Mrs. Daphne Watkins, whose husband, Adrian, was Chairman of the Monmouthshire Hunt.

It is, I think, fair to say, though, that the Nitram ladies' championship at the Melton Hunt Club fixture produced a classier winner than Star Nello. This was Honourable Enoch, an eight-year-old from the Albrighton who was completing a hat-trick of wins in ladies' opens under his owner-rider, Mrs. Harriet Small, and had beaten Star Nello in one of them.

In a field which included Florida King, who started favourite and was still in the lead at the downhill third last, Honourable Enoch took up the running between the last two fences; and although he was given a good race by Rosemary Barnett's mount Night Ride, who tried desperately hard to get to him, he crossed the line with a length and a half to spare. Empress Victoria, the third horse home under Clare Mair, went by Florida King on the run-in.

This was Mrs. Small's fourth success on Honourable Enoch, a first winner for her when the 24-year-old rider won on him at the Meynell & South Staffs. The horse was bought in the summer of 1979 from the Shifnal trainer Roy Cambidge, for whom he won over hurdles and was placed in two novice chases.

A class fixture deserves a class winner and Melton certainly got one when Dick Saunders won the men's open on a future Grand National winner, Frank Gilman's home-bred Grittar, bred from a mare, Tarama (by Tamerlane), who won two novice chases for her owner.

It is true that the seven-year-old Grittar, a winner of two hunter chases with Caroline up on his five previous appearances during the season, and placed in two others at Cheltenham, had only four opponents to beat; but he couldn't have won more convincingly, and the horse that he beat in much the fastest time of the day, Joey Newton's mount Church Newton, had won five open races and a hunter chase at Uttoxeter.

Another of Frank Gilman's, the five-year-old Towtame, a half-brother to Grittar, also with Dick Saunders up, crowned his promising season with a win in the Marie Curie novice championship.

There is not much doubt, however, that of all the five-year-olds seen out during the season the most promising was Derrick Llewellin's Carmarthenshire mare National Clover, bred from the mare he won a division of the 1959 Dudley Cup on, Clover Bud, who went on to win the Welsh Grand National when sent into training with Fred Rimell.

After a slow beginning in maiden races, National Clover ended her season winning three ladies' opens with a novice rider up and looking better and better each time.

Two other young horses who finished the season with hat-tricks after starting it as maidens were Persian Scimitar, a seven-year-old from the Devon & Somerset Staghounds, and Fling Ding, a seven-year-old from the Belvoir; and both of them went into quite a few people's notebooks.

Among the 16 starters for the four-mile race at the Heythrop were at least four horses with the right credentials, Long Lane, Sparkford, Man Of Europe and Headmaster. But they were all outstayed and outfenced on the soft ground by the hobdayed Spartan Scot, a nine-year-old from the Ledbury.

Patiently ridden by Tim Houlbrooke, the son of Spartan General had mastered Sparkford by the time the latter fell at the last fence, and he went on to win by eight lengths from the Dufosee-ridden Ballytartar, who stayed on to take second place off the tiring Man Of Europe, joint favourite with Sparkford.

A winner of the men's open in soft ground at Mollington, Spartan Scot was bred by his owner, Mrs. Hilary Wellon, from Scot Crest, a Jock Scot mare on whom her husband, Harold Wellon, had won 11 point-to-points. Mrs. Wellon described her winner as "just one of the family, a real character."

Headmaster, who had run a disappointing race in the Heythrop four-miler, finishing 8th of the 13 finishers, ran a much better one in the Dudley Cup, for which the going at Chaddesley Corbett was hard. But not a good enough one to win it.

There were only five runners for the race, and one who remained in his box on account of the going, after coming all the way from Yorkshire for it, was the 1978 winner, Sporting Luck. But the going was no problem for Roger Everall's home-bred nine-year-old from the North Shropshire, Major Star, out of a mare who shared the same granddam as Captain Christy, the Cheltenham Gold Cup winner of 1974.

Expertly ridden by Steven Brookshaw, the third member of the Brookshaw family to ride a Dudley Cup winner, Major Star was too speedy for Headmaster in the closing stages and beat him by five lengths. At this stage of the season, he was unbeaten with four wins to his credit; but in his final race of the season, the men's open at the Albrighton Woodland on the same course but over a shorter trip, he failed to give 71b. to the horse that had finished third to him in the Dudley Cup, the Worcestershire-hunted Extra Fine, a winner of five of his seven races with Bob Woolley up. This race, too, was run on hard ground.

The third of the season's classic point-to-points, the Grimthorpe Cup at the

Middleton, was also run on hard ground, and for this there was a field of eight and another home-bred winner in Arthur Johnson's Scalby Cresta, an 11-year-old half-brother to his good mare Saucy Polly, from a dam, Golden Mitre (by Bobsleigh), who had produced a number of winners for him.

Confidently ridden by Gordon Halder, and putting in a superb jump at the second last, Scalby Cresta, a horse hunted in Yorkshire with the Staintondale, made every yard of the running and passed the post half a length ahead of the favourite, Hal's Slave, the winner of the four-mile men's open at the Percy. Scalby Cresta's previous success was in the men's open at the Bedale & West of Yore, where he had a different rider up.

But, to set Scalby Cresta's Grimthorpe Cup win in perspective, it is worth taking a look at the men's open at the Staintondale, in which he finished fifth to Whiggie Geo. The horses who took the second, third and fourth places in this race, Tilston, Border Mark and Waggoners Walk, were all winners under Rules during the season. Tilston, an eight-year-old from the York & Ainsty, won three hunter chases in a row under Jack Peckitt, giving Hal's Slave 101b. in one of them and beating him by 12 lengths. Border Mark, a 12-year-old from the Bedale, ended a successful season under his owner-rider, Capt. James Evetts, with a win at Wetherby, where he beat Tilston and Scalby Cresta; and the three races in a row won by Waggoners Walk under Rules included the Eider handicap chase at Newcastle and the Kim Muir at Cheltenham, where he was ridden by Chris Cundall.

Graham Pidgeon introduced a very promising newcomer to the point-to-point scene in his Grafton seven-year-old Zarajeff, a winner on the Flat in Belgium and subsequently over fences and hurdles in this country. In his first season carrying the well-known Pidgeon colours, Zarajeff won six ladies' opens on the trot, ridden in the first two of them by Didi Morris, and in the other four by Graham's daughter, Jenny, a future ladies' champion.

It was interesting to see a new rider being tried on Eric Covell's wayward Flintstone in the shape of Mrs. Pat Palmer, one of the strongest lady riders in the South East; and her initial appearance on this ten-year-old from the Crawley & Horsham was well rewarded when she induced him to beat Scarlett French's mount Prince Tacitus in the ladies' open at the Eridge. It was Flintstone's first appearance at Heathfield, and a huntsman was heard to remark, "He had so much to think about that he hadn't time to think about stopping."

Mrs. Palmer won two other ladies' opens on him this season. He was, however, still doing some thinking. On the sharp Hampshire track in Hackwood Park, he was closing on the eventual winner, Dick Baimbridge's Silvertown, with the splendid Alison Dare up, as he successfully negotiated the bend leading to the fourteenth when he suddenly dug his toes in and declined to proceed any further. Mrs. Palmer then decided to call it a day; but Flintstone developed other ideas and started racing again from his position at the rear of the field; and giving his rider no further cause for alarm, he went on to finish third, some 25 lengths behind the winner.

In his next race, the ladies' open at the Old Surrey & Burstow, he was on his best behaviour, well almost. He faltered only once, at the fifth, where Mrs. Palmer bellowed into his ear; and from that moment onwards he was the perfect gentleman, winning by a distance. Eric Covell, visibly moved, said afterwards, "My greatest pleasure is to see that horse win."

It was a similar story in the ladies' open at the East Sussex & Romney Marsh when Flintstone had another win at the expense of the horse he had beaten in his previous race, El Padre, the eight-year-old Mrs. Ann Blaker had bought from Joe Turner in East Anglia.

But when he started favourite for the ladies' open at the PPOA fixture, he attempted to refuse at the open ditch the last time he came to it; and after being persuaded by Mrs. Palmer to clamber over it, he stopped altogether. His determined rider did, though, manage to get him going again; and he was travelling so sweetly over the remaining fences that he had moved up into third place by the time he reached the post, 6.5 lengths behind the winner, Night Ride, on whom Rosemary Barnett broke the Kingston Blount course record with a time of 6 mins. 8.5 secs., which was 5.5 seconds faster than the previous record set up in 1979 by Joan Barrow on Chris Glyn's home-bred Pacify at the Vale of Aylesbury fixture.

Flintstone's last race of the season was a hunter chase at Fontwell; and in this, he refused at the fourteenth, and although Mrs. Palmer managed to get him going again she was compelled to pull him up after he had jumped two more fences in the rear. Amazing to think that, after changing ownership, the old horse would still be appearing on a course for three more seasons, and that he actually managed to win another race in 1981, without the assistance of either David Evatt or Mrs. Palmer!

A word now about Mrs. Sue Reynard, in my book the heroine of the Cheltenham Foxhunters', who finished third on her Wiener Chic to the two professionally-trained horses, Rolls Rambler and Remigio, and wasn't overhauled by them until the run-in when they went by up the final hill. She was unlucky, too, in another respect with the horse she trained herself on Dartmoor. Nine days after the Cheltenham race she broke her leg. So Wiener Chic had his season cut short, after winning two more ladies' opens and being beaten a head by Hargan on his first appearance.

When a horse starts at 4-1 on in a three-horse race run at a false pace there is bound to be a stewards' enquiry; and this is what happened at the Belvoir when Capt. Bryan Parry's good horse Cheekio Ora got beaten a short head by Joey Newton's mount Church Newton in the men's open. Asked for an explanation, Cheekio Ora's rider, Peter Greenall, replied splendidly, "My owner doesn't like his horses abused unnecessarily." Collapse of all parties.

Peter's younger brother Johnny, aged 19, rode his first winner when scoring in the restricted open at the Brocklesby on Melivan, a horse he had bought as a schoolmaster for 2,000 guineas at Doncaster and was sitting on in public for the first time.

George Dudley, the long-serving groundsman at Tweseldown, retired (officially) on June 1st, the day the Army gave up running the course and put the future of Tweseldown in doubt.

Tailpiece:
"My winners don't quite keep pace with my years," said the 51-year-old Dick Woodhouse after riding his 50th winner, his own horse Exhibit B, in the members' race at the PPOA meeting.

1981

*In which Tweseldown is saved, a new novice championship is
introduced, Scotland produces another outstanding performer, the
professionals are given food for thought, and Bill Shand Kydd
speaks up for hunting.*

The first thing to say about this season is that, with the Army having given
up its lease of Tweseldown, a course over which Edward, Duke of Windsor
was to be seen riding in the days when he was Prince of Wales, the
Hampshire course was rescued from oblivion by a consortium of local enthusiasts
who purchased the 21-year-old lease and formed Tweseldown Racecourse
Company Ltd. The five members of the consortium were Philip Scouller, Mark
Davies, Sally Bullen, Guy Luck and Toby Ward.

Invitations for shares in the new company were asked for, with a suggested
minimum of £200, and there was no lack of applicants when the appeal was
launched at a public meeting at Hartley Wintney. Graham Pidgeon, representing
the Point-to-Point Owners' Association, staked a claim for £1,000-worth of shares;
and among other major shareholders were the Royal Naval Equestrian Association,
Ken Goschen M.F.H., who hunted across Tweseldown with his own private pack
of foxhounds (Mr. Goschen's), and Capt. Bobbie Norris, who had ridden his first
winner over the course between the Wars.

The Army point-to-point continued to be held at Tweseldown, where it was
being run by the Army Saddle Club, but it was now combined with the Sandhurst
Draghounds (a supposedly civilianised organization) so as not to be a drain on the
Military, who were under pressure to make spending cuts and having to do some
re-thinking.

There was also some good news from the Levy Board, with the increase of its
grants for point-to-points from £83,500 to £111,000; and from the Jockey Club,
with a rise in the ceiling of prize money to £150 for open events and £100 for all
other races.

Other amendments to the Rules included a declaration on hunters' certificates
that the horse had been *properly* hunted; and the definition of a 'maiden' extended to include horses that had never won a race of any decription on the Flat,
including bumpers' races. Other, that is, than a match or a private sweepstake.

It was now obligatory, too, as from March 26, that all horses running in hunter chases must have a passport showing that they had been vaccinated against equine influenza, although this didn't apply to horses running exclusively in point-to-points.

With the prize money going up to £8,500, the Cheltenham Foxhunters' was now the richest hunter chase, relegating the Jeep-Christies' men's final at Chepstow to second place at £6,000, alongside the Land Rover Champion Hunter Chase at the Cheltenham evening fixture in May.

The season also saw the inaugural running of a novice championship sponsored by the tractor firm of Massey-Ferguson, with 40 qualifying races for maidens at various point-to-points culminating in a £5,000 final at Wetherby towards the end of May.

And at the Melton Hunt Club fixture in mid-May, I.C.I. having opted out of their Nitram ladies' championship, this championship was being taken over by the agricultural merchants Albright & Wilson and named accordingly.

There was a very exciting race, on good to soft ground in a field of 13, for Lord Ashton of Hyde's Cup at the Heythrop, with Nostradamus a nine-year-old from the Bicester, owned by John Sumner, a steward of the Jockey Club, and ridden by his son-in-law, Ian McKie, holding off the fast-finishing Long Lane by a head.

This was the fifth win of the season by Nostradamus, who remained unbeaten', winning all nine of his races and ending up as the winner of the Grand Marnier Trophy. Although Nostradamus's win in the Heythrop four-miler was a narrow one, it was also a clever one, fully reflecting McKie's remark that this prodigious stayer, by Normandy out of the Javelin mare Nostra, a winner over hurdles and fences, never did more than he needed to do. He proved this once again later in the season at Kingston Blount when, under McKie's strong driving, the horse who was named after the Prophet, and ran with the confidence of one, beat Armagnac Princess by a neck.

And it was Armagnac Princess, a nine-year-old mare from the West Country, who went on to gain an effortless success under Jimmy Frost in the Jeep-Christies' men's final at Chepstow, where she was recording her fifth win of the season.

The Jeep-Christies' ladies' final also produced a West Country winner when Katie Halswell, who had fasted for three days to make the low weight of 9-11, won it on John Weldhen's Moon Step, a nine-year-old from the Four Burrow in Cornwall, where he was trained by his owner. This was Katie's second winner under Rules, and her first since she had a bad fall 13 months ago and, as Geoff Lester reported in the *Sporting Life*, was told by her doctors that she would never walk again.

Night School and Wiener Chic, the two who finished second and third to Moon Step at Chepstow, cut each other's throats with the furious pace they set in the heavy ground.

But it was nevertheless another good season for Sue Reynard (née Foale) and her German-bred Wiener Chic. They won three ladies' opens, beating Moon Step in one of them, and accounted for two of Oliver Carter's best horses, Ottery News and Otter Way, in hunter chases at Devon & Exeter and Newton Abbot.

The Lady Dudley Cup at the Worcestershire was run in a near-blizzard, and was won in a field of eight by a mare who was bought for a mere 430 guineas at Ascot as a three-year-old. In the capable hands of Nigel Oliver, Bill Price's Petite Mandy, a nine-year-old from the Radnor & West Hereford, was never in any danger after jumping past the pace-making Hemay at the last open ditch.

Stabled near Leominster, where she was trained by Bob Davies, the champion point-to-point rider of 1971, Petite Mandy, a winner of three adjacent hunts' races in 1980, was recording her third win of the season, having won an open point-to-point at the Golden Valley and beaten Sparkford in a hunter chase at Worcester; and she was to win another hunter chase afterwards when defeating Royal Air at Hereford.

In the last season that it was to be run over the full Grand National distance of 4.5 miles, the Middleton's Grimthorpe Cup race was won in the slowest time in its history, 10 mins. 14 secs. The horse who had this dubious distinction was the one-paced Mountain Lad from the Sinnington who had lost his maiden certificate at the Holderness and won a three-horse men's open at the Bedale & West of Yore. Ridden by Jack Peckitt, his rider when he won his maiden, and relishing the soft going at Whitwell-on-the-Hill, Mountain Lad won easing up by a length from Bonabrig, the winner of the men's open over the stayers' course at the High Peak & N.E. Cheshire Drag fixture at Flagg Moor.

Mountain Lad made three more appearances after his Grimthorpe Cup win, scoring in a men's open on soft ground at the Badsworth before being pulled up in the Jeep-Christies' men's final at Chepstow and finishing sixth of eight in the John Corbet Cup at Stratford won by Alison Dare on Precipitous, one of the horses trained by Dick Baimbridge.

In view of the ill feeling stirred up in 1980 by the domination exercised in the season's top hunter chases by horses from professional yards, and the suggestion made by Jim Mahon at a PPOA meeting that, for a trial period, one third of the season's hunter chases should exclude horses from professional yards (unless owned by the trainer), and that for prestige races such as the Cheltenham and Liverpool Foxhunters' a complete ban should be imposed on horses who had won any kind of race under Rules other than one confined to hunters, it was good to see the wind blowing in the right direction, with the Leicester executive, under the command of Capt. Nick Lees, confining one of the races at their hunter-chase meeting to horses that had not won any race other than one for hunters, and two others to horses that had been placed in point-to-points.

At the same time, it is interesting to recall that, in 'the good old days' when the Cheltenham Foxhunters' was run over four miles and the Liverpool Foxhunters' over the full Grand National distance, winners of races other than those confined to hunters were not eligible to compete in them, nor were they in the majority of hunter chases.

It is also worth remembering that, although four of the best hunter chasers of the post-war years, The Callant, Merryman II, Baulking Green and Credit Call, were professionally trained when they won their prestige hunter chases, the first three came up through the point-to-point ranks and Credit Call had never won under Rules before he went hunter chasing.

Having got that off my chest, I can now recall with the greatest pleasure that, in 1981, the big double at Cheltenham and Liverpool was brought off by Grittar, owned, trained and bred by Frank Gilman and ridden by the veteran Dick Saunders, a feat which caused him to be promoted from a lowly position in 1980 to second place behind Spartan Missile (now on 12-7) in Mackenzie & Phillips' handicap, at 11-11.

In his Cheltenham race, for which he started at 12-1, despite having been a winner at Leicester, Grittar, left in the lead when Whiggie Geo came to grief eight fences from home, continued merrily on his way and won with his ears pricked by 12 lengths from Geordie Dun's mount, Mrs. Patricia Russell's Honourable Man, who was bidding for his fourth win in a row, having won hunter chases at Stockton, Newcastle and Market Rasen with Tony Fowler up.

The favourite for the Cheltenham Foxhunters' was the professionally trained Shannon Bridge, who was pulled up by Oliver Sherwood before the second last after his chance had gone. The first professionally-trained horse home was Robert Waley-Cohen's owner-ridden Sun Lion, who finished a well beaten third, but was subsequently the winner of the 4-mile Range Rover Trophy hunter chase at the Cheltenham evening fixture in May when Chris Bealby rode him.

After his Cheltenham win, Grittar was the natural favourite for the Liverpool Foxhunters', and he obliged in the manner expected in a field of 25. Taking up the running at the fifteenth, he drew quickly clear and scored by 20 lengths from Sydney Quin, on whom Paul Webber had made a great recovery after a bad mistake at Becher's. In his last race of the season Grittar had a comfortable win in a hunter chase at Southwell to make it four wins in a row.

Spartan Missile had a relatively quiet season, winning two races in seven appearances and finishing lame after one of them. But he was fourth to Little Owl in the Cheltenham Gold Cup and ran a fine race in the Grand National, beaten only by Aldaniti in a field of 39. He would no doubt have gone closer but for a couple of jumping errors.

One professionally-trained horse who did well in hunter chases was the Josh Gifford-trained Roadhead, an eight-year-old from the Crawley & Horsham who was acquired by his owner, John Wilson, for his 21-year-old daughter, Margaret, to ride in exchange for two cows he passed on to her uncle. On this horse, Margaret won four hunter chases, and in one of them, at Ascot, she beat John Thorne on Spartan Missile.

Queensberry Lad continued to shine in the North, winning hunter chases at Kelso (twice), Ayr, Perth and Hexham, though he didn't do quite so well on his ventures South. He was pulled up in the Cheltenham Foxhunters' and beaten, but only by a head, by Ottery News in the *Horse and Hound* Cup at Stratford.

The eight-year-old Ottery News, a mare by Pony Express, did rather better for Oliver Carter than his old favourite Otter Way, now 13 years old. Otter Way won a hunter chase at Ascot and a handicap chase at Devon & Exeter; but Ottery News was the more consistent. Never out of the first three in eight appearances, she won two hunter chases with Chris Down up, the *Horse and Hound* Cup with Jim Wilson up, was a runner-up in two other hunter chases and two handicap chases, and finished third to Diamond Edge in the Whitbread Gold Cup at Sandown, with John Francome putting up 71b. over-weight.

138

But, for sheer consistency, especially at the age of 16, Devon Spirit, the South Devon star bred by Mrs. Dinah Pook from her successful point-to-point mare Seventh Symphony, took some beating. A winner in 1981 of five of his seven point-to-points with Mrs. Pook's son Keith up, and placed in the other two, the son of Spiritus enjoyed a splendid swan song winning a hunter chase at Newton Abbot with Jimmy Frost replacing Keith, who had broken his ankle in a fall the previous week.

In a career which began for Mrs. Pook in 1970, when he lost his maiden certificate as a five-year-old, and during which, never missing a season, Devon Spirit ran in well over 100 races, winning 32 point-to-points and six hunter chases; and he was placed in a further 50 races. In the opinion of my West Country correspondent, Peter Wakeham, Devon Spirit was "a much better racehorse than his dam." Which is saying something.

In a good season for novice horses, there was an outstanding one in Scotland in Willy Hamilton's home-bred Earls Brig, a six-year-old from the Jedforest by New Brig out of a Black Tarquin mare, Naughty Tara, who won the Heart Of All England at Hexham for Mr. Hamilton in 1972.

Ridden in all his races by Peter Craggs (a Master of the Morpeth in later years), Earls Brig, who lost his maiden certificate at the Cumberland Farmers, was unbeaten in his five races; and for much of the season, as late as April 20, Craggs was in the lead for the *Daily Telegraph* Cup when a double at the Tynedale, following a winner at the Braes of Derwent two days earlier, brought his score up to 11.

In East Anglia, a rival to General Confusion (who won four more open point-to-points and a hunter chase at Leicester for George Cooper) was continuing to make her presence felt. This was David Wales's seven-year-old mare Swift Wood, a daughter of Precipice Wood out of a mare by Court Martial. A winner in 1980 of three open point-to-points and two hunter chases, including the John Corbet Cup at Stratford, with David's son William up, Swift Wood enhanced her reputation in 1981 with the same rider up, winning five open races (with General Confusion behind her in two of them) and two hunter chases.

But the two best horses in East Anglia (and there was no more than 11b. between them in Mackenzie & Phillips' handicap) were the pair who had lady riders up, Mr. Mellors and Ronnie Bulgin's newcomer, Mac Kelly, a spectacular performer who had won on the Flat and over hurdles and was even better as a point-to-pointer. They met only once, when Mac Kelly, ridden by Mrs. Jane McMath, beat Mr. Mellors, with Lucy King up, by a neck in holding ground at Cottenham; and had the going been more to Mr. Mellors taste, the result would probably have been reversed.

Mr. Mellors,won a ladies' open at Cottenham ridden by Mrs. Didi Powles (née Morris) and four hunter chases with Lucy King up, beating Cheekio Ora a length at Cheltenham in one at a difference of 41b. Mac Kelly won four of his five ladies' opens, ridden in three of them by Didi Powles after Jane McMath had broken her collar-bone when she was unseated at Higham.

Zarajeff was still going great guns for Jenny Pidgeon, winning six ladies' opens in different parts of the country; and another very useful ladies' horse was the seven-year--old Seine Bay produced by Tony and Charlotte Perry in the Albrighton country.

Having won twice for her in 1980, Seine Bay won six of his nine races in 1981 with Charlotte up, beating the 1980 Nitram winner Honourable Enoch in two of them, though the latter got the better of him on another occasion in a hard-fought ladies' open at the North Staffs & Meynell & South Staffs; and in his last race of the season, the first running of the Albright & Wilson ladies' championship which had replaced the Nitram at Garthorpe, Seine Bay found two that were going too well for him.

This championship was a good race, even though there were only eight contestants for it; and in it Lucy King was seen at her best on the 14-year-old Clonmellon, who was easy to back at 6-1 despite having already won four ladies' opens and a hunter chase at Fakenham. This was because of the weight of money for the favourite, Ridley Lamb's Bedale-hunted Shore Captain, on whom his daughter, Peta, had won three ladies' opens and finished second to Cheekio Ora in a hunter chase at Nottingham.

Seine Bay was showing the way going downhill to the third last, but Shore Captain and Clonmellon were both closing on him; and in a desperate finish, and owing a lot to Lucy's brilliant riding, Clonmellon got home from Shore Captain by threequarters of a length, with Seine Bay three lengths away in third.

Clonmellon and Shore Captain both ended their season with another point-to-point win. After finishing a runner-up to Swift Wood in a hunter chase at Fakenham, where he was giving the mare 31b., Clonmellon had his seventh win of the season in the ladies' open at the Exmoor, and Shore Captain his fourth in the ladies' open at the Blankney. Since she got Clonmellon out of Roddy Armytage's yard and started him point-to-pointing in 1978, Libby Lees had now won 11 point-to-points and seven hunter chases with him.

Yorkshire Mariner, who was show jumping in 1980 for his former owner, crowned a successful first season in point-to-points with a satisfying win in a field of 14 for the Marie Curie novice championship. It was the eight-year-old's fourth win with 28-year-old Michael Dawson up. But when he lost his maiden certificate in the hunt race at the Brocklesby on his second appearance in a point-to-point it was Michael's father, the horse's 61-year-old owner, Cliff Dawson, a Joint Master of the Brocklesby, who was riding him. Cliff Dawson bought Yorkshire Mariner after seeing the way he went across plough in the hunting field.

Yorkshire Mariner wasn't the only novice to catch the eye at Melton. Another was Cherry Easterby's five-year-old King Appollo, on whom Peter Greenall, riding him for the first time, completed a double in division two of the restricted members', in which King Appollo's time was only half a second slower than that recorded by his earlier winner, Cheekio Ora, whose win in the men's open was his fifth of the season, the other four all being in hunter chases.

Shamefully, King Appollo was one of two exceptionally promising five-year-olds to be balloted out of the first running of the Massey-Ferguson novice final at Wetherby. The other was Colonel Henry, a five-year-old from the Fife who had followed a win in a maiden race at the Dumfriesshire with an impressive performance in a restricted open at his home meeting, where his time was the fastest of the day.

Desert Victor, the 25-1 winner of the Massey-Ferguson final in a field of 19, was recording his first-ever win, and so was his rider, 28-year-old John Swiers. An eight-year-old from the York & Ainsty, Desert Victor disappeared into obscurity afterwards.

It is a remarkable fact that nearly all the successful horses that the East Anglian owner Joe Turner has sold on have done well afterwards for their new owners. None, I would wager, more so than Even Harmony, who won 41 point-to-points and five hunter chases at Fakenham for him.

Before the start of the 1980 season, Joe sold Even Harmony to the Leicestershire owner-rider Andrew Berry, for whom he won a men's open at Cottenham that season. And in 1981, by which time Even Harmony had reached the age of 14, he won seven races, six of them open events, in his nine appearances; and when he ended his season winning the men's open at the Blankney, his grand total of wins had risen to 54, just 11 fewer than the record total of 65 attained by the West Country pony Lonesome Boy by the end of his last season in 1961. Whilst Even Harmony was never to reach Lonesome Boy's phenomenal total, he wasn't finished yet, and he was to come pretty near to doing so.

Spartan Lace, one of the many horses bred in the Grafton country by "Bunny" Tarry from the mares he acquired from Lucy Jones, was a good winner of the Leyland Tractors farmers' championship at the PPOA fixture at Kingston Blount, easily accounting for the Portman mare Morning Heather. Jimmy Tarry was looking round on the run-in. It was the daughter of Spartan General's fourth win of the season, including one in a hunter chase at Wolverhampton; and the points she gained from it secured the £550 bonus for her owner as well as the £60 on offer for winning the race.

Persian Scimitar confirmed the promise he had shown the previous season as a seven-year-old, winning five hunter chases and the men's open at his home meeting at Holnicote, ridden by Nicky Bush on four occasions and by Mike Trickey on two. One of the hunter chases he won with Nicky Bush up was the valuable Land Rover Champion Hunter Chase at Cheltenham, where he had a comfortable win at the expense of The Drunken Duck and Wiener Chic.

Cheekio Ora, paying more tributes to the skilful training of Capt. Bryan Parry, won five of his nine races under Peter Greenall, four of them hunter chases and the other the men's open at the Melton Hunt Club. Also in Capt. Parry's yard, at the start of the season, was Loyal Partner, a winning hurdler bought out of Mick Easterby's yard. This seven-year-old won six open races in succession, ridden by three different riders, his first two with Peter Greenall up; and then, after he had changed hands again and gone into the South East, two with Tony Clay up and two with David Evatt riding him.

And among those who started the season as a maiden was a seven-year-old mare by Spartan General called Greek Vixen, owned by Mrs. Diana Baylis and produced in the Berkeley country by that master of the art Dick Baimbridge to win four races on the trot, one of them owing much to the shrewdness of his rider, Nicky Bush. This was a men's open in Hackwood Park, where Greek Vixen passed the post in third place. She was, however, the only one of the six finishers not to be disqualified, the other five having all missed out a fence on the second circuit after being waved round it by a huntsman on account of a horse lying prostrate on the landing side; while Greek Vixen's rider had the good sense to disregard what he knew were unauthorised instructions, however well intended.

Ian McKie and Lucy King both retained their riders' titles. McKie, owing most to Nostradamus, whose nine successes in point-to-points netted the Grand Marnier Trophy for John Sumner, rode 18 winners, not quite as many as he had ridden in 1980 when he shared the *Daily Telegraph* Cup with David Turner, but two more than his chief rivals, Peter Greenall and farrier Tim Rooney, behind whom came the Northumbrian rider Peter Craggs with 13.

Lucy King, with her 14 winners in point-to-points, most of them for Libby Lees, was also the leading rider in hunter chases, with six winners, one more than Graham Macmillan. "The nicest thing about Lucy," said Libby Lees, paying her a well-deserved compliment, "is that her horses mean more to her than titles."

The runner-up for the *Sporting Life* Cup was Jenny Pidgeon with ten wins on three of the horses owned and trained by her father, Zarajeff making the biggest contribution with his six wins.

The Grand Marnier novice riders of the season were 17-year-old Mark Richards, an Abergavenny scholboy, who rode eight winners, and 25-year-old Peta Lamb from Yorkshire with her six wins, four of them on her father's Shore Captain.

Mark Richards, who had a highly successful season on his father's Dempsey, winning six open races in a row on this nine-year-old from the Monmouthshire, was also the recipient of the Wilkinson Sword for the leading rider under 21; and it is interesting to note that the runner-up for this award, with seven winners, was a certain Nigel Bloom, who was also a 17-year-old at this time. This was the season he had his first winning ride in a point-to-point and his first winner under Rules.

Only one rider, Herefordshire's John Bryan, had the distinction of riding four winners at the same meeting. He did so at the North Hereford, where he won all three divisions of the restricted open, on Fonmon, Little Bilsham and Dainty Dolly, and a division of the men's open on Sparkford.

Stuart Jeanes, a rider who was very well known in the South East before moving West, landed his 100th career winner when scoring on the eight-year-old Easter Express in the maiden race at the Devon & Somerset Staghounds; and at the Portman, Richard Miller, who had ridden well over 150 winners by this time, had his 50th win over his home course at Badbury Rings.

A bizarre incident occurred in the course of the maiden race at the Lanarkshire & Renfrewshire at Bogside when Master View unseated his owner-rider, John Church, and made straight for the sea. Mr. Church promptly took off his jersey and boots and plunged straight into the sea after him. His troubles, however, did not end there, although he managed to turn the horse round. Master View responded by making for a heavily-guarded chemical works filled with high explosives, and had to be rescued by the police.

An ingeniously-framed race at the Cambridge University United Hunts' Club fixture at Cottenham was a restricted riders' farmers' race confined to riders who had not ridden more than ten winners. There were two divisions of it, with 16 in the first and 18 in the second; and the two winners were Simon Sherwood, riding his father's Stoic Yarn in the faster division, and Nicola Barber up on her grandfather's David Tudor in the other. Both horses started favourite.

Larkhill had the distinction of being the first point-to-point course on which as many as 11 races were run. This was at the United Services meeting early in the season; and there was one very ill-made fence, the fifth and also the last, which caused a great deal of havoc. As one rider said, the fence was too upright and leaned in the direction of the horses approaching it, so that they tended to get under it. It was also bigger than any other obstacle on the course, and not yielding enough at the top, with pieces of birch as big as a man's wrist.

The last race of the day here was run in fading light, and there were as many as four ambulances parked near the final obstacle, with a lot of people gesticulating and shouting instructions. It was hardly surprising, therefore, that several horses and riders ended up on the floor. Needless to say, the offending fence was drastically re-structured for later meetings.

There are occasions, as I feel sure every punter would agree, when point-to-point bookmakers fail to come up to scratch. One such case in 1981 was at the Talybont, where only four bookmakers were operating and prices, to put it mildly, were constricted. For a nine-runner ladies' open, two of the runners were being offered at odds on. Neither of them won.

The other side of the picture was seen at the South & West Wilts fixture at Larkhill, where a little-patronised hunt tote returned every winner at odds on, in contrast to the prices chalked up on the bookmakers' boards, with two of these winners on offer at 5-1 and 7-1.

At the national point-to-point dinner in London, the retirement of Chris Glyn as Chairman of the function he had founded 15 years ago was marked by a presentation to him of two Michael Lyne racing prints subscribed to by his friends in the point-to-point world. Bill Shand Kydd, the proposer of the toast to the sport, drew the attention of his audience to the close links between point-to-point racing and hunting, and the need to defend hunting. "Don't wait for others to fight," he said. "Do your best to put the truth in front of people so that your sons and daughters can continue to enjoy the sport we love."

In March, Edward ("Ruby") Holland-Martin died in Cheltenham General Hospital at the age of 81. One of the leading point-to-point riders of the pre-war years – he was joint-champion with Mr. E.W.W. Bailey, the owner-rider of Pucka Belle, in 1936 – and a noted amateur under Rules, Ruby Holland-Martin was equally successful as an international show jumper. He was a particularly elegant horseman, riding, I recall, in a monocle. One of his horses, Hefty, won the Dudley Cup of 1946 with his brother, Thurstan, up. Ruby's riding career came to an end when he was crippled in a hunting accident in 1952. But the family tradition of race-riding was carried on by his nephew, Tim.

And in September, the much-loved Reading bookmaker, Charlie Ball, who was still operating his book at point-to-points when he was well into his late eighties, died at his home at the age of 89. A man highly respected in his profession, and as fearless at laying the odds as the late Albert Dimes, Charlie was the recipient of a special award at the national point-to-point dinner three years before his death. He was everyone's favourite bookmaker in the South Midlands.

Tailpiece:
"My father told me that I couldn't go wrong if I remembered not to break the rules of the two great authorities, the Vatican and the Jockey Club," Jim Mahon speaking at the PPOA dinner in Stratford.

1982

In which tragedy is mixed with inspiration, the natural-country races begin their limited life-span, Iain Mackenzie has a new partner, the distance of the Grimthorpe Cup is reduced, and legal history is made at Kimble.

L ook at it how one will, the 1982 season was at once tragic and inspiring. Two riders died as the result of falls, one of them instantly; and a former point-to-pointer won the Grand National.

John Thorne, a rider who didn't know the meaning of fear, died in hospital in March the day after a fall on one of his novices in a maiden race at the Bicester & Warden Hill point-to-point at Mollington. He was having only his second ride in a race (his first was on another novice in an earlier race at the same meeting) since breaking his leg the previous November; and Bend A Knee, the young horse he was riding, had been on the floor in his two previous races this season with another rider up on him in hunter chases.

A great deal was written about John after his fatal accident, and there is little more that I can add. Except to express my sorrow at the death of a great man whose name will live on. But I would like to record what Dick Saunders said to me at the time: "John was one of the bravest men I have known, and always so generous in defeat. His attitude towards life in general was an inspiration to us all, and particularly perhaps to the younger riders. As a member of the Jockey Club, he had so much to offer to the future of jump racing and point-to-pointing, and he cannot be replaced."

The bookmakers felt the same way about him; and one of them, Desmond Gleeson, wrote in a letter to the *Sporting Life*, "John Thorne was the focus of all things good in the sport – loyalty, bravery, a love of horses and complete dedication to the sport he adorned with such distinction and honour... The racing public will remember him with his Grand National second on Spartan Missile. We of the point-to-point world will equally remember him trying to win a £50 Open at the Vale of Aylesbury."

The other rider who died in the cause of the sport he loved was 19-year-old Robert Wales, the younger son of David Wales. He was killed instantly in a fall on his father's Papillon in the hunt race at the West Norfolk point-to-point at Fakenham in May. Robert had already ridden a winner during the season; and he had ridden eight before then. Nicholas Barber, the Hon. Sec. of the East Anglian Area Point-to-Point Association, described him as "an unassuming young man and a very good horseman."

I was at the Grafton point-to-point on the Oakley course at Newton Bromswold on the day Grittar won the Grand National with Dick Saunders up, and watched the race, along with a great many others, on a television screen there. I have rarely seen such enthusiasm when it became clear that Grittar was going to win by a street and add his name to the select band of ex-point-to-pointers who had won the National in the post-war years, the others being Russian Hero in 1949, Teal in 1952, Oxo in 1959, Merryman II in 1960 and Highland Wedding in 1969; and there would be others still to come.

It was a moment to savour when Grittar passed the post at Aintree, made all the more so by the fact that Dick's daughter Caroline had won the adjacent hunts' race at Newton Bromswold not long before on Rugy. To no one's surprise, Dick Saunders decided to make this latest success on Grittar the crowning achievement of his distinguished career as a race-rider, and at the end of May when Buchanan's Whisky celebrated the inauguration of their natural-country races with a memorable dinner at the Honourable Artillery Company's imposing headquarters at Armoury House in the City of London, he was presented with a special award by James Macdonald Buchanan "for riding the winner of the Grand National at an advanced age." Dick was 48.

That dinner, I may say, as one who attended it, was some occasion, complete with a gunners' orchestra situated on a balcony and playing some marvellous stuff on the post-horn. Chris Collins, proposing the toast to the sport, described the venture as "a great new concept that has brought back some fun into what we do"; and the response came from Michael Clayton, the Editor of *Horse and Hound*, who said that he had arrived at Armoury House on his "traditional mode of transport," which turned out to be not a horse but a bicycle.

Buchanan's had put up £2,000 of sponsorship for their innovatory series of natural-country hunt members' races, which had hitherto been the sole prerogative of the High Peak & N.E. Cheshire with its traditional members' race at Flagg Moor over stone walls. The ten meetings selected by Buchanan's were: the Beaufort, Percy, Cottesmore, Spooners & West Dartmoor, High Peak & N.E. Cheshire, the Cattistock, Cleveland, Fife, Worcestershire and the Lauderdale. All of them had specially constructed courses for it, with the obstacles ranging from hedges and ditches to post and rails, stone walls and banks. So there was plenty of variety; and also plenty of runners, an average of 20 per race, with as many as 39 going to the post in appalling weather conditions at the Beaufort, where 30 completed the course and the winner was a horse bred in Ireland by Celia Conolly-Carew, Paddy Too, making his first-appearance on a course, and ridden by a 29-year-old rider, Mrs. Caroline Shearing, riding her first winner and doing remarkably well to beat a horse ridden by Sue Horton.

But the most dramatic finish to one of these races was in a field of 24 at the Cottesmore, where Joey Newton got his Southern Favour up to win by a head from the five-year-old Miss Chief, whose owner-rider, Joss Hanbury, a Joint Master of the Hunt, had won the cross-country ride at Market Harborough on her a few weeks beforehand.

Southern Favour, a winner of a novice chase when trained by Arthur Stephenson, had finished fifth in a men's open earlier in the season; and the appearance of this rather moderate performer in a natural-country race was described in the famous annual of Hunter Chasers and Point-to-Pointers as "an unsporting piece of pot-hunting." Does one, I wonder, detect the hand of Terry Selby in this description? The exuberant Terry, a man never at a loss for words, even if they are not always the right ones, had now replaced David Phillips as Iain Mackenzie's partner, though the annual was still appearing under the auspices of *Horse and Hound*.

In order to bring point-to-pointing into line with racing under Rules, a new rule was introduced this season to the effect that all horses running in point-to-points had to be vaccinated against equine influenza and needed to have passports. It was not a ruling that pleased everybody. The Dorset rider Richard Miller, a Joint Master of the Portman, having got wind of it before the start of the season, remarked feelingly at the national point-to-point dinner in September 1981, that he did not see any necessity for extending this ruling to point-to-points. "The small owner," he said, "perhaps running his horse once or twice, would be put to a great deal of trouble and expense, while there would also be an additional burden of supervision on already hard-worked amateur officials."

In a season when injuries to riders, including the two that proved fatal, were proving a cause for concern, it was unanimously agreed at the PPOA A.G.M. at Stratford in June that there should be mandatory insurance for all riders. Three months later, at the national point-to-point dinner in London, Major Malcolm Wallace, at that time the Commanding Officer of the King's Troop R.H.A., and the chef d'equipe of our Three-Day Event team, revealed that the fund set up for the amateur rider Mikey Heaton-Ellis, who was confined to a wheel-chair as the result of a fall at Huntingdon, had topped the £20,000 mark.

There were some other major changes on the sponsorship front. Leyland Tractors, having opted out of their farmers' championship race at the PPOA fixture at Kingston Blount, Ready Mixed Concrete stepped in with £20,000 sponsorship embracing 28 qualifying races for their RMC Group Magnum Championship for the Hugh Sumner Cup at the meeting. The conditions were virtually the same as before, except that the race was not now confined to farmers' horses. There was still a points championship attached to it with the usual £550 first prize and £100 and £50 for the second and third.

The Grafton mare Spartan Lace repeated her success in the race, although not in the points championship. For this she was pipped, by a single point, by the runner-up to her in the Magnum race, the Carmarthenshire mare National Clover, who was also leading horse in the PPOA'S Sean Graham young horse awards, and the winner for her owner-breeder, Derrick Llewellin, of a new challenge trophy presented by Mrs. Judy Frank to the breeder of the leading young horse on a points basis.

Spartan Lace and National Clover both had another good season, the Grafton mare winning four open races and a hunter chase at Hereford with James Tarry up; and National Clover winning six ladies' opens with Shan Morgan up.

The star ladies' performer of the season, however, was Ronnie Bulgin's Essex Farmers' eight-year-old Mac Kelly, a winner of eight ladies' opens, most of them by a distance, with the brilliant Didi Powles up; and it was Mac Kelly who ended up as the winner of the Grand Marnier Trophy.

But it wasn't so much the number of races Mac Kelly won that marked him out as the incisive manner in which he recorded them, on all types of going, from firm to holding. More often than not, he was never headed. Moreover, he didn't stick to his own neck of the woods, winning in seven different counties; and when he was taken up to the South Durham, he won by a distance in the fastest time of the day. But for unseating his rider at his home meeting and falling three out at the West Norfolk, he would have got into double figures. It is true he disappointed in his last race of the season, the Albright & Wilson ladies' championship at the Melton Hunt Club, where he weakened rapidly after jumping the downhill third last and finished fifth of the six starters. But even a champion must be allowed the occasional lapse; and although he didn't break down, he was looking distressed when he came in.

The Albright & Wilson championship was won in a field of six, by the youngest horse ever to win this ladies' championship since its inception under the umbrella of Goya in 1972. Just as Mac Kelly looked to be running away with it, Pitskelly Blues, a mare from the Bedale, shot into the lead approaching the penultimate fence under her 27-year-old rider, Jane Ramsay, riding her 21st winner, and won by three lengths from Lucky Rew, whose only previous success during the season was in a ladies' open at the Quorn over the same course. He had, however, won four chases when in training with Arthur Stephenson. So even though Mac Kelly would almost certainly have romped home had he been himself, one can't really say that the five-year-old Pitskelly Blues had nothing to beat.

Moreover, this mare from the bargain basement, who had cost his owner, Henry Clarke, a Thirsk businessman, no more than 1,500 guineas at the Doncaster Sales in 1981, had started the season as a maiden and was recording her sixth success in a row, four of them with Jane Ramsay up, and in one of which she had beaten Shore Captain, the winner of the *Sporting Chronicle* northern ladies' championship at Sedgefield.

It was a pity, though, that Jacksway wasn't able to meet his engagement owing to a strained ligament. This little nine-year-old from the East Sussex & Romney Marsh was the outstanding ladies' horse in the South East and was unbeaten in seven ladies' opens with 25-year-old Clare Mair up. He had twice beaten Lucky Rew; and at the Easton Harriers at Higham, where he won the ladies' open in 5 mins. 47 secs., the fastest over the course since Even Harmony recorded 5 mins. 45 secs. over it in the same race in 1976, he had two of the best ladies' horses in East Anglia, Mr. Mellors and Pelant Barle, behind him.

Mr. Mellors was by no means on the downgrade at the age of nine. He gave Mac Kelly his hardest race when running him to a neck at Cottenham and won four hunter chases, ridden by Lucy Gibbon (née King) in the first two of them and in the other two, which included one in memory of Ruby Holland-Martin at

Cheltenham, by Simon Sherwood. The 12-year-old Pelant Barle completed a hat-trick in ladies' opens with Joanna Hodge up.

The leading lady rider of the season, and winner of the *Sporting Life* Cup for the first time, was Jenny Pidgeon, 13 of whose 18 successes were gained on two of her father's horses, Zarajeff and French Peacock, the latter a ten-year-old half-brother to Persian Scimitar. On Zarajeff she won seven ladies' opens, six of them in succession; and on French Peacock she was in the winner's enclosure six times riding against the men. Three of Zarajeff's wins were gained outside his area at Badbury Rings over a course on which he had never been beaten in his six appearances there.

The runner-up to Jenny Pidgeon for *The Life* Cup, with 15 winners, was Mrs. Jenny Hembrow, who achieved her successes on a variety of horses without having anything particularly outstanding to ride, and did remarkably well to win four races in a row (three of them adjacent hunts' races) on a horse who had a reputation for being unreliable under Rules, 13-year-old Lucky Victory from the Taunton Vale.

There were two very exciting ladies' races in the Northern Area at the Berwickshire and the Percy. Brig Park, a Friars Haugh course specialist, broke the Friars Haugh course record at the Berwickshire when winning under Mrs. Jane Clarke by half a length and a short head from Pop's Girl and Royal's Green in a time of 6 mins. 42 secs. Turning into the straight with one more fence to jump, there were six horses in with a chance, and Brig Park was the last of them; but the 11-year-old daughter of New Brig produced such acceleration that, despite a bad blunder at the last, he got up to record the second of his three wins in ladies' opens during the season, helped to some extent by Lucy Dun (Geordie's younger sister) having lost an iron on Pop's Girl.

In a blanket finish at the Percy at Alnwick, Kings Or Better, an 11-year-old from the Jedforest, held on to the lead he had established at the last under Gillian Minto to score by half a length and a neck from Royal's Green and Halion, with Pop's Girl close up in fourth in the field of 16, and Brig Park, who had started favourite, finishing fifth. This was the first win of the season for the combination, and they were to have three more afterwards.

Although the going for the ladies' national championship at Chepstow was hard, there were 16 contestants for it. The favourite was Jenny Hembrow's mount Withen Wood, a horse who had given her three wins in ladies' opens. But this nine-year-old from the Taunton Vale ran a lifeless kind of race and was never in a position to challenge the leaders. The winner was a horse who started the season as a maiden, Pastry Brush, an eight-year-old from the Clifton-on-Teme who had won three races on the trot under his schoolteacher rider Margaret Kimnell before coming to Chepstow.

Pulling hard for most of the way, Pastry Brush took up the running seven fences out and ran on well to hold off Karafair, his only serious challenger, by three parts of a length. He was a first winner under Rules both for his rider and his owner-breeder, John Hornblower.

For the second time in three years, the Albert Sanderson-Nigel Tutty combination (not forgetting Sanderson's daughter, Jean, who trained the horses for him) carried off the men's championship at Chepstow, this time with the home-bred mare Lady Buttons, a daughter of New Brig out of a Pinicola mare.

Taking up the running two fences out, Lady Buttons won very comfortably from Mike Felton's mount Buck Royale, in a field which included such stalwarts as Sparkford, Carndonagh and Sir Bryn. The last-named, who started favourite at a fraction of odds on and finished fifth, had won five open events and a hunter chase at Worcester with Jimmy Tarry up.

Lady Buttons' three previous wins during the season had included a Vaux restricted at the Derwent and a men's open at the Cleveland, her home meeting; and she ended her season beating Housemistress (a winner of five ladies' opens in a row with Rosemary Harper up) in the John Corbet Cup at Stratford.

Peter Greenall, a dual winner of the amateur riders' titles (in the 1975-76 and 1976-77 seasons) fulfilled a life-time ambition when becoming the first rider to win both the amateur riders' title and the point-to-point crown, which he did in 1982 with his 24 winners in point-to-points. He arrived back from his honeymoon in time to collect the *Daily Telegraph* Cup at the national point-to-point dinner in September. Greenall achieved his wins on 12 different horses, five of them his own; and 16 of his point-to-point winners were trained by Capt. Bryan Parry, the owner of Cheekio Ora, on whom he also won two hunter chases; and on John Docker's home-bred Lone Soldier he won the Liverpool Foxhunters', in which the runner-up was the professionally trained Rolls Rambler.

Of course, he had the right kind of pedigree behind him. His great grand-father, Sir Gilbert Greenall, was Master of the Belvoir for 17 years between 1896 and 1912: and at his stud in Ireland he bred the 1921 Oaks winner, Love In Idleness. Peter's grandfather, the second Lord Daresbury, was Master of the Belvoir from 1934-1947, and of the County Limerick Foxhounds in Ireland from 1947-1977; and Peter's grandmother, the former Joyce Laycock, later the Hon. Mrs. Edward Greenall, one of the best lady riders of her day, was the champion lady point-to-point rider of 1934 and 1938 and a joint champion in 1935. It is also interesting to reflect that as long ago as 1982 Peter was an advocate of Sunday racing, seeing it as something that "would revive the sport's potential as a fund-raising exercise for the hunts by increasing attendances."

The runner-up to Peter Greenall for the men's title, with 18 point-to-point winners, riding 12 different horses, was Jimmy Frost, who also won a maiden hunter chase at Hereford on Lucky Friday. The best horse Frost rode was his father's Dartmoor mare Armagnac Princess, on whom he won four open races and was twice a runner-up, to Cheekio Ora in a hunter chase at Hereford and to Mrs. Rame Fell's dual hunter-chase winner Bararden in the men's open at the Tetcott.

Seventeen-year-old Willy Bryan (the younger brother of John) was the Grand Marnier male novice rider of the season with his seven winners and nine second places, and he also shared the Wilkinson Sword with two other riders who rode seven winner, 18-year-old Mark Richards and 19-year-old Philip Mathias. The 17-year-old Lucy Crow was the winner of the Grand Marnier female novice riders' award with her six winners.

Robert Hacking rode his 150th winner in point-to-points when scoring in an adjacent hunts' race at the Tickham on the eight-year-old Mark's Methane, a horse who would be proving a veritable money-spinner for his owner-breeder, Mrs. Jean Campbell in the East Sussex & Romney Marsh country, and had started his racing career with a hat-trick of wins. Robert Alner landed his 100th point-to-point winner when scoring on Woodhay in a division of the Coronation Cup mixed open at Larkhill, where another of the winners was Nostradamus, a winner during the season of five open races (two of them ladies' opens with "Tocky" McKie up) and a novice hunter chase at Cheltenham in May.

And at the Pegasus Club (Bar) meeting at Kimble legal history was made when 19-year-old Sara Lawrence (the daughter of John Oaksey), who was reading Law at London University, became the first lady, not only to ride in the Bar members' race, but to win it. The horse she was riding was Edward Cazalet's Quilteven, who scored by a distance.

Spartan Scot, with Tim Houlbrooke up again, won the Heythrop four-miler for the second time in three years. At the half-way mark, the 11-year-old had six horses in front of him; but he was left in a clear lead when the front-runner, The Spud Centre, a ten-year-old from the Isle of Wight, who had been holding on grimly to a half-length lead, parted company with his rider at the last. This saw Spartan Scot coasting home from the Meynell & South Staffs mare Athenmore Lass, whose half-sister, Dunsbrook Lass, had won the race in 1972. Sadly, 1982 was the last occasion that the Heythrop fixture was being held on Bing Lowe's land at Fox Farm, Stow-on-the-Wold, where it was in its 30th year.

The going was firm at Chaddesley Corbett on Dudley Cup Day, and no more than eight lined up for the race. Seven of the runners, however, were previous winners this season; and one of them was the seven-year-old from Wales who won it unchallenged, Tenby farmer Dennis Reed's home-bred Norman Case, the third horse from the Principality to win the race since its inception in 1897. The winning rider was 19-year-old Philip Mathias, whose father, Fred Mathias, was a joint winner of the men's title with the Cheshire veterinary surgeon Ted Greenway in 1956; and it was Philip's sixth win on Norman Case, three of them in 1981, when the horse was making his début.

The horse's owner-breeder said that it had been a lifetime ambition of his to win a Dudley Cup; but that he had only brought Norman Case to Chaddesley Corbett to avoid meeting Brigadier Mouse, who had beaten him four times in Wales. One might add, as a postscript to this statement, that, on the same day the Dudley Cup was run, Brigadier Mouse was in action in the men's open at the Pentyrch, where he unseated his rider. But this nine-year-old, who was to distinguish himself three years later when winning the Grand Marnier Trophy, was a winner of five men's opens in the 1982 season.

In a year when the distance of the fabled Grimthorpe Cup at the Middleton was reduced to 4.25 miles, there was hard ground and a howling gale at Whitwell-on-the-Hill. But the seven runners included last year's winner Mountain Lad, a useful horse from East Anglia in Purple Haze, the mount of Michael Bloom; and the Meynell & S. Staffs mare Athenmore Lass.

There was a dramatic finish to the race, which developed into a match between Purple Haze and Border Mark, a 14-year-old from the North Cotswold, on the final circuit, with neither giving an inch and Border Mark, with his owner-rider Capt.

James Evetts up, just holding Purple Haze off by a neck. Mountain Lad was eight lengths away in third. Athenmore Lass unseated her rider at the seventh.

Border Mark, who had now won five races during the season, including two open events, for his owner-rider, and been placed in all his others, was quick to frank the form, winning another men's open over the much shorter trip at the Albrighton Woodland and running Otter Way to four lengths in a hunter chase at Hereford. Earlier on, James Evetts had said, "I want Border Mark to be the first horse to beat Nostradamus." He didn't achieve this. Perhaps because he never came up against him.

There were 15 starters for the Massey-Ferguson novice championship at Wetherby, where horses that had been hunted in Yorkshire filled the first three places and there was no outstanding novice from southern parts in the field. The seven-year-old Sealed, who won this race by 20 lengths with Chris Cundall up, had previously been a runner-up in a novice hunter chase at Nottingham; and before that he had won three of his six point-to-points, finished third in another and fallen twice.

A better prospect for the future was the horse who won the Marie Curie novice championship at Garthorpe, the Hon. Mrs. R.L. ("Urky") Newton's seven-year-old John Bunyan, hunted locally in Leicestershire with the Belvoir and ridden by her son Joey.

John Bunyan, who was completing a hat-trick of wins in an unblemished season, was still on the bridle when he came in eight lengths ahead of Kitchen Boy, an eight-year-old from David Tatlow's yard in the North Cotswold country who had won all four of his previous races.

Bought unbroken from Arthur Stephenson as a three-year-old, John Bunyan, a son of Menelek, from sprinting stock on his dam's side, was a horse who suffered from sore shins, hence his limited appearances. But he was firing on all cylinders whenever he appeared on a course; and I think it is fair to say that he was the best novice seen out during the season.

It was good to see Brod Munro-Wilson winning the Cheltenham Foxhunters' on his own horse The Drunken Duck, the horse he had won the Grand Military Gold Cup at Sandown on last season after buying him for 8,600 guineas out of Alan Smith's yard at the Ascot Sales in June 1980. There was no rider who tried harder than Brod, and few that were more unorthodox; and at Cheltenham he won by a head from Tony Fowler on Honourable Man.

It was also good to see the Sussex rider Tony Clay ending a memorable season with a win in the *Horse and Hound* Cup at Stratford on Loyal Partner, the horse the Clays acquired from Bryan Parry mid-way through the 1981 season. Clay had four more wins on Loyal Partner in 1982, and at Stratford, where he got the eight-year-old up on the post to beat Jim Wilson's mount Otter Way by a short head, with Mr. Mellors close up in third, the partnership were having their third success of the season in hunter chases. Another good family horse that Clay rode was the 11-year-old Dancing Brig, on whom he won four hunter chases, with The Drunken Duck behind him in one of them; and with his seven wins in hunter chases, Tony Clay was the joint leading rider in these races with Simon Sherwood and Dermot Browne.

Dermot Browne, Michael Dickinson's amateur, was the champion amateur rider of the season with 28 winners, seven more than Tim Easterby and Jim Wilson. The best horse Browne rode in hunter chases was the Dickinson-trained Compton Lad, who was unbeaten in these races, and whose five wins included one in the four-mile Range Rover Trophy at Cheltenham in May. The nine-year-old Compton Lad, who had done his hunting with Sir W.W. Wynn's in Cheshire, was bred in the Cotswolds by Mrs. Jackie Brutton and was by an Ascot Gold Cup winner, Precipice Wood, out of Mrs. Brutton's great point-to-point mare Snowdra Queen, the 1965 winner of Lord Ashton of Hyde's Cup at the Heythrop and the Lady Dudley Cup at the Worcestershire, and a dual winner of the United Hunts Cup at Cheltenham among other races in the 'sixties.

Ten Up, a winner this season of two hunter chases, was not the only former winner of a Cheltenham Gold Cup to be running in hunter chases in 1982. Another was Mrs. Olive Jackson's Midnight Court, the 1978 winner when trained by Fred Winter. Still in Winter's yard, Midnight Court, who had been hunted with the Belvoir, was unbeaten in his three appearances in hunter chases with Oliver Sherwood up. The 11-year-old also ran in a three-horse chase at Doncaster with the same rider up; and on that occasion he did get beaten, by Night Nurse, a horse ridden by Jonjo O'Neill. So perhaps he wouldn't have swept the board had he run in point-to-points.

Otter Way (now 14 years old) and Ottery News continued to do well for Oliver Carter, winning 10 races between them, Otter Way's six wins including two in hunter chases. Ottery News won two hunter chases (one of them at Newton Abbot on the disqualification of the horse who passed the post first), two handicap chases and was a runner-up in the Whitbread Gold Cup at Sandown, beaten 21 lengths by Shady Deal who was receiving 8lb. from her; and at Hereford on the last day of May, Ottery News won one division of the hunter chase and Otter Way won the other, both of them ridden by Polly Curling on that occasion.

With two wins in men's opens with his owner up and two wins in ladies' opens, in which he was ridden by Helen Roberts and was a first winner for her when scoring at the Brocklesby, the 15-year-old Even Harmony advanced his grand total of wins to 57 in 94 appearances since he first started in hunt racing carrying the colours of Joe Turner. He was to have one more season in 1983 but it ended in his death, doing what he loved best, when he collapsed and died after finishing second in the ladies' open at Brocklesby. By that time, his 57 wins in 96 appearances had included 25 in men's opens, 17 in ladies' opens and five in hunter chases at Fakenham.

Sporting Luck, who had broken down once since winning the Dudley Cup of 1978 for his Yorkshire owner, had a much revitalised season in 1982 and was unbeaten in his four races as a 15-year-old, winning the men's opens at the South Durham, the Brocklesby, where he kept on pulling out something extra when tackled by Cheekio Ora, the Holcombe Harriers and the Vale of Lune, ridden in all of them by his Dudley Cup rider Tim Smith.

In Wales, Mrs. Rose Harry's 16-year-old Fitz reached a grand total of 30 wins when recording his third win of the season in the men's open at the Tredegar Farmers with the Welsh champion John Llewellyn up; and the son of Manicou out of a mare by Brightworthy hadn't finished yet.

Three of farrier Richard Lee's four runners at the Golden Valley were in the winner's enclosure; and one of them, Majetta Crescent in the ladies' open, was a first winner for the trainer's wife Carol. This nine-year-old grandson (on his dam's side) of a St. Leger winner, Sayajirao, won four of his six ladies' opens with Carol Lee up, Majetta Crescent, the horse Jonjo O'Neill broke a record on recording his 126th win of the 1977-1978 N.H. season when winning a handicap hurdle at Perth, was subsequently bought for £300 out of a knacker's yard shortly before he was about to be put down.

Michael Tory's Portman mare Morning Heather won the four-mile men's open for the Tedworth Gold Cup at Larkhill for the second time in three years; and despite the fact that she was carrying a 7 lb. penalty this time, the mare's time of 7 mins. 55 secs. was a course record for the distance. Admittedly it was recorded on a fast surface; but it was 11 seconds faster than the time she took to win the race on firm ground in 1980. Mike Felton rode her on both occasions.

Tailpiece:

Warwickshireman Tony Perry, having his first ride in a race at the age of 46 on his own horse Phred O'Reilly (an animal of unknown parentage and equally unknown form) in the hunt race at the North Warwickshire, and putting up 10lb. overweight, got as far as the last open ditch before being unshipped. Informed by a kind friend that the clerk of the scales had credited him with carrying 13st. 3lb., he replied, "Good Heavens! I was under the impression that I weighed more than that when I got out of bed this morning."

1983

*In which the Heythrop has a change of venue, the men's and ladies'
finals at Chepstow have new sponsors, Irish invaders capture the prizes
at Cheltenham and Liverpool, and a champion hurdler appears on
the point-to-point scene.*

T he 1983 season was prefaced by a furore on the subject of hunting, sparked
off by the Jockey Club expressing its concern at the price racing would have
to pay if the threat to the sport became a reality. The anti-hunting voice
made itself heard when the *Sporting Life*'s breeding expert, Tony Morris (who was
later to defect to the *Racing Post*), cast doubts on the morality of hunting. He was
supported, in an absurd letter from a Mr. F. Marstin, who (need one say it?) was
writing from London, and delivered himself as follows:

> "I do not believe banning fox-hunting would have any serious effect on
> steeplechasing... Furthermore, the vast majority of the hunter-chase and
> point-to-point fraternity are nothing less than part of an inner social circle that
> perpetuates the idea of class distinction and purely wishes to retain its tradi-
> tional lifestyle, part of which happens to be fox-hunting."

Messrs Morris and Marstin were, however, in the minority, and among those
expressing more civilised views were the amateur riders James Bealby and Joey
Newton; whilst Elizabeth M. Brooks, writing from Bideford, Devon, and describing herself as "a small permit holder," made the very valid point that "hunting is
ideal for schooling young horses, rejuvenating jaded ones and providing a useful
life for retired or too-slow ex-racehorses."

Joey Newton remarked in his letter that there was an excellent case for hunting on moral grounds, in that "it is the most efficient method of fox preservation
and control in its natural environment, since the sport confers nothing but bene-
fits on wild life through the preservation of habitats"; and stud owner Neville
Dent effectively exploded the myth of class distinction with his remark that well
over 60% of the 80 jumping mares that had passed through his hands "have been
owned by genuine working farmers who hope to breed a horse good enough to
point-to-point and, if they are even luckier, to go on to race under N.H. rules."

And I am not ashamed to say that I also joined in the controversy, quoting Lester Piggott. "To lose hunting," said Lester, "would be the beginning of the end for country sports as we have known them for hundreds of years."

The militant side of the anti-hunting mania was much in evidence at Hackwood Park on the night before the Vine & Craven point-to-point was due to take place there. The fanatics did everything but cause damage to the fences, cutting the guy ropes to the tents, sabotaging the wiring of the public address system, severing the tapes marking the course and putting sugar in the water supply. But they didn't succeed in preventing racing from taking place the next day. It went ahead half an hour later than scheduled; but this was following an inspection on account of the weather.

The weather, in fact, was far from kind this season, causing the abandonment of 23 fixtures, many of them after postponements. One other meeting, Mr. Goschen's at Tweseldown, was abandoned as a result of the course being covered with treated sewage! A further 18 meetings took place after postponements. 28 of the season's hunter chases were also victims of the weather, fortunately none of them major ones. Even so, there were a record number of runners in point-to-points, no fewer than 14,250, if one includes the 250 appearing in the natural-country races.

A tightening up of the mandatory vaccination of point-to-pointers was initiated with a clause in the regulations stipulating that "any horse which is not correctly vaccinated or whose passport is not correctly endorsed, will not be allowed to run." Safety precautions were also stepped up with a regulation insisting that there must be "at least one ambulance on the course, preferably two."

And there were some significant changes of venue, as well as in sponsorship. The Heythrop's traditional Tuesday fixture was transferred from Stow-on-the-Wold to its present venue at Dunthrop Farm, near Chipping Norton, following the sale of its old home at Fox Farm.

The Heythrop was one of five executives to be granted an extra meeting in aid of the Grand National Appeal Fund, the others being the East Anglian Area with one at Horseheath, the Midlands Area with one at Thorpe Lodge, near Newark, the combined PPOA & North Western Area meeting at Whittington in Lancashire, and the South East Area at Detling, near Maidstone. None of them was a victim of the weather and all were successful in raising substantial sums for the cause.

On the national front, the Massey-Ferguson Gold Cup maiden-series final was switched from Wetherby to Worcester – a change which enabled a more representative field to go to the post for it, with 19 runners; and the men's and ladies' championships at Chepstow both had new, and different sponsors, Webster's Yorkshire Bitters taking over the men's final and the RMC Group making itself responsible for the ladies' final.

The two most prolific point-to-point winners of the season were Mrs. Barbara Perry's Seine Bay, from the Albrighton, and Roy Cake's Tawny Myth, from the South Dorset. Each of them won eight races. But it was Seine Bay who took the Grand Marnier Trophy on account of a second and a third placing as against Tawny Myth's single second place.

Charlotte Perry won five ladies' opens on Seine Bay; and, after she had been injured in a fall, Sally Aston won three more. Tawny Myth, however, had the more remarkable season, carrying a lot more weight. He was beaten only once, on his initial appearance. Ridden each time by Richard Cake, the nine-year-old son of Armagnac Monarch, six of whose eight wins were in open events, was carrying a 7lb. penalty when he won the 4-mile men's open at the Tedworth in one of the best fields that had gone to the post for this race, and one of the other runners was Nostradamus, who finished sixth. Tawny Myth and the favourite, seven-year-old Brent Mystery, had the race to themselves from four fences out, and there was little between them as they approached the last, from which point Tawny Myth produced much the better acceleration and drew away to win by five lengths, with Lochage, a winner over four miles at Tweseldown, finishing a distance away in third.

This was the 21st winner for Richard Cake, who farmed 350 acres with his father at Plush, near Dorchester, and looked after Tawny Myth when not doing the farming. The Cakes bought Tawny Myth for a comparatively modest sum from John Felton, the father of Michael, who won a maiden race on him at Larkhill in 1981. The following season, Richard Cake won three races on the horse.

It is interesting to note that Mackenzie & Selby rated Tawny Myth and Seine Bay within 5lb. of each other in their annual, which had now lost the umbrella of *Horse and Hound,* but none of its sparkle. They rated Tawny Myth at 10-11 and Seine Bay at 10-6.

With the possible exception of Cheekio Ora, a winner, under Peter Greenall, of three men's opens, one of them on the last day of the season at the Torrington Farmers in the West Country, and three hunter chases, I would rate Tawny Myth the best point-to-pointer of the season – which doesn't necessarily mean that he was the best horse seen out in a point-to-point, since amongst others to appear in these races were Earls Brig and Queensberry Lad, whose appearances were more limited.

Earls Brig, rated not far from the top at 11-4 in Mackenzie & Selby, won twice in his five appearances, winning the men's open at the Morpeth on his only appearance in a point-to-point and beating Queensberry Lad (rated at 11-1) in a hunter chase at Kelso. On his three other appearances under Rules, he was a runner-up to the-Irish winner of the Cheltenham Foxhunters', a faller at the last in the Scottish Grand National at Ayr when his chance had gone, and fourth to Prominent King in the Land Rover Champion Hunter Chase at Cheltenham. Queensberry Lad, on his only other appearance at the age of 11, was a facile winner of a poor men's open at the Dumfriesshire.

Three horses won seven point-to-points during the season. The highest-rated by Mackenzie & Selby at 10-9, was Mrs. Rame Fell's Frevolity, an 11-year-old from the Spooners & West Dartmoor who won four of the West Country men's opens with David Wonnacott up and three ladies' opens, including one at Umberleigh on the last day of the season, with Mrs. Janine Mills (née Evans) up.

National Clover (10-5) won all seven of her races in Wales with Mandy Lingard up, was placed in four of her six other races and failed to complete the course in the other two.

The third horse to win seven races was a future megastar, the horse that was to prove Scotland's pride and joy, and had a book written about him, Adam Calder's home-bred seven-year-old from the Berwickshire, Flying Ace, by Saucy Kit out of Flying Eye, a prolific point-to-point winner by Vulgan. Ridden in all his races by his owner's daughter, Doreen Calder, who was hardly ever off him during his illustrious career, Flying Ace was unbeaten in his first season, beginning it in the hunt race at his home meeting. He then won a restricted open at Alnwick and five adjacent hunts' races, earning a rating of 10-7 from Mackenzie & Selby.

High up in Mackenzie & Selby's handicap were the Irish winners of the Cheltenham and Liverpool Foxhunters', Eliogarty top-rated at 11-10 and Atha Cliath, fourth rated, behind Prominent King and Spartan Missile, at 11-5.

Eliogarty, owned and ridden by the 24-year-old Shropshire-born Caroline Beasley, who went to Ireland for a hunting holiday and stayed there, was a prolific point-to-point and hunter chase winner for Caroline in Ireland; and on his first visit to England the eight-year-old, now trained by Barry Kelly in Co. Meath, gave her a comfortable win in the Cheltenham Foxhunters' at the expense of Earls Brig and Compton Lad. The first woman ever to ride a winner at the Cheltenham festival, whilst she was in Ireland Caroline had the choice of buying either Eliogarty or Gaye Brief, the 1983 Champion Hurdle winner. She chose Eliogarty; and it was a choice she never regretted.

Despite being nearly brought down at the first and not far from the floor again at the Canal Turn, the eight-year-old Atha Cliath, trained by Patrick Mullins at Gorsebridge, Co. Kilkenny, and ridden by his son Willie, was an equally easy winner of the Liverpool Foxhunters' after being led into the last by Gayle Warning. A failure in the Cheltenham Foxhunters', Atha Cliath beat Eliogarty by a short head at Punchestown when giving him 7lb., but went under to him in the Sweet Afton hunter chase at Punchestown by 1.5 lengths when also giving him 7lb. So there would have been quite a strong argument for ignoring his lapse in the Cheltenham Foxhunters' and rating him above Eliogarty. It was, I can add, the first time that horses from Ireland have won the Cheltenham and Liverpool Foxhunters' in the same year.

Nostradamus was the winner of the four-mile men's open for Lord Ashton of Hyde's Cup at the Heythrop for the second time in three years. Adapting himself splendidly to the new course on a sharper track, and comparatively easy to back at 5-1, with most of the money coming for Spartan Scot in the field of 14, the 11-year-old was always in a handy position; and from the downhill fence two fences out he and the Meynell & South Staffs mare Athenmore Lass had the race to themselves. Athenmore Lass stuck to him resolutely, but Nostradamus jumped the last fence in front and had no difficulty holding her off.

What made this performance so satisfying for Ian McKie was that his despondence when Nostradmus was beaten half a length by More Culture in his previous race at Lockinge was turned into joy at finding More Culture finishing seven lengths behind him in third place.

It was not otherwise the most brilliant of seasons for Nostradamus. John Sumner's good old stayer managed to win only one other race in his eight appearances, a ladies' open over the sharp track in Hackwood Park with Tocky McKie up; but he was a runner-up to good horses on three occasions, so it was a bit early to say that *Anno Domini* was taking its toll.

There were 12 runners for the Dudley Cup in the heavy ground at Chaddesley Corbett. It was not a vintage field. The favourite was the locally-trained Rockin' Berry, who had lost her maiden certificate the previous season and was a winner of a restricted open at the North Hereford,the members' ladies' race at the Harkaway Club fixture over the shorter trip at Chaddesley Corbett and a ladies' open over the former Dudley Cup course at Upton-on-Severn. But the mare wasn't quite good enough to win on this occasion.

The winner was a horse from the North Hereford, Clear Pride, who very nearly didn't run, owing to the heavy going. The decision to let this 12-year-old winner of the men's opens at the Wheatland and the Holcombe Harriers take his chance in the Dudley Cup wasn't made until a few minutes before the declarations closed. However, well ridden by his usual pilot, Duncan Trow, who was having his first ride in the race, he was a convincing winner. It was Clear Pride's 15th win, including two in hunter chases, in 46 appearances.

Joining Rockin' Berry at the "Rushton" fence four fences out, Clear Pride quickened to take a clear lead approaching the penultimate fence and held off a renewed challenge from Rockin' Berry by a length. Owned by Mrs. Phil Jones, Clear Pride was a first Dudley Cup winner for his trainer, Richard Lee, who had sent out a long string of winners from his successful livery yard at Presteigne on the border of Wales and in another four years would be taking out a licence as a public trainer.

Albert Sanderson's home-bred mare from the Cleveland, Lady Buttons, trained by his daughter Jean and ridden by Nigel Tutty, was a very convincing winner of the 4.25-mile Grimthorpe Cup on the testing going at Whitwell-on-the-Hill. Drawing three lengths clear three fences out in a field of 16, she had doubled this advantage over the useful Waggoners Walk by the time she reached the winning post. Yorkshire Mariner, the favourite for the race, finished a further four lengths behind in third. But it was not nearly so spectacular a season for Lady Buttons as the previous one. The only other race she won in her eight appearances was the men's open at the Cleveland, where she beat Mountain Lad.

The 14-year-old Waggoners Walk was having his last race before retirement. He will be remembered particularly as the winner of the four-mile National Hunt Chase at Cheltenham in 1980 and the Kim Muir there in 1981; and among the other races he won was the Eider Chase at Newcastle.

It was good to see the Welsh champion John Llewellyn rewarded with the *Daily Telegraph* Cup at last, in the year after he had ridden his 100th winner in point to-points. The 37-year-old rider rode 19 point-to-point winners in 1983, two more than Peter Greenall. Both riders were in action on the last day of the season at the Torrington Farmers, where they won the two divisions of the men's open, Llewellyn getting two spectacular leaps out of the 14-year-old East Of Eden to win division one from the West Country favourite, Jimmy Frost's mount Blue Beans by a length, and having to survive an objection afterwards. Greenall finished third in this race on Killinick Buck. East Of Eden, owned by Jim Shaw, a retired Worcestershire farmer, was trained by Richard Lee, saddling his 13th winner of the season.

In the other division, Peter Greenall's mount Cheekio Ora displayed his class by cutting down John Llewellyn's mount Master Straight (who had completed a hat-trick in Wales) and winning on the bit. It was the ten-year-old Cheekio Ora's 24th win since Bryan Parry bought him for 1,600 guineas off a Billingshurst newsagent at the Ascot Sales in December 1977.

For the second year running, Jenny Pidgeon won the *Sporting Life* Cup, with the same number of point-to-point winners that she had the previous season, 18. The three best horses she rode during the season, French Peacock, a winner of six of his seven races, Zarajeff, a winner of five of his eight, and Random Leg, on whom she had three wins in point-to-points and her first win under Rules in the John & Nigel Thorne Memorial Hunter Chase at Stratford, where the runner-up to Random Leg was Spartan Missile, ridden by Mrs. Diana Henderson, the former Diana Thorne, who was now married to the Lambourn trainer Nicky Henderson.

French Peacock, Zarajeff and Random Leg were all trained by Jenny's father, Graham. The first two were owned outright by him and Random Leg, a former inmate of Josh Gifford's yard, he owned jointly with Mrs. Gillian Brazier.

The two joint runners-up for the ladies' title were Mrs. Lucy Gibbon (née King) and Mandy Lingard, each with eight wins; and the 23-year-old Mandy Lingard was the Grand Marnier leading novice rider on the distaff side. The Grand Marnier leading male novice rider was the West Country farrier 21-year-old David Wonnacott. One of the riders associated with Tawny Myth, he rode ten winners, the same number as the 19-year-old Mark Richards, the recipient of the Wilkinson Sword at the PPOA dinner in Stratford. The award for special services to the Sport presented at the national point-to-point dinner also went to a West Countryman, Grant Cann.

And the leading rider in hunter chases, and first recipient of Peter Greenall's new cup for this at the national point-to-point dinner in London, was Alison Dare with her six wins in this field, four of them on Mrs. Joyce Baimbridge's seven-year-old Kentigern and the other two also on horses trained by Dick Baimbridge in the Berkeley country. Greenall also rode six winners in hunter chases; but naturally he didn't want to share in the trophy himself.

Had there been a trophy for the riding performance of the season, I would have given it to the 19-year-old Polly Curling for her masterly performance on Oliver Carter's Fishleigh Gamble in the ladies' open at the Wilton. After breaking a leather at the seventh, she rode the next 12 fences without irons and won by a distance. They were all talking about her in the West as another Sue Aston. She was, however, still a long way off winning her first *Sporting Life* Cup.

But, with Ottery News on the sidelines, the star of Oliver Carter's yard was still his home-bred Otter Way, who, although he had now reached the age of 15, ended his season as he had begun it, with a win; and this time it was in the *Horse and Hound* Cup at Stratford which he was winning for the second time in eight years. Despite having been beaten a short head in this end-of-term championship last year, he started at 20-1. However, with Jim Wilson up, he kept on pulling out something extra to get the better of Gill O'Whiskey and the favourite Honourable Man.

"What a trier!" said Jim Wilson afterwards. Amazing to think that Otter Way was bred from a mare of unknown parentage who cost Oliver Carter no more than £150.

When Otter Way won his first *Horse and Hound* Cup in 1976 he was ridden by Grant Cann, who landed his 200th point-to-point winner at the age of 40 when scoring on an untried five-year-old, Speedy Surprise, in a two-horse hunt race at the Stevenstone on May 30. Cann was the second West Country rider to reach a double century of point-to-point winners. The first was Frank Ryall in 1968.

There were 13 runners for the Webster's Yorkshire Bitter men's final on the soft ground at Chepstow, where the favourite was Brent Mystery, the runner-up to Tawny Myth in the Tedworth four-miler; and the winner, Little Bilsham, started at 14-1. Brent Mystery, who led from the eleventh until after the seventeenth, fell three fences out when weakening; and at this stage Little Bilsham was disputing the lead with the Yorkshire runner Urser, who fell at the second last when still in with a chance; but his fall left Little Bilsham clear under 18-year-old Willy Bryan (the brother of John), who was riding his first winner under Rules. But this win had its downside with Bryan being fined £20 by the stewards for excessive use of the whip, which he didn't need to employ anyway.

Just exactly why Little Bilsham was allowed to start at such a long price is a mystery, since he was in a top point-to-point yard (Bill Bryan's) and Gordon Spratt's nine-year-old son of Armagnac Monarch had already won four races, three of them open events. Had Little Bilsham run in the Dudley Cup, he would undoubtedly have taken a great deal of beating.

The RMC Group ladies' final also produced a 14-1 winner; but in this case the price was easier to understand, with such horses as Nostradamus, Seine Bay, Sporran Lad, Master Straight and Moonstep in the field.

The eight-year-old Baulking Byway, out of a dam who was a half-sister to Baulking Green, proved more than a match for all of them. Nostradamus and Seine Bay were big disappointments, though they both completed the course. Bred by his owner, Mrs. Ann Bray, a Gloucestershire permit holder, Baulking Byway had only one previous success during the season, in a restricted open at Larkhill; but, in the experienced hands of Rosemary Harper, he delivered his challenge at Chepstow approaching the last and sprinted away on the run-in to win by 15 lengths from the Delahooke runner Sporran Lad, a winner of three ladies' opens and a novice riders' contest at the East Anglian Grand National Appeal fixture at Horseheath.

Neither Baulking Byway nor Sporran Lad was in the field for the Albright & Wilson ladies' championship at the Melton Hunt Club; but both of them would have been hard pressed to beat the very easy winner, Highgate Lady, who handled the heavy going exceptionally well, never putting a foot wrong in winning her fifth ladies' open of the season, ridden in the last three of them by Emma Newton, the wife of Joey, who had bought the six-year-old mare for £10,000 off her owner-rider, Mrs. Sheena Scott, after the latter had won on her at the Quorn.

The Newtons also carried off the Marie Curie novice championship with the six-year-old Ryedale, who was recording his sixth success of the season, the last five of them in a row. Ryedale, by Little Buskins out of a mare by Arctic Slave, had been bought for Joey Newton by David Minton (who was then with the Curragh

Bloodstock Agency) for 5,000 guineas as an unbroken four-year-old at the Dublin Sales in June 1981; and his win at Melton saw him following in the footsteps of John Bunyan, then in process of fulfilling his promise.

Having graduated from novice class, the eight-year-old John Bunyan won five of his seven races in 1983, including two hunter chases, in one of which, at Huntingdon, he gave weight and a beating to Highgate Lady when she was in her former ownership.

Although he had qualified for it, Ryedale was not in the field for the Massey-Ferguson final at Worcester, where there was a field of 19 and a 20-1 winner in Apixy Apaxy, a seven-year-old mare from the Berkeley who was winning for the second time, having won her qualifier, the maiden race at the West Somerset Vale.

Apixy Apaxy, a first winner under Rules for 30-year-old John Tuck, whose mother, Mrs. Jill Tuck, bought the mare for 925 guineas at the Ascot Sales a year ago, was a ten-lengths winner at Worcester, though she might have had rather more to do if the runner-up, Stephen Swiers' mount Exit Only, hadn't broken down. "We bought her to have a bit of fun with, hoping to win point-to-points," said John's father, Bill Tuck.

My idea of the most exciting five-year-old seen out this season was Brockie Law, who had won twice over hurdles as a three-year-old and been qualified for point-to-point racing with the Jedforest in Scotland, where he was found for Teresa Webber by Colin Wares. When Brockie Law came South into trainer John Webber's yard in the Bicester country to start his point-to-point career, he won three ladies' opens in three different counties with the trainer's daughter up and was placed on three of his other four appearances. It was the beginning of a highly successful partnership for Teresa, who had ridden her first winner the previous season when scoring on another of her father's horses, White Paper, in the adjacent hunts' race at the Old Berkshire.

Among the veterans, one who certainly deserves a mention is Forbidden Fruit, who made a miraculous recovery after severing a tendon in two places. A winner over fences and hurdles from Tim Forster's yard, this 13-year-old from the North Cotswold, owned by David Smyly and ridden by his 17-year-old son Giles, a schoolboy at Eton, was a winning ride for Giles the first time he sat on him in public, in the adjacent hunts' race at the Heythrop; and this was the first of three consecutive winning rides for the partnership.

The next one came in the novice riders' race at the Heythrop Grand National Appeal meeting, where Brockie Law and Teresa Webber were the runners-up; and this was followed by a win in a men's open at Tweseldown. In this last race of the season, with Giles detained at school, Forbidden Fruit, carrying a 7lb. penalty, was a comfortable winner of the men's open at the Cotswold Vale Farmers with James Evetts riding him. So it was four wins in a row for the 13-year-old.

Another valiant pairing was the Beaufort combination of two veterans, David Bennett and his 12-year-old Dorset Farmer. In his best season ever, Bennett won six races on Dorset Farmer. Four of these successes were in open events, and the partnership's last four wins were consecutive ones. On another of his horses, Blickling Hall, an 11-year-old son of Blakeney, Bennett, a businessman who liked to spend his leisure time abroad in the sun, won the four-miles men's open at the

Dartmoor; and he completed his first-ever double with a win on Dorset Farmer in the British Field Sports Society race.

The Dartmoor race was one of two four-mile races that took place in the Devon & Cornwall Area. The other, now in its sixth year, was the four-mile men's open at the Exmoor; and in this Blickling Hall finished fourth to Village Green, an 11-year-old from the Lamerton who was giving his owner-rider, Cornish farmer Roger Eggins, his second win of the season on him.

The South East Area had the bright idea of marking its Grand National Appeal fixture at Detling with its first four-mile race and grandly describing it on the race-card as the 'Kent Grand National'. The going was so holding at Detling that one fence was omitted. But this 12st. race attracted 11 runners and was well won by one of the three horses carrying a 7lb. penalty, Leslie Vine's No Justice, a ten-year-old from the East Sussex & Romney Marsh who was completing a hat-trick of wins with John Hickman up and made it four wins in a row afterwards with a win in another open race. The two horses who followed No Justice home at Detling, The Four Hundred and Casamayor, were also carrying 7lb. penalties.

The Heythrop found another way of celebrating their Grand National Appeal fixture. They had some very distinguished company on parade, along with their jockeys and trainers, including five Grand National winners in Well To Do, Red Rum, Aldaniti, Grittar and Corbiere, the runners-up Crisp and Spartan Missile, a Cheltenham Gold Cup winner in The Dikler, and another old favourite in Spanish Steps.

In celebrating the 50th anniversary of the Robarts family's ownership of their course at Kimble on Easter Saturday, the Vale of Aylesbury also had some distinuished company present at their meeting. Among those seen on this occasion were three star lady riders of former days: Mrs. Joyce Newland (née Seaton), who came from the same village as Golden Miller's rider, Gerry Wilson, and was described by the late Len Coville as a rider cast in the same mould; her sister, Mary Seaton, who was riding against the men in the 'twenties; and Ruth Rhodes, a very familar figure on the course at Kimble.

There were, however, no winners for the Robarts family this time. John Robarts's two fancied runners, Random Lad and the home-bred General Cherry, both finished third in their races. The star performer was Graham Pidgeon's French Peacock, who beat Nostradamus in the adjacent hunts' race in seven seconds faster time than Housemistress took to win the ladies' open for Rosemary Harper.

It is not often, indeed hardly ever, that winners of high-class hurdle races are to be seen contesting point-to-points. But one who was doing so in 1983 was Meladon, the winner of the *Daily Express* Triumph Hurdle at Cheltenham in 1977. Bought in 1980 by Mrs. Beverley Formby to act as a pacemaker for Pollardstown (a runner-up to Sea Pigeon in the Champion Hurdle of 1981), the ten-year-old, now trained by Anthony Perry in the Albrighton country, made a winning point-to-point début under Steven Brookshaw in the men's open at the South Shropshire, where he was having his first race since breaking down for the second time in 1981.

The idea had been to send Meladon hunter chasing if his legs stood up to it.

Apparently, they didn't, as this one race was his single appearance in hunt racing.

In Scotland, Colin Hall's Foolish Hero, a hobdayed seven-year-old by the American sire Run The Gantlet, was proving himself to be the best ladies' horse after Flying Ace, winning six ladies' opens with Gillian Minto up. He was also the joint leader with the seven-year-old Ryedale in the Midlands Area in the contests for the PPOA's Sean Graham young horse awards with 60 points, two more than Flying Ace attained.

Although General Confusion (now 12) and Swift Wood were stll going strong in East Anglia, the former with four wins in open events and the latter including four wins in hunter chases among her six successes, there was a rising star in this area in George Barber's seven-year-old Drakes Pinnacle, who had lost his maiden certificate the previous season and won six races on the trot under Roy Barber in 1983, the last three of them hunter chases; and he was third, behind the Bedale horse Casa Knipe and Housemistress in the John Corbet Cup at Stratford.

But the horse rated highest in East Anglia by Mackenzie & Selby, at 11-0, was one who sometimes suffered from a deficiency of oxygen, the reliable Mr. Mellors, whose four wins under Simon Sherwood comprised one in an open point-to-point, in which he had General Confusion behind him, and three in hunter chases.

Mr. Mellors was not the only well-known performer to have oxygen problems. Another was Richard Lee's charge Majetta Crescent, who was often in danger of collapsing from a shortage of oxygen after a race and had to have an oxygen bottle standing ready for him in the unsaddling enclosure. But the problem didn't prevent the ten-year-old from continuing his majestic progress. In his ten appearances during the season he was in the winner's enclosure five times with Carol Lee up and placed on a further four. One of his victims was Pastry Brush in the ladies' open at the Wheatland, and another was Frevolity, beaten a short head at the Exmoor in his last race of the season.

In Wales, Fixed Price, a nine-year-old from the Talybont, was proving a horse from the bargain basement. Bought for 725 guineas at Ascot from Mrs. Mercy Rimell (for whom he had won two chases) by the Abergavenny glazier Grenville Richards, Fixed Price started with a win under Mark Richards in a good open race at the Beaufort and then won three of his next four races, beating Clear Pride in the last of them. His only defeat was by Little Bilsham in the men's open at the Albrighton Woodland. Grenville Richards trained Fixed Price at the foot of a mountain in Wales.

At the Southdown & Eridge fixture at Parham, Mrs. Sheilagh French and her three daughters all had rides in the ladies' open, Sarah won the race on Leslie Vine's Barb's Beau and her mother finished third on her own horse Cairn Royal. But Scarlett and Lucy failed to get into the money.

Mrs. Jean Campbell's nine-year-old Mark's Methane continued to have things more or less his own way in these parts, winning six of his nine races with Bob Hacking up and beating No Justice by a distance in one of them. He finished his season winning a hunter chase at Fontwell by half a length from the Old Berks contestant Wellands Copse, who was being ridden by a certain Richard Dunwoody!

Another big name under Rules riding in point-to-points in these days was Ian Balding, who had a useful old horse in Ross Poldark. Used as a lead horse for the stable's hurdlers, the 12-year-old Ross Poldark had won both his point-to-points when he began his career between the flags in 1982; and in 1983 horse and rider started with a hat-trick of wins, following success in an open race at Tweseldown with wins in hunter chases at Leicester and Folkestone. In their other races they were runners-up in a hunter chase at Lingfield and fourth to Atha Cliath and Willie Mullins in the Liverpool Foxhunters'. Ross Poldark, who hadn't seen a course before he won his first race at Tweseldown the previous season, was bought out of the hunting field.

It was becoming the fashion in certain circles to run down the Buchanan's natural-country races, and certainly they were usually regarded as a bit of a nuisance by the racing Press, who tended to ignore them. But there was no doubt of their popularity with the contestants, especially in the case of the ones at the Beaufort and the Cottesmore. There were 34 runners for the former and 20 at the Cottesmore, where there was a ding-dong battle from five fences out, with the first three going past the post within a length of each other.

This race produced a first winner for a 20-year-old farm secretary, Karen Wright, who was having her first ride in a race on a 15-year-old gelding of doubtful parentage, Southside Hobo, owned by a Lincolnshire farmer, Ross Haddow, who bought him for £500 and let him earn his keep seven days a week in a riding school. Surely the kind of combination such races were devised for?

For Katie Halswell, the West Country rider associated with such good horses as Galloway Fabulous, Star Express and Moonstep, the 1983 season was her last. Twice the leading lady rider in the West Country and a runner-up to Pip Fisher for the *Sporting Life* Cup in 1979, she had been troubled with back problems for some years; and she announced her retirement after a fall on Moonstep in a hunter chase at Taunton in the third week of April.

In July, Richard Woodhouse died at the age of 54. A Joint Master of the Portman from 1969 to 1980, Dick was a much-loved character and a fine amateur rider who won the Cheltenham Foxhunters' twice on his own horses, Woodside Terrace (a horse he paid 360 guineas for at the Ascot Sales as a ten-year-old) in 1965, and Highworth in 1970. His memory is kept alive today by his widow, Susan, with the trophy she presents annually at the PPORA luncheon at Stratford Racecourse to the leading owner-rider of the season; and also by the hunter chase at Wincanton that has been named after him.

1984

In which mares get preferential treatment, the Audi Grand Prix de Chasse takes shape, walk-overs abound, David Turner rides his 300th winner, and the national point-to-point dinner moves to The Belfry.

This was the year that the 51b. allowance for mares (of six years old and upwards) was introduced to the point-to-point scene. It was made on the recommendation of the Thoroughbred Breeders Association, whose spokesman, Neville Dent, had remarked in a letter to the *Sporting Life* that "mares were not winning the number of races to which they were numerically entitled." Be that as it may, mares of the quality of National Clover, Lady Buttons, Highgate Lady and Swift Wood, to name but four, hardly seemed to be in need of such an allowance; and in 1984 Derrick Llewellin's South Pembrokeshire mare National Clover was the Grand Marnier winner with nine wins to her credit.

Not everyone was in agreement with the concession, and there were those who were strongly opposed to it. One of them was David Thomson, the Chairman of the Northern Area Point-to-Point Association, who referred to it at the Association's annual dinner at Kelso in November 1983 as "more unnecessary legislation, when we had just got used to coping with passports and the like"; and I have to admit to describing it at the same dinner myself as "a case of sex discrimination gone mad." But it had, of course, come to stay; although it is true to say that, in its first year, while there was certainly an increase in the number of mares running in point-to-points, the 231 point-to-points and 16 hunter chases won by them was not much above the average.

Prior to National Clover's success, the last mare to win the Grand Marnier Trophy was Hargan, the 1979 winner with her ten wins. The other mares to win this trophy since its inception in 1970 were Pensham in 1972 with 11 wins and Little Fleur in 1978 with her 12.

Eight of National Clover's nine wins, all with Mandy Lingard aboard, were in ladies' opens; the other was in the mares' race at the PPOA fixture on the Berkeley course at Woodford. The only other horse to win nine point-to-points during the season was Flying Ace, who came within a whisker of winning the Grand Marnier Trophy but lost it with fewer placings than National Clover.

Flying Ace did, however, undergo defeat in his last three races. His first was in the ladies' championship at the Melton Hunt Club, where BritAg fertilisers had taken over the sponsorship of this championship from Albright & Wilson. After 17 wins on the trot, the Scottish ace was beaten by the front-running Witchin, who, in his first season of point-to-point racing, had won two of his four previous races and been beaten in a race over the Garthorpe course by Highgate Lady.

Having lost several lengths through a slow start, Flying Ace was in hot pursuit of Witchin after jumping the third last but, hard though he tried, he was unable to reach him and went under by a length and a half. Brockie Law, running on strongly under Teresa Webber, was no more than a head behind in third.

Witchin's time of 6 mins. 9 secs. under the 29-year-old Jill Grinyer (who was later to become Mrs. Michael Dawson) was the fastest for the course since the Warwickshire mare Zanetta broke the record with a time of 6 mins. 4 secs. in the 1978 race.

An eight-year-old by Chou Chin Chow out of Chevaliers Witch, by Arctic Chevalier, Witchin was bred in Ireland and was a winner twice over hurdles when trained by the Carlisle permit holder John Henderson. He was bought in the autumn of 1983 by Cliff Dawson, a Joint Master of the Brocklesby, on the advice of Jonjo O'Neill. The BritAg race was his last of the season.

Flying Ace's next race was the new RMC Group ladies' championship at Chepstow; and I have to say that Doreen Calder was not seen at her best on this occasion, to put it mildly. It was not entirely surprising that she was fined £25 by the stewards for failing to acquaint herself with the course. Flying Ace, carrying the top weight of 11-0, was left with an enormous amount of ground to make up over the last four fences; and although he made up a considerable amount of it in the closing stages, he could get no nearer than fifth of the 11 finishers in the field of 18.

The race was won by a horse carrying 10-4, Cobley Express. Given an exemplary ride by the experienced Mrs. Janine Mills, who was riding her 50th winner, Cobley Express, an eight-year-old by Pony Express whose only previous win during the season had been in the ladies' open at the East Devon, took over from Rednael on the run-in and sped away from the Belvoir mare to win by five lengths.

Flying Ace's last race of the season was the *Horse and Hound* Cup at Stratford. He was always prominent this time and had taken up the running five fences out, but a bad mistake at the third last destroyed whatever chance he might have had and he finished fourth to Tim Easterby's owner-ridden Prominent King, who was winning his third hunter chase of the season.

The unsatisfactory thing about this race was that one of the horses who would certainly have given them all something to do, Willy Hamilton's Jedforest nine-year-old Earls Brig, a winner of two hunter chases and an amateur riders' handicap chase at Kelso, was a victim of the random balloting-out system that was in force.

This beastly balloting-out was a consistent bugbear. It happened too, and not for the first time, in the final of the Massey-Ferguson maiden-race series at Worcester, from which the 11 horses balloted out included Mrs. Ivy Frank's six-year-old Macnab's Quest, a winner, with Grant Cann up, of four of his six races, three of them in a row before the Massey Ferguson was due to be run.

But at least we had a good winner of the Worcester race in Trevor Marks's home-bred Stanwick Lad, who had distinguished himself under John Sharp with three wins beforehand, the last of them in the Marie Curie novice championship at Garthorpe, where Sharp was sitting pretty all the way, with Peter Greenall struggling to keep pace on the dual winner Naughty Niece, who took the runner-up's spot.

At Worcester, Stanwick Lad had a lot more to do in a field of 20; but he went about his task in fine style and was an impressive winner from two decent horses, Le Jour Fortune (claiming the 5lb. mares' allowance) and Political Whip.

Marks bred the seven-year-old Stanwick Lad on his farm in Northants from a mare, Princess Astra, who died the year after he was foaled; and Stanwick Lad's sire, Netherkelly, stood at Richard Bowers's Elms Stud at Denton, near Northampton. In years to come, Stanwick Lad was to prove his worth in gold.

One new rule that nobody could quarrel with was the introduction of mandatory insurance for all riders in point-to-points, including those taking part in natural-country races.

But another one, demanding that "No rider may be declared for more than one horse in any one race" was far from popular with the owners of well-filled stables, especially those which were short of riders to call on, since it meant that, in the event of a race being divided after declarations, a second ride for the stable jockey was not permitted, save in exceptional circumstances such as illness or injuries from a fall.

The object of this ruling was to remove the temptation to take extra horses to a meeting in the hope of divisions on the day of racing. This caused one hunt, the Oakley, to cut out their restricted open, which had to be divided four times in 1983, three times when the entries were received and once more after declarations.

There were 17 runners for the Heythrop four-miler on the good to firm ground at Dunthrop Farm; and the favourite, Lay-The-Trump, a nine-year-old inmate of Richard Lee's Presteigne yard who had won three of his four previous races under his 20-year-old rider, Bruce Dowling, and been beaten a head on the other occasion, justified his market position with a gutsy performance.

Starting off in the lead, Lay-The-Trump never saw another horse during the race and, despite a mistake at the last, where Dowling lost one iron and kicked the other out, he held off a challenge from Spartan Scot to score by half a length, with the virtually friendless Unbeatable Hand close up in third under Lawrence Lay, ahead of The Vintner (a veteran of four Grand Nationals and a winner this season of three open point-to-points).

By Laurence O out of a mare by Portmanteau, Lay-The-Trump won three point-to-points in Ireland before coming over to England and finishing sixth in the Newmarket Town Plate ridden by Bruce's father, Dr. Bob Dowling. After his success at the Heythrop he won four of his remaining six races, bringing his score for the season up to eight.

The distance of the ladies' open for the Lyon Trophy at the Heythrop had now been increased from 3.5 miles to 3 miles 6 furlongs; and this year's race was smoothly won by chiropractor Teresa Webber on her father's Brockie Law, a winner of four of his six ladies' opens during the season.

The Old Harrovian & Old Etonian race which has been a feature of this meeting and, more often than not, been won by an Etonian combination, saw Colin Gee striking another blow for Harrow with his fourth win in the race, this time on his eight-year-old Egbert, a winner on the Flat in France and over hurdles and fences in England before Gee bought him for 4,600 guineas. The horse had already won once before during the season and was to win twice more after his Heythrop success, proving himself to be a worthy successor to Gee's good horse Crystal Gazer.

It was firm going on Dudley Cup day at Chaddesley Corbett, despite the release of 200,000 gallons of water onto the course from three tankers. Eleven of the 36 starters stood their ground for the big race, with the triple open-race winner Little Bilsham from Bill Bryan's yard heading the market at 6-4.

But it was the superior finishing speed of the locally-trained Darlingate, a 6-1 shot, that decided the issue between the last two fences. Taking the lead off Little Bilsham, whose rider, Willy Bryan, had made full use of the horse's stamina, Darlingate went on to beat him by three lengths. Tommy Jackson had ridden a blinder on this nine-year-old winner, who had a tendency to run out over left-handed tracks. Kept to the outside all the way, Darlingate, who was recording his second win of the season over a left-handed track, behaved impeccably.

Owned by Michael Howard, a Worcestershire farmer, who bred him from a point-to-point mare called Somebody's Darling (a half-sister to Chris Collins's top hunter chaser Titus Oates) acquired from Mrs. Harold Rushton, Darlingate was a maiden at the start of the season when he won a restricted open and had the first of his three wins in open events.

For the first time in its long history, the Middleton fixture had to be abandoned owing to the hardness of the ground at Whitwell-on-the-Hill. So there was no Grimthorpe Cup race in 1984.

But it was a horse from the Middleton, Mick Easterby's home-trained Urser, who won the new Diners Club men's final at Chepstow. Carrying the top wieight of 12-7, and with the experienced Tim Thomson Jones in the saddle, the ten-year-old Urser, travelling much the best in a field of nine from a long way out, was never headed after hitting the front three fences from home; and he won by three lengths from one of Wales's best, Brigadier Mouse, to whom he was giving over a stone. This was the climax to a season which netted Urser four wins in hunter chases, one in an open point-to-point and four runner-up's spots in ten appearances.

Another Easterby horse to put himself bang up amongst the top hunter chasers since he started in hunt racing in 1983 as an 11-year-old after a successful career on the Flat and over hurdles in Ireland and later over hurdles and fences in England, was Prominent King, trained at Malton by Mick's brother, Peter, and owned by Peter's 21-year-old son Tim, who was up on him when he had the last of his four wins on the trot in the 1983 season in the Land Rover Champion Hunter Chase at Cheltenham.

In 1984, Prominent King won three of his five hunter chases, the first of them at Sedgefield, with Ronnie Beggan up, and the other two with his owner aboard. In his win at Market Rasen it was Urser who was the runner-up, beaten half a length at a weight advantage of 91b; and once again he finished his season on a high note, giving Tim Easterby a great ride in the *Horse and Hound* Cup at Stratford, where he quickened impressively to take the lead off Brent Mystery at the last fence and score by five lengths, with the third horse, Whiggie Geo, 20 lengths behind. Considering that he was beset with leg problems and wasn't the easiest horse to train, Peter Easterby did wonderfully well with him.

One of the few horses to beat Prominent King was the very promising John Bunyan, who did so by five lengths in the hunter chase at Sedgefield that he was winning for the second year running. As John Bunyan was receiving 51b. from Prominent King in this race, there wasn't much to choose between them. Mackenzie & Selby had Prominent King at 11-5 and John Bunyan at 11-3.

But the season was to end most unfortunately for Urky Newton's nine-year-old from the Belvoir, after he had won two open point-to-points and four hunter chases and been placed twice. He was in the process of winning another hunter chase at Fakenham when he slipped up on the flat approaching the last and broke his shoulder. This was a very sad loss for the Newtons, who had done so brilliantly with the son of Menelek. They still had Highgate Lady, however, and the mare won four of her nine races with three different riders up. In one of these races, the ladies' open at the Belvoir, where Julia Dean was deputising for Emma Newton, who was expecting a baby in August, Highgate Lady convincingly beat Witchin.

Another top performer lost to the scene, after adding six more open-race wins to his score, was the West Country horse Frevolity, who broke down so badly in the men's open at his home meeting, the Spooners & West Dartmoor, that he couldn't be saved. Mrs. Rame Fell's 12-year-old had run in 65 races and won 26 of them, including a hunter chase.

There was a good field of 14 for the inaugural running of the £5,000 Audi Grand Prix de Chasse at Sandown for which there had been qualifying opportunities in adjacent hunts' races at 20 point-to-points up and down the country. And a most satisfying result. Elmboy, the six-year-old winner, ridden by the long-legged Alan Hill, was not only the youngest horse in the race, but he was carrying top weight of 12-7 and recording his fifth win in a row, three of them in hunter chases, for his owner, Norman Mawle, the tenant farmer who bred him in the Bicester country. By Chris Sweeting's stallion Sunyboy, Elmboy was out of Elmolyn (by St. Elmo). On his only defeat in 1984 he was a faller on his first appearance of the season in an adjacent hunts' race at Kingston Blount.

Amidst rumbles of discontent from the point-to-point fraternity, the professional-trained (by Fred Winter, no less) Venture To Cognac, who had never seen a point-to-point course in his life, though he had run in bumpers' races in Ireland in his younger days, proved too smart for the opposition in the Cheltenham Foxhunters', the field for which included other professionally-trained horses in Compton Lad (4th) and Prominent King (5th).

Ridden as usual by Oliver Sherwood, the 11-year-old Venture To Cognac, who was in fact bred from a point-to-point mare in Ireland (Venture More, by Eastern Venture), was beating Spartan Missile (now trained by Nicky Henderson for John

Thorne's widow, Wendy) for the second time this season; and it was the son of Hot Brandy's third win in a row in a light season which saw him making only four appearances. His only defeat was in his first appearance of the season, when Further Thought (who was pulled up in the Cheltenham race) beat him in a hunter chase at Windsor.

Inevitably, there were a number of protests after Venture To Cognac's success at Cheltenham. Brian Beel, the point-to-point correspondent of *The Times,* made his views clear in an article for the *Sporting Life* headed "Let's penalise the professionals..." Trainers Tom Jones and Jim Old were among those who spoke up for them in letters to the paper.

But the most virulent protest came later from an Essex reader, Chris Cashmore, who had this to say: "It seems the hunter chase season has finished on a depressing note. It was bad enough when a professionally-trained horse won the Foxhunters' at Cheltenham. It was even worse when the same happens in the *Horse and Hound* Cup at Stratford, and diabolical when it happens in the Gentleman's Championship at Chepstow, which above all should be the day of the local point-to-point enthusiast"; and to this he added, "When will the Jockey Club take action? I think we can confidently say 'never' unless the Point-to-Point Owners' Association makes strong representation."

But really, of course, as Brian Beel had suggested, it was up to those who frame the conditions for the top hunter chases to impose a penalty system which would make it difficult for professionally-trained horses to win them. I think, though, that family horses, such as those trained by the Easterbys, should be exempt from swingeing penalties.

At least the Liverpool Foxhunters' wasn't won by a professionally-trained horse. This went to the Lauderdale-hunted Gayle Warning, owned and trained by John Dudgeon and ridden by his 26-year-old son Sandy, a very skilful pilot.

The runner-up to the Irish horse Atha Cliath in last year's race, and third to Lone Soldier and Rolls Rambler in the one before, the ten-year-old Gayle Warning, despite jumping to the right over the last, ran on strongly to master Peter Greenall's mount Lone Soldier, with Brod Munro-Wilson taking third place again, this time on Talon, another of the horses he owned himself.

The winner of the men's open at the Lanarkshire & Renfrewshire on his only point-to-point appearance during the season, Gayle Warning was winning his third hunter chase of the season, and he was to win two more before the end of it. His single defeat in his seven appearances was occasioned by Colonel Henry, running over his favourite course at Kelso.

One of the best open races seen in Yorkshire for some time was the men's open at the Derwent fought out by Urser and Whiggie Geo. Having beaten Midnight Court (the Cheltenham Gold Cup winner of 1978) in an open race at the South Durham, Whiggie Geo was the favourite in a field of 13; and when he jumped the last in the lead, with Nigel Tutty looking round on him soon after he landed, he looked home and dried; but Keith Reveley got a tremendous late run out of Urser to score by a neck and put Mick Easterby's ten-year-old in fine fettle for the three hunter chases he was to win later.

The Derwent meeting at the well-named Charm Park also saw the appearance of one of the best novices of the season in Flash Deal, a seven-year-old produced in the Bramham Moor country by Peter Beaumont. With Anthea Beaumont up, Flash Deal won the faster division of the restricted open unchallenged, losing his maiden certificate in the process. It was the first of four easy wins on the trot in a season which saw the son of Harwell unbeaten. Flash Deal's dam, Gorteen (by Straight Deal), bred five winners under N.H. Rules, and Flash Deal was to be another of them.

National Clover was not the only outstanding point-to-pointer in Wales this season. Another was Brigadier Mouse, owned and trained at this time by Bob Reynolds, the Hon. Sec. of the Tivyside point-to-point. This 11-year-old by Zulu was out of the frame only once in his ten appearances. A runner-up on five occasions, he was in the winner's enclosure three times under Barry Thomas, the last of them at Stratford, where he beat Spartan Scot and Cobley Express in the John Corbet Cup. And there was more to come from him. His owner, however, was not so fortunate. The hotel he owned at St. Dogmaels was devastated by fire during the season.

In the South East, Mark's Methane, whose pedigree went back on his dam's side to that prodigious stayer Whiteway, the Cesarewitch winner of 1947, and who was used by his owner-trainer, Mrs. Jean Campbell, to get the cattle in on her farm at Ashford during the summer, was continuing to progress under the Hackings, father and son, Bob Hacking winning four open point-to-points and a hunter chase at Fontwell on him; and, when he was out of action with a broken rib, 18-year-old Paul, a pupil assistant with Josh Gifford, having his first win under Rules on him in a Fontwell hunter chase.

At the West Kent fixture at Penshurst, where Bob Hacking won the men's open on Mark's Methane, Paul completed a double, winning the adjacent hunts' race on Fancy Fellow and a division of the restricted open on Disturbed, a promising six-year-old that had been bought as a family horse for 2,900 guineas at the Doncaster Sales the previous August.

The Hackings were not the only family heavily involved at the West Kent. John Hickman and all three of his sons were all riding in the race won by Fancy Fellow. But they did not fare as well as the Hackings, who took two of the first three placings in it with Bob finishing third on Mrs. Campbell's Jess Jim. In fourth place in the field of 19 was 19-year-old James Hickman on Leslie Vine's Yung Cheng. Nigel Hacking was ninth on Lord Of The Rings. But the other members of the Hickman family were among the also-rans. 22-year-old Peter Hickman was on a faller. 17-year-old Andrew Hickman was compelled to pull his mount up; and father John failed to induce his horse Azd (another of Leslie Vine's) to move off with the others. How's all that for family enterprise?

The United Services meeting at Larkhill is invariably a high-class early season fixture; and it is especially noted for the Coronation Cup, which was first presented in 1953 for the open race, which is almost always divided. In 1970, 1977 and 1981 there were as many as four divisions; and in 1984, there were three, all of them won by good horses in Ballytartar, Tawny Myth and Balbeg. Tim Holland-Martin's eight-year-old Balbeg, a son of Ladybank, was much the fastest of the three in beating The Vintner in a time of 6 mins. 8 secs. But even this was outshone by another of Holland-Martin's owner-ridden horses, the six-year-old Hot Fever, who had lost his maiden certificate at Andoversford the previous season. Despite needing the race, he put up a time of 6 mins. 3 secs. when taking the U.S. past & present race in impressive style. But he was evidently not a horse who stood up to a lot of racing, as he made only two appearances. The other was in a hunter chase at Sandown, where he looked to be trotting up when he came down two fences out.

In later editions of their annuals, when listing the winners-of the major point-to-point races of the season, Mackenzie & Selby have been doing their best to elevate the Coronation Cup mixed open at Larkhill to classic status at the expense of the Middleton Hunt's Grimthorpe Cup. Personally, I don't think this is on, for more reasons than one. Firstly because the Larkhill race has a much shorter history, secondly because it takes place too early in the season; and thirdly, and perhaps most important of all, because with its frequent divisions it produces too many winners. But it is, of course a matter of opinion; and certainly there have been some truly outstanding winners of the Coronation Cup over the years.

Tweseldown was celebrating its 100th anniversary as a racecourse in 1984 at the Tweseldown Club fixture in May; and to mark the occasion, Aldaniti, the 1981 Grand National winner, was on parade with Bob Champion up. There was, too, some blood-stirring music from the trumpeters of the King's Troop of the Royal Horse Artillery, in full regalia; while at the celebratory supper on the course which followed the racing, Richard Pitman and Josh Gifford engaged in some public cross-talk which would have done credit to Morecambe and Wise.

As to the racing itself, whilst it failed to match the occasion in quality, there was a highly appropriate winner of the opening club members' race when it was won by the man who has ridden more winners at Tweseldown than anyone else in its history, Philip Scouller, riding his Pride Of Down, who was completing a hat-trick of wins for him.

An exciting new inmate of Libby Lees's Bury St. Edmunds yard this season was the five-year-old Corked, a very speedy customer who had won two races on the Flat as a three-year-old. Making only his second appearance over fences, Corked demonstrated his speediness in a restricted riders' farmers' race at Cottenham when winning it under Simon Cowell in a time of 6 mins. 2 secs., only a second slower than the time taken by Lucy Gibbon to win the ladies' open on Aingers Green and Peter Greenall in winning a division of the men's open on Cheekio Ora. Corked won three other races during the season, the last two of them hunter chases at Folkestone and Fakenham.

There were 18 walk-overs in 1984; and four of them were at the Burton fixture at The Carholme, the former home of the Lincolnshire. The entire meeting, for which the going was bone-hard, produced no more than four active runners. Two more of the season's walk-overs, those for the hunt race at the Suffolk and the club members' race at the PPOA fixture at Woodford towards the end of the season, were instrumental in securing the men's title for David Turner. As the latter was on a horse from outside the Turner yard, Pam Saunders, Harringworth in the Pytchley country, it sparked off a certain amount of controversy; and maybe it wouldn't have been allowed to happen had not Dick Saunders been away at

Windsor Horse Show judging hunters.

Three of the national titles were decided at the Torrington Farmers fixture at Umberleigh on the last day of the season. Peter Greenall and David Turner were dead level for the men's title with 19 winners apiece before the start of this meeting. Mandy Lingard was one behind Jenny Pidgeon for the ladies' title with 12 winners; and National Clover was one behind Flying Ace for the Grand Marnier Trophy on a total of eight.

David Turner's win on his father's Swarm in the men's open, in which Greenall was fourth on Royal Missile, gave him his 20th winner; and although Greenall had a chance to draw level again, having secured a ride in the restricted open on Canford Lad, by courtesy of Eddie Whettam, who gave up his prospective ride on this seven-year-old from the South Dorset to him, it availed him nothing, as the horse's dislike of the firm ground became so apparent on the final circuit that Greenall felt impelled to pull him up.

So, while David Turner's score for the *Daily Telegraph* Cup rose to 20, Peter Greenall's remained at 19; and behind them in third place was West Countryman Grant Cann with 16, two ahead of Eddie Whettam.

It was the eighth time that David Turner had been the leading point-to-point rider of the season, including the occasion in 1980 when he shared the men's title with Ian McKie; and his success in 1984 came in a season which saw him riding his 300th winner in point-to-points at the age of 36. This came up at his home meeting at Ampton when Courtneigh came out for the second time during the afternoon to win the men's open at the Suffolk after having given David a walk-over in the hunt race. Five of the six races at this meeting were won by members of the Turner family, four of them going to David and another, the ladies' open, to his sister Josie Sheppard riding Swarm.

It was also a tremendously satisfying season for Peter Greenall, despite his failure to land the *Daily Telegraph* Cup. He rode his 100th winner under Rules when scoring on James Delahooke's Border Burg in a hunter chase at Leicester in February; and his 100th winner in point-to-points when winning the maiden race at the Grove & Rufford in April on Commander Joe Newton-Taylor's mare Naughty Niece.

Jenny Pidgeon was without a ride at Umberleigh; but Mandy Lingard had two, and one of them was National Clover, who made short work of the opposition in the ladies' open to put the Warwickshire-born Mandy on the same mark as Jenny with 13 winners and thus enable her to share the *Sporting Life* Cup with her, two ahead of Doreen Calder.

The national point-to-point dinner was now in its first year at The Belfry (that golfing hotel in Warwickshire) after 17 years in London; and it was here, where the toast to the sport was proposed by the first rider to win a race on The Dikler, Capt. Brian Fanshawe, a Joint Master of the Cottesmore, that Derrick Llewellin, the owner of National Clover, received the Grand Marnier Trophy from the hands of Michael Dickinson.

The Grand Marnier novice riders of the season were two 20-year-olds, Bruce Dowling from Herefordshire, eight of whose ten wins had been on Lay-The-Trump, and the West Country's Mandy Turner with six wins on three different horses. Bruce Dowling was also the recipient of the Wilkinson Sword presented at the PPOA dinner in Stratford.

Peter Greenall's trophy for the leading rider in hunter chases went to Tim Thomson Jones with his seven wins, three of them on Mrs. Vanden Bergh's nine-year-old Further Thought, trained by Mrs. Anne Underwood in the East Sussex & Romney Marsh country and two apiece on Urser and the 12-year-old Mauritius. The latter was a horse Thomson Jones had to work hard on; but it was on this veteran performer that the great nephew of Jim Joel had his 100th win under Rules when getting him home by a head from Dr. David Chesney on Glencarry in a hunter chase at Sandown in March.

Robin Greenway rode his 99th winner in point-to-points when scoring on the 11-year-old Cherry Foot in the adjacent hunts' race at the Vale of Lune. Devon's Michael Williams had his 99th when winning the maiden race at the East Cornwall on the six-year-old Spartan Mariner (a daughter of Spartan General); and there were 50th winners for Peter Craggs and Ron Treloggen, the former on the nine-year-old Wellhill in the maiden race at the Morpeth and the latter when he won the four-mile race for the Tedworth Gold Cup at Larkhill on Highland Drake by a head from Philip Scouller on his Cashea.

And there was a first winner for Tim Jones, who was an 18-year-old schoolboy when he won an adjacent hunts' race on Turn Tale at the Llangeinor, the meeting that his father, Lloyd Jones, had been killed at 12 years earlier.

Several notable personalities in the point-to-point world died after the season was over; and two of them were point-to-point journalists. Ian Reid, who died in July at the age of 68 and was a serving officer in the Black Watch during the War, afterwards writing a book about his escapes from prisoner of war camps in Italy, wrote on point-to-points for the *Reading Evening News* and later became the first writer to write regularly for *The Times* on the subject.

Desmond Hill, who died in September at the age of 64, was both the rowing correspondent and the point-to-point correspondent of the *Daily Telegraph*. When he was a schoolboy at Radley he rowed in the Ladies' Plate at Henley. In later years, he gained a blue when rowing for Oxford; and it was for his services to rowing that he was awarded an O.B.E. in 1983. A man who enjoyed life to the full, he was a delightful companion with a great sense of humour. He was also one of the founders of the national point-to-point dinner, along with myself, John Wood, and the prime instigator of it and first Chairman, Chris Glyn, who subsequently became Lord Wolverton.

In August the German-born Inge Parry (the second wife of Bryan) died at the age of 57. She was a woman who had a special way with horses, and an inestimable help to Bryan with his training. She came from a long line of Prussian aristocrats. Her father, Graf Hans Georg von Kalneis, was head of two German national studs, and his horses won the German Derby six times. Inge's brother-in-law, Graf Heinrich von Lehndorf, achieved fame of a different sort. He was one of those hanged for his part in the conspiracy that so nearly ended Hitler's life.

Inge was not short of bravery herself. Attempting to escape from the Russians when they were trying to gain control of East Prussia, she crossed a half-frozen river with two horses, riding one and leading the other; and got shot at by the

Americans on the other side of the river. In or out of the saddle, she was equally fearless. I felt extremely privileged to be invited by Bryan to deliver the address at her funeral service in Rutland; and to be doing the same thing at Bryan's four years later.

In July, Kenneth Dale, the Gloucestershire farmer who produced a string of point-to-point winners in his day, the most famous of them being Tenor, the horse he discovered in a field by the railway line at Moreton-in-Marsh, died at the age of 78. In later years, Tenor lived out his long life on the Berwickshire farm of Kenneth's elder son, Peter.

Tailpiece:
"He jumped so well it was almost an embarrassment to sit on him," said the 6ft. 5in. Chris Coyne after winning for the third time on his six-year-old Nord Hinder when scoring in the men's open at the Vale of Aylesbury's Kingston Blount fixture.

1985

*In which the balloting-out system is improved, Flying Ace has his best
season to date, a New Zealand-bred horse wins a point-to-point classic,
and a future Grand National winner loses his maiden certificate.*

T his was the season that the PPOA, under its adventurous Chairman, Jim
Mahon, made a bold bid to hold the first Sunday point-to-point at its club
fixture on the Warwickshire course at Ashorne. At this time, however, no
betting facilities were available on Sundays; and the application was turned down
by the Jockey Club on the recommendation of its Point-to-Point Liaison
Committee. The main reason for this was that the Jockey Club stewards felt it premature to grant a Sunday fixture before the Home Office Inquiry into shopping
hours had published its findings.

But there was some good news on the balloting-out front which, in the past
had seen so many good horses balloted out of hunter chases in which they were
eminently well qualified to run. The new system gave preference to horses which
had won qualifying races at point-to-points over those which had finished second
or third in them; and, in the case of the *Horse and Hound* Cup at Stratford from
which the Scottish horse Earls Brig was so unfairly balloted out in 1984, it was now
the handicapper's decision that would determine any eliminations.

Although Buchanan's had decided to cease their sponsorship of the hunt mem-
bers' natural-country races, others came forward to take their place, notably the
Colt Car Company, which were sponsoring most of them; although the highly-
successful one at the Cottesmore, which again attracted a good field of 21, was
being sponsored by Holiday Inns. This race was won by the 63-year-old Sir
Stephen Hastings riding his hunter Charlie, the winner of a cross-country race. Sir
Stephen, a Tory M.P. for 23 years, was the Chairman of the British Field Sports
Society and Joint Master of the Fitzwilliam. So it was an appropriate success.

The outstanding performer of the season, even if he wasn't the winner of the
Grand Marnier Trophy, was Scotland's Flying Ace, a winner of all 11 of his races
under Doreen Calder, although he lost one of the three hunter chases that he won
when he was disqualified at Kelso on account of his rider failing to draw the
weight. The weight cloth came off just short of the winning post.

Flying Ace's last two races of the season were the RMC Group ladies' final at Chepstow and the *Horse and Hound* Cup at Stratford. In the former, he got home by a short head from Majetta Crescent, to whom he was giving 101b; and in the *Horse and Hound* Cup, in which Doreen Calder was the first woman to ride the winner, he passed the flying Miss Crozina on the run-in and beat this very useful York & Ainsty mare, who had won her four previous races, which included the Heart Of All England at Hexham and another hunter chase at Stratford, by two lengths, giving the mare 51b. and despite drifting to the left on the run-in. Another horse Flying Ace beat during the season was that spectacular front-runner J-J-Henry, a winner of five races on the trot with Anthea Beaumont up.

But since three of Flying Ace's 11 wins were in hunter chases, he lost the Grand Marnier Trophy to a horse who had previously done his hunting in Wales but, having changed ownership, was now being hunted with Mr. Goschen's pack and being trained by Keith Podger at Liphook, Hants, the 12-year-old Brigadier Mouse, whose new owner, Mrs. Clare Foote-Forster, was a fashion model.

In addition to winning a hunter chase at Fontwell with Simon Sherwood up, Brigadier Mouse won nine point-to-points, ridden in five of them by Tom Grantham, in three by Mrs. Nicky Ledger and in one by Eddie Whettam. One of the horses Brigadier Mouse beat during the season was the 1982 *Horse and Hound* Cup winner Loyal Partner; and he was never out of the first two in all 13 of his races.

If ever there was a horse who must have got fed up with coming up against Flying Ace so often, and whose connections deserved a medal for their perseverance, it was Colin Hall's Jedforest nine-year-old Foolish Hero, who won five races with Gillian Minto up, but was the runner-up to Flying Ace on no fewer than six occasions. But Foolish Hero got a fitting reward in his last race of the season when he won the ladies' championship at the Melton Hunt Club. There were six starters for this on the good to firm ground at Garthorpe, and two of the most fancied runners, Witchin and Highgate Lady, unseated their riders, Witchin at the open ditch the second time round and Highgate Lady at the last fence when the Belvoir mare was a length and a half up on Foolish Hero, who went on to win unchallenged.

There was a good finish to the Marie Curie novice championship at this meeting, fought out by two home-bred horses. Alastair Gilchrist was just in front at the last on his eight-year-old West Shropshire mare Catherine Tudor; but David Jeffries got a great late burst out of his seven-year-old Castle Andrea to score by half a length.

A winner of two of his five previous races, Castle Andrea, bred on his owner's farm in the Bicester country, was out of a mare, Carswell, who had acted as a foster mother to a foal at the Harwood Stud at Newbury; and for this service, Jeffries was offered a free nomination either to Andrea Mantegna or Reliance II. He chose Andrea Mantegna, an Italian Derby winner, and Castle Andrea was the result.

The Massey-Ferguson maiden-race final at Worcester was also won by a good young horse, in this case a five-year-old recording his fourth win of the season, the grey Able Sailor, owned by James Dean, a London estate agent, and trained for him by Charles Smith in his Lincolnshire livery yard. Confidently ridden by Robert Morris, a Leicestershire veterinary surgeon, Able Sailor won the Massey-Ferguson unchallenged from pillar to post in a field of 19.

Another promising youngster to make his point-to-point début was John Wilkinson's home-bred six-year-old Rattlin' Jack, trained by Dick Saunders in the Pytchley country. Rattlin' Jack began by losing his maiden certificate at Mollington and went through the season unbeaten, following his initial success with wins in the fastest of three restricted opens at the Cottesmore and the adjacent hunts' race at the Woodland Pytchley. This imposing youngster, who was ridden in all his races by Wilkinson's son Mark, an assistant trainer to Fulke Johnson Houghton at Blewbury, and later to become a professional trainer in his own right, was by True Song out of Wilkinson's point-to-point mare Marinella (by Manicou). Manicou, of course, was the first horse to carry the colours of The Queen Mother.

For the third time in five years, and at the age of 13, Nostradamus emerged as the winner of the Heythrop four-miler. The only other horse to achieve such a feat was Lord Fortune, who won it in 1970, 1976 and 1977. Ridden as usual by Ian McKie, John Sumner's veteran, starting third favourite at 7-2, behind Lay-The-Trump (now owned by Peter Greenall but still trained by Richard Lee) and Court Papers (who had beaten National Clover at the West Shropshire), had brushed off the attentions of Lay-The-Trump before the third last and was being hotly pursued by Court Papers on the downhill run to the last. But a superb jump there settled the issue and he went on to win by three lengths, with Lay-The-Trump toiling in a tired third in the field of seven, the smallest since the race's inception in 1953.

McKie said afterwards, "The only reason I rode the old horse, instead of letting Tocky ride him in the ladies', was that she hurt her back while team-chasing last summer." Mrs. McKie did, however, ride him in two later races, finishing second on him to Jenny Pidgeon on Random Leg in a ladies' open at Kingston Blount and winning a ladies' open at Andoversford on him.

The Heythrop was also an interesting meeting in other respects. Teresa Webber, who was to become the wife of helicopter pilot Robert Elwell in June, repeated her 1984 success on Brockie Law in the 3m 6f ladies' open for the Lyon Trophy, this time at the expense of the East Anglian combination of Lucy Gibbon and Aingers Green. The Old Etonian combination of Paul Webber and Col. Arthur Clerke-Brown's Britway won the Old Etonian & Old Harrovian race after a duel with Giles Smyly and Forbidden Fruit; and Mark Chamberlayne and his promising Whitsunday completed a hat-trick of wins (the first of them the previous season) in the adjacent hunts' race, winning it by a distance.

The six-year-old Whitsunday, by Chris Sweeting's Conduit Stud stallion Sunyboy, was bred by Chamberlayne from Boxing Day II, a winning point-to-point mare given to him by his father, Col. John Chamberlayne, who bred both this mare and her dam, Bank Holiday IV.

Sunyboy was given another boost as a prolific sire of winners when Norman Mawle's Elmboy fulfilled the promise he had already shown by adding the Cheltenham Foxhunters' to his tally under Alan Hill, comfortably beating Border Burg in a field which included such horses as Compton Lad (4th), Eliogarty (5th), Spartan Missile (6th), Further Thought (ur at the fifth), Urser (ur at the 12th) and Prominent King (well behind when pulled up three out).

But it was not Elmboy's day in his last race of the season, the Audi Grand Prix de Chasse at Sandown. In this race, he broke down when finishing fourth to the unconsidered Yellow Jersey and being promoted to third when the runner-up, Mister Bosun, was disqualified for losing his weight cloth. Elmboy's break-down, however, was not bad enough to prevent him from winning a handicap chase at Cheltenham in November.

Considering that the eight-year-old Yellow Jersey had won three races on the Flat in his younger days and two open point-to-points before he came to Sandown, his starting price of 25-1 was certainly a generous one; and in finishing a neck ahead of Mister Bosun he did not come under pressure, since his 25-year-old rider, Paul Hamer, was well aware of the situation, having been hit on the head by the runner-up's flying weight cloth.

The Audi was a family triumph for the Hamers. Yellow Jersey was owned by Paul's brother, Geoff, who bought him for 850 guineas at Ascot before the start of the 1983 season and had now trained him to win five point-to-points and the Audi final from his base at Bridgend in South Wales.

Dudley Cup Day at the Worcestershire was prefaced overnight by the senseless activities of the anti-hunting vandals, who burned down what would have been the sixth fence from home. So there were 18 fences to jump instead of the usual 20.

The ready-made favourite in a field of eight for the big race was Richard Lee's charge Sliebemore, who had won his two previous races and had Peter Greenall up on him again. This time, however, the seven-year-old was put well and truly in his place by a horse four years his senior, Ridgeman, who became the first horse bred in New Zealand ever to win a Dudley Cup.

Ridden by the 36-year-old Keith Johnson, who farmed with his father at Madeley, near Hereford, Ridgeman, a horse with a tendency to break blood vessels, showed every sign of delighting in the fast going. Taken to the front straight away, he galloped his seven opponents into the ground and the race was really for second place, with Sliebemore securing it by half a length from the previous year's winner Darlingate, who had been running below form all season. The time for the race, with two fences fewer to jump, was exactly the same as Darlingate's in 1984, 6 mins. 38 secs.

It was Ridgeman's second success of the season. His first was a dead-heat with Greenall's mount Naughty Niece in a division of the men's open at the Harkaway Club over a shorter trip at the same venue. In his race before the Dudley Cup he had been beaten by Song Of Life, ridden by Peter Greenall; and, ironically enough, Greenall had been offered the choice of riding either Song Of Life or Sliebemore in the Dudley Cup.

Bought out of Stan Mellor's yard by Herefordshire farmer Roger Phillips and hunted with the Radnor & West Hereford by him, Ridgeman was recording his fifth win since his departure from Mellor's yard prior to the 1981 season.

Salkeld, a horse formerly trained by Neville Crump, for whom his successes included the 1980 Scottish Grand National at Ayr, was a narrow winner of the Grimthorpe Cup at the Middleton. Ridden by David Kinsella, the 13-year-old son of David Jack made all the running and managed to hold on just long enough over the 4.25-mile trip to ward off the close attention of Stephen Swiers's mount Its A

Capper by half a length in the field of 13.

A gift horse to John Jemmeson, a blacksmith in the Bedale & West of Yore country, the old horse made eight appearances in 1985, and the Grimthorpe Cup was his second success in his new colours. Although he failed to shine in the 1986 Grimthorpe Cup, he was to have one more success that season in the men's open at the Pendle Forest & Craven before his retirement from the scene at the age of 16 after a single token appearance in 1987 in his own hunt race, in which he finished third.

The Liverpool Foxhunters' went to a horse from the East Sussex & Romney Marsh, the ten-year-old City Boy, owned by Mrs. Josephine Mann and trained by her at Winterbourne, Sussex, in the same yard that her sister, Mrs. Anne Underwood, trained Further Thought, who was rated equal top of their handicap at 11-9 by Mackenzie & Selby with another horse hunted with the East Sussex & Romney Marsh, Royal Judgement. City Boy and Further Thought were by the same sire, Ginger Boy.

In terms of wins, City Boy (rated at 11-4) had a better season than either Further Thought or Royal Judgement, winning six hunter chases with Tim Thomson Jones up; and he ended his season running away with the John Corbet Cup at Stratford.

Further Thought, who was also ridden by Thomson Jones, won three hunter chases in four appearances, beating Royal Judgement in two of them and giving him weight each time. Mrs. Jean Campbell's home-bred 12-year-old Royal Judgement, in his seven appearances, won five hunter chases with Paul Hacking up.

Needless to say, Tim Thomson Jones was the leading rider in hunter chases with his 13 winners, and the winner of Peter Greenall's Cup for the second year running. But the leading amateur of the 1984-1985 season was Simon Sherwood with 30 winners.

Mick Easterby's Urser (rated at 11-6 by Mackenzie & Selby, on the same mark as Border Burg and Miss Crozina), had another good season, winning five of his six races, two hunter chases and the men's open at the Derwent with Keith Reveley up and his last two hunter chases with Tim Thomson Jones in the saddle. His final appearance of the season was in the Diners Club men's final at Chepstow, where he won very easily from Fixed Price and the East Anglian star General Rule, giving 9lb. to the former and a stone and 4lb. to General Rule, who had won five of his six open point-to-points, the last four of them under George Cooper including one over four miles at Marks Tey.

Thomson Jones said after his Chepstow race that he had never known Urser fence better, and that he won with two stone in hand.

Another very useful horse in Yorkshire, though not in the same class as Urser, was the Malton permit holder Ralph Brader's home-bred Political Whip. This seven-year-old by Politico out of a mare by a Derby winner, Hard Ridden, won three point-to-points and two hunter chases in his seven appearances with Tim Walford up, finishing his season on a high note when demolishing his 14 opponents in the Vaux final at Sedgefield.

In Lincolnshire, Cliff-Dawson was in process of producing an outstanding performer in ladies' races in his six-year-old mare Sweet Diana, a former selling hurdler. Ridden each time by his future daughter-in-law, Jill Grinyer, Sweet Diana started her point-to-point career with a win in the ladies' open at the South Durham; and, after finishing third to Mac Kelly at the Cottesmore, the mare went on to win three more ladies' opens, the only horse beating her on the way being Highgate Lady. In her last race of the season, the ladies' open at the Fernie, horse and rider were surprised in the closing stages by Caroline Saunders and Frank Gilman's home-bred Towtame (a half-brother to Grittar), who caught them napping on the run-in. But there was much more to come from Sweet Diana in the future; and Towtame was certainly no mug. This was the ten-year-old's fourth win of the season.

As for Mac Kelly, although this 11-year-old was temporarily toppled from his East Anglian throne on the heavy ground at Marks Tey by Bush Lady, a ten-year-old mare from the Southdown & Eridge who was a first winner for her owner-rider, equestrian artist Joanna Henry, he won all six of his other races, ridden in all of them by his trainer, Mrs. Jane McMath; and among the horses he had behind him during the season were Sweet Diana, Brockie Law, Mr. Mellors, Random Leg, Highgate Lady, Towtame, Aingers Green and Joe Turner's Swarm.

Meanwhile, in the South East another star performer in ladies' race, the 12-year-old Jacksway, a winner of 16 races with Clare Mair up, was making his farewell appearance as a faller in the ladies open at the Tickham won by Mrs. Ann Blaker on her gallant old 13-year-old E1 Padre, for whom there was no question of retirement.

E1 Padre, of course, was the horse Mrs. Blaker bought from Joe Turner in 1979 with a contingency clause that she paid Joe £500 for his first two wins. The first had come for her in 1980 and the second in 1981; and in 1985 E1 Padre was a winner of four races, with Mrs. Blaker up on him in all of them. Her proudest moment on him, she said, was when he beat Brigadier Mouse this year in the ladies' open at the Surrey Union meeting at Peper Harow.

In the same area, Mark Davies', good old 17-year-old Helpex, the horse he had been hunting with the Crawley & Horsham and won 22 races with, riding him in most of them himself, made his last appearance before retirement when finishing fourth in an adjacent hunts' restricted at the Isle of Wight fixture at Tweseldown, where he was being ridden by 19-year-old Carolyn Grantham, the daughter of his trainer, Tony Grantham. But Davies had an excellent replacement for him in Colonel Henry, the horse he had recently acquired from Scotland. This nine-year-old was being trained for him by Clare Mair in the East Sussex & Romney Marsh country, and Davies started off with two wins on him in 1985.

Mrs. Rosalyn Bratchley's East Cornwall seven-year-old Phil Grey, a doughty stayer who had lost his maiden certificate in the hunt race for local residents at his home meeting the previous season, when he won two other races, was progressing by leaps and bounds in the West Country, where he was the most prolific winner. Ridden by his usual jockey, Stephen West, he won seven of his 11 races in 1985, and five of them were open events.

Visitors to the Staintondale in Charm Park had a treat in store for them, did they but know it. In watching the six-year-old Mr. Frisk giving a front-running performance as he trotted up under Robin Tate in his division of the maiden race they were looking at a future Grand National winner. So were those later on at the York & Ainsty when this horse from the Cleveland, bred from a winning point-to-point mare, Jenny Frisk, won the restricted open by a short head from the Sinnington seven-year-old Whistling Jim. "May prove quite useful in the years to come," said Mackenzie & Selby in their annual. They can say that again!

But for visitors to the Burton at The Carholme there was a shock. The meeting began with a bomb scare; and it had been preceded in the early hours of the morning by the burning down of the first fence in the straight by the people posing as animal lovers. Racing, however, went ahead, with one fence less to jump on each circuit.

Following the example set some years beforehand by the United Services with their Coronation Cup at Larkhill, the Garth & South Berks turned the four-mile race that they were introducing to their meeting at Tweseldown into a mixed open, but it didn't make much difference to the result, as the first three past the post were all ridden by male riders.

The winner, Michael Portman's owner-ridden Lochage, a horse hunted with the V.W.H., was a remarkable old horse. A 14-year-old son of Spartan General, he had been written off by the vet after being badly struck into in a hunter chase at Lingfield in 1984. Yet here he was, recording his fourth success of the season, and his seventh at Tweseldown, including one in another race over four miles.

Of all the races that Lochage won during the season, I think it can safely be said that his finest performance came when, in his first race of the season at Tweseldown, he got up on the run-in to score by a head from the very useful Mister Bosun, on whom Jenny Litston won four races during the season and was unlucky enough to lose her weight cloth when finishing second in the Audi final at Sandown.

Michael Portman, who worked for estate agents Strutt & Parker at Lewes and rode out there for Bobbie Beasley, was always keen to give the credit for Lochage's successes to his mother, Mrs. Penny Portman, who looked after this tough old campaigner.

The postponed Cambridgeshire Harriers fixture at Cottenham was the first evening fixture to be held in East Anglia; and very successful it was, both as regards attendance and the quality of the racing, which reached its peak with a high-class ladies' open, in which the first three past the post were Aingers Green (Lucy Gibbon), Corked (Jane McMath) and Zarajeff (Jenny Pidgeon).

This meeting marked the 40th anniversary of involvement with the course of Mrs. Betty Gingell, the very popular Master and Huntsman of the harriers pack, and of her husband, Hugh, who looked after this beautifully-appointed venue with such tender care.

Peter Greenall was again the leading point-to-point rider of the season, and winner of the *Daily Telegraph* Cup for the second time in four years, this time with 23 winners as against the 15 recorded by his nearest rival for the trophy, David Turner, whose grand total of point-to-point winners had risen to 321, while his career total, with his 30 winners under Rules, had passed the 350 mark.

The vast majority of Greenall's winners were trained by Richard Lee, no fewer than 17 of them, and these included his two most prolific ones, Lay-The-Trump and a very promising seven-year-old in Highland Blaze, on each of whom he won four races. Highland Blaze was beaten only once in his six appearances, and that was when he was on the floor in a restricted open at the West Shropshire on his first appearance of the season. At the Harkaway Club fixture at Chaddesley Corbett Greenall brought off a four-timer which included two dead-heats, on Naughty Niece and Pride Of Tullow, both of whom were unlucky not to get an outright verdict.

Jenny Pidgeon, with her 18 wins, 16 of them on four horses owned by her father and the other two on Matchplay, owned by her mother, was the winner of the *Sporting Life* Cup for the fourth year in succession. Her two most prolific winners with five wins apiece, were Random Leg and the 12-year-old Zarajeff; and when Zarajeff won the ladies' open at the Whaddon Chase fixture at Little Horwood Graham Pidgeon was saddling his 100th winner in point-to-points.

The joint runners-up for the ladies' title, each with 13 wins, were, Alison Dare and Lucy Crow; and Lucy, who had not yet reached the age of 21, was also the winner of the Wilkinson Sword.

The Grand Marnier novice riders of the season were Scotland's 18-year-old David Mactaggart with six wins (four of them on his father's mare Olive Press, who had given him his first win when he won the men's open at the Berwickshire on her) and 22-year-old, Karen Dowsett from West Wales with eight wins, six of them on Mickley That, a mare from the famous Mickley line.

John Llewellyn rode his 150th winner (ten of them under Rules) when scoring on Mr. Money Banks at the Llangeinor. Tim Rooney had his 100th (91 of them between the flags) at the Pentyrch. Robin Greenway, John Sharp and Devon's Michael Williams all reached their century of point-to-point winners; and Lucy Gibbon, who was on a total of 72 point-to-point winners, had her 100th career winner when scoring on Janet Harris's Graiguewell in the ladies' open at the North Norfolk Harriers.

Richard Lee saddled four winners with his four runners at the Teme Valley & United meeting at Brampton Bryan. One of them, on whom Carol Lee won the ladies' open, was Bob Murrin's Majetta Crescent, a winner of six races during the season; and when this 12-year-old won the ladies' open at the Tedworth in a time of 5 mins. 55 secs. he was equalling the Larkhill course record that had been set up by Marshalsland in 1978 and maintained by Alsirat in a men's open there three years later.

But for one hardy rider, the former coalminer Bob Woolley, who had never had a riding lesson in his life when he rode his first winner in 1960 at the age of 20, there was a tragic accident at the Berkeley when he was one short of riding his 100th winner in point-to-points. A fall on a very dicey jumper, Angus Ovada, at the first open ditch in a division of the restricted open, saw him ending up in Frenchay Hospital at Bristol with serious spinal injuries which were to confine him to a wheel-chair. A Trust Fund was set up for him under the chairmanship of Tim Holland-Martin, and this raised £700 when a collection was taken at Stratford on *Horse and Hound* Cup Day.

A feature of the national point-to-point dinner in its second year at The Belfry, where Jim Mahon was the very worthy recipient of the engraved salver for special services to the sport, was the auctioning by the Jockey Club's James Weatherby of a quarter share in Gerald Probert's successful West Country point-to-pointer White Supreme (a five-year-old winner of five races during the season) in aid of the Bob Woolley Trust Fund. The successful bidder, at £1,000, was the Leicestershire permit holder Frank Gilman, the man who trained his own horse Grittar to win the 1982 Grand National.

The proposer of the toast to the sport at this dinner was the distinguished trainer (and coursing enthusiast) Sir Mark Prescott, who amazed his listeners by speaking without a note; and the entertaining responder was the Old Berkshire's Ron Liddiard, author of a splendid biography of Baulking Green, one of the great hunter chasers of former days.

When Dorian Williams, the voice of show jumping, died in July at the age of 71 it was a bleak day for the entire horse world. If ever a man was irreplaceable, Dorian was. It was almost unbearable to envisage another voice declaiming the words of Ronald Duncan's moving poem on the last night of the Horse of the Year Show at Wembley. Master of the Whaddon Chase from 1954-1980, Dorian was a familiar figure at the Hunt's point-to-point when it was held at Great Horwood.

I also recall with sadness, shortly before the start of the season, the death of Major Bernard Loraine-Smith at the age of 72. This distinguished soldier and holder of the M.C. was a pillar of the Heythrop point-to-point, and an acting steward at Stratford, Leicester and Warwick. I shall remember him in particular as a voice on the telephone saying in gentle rebuke, "Steady The Buffs, Michael."

1986

In which the Tote has withdrawal symptoms, per capita admission charges are introduced, the Worcestershire celebrates its 150th anniversary, Pat Tollit's record is broken, a future Cheltenham Gold Cup winner makes-his début in point-to-points and a coup is landed at the Quorn.

Apart from the fact that 17 of the 193 point-to-points scheduled for 1986 were lost (16 of them on account of the weather, and the Beaufort because the new date they had chosen for their postponed fixture was objected to by the Chepstow executive owing to a clash of dates), the season might justifiably be described as a vintage one for the sport, with outstanding winners of the first two point-to-point classics in Paddy's Peril and Highland Blaze, and Land Rover taking over the men's final (at Chepstow) that they have been sponsoring ever since.

The Cheltenham Foxhunters' continued to lead the pecking order as the richest hunter chase of the season with total prize money amounting to £13,620, and was followed by the Liverpool Foxhunters' with £10,464, the *Horse and Hound* Cup at Stratford with £8,568, then, somewhat surprisingly, by the Audi 'Grand Prix de Chasse at Sandown with £7,596, the Land Rover men's final with £7,500 and the Massey-Ferguson final at Worcester with £6,330.

But there was some more bad news from the Horserace Totalisator Board with the announcement that they would be withdrawing their facilities altogether from point-to-points, except when it came to offering advice to those hunts – an increasing number – who would be running their own Totes, in some cases with enterprising variations, such as tricasts in the South East Area and a jackpot at the Melton Hunt Club fixture.

For the first time since the days of the old bona-fide hunt meetings, the Jockey Club sanctioned per capita admission charges to point-to-points. Not a great many hunts took advantage of this concession; but those that did included all three of the meetings held at The Carholme in Lincolnshire; and was it, I wonder, a mere coincidence that two of the fences at the Blankney were vandalised, presumably by people arriving too early to be charged for admission?

The first hunt to charge for admission was the Cumberland Farmers at Dalston, where there was a £1 admission fee for pedestrians, but a £6 car-park charge which rather defeated the object of the exercise.

To begin with the horse who ended the season occupying the top spot in Mackenzie & Selby's handicap at 11-12, James Delahooke's good hunter chaser Border Burg, bred by his head lad, George Cook, in the Whaddon Chase country, let's examine the progress of this nine-year-old son of Perhapsburg out of a mare by Border Legend.

After an uncharacteristically dismal showing in the Cheltenham Foxhunters', for which the weather prevented him from getting a preliminary run, Border Burg's impressive sequence of wins began under Peter Greenall with a neck defeat of Eliogarty (to whom he was giving 10lb., with Greenall putting up 3lb. over-weight) in a hunter chase at Ludlow. He then returned to point-to-points to qual-ify for the Audi final in the adjacent hunts' race at the Vale of Aylesbury Easter meeting at Kimble, where he duly obliged under Alan Hill. His next race, with Peter Greenall returning to the saddle, was a hunter chase at Ascot, where he sum-marily disposed of Royal Judgement, giving him weight.

Then came the Audi Grand Prix de Chasse at Sandown, with Greenall up again; and here he shot into the lead at the fourteenth and went on to score unchal-lenged from Game Trust in a field of 18 which included Phil Grey (3rd), Tawny Myth (4th), Fixed Price (7th), General Rule (8th) and Brigadier Mouse (12th), with City Boy and Yellow Jersey among those who failed to complete the course.

Border Burg had one more outing this season, at the Cheltenham evening fix-ture in May; and here, in another hunter chase sponsored by Audi, Greenall had to exert himself to get the better, by a length and a half, of Paul Hacking on Royal Judgement, who was receiving 7lb. from the winner.

A tribute to Border Burg was paid when Eliogarty, now trained for Caroline Beasley by David Murray-Smith at Lambourn, easily beat Venture To Cognac in the Liverpool Foxhunters'. The 27-year-old Caroline Beasley, who had been the first woman to ride a winner of the Cheltenham Foxhunters' in 1983, was now also the first woman to ride a winner over the Aintree fences.

In this year's Cheltenham Foxhunters' there was another winner from Ireland when the six-year-old Attitude Adjuster, ridden by the accomplished Ted Walsh and trained by Mouse Morris in Co. Tipperary, ran on strongly to hold off a chal-lenge from the best that England could produce in Further Thought, with anoth-er Irish invader, Mister Donovan, taking third place.

Attitude Adjuster, who was running in blinkers for the first time, and was bought for 12,000 guineas in the autumn of 1984, had a remarkable record for a young horse. A Winner of all five of his point-to-points in Ireland and three of his five hunter chases there, including one at Fairyhouse after his success at Cheltenham, by the end of the 1986 season he had amassed a total of nine wins in 11 appearances. The only horse to beat him when he failed to complete a course (as he did on one occasion)was Ah Whisht, who did so on his last appearance of 1986 in a hunter chase at Punchestown.

In the first of the point-to-point classics, the four-mile race for Lord Ashton of Hyde's Cup at the Heythrop, for which there was a field of 16 on the good to soft ground, we saw a winner who was easing up under John Deutsch as he passed the post four lengths ahead of another horse from the North Cotswold, Ladnek, who had taken second place off Peter Greenall's mount Boonabaroo rounding the bend before the last.

The ten-year-old Paddy's Peril, a horse who had won four point-to-points for Peter Greenall as a six-year-old, and seven novice chases for Rex Carter in East Anglia after being sold to him for 7,200 guineas, was bred by Harry Bell in Scotland. He was now jointly owned by Tony Perry and his trainer-rider John Deutsch, having been bought for them by David Smyly for 6,000 guineas at Ascot in September 1985; and the Heythrop race was the fourth open race he had won for them. There was to be one more open-race success for him before the season was out, in the new Nitracc championship race at the Melton Hunt Club fixture at Garthorpe.

But the coveted Lady Dudley Cup at the Worcestershire Hunt's 150th anniversary fixture, which was being celebrated at Chaddesley Corbett, eluded him, although he started favourite for it. In this race he came up against Peter Greenall's eight-year-old Highland Blaze. Looking every inch a winner on his way to the second last, with John Deutsch looking over his shoulder, Paddy's Peril was beaten for pace, and by the combined brilliance of Peter Greenall and Highland Blaze, who shot past at the last and won this vintage Dudley Cup race by three lengths. In third place, a further eight lengths away, was another of Richard Lee's charges, Sliebemore.

This was the fourth win of the season for Highland Blaze, and he was to win two more races afterwards before being sold at Doncaster in August to David Naylor-Leyland for 16,000 guineas. His only defeat of the season was in the men's open at the Ledbury, where he was a faller at the first fence.

Bred by Roger Lyles in East Anglia, Highland Blaze was by the Norfolk stallion Barolo out of Venturous Trout, a mare Lyles bred from Highland Trout after acquiring her from the late Walter Wales in exchange for a point-to-pointer, Master Fifty, a prolific winner between the flags.

Highland Blaze and Paddy's Peril were both found for Peter Greenall by Capt. Bryan Parry and trained by him until the latter was sold and Highland Blaze joined Richard Lee's yard, from which he won 11 of his 13 races. All of those he stood up in, in fact.

With the distance of the Grimthorpe Cup further reduced to four miles and a furlong, and only nine runners on the good to soft ground at Whitwell-on-the-Hill, it was anything but a vintage Grimthorpe, with only the winner, Freddie Teal, an eight-year-old from the Brocklesby, having won a previous race since the start of the season, and that an adjacent hunts' race.

Well ridden by Paul Strawson, however, Freddie Teal took up the running three fences out and never came off the bridle in scoring by five lengths from the Grove & Rufford contender, Shackin Brig. Last year's winner, Salkeld, although prominent for much of the way, was last of the five finishers. He would have been much better suited by firmer ground. But at least the winner was to win a hunter chase at Southwell afterwards.

Land Rovers' initial sponsorship of the men's final at Chepstow produced a field of 18 and saw Urser making a bid to complete a hat-trick of wins in this race. But the 12-year-old had not been showing his best form during the season, although he had won three of his five point-to-points and a hunter chase at Ayr, and he finished nearer last than first.

The winner, Grenville Richards's 12-year-old Fixed Price, ridden by John Llewellyn, was well suited by the going and finished four lengths clear of the West Country stayer Dicky Blob. The unlucky horse of the race was another from the West Country, Chris Down's mount Culm Valley, who was travelling very sweetly when she fell at the last with every chance.

Fixed Price, though, was a very useful sort, and this was his fifth win of the season in his seven appearances. A winner of his first four races on the trot and the runner-up in a hunter chase at Cheltenham, this grandson of the 1948 St. Leger winner Black Tarquin was also a winner on his last.

John Deutsch, who finished fourth in the Land Rover final on Paddy's Peril, had weighed in 4lb. heavier than he weighed out and was fined £40 by the stewards for changing his equipment after doing so, as well as having his attention drawn to the fact that he was carrying a whip that did not conform to Jockey Club standards.

Mrs. Mercy Rimell's home-trained Three Counties was a good winner of the RMC Group ladies' final in a field of 14. The nine-year-old was being ridden for the first time by Gee Armytage, Katie Rimell who had been up on him when he won all three of his ladies' opens before coming to Chepstow having been sidelined with a broken jaw. Gee, who was riding her tenth winner of the season under Rules, proved a thoroughly efficient deputy, driving Three Counties out to score by two lengths from Crested Grebe, who was receiving 10lb. from the winner. Brockie Law, carrying the same weight as Three Counties, ran well under Teresa Elwell, finishing 2.5 lengths behind the runner-up.

Mrs. Rimell had bought Three Counties for her 22-year-old granddaughter to ride after seeing him in a field in Tipperary the previous summer. A winner over fences and hurdles in Ireland, he was to prove a good investment.

Although there were only four runners for the Nitracc ladies' championship on the soft ground at Garthorpe, three of them, Sweet Diana, Brockie Law and Red Shah, who finished in that order, were class horses. From the way she won, however, Sweet Diana looked to be in a class of her own. Taken to the front straight away under Jill Grinyer, the mare from the South Wold won unchallenged, recording her eighth win of the season in the process. On the only occasions she was beaten, she was carried out at the fourth by a loose horse at the Badsworth and unseated her rider at the last in the ladies' open at the Quorn when 15 lengths clear. With her nine wins in eleven appearances, Cliff Dawson's mare was an outright winner of the Grand Marnier Trophy.

In the Marie Curie novice championship at Melton there was another triumph for the Newtons when Joey Newton's owner-ridden Periscope, a six-year-old son of Deep Run, gave them their fourth win in this championship, three of them with Joey up, and the first, in its inaugural running in 1968, with Tommy Philby winning on Lance Newton's Roving Lad.

In the field of 19 for this year's race, Periscope, a winner of two of his five previous point-to-points, was never in any kind of danger after jumping the downhill third last in the lead. The runner-up, Better Spoken, a nine-year-old mare trained by John Sharp in the Oakley country and ridden by Paul Taiano, finished a good 15 lengths behind the winner.

This was Periscope's first season of point-to-point racing. Previously trained by Nicky Henderson, he had broken a bone in his foot and had a plate inserted in it before he was bought for Joey Newton by David Minton, since when he was hunted hard with the Belvoir before beginning his point-to-point career.

Worcester's Massey-Ferguson maiden-race final went to a horse from Wales, John Parfitt's eight-year-old Tarville. Given a strong ride by Tim Jones, this winner of the maiden race at the South Pembrokeshire got up on the run-in to score by a neck from a 33-1 shot, the Morpeth five-year-old Paddy Murphy, who was in with a chance under Peter Craggs when he was hampered by the fall of the favourite, Old Applejack, two fences out. But it was the six-year-old Old Applejack who was the really unlucky one. This facile winner of four races on the trot, three of them with Robin Tate up, was looking all over a winner at the time of his fall; and in their ratings at the end of the season Mackenzie & Selby had this contender from the Bedale rated llb. above Tarville at 10-8.

My idea of the pick of the novices in 1986, however, though he would not have been eligible for the Massey-Ferguson, as he had lost his maiden certificate when he appeared on a course for the first time the previous season, was James Delahooke's I Got Stung. This grandson (on his dam's side) of the Italian Derby winner Macherio won four hunter chases in effortless style under Alan Hill, and the last of them was the John Corbet Cup at Stratford.

Not for the first time, the *Horse and Hound* Cup was won the following day by a horse from a professional yard, The Pain Barrier, trained by Oliver Sherwood at Upper Lambourn for Jeremy Langton, the Chairman of a Lloyds syndicate, and ridden by his daughter, Amanda, who had her own livery yard at Cheltenham and was riding her third winner under Rules, her other two wins being on the same horse at Plumpton and Towcester.

In a field which included Ladnek (a winner of four races during the season), Majetta Crescent and Yellow Jersey, The Pain Barrier drew clear from two fences out and easily accounted for Culm Port (a full sister to Culm Valley and the winner of her four previous races on the trot, including two West Country hunter chases and a handicap chase at Newton Abbot). Three lengths behind Culm Port came an over-the-top Flying Ace, a winner during the season of three hunter chases and six point-to-points.

One horse was killed in this race. Oliver Carter's Athford, who was in the winner's enclosure twice during the season, broke his back when he fell at the third last, the same fence at which Caroline Beasley parted company with Eliogarty.

A real old-fashioned coup was brought off at the Quorn when Gerald Probert's West Country mare Queen Beyan, backed down from 50-1 to 10-1 for the restricted open, got home under Ashley Bealby from John Sharp's mount Better Spoken by a hard-earned half length in a field of 19 and an estimated £5,000 was taken out of the books.

Having taken a good look at Queen Beyan's previously dismal form, the stewards were right on the ball and convened a hurried informal enquiry. Probert, however, came up with the novel explanation that he himself was an extremely bad rider and had ridden the mare in most of her previous races putting up lumps of over-weight. He also pointed out that on the occasions when he hadn't ridden her, she ran twice on the same day in heavy going at the Dulverton West, falling in a ladies' race there and being pulled up in a division of the PPOA race; but that at Garthorpe she had the firm ground that suited her. When he brought her there, he added, he was determined to get "a good local jockey" to ride her. And who could fail to be disarmed by such a convincing explanation?

Probert, who trained Queen Beyan himself in his yard near Exeter (whilst keeping his other horses with Keith Cumings at Bishops Nympton), acquired Queen Beyan in Ireland from Ted Walsh around Christmastime. She had run in three point-to-points there and finished a distant third in the hunt race at the Westmeath point-to-point in 1984.

Queen Beyan wasn't Probert's only winner at this Garthorpe fixture. He had another one when White Supreme, in whom Frank Gilman now owned a quarter share after bidding for it in aid of the Bob Woolley Trust Fund at last year's national point-to-point dinner, won the ladies' open with Caroline Saunders up. The six-year-old was handed the race when Sweet Diana unseated her rider at the last.

When Tim Jones won a division of the maiden race at the Ystrad fixture in South Wales on Norton's Coin, a five-year-old bred by his owner, Percy Thomas, in the Pentyrch country from a mare by the Tarrys' stallion St. Columbus, he was riding a horse who was to win the Cheltenham Gold Cup four years later and join the select band of former point-to-pointers who had achieved the same feat in the post-war years. The others were Four Ten in 1954, Limber Hill in 1956, Linwell in 1957, Woodland Venture in 1967 and The Dikler in 1973.

Today, the perpetual challenge cup presented annually by Mrs. & Mrs. Sirrell Griffiths (the owners of Norton's Coin when he won at Cheltenham) to the owner of the leading point-to-pointer of the season in West Wales is called 'The Norton's Coin'.

A new 'City of London' race was introduced at the Tweseldown Club fixture, open to members of various City institutions, including the Stock Exchange, Lloyds of London, the London Discount Market and the Baltic Exchange; and the race developed into an interesting match between Richard Russell on his home-bred Desert Fox and Mark Davies on his Colonel Henry, with Desert Fox staying on the better to score by a length and a half in a field of nine. Desert Fox, a Spartan General eight-year-old bred by Russell from a winning point-to-point mare by Wily Trout that he bought from Michael Dickinson, was unbeaten in his five races during the season, and these included three hunter chases. Two of them were at Cheltenham, in the first of which he beat Eliogarty over 3 1/4 miles. The other was at the Audi evening fixture there, where he was successful over four miles in a field of 22. Desert Fox was trained by "Bunny" Tarry in the Grafton country.

The seven-year-old Rattlin' Jack continued to show good form for John Wilkinson and his trainer Caroline Saunders in the Pytchley country, with Mark Wilkinson winning three more point-to-points on him in his last season before taking out a licence to train under Rules and saddling him to win a novice chase at Leicester in March the following season with Tim Thomson Jones up.

And in Scotland, Foolish Hero, the horse who had been condemned to playing second fiddle to Flying Ace for so long, was enjoying a heyday. Now owned by Gus Minto, the ten-year-old, freed from his shackles, won five ladies' opens on the trot under Gillian Minto, who also won an adjacent hunts' race on him. Three of his wins were particularly spectacular, proving his gutsiness up to the hilt. At the Haydon, he got up on the line to score by a head from Charons Daughter, to whom he was giving 15lb. At the Eglinton, he won by a short head from Loch Brandy, who was claiming the mares' allowance; and at the Tynedale, over a distance of 3m 5f in the ladies' open, he won in the last stride from Upesi. Perhaps this says as much for his rider as it does for the horse. But both of them deserve the utmost credit.

Although failing to land the ladies' title again, Jenny Pidgeon had another good season with ten wins on four different horses. Her most prolific winner was her father's Matchplay, on whom she won four races and had her 100th win in point-to-points when scoring on him in the PPOA club race at the Hursley Hambledon at Badbury Rings, where he was the second leg of a double for her, the first coming up in the ladies' open on Zarajeff, who was maintaining his unbroken sequence of wins over the course, this being his eighth win there. Matchplay, who won five of his six races during the season, was ridden by Mark Wilkinson when he won an adjacent hunts' race at the Grafton.

Josephine Sheppard, who was even less in contention for the ladies' title than Jenny Pidgeon, was rewarded for her sterling contribution to the sport when a win on her father's Swarm in the ladies' open at the Puckeridge & Thurlow saw her riding her 172nd winner in point-to-points and breaking Mrs. Pat Tollit's previous record of 171 for a lady rider. With Josie's brother David having already put himself at the top of the tree with 327 winners by this time (and he was to make it three more by the time the season was over), this caused the Newmarket trainer David Ringer to remark, "Joe Turner should have gone to stud earlier and produced more than two offspring." Even so, Joe had managed to saddle a grand total of nearly 700 winners; and his services to the sport were recognized in appropriate style when he was presented with the dinner committee's special salver at the national point-to-point dinner in September.

Dick Baimbridge's No. 1 rider Alison Dare, with her 19 winners during the season, was the winner of the *Sporting Life* Cup for the leading lady rider for the first time at the age of 28, in a season when she rode her 50th winner, a target achieved on Baimbridge's charge Dawn Street in a high-class ladies' open at the South & West Wilts fixture at Larkhill, where she beat Jenny Litston on Mister Bosun by a head, although there were those who contended, Mackenzie & Selby among them, that the verdict should have gone the other way. Two lengths behind the runner-up came Brockie Law.

This meeting marked a 50th anniversary of point-to-point racing for the South & West Wilts. So there was cause for a double celebration.

The runner-up for the *Sporting Life* Cup, with 14 winners, was a rider in her first season of point-to-point racing, 16-year-old Amanda Harwood, the daughter of Flat-race trainer Guy Harwood, a former point-to-point rider himself.

Amanda was also the winner of the Grand Marnier female novice rider's award and of the Wilkinson Sword. One of her two prolific winners was her father's Red

Shah, a winner of two point-to-points in Ireland who had finished fourth in the four-mile National Hunt Chase at Cheltenham last year before Harwood bought him. On this nine-year-old from the Crawley & Horsham who was never out of the first three in his 11 races, Amanda's seven wins included one in the four-mile unisex open at the Garth & South Berks, where he beat Lochage by four lengths.

Amanda's other prolific winner, also a winner of seven races for her, was another horse owned by her father, the 11-year-old Lawn Meet, a horse bred by Diana Henderson (née Thorne) from Bright Daisy, a mare she won four point-to-points on. In his three other races Lawn Meet was a runner-up. On no fewer than five occasions Red Shah and Lawn Meet were both in the winner's enclosure at the same meeting, and one of these was way out of their county at the South Devon.

Another 16-year-old in her first season of race-riding, Pip Jones (the sister of Tim), gave us a taste of things to come from her when she rode her first winner, scoring with perfect timing in the ladies' open at the Llangibby on John Parfitt's eight-year-old Eggington. Led into the last by Magic Rock, Eggington drew away on the run-in to win by two lengths. Earlier in the day, Pip, a junior international show jumper, had been in action at the Wales & West Show. It is not often that one sees two 16-year-olds of such class as Amanda Harwood and Pip Jones.

As a complete contrast, Lt. Col. Dick Bromley-Gardner was 65 when he won the United Services past & present race at Larkhill's New Forest Buckhounds fixture on his own Young Pretender, a horse he bred himself from a 22-year-old mare who was shortly to deliver her fifteenth foal.

For the third time in five years, and in his last season before he hung up his racing boots for ever, Peter Greenall collected the *Daily Telegraph* Cup with his 28 wins in point-to-points, the highest score since John Bryan's 32 in 1978. Greenall's grand total of point-to-point winners had now reached 160; and he had ridden over 100 winners under Rules, those in 1986 including Border Burg, a winner of four hunter chases. His combined total of 32 wins this season was achieved on 11 different horses, all but three of them his own.

26 of Greenall's 28 wins in point-to-points this season were on horses trained for him by Richard Lee, who had saddled 34 winners in his best season ever out of a grand total of 137, including two in hunter chases, and was departing from the point-to-point scene to take up a new career as a professional trainer. He had gone a long way since coming up through the South Hereford Pony Club, though not quite in the direction his parents had hoped for. "They wanted me to lead a respectable life," he said, "but I ended up being neither respectable nor a jockey." He did, though, ride his fair share of winners as an amateur; and after leaving school he took his first hesitant step towards respectability by becoming an articled pupil to a firm of estate agents. But four years of trying saw him passing no exams; and instead he became a farrier, serving his apprenticeship with Fred Winter's farrier, John French.

The runner-up to Peter Greenall for the men's title was Mike Felton. Riding 15 different horses, he rode 24 winners; and on the eight trained by Henrietta Knight he won 13 races, Henrietta's own Matt Murphy, a ten-year-old by Deep Run, giving him four of them and winning another race with Paul Webber up. Nine more of' Felton's wins were on five horses trained by John Dufosee, Jane Dufosee's nine-year-old Just Dai contributing four of them.

The Grand Marnier award for the leading male novice rider of the season was jointly won by Anthony Tory, a 19-year-old pupil assistant to Tim Forster, and 31-year-old Ian Dowrick from the West Country. Each of them rode six winners in point-to-points; and Anthony Tory, who was later to turn professional, rode his first winner under Rules when scoring in an amateur riders' handicap chase at Fontwell on Kilton Jim, a horse owned and trained by his father (Michael), and who had given him four wins on the trot in point-to-points.

Peter Greenall's trophy for the leading rider in hunter chases was also shared, by Alan Hill and Johnny Wrathall, with five wins apiece in these races.

In the West Country, Norman Down had a nice little family trio that he bred himself, at Cullompton in East Devon, the two full sisters Culm Port and Culm Valley (by Port Corsair out of Copper Plate II, by Spiritus) and their half-sister River Culm (by Royal Salmon). They won eight races between them in 1986, with Norman Down's son Chris up in all but one of them.

The 12-year-old Culm Port had the most impressive form, with her four wins in a row including three under Rules, in one of which she was ridden by Venetia Williams; but the ten-year-old Culm Valley, who won both her open point-to-points, may have been unfortunate not to go through the season unbeaten in view of her last-fence fall in the Land Rover men's final at Chepstow; while the nine-year-old River Culm, who started the season a maiden, won both her races.

Roy Cake's 13-year-old Tawny Myth, who was to retire without adding to his score in 1987, along with his rider, Richard Cake, made the 1986 season a memorable one for him, winning four races in a row, three of them open events; and this brought his grand total of wins up to 24, including three in hunter chases.

Another veteran performer who was to call it a day in 1987 without any further wins was East Anglia's 13-year-old Mr. Mellors, whose four wins on the trot in 1986, the second of them in the hunt race at the Suffolk, where he was ridden by his trainer's husband, Alan Heath, and the others, including a hunter chase at Folkestone, with Simon Cowell up, gave him a grand total of 33 wins, which included 21 in hunter chases. "I shall never have another horse like him," said his owner, Mrs. Clare Villar, who has had more than her fair share of good horses, thanks in no small measure to her trainer, Libby Heath (formerly Lees).

The Point-to-Point Owners' first annual luncheon, held in a marquee on Stratford Racecourse, and now the setting for their young horse awards, topped this year by the seven-year-old Sweet Diana in the Midlands Area, was rather a sad occasion in another respect. It marked the retirement of the Association's founder, Jim Mahon, from his position as Chairman; though they couldn't have chosen a better man as his successor than Dorset's Percy Tory. Jim, of course, moved upstairs to become President, and was as active as ever in that capacity.

An interesting report prepared this season by a Working Party set up by the Jockey Club had much to say on the subject of livery yards, which were proliferating at a rate of knots. This is the conclusion it reached: "After taking careful note of the opposing view that these establishments may be felt to be more akin to professionally licensed yards under the Rules of Racing, and thus contrary to the amateur nature of the sport, in general the livery yards have contributed greatly both to the welfare of hunting and point-to-pointing," and it recommended that no restriction should be imposed on them. Considering how much these yards were doing to improve the quality of the racing, this was clearly the right attitude to take. Where indeed would we be today without the livery yards!

The report also came out against allowing grooms and hunt servants to ride in point-to-points, whilst expressing approval that assistant trainers were allowed to do so.

Among the deaths that occurred this year was that of the distinguished trainer Ryan Price, who was in a class of his own as a rider of point-to-pointers in the days before he became a public trainer. I was privileged to see him in action on numerous occasions in pre-war days, once when he rode five winners at the same meeting; and I am not ashamed of having committed myself to saying in print that he would have won on a cart-horse had he been put up on one. So successful was he as an amateur that he was told by the stewards of the National Hunt Committee to turn professional or else... His death came four years after Peter Bromley's splendid book on him was published.

Gregory Blaxland, who died in February at the age of 67, was a valued writer on point-to-point racing in the South East and, despite being confined to a wheelchair with polio, contracted in 1954 when he was serving with his regiment in Kenya against the Mau Mau, he was a much respected regular reporter of point-to-points in Kent and Sussex for local papers.

In October, Bill Tellwright died at the age of 58 as the result of a schooling accident. Formerly well-known as an amateur rider of quality, and as a steward at Uttoxeter for more than 20 years, he won the Kim Muir at Cheltenham on Nicolaus Silver in 1961. The best horse he rode in hunt racing was the Cheshire mare Happy Morn 11. On this winner of 25 hunter chases, with Bill up in quite a number of them, he won the race that is now known as the *Horse and Hound* Cup, the Final Open Hunters' Chase at Stratford in 1955.

But the youngest to die was Sue Horton in April. She was found dead in her car in the garage of her Wiltshire home, having dropped off to sleep in it with the engine running and being overcome by fumes. The coroner's verdict was accidental death from carbon monoxide poisoning. One of the all-time greats, whose skill in the saddle was matched by her generosity of spirit – she never had an unkind word to say about anyone. Sue, who rode 145 point-to-point winners, was 43 at the time of her death. Which means that when she had her first win on My Milly at the Mid Devon point-to-point at Moretonhampstead in 1960 as Sue Aston she was 17, and not 14 as was generally supposed. As someone once said of her, "Sue is as sweet as a field of clover."

Tailpiece:
After an unsuccessful ride in the last race at the Tedworth's Larkhill fixture, where he rode a winner for Henrietta Knight in the second, Mike Felton departed for the Vale of Aylesbury meeting at Kingston Blount in a helicopter piloted by Robert Elwell and rode another winner for her, Tough And Rugged in the men's open. He wasn't, however, by any means the only rider to make use of a helicopter in

order to ride at two meetings on the same day. I think Sue Aston must have been the first; but in later years Peter Greenall did so quite often, and there were certainly others.

1987

In which prize money is raised, two point-to-point classics acquire a new sponsor, The Times enters the scene with a restricted open championship, the Audi final moves its home, Kimble celebrates an anniversary, and a London taxi-driver rides a winner.

I suppose the most significant change in the rules this season was the Jockey Club's decision to increase the permissible level of prize money for point-to-points, even if it was rather a modest one. The prize money for open events (including restricted opens) went up from £150 to £200, and that for all other races from £100 to £125. These ceilings were, of course, optional, and some of the less affluent hunts could not rise to them.

Another concession was a decrease in the minimum weights for adjacent hunts' races, other than those confined to maidens. These races could now be 12st. ones, with 11-7 for five-year-olds and 11-9 for mares aged six or over. But there had to be a cumulative penalty system for previous winners in all such races.

For the first time in its 200-year history, *The Times* newspaper, largely at the instigation of its point-to-point correspondent, Brian Beel, entered the field of equestrian sponsorship with a series of restricted open races at point-to-points culminating in a £2,500 final at Towcester in the third week of May.

And this wasn't the only first venture into point-to-point sponsorship by a national newspaper. This was the season that the *Sporting Life* took on the sponsorship of the first two point-to-point classics, the four-mile race for Lord Ashton of Hyde's Cup at the Heythrop and the Lady Dudley Cup at the Worcestershire. The paper was now also the sponsor of the 3m 6f ladies' open for the Lyon Trophy at the Heythrop, whilst its stablemate, the *Sporting Life Weekender*, assumed the sponsorship of the ladies' open at the Worcestershire, where The *Life* was also sponsoring the restricted open.

Some of the major sponsors, however, dropped out, among them Massey-Ferguson, whose maiden-race series, with its final at Worcester, was a sad loss, as was the cessation in the North of the Vaux sponsorship at Sedgefield, although in this case there was still a Northern point-to-point champion hunter chase there.

The Times series embraced qualifying. races at the Cumberland Farmers, Bedale & West of Yore, the Staintondale and the Linlithgow & Stirlingshire, among others. So it was not doing too badly for northern fixtures.

Although Nitracc had relinquished their one-off attempt to create a men's final at the Melton Hunt Club fixture at Garthorpe, where the men's open race was now being sponsored by the *Racing Post*, their ladies' championship was still going strong there.

With the retirement of Peter Greenall, speculation was rife as to who would be the winner of the *Daily Telegraph* Cup. The Middlesex bookmaker Desmond Gleeson, the pioneer of ante-post betting on the riders' championships, was going 2-1 Mike Felton for the men's title, with David Naylor-Leyland next in the betting, followed by David Turner at 6-1. He was to prove bang on the mark with Felton and not far off it with Naylor-Leyland.

Mike Felton, with the might of John Dufosee's yard to call upon, as well as some of Henrietta Knight's charges, looked to be particularly well served; while for Naylor-Leyland there was that star performer Highland Blaze, now being trained by Henrietta Knight.

The 31-year-old Naylor-Leyland made an auspicious start when, on the opening day of the season at Tweseldown, he brought off a treble. One of his winners there, and a most impressive one in the fastest time of the day, was Highland Blaze in the second division of the three mixed opens, which he won very easily from Mike Felton's mount Sutton Prince. Considering that he had been troubled with arthritis and that Henrietta Knight had been dubious about running him, Highland Blaze's performance was even better than it looked. Unfortunately, it proved to be his only appearance of the season, as he went wrong afterwards and had to be pin-fired.

Naylor-Leyland's other two winners were Reynard's Bow, another of the horses trained by Henrietta Knight, in the Army saddle club race, in which he was eligible to ride by virtue of being a Territorial officer in the Life Guards, and Mrs. Jackie Porter's six-year-old Crayke in the maiden race, the latter a former inmate of Andy Turnell's yard now trained by John Porter.

Mike Felton had to wait until the following week to ride a winner. It came when he scored on Lord Vestey's Goldspun, also trained by Henrietta Knight, in a division of the mixed open for the Coronation Cup at Larkhill's United Services meeting, where Naylor-Leyland rode his fourth winner of the season when scoring on Reynard's Bow in the past & present race.

The contest between the two riders for the men's title continued apace; and in the fourth week of the season, at Tweseldown's Army fixture, both riders completed doubles, with Naylor-Leyland having his third win on Reynard's Bow in the serving members' race and following it with a win on Tough And Rugged in the first of the three Land Rover qualifiers there; while Felton won the adjacent hunts' race on Lothian General, a nine-year-old son of Spartan General owned by Henrietta's mother, Mrs. Guy Knight, and the third division of the men's open on Delius, a high-class horse under Rules whose career was blighted with leg problems.

The following week, Naylor-Leyland had his fourth win on Reynard's Bow in a PPOA club race at Badbury Rings, and Felton completed a double on the Dufosee-trained Firmament in a restricted open and his wife's Upper Blackhall in the maiden race, which was handed to him on a plate when Naylor-Leyland's five-year-old Broonie's Taing fell at the last.

At this stage of the season Felton had ridden six winners and Naylor-Leyland seven. But the pattern was soon to change; and by the time Felton had landed his first-ever four-timer on four of Henrietta Knight's charges at the Old Berks on Easter Monday, he had ridden 19 winners as against Naylor-Leyland's 14; and, in the meantime, the Devon-based Philip Scholfield, who had been rapidly making up ground, was on the 13 mark.

None of the three riders had any winners at the Torrington Farmers on the last day of the season; and by then Mike Felton had made certain of securing his first *Daily Telegraph* Cup, having won 26 point-to-points riding 17 different horses, and never more than three on the same horse, a score achieved twice, on Lothian General and Sutton Prince.

Philip Scholfield, who completed trebles at the Eggesford and the Dulverton West, was the runner-up for the title with 18 wins on 12 different horses. His most prolific winner was Ken Dunn's Eggesford nine-year-old Cal Mal, on whom he won four point-to-points and the Land Rover men's final at Chepstow, where the runner-up, beaten 20 lengths, was Paddy's Peril.

But there is no doubt that David Naylor-Leyland, with his 16 wins on six different horses, was very unlucky not to go closer. His bad luck began with Highland Blaze going wrong and continued when Reynard's Bow (his most prolific winner with five wins) had his season shortened by injury and Tough And Rugged (on whom he won four races) broke his leg on the flat at Kimble and had to be put down.

Alison Dare, superbly mounted on the horses trained by Dick Baimbridge in the Berkeley country, was always looking the winner of her second *Sporting Life* Cup; from the moment, that is, when she completed a four-timer with all four of her rides at the South Herefordshire fixture at Garnons on March 16. Her first winner there, the nine-year-old Fennelly in the adjacent hunts' race, was the fastest of the day, carrying a 31b. penalty and winning as he liked; and Mrs. Joyce Baimbridge's eight-year-old Kiltra Boy was almost as impressive winning much the faster division of the PPOA club race. Another good winner for Alison was Mrs. Patsy Willis' Mendip Express, the nine-year-old son of Pony Express who won the Nitracc ladies' open easing up; but Alison had to work harder to win the faster division of the maiden race on a horse she owned herself, seven-year-old Tudor Pageant.

Alison's 17 wins were gained on six horses, with the unbeaten Dawn Street, a nine-year-old owned jointly by Roger Willis and Mrs. Jennifer Cooper, her most prolific winner. Dawn Street's five successes included a convincing defeat of Tough And Rugged in the fastest-run division of the Coronation Cup mixed open at Larkhill.

It is tempting to say that it was a case of Alison first and the rest nowhere for the ladies' title, the joint runners-up for which, Lucy Gibbon and Jenny Pidgeon, finished their season seven winners behind her.

The two Grand Marnier novice riders of the year were Yorkshire's 21-year-old Chris Wilson and 17-year-old Pip Jones from Wales, the former with six wins on four different horses and Pip Jones with five. All Pip's wins were in Wales, and four of them were on John Parfitt's nine-year-old Eggington. The winner of the PPOA's Wilkinson Sword award, with eight winners, was a former winner of a Grand Marnier novice rider's award, 20-year-old David Mactaggart.

The best horse that Mactaggart rode was his father's home-bred Buccleuch mare Olive Press, on whom he won the men's opens at the Haydon and the Berwickshire but had a disappointing time on her afterwards when her form suggested that not all was well with her.

Another home-bred mare, Mrs. Caroline Nicholas's eight-year-old Mantinolas, from the Tiverton Foxhounds, was the winner of the Grand Marnier Trophy, with her eight wins in 11 appearances, ridden each time by Ron Treloggen. Mantinolas, a winner on all types of going, was the first horse from the West Country to win this trophy since Paul Tylor's mare Hargan in 1979.

Mrs. Nicholas is the daughter of Tom Smith, after whom the famous Tom Smith's Walls on the Badminton Three-Day Event cross-country course are named. Mantinolas, by Mandamus, was bred by Tom Smith at Badminton from Happy Tino, a mare by Rugantino; and she was given to Caroline as a five-year-old, together with her dam.

"If you want to bankrupt a friend you give them a brood mare" was one of Tom Smith's sayings; and he had given Ken and Caroline Nicholas two! But there is no evidence that they suffered from it, and they had others of the same stock at home, including a six-year-old half-brother to Mantinolas by Pony Express called Happy News, who was to lose his maiden certificate the following season, when he won two of his three races with Ron Treloggen up.

The next most prolific winner after Mantinolas was John Gray's Kintbury, a 12-year-old former hurdler (by Ballymoss) from the Meynell & South Staffs who was unbeaten in his seven point-to-points under Steven Brookshaw and finished fourth to Mister Bosun in a hunter chase at Ascot.

Flying Ace added six more wins in hunter chases to his score but didn't appear in a point-to-point. Doreen Calder, however, missed out on Peter Greenall's trophy for the leading rider in hunter chases. This went to the South Midlands rider Alan Hill, who won it outright this time with eight wins, three of them on Border Burg, who ended his season beating Eliogarty in the Liverpool Foxhunters' and, despite having run way below par in the Cheltenham Foxhunters', finished up at the top of Mackenzie & Selby's handicap on a mark of 11-8, llb. above Mrs. Angela Sheppard's Vale of Aylesbury eight-year-old Risk A Bet, who was unbeaten in his three hunter chases under Ian McKie.

The Cheltenham winner was a horse from a professional yard, the Fred Winter-trained 11-year-old Observe, who made all the running under Winter's assistant, 25-year-old Charlie Brooks (who was later to become a trainer in his own right), and won by a length and a half from Three Counties.

Three Counties was not long in gaining compensation for this defeat. After winning a ladies' open at Kimble on him, Katie Rimell went on to a resounding success on him in the *Horse and Hound* Cup at Stratford, where Flying Ace was the runner-up, 20 lengths behind.

Needless to say, the success in the Cheltenham Foxhunters' of Observe, a winner of some £75,000 in high-class races under Rules, provided fresh fuel for those who maintained that such horses ought not to be running in hunter chases.

Among those who spoke out strongly against such opportunism by professional trainers was bloodstock agent David Minton. A guest speaker at the PPOA annual lunch at Stratford Racecourse, he asserted that horses of the calibre of Observe should not be permitted to run in the Cheltenham Foxhunters' until at least two years had elapsed since they were competing in a higher class of race.

Similar sentiments were expressed by David Nicholson, the proposer of the toast to the sport at the national point-to-point dinner. His view was that any horse with a handicap rating of 50 or over under Rules should be barred from hunt racing until at least a full year had elapsed.

There were, though, some dissenting voices. Roger Roberts, responding to Nicholson's toast from inside the sport, had this to say: "Why shouldn't the old horses enjoy themselves in point-to-points?" and he cited Plummers Plain as one doing just this in the 'sixties. My own view is: Provided that they have been *properly* hunted, let them all come, but bring in a swingeing penalty system for them.

On a day of atrocious weather, at a meeting which did well to survive, the Heythrop four-miler was dominated by the two market leaders, Paddy's Peril and Political Whip, the latter now owned by David Naylor-Leyland and trained by Henrietta Knight. The very soft ground, however, was against Paddy's Peril, and in the end he was comfortably beaten by Political Whip, whose new owner was enjoying his second success on him and was to have a third in the men's open at the Croome & West Warwickshire three weeks later.

On the day of his triumph in the first of the season's classics, Naylor-Leyland completed a double in the Old Etonian & Old Harrovian race, beating Harrow's Colin Gee on Chalk Pit; and at the same meeting there was a double for Teresa Webber on Brockie Law in the ladies' race for the Lyon Trophy and White Paper in the adjacent hunts' race.

For the second time in four years, the Middleton fixture had to be abandoned, this time owing to waterlogging. So there was no Grmthorpe Cup race. But the Dudley Cup was able to go ahead on the firm ground at Chaddesley Corbett. Paddy's Peril was a hot favourite for it at 2-1 on in the field of seven. But he had to be content with a dead-heat for second place behind a 33-1 outsider in Pride Of Tullow.

A horse formerly owned by Peter Greenall, and bought for 2,300 guineas at Doncaster the previous August, the nine-year-old Pride Of Tullow was now owned by a syndicate of five headed by Jim Harris, a farmer and butcher in the North Hereford country, and trained by John Evans on his farm at Bromyard. Hitting the front after the last open ditch, Pride Of Tullow was never headed thereafter under Tim Bowen, on whose advice he was bought. This was Pride Of Tullow's only success of the season, and he never won another race afterwards.

Once again, Cliff Dawson's Lincolnshire mare Sweet Diana was the top performer in ladies' races: winning five of them on the trot with Jill Grinyer up until blotting her copybook with a fall at the twelfth in the Nitracc ladies' championship at Garthorpe. This was won by Teresa Elwell on Brockie Law, recording his seventh win in an unbeaten season which included success in a hunter chase at Southwell.

But Sweet Diana was right back on form when it mattered most, in the RMC Group ladies' championship at Chepstow, making all the running and winning unchallenged from Carol Lee's Majetta Crescent.

Now in the twilight of his career at the age of 14, Majetta Crescent had been given to Carol by his previous owners, Bob Murrin and John Ayres, following her husband's decision to set up as a public trainer, and she was training the horse herself. The partnership had already won four of their six previous races this season and they were to win a fifth on their last appearance of the season at the Torrington Farmers', where they mastered Eggington and Pip Jones in the ladies' open. This was their 27th win together, and the 28th for Majetta Crescent. Richard Lee considered Majetta Crescent to be the best point-to-pointer he ever trained, describing him as "very classy."

Another bright shiner in ladies' races was the Grafton 12-year-old Random Leg, who won six races with Jenny Pidgeon up and was a runner-up in his other two. The two horses who beat him were Brockie Law at Kingston Blount and Sheenagh Lamont's owner-ridden Brigadier Hathi at the Oakley. A winner of three of his five races during the season, Brigadier Hathi, a horse bought for £460 at Ashford market in Kent, broke down at the East Sussex & Romney Marsh on his last appearance of 1987.

In its first year at the Cheltenham evening fixture in May, the Audi Grand Prix de Chasse was a triumph for Jenny Litston and the 14-year-old Mister Bosun, the horse that had served her so faithfully over the years. Riding an exemplary race on him, Jenny took him clear four fences out, and the old horse responded by running on strongly to hold off Alison Dare's challenge on Fennelly, who was receiving 121b. from him. It was Mister Bosun's fourth success of the season; and one that Jenny won't have forgotten as she looks back from the wheel-chair that was to claim her six years later.

The inaugural running of *The Times* restricted open final at Towcester produced a field of 15, despite the firmness of the ground; and it was satisfyingly won by a horse who can justifiably be described as a reformed character since he entered the Haverfordwest yard of Bert Lavis in the Carmarthenshire country before the start of the season. In the confident hands of Philip Mathias, Ralph Morgans' seven-year-old Sea Express, who had narrowly escaped being banned for unruly behaviour in his previous ownership, was never headed after jumping the second and ran his race out well. Having lost his maiden certificate at the Tivyside and followed this with a win in the restricted open at the South Pembrokeshire, Sea Express was completing a hat-trick of wins.

There was no Newton runner in the Melton Hunt Club's Marie Curie novice championship this time; and in a field of 11 on good to firm ground, Johnny Greenall's owner-ridden Father Brady, an eight-year-old by The Parson trained for him by Caroline Saunders, had things all his own way after the favourite, Jeremy Hindley's Rhusted, with James Fanshawe up, had broken down when in a commanding lead approaching the third from home. This was a sad blow for Rhusted's connections, including his trainer, Gillian Duffield, who had trained him to win four point-to-points in a row before he came to Melton.

But although Father Brady was a lucky winner on this occasion, he was also a good one. One of the two races he had won beforehand was a novice hunter chase at Cheltenham, where he was a comfortable winner in a field of 17.

Among the other good horses to win at Melton, where Brockie Law and Paddy's Peril were also successful, was another who started the season as a maiden, Mrs. Helen Vergette's Perroquet, a seven-year-old by Precipice Wood trained by George Vergette in the Cottesmore country. When beating Able Sailor by three-quarters of a length in the club members' race, Perroquet was recording his fifth win in a row with his owner up; and his time of 6 mins. 20 secs. was two seconds faster than Father Brady's in the novice championship, for which Perroquet would have been eligible.

The Vale of Aylesbury fixture at Kimble on Easter Saturday was celebrating the 75th anniversary of point-to-point racing on the Robarts family's course, where racing first took place in 1912 when the Old Berkeley (one of the three former packs that were later combined with the Vale of Aylesbury) held their meeting there. It was on this course at Kimble that Lord Oaksey (The Hon. John Lawrence, as he was at the time) and Chris Collins had their first rides in a race.

John Oaksey was riding a mare called Next Of Kin in a race for members of the legal profession at the Pegasus Club (Bar) point-to-point in 1951, and I am making no excuses for re-quoting what he wrote with amusing relish about his experience in an article for *The Field*: "She fell over backwards twice in the paddock, but the others fell over in the race itself. Next Of Kin came home alone carrying a bewildered blissful burden, and in that moment, I suppose, my immediate future was settled. The distinguished judges and barristers who organized the Bar point-to-point had, quite unwittingly, deprived their profession of my services."

It can't be often that one sees a London taxi-driver riding a point-to-point winner. In fact, I think that the 31-year-old Dennis Turner, who did so at the Oakley on a horse he bought at the Ascot Sales for 875 guineas and had been hunting with the Fitzwilliam, might well be the first one to do so. Dennis, who hadn't ridden in a point-to-point for seven years, and was once an apprentice with Verly Bewicke, was riding his wife's Samalaja in a division of the maiden race, and he got the nine-year-old home by two lengths from Alan Hill's mount Cheekie Chappie in what proved to be the faster division. Nor was this his only win. A fortnight later, riding the same horse, he won the hunt race at the Fitzwilliam.

Two riders rode their 100th point-to-point winners during the season, Tim Rooney when scoring on Mrs. Rose Harry's Suikerbos in a division of the men's open at the Brecon, and Chris Down riding River Culm in the restricted open at the Eggesford; and in Scotland, Doreen Calder was riding her 50th winner when Flying Ace recorded his 37th win in a hunter chase at Edinburgh.

Meanwhile, in East Anglia, another George Cooper 'special' was beginning to make a name for himself in the shape of Carl's Choice, a six-year-old grandson of Spartan General who had lost his maiden certificate the previous season at Marks Tey when making his first appearance on a course after being bought for 4,500 guineas at Doncaster.

Ridden each time by his owner, Carl's Choice won two of his four races in 1987, beating Stanwick Lad by half a-length in the second of them, a men's open at Cottenham. This was his second win over a course he was to make virtually his own in future years.

The outstanding ladies' horse in East Anglia was now point-to-point journalist Carolyn Tanner's ten-year-old Kula, from the Puckeridge & Thurlow, a winner of five races with Lucy Gibbon up.

It is true that another horse from the same hunt, David Claydon's eight-year-old Martineau, ridden by his 19-year-old daughter Paula, won as many races as Kula, but he was beaten three times by him before Martineau gained his revenge by a short head in a ladies' open at Cottenham when Lucy Gibbon lost an iron at the last. Martineau, however, with a time of 5 mins. 58 secs., was the first horse to break the six-minute barrier at Cottenham since Fizz Chown's mare Cherry Blossom recorded an identical time when winning the same race at this meeting in 1976. But even this time wasn't a course record. This was still held by Vasser Rowe's Bitter Lemon, who won the men's open with David Wales up at the Cambridgeshire Harriers' fixture in 1968 in a time of 5 mins. 55 secs.

In the North West, the star performer in ladies' races was Zena Brookshaw's North Shropshire mare Pennyazena, one of the horses (Kintbury was another) trained by her husband, Steven. Ridden on each occasion by the accomplished Stephanie Baxter, this eight-year-old mare won five of her six ladies' opens and would no doubt have been unbeaten but for Stephanie Baxter losing her irons in another and having to pull her up.

Four of the horses sent out, by Ann Blaker from her small yard at Nutley in Sussex were winners at the Old Surrey & Burstow fixture on her home course at Penshurst; and one of them was the evergreen El Padre, now aged 15. Mrs. Blaker displayed perfect timing to win the ladies' open on him. Applejo, another of the horses she bought from Joe Turner, though not one owned by her, won a two-horse men's open with Trevor Head up. Team Spirit won the natural-country race here for the second year running, with his owner, David Pinsent, a 44-year-old company director who owned a vineyard in California, putting up over-weight again; and another of Mrs. Blaker's charges, Peter Webb's owner-ridden Kerry Street, was successful in the ordinary hunt race.

That doughty West Country stayer, John Nicholls's 12-year-old Dicky Blob, was recording his 20th win when he won the men's open at the Dulverton West with Stephen Long up. This was his fifth win of the season, and it would have been his sixth but for a disqualification at the Bolventor Harriers when his rider failed to weigh in. Among the races Dicky Blob won this season was the four-mile men's open at the Dartmoor which he was winning for the second year running with a 7lb. penalty. He was also the runner-up to Border Burg in a hunter chase at Leicester.

Nicholls bought Dicky Blob as a four-year-old from his breeder in Wales, Mrs. Rose Harry, with eventing in mind for him; and the horse didn't see a racecourse until he was eight, when he lost his maiden certificate with Stephen Long riding him in an adjacent hunts' race at the Lamerton, and then won three more races with his owner up.

In the same yard that housed Border Burg and I Got Stung was another good horse, George Cook's speedy King Neon, bred by him from Ditchling Beacon, a High Line mare given to him by his boss, James Delahooke. King Neon, who had started to show promise when running Mac Kelly to a length and a half in a ladies' open at Cottenham last season as a six-year-old, and was being ridden again by the Edinburgh-born Joan Johnston, won a ladies' open at Cottenham and two novice hunter chases at Stratford, the second of them the John Corbet Cup.

In Yorkshire, Whiggie Geo was continuing to defy his years at the age of 15, winning three men's opens in a row under Nigel Tutty, having amassed a grand total of 23 wins, including five in hunter chases; and this was also the last season of racing for another Yorkshire veteran, Mrs. Patricia Russell's 14-year-old Honourable Man, who made his swan song with his 15th win, including eight in hunter chases, when scoring in an adjacent hunts' race at the Bramham Moor with David Kinsella up.

But for the York & Ainsty mare Miss Crozina there was not such a happy end to her racing career. After never coming off the bridle when winning the men's open at the Hurworth under Tim Smith, she broke down badly in the men's open at the Bramham Moor.

In East Anglia it was the turn of the 14-year-old Mr. Mellors for retirement; but he wasn't, unfortunately, able to go out with anything more to add to his 33 wins, which included 21 in hunter chases since the day he entered Libby Heath's yard in 1978.

Some horses, however, seem to go on for ever; and one such was the Bicester 15-year-old White Paper, a winner of three more races with Teresa Elwell (née Webber) up and of a men's open with Robert Elwell aboard; and when winning the ladies' open at the Vale of Aylesbury fixture at Kingston Blount in a time of 6 mins. 3.5 secs. White Paper was putting up a time that was five seconds faster than Night Ride's record time in the corresponding race at the PPOA fixture there in 1980.

It was a good season for the livery yards, with Henrietta Knight saddling 25 winners, Dick Baimbridge 21 and John Dufosee 20.

In May, Mrs. Philip Marshall died. She will be remembered in particular as the former Ida Croxon, who engaged in so many memorable duels with the great Pat Tollit in the 'fifties and 'sixties, especially for her performances on Mrs. Cecily Gaskell's spectacular grey, almost white, Don Isle, on whom she won 14 races and gave spectators so much pleasure.

At the national point-to-point dinner in October, the dinner committee's engraved salver for special services to the sport was presented to the Tory family of Dorset; and there to receive it from the hands of Hugh Condry was Percy Tory, son of Stewart, brother of Michael, and uncle of Anthony. This was the first time that the salver had gone to an entire family.

Speaking at this dinner, David Nicholson added his name to those who had been campaigning for point-to-point racing on Sundays. "You can do it," he told the audience of 280. "It is essential we have racing on a Sunday, and point-to-point racing is the obvious place to start."

Tailpiece from John Hislop's book on Flat-race riding:
"Jockeys who appear to be doing least are often putting in the most, and vice versa."
What an admirable text to hang up in Portman Square!

1988

*In which an Irish maestro pays a visit to the Beaufort, Philip Scholfield
sets a new record, Cliff Dawson produces another star in Lincolnshire,
and a rank outsider wins the Liverpool Foxhunters'.*

If one includes the horses running in natural-country races, in which the
Beaufort led the way with 19, there were a record number of runners for the
193 point-to-point races that took place this season. Postponements and aban-
donments were few and far between; and only three meetings, the Eglinton, Flint
& Denbigh and the first of the two Eridge & Southdown fixtures, were lost altogether. In the early part of the season at least a dozen meetings had over 100 runners, the North Hereford showing the way with 162 for its ten races, followed by
the Beaufort with 142 for nine and the Brecon with 139 for 11.

One new rule that caused a few problems was the Jockey Club's insistence that
the checking of horses' passports, which had hitherto been done by local vets,
must now come under the direct control of the Jockey Club's veterinary officers.
This took some time to sink in and resulted in quite a number of intended runners having to be withdrawn for passport infringements, as many as four at the
West Shropshire Draghounds fixture at Weston Park, where their owners were all
fined £65.

I have it firmly fixed in my mind that the best horse seen out in point-to-
points this season was the eight-year-old Curaheen Boy, owned and ridden by
David Naylor-Leyland, and trained for him by Henrietta Knight in the Old Berks
country.

A winner of nine point-to-points and a hunter chase in Ireland when owned
and trained by the great Pat Hogan, from whom he was bought afterwards,
Curaheen Boy made a winning English début when trotting up in an adjacent
hunts' race at Tweseldown; and he would have ended his season winning all of his
six races without coming off the bridle but for being disqualified on his sixth
appearance in the adjacent hunts' race at the Heythrop when Naylor-Leyland for-
got to weigh in.

On his dam's side, Curaheen Boy traced back to Bright Cherry, the dam of
Arkle; and when he beat Dawn Street in a classy adjacent hunts' race at the

Beaufort in a time that was only two seconds outside the Didmarton course record, Pat Hogan was there to see him do so; and also to see Dromin Joker, another of the horses he had sold to Naylor-Leyland, undergoing his only defeat of the season when beaten by Paddy's Peril in the men's open. Another good winner for Hogan in Ireland, the eight-year-old Dromin Joker, named after one of the best coverts in Limerick, was a winner of four races during the season.

Curaheen Boy was not, however, the occupant of the top place in Mackenzie & Selby's annual, which had now expanded from 697 pages to 771. This went to a horse who had confined his appearances to hunter chases and won four of them with Paul Hacking up, Mrs. Jean Campbell's ten-year-old Certain Light, who had been hunted with the Tickham. He was rated at 11-11; and next to him at 11-10 was another hunter chaser, Three Counties. Curaheen Boy's rating was 11-9.

Certain Light, by the American sire Lucifer out of a mare by Primera, included among his wins the Cheltenham Foxhunters', in which Hacking was seen at his best when driving him home to win by two lengths from Katie Rimell's mount Three Counties. The two horses met again in the Audi Hunter Chase at the Cheltenham evening fixture in May when Certain Light confirmed the form with a six-lengths win. On the one occasion that Certain Light failed to win, he unseated Hacking with a bad mistake in the early stages of a hunter chase at Ascot won by I Got Stung. A gift horse from Lady Rootes to the Kent permit holder Jean Campbell, Certain Light, a winner over hurdles from Josh Gifford's yard in March 1984, had now won six hunter chases and an open point-to-point since he started hunt racing for Mrs. Campbell in 1986.

The firmness of the ground at Stratford kept Certain Light out of the *Horse and Hound* Cup, for which he had been declared; and this left the way clear for Three Counties, although he had to earn his success the hard way, as his fencing was far from fluent and he had to make up a great deal of ground in the closing stages. However, he did so with his usual gameness, coming with a great run at the finish and getting up to score by half a length from Bajan Sunshine, a winner over hurdles and fences whose six wins on the Flat had included the 1983 Cesarewitch.

Three Counties was the second training success for Mrs. Mercy Rimell on consecutive days at Stratford. The first was her nine-year-old Deep Prospect, on whom her pupil assistant, Matthew Sheppard, won the John Corbet Cup novice hunter chase the previous evening, beating two other useful novices in Double Turn and Paddy Murphy. The son of Deep Run was winning his fourth race on the trot, two point-to-points and two hunter chases, and finishing his season unbeaten.

The Liverpool Foxhunters' produced a result that was both highly dramatic and immensely satisfying for the point-to-point fraternity, notably in East Anglia; and the finish was fought by two horses who weren't given a snowball's chance in Hell in most people's minds.

After two of the more fancied contenders, Three Counties and Eliogarty, had both come to grief at Becher's, Nigel Ridout moved the 66-1 shot Shylocks Retreat into the lead three fences out, taking over from Simon Andrews on the 50-1 Newnham. But in a desperate race all the way to the line, Newnham got back again to score by a head. David Naylor-Leyland was 20 lengths behind on the third horse, Beamwam; and the favourite, Marcus Armytage's mount Acarine, a winner of hunter chases at Nottingham and Fakenham on his two previous appearances, finished fourth.

Michael Johnson's Newnham, an 11-year-old by Cantab trained by his owner on the borders of Luton Airport and hunted with the Puckeridge & Thurlow, was up to this point the longest-priced winner of the race since pre-war days, and this was his second win of the season. His first was in a ladies' open at Horseheath with Bridget Rowe up; and he was to have another after his triumph at Aintree when the 27-year-old Andrews won a men's open at Cottenham on him.

Bought in Ireland as a yearling by Josie Sheppard, Newnham had his initial win in the maiden race at the Enfield Chace in 1982 as a five-year-old with Gurney Sheppard up. The following season he won two races with Josie up and another with Gurney up. It was after that that the horse was sold to Michael Johnson, for whom his first win was in the hunt race at the Puckeridge & Thurlow in 1985 with Simon Andrews up. In 1986 he won the adjacent hunts' race at the Suffolk; and the two races Andrews won on him in 1987 included one right out of his country, the four-mile men's open at the Exmoor. So his chances of winning at Aintree were not quite as forlorn as his price suggested.

The most prolific winner of the season, and the recipient of the Grand Marnier Trophy, was Trevor Marks's home-bred Stanwick Lad. A winner of ten open point-to-points with John Sharp up, the 11-year-old son of Netherkelly would have been unbeaten in these races but for slipping up on a bend when in process of cantering home in another. He was a winner over a wide variety of courses ranging from the stayers' course at Newton Bromswold to the sharp course at Higham; and he wound up his season finishing third to Arizona Belle and Mademist Susie in the Land Rover men's final at Chepstow. Good horses though they were, the winner and runner-up in this race were both rated below Stanwick Lad in Mackenzie & Selby's handicap. The former was receiving 12lb. from him at Chepstow, and the latter over a stone.

Arizona Belle, an 11-year-old mare from the Seavington, owned by David Kellow and trained by her rider, Robert Buckler, was recording her second win of the season; and horse, owner and rider were all enjoying their first success under Rules. Mademist Susie, a seven-year-old mare from the Hurworth, was unbeaten in her four point-to-points under Nigel Tutty, three of then open events.

Tarville, the winner of the RMC Group ladies' final, was also being ridden by a rider having her first win under Rules, 21-year-old Heather McCaull. Formerly trained by John Edwards and now with John Parfitt in Wales, the ten-year-old Tarville, the winner of the Massey-Ferguson final for Parfitt in 1986, was recording his fourth win of the season, having had three different riders up on him.

But of rather more interest as a Future Prospect was the horse who finished second to him, Cliff Dawson's up-and-coming star Roscoe Boy, a horse bought out of a field as a four-year-old. Roscoe Boy, who had lost his maiden certificate when making his first appearance on a course as a five-year-old in 1987 and was a stablemate of Sweet Diana's, was a winner of three of his six races in 1988 and a runner-up in the other three, ridden each time by Jill Dawson (née Grinyer). One of the races he won was the Nitracc ladies' championship at Garthorpe, where he got home by a neck from Penny Falls (a mare he had beaten quite easily at the

Blankney) and had to survive an objection after hanging left on the run-in. The stewards decided that, although there had been a degree of interference, it was accidental and hadn't affected the result.

The Dawsons also had another good season with Sweet Diana, their premier star. The mare won all five of her ladies' races; and in her only other race, a hunter chase at Towcester, she divided Whitsunday (now in training with Nicky Henderson) and King Neon.

Before he started in point-to-points, Roscoe Boy had won show-jumping competitions and competed successfully in hunter trials for Dawson. The Dawsons bought his dam, Hayburnwyke (by Pretty Form), soon after the mare had foaled him.

The most prolific point-to-point winners after Stanwick Lad, each with seven wins, were Mick Easterby's six-year-old Karakter Reference, from the Middleton, Lisa Smithson's eight-year-old Lislary Lad, ridden by Tim Jones and trained in Wales, and Chris Marriott's home-bred Prince Pippin, a nine-year-old from the Heythrop who had his owner up in all his races.

And since Karakter Reference, a winner of four races with Susan Easterby up and three with Howard Brown in the saddle, started the season as a maiden, and underwent his only defeat when slipping up in his last race at the York & Ainsty, he must be accounted the leading novice of the season.

It seemed a pity that Karakter Reference didn't meet his engagement in the Marie Curie novice championship at the Melton Hunt Club. Had he done so, I am confident that he would have won it. Another who failed to meet his engagement in this championship, and no doubt would have gone very close, was the North Shropshire six-year-old Mount Argus, who completed a hat-trick of wins in his last three races under his trainer, Steven Brookshaw.

In the event, the race was still won by a horse from Yorkshire, the six-year-old Jelupe, owned, bred and trained by his 45-year-old rider, Robin Sandys-Clarke, a land agent on the Raby Castle estate in Co. Durham, who broke the horse in himself and hunted him with the Zetland.

The winner of a restricted open at the Bramham Moor, Jelupe quickened well to go clear of the Warwickshire mare Gibraltar Girl approaching the second last and won by a comfortable four lengths in a time that was only five seconds slower than Roscoe Boy's in the ladies' open.

The best novice in the Northern Area was Mrs. Pat Shrubsole's home-bred six-year-old Ready Steady, a horse hunted with the Percy in Northumberland. A ready winner of six point-to-points, Ready Steady was ridden in five of them by his owner's niece, the intrepid Gay Smalley, a member of the Dangerous Sports Club.

The 27-year-old Gay, who had broken both her legs in a very bad car crash two years before and made a miraculous recovery, was riding in only her second point-to-point when she won a maiden race at the Haydon on Ready Steady in February. But after her five wins on him, and finishing a runner-up in the Heart Of All England at Hexham with her only ride in a hunter chase, she was unable to ride the horse in the last of his ten races because she had injured herself in another motor accident when returning home from the Lauderdale two days earlier. So Ready Steady was ridden in the ladies' open at the Zetland in May by Kerstie

Barnett and was a first winner for her.

But, by the time the national point-to-point dinner came round at The Belfry in September, Gay Smalley was there to receive from Peter Scudamore the Grand Marnier female novice rider's award for the five point-to-point winners she rode during the season. The winner of the male novice rider's award was a 29-year-old rider from Worcestershire, Simon Grundy, whose eight wins included six on Michael Low's 12-year-old Dingbat, an experienced campaigner under Rules who proved a wonderful schoolmaster.

It was certainly a season that the 30-year-old Philip Scholfield will remember. Not only did he win the *Daily Telegraph* Cup for the first time, but he did so with a record-breaking total of 37 winners, smashing John Bryan's previous record of 32 in 1978.

Scholfield's wins were on 17 different horses, and 28 of them were on horses owned and trained by Ken Dunn in the Eggesford country. His most prolific winners were Dunn's pair Golden Hornet and Foxe's Castle, the two he completed a double on at the Torrington Farmers on the final day of the season. Both of them won six races. The youngest of Scholfield's winners was another of Dunn's, the five-year-old Spireslake, who was unbeaten in his three races.

The runner-up for the men's title was Mike Felton, who rode 28 winners, with his mother's Sutton Prince, one of the horses trained by John Dufosee, doing most to help him on his way with six wins. Behind Felton came John Llewellyn with 20 winners, Tim Jones with 18, John Sharp with 15 and the luckless David Naylor-Leyland, whose bid for the men's title came to an abrupt end after he had ridden 13 winners when a bad fall on Young Lover in the Old Etonian & Old Harrovian race at the Heythrop on April 12 put him out of action for the remainder of the season.

The contest for the *Sporting Life* Cup was very closely contested; and it wasn't resolved until Umberleigh on the last day of the season, when the two leading contenders, Jenny Litston and Amanda Harwood, came up against each other in an absorbing ladies' open. Mrs. Litston was riding Richard Barber's Gerry Doyle in this and Amanda was up on quintuple winner Hurry Up Henry. Although the ten-year-old Gerry Doyle had won three of his previous seven races and been a runner-up in three others, this was the first time that Mrs. Litston had ridden him; but he ran as sweetly for her as he had done for Jane Southcombe.

It was a two-horse race from three fences out, with Gerry Doyle the better of the two as he sped up the hill to the second last, where he had an advantage of almost four lengths, which he had more than doubled by the time he reached the post.

A winner over fences and hurdles in Ireland, Gerry Doyle was bought by Barber for 1,800 guineas from the Irish trainer Tom Nicholson outside the ring at Doncaster after being spun by the vet for a dicky heart, and this was the fifth race he had won for his new stable. He was the 16th winner of the season for the 24-year-old Jenny Litston, and she ended up with one more winner than Amanda Harwood.

Backed at ante-post odds of 20-1 for the ladies' title with the Middlesex bookmaker Desmond Gleeson, Jenny Litston achieved her 16 wins on six different horses. Her most prolific winner was the Weston & Banwell 12-year-old Gathabawn, on whom she won six ladies' opens, beating Gerry Doyle in one of them, and was unlucky not to win a seventh. But the best horse she rode was the 15-year-old Mister Bosun, whose sire, Deep Run, was the leading point-to-point sire of the season, producing 24 winners in this field, plus his three in hunter chases. Jenny's four wins on Mister Bosun included a record-breaking-performance in the ladies' open at the South & West Wilts, where the combination broke the Larkhill course record with a time of 5 mins. 51.6 secs.

Although Amanda Harwood was without the services in point-to-points of Red Shah, on whom she won a handicap chase at Fakenham in December, she was very well mounted on three more of her father's horses, Hurry Up Henry, Betty's Pearl and Only For Love; and at the Crawley & Horsham in March she won on all three of them. Between them, these three horses gave her 14 of her 15 successes, Hurry Up Henry and Betty's Pearl contributing five each, and the other four coming from Only For Love.

Three other lady riders reached double figures during the season. Jill Dawson, who finished third in the table with 13 winners, had been receiving major assistance from Sweet Diana and Roscoe Boy, but five more of her wins came from two other horses owned by her father-in-law, the 12-year-old Cawker Dyke giving her four of them.

Alison Dare and Teresa Elwell both rode ten winners. Alison's most prolific winner was Mendip Express, who went through the season like a dose of salts and was unbeaten in his six races, which ended with his trouncing of Gerry Doyle in the 3.5 mile ladies' open at the Exmoor, where the horse who finished third, John Weldhen's six-year-old For A Lark from the Four Burrow in Cornwall, was going to make a big name for himself in these races and had already won two of them.

Teresa was sadly handicapped by the loss of Brockie Law, who, after winning at Kingston Blount on his single appearance, succumbed to colic and failed to recover from an operation. The ten-year-old had won 20 point-to-points and two hunter chases for her during his distinguished career. But she still had the 16-year-old White Paper, and won four more races on him. The others she won on were Mister Skip and Tormore. Neither was owned by her but both were trained by her.

The Middleton Hunt's Grimthorpe Cup was the first of the season's three point-to-point classics this season, preceding the four-mile men's open for Lord Ashton of Hyde's cup at the Heythrop by four days. On the good to soft ground at Whitwell-on-the-Hill, there were ten starters for this 4m 1f race, all of them from within the Yorkshire area. No more than three of them completed the course. The winner, by a distance, in the comparatively slow time of 9 mins. 28 secs., was a horse who had lost his maiden certificate the previous season, Mrs. Sue Frank's home-bred nine-year-old Ingleby Star, who was making his seventh appearance of a season in which his only previous success was in the men's open at the Derwent.

Ridden again by Nigel Tutty, Ingleby Star, relishing the longer trip and ground with a cut in it, made all the running and won by a distance from Tacroy, who had beaten him by a length over a shorter trip on their previous encounter in the men's open at the Staintondale. But it can't, by any stretch of the imagination, be called a vintage Grimthorpe.

But there was certainly a vintage winner of the Heythrop four-miler in Paddy's Peril, who was winning it for the second time in three years, and in most impressive style. John Deutsch was sitting pretty on the 12-year-old all the way, and from four fences out he started to go right away from Henrietta Knight's charge Goldspun, on whom Mike Felton was having to work hard to keep in touch. Paddy's Peril won unchallenged by 20 lengths; and I thought Tony Perry, his joint owner, was going to burst with pride. It was the fourth successive win of the season for Paddy's Peril, and as memorable in its way as his harder-earned win at the Beaufort, where he was responsible for Dromin Joker's only defeat in this eight-year-old's five appearances.

It was a different story in the Dudley Cup 11 days later, however. Paddy's Peril was an evens favourite for this in a field of nine. But the race had always been a positive jinx for him and this time he even robbed himself of the second place he had occupied in the last two years by unseating John Deutsch with a bad mistake at the last fence when he still had a length to make up on the very fluent winner, North Key, an eight-year-old from the Ludlow whose rider, 29-year-old Alistair Ulyet, was having his 50th win in a point-to-point.

A horse who traced back to the 1962 Derby winner Larkspur on his dam's side, North Key had won a hunter chase at Ludlow on his previous appearance, and he was to complete his hat-trick in another one at Warwick after his Dudley Cup win. A winner over hurdles as a three-year-old, he was a horse from the bargain basement. His owner, Jeffrey Palmer, who farmed at Clent, near Ludlow, bought him privately for £300 and sent him to be trained by Margaret Kimnell, who won a ladies' open on him the previous season at the South Shropshire. Alistair Ulyet described him as "a hell of a decent hunter and a brilliant jumper."

For the second year running, the final of *The Times* restricted open series at Towcester was won by a horse from Wales when the six-year-old St. Helens Boy, owned and trained by John Tudor at Bridgend in the Llangeinor country and ridden by his nephew, Jonathan Tudor, made all the running in a field of 13 and easily held off the favourite, the Seavington mare Fool's Pleasure.

A maiden at the start of the season, St. Helens Boy, who cost his owner just 625 guineas at Ascot, and whose dam, Cullen, won the Great Metropolitan at Epsom in 1966, was winning for the third time in his seven appearances.

While Flying Ace was still-very much the King in the Northern Area with his nine wins in hunter chases enabling Doreen Calder to collect Peter Greenall's Trophy for the first time, a budding star in this area was the winner of the Heart Of All England at Hexham, Paddy Murphy. This Irish-bred seven-year-old, a son of Pollerton standing 17 hands high, won four point-to-points and two hunter chases under Charlie Sample, and was the runner-up to Flying Ace on a second appearance at Hexham.

His greatest triumph, albeit a fortunate one, was in the Audi Grand Prix de Chasse at the Audi evening at Cheltenham in May, when he was left out on his own in a field of 20 after Allen Lad, owned by the *Daily Telegraph*'s David Welch and trained for him by Dick Baimbridge, had been fatally injured in a fall at the second last with the race seemingly in the bag.

Bought as an unbroken three-year-old for 4,100 guineas at Ballsbridge by his accountant owner Tony Lapping, Paddy Murphy was trained for him by Geoff Coatsworth at his successful livery yard in the Morpeth country.

Two of the livery yards had their best seasons ever. Henrietta Knight sent out 27 winners (two more than in 1987) from her Lockinge yard; and John Dufosee went one better than the previous season with 21 winners from his Dorset yard; while Libby Heath, in her last season before going public, saddled seven point-to-point winners and seven in hunter chases, most of them owned by her chief patron, Mrs. Clare Villar.

Alison Dare, Mike Felton and Steven Brookshaw all rode their 100th winners, Alison's including 14 in hunter chases. Brookshaw, who was on a total of 97 point-to-point winners, had also ridden five under Rules. True Dowry's win in the club members' at Melton gave Joey Newton his 99th point-to-point win, but he had passed the 100 mark with his successes in hunter chases.

Jamie Jukes, a future men's champion, rode his first winner at the age of 17 when dead-heating in the hunt race at the Carmarthenshire on Sparcon, a 14-year-old son of Spartan General, with Philip Mathias, who was riding his 50th point-to-point winner, Rocks Of Bawn, the first leg of a treble for him.

There were also first winners for young members of two well-known East Anglian families. Lisa Rowe, the 16-year-old daughter of Hunter and Pat Rowe who was to become Manager of Warwick Racecourse in later years, had her first success when scoring on her grandfather's pony-sized mare Shedid in the maiden race at the Dunston Harriers; and 18-year-old Sarah Sheppard had hers on her stepmother's General Wrekin in the ladies' open at the Grafton before going on to complete a hat-trick of wins on this eight-year-old grandson of Spartan General.

But for Sarah's father, Gurney Sheppard, it was his last season of race-riding. He made his final appearance before retirement at the age of 50 when narrowly beaten on his Rubie's Choice (a horse who gave him four of his six wins during the season) by Philip Scholfield on Foxe's Castle in an exciting men's open at the Torrington Farmers. He was finishing with a grand total of 55 point-to-point winners. He was, of course, to send out many more from his Hertfordshire yard.

Over the years, an extraordinary variety of professions have been represented on the point-to-point scene, one of the few remaining bastions of amateur sport; and just about the only profession unrepresented so far was that of gravedigger. Among those riding winners in 1988 were a number of farm workers (the most notable being Philip Scholfield), two Newport dockers in Steve Shinton and Richard Williams, a Welsh steel worker in Joe Price, a tree surgeon (Warren Marshall), a Hereford van driver (Robert Harris), a Wolverhampton plumber (David Robinson), a helicopter pilot (Robert Elwell), a deep-sea diver (Malcolm Batters), a carpenter (Paul Staples), a Jockey Club official (Simon Claisse), a doctor (Philip Pritchard), a barrister (Michael Connell) and a milkman (Willy Bryan).

Lest we forget, I must also record that this was the last season of point-to-point racing for the future Cheltenham Gold Cup winner Norton's Coin, at this time still running in the colours of his breeder and trainer, Percy Thomas in the Pentyrch country. A winner of three of his six races, Norton's Coin won two races with Tim Jones up, including a hunter chase at Chepstow, and the adjacent hunts' race at the Vale of Clettwr with Pip Jones up.

It is interesting to recall that, in proposing the toast to the sport at the national point-to-point dinner at The Belfry, Nicky Henderson came out as being 100% against racing on all-weather courses. "God help the day," he remarked, "when we finish up with all-weather racing at Kempton Park in January."

Responding to the toast was a High Court Judge, Sir Bernard Caulfield, who proved to be one of that rare species, a speaker who held his audience in the palm of his hand as soon as he opened his mouth. He delivered one of the most attention-grabbing speeches that has ever been heard at this dinner. As the producer of a son, Michael Caulfield, who was shortly to become the Secretary of the Jockeys' Association of G.B., Sir Bernard was well acquainted with the racing scene; and, in the 'seventies, he had presided over the Gay Future trial, which featured a notorious betting coup at Cartmel. In the public mind, however, he was the Judge who immortalised himself with his reference in the Jeffrey Archer libel case to the "fragrant" Mary Archer.

In January, a few months after the award for special services to point-to-point racing had gone to the Tory family at the 1987 dinner, Stewart Tory, the senior member of the family, died when in reach of his 83rd birthday. Percy Tory had said that the first thing he did when he got home to Dorset with the salver was to take it to his old man, who wrote in a letter afterwards, "No one appreciates it more than I do." And one can say, with complete justification, that no one deserved it more. Master of the Portman from 1959-64, and later a Joint Master, Stewart returned to sole mastership in 1983; and he remained in it right up to the time of his death, three days before which he was joyfully shouting instructions from a car, having been cub hunting from the saddle for six hours in October.

Successful as both owner and rider in point-to-points, Stewart was running a good horse in the early 'fifties called Reverent Mother. I have every reason to remember this mare because I was eagerly awaiting the day when I would be able to write in the *Sporting Life* that Reverent Mother was being chased home by The Wicked Uncle. Stewart, I discovered, was also waiting for it. But, alas, the opportunity never came, although both horses were winners and sometimes runners-up in the same area in the same period. Stewart Tory's maxim was: "Hunting and point-to-points are a foundation for good chasers." And how right he was!

After the was over, Capt. Bryan Parry, who had trained so many winners for Peter Greenall, and not a few of his own, died on September 23 at the age of 74, after losing a long and courageous battle with multiple sclerosis and cancer. A noted point-to-point rider in the 'thirties, he played a major part in enabling Greenall to capture the *Daily Telegraph* Cup in 1982, and also in 1985, the year of his retirement as a trainer. He was also a Master and Huntsman of four packs of hounds in his time.

Bryan had a piercingly fine eye for a horse. The two best horses that he owned himself were Blue Cascade, on whom Malcolm Arthers won 12 point-to-points and a hunter chase for him, and Cheekio Ora. The latter was his brightest star, winning 18 point-to-points and 18 hunter chases, ridden in most of them by Peter Greenall, who said of his owner: "Only the best would do for Bryan."

I have two vivid last memories of Bryan Parry. The first was when I saw him struggling painfully down the steps from the paddock at the Cheltenham evening fixture in 1987. I remember thinking, What tremendous gallantry! The second was at his home at Somerby on the day of the Melton Hunt Club point-to-point in the year of his death, when he told me gleefully that he was having gourmet meals sent into him from a nearby restaurant. When I asked him how he felt, he said drily, "Apart from my multiple sclerosis and cancer, I feel fine."

Others who died this year were Dick Black, one of the very few amateurs to win the Cheltenham Cold Cup, a feat achieved on Lord Grimthorpe's Fortina in 1947; Pat Wint, one of the top lady riders of the 'fifties, who will be remembered for her fearlessness and the run of successes she had on Jack Spurrier's horses, Tartine, Joyess and Icy Steel, some of them when returning to the fray two years after breaking her back in 1957; Tom Smith of Badminton, who passed on his skills to his two daughters, Caroline Nicholas and Kathy Turnell, and bred Mantinolas, the 1987 Grand Marnier winner; and Charlie Smith, who rode over 50 winners as an amateur, including Kitty Brook, the mare from the Vine who went up to Yorkshire and won the Grimthorpe Cup in 1954. Charlie was the elder brother of the Flat-race jockeys Eph and Doug Smith; and, said Doug, "He had the best hands of the lot."

Tailpiece from Tim Forster:
"If you haven't been to the Torrington Farmers', you haven't lived."

1989

*In which a great man is remembered, the men's and ladies'
championship races switch to new venues, the distance of the
Grimthorpe Cup is reduced again, Johnny Greenall wins his brother's
trophy for the first time, and John Bowles loses an Appeal.*

In view of the fact that he died in January, at the age of 77, I feel it is appropriate to begin this chapter with some recollections of the man most people with
long enough memories, myself included, would regard as the greatest of all
point-to-point riders, Sir Guy Cunard.

During his long and distinguished career as a race-rider, which began with a
loser when he was a schoolboy at Eton and ended with his retirement in 1968 after
another of those bad falls that, in later years, caused him to take painkillers whenever he was about to get up on a horse, 'The Galloping Major', as he became
known throughout Yorkshire, was the leading point-to-point rider on six occasions between 1949 and 1964, in the days before the *Daily Telegraph* came on the
scene with its cup for the men's title.

Sir Guy's total of 268 point-to-point winners had so far only been surpassed by
the legendary Willie Rooney in Ireland and David Turner in this country. He also
rode 61 winners under N.H. Rules, his successes in this sphere including a notable
double in 1948, when he won the four-mile National Hunt Chase at Cheltenham
on Bruno II and the Liverpool Foxhunters' over the full Grand National distance
on San Michele.

So successful was Guy as a point-to-point rider that he was a positive embarrassment to officialdom in the Yorkshire Area, where, in 1950, they introduced a
7lb. penalty for any rider who had ridden 15 winners under N.H. Rules. Guy was
about the only rider affected by this; but it didn't prevent him from riding 17 winners that season and, assuming his normal position as the area's leading rider, with
just two fewer winners than Bertie Hill had for the national title. The following
year, the Yorkshire Area had second thoughts and dropped their brilliant idea. This
saw Guy winning the national title again; and he maintained it for the next two
seasons, resuming it again in 1963 and 1964.

But it wasn't so much the number of his successes that made Guy so memorable, nor even the brilliance of his riding, and the ruthless treatment meted out

to any opponent attempting to come up on his inside. It was a combination of his utter dedication to the sport and a personality that made its mark on every individual that it touched. All this with a wonderfully dry sense of humour and a kind of inspired pessimism. When his good old horse Trianon broke his leg on the flat at the Goathland in 1953 he was writing to me in the following terms: "I have several times thought that when Trianon was finished, it would be time to stop... The banking account is about empty. So it looks about the end."

But it wasn't, of course. There were still such horses as Calypso Mio, Puddle Jumper, Young Rohan, and numerous others to come. I think it would be true to say that Guy loved horses rather more than he loved people. He was not exactly one for the social life. His memory is commemorated today with trophies at the Heythrop and Melton Hunt Club point-to-points and hunter chases named after him at Sedgefield and Wetherby; and at Huntingdon there is a race named after his favourite horse, Puddle Jumper.

It seems a pity, though, that they haven't as yet named one after him at Folkestone, to which he was a frequent visitor for the hunter-chase meeting; and where, on one occasion, when he opened the ancient cricket bag in which he kept his riding gear, a mouse jumped out.

There was a death in tragic circumstances at the East Essex at Marks Tey on April 1. Nineteen-year-old Sarah Sheppard, the daughter of Gurney and the stepdaughter of Josie, was killed instantly when Quick Vision, the horse she was riding in the ladies' open, came down two fences from home when up with the leaders and rolled on her. She had ridden three more winners during the season and won a hunt race at Horseheath on Quick Vision.

Sarah is now commemorated with a trophy presented annually to the leading young rider in the East Anglian Area "who, in the opinion of the Judges, would make the area's best ambassador for the sport."

For some years, the finals of men's and women's point-to-point championships had been held on a course where they were the only jump races at an otherwise all-Flat meeting. In 1989, however, the Land Rover men's final moved to Towcester and the RMC Group ladies' final to Warwick, both jump meetings.

It has to be said that the top point-to-pointers of the season were conspicuous absentees from the Land Rover final, which was won on firm ground in a field of nine by the horse who had won the Marie Curie novice championship at Melton in 1985, David Jeffries's 11-year-old Castle Andrea. Ridden this time by Tom Illsley, he was having his only success of the season. But he ran his race out well in beating two rather moderate performers in Blue Ravine and Potterway, to both of whom he was giving weight. The big disappointment was the second favourite, Charlie Sample's mount Tartevie. This 11-year-old from the Morpeth who was never in a challenging position and finished fifth, was a winner of five of his nine previous races, and his successes during the season had included the Heart Of All England at Hexham and a 4-mile hunter chase at the Audi evening fixture at Cheltenham, where he beat his stable companion Bentom Boy by a length.

The RMC Group ladies' final, run three days earlier on good to firm ground, attracted a field of seven and saw Jane Southcombe completing a hat-trick of wins on Ron Fear's home-bred Air Strike, an eight-year-old trained by his owner and hunted with the Weston & Banwell Harriers. Air Strike collected a notable scalp in drawing away from the front-running Sweet Diana, who was attempting to give him 121b. and went under by seven lengths.

Sweet Diana's only other defeat in her eight appearances under Jill Dawson was in her first appearance of the season at Cottenham, where she had a lead of ten lengths when she fell at the fourteenth; and her successes included three wins in ladies' opens at Garthorpe and an all-the-way win in a hunter chase at Southwell in heavy ground. Jill Dawson also won six races on Sweet Diana's stable companion Roscoe Boy, whose only defeat in his seven appearances was administered by Highgate Lady, who beat him by half a length in the ladies' open at the South Notts at a difference of 51b.

But the most prolific point-to-point winner of the season, and the collector of the Grand Marnier Trophy for his Cornish owner John Weldhen, was the seven-year-old For A Lark, a winner of ten ladies' opens, with Janine Mills up in the first of them and, after she was injured, the 25-year-old Mandy Turner riding him on the other nine occasions. It was the fourth time since its inception in 1970 that the trophy had gone to a horse from the West Country; and only three other horses as young as seven had won it, Boy Bumble in 1974 Little Fleur in 1978 and Sweet Diana in 1986.

It must, I think, be the first time that a point-to-point winner has been bred by an Arab Sheikh; and this one, as his name suggests, was bred for a lark by Sheikh Ali Abu Khamsin from a £3,000 mare. For A Lark is a horse with an international pedigree. By the American sire Imperial Fling out of Good Larker (by Some Hand), he traces back to the Swedish mare Tit Lark, whose sire, Hornbeam, had the same capacity for stamina plus the ability to act on firm ground. For A Lark acted on all types of going from firm, over which he accounted for Gerry Doyle, to holding, on which he beat the staying Dicky Blob.

A dual winner on the Flat as a three-year-old when trained by John Winter, and twice over hurdles as a four-year-old, For A Lark was bought for 1,300 guineas by John Weldhen at the Ascot Sales in June 1987; and he was winning his 13th race for him when he scored in the ladies' open at the Stevenstone on his last appearance of the season.

The nearest rival to For A Lark for the Grand Marnier Trophy was Bruce Andrews' East Anglian performer Noan Wood. This ten-year-old by Precipice Wood won eight ladies' opens (seven of them on the trot) under 21-year-old Paula Claydon, who also won a hunter chase at Fakenham on him when he was making his last appearance of the season.

The remarkable thing about Noan Wood was that four of his wins were achieved after he had broken a splint bone, which was later successfully operated on at the Equine Research Station at Newmarket. As late as April 22, Paula Claydon was sharing the lead for the *Sporting Life* Cup with Lucy Crow on a total of nine winners, while Noan Wood still held a lead of two over For A Lark for the Grand Marnier Trophy.

After that, however, there were no more wins in point-to-points for either Noan Wood or Paula Claydon. So For A Lark went on to make the Grand Marnier Trophy safe with four more wins; and the contest for the ladies' title developed into a match between Mandy Turner and Shropshire's Lucy Crow. Both riders were in action on the last day of the season at the Torrington Farmers, with Lucy Crow on a total of 15 winners and Mandy Turner on 14.

Mandy had four rides at Umberleigh and Lucy two. Neither of them managed to add to their scores. Mandy came nearest to doing so with two third places, on Lydacott Moon in the hunt race and Home Hill in the restricted open. But Lucy, though now in an impregnable position for the title, was probably the more disappointed. Saddle Lake, who had given her her 15th win in the 3.5 mile ladies' open at the Exmoor the previous week, found the course much too sharp for him, was always struggling to go the pace, and was pulled up two out in the ladies' open. Mandy didn't have a ride in the race.

Lucy Crow, who had celebrated her 25th birthday the day before she was presented with the *Sporting Life* Cup on November 17 at the national point-to-point dinner by a distinguished Judge (the legal kind), Sir Sanderson ("Sandy") Temple, who was also a point-to-point rider in his younger days, achieved her 15 wins on seven different horses, all but three of them owned by her father, Edward Crow. Her most prolific winner, however, was Mrs. Whiteway's eight-year-old Singing Seal, who was unbeaten in his four races.

Mike Felton was a comfortable winner of the *Daily Telegraph* Cup for the second time in three years, with 26 wins on 13 different horses, the eight from John Dufosee's yard netting him 19 wins, and the three trained by Henrietta Knight giving him five. His most prolific winner was Dufosee's charge Sutton Prince, on whom he won six races, five of them open events. The best novice he rode was another inmate of the Dufosee yard, Jock Cullen's eight-year-old grey Polar Glen, who gave him three wins on the trot. But when Polar Glen won the Audi Grand Prix de Chasse at Cheltenham in May he was ridden by Anthony Tory, who had just drawn level with Philip Fenton for the amateur riders' title with his 14th winner under Rules. although he was to lose out to Fenton in the end.

The runner-up for the *Daily Telegraph* Cup with 18 winners was John Llewellyn, who was riding his 200th point-to-point winner when he scored on Remember Dewy in a maiden race at the Brecon in the course of completing a four-timer, a feat also achieved by Steven Brookshaw at the South Shropshire and Charlie Sample at the Morpeth.

Joey Newton, Charlie Macmillan and Steven Brookshaw all rode their 100th point-to-point winner during the season; and Ron Treloggen's win on Brians Boy in the restricted open at the Tedworth gave him his 100th career winner, including 20 under Rules.

With the distance of the Grimthorpe Cup reduced to three miles and a furlong, and the race run on Easter Saturday, there were 12 runners on the soft ground at Whitwell-on-the-Hill, where racecards were sold out after the first race.

Nigel Tutty's mount Bally Way, a winner of open races at Witton Castle and Duncombe Park on his first two appearances of the season, and a runner-up in an open at Charm Park on his third, started favourite at 5-2, but neither he nor the second favourite, last year's winner Ingleby Star, could hold a candle to the eight-year-old gift horse Old Nick, who led from the thirteenth under Simon Whitaker and won by seven lengths from Bally Way, with Ingleby Star a length further behind in third.

Owned by Mr. & Mrs. Tom Bell and qualified by Whitaker with the Bedale & West of Yore, Old Nick was given to the Bells by the Wetherby trainer Jack Hanson after he had broken down during the 1987 season; and this was the horse's first success since winning three novice hurdles for Hanson in the 1985/86 season. Trained for the Bells by David Smith, he was to win another open race at the Bramham Moor on his next appearance and become a factor in hunter chases in later years.

On a blustery day at the Heythrop, with the ground becoming increasingly holding, 13 lined up for the second of the season's classic point-to-points, the 4-mile men's open for Lord Ashton of Hyde's Cup; but there was only one horse running on at the finish, Charlie Main's owner-ridden Lolly's Patch, a horse trained by Caroline Saunders in the Pytchley country.

Mike Felton's mount Fredwell was looking all over a winner three fences out. He was a long way ahead of Lolly's Patch on the downhill run to the last; but Lolly's Patch, an out and out stayer if ever there was one, was eating up the ground behind him; and with Fredwell dying on his feet, he swept past him to win by eight lengths. The favourite for the race, Okayso, another of the horses trained by Caroline Saunders, with three consecutive wins behind her, failed to get the trip and finished a toiling fourth.

Asked whether he had expected his nine-year-old Lolly's Patch to win such a race, Charlie Main said, "Not exactly, but I am convinced he knows where the finishing post is." This was the third successive win for Lolly's Patch; and he was to have another in his next race, the men's open at the Clifton-on-Teme, where he accounted for Able Sailor.

A competitive Dudley Cup, the third of the season's classics and, like the Heythrop race, in its third year of sponsorship by the *Sporting Life*, was contested on good going by 12 horses from as many different hunts; and it was won by a horse who started the previous season as a maiden and was winning his first open event, Peter Deal's Border Sun an 11-year-old by Sunyboy (out of a mare by Border Chief) completing a hat-trick of wins under Simon Sweeting, the elder son of his trainer in the Heythrop country, Chris Sweeting, who had Sunyboy at his Conduit Stud. Starting second favourite at 9-2 to Macnab's Quest, a winner of a hunter chase at Stratford and two open point-to-points, Border Sun was settled down in the rear until he reached the half-way mark and began to make swift progress. Reaching the pacemaking Norman Case just before the last fence, Border Sun ran on strongly to win by six lengths. Macnab's Quest, who found the fast pace too hot for him, finished fourth, half a length behind Carneades, on whom Giles Smyly had won an open race at the North Cotswold and the Old Harrovian & Old Etonian race at the Heythrop.

Bought from Bob Nicholas, his breeder in Somerset, Border Sun had now won six races, ridden in all of them by the 23-year-old Simon Sweeting, who was in his last year as a student at the Royal Agricultural College in Cirencester.

The three top-rated horses in Mackenzie & Selby's handicap, Call Collect at 12-0, Three Counties, and Mystic Music, both at 11-12, had all confined themselves to hunter chases; and between them, they wiped up three of the major ones, the

Cheltenham and Liverpool Foxhunters' and the *Horse and Hound* Cup at Stratford.

I wouldn't want to quarrel too much with these ratings. Except to echo this qualifying remark made in the famous annual: "All Scotland would claim Mystic Music for 1989's top hunter chaser." Indeed they would. And so would I. This ten-year-old mare from the Dumfriesshire, owned by Miss Helen Wilson, trained by her sister, Kate Anderson, and ridden in all her races by Kate's husband, Kevin, was in the winner's enclosure on six of her seven appearances; and in heavy ground at Haydock she beat Call Collect by 15 lengths. On the only occasion the mare failed to win she was unlucky to lose. She was still on the bit, and cantering over her rivals, when she fell two fences from home in her hunter chase at Newcastle. People in Scotland were saying that she was the best hunter chaser produced there since Earls Brig and Flying Ace. The latter was still running in 1989. but on the downgrade at the age of 13, though he was a winner of two hunter chases at Hexham.

Mystic Music's greatest triumph this season was in the *Horse and Hound* Cup at Stratford, where she romped home by 20 lengths from Sharp Jewel in a field of 16 which included, amongst other good winners, Certain Light, Contradeal, Stanwick Lad, Huntworth, Air Strike and Macnab's Quest.

Call Collect, in his four appearances, was a winner of a novice hunter chase at Wetherby before going on to win the Liverpool Foxhunters' in impressive style by 20 lengths from Ian McKie's mount Risk A Bet, a winner beforehand of a hunter chase at Nottingham. The horse who finished third at Aintree, half a length behind the runner-up, was the winner of the Cheltenham Foxhunters', Three Counties.

Bred at the Ardenode Stud in Co. Kildare, the eight-year-old Call Collect, a winner of two point-to-points in Ireland the previous season, was owned by Jim Clements, a timber merchant in Co. Down, who sent him to be trained in England by John Parkes at Malton. But the horse was still being ridden by his Irish rider, the 44-year-old Raymond Martin, who was training him when he won his point-to-points in Ireland.

It was a different story in the Cheltenham Foxhunters', even though the going was similarly heavy; and it was a case of third time lucky for Three Counties, who had been a runner-up in it twice. Katie Rimell always had the 12-year-old in a handy position and he had already mastered Certain Light when last year's winner unseated Paul Hacking with a blunder at the last.

This was Three Counties' second hunter-chase win in a season which saw him making three appearances. It was also the year that marked Mercy Rimell's retirement as a trainer.

It was good to see Jelupe fulfilling his promise on the hunter-chase scene and giving a boost to the Marie Curie Foundation novice championship in the process. Ridden again by his veteran owner, Robin Sandys-Clarke, the seven-year-old won both his point-to-points; and his three wins in hunter chases reached a triumphant climax when he beat Tartevie in the John Corbet Cup at Stratford; while his win in the men's open at the Melton Hunt Club fixture enabled his 46-year-old owner-rider to become the first recipient of one of Guy Cunard's earliest polo trophies, the King's Coronation Cup that was first presented at the Ranelagh Club in 1913 and won outright by Guy in later years. In 1989 this challenge trophy was awarded to the oldest winning rider at the Melton Hunt Club fixture. Sandys-Clarke was an appropriate first winner of it because he rode Guy's horse Bountiful Charles on a couple of occasions in 1970 and finished fourth on him in an amateur riders' hurdle at Wetherby.

The big disappointment of the season was Curaheen Boy, who failed to train on and gave an unaccountably poor showing in all four of his races, three of them hunter chases and one an open point-to-point at Lockinge. Clearly, all was not well with him.

It was also a comparatively disappointing season for Curaheen Boy's trainer, Henrietta Knight, in her last season before going public. Although she saddled 17 winners, including three in hunter chases. Dromin Joker finished lame at Larkhill after winning three more races. Mahon Bridge, another of her purchases from Ireland, broke down irretrievably on his only appearance. Gambir, a newcomer to the yard of whom high hopes were held, broke a blood vessel running in the same race at Larkhill as Dromin Joker.

She was, however, soon to get off the mark in her new role as a public trainer; and she had finished her five-year-long point-to-point career training over 100 winners.

Johnny Greenall, the leading rider in hunter chases, and first-time winner of his brother's trophy, had his seven successes in these races on six different horses at seven different venues. All his wins were on his own horses, four of them trained by Caroline Saunders and the other two by Arthur Stephenson, including the only horse on whom he won twice, Water Wagtail at Wolverhampton and Kelso.

With 28 winners in point-to-points and five in hunter chases, Caroline Saunders's Pytchley stable was the leading livery yard of the season; and it also did most to produce the leading novice rider of the season and winner of the Grand Marnier male novice rider's award, 21-year-old Andrew Sansome, who rode 14 winners, the highest number for a novice since Amanda Harwood's 14 in 1986.

Thirteen of Sansome's wins came on the three horses he rode for the Saunders's yard; and the most prolific, with five wins, was also a novice, nine-year-old Ballinaveen, owned by Caroline's 83-year-old grandmother, Mrs. Kathleen Saunders. Beaten only twice in his seven races, in one of them going under by a neck to the Pidgeon horse Scotch On The Rock (who went on to win a novice hunter chase at Cheltenham), Ballinaveen was the winner of the Marie Curie novice championship at the Melton Hunt Club.

Another of the Saunders winners, with Andrew Sansome up, was a horse prone to breaking blood vessels. The eight-year-old Golden Wings lost his maiden certificate in an open race at Cottenham, and his four wins included a dead-heat with Stanwick Lad in the men's open at the Oakley.

But the brightest star in the Saunders yard so far as the future was concerned was Richard Russell's owner-ridden Teaplanter, giving evidence of the shape of things to come when this massive six-year-old, standing over 17 hands high, lost his maiden certificate at the Pytchley.

George Cooper's Carl's Choice was the most prolific winner turned out in East

Anglia, with four wins in open point-to-points and two in hunter chases; and Cooper's four wins in point-to-points on him, and one further one on another of his horses, enabled him to receive the *Horse and Hound* Cup for the leading owner-trainer-rider, with not more than three horses in his yard, that was in its second year of presentation at the national point-to-point dinner. In its first year, this trophy had gone to a Yorkshire owner-rider, Clive Musgrave, with three wins on his Courageous Owl.

For the outstanding five-year-old of the season I would plump unhesitatingly for Mrs. Helena Johnson's Khattaf, who had joined Keith Cumings's Bishops Nympton yard the previous July from Jim Old's stable. Although placed on the Flat as a three-year-old, and fourth three times over hurdles, Khattaf was losing his maiden certificate when he won a ladies' open in heavy ground at the Mendip Farmers with Rosemary Vickery up on his first appearance in a point-to-point, scoring by some 40 lengths. With the same rider up, he won his next three ladies' races before undergoing his only defeat of the season, when he was beaten a length by For A Lark at Bratton Down. A son of Kris, Khattaf was out of a mare by Busted.

Capt. Cumings also produced one of the most exciting seven-year-olds of the season in John Keighley's And Theres More, who, after being pulled up on his first appearance in a point-to-point, won his remaining five races in tremendous style with Justin Farthing up, the last of them a men's open at Bratton Down. And Theres More was bought in the summer of 1988 out of Mouse Morris's yard in Ireland, but didn't lose his maiden certificate until Keith Cumings had him.

Another exciting seven-year-old was the Northumberland mare Dun Gay Lass, a winner, under Martin Claxton, of three point-to-points and a hunter chase at Kelso. Of the six-year-olds, there was no more impressive performer in point-to-points than Mrs. Cynthia Higgon's Sir Noddy, home-trained in Pembrokeshire and bred by Lady Boothby in Glamorgan. By Tom Noddy, a sire I confess never to have heard of, Sir Noddy was foaled by a Pinzan mare called Pinzarose, who was never raced and was used by Lady Boothby solely for breeding. At the end of the season, his first on a course, after winning three races on the trot under Tim Rooney, and blotting his copybook in two others, Sir Noddy was sold for a five-figure sum to go racing under Rules.

There were first winners this season for members of three well-known point-to-point families. Sixteen-year-old Gaye Harwood, the younger sister of Amanda and the second of Guy's three daughters, rode her first winner when scoring on her father's Star Of Screen (already a good winner for Amanda) in a ladies' open at Hackwood Park, and completed a double on Lawn Meet, another of her father's runners there. Guy was there to see her do it, and looked suitably chuffed as he helped lift half her own weight of eight stone onto the scales.

Michael Miller, the 17-year-old son of a famous father, rode his first winner when scoring on 'The Jolly Miller's' eight-year-old Levantage Lad in an adjacent hunts' race at Larkhill's United Services fixture in the sort of style which Richard might have said afterwards, but refrained from doing so, makes him a chip off the old block. Levantage Lad was a relation, on his dam's side, to Debonair Boy. It was a case of family beating family. The runner-up, Flaming Blaze, was ridden by

Michael Tory's son Anthony.

In the hunt race at the Suffolk, one of Joe Turner's granddaughters, Nicola Bothway, rode her first winner when scoring on her grandfather's As You Were at the expense of her uncle, David Turner, on another family horse, Bit Of A Dandy.

There was also a first success for another up-and-coming rider, 18-year-old Tim McCarthy, who rode his first winner with his fourth ride in a race, when scoring in an open race at Tweseldown on the staying Namoos, a horse owned and trained by his mother, Mrs. Christine McCarthy, in the Old Surrey & Burstow country. The young McCarthy had three more open-race wins on the eight-year-old Namoos this season, one of them in a 4-mile race at Tweseldown.

I can also record that Polly Curling, 24 years old at the time, had her first success as a trainer when winning the adjacent hunts' race at the Blackmore & Sparkford Vale on bookmaker Chris Smith's five-year-old Pastoral Pride. Smith was there taking bets on the race under his trade name of Dick Reynolds. He must have had a killing, because Pastoral Pride, his first winner, started at 33-1. What price a horse ridden by Polly Curling starting at that price these days?

The American rider Bruce Davidson, a dual Three-Day Event world champion, had his first ride in a point-to-point over here when he rode his own horse Dashing Fred, a six-year-old son of Deep Run trained for him by Henrietta Knight, in a division of the mixed open Coronation Cup race at the United Services meeting at Larkhill, and finished second to Alan Hill on Border Burg. Before the season was out, Davidson rode his first winner under Rules when getting Dashing Fred up on the line to beat James Tarry's mount True Bloom by a neck in a hunter chase at the Cheltenham fixture in May.

Mark Barlow's Military Two Step, a former inmate of Toby Balding's yard, was quite a flying machine in the South Midlands. Produced from Robert and Teresa Elwell's yard, this seven-year-old lost his maiden certificate at the Oakley with Ian McKie up, then won a restricted open with the same rider before progressing to ladies' opens and winning three of them from the front with Teresa Elwell up. He was the leading points scorer in the South Midlands, where Teresa was the leading lady rider.

In the North Western Area there was Pennyazena, a ten-year-old mare bred from Pennyalina, a winner of four point-to-points on the trot. Owned and trained by Steven Brookshaw's wife Zena, and admirably ridden by Stephanie Baxter, Pennyazena won all four of her point-to-points and ended her season winning the area championship at Bangor.

Point-to-point bookmakers are frequently accused of a reluctance to lay realistic prices and accept major bets. But there is a reverse side to this. At the Axe Vale Harriers in Devon, for instance, a memorable coup was landed when Katesville, a mare owned and trained by Lee Bowles in Wales and ridden by Tim Jones, was responsible for between £10,000 and £12,000 being taken out of the books after winning the men's open on her first appearance of the season. One bookmaker was said to have laid a bet of £7,500 to £300 about this eight-year-old.

As Lee Bowles was the son of John Bowles, who had been warned off for 20 years in 1980 for the part he played in a horse-ringing incident at Newton Abbot in 1978, all sorts of rumours were floating around after Katesville's win. But although it is true that the mare was showing great improvement on her form of the previous season, it appeared that she had been suffering from a virus that season. Moreover, she had shown pretty decent form in the past when she was in Gurney Sheppard's East Anglian yard; and she was, in fact, unbeaten in her four races in 1989 though she was to lose one of them on a technical disqualification connected with an error in the recording of her sire's name, which was eventually corrected from Crozier to Slippered.

John Bowles, incidentally, had been appearing on several point-to-point courses, despite being warned off, and already been fined for doing so by the Jockey Club. Presumably he was a believer in the maxim, 'You can't keep a good man down'.

Another 20-year warning-off took place in October. Chris Willett, one of the leading point-to-point riders in the South East, had been found guilty at Maidstone Crown Court of taking part in a 'ringing' operation in an Arab horserace and given a gaol sentence. The Jockey Club took the appropriate action.

An unusual coup was brought off at the Belvoir by William Dixon, the 39-year-old managing director of a printing firm in St. Albans. He had backed himself to win £2,000 by completing a course within five years on his horse Carry On Again, bought with the intention of giving him his first ride in a race; and he landed the wager at his third attempt, but not without some degree of difficulty. At his first attempt, at Horseheath, he fell off and broke his collar-bone. At his second, an open race (brave man!) at Cottenham, he had a refusal at the second last. But, at his third, in another open at the Belvoir, after a refusal at the fifth, and falling off on landing when he eventually persuaded his horse to jump the fence, he remounted to finish a distant last in the field of four. Nice one, William.

The new official Totemobile made its first appearance on a course at the Grafton point-to-point at Mollington on April 1, and it proved highly remunerative with takings of £6,333 on the meeting, plus £650 on the televised meetings at Newbury and Doncaster. The machine was operating with each way bets and dual forecasts, the one for the first division of the maiden race paying out an astonishing £72.70 for a place bet on the runner-up (considerably more than the dual forecast) and returning the 33-1 winner at odds of 61-1.

Four well-known performers made their final appearances this season. The first to do so was the 13-year-old Paddy's-Peril, who made a single appearance in a mixed open at Tweseldown on the first day of the season and got up near the line to score by half a length from Nearly Handy in the fastest time of the day. It was the fourth season running that Paddy's Peril had won first time out, But he paid a sad price for it, injuring his suspensory joint again, this time higher up. Since he started racing for John Deutsch and Tony Perry, Paddy's Peril had run in 25 races over the four seasons, won 14 of them and been placed in eight others, including two hunter chases; and only once was he out of the first four, when he unseated Deutsch in the 1988 Dudley Cup.

Carol Lee's Majetta Crescent made his farewell appearance at the age of 16 when finishing a disappointing last season eighth of 11 in the ladies' open at the Gelligaer Farmers in mid-May, by which time he had amassed 32 wins and been placed in a further 24 races and, in the same month, Grenville Richards's 15-year-old Fixed Price made his final appearance with a walk-over in the hunt race at the Talybont, bringing his grand total of wins in point-to-points up to 20. He was also the winner of a Land Rover men's final at Chepstow. The Talybont was one of the meetings enlivened by the presence of the warned-off John Bowles, who was seen in the sponsors' tent.

At the Bramham Moor in April it was the turn of Mick Easterby's 15-year-old Urser to make his farewell appearance with his third place in a ladies' open, after a win in a similar race at the Middleton. He was ridden on both occasions by Susan Mason (née Easterby). During a career in hunt racing which began in 1982 Urser ran in 58 races, winning 18 point-to-points and nine hunter chases (including the men's final at Chepstow twice) with seven different jockeys up on him.

This was also the year that Chris Glyn, who had recently inherited his father's title and become Lord Wolverton, retired as Secretary of the Point-to-point Secretaries' Association after a spell of 18 years; and to mark the occasion, a presentation was made to him in Portman Square by Capt. Ronnie Wallace, the Chairman of the Master of Foxhounds Association. Chris Glyn, of course, was also the man principally responsible for the foundation of the national point-to-point dinner.

Among those who died this year were Jack Bloom, E.J. ("Joss") Masters, Charlie Macmillan, Tim Molony and Bob Woolley.

Charlie Macmillan's death came at the age of 52 and was the result of a fall when out riding near his farm at Lockerbie on Jimmy Brig, the horse he had his 100th point-to-point win on at the Eglinton in March. The Northern Area point-to-point champion in 1977 and 1983, he also rode 50 winners under Rules, one of them Bright Beach, on whom he won the Cheltenham Foxhunters' of 1968. And he was the only rider other than Doreen Calder to win a race on Flying Ace.

Jack Bloom, the father of Michael, to whom he passed on his talents, died in February at the age off 77. A noted amateur rider in his day, he finished sixth in the Grand National of 1949 on Tonderman, a horse bought for £100 and described as "unrideable". On another occasion, in a point-to-point at Cottenham, he had the distinction of winning a race on a horse he was instructed by his owner not to win on, and on whom he had the good sense to invest £10. After he had given up race-riding, Jack Bloom became a successful trainer under N.H. Rules; and among the numerous winners he trained was Chambertin, the horse his son rode in the 1961 Cheltenham Gold Cup, though he was not a winner on that occasion.

E.J. ("Joss") Masters. who died in Ireland at the age of 85, was known during his days as a trainer of point-to-pointers in Kent as 'The Wizard of Tenterden'. And rightly so. He turned out winners with astonishing regularity, picking up many a future winner arriving off the train from Ireland. "Joss is waiting at the station" was a well-known saying in the South East. He was always a man with an eye for a horse.

The wheel-chair-bound Bob Woolley, who had been on a total of 99 winners at the time of his accident, lost his courageous fight for survival at the age of 50. Bob's riding style was once likened to that of "Scobie Breasley in a five-furlong sprint."

In December, the great professional Tim Molony died at his home near Melton

Mowbray at the age of 70. He will be remembered not only for his achievement in riding some 900 winners, and as a five-times champion jockey under N.H. Rules, but as the starter at the classy Melton Hunt Club point-to-point for a great many years, before giving way to George Slack in 1986.

One who continued the good fight, however, was the exceedingly popular Glamorgan bookmaker Gordon Langley, who bets under the name of Gordon Power. Gordon had been suffering badly from cancer of the bone marrow. But this didn't stop him from resuming operations as a bookmaker at point-to-points almost as soon as he had been released from hospital to walk about with the aid of sticks. He has since added the production of Vanity Pair prints to his activities.

Tailpiece and Punch-line:
Quote from James Delahooke in 1989 on how to treat the militants on the anti-hunting and coursing front: "It is impossible to have a reasoned argument with rent-a-mob and a good kicking seems to work better anyway." Reply from a letter-writer to the *Sporting Life*: "Queston: What's the difference between a Millwall yob and James Delahooke? Answer: Several hundred acres and a few grand a year."

1990

In which prize money is raised again, grooms are given the okay to ride, 2.5-mile races are introduced, the professionals have restrictions imposed on them, a dubious record is set, and former point-to-pointers make their mark at Cheltenham and Liverpool.

T his has to be the year that will be remembered most of all as the one in which both the Cheltenham Gold Cup and the Grand National were won by horses who started their racing careers in point-to-points. The biggest shock to the professional fraternity must surely have been the triumph at 100-1 of Norton's Coin in the Cheltenham Gold Cup. Now owned and trained by permit holder Sirrell Griffiths near Carmarthen, and ridden by Graham McCourt, Norton's Coin won in record time (6 mins. 30.9 secs.) on the good to firm ground and had behind him, beaten threequarters of a length and four lengths, Jenny Pitman's charge Toby Tobias and the odds-on favourite Desert Orchid. Nine days later, Norton's Coin was paraded with pride at the Llandeilo Farmers point-to-point at Resolven.

Mr. Frisk, trained by Kim Bailey and ridden by the amateur rider Marcus Armytage, was a game winner of the Grand National at odds of 16-1. Hanging on grimly from the elbow, he beat Durham Edition by three parts of a length in a field of 38; and it is interesting to note that the horse who finished fourth in this race, Bill Shand Kydd's Brown Windsor, was later to make the reverse journey to the point-to-point scene. Mr. Frisk, still being ridden by Marcus Armytage in his next and last race of the season, won the Whitbread Gold Cup at Sandown, where Durham Edition was again the runner-up to him, beaten rather more easily this time.

On the point-to-point front, where there was another modest increase in prize money, the ceiling for which went up to £250 for open races (including restricted opens) and £175 for other races, the most controversial change in the regulations was the decision to allow grooms working in livery yards, dealers' and private yards to ride in point-to-points. This was acting against the advice of the Horserace Advisory Council and the Amateur Riders' Association.

But the new regulation was welcomed in some quarters close to the sport. Percy Tory, the Chairman of the Point-to-Point Owners' Association, thought it a long time overdue. Col. Arthur Clerke-Brown in the South Midlands was particularly supportive, declaring that "It will stop cheating"; and Willy Bulwer-Long in East Anglia described the decision as "a fair one" and said that "It will suit the point-to-point world." No doubt he and The Colonel were influenced by the fact that assistant trainers were permitted to ride in point-to-points.

The decision to permit a limited number of maiden races for five, six and seven-year-olds to be run over 2½ miles worked very successfully in the earlier part of the season, when some of them attracted so many runners that they had to be run in two divisions. But not a great many hunts took advantage of the concession; and in the latter part of the season, when the going firmed up, there was a walk-over in such a race at Tweseldown and no more than two runners for the one held at Larkhill the following week.

Firm going, in fact, played havoc with the number of runners overall, reducing them from 13,836 in 1989 to 11,714 in 1990; and there was a record number of walk-overs, no fewer than 33, with as many as three at the Braes of Derwent and the Burton (where there were no more than seven active runners – which must surely have been an all-time low); while for the hunt race at the New Forest Buckhounds fixture at Larkhill in mid-March there were no declared runners at all.

The one good effect of the drought was that it drove more and more hunts to water their courses. Conspicuous example of successful watering were to be seen at the West Norfolk, the Fernie, Worcestershire, Melton Hunt Club, North Shropshire, Ledbury, the Pytchley and the Quorn. Also, it goes almost without saying, on Col. Clerke-Brown's course at Kingston Blount for the Vale of Aylesbury fixture in May.

One new regulation that had the unreserved support of the point-to-point fraternity, since it applied both to point-to-points and hunter chases, was the one stipulating that no horse running in any of these races must have won a steeplechase (other than one confined to amateur riders) during the current season, or the two preceding ones, carrying a penalty value of £6,500 or more. This went a long way towards ensuring that the Cheltenham and Liverpool Foxhunters' would be restored to their former status as championships for genuine hunters. Reverting to the old distance of four miles at Cheltenham and the full Grand National distance at Liverpool would, however, do even more.

While the four sponsors of a major point-to-point series with a final on a professional racecourse, Land Rover, the RMC Group, Audi (who raised the prize money for their Audi Grand Prix de Chasse at Cheltenham in May to £5,000) and *The Times*, all remained faithful, Grand Marnier underwent a temporary defection from the scene, leaving the *Daily Telegraph* to come up with a new trophy for the most prolific point-to-point winner of the season, and also taking over the awards for the leading novice riders of the season.

Call Collect and Mystic Music, the former a winner of three hunter chases, including the Cheltenham Foxhunters', and the latter also a winner of three, including the *Horse and Hound* Cup at Stratford, kept their positions at the head of Mackenzie & Selby's handicap, and on the same marks, 12-0 and 11-12; but Three Counties, who finished fourth on his two appearances in hunter chases as a 13-year-old, dropped down to equal fifth with the winner of the Liverpool

Foxhunters' on a mark of 11-5. The horse making the most substantial rise was Teaplanter, who rose from 9-10 to 11-7, taking third place in the handicap.

Teaplanter's advance was the result of his winning four of his five races with his owner up; and the fact, no doubt, that he would have remained unbeaten in his four hunter chases but for a fall at Nottingham two fences out when he was in process of trotting up. He had, however, yet to tackle a major hunter chase, although that day would come.

It was a bad season for accidents to riders, and two of them were fatal. Twenty-five-year-old Sarah Dench, who worked as a secretary in her father's caravan-site business at Seasalter, was killed instantly at the West Kent in April when his 16-year-old Tempestuous, who broke a blood vessel in his lung leading the field at the penultimate fence in the ladies' open, came down on top of her; and the veteran Hertfordshire owner-rider Tom Regis, who had reached the age of 50 before he rode his first winner in 1987, died in March from the injuries he received from a fall in the Fernie team-chasing event in Leicestershire. Just nine days beforehand, Tom had won the hunt race at the Oakley for the third time on his 13-year-old Can't Catch Me, the horse he had his first win on.

Simon Andrews broke some ribs and punctured a lung in a fall at Cottenham on March 3; but it didn't keep him out of action for more than a fortnight. He came back with a win on Newnham in a men's open at Horseheath, and was up on him again when finishing fourth in the Liverpool Foxhunters'.

Tim Rooney, Nigel Bloom, Paul Hamer, John Llewellyn and Philip Scholfield all had their season shortened by injury; and David Turner was out for the entire season, having broken his pelvis the previous October. Rooney was on a seasonal total of 17 winners and well in the running for the men's title when he broke two bones in his ankle and sustained a spiral fracture on the outside of his leg with a fall on Gunmetal Boy at the Ystrad on May 5. This was to drop him into fifth place in the list of leading male riders, one behind John Llewellyn and Tim Jones.

The Yorkshire rider Robert Strickland, who had a very bad fall at the Old Raby Hunt Club fixture at Witton Castle in early February and was in intensive care for a considerable time, made a marvellous recovery from being at death's door; and the next news of him from his fellow rider Nigel Tutty was that "he is as fit as a fiddle." Five years after his accident he was appointed Clerk of the Course at the Hurworth point-to-point.

The winner of the *Daily Telegraph* Cup, for the second year running and the third time in four years, was Mike Felton. He was assisted by three walk-overs, two of them at the same meeting, the Tedworth. But it didn't make any difference because he was well clear of his nearest rival with his 27 winners. Philip Scholfield, the runner-up to him, rode 20.

Felton's 27 wins were gained on 14 different horses, the most prolific of them being one of the 35 winners trained by John Dufosee in his best season ever, the nine-year-old Mischievous Monk, a winner of five of his seven races.

Dufosee was the leading livery yard proprietor with his 35 winners in point-to-points and two in hunter chases. Next to him came Richard Barber with 27 wins, nine of them contributed by the partnership of Julie Barrow and Gerry Doyle in ladies' opens. Then came Dick Baimbridge with 24 winners and Caroline Saunders with 20 winners in point-to-points and five in hunter chases.

Philip Scholfield's most prolific winners, each with three successes, were Golden Link and Cordiglia. The latter, a six-year-old mare he trained himself in the Mid Devon country, started the season as a maiden and remained unbeaten.

Scholfield was one of two riders to achieve their 100th winner in point-to-points. The other was Alison Dare, who reached her century on Dick Baimbridge's charge Russki at the Harkaway Club fixture in mid-March. And for Dorset's Robert Alner there was a 150th win in point-to-points when he scored on Harry Wellstead's Sheer Water in a restricted open at the West Somerset Vale on April 14.

Alner, who was training horses under permit, saddled 18 winners in point-to-points and rode 12 of them himself. He also won two hunter chases on his wife's Ponteus Pilot and rode a winner in Ireland on a Sunday.

Alison Dare, as usual very well mounted on the horses trained by Dick Baimbridge in the Berkeley country, was the winner of the *Sporting Life* Cup for the third time in five years with her 20 wins, six of them on the unbeaten Mendip Express, who now had nine consecutive wins to his credit; and behind Alison came a future ladies' champion, 25-year-old Polly Curling, tying with Lincolnshire's Jill Dawson for the runner-up's position with 14 winners. It seemed at first that the Somerset-based rider would be a runner-up in her own right, because a win at the Torrington Farmers on Gerald Probert's White Supreme gave her her 15th win of the season; but she lost one of her earlier ones on another of Probert's horses when Queen Beyan was disqualified in Portman Square as the result of a prohibited substance being found in her urine after the mare had recorded the first of her four wins in a row at the East Devon.

The *Daily Telegraph* novice riders of the season were two 19-year-olds, Toby Balding's assistant Hamish Rowsell and East Anglia's Nicola Bothway. The former rode six winners riding four different horses and Nicola nine. Eight of Nicola's wins in point-to-points were on horses owned and trained by her grandfather; and these included As You Were, who wound up a highly successful season for horse and rider beating Sweet Diana in the RMC Group ladies' final at Warwick.

This was Sweet Diana's second defeat of the season in her seven appearances. Her first was in the ladies' open at the Quorn, where she was well beaten by George Vergette's ten-year-old Perroquet and came in lame. Not that this was in any sense a disgrace. The grey son of Precipice Wood was winning his fifth race in a row under Helen Vergette, and these had included three in hunter chases.

Perroquet's only defeat in his six appearances was brought about by another of the Dawson horses, Roscoe Boy, who made mincemeat of him in the ladies' championship at the last of the Garthorpe fixtures and was unbeaten in his eight appearances.

Cliff Dawson also produced a highly promising newcomer in Roscoe Boy's seven-year-old full brother Herman Blake, who lost his maiden certificate in the club members' restricted at the same meeting. The two horses, by Roscoe Blake, were bred at Bangor-on-Dee by Gressley Humphreys, who also bred their dam, Hayburnwyke, later bought from him by Cliff Dawson for breeding purposes.

The winner of the new *Daily Telegraph* Trophy for the most prolific winner of the season was a horse from Wales, Timber Tool. A winner of 11 of his 12 races, all but one of them open events, and carrying a 71b. penalty in most of them, this eight-year-old son of Wolver Hollow out of a mare by Welsh Pageant had been transformed almost beyond recognition since being purchased by his Pembrokeshire owner, Bill Evans, from Mrs. Gill Jones in the Ledbury country after finishing third in an open race at the Golden Valley in March 1989. Trained by Bill's wife, Mary, he began his career from his new yard winning three of his five remaining races that season, all of them open events.

In 1990, when the only horse to beat him was Katesville, the mare he had accounted for earlier in the season at the Brecon, Timber Tool won his first seven races with Tim Rooney up, had a walk-over in another with Paul Hamer and won his last three, including two on his visits to the West Country, with John Llewellyn up.

When Bill Evans was presented with his trophy at the national point-to-point dinner, where he thanked Gill Jones publicly for selling him Timber Tool, he remarked: "What with Norton's Coin winning the Cheltenham Gold Cup, it just goes to prove it is not only sheep that we can produce in Wales!"

John Llewellyn, whose 18 wins in point-to-points this season had given him a grand total of 230 winners in these races, and moved him up above Frank Ryall and Grant Cann in the list of all-time greats, was now occupying third place in the table behind David Turner with his 343 and Guy Cunard with his 268. But all three of them, of course, were way behind Ireland's adopted Welshman, Willie Rooney, who rode his first winner in Wales in 1926 at the age of 13 and some in England before moving in the 1930's to Ireland, where he rode 367 winners, bringing his grand total of winners up to 401 by the time he was compelled to retire as the result of a stroke, having ridden in races until he reached the age of 61. He died in 1988.

The first of the season's point-to-point classics this year was the four-mile race for Lord Ashton of Hyde's Cup at the Heythrop. Run on firm ground, it produced a field of seven out of an entry 29, only three of which completed the course. The favourite, Tim Jones's mount Knock On The Head, who had dead-heated over four miles with Katesville at the Pentyrch last season, was not among them. He never showed with a chance and was eventually pulled up.

With just over a mile to go, Polar Glen, Ballyoran Star (the mount of John Deutsch) and Telf (who had had a walk-over in the four-mile race at the Tickham on his previous appearance under Paul Hacking), were out on their own. Telf was a close third when he made a mistake at the 16th and unseated Hacking. So it was left to Polar Glen and Ballyoran Star to fight it out. But it was a one-sided match. Mike Felton was looking round on Polar Glen approaching the last. This was Polar Glen's first win of the season. But Jock Cullen's eight-year-old was to win another open race at Badbury Rings on his next appearance and end his season winning a hunter chase at Fontwell, where he was a first winner under Rules for 20-year-old Jason Dufosee, the son of his trainer.

Cullen had bought Polar Glen out of Ron Hodges' yard for his daughter Belinda (the future Mrs. Anthony Tory) to ride in point-to-points; but she was unable to do so, having broken her ankle badly riding another horse at Larkhill in 1988 and not ridden since then.

Runners were in even shorter supply for the second of the season's classics, the Grimthorpe Cup at the Middleton, where the going was good and the race was still being run over a distance well short of four miles. Four faced the starter here; and the easy winner, making all the running, was Certain Rhythm, a seven-year-old from the Bramham Moor ridden by his trainer, Mike Sowersby. Certain Rhythm ran in only two races and won both of them.

The third of the classics, the Lady Dudley Cup at the Worcestershire, run on well-watered ground at Chaddesley Corbett, drew a high-class field of nine runners and produced a dramatic skirmish which ended with the success of a 20-1 outsider in Turn Mill, who was tailed off in last year's race.

Well handled by the 23-year-old Michael Hammond, an antiques dealer in Chipping Campden, Turn Mill came from behind with an impressive turn of foot to beat the dual winner Whitsunday by a head, with Katesville, who had been alternating with Whitsunday for the lead, a neck away in third. Last year's winner Border Sun found the pace too hot for him and finished fifth.

This was Turn Mill's one and only win of the season in her four appearances, but she had been a runner-up in a hunter chase at Bangor. Bred in Worcestershire by Mrs. Pat Tollit, this nine-year-old mare was owned by Mrs. Anne Potter in the Teme Valley country and trained by her daughter, Annette, who had been working for Tommy Smith, the leading trainer in Sydney, and used her return air fare to Australia to buy the horse from Mrs. Tollit as an unbroken three-year-old.

The 11-year-old Blue Ravine, trained by Ridley Lamb in Northumberland, greatly improved on his past performances with an excellent season under Simon Bell which saw him winning two point-to-points and three good hunter chases in a row, starting with the Heart Of All England at Hexham, continuing with the Land Rover men's final at Towcester and ending with the John Corbet Cup at Stratford.

The brave Simon Bell was a sufferer from cystic fibrosis; and after Blue Ravine had convincingly accounted for Dalton Dandy and Polar Glen at Towcester, he made what might be considered the understatement of the season. "It only hurts," he said, "when I injure my ribs and have to cough." Bell was also riding Blue Ravine when the horse finished sixth of 28 in the Scottish Grand National at Ayr. Blue Ravine's starting price for this race was 500-1.

Barrister Robin Mathew's 11-year-old Park Shade was a lucky winner of the Audi Grand Prix de Chasse at Cheltenham, where he started at 14-1 in a field of ten. Beech Grove, the favourite, with Mike Felton up, was looking an assured winner when he came down four fences out after taking up the running from the pacemaking Ascertalmoor; and, with Master Hardy unseating his rider at the same fence when in third place, Park Shade was left in complete charge.

A first winner under Rules for his rider, 22-year-old Henry Daly, who had been acting as head lad for Kim Bailey when Mr. Frisk followed his win in the Grand National with a success in the Whitbread Gold Cup, Park Shade had his only other success during the season in his qualifying race at the North Cotswold.

Kim Bailey, who was present at Cheltenham to see Park Shade win, said of the horse's rider, "He's had a lot of responsibility feeding Mr. Frisk and and the others in the absence of my injured head lad, and he's done a bloody good job."

The Times championship at Towcester was also won by a horse whose only other win during the season was in his qualifying race at a point-to-point, eight-year-old Eastern Chant, the winner of the restricted open at the North Staffordshire. Nicely ridden by 21-year-old Chris Stockton, a Leeds University student, Eastern Chant was a comfortable winner at Towcester in a field of ten. Bred by his owner-trainer, Isobel Dady, on her farm in Warwickshire, Eastern Chant had lost his maiden certificate in 1988 but was absent from a course throughout 1989.

Call Collect's win in the Cheltenham Foxhunters', in which he convincingly mastered Old Nick on the run-in and had West Tip, Three Counties and Whitsunday further behind him, was at least half a success for Ireland, the country of his birth. While he was trained by John Parkes in England, his owner, Jim Clements, hailed from Co. Down; and his rider, Raymond Martin, was an Irishman born and bred. Parkes said, "He gave Call Collect a beautiful ride without having to over-exert him." This was the 11-year-old's third hunter-chase win in a row, his two earlier ones being at Ayr and Kelso with Charlie Farrell up; and he was seventh to Mr. Frisk in the Grand National, his last race of the season.

Lean Ar Aghaidh, the 13-year-old winner of the Liverpool Foxhunters', was also bred in Ireland, by Patrick Cashman, and trained in England, by Stan Mellor; and he was ridden by a 41-year-old New Zealand dairy farmer, Denis Gray, who had ridden in three Grand Nationals and was riding his seventh winner under Rules this season. He had had an earlier success on Lean Ar Aghaidh in a hunter chase at Stratford.

Owned by Mrs. Georgina Tulloch and hunted with the V.W.H., Lean Ar Aghaidh was a smooth winner at Aintree. He wasn't headed after taking up the running approaching Becher's and finished with plenty in hand of the runner-up, Crammer, a winner of his only other hunter chase. The seven horses who came down in a melée at the seventh included Border Sun.

Off the course with a leg injury all the previous season, Lean Ar Aghaidh had finished third to Maori Venture in the 1987 Grand National when ridden by Guy Landau and won the Whitbread Gold Cup at Sandown the same season under him. In 1988 he ran in the Grand National again and finished ninth.

Mystic Music's second win in the *Horse and Hound* Cup at Stratford under Kevin Anderson was accomplished in the same easy manner as her first. Taking up the running three fences out, the Dumfriesshire mare quickly drew clear to win by 25 lengths from Edenspring, a winner of three hunter chases under Tommy Jackson, the last of them the Audi Champion hunter chase at the Cheltenham evening fixture, where he beat Polar Glen.

Doubtless Mystic Music would have won all four of her races but for slipping up on a bend on her only appearance in a point-to-point in the men's open at the Jedforest.

With Flying Ace making only two appearances as a 14-year-old, winning the ladies' open at the Haydon and finishing fourth to Mystic Music in a hunter chase at Edinburgh, the outstanding ladies' horse in the Northern Area was the Jedforest 14-year-old Mossy Moore, a winner of seven ladies' opens in nine appearances for his owner-rider, 19-year-old Sandra Forster.

Sandra Forster, Ken Oliver's granddaughter, trained Mossy Moore herself, and her seven wins on him enabled her to collect the *Horse and Hound* Cup for the leading owner riding and training her own horses. She was also the runner-up to Nicola Bothway for the *Daily Telegraph* female novice rider's award.

On the only occasions that Mossy Moore was beaten, he fell at the last when trying to get on terms with Roscoe Boy at Witton Castle on his first appearance of the season, and when he was the runner-up to the Berwickshire mare Willow Wood at the Lanarkshire & Renfrewshire. But the latter can probably be described as a freak defeat as the winner was put firmly in her place by Mossy Moore later in the season.

Two other horses to win seven races during the season were Stanwick Lad and Mourne Warrior, a seven-year-old from the North Shropshire. All seven of Stanwick Lad's wins were in open events with John Sharp up, six of them consecutive ones, including one well out of his country at the Badsworth. The only horses to beat Stanwick Lad after his slow start to the season in an open event over the sharp course at Higham were Beech Grove, who did so at Cottenham when Stanwick Lad finished lame, and Mrs. "Twink" Thompson's Gentle Approach, one of the stars of Caroline Saunders' yard who won five open races in a row under Andrew Sansome, four of them over his favourite course at Garthorpe, where he was receiving 71b. from Stanwick Lad in the first of them and beat him by a long-looking half length.

Mourne Warrior, a half-brother to Polar Glen, won his seven races with three different riders up, losing his maiden certificate at the Meynell & South Staffs under Simon Crank and then winning three races with Alastair Crow up and three with his sister Lucy riding him. The first horse owned by Guy Matthews, a Shrewsbury builder, Mourne Warrior, the overall winner in the PPOA young horse awards, was trained in Shropshire by Alastair and Lucy's mother, the indomitable Sheila Crow.

In the Marie Curie novice championship, however, his last race of the season, with Lucy Crow putting up a deal of dead weight on him, Mourne Warrior was not at his best and was last but one of eight finishers in a good field of nine.

The first three past the post in this race, Scaliscro, the five-year-old Bertie Boy (who was to fulfil his promise for Willy Bulwer-Long under Rules in later years) and James Tarry's mount Saybright (who was to become one of the best open-race horses in the South Midlands), had won nine races between them before they came to Garthorpe, Saybright the most prolific of them with five successes.

In a tight finish, Scaliscro held off a strong challenge from Bertie Boy to beat him by a length. Saybright, who finished 20 lengths behind the runner-up, had been in close contention until a bad mistake at the downhill third last took all the stuffing out of him.

Not only was Scaliscro a novice, but so was his rider, 26-year-old Charles Wadland, who had the first of his four wins in a row on him in a maiden race at the PPOA fixture at Ashorne in April. Bred in Yorkshire by David Barron at Thirsk, the nine-year-old Scaliscro was owned by Jock Mackenzie, a company director from the Isle of Lewis in Scotland who worked in London, and trained for him by Dennis Green in Warwickshire, where he was hunted.

Although the *Racing Post* men's open at this Garthorpe fixture attracted only four runners, the finish was fought out by two very useful horses, with Gentle Approach hanging on grimly to hold off Bernard Pike's Blackmore & Sparkford Vale mare Elver Season by a diminishing half length.

The seven-year-old Elver Season, who had lost her maiden certificate the previous season and was trained and ridden by Robert Alner, was undergoing her only defeat in 1990, during which she won five races in succession, four of them open events. She was of course, on her way to the hunter chase scene.

And one who had just reached this position was Mrs. Hilda Clarke's eight-year-old Mount Argus from the North Shropshire, who was unbeaten in his three open point-to-points and crowned his season with a win in a hunter chase at Uttoxeter in the hands of his trainer, Steven Brookshaw.

In the same yard as Mount Argus, and indeed now owned by Steven Brookshaw himself, was the veteran Kintbury; and this 15-year-old son of Ballymoss was adding to his ten wins over hurdles when the completion of a hat-trick of wins in ladies' opens under Karen Bryan gave him his 13th win in open point-to-points and a career total of 24 wins (including one in a two-mile chase).

One of the most intriguing races of the season was the four-mile men's open run on firm ground at the Exmoor, for which the six runners came from a wide vartety of areas and the only West Country runner was Bishopric, a winner this season of three races under his veteran owner, George Turner. Another was Nenni, a proven stayer who liked firm ground and had finished third to Tartevie over four miles at Cheltenham in his previous race. Also in the field were Newnham, the 1988 winner of the Liverpool Foxhunters', Foolish Hero, Political Whip and Scaliscro.

And it was Nenni, starting favourite under his usual pilot, Richard Ford, who emerged as the winner. But not without a battle. He was given a hard race by Scaliscro, who made most of the running under Charles Wadland and was looking all over a winner as he rounded the last marker in a lead of three lengths. Richard Ford, however, had timed his late run to perfection, and he got Nenni up on the long uphill run-in to score by half a length, with Bishopric 12 lengths away in third followed by Political Whip, the 1988 winner. Foolish Hero was fifth. Newnham, another previous winner of the race, in 1987, was not very interested this time and Simon Andrews pulled him up after the nineteenth. The time of 8 mins. 2 secs. equalled the record time set up by David Turner on Swarm in the 1984 race.

A French-bred 11-year-old hunted with the Vale of Lune, Nenni was owned by Mrs. Phyl Robertson and trained by her daughter, Sarah, in her livery yard at Carnforth, near Lancaster. Nenni was winning his third race of the season. Richard Ford, a horseman of some style, was attached to Thomas Tate's yard at Wetherby, and his 15 winners included six under Rules.

If there were to be a prize for the toughest performer of the season, I think I would have awarded it to Major Matthew Sample's Morpeth-hunted 12-year-old Tartevie, one of the horses trained by Geoff Coatsworth. Besides winning over four miles at Cheltenham with his owner-up, Tartevie stuck his neck out with the utmost gameness to beat Whistling Thorn by a neck in the four-mile men's open at the Percy. The previous season, when he won five races, Tartevie had won the same two four-milers when ridden by Charlie Sample. They don't come any tougher than that, even in the Border Country.

In East Anglia, the nine-year-old Carl's Choice was steadily adding to his score, winning all four of his point-to-points, one of them a ladies' open at Cottenham, where, in the first race he had ever had a lady rider on top, he was a first winner for 26-year-old Fiona Clarke. His other three wins in men's opens, two of them in Sussex, were all with his owner up; and now with a grand total of 15 (including two in hunter chases), he was well on the way to surpassing the 23 wins achieved by his illustriaus predecessor, General Confusion – something that he was to accomplish two years later.

Another prolific scorer, John Weldhen's Four Burrow seven-year-old For A Lark, was unbeaten in his five ladies' opens in the West Country with Mandy Hand up; while in Surrey, El Padre, the horse that Ann Blaker had bought, with a contingency, for £1,500 from Joe Turner, was managing to add to his score at the age of 18 with his owner winning the ladies' open at the Old Surrey & Burstow on him. By this time, Mrs. Blaker had ridden El Padre in over 100 races and won 14 on him. It was, however, to be his last season as a winner; and two years later he was put down at the age of 20, with a grand total of 17 wins behind him, including three for Joe Turner under Rules.

If ever a rider was entitled to be described as a leading course specialist it must surely be the Tweseldown maestro Philip Scouller, who rode his 50th winner over this Hampshire course when scoring in a division of the adjacent hunts' race at the Army fixture there on his French-bred Frere Hogan on February 24, the day after this working owner of a family engineering business in Reading reached his 44th birthday. It seems a pity that there hasn't been a trophy of some sort to commemorate the achievement. Especially as Scouller was one of the leading lights in preserving this much-used course when it was in danger of falling into disuse.

It happens so rarely that a horse hunted in England during the current season goes over the water to contest a race in Ireland that I feel it is worth recording the feat of Rising Sovereign, the 12-year-old from the Southdown & Eridge, who not only did this but gave his rider, 29-year-old Irish-born Matt Jones, his first winner. The achievement was made possible by the flexibility of the Irish Steeplechase Committee in permitting the presence of the horse in the special international open race at the two-day South Union Foxhounds point-to-point at Kinsale in May. Rising Sovereign who was unable to win any of his point-to-points in England, though he was a runner-up twice, battled on well to score in Ireland by half a length from Dancing Guy, a winner of two open races there.

Of the five-year-olds, two who distinguished themselves by winning maiden races at the same meeting and revealing the promise that was to be fulfilled later on, were Wall Game and Sheer Jest, both of whom won easing up at the Oakley under Alan Hill.

The American-bred Wall Game, a winner of two of his three races in his first season, was bought by James Delahooke in the United States as a Christmas present for his wife, Angela. Sheer Jest, whose time at the Oakley was seven seconds faster, was one of the horses owned by Mrs. Judy Wilson and trained by the skilful Bill Warner in the Pytchley country.

It was this season that the warned-off John Bowles, who had failed in his attempt to clear his name and was shortly to depart for Ireland, decided that enough was enough and ceased his unauthorised appearances on point-to-point courses. "I am fed up," he was quoted as saying, "with not being able to share my son Lee's success, and not being able to take part in the sport I love."

Lee Bowles, meanwhile, was doing very well, training 11 point-to-point winners during the season, among them Katesville and The Screamin Demon, who won eight races between them. Katesville won five open events, beating Timber Tool in one of them; and The Screamin Demon, a seven-year-old by Le Moss, took the PPOA young horse award in the South Wales Area with his three wins and one second place in his five appearances.

Dick Baimbridge became the first livery-yard proprietor to receive the inscribed salver for special services to point-to-pointing at the national point-to-point dinner at The Belfry, where Alison Dare was presented with the *Sporting Life* Cup by the paper's Editor, Mike Gallemore, Mike Felton received the *Daily Telegraph* Cup from Max Hastings, Johnny Greenall, with his six wins in hunter chases, collected his brother's trophy for the second year running; and Michael Clayton, the Editor of *Horse and Hound*, was there to present the magazine's cup for the leading small owner-trainer-rider to Sandra Forster.

In July, the amateur rider Johnny Wrathall was tragically killed in a motor accident at the age of 37. It happened in France when he and his co-driver (who was in the driving seat on this occasion and was also killed) were part of a convoy in an articulated lorry carrying stage equipment from London to Spain for the pop singer Madonna. At the time of his death, Wrathall was an assistant to Henrietta Knight, who had set up as a professional trainer the previous year.

At various stages of his career, during which he rode 42 winners in point-to-points and 17 in hunter chases, Wrathall worked for Dick Saunders, the Costello family in Ireland and the noted German show-jumping rider Paul Schockemöhle. Saunders said of him: "He was in the top flight of point-to-point riders, a very talented and accomplished horseman, whether it was producing showjumpers, hunters or racehorses"; and Henrietta Knight said, "He had all the right qualities and is impossible to replace." Johnny Wrathall had been the best man at the wedding of Alan and Trelawney Hill, and he was to have one of Alan's horses, My Best Man, named after him.

Permit holder Colin Nash died in June at the age of 64. Joint Master of the Old Berks from 1963 to 1986, he trained Jim Reade's great hunter chaser Baulking Green in his point-to-pointing days and was the man responsible for sending the horse into training with Tim Forster, whose first winner under Rules he was when winning the Clive Hunters' Chase at Cheltenham in April 1962.

Also this year there occurred the deaths of two people closely associated with another great hunter chaser, The Callant. Jimmy Scott-Aiton, the horse's rider, twice a winner of the Cheltenham Foxhunters' on him when the race was run over four miles in 1956 and 1957, died in March at the age of 66. He was a senior steward at Kelso at the time. And Charlie Scott, the horse's owner, and a great man to hounds with the Jedforest for over 70 years, died in July.

Tailpiece:

In December the Labour Party revealed its intention to outlaw hunting in the New Year. Fortunately, it never came to fruition. But it was an indication of the possible shape of things to come.

1991

*In which a major sponsor drops out, a new men's champion emerges,
another Yorkshire horse wins the Dudley Cup, and a rank outsider
wins the Liverpool Foxhunters'.*

A lthough eight of the 205 fixtures scheduled for this season were victims of
the weather, there was still an increase in the number of runners, which
went up from 11,644 in 1990 to 13,021; and one of the 197 meetings that
took place was an entirely new one, the Piccadilly Hunt Club fixture over portable
fences on Hereford Racecourse, which shared its date on the last day of the season
with the Torrington Farmers in the West Country.

The Piccadilly Hunt Club itself was formed in February 1949, when 43 hunting people from the counties of Worcestershire, Herefordshire and Gloucestershire
rode along Piccadilly to the House of Commons to protest against what proved to
be an unsuccessful anti-hunting bill.

The Jockey Club had modified its regulations to give its blessings to the Club's
first point-to-point on account of its being held with the specific intention of providing financial assistance to Andrew James, the 33-year-old Abergavenny farrier
whose fall in a maiden point-to-point at the Ludlow point-to-point in April had
resulted in a fractured spine and subsequent confinement to a wheel-chair.

The Hereford fixture was an immense success, both as regards the quality of
the racing and the financial assistance that came to Andrew through the Injured
Jockeys Fund, for which a sum of £23,747.05 was raised, £12,500 of it coming
from customers paying at the turnstiles.

Another well-known rider seriously injured during the season was Chris
Cundall, the Yorkshire veterinary surgeon who used to ride for Guy Cunard, and
had a good horse of his own in Ellerby Sarah. He also had a very bad fall in April,
in the restricted open at the Bedale & West of Yore, riding a horse who slipped up
on the flat, leaving him with a cerebral oedema, a broken arm and paralysis of the
cranial nerve, and causing him to spend 51 weeks in hospital. But it didn't end his
racing career. Two years later he was back with a winner at the Derwent, after
building cross-country courses as part of his therapy.

The most regrettable loss on the sponsorship front came from the decision of

Audi to withdraw their adjacent hunts' series which had culminated in the Audi Grand Prix de Chasse at the splendid evening fixture at Cheltenham in May. The fixture itself, however, still went on under other auspices; and, with one of the races divided, there were now seven races on the card.

The emergence of the 28-year-old Somerset rider Justin Farthing as the men's champion was a triumph for the third generation of a well-known point-to-pointing family. His father, John, and his grandfather, Tom, were highly proficient point-to-point riders in their day; and Justin, a rider who was always struggling with weight problems, was still using the well-worn saddle cloth that bore their signatures.

Justin's 26 wins in point-to-points were mostly on horses trained by Richard Barber, for whom he completed a four-timer at the Cattistock where one of his winners, six-year-old Rushing Wild, was a future winner of the Cheltenham Foxhunters'; and in winning the men's open race here he put up a faster time than another future winner of the Cheltenham race, seven-year-old Double Silk, took to win the adjacent hunts' race. Farthing won four races on Rushing Wild, who started the season as a maiden and was appearing on a course for the first time when he was beaten in a division of the maiden race at the Mendip Farmers fixture at Nedge in February by Double Silk.

Philip Scholfield, the runner-up to Justin Farthing for the *Daily Telegraph* Cup, rode 23 point-to-point winners (one of them on the later disqualification of the horse who passed the post first); and behind him came Robert Alner with 18 and John Llewellyn and Tim McCarthy with 16 apiece.

Mike Felton was way down the list with nine winners. No doubt he was busy putting the finishing touches to the comprehensive book on Point-to-Pointing that he had written in collaboration with Terence Brady. A *must* for all point-to-point enthusiasts, whether as participants or spectators, it was published this year by Pelham Books.

The best horses Scholfield rode were Philip Gough's seven-year-old East Cornwall mare Ballyeden and Mrs. Janita Scott's nine-year-old mare Confused Express from the South Devon. Ballyeden, trained by Ben Messer-Bennetts, was the winner of the first-ever national mares' championship, inaugurated by the PPOA and sponsored by *Horse and Hound*, which had also taken on the sponsorship of the Association's young horse awards. With her four wins and three second places in seven appearances, Ballyeden collected 58 points for this championship as against the 50 of the reserve champion Jonathan Sprake's owner-ridden Royal Buskins, whose three wins in open events included the Tedworth Hunt's four-mile gold cup race. In her other four appearances, Royal Buskins was a runner-up.

Confused Express, a noted stayer, won three races on the trot, the last of them an open event. But she was a faller in the four-mile men's open at the Dartmoor, where she started an evens favourite. Whether or not she would have won this race but for her fall must remain a matter of opinion. But the winner of it, Roy Stevens's home-bred Lucky Hanassi, won five races during the season, the last four on the trot including a ladies' open run over a similar distance.

Alison Dare, the winner of the *Sporting Life* Cup for the second year running, with exactly the same number of winners as Justin Farthing, and her highest score in a single season, had all 26 of her wins on horses trained by Dick Baimbridge, the leading trainer of the season with a total of 29 winners.

Alison's most prolific winners were those consistent 13-year-olds Mendip Express and Fennelly, on each of whom she won six races. Fennelly was beaten once, by a short head on his home course at the Berkeley after making a bad mistake two fences out. Mendip Express was a narrow runner-up twice. The most promising of Alison's rides was Dr. Paul Brown's Stephens Pet. A winner once over hurdles when trained by Jonjo O'Neill, Stephens Pet won three races on the trot in his first season of point-to-point racing.

Pip Nash (née Jones), the runner-up to Alison for the ladies' title with 22 winners, also broke the previous record for a lady rider. These two riders were neck and neck for most of the season; and Pip was actually one ahead of Alison on Easter Monday when she had her tenth win of the season in the adjacent hunts' race at the Old Berks on her husband's Four M's, on the same day that Alison had her ninth on Mendip Express in the ladies' open at the North Cotswold. Two days later, however, Alison drew level, riding a superb race on Stephens Pet in the ladies' open at the Croome & West Warwickshire, getting the eight-year-old up to beat Master Eryl by a short head after he had been three lengths down at the last.

It was still level pegging between the two riders, with 21 winners apiece, on May 18, when Alison won on Fennelly at the Dulverton West and Pip completed a double at the Melton Hunt Club, winning the family riders' race on Chris Nash's Ixor and the ladies' championship on Mrs. Sheila Nash's Jimster, who beat the best ladies' horse in the Northern Area, Pauline Robson's mount Steele Justice, easing up as he passed the post three lengths clear in much the fastest time of the day.

This was really the end of Pip's challenge for the ladies' title, as her two best rides, Ixor and Jimster, were both roughed off shortly afterwards. Both had been prolific winners. The six-year-old Ixor, who started the season as a maiden, won four races with Pip up and two with her brother Tim riding him; while the nine-year-old Jimster, a winner twice over hurdles, won five ladies' opens with Pip up and three men's opens with Tim up. Ixor was hunted with the Old Berks and Jimster with the Pentyrch in Wales; and Jimster, with his eight wins, was the nearest challenger to the winner of the *Daily Telegraph* Trophy for the most prolific winner of the season.

This trophy was won by a truly remarkable old horse, 12-year-old Fort Hall, owned by Mrs. Lucy Wadham, trained by her in Libby Heath's old yard near Bury St. Edmunds, and hunted with the Puckeridge & Thurlow.

A winner of 11 races (one of them a hunter chase at Worcester) in 14 appearances, and a runner-up in his other three, Fort Hall, who was in action on the first and last days of the season, was ridden in all his races by 25-year-old Tanya Bracegirdle, an assistant to Alex Scott at Newmarket. The only point-to-points he was beaten in were his first two races at Higham, where he was beaten on both occasions by Perroquet. His only other defeat was in Stratford's *Horse and Hound* Cup, for which he was a gallant runner-up.

Two 16-year-olds, Trevor Marks Jnr. and Guy Lewis, a Monmouth schoolboy, were joint winners of the *Daily Telegraph* male novice riders' award, with six winners each. Marks had all six of his wins on two of his father's home-bred horses, winning five races on Stanwick Lad, who was proving a wonderful schoolmaster for him, and one on the ten-year-old Stanwick Fate. Lewis, who also took the PPOA's Wilkinson Sword as the leading rider under the age of 21 who hadn't ridden a winner before the start of the season, won three races on Channel Pastime and three on Blinkin' Nora. Both of them were hunted with the Llangibby and trained by his father. Blinkin' Nora was owned by his mother.

Joanne Cumings, now aged 21, was out on her own as the leading female novice rider with 13 point-to-point wins, the highest score for a novice rider since Andrew Sansome's 14 in 1989; and the highest for a female novice rider since Amanda Harwood's 14 in 1986.

With Khattaf out of action throughout the season, Jo Cumings's major winners were the seven-year-old Starember Lad, owned by Mrs. Helena Johnson and trained by Jo's father, and Robert Alner's eight-year-old Sheer Water, trained by Harry Wellstead. On Starember Lad she won four ladies' opens and had her first win under Rules in a hunter chase at Chepstow; and on Sheer Water she won a race for novice riders and four ladies' opens in a row.

In a season which at last saw the Dumfriesshire mare Mystic Music in her rightful place at the head of Mackenzie & Selby's handicap, the Northern Area was particularly rich in talent; and it also produced the second in this handicap, the College Valley mare Dun Gay Lass, rated 31b. below Mystic Music.

After breaking a blood vessel at Kelso on her first appearance of the season, Mystic Music won her four remaining races in a canter, the open race at her home meeting and three hunter chases. Sadly, the last of these races, at Perth, proved to be this splendid mare's final appearance on a course. Whilst being prepared for another onslaught on the *Horse and Hound* Cup at Stratford, she broke a splint bone, ending her racing career under Kevin Anderson with seven wins in point-to-points and 13 in hunter chases.

This was bad enough. But something very much worse was to come. The mare's owner, the former Helen Wilson, was fatally injured in a car crash in October, just four months after her marriage to a fellow civil engineer, Adam Forster.

The nine-year-old Dun Gay Lass, a winner in 1991 of two open point-to-points and a hunter chase at Kelso, was one of the unluckiest losers of the Cheltenham Foxhunters' that we shall ever see. The only mare in the race, she had it in the bag when, half-way up the run-in, her rider's stirrup iron snapped in half and left her floundering. Martin Claxton performed a near-miracle to stay on board, and even got her going again to such effect that she almost recovered the advantage she had lost to the Irish raider Lovely Citizen. But not quite. The mare was beaten a head. If ever there was a moral winner of this race, Mrs. Phyllis Claxton's Dun Gay Lass was one. The third horse home, Crammer, was 15 lengths behind the gallant runner-up. Teaplanter, unbeaten in his three previous hunter chases, and a winner of three in a row afterwards, unseated Richard Russell at the ninth. He was the 6-4 favourite in the field of 18; and his six successes gave his owner-rider Peter Greenall's trophy for the leading rider in hunter chases.

So the traditional Irish roar went up for Lovely Citizen, owned and bred by Eugene O'Sullivan, trained by one of his sons, Eugene Jnr., and ridden by another, 23-year-old William. Before he came to Cheltenham, the eight-year-old Lovely Citizen won three open point-to-points and two hunter chases in Ireland; and he won another hunter chase at Fairyhouse afterwards.

Steele Justic, Flying Ace (now 15) and Mossy Moore were the dominant horses in the strong Northern Area ladies' races; and Willy Manners's seven-year-old Steele Justice, who beat Flying Ace at the Percy and the Braes of Derwent, and won six of his eight races with Pauline Robson up, was the only one of the three to win a race outside the area, when he won the ladies' open at the Zetland by the best part of a fence in a field of five. He was also the highest scorer of all the winners of the PPOA young horse awards.

Flying Ace won five of his ten ladies' opens under Doreen Calder and was a runner-up in four others, twice to Mossy Moore, to whom he returned the compliment at the Fife and the Lauderdale. So it was even stevens those two.

Sandra Forster's owner-ridden Mossy Moore, who was the same age as Flying Ace, was a winner of four ladies' opens in his seven appearances; and although he finished fourth to Steele Justice at the Cumberland Farmers, he had the distinction of relegating him to third place when they met again at the Jedforest, Mossy Moore's home meeting.

After Mossy Moore had beaten Flying Ace in his last race of the season, in a two-horse match at the Cumberland Foxhounds' fixture at Aspatria, Sandra Forster decided that this was the right moment to retire him. The 15-year-old was recording his 12th win for her; and it waa Sandra's 24th career winner.

Two other veterans making their final appearances were the Elwells' 19-year-old White Paper and Mrs. "Twink" Thompson's 14-year-old Gentle Approach, one of the bright stars of Caroline Saunders's Pytchley yard. Neither, unfortunately, bowed out with a win, though Gentle Approach, who broke down in his last race at Garthorpe, a course over which he had won seven times, did manage to win two more open events to bring his grand total of wins up to 20, including his successes under Rules in Ireland before he started in hunt racing.

White Paper, a runner-up twice under Robert Elwell in his four appearances, was signing off with 24 wins, most of them with Teresa Elwell riding him in ladies' opens. The 19-year-old made 42 appearances in point-to-points.

The Warwickshire amateur John Deutsch, who had won the Heythrop four-miler twice on Paddy's Peril, became the first rider to follow in the footsteps of Ian McKie and win this point-to-point classic for the third time. McKie's three wins had all been on Nostradamus; but Deutsch was having his third success in the race on a horse he was riding in it for the first time, Dromin Joker, the 11-year-old he had bought from David Naylor-Leyland before the start of the season and won the men's open at the V.W.H. on after hunting him with the North Cotswold.

The going for this year's race was firm, and the favourite for it in the field of eight, which included the 1987 winner Political Whip, was the Vale of Lune 12-year-old Nenni, who liked it that way, but proved no match for Dromin Joker, who was taken to the front by Deutsch at the second and never headed thereafter. Deutsch was looking over his shoulder on the way to the last and must have liked what he saw. Nenni, who was being hard ridden by Richard Ford, finished six lengths away in second, and eight lengths behind came the well-supported Maori Warrior, a winner of three of his five previous races. The time of 8 mins. 23 secs. was the fastest since 1988, when John Deutsch had the second of his two wins on Paddy's Peril in 8 mins. 19.2 secs., also on firm ground. Dromin Joker had two more races afterwards, finishing a runner-up to Frank Gilman's Neltama at the Quorn and winning a men's open at Andoversford with a 7lb. penalty. Nenni finished his season with a fourth to Justin Farthing's mount Archie's Nephew in the four-mile men's open at the Exmoor.

The Heythrop was an interesting meeting for more reasons than one. After James Barclay, a 17-year-old schoolboy at Radley, had won the opening hunt race on his mother's 14-year-old Contradeal, some kind person revealed that he had contravened the regulations by jumping a fence on the way to the start. The stewards sensibly turned a blind eye on this, one of them remarking off the record, "Well, he is very young, isn't he?"

They were less indulgent, however, when Marcus Armytage, the leading amateur of the season, having his first ride in a point-to-point, omitted to weigh in after finishing third in the Old Etonian & Old Harrovian race to the Old Harrovian Edward Bailey on Fell Climb. They disqualified the horse he was riding and fined him £40.

Nor was this the end of their deliberations, since they upheld an objection to the winner lodged by another Old Harrovian, Richard Russell, who had been beaten a neck on his Arctic Paddy and claimed that his horse had been leaned on after the last. This caused one of the losing Old Etonians to remark loftily, "Such a thing would never have happened at Eton." It could be he was feeling sore that, for the first time in the history of the race, no Etonian was in a position to claim the trophy on offer for the first Old Etonian past the post.

For the third time in eight years, the Middleton point-to-point was a casualty of the weather, on this occasion because there was snow on the course at Whitwell-on-the-Hill; and this meant, of course, that we had lost the classic Grimthorpe Cup race.

But at least we had a third Yorkshire winner of the Lady Dudley Cup at the Worcestershire, and a vintage one at that, in the shape of The Red One, owned and trained by Peter Haley, a building contractor from Catterton, not far from York Racecourse. The Red One's predecessors were the late Archie Thomlinson's Paul Pry in 1951 and Miss Joyce Hey's Sporting Luck in 1978.

Starting favourite at 5-4 on, on the strength of having won four open races on the trot, the seven-year-old from the Bramham Moor won on the bridle under Stephen Swiers in a field of 11, leaving Master Eryl to get the better of Karannsu in the battle for second place. The Red One's time of 6 mins. 39 secs. was seven seconds faster than that taken by Turn Mill to win last year's race on similarly fast ground, good to firm.

This was The Red One's first season as a point-to-pointer; and apart from a fall at the Cheshire Forest in his first race, he was unbeaten. A winner three times over hurdles for his former trainer, John Hanson, The Red One was given to Peter Haley by Hanson as a present. His usual rider was Haley's nephew, 19-year-old Wayne

Burnell, who, after winning four races on him, broke his femur riding another horse at the Sinnington, and put himself out of action. Otherwise he would have been up on The Red One in the Dudley Cup.

In a somewhat sub-standard Land Rover men's final at Towcester the joint favourites at 4-1 were Timlyn (a winner of two open races) and the now 14-year-old Border Burg (now well on the downgrade but the winner of an open race at Upton-on-Severn). They finished third and fourth to Granny's Prayer, a ten-year-old from the Berks & Bucks whose only previous win during the season under the strong handling of Rory Lawther had been in an adjacent hunts' race at Kimble.

The RMC Group ladies' final at Warwick was also won by a horse with no more than one previous win during the season, 13-year-old Paddy's Pond, the winner of a restricted open in Wales. Ridden again by Heather McCaull, Paddy's Pond, comfortably successful in a field of seven, had his task considerably lightened when the favourite, Nicola Bothway's mount As You Were, had all the stuffing taken out of him with a bad mistake at the fourth.

The final of *The Times* restricted open series at Towcester provided a first winner under Rules for all concerned with the success of Strong Bond, a ten-year-old from the South Dorset. Owned and trained by Mrs. Meg Cooke and ridden by 21-year-old Nick Mitchell (the younger brother of Tim), Strong Bond was recording his third win of the season when he got up in the last stride to beat Chris Coyne's mount Denstone Wanderer by a neck. Mrs. Cooke bred this winner from a quality mare she received as a gift, Windward II (by Wood Cot), who was hunted on Exmoor.

There was an even more remarkable turn-up for the book in the Liverpool Foxhunters' than the one for the 1988 race. The finish was fought out by two stable companions trained by the Royston trainer John Jenkins, with the one who started at 100-1, Double Turn, getting up under Perry Harding-Jones on the run-in to beat the 10-1 shot Brunton Park, who had Simon Andrews up, by two lengths, with the Tarrys' home-bred True Bloom taking third place under James Tarry a length behind. There were 27 starters for this race. The 7-2 favourite for it, Field Conqueror, the winner of a 2.5-mile handicap chase at Bangor 13 days earlier, was sixth of the 15 finishers.

This was Double Turn's first success since 1988, when his four wins from Libby Heath's yard, all with Perry Harding-Jones up, included two novice hunter chases and, in the autumn of that year, a handicap chase at Southwell. The ten-year-old son of an American sire (Comedy Star) out of a New Zealand mare (Pearl River) was hunted with the Puckeridge & Thurlow, the same hunt that had produced Newnham, the 1988 winner.

In the *Horse and Hound* Cup at Stratford there was a second success for the South East Area, the first since Loyal Partner won the race in 1982. This time it was Peter Bonner's Federal Trooper, trained in the Old Surrey & Burstow country by the former pro. jockey Denis McCarthy and his wife, Christine, and vigorously ridden by their 20-year-old son, Tim. In a driving finish, the ten-year-old Federal Trooper, a former inmate of Jenny Pitman's yard, from which he had won once over hurdles and once over fences, held off a strong challenge from that prolific winner Fort Hall by half a length.

It was the climax to a splendid season for Federal Trooper; and also for his new yard, which had produced 16 winners in point-to-points and four in hunter chases, all of them ridden by Tim McCarthy, whose 16 wins in point-to-points saw him finishing equal fourth with John Llewellyn in the table of leading riders. Six of McCarthy's wins came on Federal Trooper, including one in a hunter chase at Folkestone to add to his success at Stratford. The best of his wins in point-to-points came in the men's open at the Fitzwilliam, where Federal Trooper, three lengths down at the last, produced a tremendous late run to beat Stanwick Lad by a neck and broke the Cottenham course record with a time of 5 mins. 51 secs.

A true amateur, Tim McCarthy worked three days a week from 4.0 p.m. to midnight as the duty manager of the Surrey Tennis & Country Club in Croydon. And he comes from racing stock. His father rode 50 winners over fences; and his grandfather, after whom he was chistened Tim, won the 1930 Grand National Trial at Gatwick on Peggy's Pride.

Ron Treloggen and Paul Hamer both rode their 100th winner in point-to-points, Treloggen when scoring on a maiden, Silver Zip, at the Torrington Farmers in the last point-to-point race of the season, and Hamer when winning the adjacent hunts' race at the Llandeilo Farmers' on Billy Hancok's 12-year-old Vivaque in April.

East Anglia's George Cooper, who now had 81 point-to-point winners to his credit, was the winner of the *Horse and Hound* Cup for the leading small owner-trainer-rider for the second time in three years with five wins on his unbeaten Carl's Choice, who had two of his successes outside his area in Sussex and was well on the way to surpassing the the 23 wins recorded by his illustrious predecessor General Confusion.

One with more wins behind him than this, however, was John Weldhen's For A Lark, who took his score up to 28 with his six wins in eight appearances, four of them with Mandy Turner up and the other two with her deputy, Linda Blackford, riding him.

Gerald Tanner's home-bred seven-year-old Celtic Leisure (by Celtic Cone out of a Jock Scot mare) and Dick Baimbridge's charge Grademount were both unbeaten in their five races. Celtic Leisure was ridden in all his races by Mrs. Rosemary Vickery, who trained him in the Blackmore & Sparkford Vale country; and Grademount in all his by Alison Dare. The eight-year-old Grademount was one of four winners saddled by Dick Baimbridge at the Ross Harriers; and it was not surprising to see him ending up as the leading trainer of the season with 29 winners, four more than Richard Barber.

The only other trainers to turn out more than 20 point-to-point winners were permit holder Chris Nash, with 24, and Harry Wellstead, who produced 22 point-to-point winners and four hunter-chase winners from Robert Alner's old yard at Hazelbury Bryan, near Blandford. The two best horses trained by him were Bernard Pike's mares Elver Season and Gunner's Flight, both of them ridden by Robert Alner in all their races. Elver Season won three novice hunter chases on the trot and was a runner-up in two others. Gunner's Flight won three open point-to-points in a row and was a runner-up in her only other.

In East Anglia, where the most prolific winner after Fort Hall was Gurney

Sheppard's ten-year-old Rubie's Choice with six wins in adjacent hunts' races, five of them with Nicola Bothway up, Nigel Bloom, the leading rider in the area with 13 winners, was seen on a promising seven-year-old mare, Lord Somerleyton's home-bred Spartan Sprite, a granddaughter of Spartan General on her dam's side. The mare had lost her maiden certificate in 1990, and in 1991 she won five of her six races, beating Stanwick Lad in one of them. There is not much doubt that she would have gone through the season unbeaten but for being held up that much too long in a four-horse race for mares at the PPOA fixture at Ashorne and failing by a length to peg back the front-running Little Mo, a 16-1 shot. As Spartan Sprite had started at 4-1 on for this race, the stewards called Bloom up before them and asked him for an explanation. He told them that Spartan Sprite needed to be held up until after the last and he thought Little Mo would come back to her. But it was an error of judgment, to say the least, and a very rare one for so accomplished a rider. What his father, who trained Spartan Sprite, said to him, I shudder to think.

Another granddaughter of Spartan General, Bunny Tarry's Grafton mare Fine Lace, one of the horses he had bred from Grecian Lace after buying this mare as a two-year-old from Lucy Jones in Somerset, made an auspicious start to her racing career when, after losing her maiden certificate on her home course at Mollington on her third appearance, she won her remaining four races, crowning her season with a triumph in the Marie Curie novice championship at Melton.

Ridden in all her races by James Tarry, whose riding style, if not exactly elegant, is extremely effective, the seven-year-old Fine Lace started to draw clear of a good field five fences out and won unchallenged from Panicsun and Caroline Saunders's well-supported charge Joestone. The latter would no doubt have gone closer if he hadn't severed a ligament; but, from the way Fine Lace won, it is doubtful if he would have troubled her.

Another name for the future was clearly Duright. A change of stables clearly worked wonders for this eight-year-old mare from the Cleveland. Starting the season as a maiden, after being bought by Peter Sawney for 6,000 guineas at Doncaster in August of the previous year, the daughter of the American sire Dubassoff won her last four races under Nigel Tutty, culminating in the Heart Of All England at Hexham, a prime target for many a novice in the North.

While Federal Trooper was the dominant performer in the South East, his counterpart in the area's ladies' races, admittedly against much weaker opposition, was David Knowles's Prince Zeus. This 12-year-old from the East Kent won six of his seven point-to-points under his regular rider Kate Hills. Maltby Boy, who finished in front of him on the only occasion they met this season but was beaten twice by him in 1990, was his only serious rival, with his four wins in five appearances for his owner-rider, Alison Salmon.

For two well-known riders, farrier Tim Rooney, who rode mostly in Wales, and Mark Davies, the 43-year-old City banker who will also be remembered as a member of the consortium which saved Tweseldown for point-to-point racing, it was their last season of race-riding; although in Rooney's case he did have one more ride in 1992, when a neck injury sustained at the first of the Welsh point-to-points in February caused him to call it a day.

A nephew of Willie, Tim had his last win riding the Llangeinor mare Bribella in a maiden race at the Ystrad. It was his 144th winner in point-to-points; and his ten wins under Rules gave him a grand total of over 150. Mark Davies's last winning ride was on his own horse Robson (bought from Peter Greenall after the 1986 season) in the men's open at the West Kent. This was his 61st winner; and he took the 13-year-old son of Spartan General with him into retirement, along with two other old faithfuls, 15-year-old Colonel Henry and 15-year-old Why Forget.

In June there occurred the death, at the age of 69, of that great West Country point-to-point rider Frank Ryall. A rider of 218 point-to-point winners, he shared the national title twice in the days when no cup was presented for it, with John Trevisick in 1954 and Roy Edwards in 1960.

A contemporary of such giants as Ryan Price, Dick Francis, Tim Molony, Fred Winter, Tony Grantham and Bryan Marshall, Ryall, who farmed at Beera, near Tavistock, also won numerous races under Rules, winning on courses as diverse as Cheltenham and Buckfastleigh. The best point-to-pointer he rode was that fabulous pony Lonesome Boy, a winner of 65 races, with Jennifer Renfree (later Barons) riding him in most of them over banking courses.

But he also rode some very good horses that he owned himself or with his father, notably the three half-sisters that he bred, Shirley Jones, Jillian Jones and Beera Girl; and he scored freely on another outstanding pony called Jolly Girl. Peter Wakeham, for whom he rode his last winner in 1975, and who today is well known as a commentator at West Country point-to-points, said of Frank Ryall and the still very active Grant Cann, "These were the two best amateurs I have seen in the 50 odd years since racing resumed after the War."

As for Willie Rooney, the legendary 'Irishman' who was actually a Welshman, and who died in Ireland the following month at the age of 77, what more is there left to say about him; and how on earth did he manage to ride as many as 401 point-to-point winners?

Well, for a start, he was born near Cardiff and rode his first winner in South Wales at the age of 13; and it wasn't until he reached the age of 61 that he was compelled to give up race-riding following a stroke. So the long length of his riding career, which also saw him riding over 200 winners under Rules, has played its part in his phenomenal achievement. But not, of course, the whole part; and when one takes into consideration the fact that point-to-pointers in Ireland are not permitted to win more than four open point-to-points and one hunt race in a single season, Rooney's feat was even more remarkable.

Before moving to Ireland in 1937, Rooney rode 26 winners in Wales and eight in England, where he sometimes came up against his life-long friend Ryan Price. And one of his major achievements in his career as a trainer was saddling Bentom Boy to win the 1984 Irish Grand National.

In December, the *Daily Telegraph*'s much respected equestrian correspondent Henry Birtwistle died at his Lancashire home at the age of 70. He had been putting up a brave fight against cancer for some time. Henry, whose duties included covering the northern point-to-points for his paper, was the Hon. Sec. of the Pendle Forest & Craven Harriers point-to-point from 1959 to 1971; and hounds were meeting outside his house at Sawley the day after his death. He would have liked that.

Several top-class point-to-pointers were fatal casualties during the season. One of them, Richard Barber's '13-year-old Gerry Doyle, a horse with 27 wins under his belt, 21 of them when he was in Barber's yard, dropped dead on the gallops two days before he was due to make his first appearance of the season at the Beaufort; and the demise of this prolific winner seriously damaged Barber's chances of becoming the leading trainer of the season.

Blue Ravine, the horse who had been so successful with Simon Bell up, and who had won the four-mile men's open at the Percy on March 30, had to be put down after he had broken his shoulder in his next race, the Land Rover qualifier at the Sinnington. Gerald Penfold's Silverton ten-year-old John Sam, a winner of all four of his point-to-points and a hunter chase at Taunton with his owner up, and of hunter chases at Ascot and Cheltenham with Ashley Farrant riding him, broke his elbow in a hunter chase at Worcester and was also lost to the scene.

And, not long after the season was over, Nick Hargreave's Tynedale 13-year-old Douglas Brig, a winner of two races during the season, and of 11 in all, including five at Corbridge, died on his home ground from a leaking heart valve. The grey son of New Brig's finest moment, said his owner, who rode him in most of his races, was when he outjumped Mystic Music to win a hunter chase at Newcastle in 1989.

In August, the late Kenneth Dale's marvellous old horse Tenor (the horse he had found in a field) died at the age of 31. He had been spending the last eight years of his life at the Berwickshire home of Kenneth's elder son Peter, being lovingly looked after by his wife, Grania. He was a winner of 30 point-to-points in his 59 appearances, with the late Sue Horton (Aston, as she then was) winning 27 of them on him. Peter Dale had this to say of him: "Tenor always wanted to be first, and even when entering and leaving his field he wouldn't let any other horse push him out of the way."

The anti-hunting brigade were much in evidence at the Banwen Miners and the Badsworth. They destroyed two of the fences with a chainsaw at Resolven; and were only prevented from doing the same thing to a third when the chainsaw broke down. But the meeting still went ahead, with the officials doing a fine job to get the course ready in time.

At the Badsworth, the demonstrators contented themselves with distributing leaflets that were largely ignored; and one of them was heard to remark dolefully that if he'd known how poor the racing was going to be he would have stayed away. It wasn't as bad as all that, though, with Douglas Brig winning the men's open in a canter under Simon Whitaker (deputising for the injured Nick Hargreave), admittedly starting at 6-4 on in a field of three.

The recipient of this year's award for special services to the sport at the national point-to-point dinner at The Belfry was one of the most popular figures ever to set foot on a course in the South Midlands, Graham Pidgeon. A founder-member of the PPOA, and the man who did most to save that excellent course at Mollington when it was in danger of being lost to the sport, Graham trained all the horses his daughter, Jenny, had won on; and after being presented with the award he had done so much to deserve, he remarked, with characteristic modesty, "My horses and my smashing jockeys have won this trophy for me." Not really

Garthorpe 1980. Grittar and Dick Saunders in process of winning the men's open at the Melton Hunt Club Point-to-Point. *Photo: Jim Meads.*

Michael Williams being annointed by Frank Gilman (centre) and Dick Saunders at the Melton Hunt Club point-to-point at Garthorpe in May 1982 seven weeks after they had won the Grand National with Grittar as owner and rider. *Photo: Jim Meads.*

The star ladies' horse of the 1982 season, East Anglia's Mac Kelly, the Grand Marnier winner, recording the first of his eight wins under Didi Powles (née Morris) in the ladies' open at Cottenham's Cambridgeshire Harriers fixture. *Photo: Jim Meads.*

The Newton family's seven-year-old John Bunyan, ridden by Joey Newton on his home course at Garthorpe, was a classy winner of the Marie Curie Novice Championship at the Melton Hunt Club fixture in 1982. *Photo: Jim Meads.*

Jenny Pidgeon, a quadruple winner of the *Sporting Life* Cup, after her win on Random Leg at Mollington in 1983. *Photo: Jim Meads.*

Alan Hill winning the inaugural Audi Grand Prix De Chasse at Sandown in 1984 on Norman Mawle's Elmboy. *Photo: Jim Meads.*

Doreen Calder and Flying Ace, winners of the *Horse and Hound* Cup at Stratford in 1985, jumping the last with (right) the runners-up, Tim Smith and Miss Crozina. *Photo: Jim Meads.*

Nostradamus (left) winning the 4-mile race for Lord Ashton of Hyde's Cup at the Heythrop in 1985 for the third time with Ian McKie up. Behind him is the runner-up, Court Papers, with Stuart Dickin up. *Photo: Jim Meads.*

Sweet Diana at full stretch under Jill Grinyer at Garthorpe in 1986. *Photo: Jim Meads.*

Mike Felton, a triple winner of the *Daily Telegraph* Cup in 1987, 1989 and 1990. *Photo: John Beasley.*

Stanwick Lad, the 1988 Grand Marnier Trophy winner, being led in with John Sharp up after another men's open win, at Garthorpe in 1988. *Photo: Jim Meads.*

ustin Farthing, winner of the *Daily Telegraph* Cup in 1991. *Photo: John Beasley.*

Robert Alner, the leading point-to-point rider of 1992. *Photo: John Beasley.*

Anthea Farrell winning the Grimthorpe Cup at the Middleton on Bruce Heywood's Ocean Day in 1992, the first year this major test for stayers became a mixed open. Nearest the camera is the runner-up, Knocklaur, with Simon Brisby up. *Photo: Roy Parker.*

Ocean Day winning the Grimthorpe Cup for the second year running, this time with Howard Brown up. *Photo: Roy Parker.*

Jim Papworth's Melton Park, a dual Grand Marnier winner, adding to his score in the club race at the Melton Hunt Club fixture in 1993 with Nigel Bloom up. Behind him is the horse who finished third, Decent Gold, with his owner John Stephenson up.
Photo: Steve Davies.

George Cooper and his consistent winner Carl's Choice on Newmarket Heath in 1993.
Photo: John Slater.

Polly Curling, a triple winner of the
Sporting Life Cup in 1993, 1994 and
1995. *Photo: John Beasley.*

Teaplanter (winner of 27 races) being hunted with
the Pytchley by his owner Richard Russell.
Photo: Jim Meads.

Peter Craggs (left) winning the *Horse and Hound* Cup at Stratford on his
Generals Boy from Alan Hill on Sheer Jest in 1993. *Photo: Bernard Parkin.*

Johnny Manners's Killeshin (G. Brown) winning the Sidney Bailey
Hunter Chase at Leicester in 1994 at the odds of 100-1.

Alastair Crow winning the members' race at Garthorpe's Melton Hunt Club
fixture on Scally Muire in 1995. *Photo: Steve Davies.*

The Bounder winning his division of the men's open with Joe Tizzard up at the PPORA meeting at Barbury Castle on the openeing day of the 1997 season. *Photo: John Beasley.*

Pauline Robson, the leading lady rider in the Northern Area for six seasons in succession, saddled her first winner under Rules in 1997. *Photo: Roy Parker.*

Shirley Vickery, the champion lady rider of 1997. *Photo: John Beasley.*

Polly Curling riding her last winner for the Barber yard, John Keighley's False Trail, in the open maiden race at the Blackmore & Sparkford Vale in 1997. *Photo: John Beasley.*

Joe Tizzard and The Bounder after their win at Barbury Castle in 1997.
Photo: John Beasley.

Leading trainers Richard Barber (right) and Dick Baimbridge
at Bratton Down in 1998. *Photo: John Beasley.*

Pip Jones, the champion lady rider
of 1998. *Photo: John Beasley.*

Alison Dare, six times a winner of the *Sporting Life* Cup
between 1986 and 1996. *Photo: John Beasley.*

Philip Scouller, who has ridden more winners at Tweseldown than any other rider,
is seen here recording his 59th win over the course, riding his own horse Glen Cherry
in the Thames Valley Combined Hunts Club members' race at the Garth & South Berks
fixture in January 1998. *Photo: Linda Charles.*

Enda Bolger on his way to breaking the world point-to-point record with his 402nd win in point-to-points at the Ormond Foxhounds fixture at Ballingarry, Co. Tipperary, on Sunday, May 24, 1998, riding Elegant Lord for J.P. McManus in the open race. *Photo: Liam Healy.*

Proud Sun (Seamus Durack) leads the hidden Fantus over the last fence in the Land Rover qualifier at Larkhill's Army fixture in 1998. *Photo: John Beasley.*

Andrew Dalton (left) and Julian Pritchard, the joint men's champion riders of 1998 at Garthorpe, where both rode a winner at the Quorn on the last day of the season. *Photo: John Beasley.*

Cavalero (Alex Charles-Jones) beating Double Silk (right) with Joe Tizzard up, in the Colin Nash Memorial United Hunts' Cup at Cheltenham 1998.

Colonel Henry, one of the top point-to-pointers in Scotland, before being bought by the South East rider Mark Davies and going on to win 10 races for him, is seen here winning at the East Sussex & Romney Marsh point-to-point in 1987. He was one of the horses Davies took into retirement with him after the 1991 season and died in 1998 at the age of 22.

Waiting to start. The Countryside March in 1998. *Photo: John Beasley.*

true, of course. If ever a man deserved it in his own right, Graham did. And even at that time he was battling with the serious illness that was to defeat him in the end.

Percy Tory, in his Chairman's speech at the PPOA A.G.M. at Stratford Racecourse, revealed that one of the things the Association was campaigning for was for point-to-point racing to commence in January. It was to happen in due course, but not yet.

Tailpiece:

The arrival at the West Kent fixture at Penshurst of a party of Japanese businessmen in a Rolls Royce was an occasion for bemusement. But they were warmly directed to the prime car park, for which they had paid. Their chauffeur was then heard to ask, "Is this the way to Gatwick Airport?" So their money was returned to them before they proceeded on their way.

1992

*In which more records are broken, The Carholme is lost to the sport,
point-to-pointing is revived at Barbury Castle, adjacent hunts' races
are replaced by Confineds, open maiden races are introduced, and
the Grimthorpe Cup becomes a mixed open.*

In a season which saw none of the 202 point-to-point fixtures lost to the weather, and 12,715 runners at them, a record number of hunters' certificates (4,021) were issued; and, taking the hunter chases into account, runners reached an all-time record of 14,111.

Another record was broken when the North Hereford fixture at Newtown produced 190 runners for its 11 races, with the Confined, the men's open and the confined maiden all being run in two divisions and *The Times* Restricted in three.

The Working Party that had been set up under the chairmanship of Major Mike MacEwan had made a number of recommendations for the improvement of the sport. These were taken on board by the Jockey Club Point-to-Point Liaison Committee and swiftly acted upon. They were certainly instrumental in widening the variety of races on offer, particularly with the introduction of open maiden races; although not everyone, especially those riders with weight problems, were pleased with the option to run them off the 12st. mark, an option now extended to all races, provided that they adhered to a cumulative penalty system in the case of previous winners. It was interesting, in the changed circumstances, to see Land Rover sticking resolutely to 12-7 for their qualifying races at point-to-points.

The decision to replace adjacent hunts' races with Confineds had a bonus attached to it, since the qualifying area for such races was now extended to 15 adjacent hunts. A new type of race was the Intermediate, designed "to give the opportunity to horses out of restricted class to run together before racing in Opens." These were open to horses qualified in any part of the country; but they were not permitted to win more than two such races.

The former restricted opens were now replaced by Restricteds, which, although still open to horses qualified anywhere in the country, were not now classified as open events in terms of prize money and consequently had their ceiling reduced from £250 to £175. Another difference, and one that was received somewhat more warmly, was that horses were permitted to win two such races, whereas in the past it had been only one.

Not all the news was good news, however. The Levy Board grant to point-to-points was reduced by 20% to £146,000, despite a recommendation from the Jockey Club that it should remain at the 1991 level. This was not well received by the point-to-point fraternity. In the words of the highly respected Col. Arhur Clerke-Brown, the owner of the course at Kingston Blount, where four fixtures were due to be held, "We can stand it in our area but for some of the less fashionable courses in remote parts of the country it could be very serious." Especially, of course, as the Grant was strictly for the upkeep of courses.

The loss of The Carholme, owing to the intransigent attitude adopted by the anti-hunting Labour-controlled Lincoln City Council, was an indication of the way the wind was blowing in certain quarters. The old home of the Lincolnshire Handicap had been the scene of point-to-point racing ever since 1967, and in 1991 three meetings were held there, the Blankney, the Burton and the South Wold. Fortunately, they all found new homes in 1992, as did the three that were held at Nedge, the lost course in the Taunton Area.

It was great to see the revival of the sport at Barbury Castle on the Marlborough Downs, where point-to-pointing last took place in 1962 on the famous Wroughton gallops where two of the greatest hunter chasers of the post-war years, Colledge Master and Baulking Green, had their first wins in an open event.

The new course, in a setting unsurpassed for its scenic beauty, over fences superbly constructed by Willis Bros. (also responsible for those at Didmarton and Ashorne), and with excellent viewing facilities, was used for two meetings in 1992, the Tedworth (which had moved there from Larkhill) and the Avon Vale (formerly held at Nedge); and there were more Barbury Castle fixtures to come in later years, including the valuable Marlborough Cup over timber fences.

On the sponsorship front there was a major addition, with BMW rejoining the scene as sponsors of the new Confined series, culminating in a £6,000 final at the Cheltenham evening fixture on April 29, when the winner was a horse who was to make a big name for himself in future years, Double Silk.

But the highlight of the season for me, as I am sure it was for many others, was the success of Rushing Wild in the Cheltenham Foxhunters'. To say that Richard Barber's charge pulverised a field which included such horses as Lovely Citizen, Dun Gay Lass, Federal Trooper and The Red One would be an under-statement.

Justin Farthing always had John Keighley's seven-year-old lying handy; and once he had hit the front five fences out it was a case of Rushing Wild first and the rest nowhere. He won by 25 lengths from the 100-1 shot Ardesee, with Federal Trooper two lengths away in third, followed by The Red One, Wall Game and Lovely Citizen. Dun Gay Lass, who started favourite at 5-2, was showing them the way at the fourteenth, but the mare's fencing was far from fluent this time and a particularly bad mistake five fences out caused her to be dismounted.

Rushing Wild's Cheltenham win was preceded by two wins in open point-to-points, at Ottery St. Mary and Didmarton. He was unlucky in his next race after Cheltenham, the Liverpool Foxhunters', in which he came down five fences from home when holding every chance; but he ended the season beating Fiddlers Pike (whose three wins on the trot for Rosemary Henderson had included two hunter chases) in a hunter chase at Chepstow.

This was Rushing Wild's last season of hunt racing. In 1993, when he was running in new ownership from Martin Pipe's yard, he won two handicap chases and finished a good second to Jodami in the Cheltenham Gold Cup. But in his next and last race, the Irish Grand National at Fairyhouse, the worst happened. After leading from the third until the approach to the sixteenth, he was pulled up on the flat with a broken pelvis and had to be put down. A sad end for a potentially great horse!

The Liverpool Foxhunters' was a triumph for a 13-year-old veteran who had never seen a point-to-point course in his life but had run in some 80 races under Rules, Geoff Hubbard's Gee-A, trained by his owner at Woodbridge in Suffolk. Very well ridden by 17-year-old Paul Murphy, having his first-ever success, and the youngest rider ever to win the race, he won by a length in a driving finish from Andrew Sansome on Raise An Argument and Paul Hacking on Glenavey. Although he had won quite a number of races under Rules in his time, including two over the Mildmay course at Aintree and five handicap chases in the 1986-87 season with Gee Armytage up, this was Gee-A's first win since he was successful in an amateur riders' handicap chase at Cheltenham in October 1990. His starting price at Aintree was 66-1. The following season, which turned out to be his last before retirement, Gee-A won his first point-to-point, a men's open over the stayers' course at Ampton, with his Aintree rider up.

The top-rated horses in Mackenzie & Selby's handicap after the season were Rushing Wild and Teaplanter, both on the 11-7 mark; and behind them came Once Stung, Roscoe Boy and Sheer Jest, all on 11-5. Although Teaplanter, still the star of Caroline Saunders's yard, if not her most prolific winner, seemed rather flattered by being equated with Rushing Wild, since he made only two appearances. He did nothing wrong on either under Marcus Armytage, and certainly enhanced his reputation when giving Starember Lad 71b. at Newbury and beating him comfortably.

The six-year-old Once Stung, one of the horses Johnny Greenall had in training with Arthur Stephenson, and also the one who did most to help Johnny win his brother's trophy for the third time, can also be said to have enhanced his reputation. A winner of three point-to-points in Ireland, Once Stung was having his first season in England; and he acquitted himself pretty well, winning four hunter chases with his owner up, including one over four miles at the Cheltenham evening fixture. He was, however, beaten a neck by Sheer Jest, at a difference of 21b., in the John Corbet Cup at Stratford on his last appearance of the season.

The seven-year-old Sheer Jest, who had lost his maiden certificate two seasons ago, was living up to expectations, following his two wins in point-to-points with two wins in novice hunter chases at Stratford; and he was a runner-up in his other two hunter chases with Alan Hill up.

The most prolific winner of the season, and an outstanding winner of the *Daily Telegraph* Trophy, with 12 wins in 12 appearances, all but one of them in open events, was the grey Brunico, point-to-point racing's nearest equivalent to Desert Orchid. His 12 wins were the highest in a single season since the unbeaten Boy Bumble first achieved this score in 1974 and Little Fleur (who was not unbeaten) equalled it in 1978. Amazingly, with a rating of no more than 10-8, Brunico failed to make it into Mackenzie & Selby's top 28. But then, of course, he hadn't run in a hunter chase; although one of his two successes on the Flat was the classy Ormonde Stakes at Chester and he was a winner twice over hurdles.

A nine-year-old son of Bruni, with mixed French and American blood on his dam's side, Brunico first made his appearance in point-to-points for the Dorset owner-trainer Eddie Swaffield in 1989, when he was a faller in his only race and earned the comment "Does not look a natural for Pointing and may well continue to disappoint" from Mackenzie & Selby. But he won two open point-to-points with the Somerset rider Ron Treloggen up in 1990, and after one unsuccessful appearance in 1991 he was acquired for the modest sum of 3,800 guineas and passed into the ownership of Rowland Mansell, a garage proprietor in the South Pembrokeshire country whose trainer was the brilliant Peter Bowen, at this time a livery-yard proprietor.

It seemed entirely fitting that one of the races won by Brunico should be the classic Dudley Cup race at the Worcestershire, where he was ridden by his regular pilot Ron Treloggen. After drifting out to as much as 3-1 in the makket, his price hardened to 7-4 in the select field of six. The favourite, however, was Julian Pritchard's mount Sams Heritage, who had completed a hat-trick of wins in a Restricted and two Confineds. But on the way to the second last the race had become a match between Brunico (who had recovered well from a bad mistake at the open ditch) and the horse who was doomed to become a perpetual runner-up in the race, the locally-hunted Treyford. Despite his mistake at the last open ditch, where Treloggen did well to stay aboard, Brunico accomplished this win as smoothly as all his others, speeding away from Treyford after leading the 12-year-old son of Deep Run into the last and scoring by three lengths, with Sams Heritage two lengths further away in third. Turn Mill, the winner in 1990, was never a factor and was pulled up by Michael Hammond three fences out. Brunico's time of 6 mins. 45 secs. on the well-watered ground was six second's slower than The Red One's on good to firm ground in last year's race. Ron Treloggen said afterwards, "The credit goes to the horse, not to me."

The horse that came nearest to Brunico's total of 12 wins was Carl's Choice, whose ten wins in open events were more than sufficient to give George Cooper the *Horse and Hound* Cup for the leading owner-rider training his own horses for the third time in four years. Carl's Choice's only defeat was in his last race of the season, when, with Lisa Rowe up on him in the ladies' open at the Cambridge University United Hunts Club fixture over his favourite course at Cottenham, he was beaten half a length by the evergreen Fort Hall with Tanya Bracegirdle up. But by this time he had already surpassed the total of 23 (including three in hunter chases) wins amassed by his predecessor General Confusion and was on a grand total of 30 wins, including two in hunter chases, with 18 of them consecutive.

The Heythrop four-miler produced the first success in it for a horse from the much-maligned South East Area when Speedy Boy, a ten-year-old from the Old Surrey & Burstow ridden by Tim McCarthy, just managed to foil the attempt of Tim Jones to make all the running on The Humble Tiller, getting up on the post to snatch the judge's verdict by a short head. McCarthy remarked afterwards that he would not have been surprised had a dead-heat been announced; and it is quite true that neither horse deserved to lose. In soft ground and incessant rain that left most of the ten runners floundering, the third horse home, John Sharp's mount Good Waters, finished 25 lengths behind the runner-up, and behind him came Turn Mill. The well-backed Border Burg fell at the eleventh.

The Heythrop race was the second leg of a four-mile double for Speedy Boy, as well as the completion of a hat-trick. He had previously won the 'Kent Grand National' run over four miles at the West Street-Tickham fixture at Detling, and followed this with a win in a two-horse men's open at the Southdown & Eridge meeting in heavy ground at Heathfield. After his success at the Heythrop, he beat the triple winner Magical Morris in a three-horse men's open at the Surrey Union. A winner over hurdles, and of three adjacent hunts' races in 1991, his first season of point-to-pointing, Speedy Boy was found by Denis and Christine McCarthy for Mrs. Marion Terry (née Borland).

The Heythrop was also notable for producing a first point-to-point winner for Oliver Sherwood when Henrietta Knight's Dromin Leader, another of the horses bought from Pat Hogan in Ireland, trotted up for him in the British Field Sports Society race for the Guy Cunard Trophy. Sherwood got this ride as the result of a chance remark made at a dinner party when he told Henrietta that his one regret was that he had never ridden a point-to-point winner. "Well," she replied, "I've got just the horse for you." Later in the season, during which he won one other race, the men's open at the Teme Valley with Julian Pritchard up, Dromin Leader was sold to Joe Turner in East Anglia.

In its first year as a mixed open, and returning to four miles for the occasion, the Grimthorpe Cup was won by a woman rider when Anthea Farrell scored on the staying nine-year-old Ocean Day, who made every yard of the running in a field of eight to beat the penalised Knocklaur by a couple of lengths. This was a good performance by the Holderness-hunted Ocean Day, a son of Chris Sweeting's stallion Balinger, as Knocklaur was no mean performer, having won four of his five previous races and been a runner-up to Many A Slip in a novice hunter chase at Newcastle; and he was to win two more races afterwards.

The two best ladies' horses in Yorkshire, however, were Northumbrian King and Ellerton Hill. Northumbrian King, a six-year-old qualified with the West of Yore, won both his ladies' opens, with Jill Dawson deputising for Anthea Farrell in one of them, and also two of his three novice hunter chases with Marcus Armytage up; and the only time he came up against Ellerton Hill, in the ladies' open at the Derwent, where Anthea Farrell rode him, he beat him by half a length. A winner twice on the Flat, and of five hurdle races when in training with Chris Thornton, Northumbrian King was given by his former trainer to Mrs. Kate Walton (daughter of the late Sam Hall, to whom Thornton was an assistant for some time). Mrs. Walton rode him in the hunting field and trained him herself.

Ellerton Hill, a nine-year-old from the Farndale Hunt in the North Riding, was a winner of four of his six races, ridden each time by his trainer at Helmsley, Mrs. Jeannie Brown. Three of his wins were at Garthorpe, and the last of them was the Darley Stud ladies' championship for the Lord Astor Cup at the Melton Hunt Club, where he proved much too smart for the front-running Military Two Step, going clear of him from the thirteenth and winning in a canter with his rider looking over her shoulder.

Bred by his owner, Thomas Thompson, on his farm near Richmond, Ellerton Hill was produced from a mare, Kenya Park, who won 13 ladies' opens, including the four-mile ladies' open at the Middleton in 1968, when she was ridden by Mr. Thompson's daughter, Mrs. June Dent.

The Land Rover men's final at Towcester was also won by a horse from Yorkshire, Doug Jemmeson's Glen Lochan, a 12-year-old from the West of Yore who was completing a hat-tick of wins under Nigel Tutty after finishing third to Ocean Day in the Grimthorpe Cup. The favourite for this race in a field of 12 was the 13-year-old Mighty Mark. A winner of his Land Rover qualifier at the Haydon, his wins under Rules had included the four-mile National Hunt Chase at Cheltenham in 1987 and the Scottish Grand National at Ayr in 1988. Headed approaching the last by Glen Lochan in his attempt to give him 101b., he was beaten four lengths.

I do not myself think that there were any horses of the quality of Northumbrian King and Ellerton Hill in the RMC Group ladies' final at Warwick; although the easy winner of this championship, Joe Turner's 11-year-old Skygrange with Zoe Turner having her first ride under Rules on him, was rated above both of them in Mackenzie & Selby's handicap at 11-2, the same mark as Mighty Mark and, interestingly, as Dun Gay Lass and Double Silk. This was Skygrange's third win of the season, including one in a hunter chase at Fakenham; and he was to win another hunter chase at Fakenham afterwards.

In what proved to be the last year of *The Times* Restricted series, the final at Towcester attracted a field of 11 and was very well won by the South Midlands farrier Rory Lawther on Astroar, who had been headed two out by Final Spring but got back again on the run-in to beat him by a length.

This was the 11-year-old Astroar's second win in three appearances. His first was in his hunt race at the Vale of Aylesbury's Kimble fixture, where he was ridden by his owner, John Perry, who trained him in Angie Murray's yard at Kingston Blount. Perry, a contract worker for Wycombe District Council, had some difficulty pulling the horse up so full of running was he.

The new BMW Confined final at the Cheltenham evening fixture could hardly have produced a more impressive winner than Reg Wilkins's eight-year-old Double Silk, by the American sire Dubassoff out of Yellow Silk, by Counsel. Ridden with the utmost confidence by Ron Treloggen, Double Silk turned the race into a procession, romping home by 30 lengths from Paul Hamer's mount Willie McGarr, a winner of three of his six previous races. This was Double Silk's fourth win in his seven appearances, including one in a hunter chase at Ascot; and altogether, with his three wins in 1991, which he started as a maiden, he had now won seven races.

But he would doubtless have had more to do at Cheltenham had not the favourite, Peter Craggs's owner-ridden ten-year-old Generals Boy come down at the seventeenth when up alongside him. This was the first defeat for Generals Boy in a season which saw him winning five point-to-points in a row, although he was beaten in his last race of the season, the men's open at the Cumberland, by the Dumfriesshire mare Palmahalm, who went on to complete a hat-trick of wins in a hunter chase at Cartmel.

For the first time in its 34-year-old history, the last big hunter chase of the season, the *Horse and Hound* Cup at Stratford, was a victim of the weather, as a result of snow on the course.

The Dorset rider Robert Alner at last got his just reward when he was a runaway winner of the *Daily Telegraph* Cup at the advanced age of 48, with 31 point-to-point winners as against Julian Pritchard's 19. Alner's most prolific point-to-point winners were four of the horses trained by Harry Wellstead in his old yard, Spring Fun, Mr. Murdock, Elver Season and Ocean Link, on each of whom he won five point-to-points; and the nine-year-old Spring Fun was also one of his four winners in hunter chases, the others being Gunner's Flight (another of Harry Wellstead's), Last Extravagance and Ballyeden. Another of his rides, and perhaps the most promising of all, in view of what she achieved under Rules in future years, was Hops And Pops, the five-year-old mare bred by Sue Woodhouse from her pony-sized point-to-point winner Panda Pops. Hops And Pops, a mare Alner had recently bought from Mrs. Woodhouse, made her début with a single appearance in 1992, when she was a most impressive winner of the open maiden at the Old Berkshire at Lockinge on Easter Monday.

In third place behind Alner and Pritchard for the men's title, with 18 winners, was the South Midlands rider James Tarry, who would not be given many marks for style but deserves top marks for effectiveness and the determination to win. The vast majority of his wins were achieved on horses bred on the Tarry farm at Preston Capes in Northants, where the two major stars were Fine Lace and True Bloom, with five wins apiece.

Alison Dare, with her 21 wins, was the winner of the *Sporting Life* Cup for the third year running, and she had now equalled Josie Sheppard's record in winning this trophy five times. All her wins were on horses trained by Dick Baimbridge, who saddled 25 winners and was the runner-up to Harry Wellstead with his 35 as the leading livery yard proprietor. All but one of the ten horses Alison rode during the season were in the winner's enclosure for her; and the one who got away, Kelly's Pal, won two races with Julian Pritchard up.

Two of the horses Alison won on, Le Kingdom and Russki, were off the course throughout 1991; and two others, Hazeleels Delight and Sleepline For Pine, were newcomers to the yard, strengthening Dick Baimbridge's claim (not made by him, of course) to be considered a master of the art of producing something out of nothing.

The unbeaten Grademount, jointly owned by Dick Baimbridge and Mrs. Patsy Willis, was Alison's most prolific winner. The nine-year-old was unbeaten in his five races (none of them a race confined to lady riders!). Stephens Pet, unbeaten in his three, put up a particularly fine performance in the ladies' open at the North Hereford when comfortably accounting for Let Me Think, who went on to win five races on the trot under Candy Thomas. Another of Alison's rides was the 14-year-old Mendip Express, who was in his retirement season and went out on a winning note when recording his fourth win of the season in the ladies' open at the Berkeley. This took the total number of wins achieved by Mrs. Patsy Willis's grand old servant up to 38, all of them with Alison up.

The runner-up to Alison for the ladies' title was the West Country's Linda Blackford, who rode 16 winners, scoring at the North Cornwall on the opening day when winning the ladies' open on Roving Glen and at the Torrington Farmers' on the last day when winning the Confined on Clear Call.

The leading novice riders were 21-year-old Jamie Jukes from Wales with 11 wins and the 25-year-old Suffolk rider Gi Chown with eight wins all on her own horse, the 11-year-old Mountain Crash, trained for her by George Cooper. Mountain Crash's best performance was in his penultimate race at the Enfield Chace, where this half-brother to Rolls Rambler made most of the running and beat Gurney Sheppard's very useful Rubie's Choice, who was undergoing his only defeat in seven appearances, by 20 lengths.

But it was the 20-year-old Zoe Turner, the rider of Rubie's Choice on this occasion, who collected the Wilkinson Sword for the leading novice rider under the age of 21 with her six wins on five different horses, one of them, Takeover Bid, providing her with a walk-over in the hunt race at the Suffolk.

Three riders rode their 100th winner during the season: Ian McKie, a Joint Master of the Bicester with Whaddon Chase, on Radical Views at Mollington on March 7, Justin Farthing on Society Member at the West Somerset Vale on April 11, and Tim Jones (still five short of his century in point-to-points) with his 100th career winner, Carrickmines, at the Curre on March 28. Tim was the first-ever Welsh amateur to achieve his century so quickly, having ridden his first winner in 1984 at the age of 18.

Another Welsh rider, John Llewellyn, reached his 250th win in point-to-points when scoring on Durzi at the Llangeinor on May 2; and his services to the sport were recognized at the national point-to-point dinner at The Belfry when he was presented with the dinner committee's inscribed salver. Robert Alner had his 200th win in point-to-points when scoring on Mr. Murdock in the Confined at the Cotley on May 4. Alner landed four trebles during the season; but the only rider to bring off a four-timer was Andrew Hickman, who did so at the Mid Surrey Farmers at Charing on February 29 with Pike's Glory, Profligate, Sir Wager and The Lager Lout.

Mike Trickey achieved a similar feat as a trainer when four of his charges won at the Devon & Somerset Staghounds fixture at Holnicote, three of them, Tangle Jim and Tim Forster's pair The Doormaker and Brimstone Hill, ridden by Polly Curling, who also won three hunter chases on bookmaker Chris Smith's Pastoral Pride, a horse she trained herself.

In a particularly good season for the emergence of young horses with promise, I don't think there was much doubt that the outstanding five-year-old, even though he made but a single appearance, was Davy Blake, who made a deep impression on all who saw him when he made his first appearance on a course in a 17-runner open maiden in soft ground at the Cumberland Foxhounds fixture at Aspatria, where he made all the running under Michael Dun and won by a distance in a time that was bettered only by Palmahalm in beating Generals Boy in the men's open. One highly experienced observer was moved to remark that this was the best performance by a five-year-old that he had ever seen. Bought for 4,200 guineas at Doncaster Sales the previous November and hunted with the

Border pack on the Scotland–England border, Davy Blake, by the American sire Cool Guy out of a mare by Klairon, was owned by Norman Dalgetty, a retired hotelier, and trained by him at Jedburgh.

Of the six-year-olds that I saw myself, three who stood out were Mere Class, Blue Cheek and Sunny Mount. Mere Class, owned and bred by Mrs. Tessa Stuart-Evans in Hampshire, ran three times, falling in his first race and then losing his maiden certificate under James Grassick in a field of 15 at the Ledbury before winning a Restricted in style over the Dudley Cup course. He was later to do well under Rules when trained by Charlie Brooks.

Blue Cheek, a son of Strong Gale, had lost his maiden certificate in Ireland with Adrian Maguire up on him in 1991, and in 1992 he was in the winner's enclosure twice, once with Noel Bradley riding him and once with Simon Sweeting up. Jointly owned by Jim Mahon and Mrs. Brenda Graham (widow of the Irish bookmaker Sean Graham, who was associated with the PPOA since its foundation), and trained by Jim in Warwickshire, he was still going strong in 1997, when, to the huge delight of the point-to-point fraternity, he won the Liverpool Foxhunters'.

Johnny Greenall's Sunny Mount, who lost his maiden certificate at the Grove & Rufford, and won three other races, was to become one of the stars of Caroline Saunders's yard, though perhaps not quite in the same class as Greenall's Once Stung.

Another six-year-old to make his mark was the Dumfriesshire-hunted Tartan Tyrant, owned by Mrs. Alix Stevenson, wife of the Managing Director of Edinburgh Woollen Mill. A full brother to Tartan Takeover (a distinguished performer under Rules), Tartan Tyrant won four races on the trot under Kevin Anderson before his defeat by Glen Lochan at the Zetland. Mackenzie & Selby had Tartan Tyrant on the same mark as the experienced Steele Justice, at 10-9, so they must have thought a lot of him.

Willy Manners' Steele Justice enhanced his reputation in 1992. A winner of six races in his eight appearances, the Morpeth eight-year-old included among his wins hunter chases at Kelso and Perth, and at Kelso he beat Once Stung by a length, receiving 71b. from him. Pauline Robson was seen at her brilliant best on him in the ladies' open at the Jedforest when, after he had been all of 30 lengths behind the front-running Fish Quay (a runner-up in four handicap chases the previous season), she reached the front on him before the third last and scored easing up.

For the great Flying Ace it was his retirement season; and if the occasion was not marked by success on the course at the age of 16, it *was* marked with the publication this year by a book about him, *Flying Ace, The Story of a Racing Legend*, by Neil Clark, with a foreword by Graham Macmillan.

In a racing career which began for him as a seven-year-old in 1983, Adam Calder's home-bred Flying Ace, by Saucy Kit out of the Vulgan mare Flying Eye (a winner of two hunter chases and 13 point-to-points), ran in 88 races and won 59 of them, comprising 36 point-to-points and 23 hunter chases, ridden in all but one of them by Doreen Calder; and if he hadn't been disqualified for failing to draw the weight in one of his races when his weight cloth came off just before he reached the post in a hunter chase at Kelso, he would have reached the 60 mark.

Another Northern Area horse to retire this year was Peter and Rhona Elliot's 14-

year-old Fallalaw, after recording his third win of the season in the ladies' open at the Border fixture at Corbridge. Like Flying Ace, the Jedforest-hunted Fallalaw began racing in 1983. Trained by Peter and ridden by Rhona, who broke him in as a three-year-old, Fallalaw won 16 races in his 64 appearances; and his successes included the Vaux final at Sedgefield in 1986.

Also retiring at the age of 14 was Freddie Teal, the Grimthorpe Cup winner of 1986 in the same year that he won a novice chase at Southwell. The son of Bivouac was a winner of 12 races for the Strawsons of Lincolnshire.

But for another Lincolnshire family, the Dawsons, there was some appalling bad luck. Sweet Diana, the mare that had won 34 point-to-points and two hunter chases for them, collapsed and died of an aneurism in the course of contesting the ladies' open at the Badsworth; and in the very next race, division one of the PPOA Restricted, their rising star, Roscoe Boy's full brother Herman Blake, met with the same fate.

Nor was this the end of the stable's misfortune. Stisted Park, a winner of two ladies' opens at Higham on his only appearances during the season, damaged a tendon so badly on the gallops that no more was seen of him; while Roscoe Boy, as big a star as Sweet Diana, departed from the scene after winning two more ladies' opens and a hunter chase at Fakenham.

Peter Bonner's Federal Trooper, the brightest prospect in Denis and Christine McCarthy's Old Surrey & Burstow yard, died of colic on the night of April 9 when in process of recovering from a leg operation at the Animal Trust Centre at Newmarket. On his three appearances during the season, the 11-year-old had won two men's opens and finished third to Rushing Wild in the Cheltenham Foxhunters'.

John Deutsch's Dromin Joker died of a heart attack when out with the Warwickshire hounds two days after completing the course in the Cheltenham Foxhunters'. A winner on his only other run in 1992, this 12-year-old was a winner of 12 point-to-points in England following his successful career in Ireland, eight of them for David Naylor-Leyland and the other four for Deutsch.

Gerald Penfold, who lost his good horse John Sam last season, lost another in 1992 when his 11-year-old Seal Prince, a winner of two Confineds and two hunter chases, had a fatal heart attack after winning the same race at Worcester that had seen the end of John Sam.

For some top riders the season was cut short as a result of injury. The East Anglian rider Tim Moore was out for the rest of the season after injuring his neck and sustaining a fractured pelvis and severe concussion in a fall at Cottenham in February. Anthea Farrell had two spells on the sidelines, breaking her leg at the Badsworth in mid-February and her collar-bone (not for the first time) in a fall at the Holderness five weeks later; but she came back in between to win on Northumbrian King at the Derwent and ended up as the Yorkshire ladies' champion yet again. Pip Nash (née Jones) was out of action after a very bad fall in a hurdle race at Nottingham in March and was on a life support machine for some time.

And for two prominent riders it was time for retirement. David Kinsella, four times the Yorkshire champion and twice a runner-up for this title, announced his final retirement after coming out of semi-reitirement to win the hunt race at the

Sinnington on Demi Cheval. He was finishing with 74 winners in point-to-points and 13 under Rules in his 20 years of race-riding. The West Midlands rider Alastair Ulyet, who had his last winning ride on Dinner Suit in the Confined at the Golden Valley, went out with a total of 81 point-to-point winners.

It was a good season for Sir John Barlow's three sons. All three of them rode winners. William Barlow, the eldest, was top scorer among them with ten winners; and he and David, the middle son, both rode winners at the Cheshire Forest, where William completed a double. William and the youngest of the three, Charles, were both in the winner's enclosure at the North Shropshire. David brought off a double at Sir W.W. Wynn's, where William was also in the winner's enclosure; and these two also rode winners at the Cheshire. Between them, the three Barlows rode 17 winners, seven more than in 1991.

Two of the best horses to lose their maiden certificates this season were Graham Roach's East Cornwall pair of seven-year-olds Moorcroft Boy and Wheal Prosper; and they had good men on top in the two Ians, Dowrick and Widdicombe. Moorcroft Boy, by the French sire Roselier, won five of his seven races under Ian Dowrick, the last four of them on the trot; and he was a runner-up in his other two. Wheal Prosper, a son of Strong Gale, won four of his seven under Ian Widdicombe, getting up on the run-in in the last of them to beat Timlyn in a men's open at Holnicote. Moorcroft Boy was the overall champion in the PPOA/*Horse and Hound* young horse awards, and Wheal Prosper was the runner-up to him.

Both horses were on offer at the new sales at Cheltenham at the end of May; but neither changed hands there, though 25,000 guineas was bid for Wheal Prosper and 18,000 for Moorcroft Boy. But they were to change hands later; and when Moorcroft Boy went into David Nicholson's yard this prodigious stayer was to do wonderfully well under Rules, excelling in the 1994 Grand National when running a terrific race under Adrian Maguire to finish third to Minnehoma. Two years later he won the Scottish Grand National at Ayr.

Another up-and-coming seven-year-old, also a maiden at the start of the season, was the Middleton-hunted Many A Slip from Tim Walford's yard. His three wins in a row encompassed a novice hunter chase at Newcastle, where he comfortably accounted for Knocklaur.

The champion mare of the season was Mrs. Janita Scott's South Devon ten-year-old Confused Express. A winner of six of her eight races with Philip Scholfield up, her successes included a resounding win in the four-mile men's open at the Dartmoor. The runner-up to her for the mares' title was Bernard Pike's Elver Season.

Caroline Saunders was the leading trainer of hunter chasers, with her nine wins in this field making her the first recipient of the new challenge trophy which was being presented at the national point-to-point dinner at The Belfry by Richard Russell and Johnny Greenall.

A very strong candidate for the most bizarre race of the season would be the ladies' open at the North Ledbury in which seven horses were disqualified for missing out the 12th fence after being waved round it by some well-meaning person who had seen a rider lying prostrate on the landing side. The one rider sensible enough to take note of the correctly-placed marker was Alison Dare, who had already got things well wrapped up on Stephens Pet.

For one much-used course there was a change of management before the start of the season, with the British Horse Society taking over the lease of Tweseldown and installing course builder Paul Cabrol as the new Manager. Fortunately, the prize money for the five meetings held there remained at the maximum level, though the entry fees for the two military fixtures went up by 100%, to £20 per horse per race.

The death in February of Angela, the Dowager Lady Grimthorpe, at the age of 90 removed a remarkable character from the scene. A noted sea-diver, she was still diving from great heights in her eighties; and five years before her death she was writing to *The Times* in defence of riding side-saddle. She was also a great rider to hounds with the Middleton; and the name of Grimthorpe, of course, speaks loudly for her connections with point-to-pointing and racing under N.H. Rules. The best point-to-pointer she owned was Starlit Bay. A horse bought from his breeder as a yearling, Starlit Bay lost his maiden certificate as a five-year-old in 1949, and his seven successes over the next two seasons included four open point-to-points and two hunter chases. And when Fortina won the Cheltenham Gold Cup of 1947 for the Grimthorpes as an entire he was the first six-year-old to do so in the post-war years.

In June there filtered through news from America of the tragic death of the Abergavenny amateur Mark Richards at the age of 29. He was killed in a shooting incident whilst tracking down drug barons. The winner of the Grand Marnier male novice rider's award in 1981 as a 17-year-old Monmouthshire schoolboy, he also won the Wilkinson Sword trophy twice.

In August, John Farthing (the father of Justin) died in Yeovil Hospital at the age of 57 following a major stroke. One of John Farthing's ambitions was to win a race on his local course at Wincanton. He never quite managed it, but he was on a runner-up there eight times. The success that gave him the most pleasure, he said, was beating Fred Winter at Exeter.

And in December, the Bishop Auckland trainer Arthur Stephenson died at the age of 72. One of the greatest of all point-to-point riders, and a contemporary of Guy Cunard, Stephenson included amongst his innumerable successes in point-to-points three Grimthorpe Cups, two of them on horses he owned and trained himself, General Ripple in 1950 and Mr. Gay in 1955; and in 1951 he won both the Dudley Cup and the Grimthorpe Cup on Paul Pry. He never kept any account of his winners in point-to-points; and I am convinced that, had he done so, he would have been found a prominent place in Mackenzie & Selby's table of leading point-to-point riders of the post-war years.

Tailpiece:

A bizarre incident occurred an the Surrey Union's much-loved course(!) at Peper Harow when the wind blew down the numbers board and one of the stewards, Desmond Donegan, was knocked out cold. As one interested onlooker remarked, "It couldn't have happened to a nicer man."

1993

In which the season opens a fortnight earlier, the PPOA stages the first Sunday meeting, an heroic coup is attempted, Grand Marnier returns to the fold, and Double Silk brings off the big double.

Although the 1993 season was notable for the innovation of point-to-point racing in January and racing on a Sunday, as well as for an increase in the record number of hunters' certificates issued, now up to 4,210, I feel impelled to give pride of place in this chapter to an unparalleled example of private enterprise on the part of a veteran rider barely out of the novice class backing himself to win the men's title and take half a million pounds out of the books.

The instigator of this venture was a 48-year-old West Countryman, Bernard Heffernan, who rode his first winner in 1992 and finished that season riding five more – which must clearly have sent a rush of blood to his head, pumped up no doubt by the fact that one of the horses he had acquired to ride in 1993 was Yahoo, who had run in three Cheltenham Gold Cups and was the runner-up to Desert Orchid in the 1989 race.

One of the bookmakers that Heffernan made his bets with was our old friend Desmond Gleeson, who, after accepting a bet of £10,000 and laying him 40-1, took the precaution of laying about 90% of it off with his Irish friends, and must have regretted it ever since. Especially as I had told him when asked for advice that Heffernan had about as much chance of winning his wager as a snowball in the Sahara Desert.

And so it proved. But it was a brave try. Heffernan actually managed to ride 11 winners (half as many as it took Alastair Crow to secure the men's title); and seven of his wins were on Yahoo. After the season was over, and before disappearing to foreign parts, Heffernan sent all his horses up to the Russell, Baldwin & Bright Sales at Malvern and got £51,770 for them, Yahoo fetching the highest price of 10,000 guineas. So at least he got some of his money back; and, really, he had done better than most people thought he would, and provided a great deal of entertainment in the process. His enterprise was certainly missed in subsequent years, and not only by the bookmakers.

Only five point-to-point committees took advantage of the Jockey Club's concession to hold point-to-points in January, and three of them were in East Anglia, where the season opened with a single fixture, the Waveney Harriers at Higham, where there were 82 runners for the eight races, two of which, the maiden and the Intermediate, had been split into two divisions.

All that was lacking from the PPOA's brave venture in holding their meeting at Ashorne on a Sunday was atmosphere. As one of the winning riders remarked, "There was so little response when my horse passed the post that I thought I had to go round again." But at least we were spared any of those dreadful cries of "Come on my son." And the quality of the racing, despite unfavourable weather, was not in doubt. There were 105 runners for the eight races, with the club maiden being run in three divisions, and such horses as Fine Lace, King Neon, Good Waters, Cool Relation and Grecian Lace among the winners; while the razzmatazz included the sight of Johnny Greenall riding Desert Orchid down to the start.

Another first deserving of mention was the first-ever bloodhounds point-to-point, with the Windsor Forest Bloodhounds holding a meeting at Tweseldown, thanks largely to the initiative of their Senior Joint Master, Chris Coyne, who was suitably rewarded with a win in the open maiden on Game Fair, a six-year-old he trained himself and owned in partnership with Chris Shankland.

There were also two first-time winners of the *Daily Telegraph* and *Sporting Life* Cups in the 25-year-old Shropshire rider Alastair Crow and the 28-year-old Somerset-based Polly Curling.

Most of Alastair's wins were on horses trained by his mother, the redoubtable Sheila Crow; but it was his uncle, Gordon Edwards, who owned and trained his most prolific winner, the home-bred nine-year-old Scallywag mare Scally Muire, whose dam Coroin Muire won six point-to-points for Edwards. Scally Muire was a winner of five of her ten point-to-points and a runner-up in three others. On each of two other horses, Equity Player and Call Me Citizen, both of them trained by his mother, Alastair, who rode his 50th winner during the season, won four races. The last of his 22 wins was on another horse trained by his mother, Mrs. Whiteway's River Melody in a Restricted at the Golden Valley in mid-May. Before the start of the season, Alastair could have been backed for the title at 50-1 with the Middlesex bookmaker Desmond Gleeson.

There were two close runners-up to Alastair Crow for the men's title, Julian Pritchard and Nigel Bloom, each with 20 wins. Pritchard, whose services were much in demand, was a winner on 16 different horses, with six of his wins coming on horses trained by Dick Baimbridge and another six on horses from Peter Warner's yard at Ross-on-Wye.

Nigel Bloom had some marvellous rides on Jim Papworth's nine-year-old Melton Park, one of the horses trained by his father in Norfolk. On this true stayer, who was at his best coming from behind and producing a searing late run, his 12 wins included a walk-over in a hunt race at Ampton which helped Melton Park win the *Daily Telegraph* Cup with one more win than Brunico.

Melton Park, who started the season as a maiden, did not keep entirely to his own neck of the woods either. He paid three visits to the West Country and won on two of them, beating Brunico a short head at Bratton Down; and, over a course which would hardly have suited him, sprinting away from Radio Cue at

Umberleigh. A winner in January, he was also a winner in June. The only horses who succeeded in lowering his colours were Blakes Orphan, who held him off by threequarters of a length in an early race at Horseheath, and Searcy, who beat him a length at the Tiverton; and it is highly probable that he would have won both these races had he consented to start his run earlier.

Bred in Ireland and bought in January 1992, Melton Park had never set foot on a course before he entered Michael Bloom's yard. "He was bought," said his trainer, "because nobody else would have him." Which speaks volumes both for Michael Bloom's eye for a horse and his skill as a trainer.

Robert Alner, who rode no more than seven point-to-point winners, plus one in a hunter chase, and was looking forward to celebrating his 50th birthday in November, can be considered unlucky not to have been in the swim for his second men's title. Having ridden his seven winners by February 13, and being very well mounted on the horses trained by Harry Wellstead, he had his season brought to an abrupt close when a freak collision in mid-air on the hitherto unraced Young Brave at Larkhill gave him a badly broken leg in two places. Before the season was out, he had taken out a full licence as a public trainer; and he saddled his first winner in this capacity when Court Rapier, with Adrian Maguire up, won the Superform N.H. Handicap Chase at Plumpton in August.

After being runner-up for the ladies' title in 1990 and third in 1991 and 1992, Polly Curling was not winning her first *Sporting Life* Cup out of turn, and as well as her 25 winners in point-to-points she rode two winners in hunter chases. This was in the days before she rode so many winners for Richard Barber, although she did have four of her wins on three horses trained by him, Rural Outfit, Cream By Post and Island Forest. But most of her wins were on horses trained by Mike Trickey on Exmoor, 16 in fact, with five of the horses from this source, Henley Wood, Tangle Jim, Thrales and two of the horses owned by Capt. Tim Forster, The Doormaker and Brimstone Hill, each providing her with three wins; and three more of her wins were on two horses she trained herself, Society Member and Taftazani.

The win that must have given Polly most pleasure came in the John Corbet novice hunter chase at Stratford, where, riding Grant Cann's mare Friendly Lady for the first time, she rode a terrific race to get her past Moorcroft Boy at the last and score by a length and a half in a race which saw Mr. Murdock and Fine Lace finishing third and fourth. This was the completion of a hat-trick for Friendly Lady, with three different riders up.

The runner-up to Polly Curling for the ladies' title was Mandy Turner, whose 20 wins included three more on John Weldhen's For A Lark and five in a row on the same owner's Oriental Plume. Third in the ladies' table, with 19 wins, was Alison Dare, and behind her came Jo Cumings with 17 wins. Four of Alison's wins were on Tudor Thomas's nine-year-old Scallywag mare Scally's Daughter, who won another open event with Julian Pritchard up and ended her season as the PPOA *Horse and Hound* champion mare. The reserve champion, two points behind her, was Peter Clarke's Flame O' Frensi, a winner of four Confineds and two Intermediates under Jo Cumings, who also won five ladies' opens in a row on Khattaf and four races on Starember Lad, two of the other horses trained by her father at Bishops Nympton.

But for one top-class lady rider there was a tragedy. Jenny Litston sustained serious head injuries in a fall on a five-year-old maiden at Larkhill in February on the same day and at the same meeting which put Robert Alner out of action for the rest of the season. An appeal for donations on her behalf initiated by Polly Curling raised £450 at the national point-to-point dinner in November.

With Grand Marnier returning to the fold as a sponsor (although not yet with their Trophy) after a three-year absence, this dinner was now enjoying the combination of four sponsors for the first time, the others being the *Daily Telegraph*, the *Sporting Life* and *Horse and Hound*.

The *Daily Telegraph* male novice riders of the season were Andrew Parker and Alan Phillips, each with 12 winners; and the female novice rider of the season, with five wins, was a 16-year-old Yorkshire schoolgirl, Ruth Clark, four of whose wins in her first season of race-riding were gained on her father's ten-year-old Waltingo, who had won four times over fences and once over hurdles when in training with the late Arthur Stephenson and proved an admirable schoolmaster.

The 24-year-old Andrew Parker, son of the Lockerbie trainer Colin Parker, was the second Scottish rider to win the male novice rider's award since its initiation by Grand Marnier in 1979. The first was David Mactaggart in 1985. A former conditional jockey who rode his first winner in an amateurs hurdle at Carlisle the previous season, Parker was particularly well mounted on the eight-year-old King Spring, winning three races in a row on this maiden at the start of the season; and on the more experienced Jimmy River. The second leg of a treble for him at the Dumfriesshire, Jimmy River won three open point-to-points and a hunter chase at Perth with Parker up.

The two best horses the 23-year-old Alan Phillips rode were Cool Relation and Cape Cottage, both owned by Denis Caro, a Jersey hotelier, the former trained for him by Penny Grainger, who supplied Phillips with six of his winners from her yard near Kidderminster, and the latter by Caro himself at his Oaksey farm near Marlborough.

The leading novice rider under the age of 21, and the recipient of the Wilkinson Sword, was 18-year-old Ben Pollock. Riding five different horses, he had the same number of winners as Ruth Clark but one more second place.

Johnny Greenall won his brother's trophy for the fourth time, with 12 winners in hunter chases, his best total so far; and the Richard Russell-Johnny Greenall trophy for the leading trainer of hunter chasers went to Caroline Saunders again, with her 16 winners in this field. Caroline also trained 25 point-to-point winners, taking her into equal third place with Dick Baimbridge as a trainer of point-to-point winners, behind Peter Bowen with 27 and Richard Barber with 26. Harry Wellstead didn't do quite so well this season, being without the services of Robert Alner for the greater part of the season; but he trained 23 point-to-point winners, plus five in hunter chases.

The *Horse and Hound* Cup for the leading small owner-trainer-rider went this time to Mrs. Alison Hickman in the East Sussex & Romney Marsh country. Riding her ten-year-old Maltby Boy, the outstanding ladies' horse in the South East, she won seven races and was a runner-up twice. She was beaten a neck out of her country at Marks Tey by Katie Ellis on the Vale of Aylesbury 11-year-old Rusty Law, a winner of five of his six ladies' opens, and by Simon Andrews on No Rebasse in a hunter chase at Folkestone.

Several riders reached landmarks of one sort or another. Mike Felton rode his 200th point-to-point winner when scoring on Mrs. Betty Whettam's Sonofagipsy in the Tedworth men's open at Barbury Castle. Tim Jones had his 100th win in point-to-points in a division of the maiden race at the Monmouthshire on Zephyr Nights. James Tarry achieved a similar feat when scoring on his father's home-bred St. Laycar in an Intermediate at the Quorn, as did Lucy Gibbon on Van Dyke Brown at the Enfield Chace.

Three riders had their 100th career winners, Nigel Tutty at the Derwent, Paul Hacking at the South East Hunts Club fixture at Charing, and Alan Hill, in his third year as Joint Master of the Vale of Aylesbury, at the Pytchley. The Yorkshire rider Stephen Swiers was bidding for his career century when he broke his collar-bone in a last-fence fall on the five-year-old Prospecting in the Marie Curie novice championship at the Melton Hunt Club fixture on May 22. Swiers was convinced that Prospecting, who was challenging the winner at the time, would have won but for this. His view was not, however, shared by the winner's rider, Julian Smyth-Osbourne, a former Joint Master of the Cambridge University Draghounds who was riding the six-year-old Dalametre (one of the horses trained by Jenny Pidgeon) for his mother, a Joint Master of the Grafton.

Alison Dare reached an important landmark when a win on David Willis's ten-year-old Russki in the ladies' open at the Harkaway Club fixture at Chaddesley Corbett bumped her grand total of wins up to 174, breaking the previous record of 173 for a lady rider set by Josie Sheppard. By the end of the season Alison's total had risen to 181.

Caroline Saunders broke her own record when she trained five of the six winners at the Harborough Hunt Club's first point-to-point fixture at Dingley, three of them owned and ridden by Johnny Greenall. All six winners at this meeting had been hunted with the Pytchley.

Two trainers brought off four-timers twice, Richard Barber at the Cotley and the Seavington, and the Haverfordwest trainer Peter Bowen at the Tivyside and the Gelligaer Farmers; and at the Tivyside four of the winners were ridden by John Llewellyn, including Brunico in the men's open.

A competitive field of 14 for the first of the season's classic point-to-points, the four-mile men's open at the Heythrop, included the 1992 winner Speedy Boy, now owned by the Wiltshire garage proprietor Ray Geddes, who had bought him out of the McCarthy yard for 6,000 guineas and was looking for a first win with him. Also in the field, which saw Johnny Greenall's dual hunter-chase winner Alpha One starting favourite at 5-4, was the McCarthys' Namoos, a proven four-miler who had won twice over the distance.

Alpha One, however, failed to get the trip after being prominent for much of the journey, and Speedy Boy was unable to live up to his name this time. Approaching the last, four horses were in with a chance, and Blakes Orphan with Tom Illsley up, was just showing them the way on the downhill run. But it was Uncle Raggy who jumped the last in front under the South Midlands farrier Rory

Lawther; and the ten-year-old son of Monksfield ran on well to score by two lengths from Blakes Orphan, with Mirage Day half a length away in third, followed by Namoos, still running on.

Although this was Uncle Raggy's first win of the season, he had been a runner-up in his three previous races, the last of them a 3m 3f hunter chase at Sedgefield. Owned by Mrs. Penny White, trained by N.H. trainer John White and hunted with the Vale of Aylesbury, Uncle Raggy was bought the previous summer out of David Nicholson's yard "to have a bit of fun with," and he was the only point-to-pointer in training amongst the 50 or so horses White had in his Wendover yard. The horse ran once more during the season, when he finished third to Harley in a 4m lf hunter chase at the Cheltenham evening fixture in May.

Ocean Day, ridden this time by Howard Brown, deputising for the sidelined Anthea Farrell, won the four-mile mixed open for the Grimthorpe Cup for the second year running. The race was run on quite heavy ground and there were no more than nine starters for it. Despite having to concede 7lb. to most of his rivals, and 12lb. to some, Ocean Day made the running from pillar to post and won easing up by seven lengths from Level Quay. It was not, however, a vintage Grimthorpe. But, in a previous race, when ridden by Anthea Farrell, Ocean Day had beaten Knocklaur in a field of 16 at the Badsworth.

Before the start of the Grimthorpe there was a scene worthy of a Dick Francis novel when an attempt was made to get at Sue Bramall's intended runner Now And Then in his box with a syringe. It transpired later that the substance was Frusemide (trade name Lasix) and the culprit was a former stable boy holding a grudge. The Stewards of the Jockey Club warned him off for eight years. Now And Then, of course, was withdrawn from the race.

The Dudley Cup was also won by the same horse for the second year running, in this case Brunico, now owned by two Welsh dairy farmers, Michael Morris and William Raymond, who had acquired him at the end of last season; but still trained by Peter Bowen, and ridden by Ron Treloggen.

Starting favourite at evens in a field of 11 and ridden with exemplary patience by Treloggen, Brunico shot past Treyford approaching the last and beat him just as convincingly as he had done last time. There were good horses behind them. Steven Brookshaw was ten lengths further away on Konrad Wolf, and behind him came Tim Jones on Carrickmines and Jimmy Tarry on Saybright. Julian Pritchard's mount Sams Heritage, a winner of his two previous races and a well-backed second favourite, was barely seen with a chance.

This was Brunico's seventh win of the season; and when he and Melton Park went down to the Exmoor at Bratton Down to contest the British Field Sports Society race there on May 29 they were dead level on a seasonal total of 11. There was very little between the two as they approached the last; and on the long uphill run-in they were going neck and neck. It was an epic battle, and it resulted in Melton Park getting the verdict by the narrowest margin. But, unfortunately, Brunico finished lame in the process. So this was the end of his bid for the *Daily Telegraph* Cup, which Melton Park went on to capture with his 12th win at the Torrington Farmers on the last day of the season.

Both Melton Park and Brunico had a quirky side to their character; and Brunico had displayed his earlier in the season in an extraordinary three-horse men's open at the Gelligaer Farmers, where he showed his distaste for being left in front with a refusal at the second. The race continued at a funereal pace, with neither Tim Jones on Zephyr Nights nor Robert Rowsell on Alf Marhaba anxious to make the running. By the seventh, Brunico was in front once more when he refused again, causing the other two to do likewise. When, eventually, the three of them jumped the fence, Tim Jones had Zephyr Nights in front at a hack canter. This suited Brunico, and in the sprint for the line he got up to win the race by a length from Alf Marhaba, with Zephyr Nights trailing in third.

A report on this remarkable race, which took 9 mins. 30 secs to run, was sent to the Jockey Club; but I do not recall any action being taken over it. Nor perhaps should it have been. Some dogs are best left to lie sleeping. Certainly the vociferous crowd was in no doubt who the hero was. The cheers were exclusively for Brunico and his partner. My South Wales correspondent, Brian Lee, reported afterwards that, in his 26 years of covering point-to-point racing in Wales, he had never seen anything else like it. And I don't think he was joking.

In the Land Rover men's final at Towcester, for which there was a field of 11 on the good to firm ground, there was a win for a horse who was recording his first success under Rules since winning the Scottish Grand National at Ayr in 1988, 14-year-old Mighty Mark, owned by Frank Walton and trained by him in Northumberland. Somewhat surprisingly, as he had failed to win any of his four point-to-points during the season, Mighty Mark was an effortless winner under Peter Johnson at the expense of the 13-year-old Good Waters, a winner of three open races under John Sharp.

The ladies' championship had a new sponsor in Champagne Taittinger, and a new venue for the final at Huntingdon; and it was won by a very speedy customer indeed in Qannaas. After being well beaten by Russki at his home meeting, the Hursley Hambledon at Badbury Rings on his first appearance of the season, this nine-year-old by Kris had made all the running in a three-horse ladies' open in Hackwood Park under Lisa Parrott; and he did so again over the 3-mile track at Huntingdon with Pip Nash up, winning unchallenged from Fort Hall and Military Two Step, with Maltby Boy further behind in fourth.

A winner of two races on the Flat, four over hurdles amd two over fences before he started point-to-pointing last season, Qannaas was recording his fourth win (three of them in point-to-points) since joining the Hampshire yard of the former pro. jockey and later television pundit Bill Smith, an adviser to the Maktoum family. A very difficult horse to beat over a fast track, Qannaas was still winning races in 1997. His owner, Mrs. Ann Leat, is the wife of the Maktoums' racing supremo, John Leat.

In the equivalent championship with a final over a point-to-point course at the Melton Hunt Club fixture at Garthorpe, Mrs. Janet Spencer's Clifton-on-Teme nine-year-old Let Me Think, a son of Pollerton out of a French-bred mare, showed his mettle in recording his fifth win of the season (one of them a walk-over) on the trot under Candy Thomas. Making all in a field of nine, he flew home in the fastest time of the day to win as he liked from Van Dyke Brown and Fedneyhill, both good winners during the season, Van Dyke Brown's three wins in point-to-points under Lucy Gibbon being followed, after Melton, by success in a hunter chase at Fakenham with William Wales up.

Wild Illusion, a horse owned in partnership by Col. Arthur Clerke-Brown and Graham Pidgeon, whose daughter trained him, was a very worthy winner of the BMW challenge final at the Cheltenham evening fixture. Produced with a perfectly-timed late run by Ian McKie, he got to Blue Danube on the run-in and beat him by 2.5 lengths. This was the fifth win of the season for the nine-year-old son of True Song, the other four being in point-to-points, with Jon Trice-Rolph up on the first three occasions.

Wild Illusion was beaten only twice during the season, both times over the stayers' course at Mollington, on the first occasion going under by a neck to Johnny Greenall's seven-year-old Sunny Mount, who, with his seven wins, ended up as the national champion in the PPOA *Horse and Hound* young horse awards; and, on the second, by Bright Burns in his qualifying race at the Grafton, where he found his 61b. penalty too much for him.

The final of the first Russell, Baldwin & Bright maiden-race series attracted a field of 15 on the soft ground at Chepstow. No more than five of the runners completed the course; and the 4-1 favourite, Hill Royale, a winner of two of his three previous races, was not among them. He had already been headed by the eventual winner, the Llangeinor mare Doubting Donna, when he came down two out. Doubting Donna, a comfortable winner under Vivian Hughes (putting up 21b. over-weight for his first win under Rules), was bred by Lady Ann Boothby and trained by her owner, Mrs. Donna Hughes, the rider's sister-in-law. When winning her qualifying race at the Llandeilo Farmers Doubting Donna had recorded a time that was 13 seconds slower than that taken by Hill Royale to win a Restricted there.

By this time *The Times* had replaced its Restricted series with a new 'Rising Stars' hunter-chase series confined to six, seven and eight-year-olds; and one of the conditions for it, thanks to its instigator, the admirable Brian Beel, was that the contestants must have been placed in point-to-points. The final, run over 2m 7f on heavy ground at Worcester in mid-April, was contested by a field of ten; and it was won by a top-class point-to-pointer in Gold Shot, a seven-year-old from the Carmarthenshire owned by Rowland Mansell and trained by Peter Bowen. Well ridden by Tim Jones, this half-brother to Brunico (the reason he was bought) got home in a dramatic finish by a length and a half and a neck from Tamar Lass (to whom he was giving 121b.) and the penalised Royal Day, the winner of a hunter chase at Towcester on his previous appearance.

A winner of four point-to-points in 1991, when he lost his maiden certificate on his first appearance on a course, Gold Shot was off the course throughout 1992; but he returned to the fray with a vengeance in 1993, winning both his point-to-points and three hunter chases.

It seems amazing, in retrospect, that permit-holder Reg Wilkins's Double Silk should have been allowed to start at 12-1 for the Cheltenham Foxhunters'. Especially as the son of Dubassoff had already beaten Moorcroft Boy a neck at Warwick giving him 91b. And from the way the nine-year-old demonstrated his superiority, he must have thought so too. Admittedly he was given a good race by the Irish invader Kerry Orchid, a winner of two open point-to-points and a hunter chase in Ireland before coming to Cheltenham; but although there was no more than a length and a half between the two as they passed the post, the result was a decisive one, and Double Silk was giving the five-year-old Kerry Orchid 101b. Double Silk's rider, Ron Treloggen, had admitted being slightly worried about the fast ground (described as good to firm) when he was on the way to the start; but he was quoted in the *Sporting Life* afterwards as saying he "was happy once the race was under way and quite confident coming down the hill for the last time." Five lengths behind Kerry Orchid came another top hunter chaser, Once Stung, who was followed by Toureen Prince, a winner of both his open point-to-points and two hunter chases afterwards, and Moorcroft Boy.

Double Silk's triumph at Cheltenham was followed by another at Aintree, when he won the Liverpool Foxhunters' on his next appearance. Ridden again by the reliable Treloggen, and fencing as superbly as usual, he won this race with even greater assurance in a field of 17; and although he started favourite this time, it was at the generous price of 5-2. The horse that followed him home was one of Johnny Greenall's stars, the nine-year-old Dark Dawn, trained by Peter Cheesbrough in Arthur Stephenson's old yard at Bishop Auckland.

By the end of the season, Double Silk had won five of his six hunter chases, beaten only on his first appearance at Wincanton; and in the process he had become the first horse since Grittar in 1981 to complete the Cheltenham and Liverpool hunters' double in the same season.

Only six went to the post for the *Horse and Hound* Cup on the good to firm ground at Stratford, and Double Silk wasn't among them. The favourite, at 6-4 on, was Alan Hill's mount Sheer Jest, a winner of his previous five hunter chases, including two last season, an earlier one this season at Stratford, and one over 2m 110yds at the Cheltenham evening fixture in May. But he was soundly beaten by Peter Craggs's home-trained Generals Boy. With his owner up, this 11-year-old from the Morpeth was crowning a splendid season in which he was unbeaten in his five races, four of them open point-to-points. Ten lengths behind Sheer Jest came Johnny Greenall's Once Stung, a winner of four hunter chases during the season.

In one respect, it was an unfortunate season for Johnny. He lost one of his promising young horses when the six-year-old Overheard, a winner of all three of his races, broke down so badly in the course of winning the last of them, a hunter chase at Bangor, where he beat Gold Shot by three parts of a length, that he had to be put down.

There were, of course, other misfortunes; and one of them befell the Dawsons' Lincolnshire yard when Roscoe Boy, a winner of 21 races for them, and all set to return to the fray in 1993, shattered a sesamoid bone on the gallops a few days before Jill Dawson completed a treble riding three other horses at the Brocklesby on March 6. It was the end of the road for him at the age of 11.

Another horse to damage a sesamoid bone, although not so badly, was Carl's Choice, who was making what proved to be the 12-year-old's swan song when completing a hat-trick of wins in a men's open at Parham on March 6. By this time he had amassed a grand total of 33 wins, 29 of them in open races and two in hunter chases. Ten of his wins were achieved on his favourite course at Cottenham, where he was the most prolific of all the winners over that course.

No fewer than 18 of the wins recorded by Carl's Choice *in open events* were consecutive ones; and this is something that even that fabulous West Country pony Lonesome Boy, with his 65 wins, never managed to achieve. In November 1994 George Cooper gave Carl's Coice to a friend of his for team-chasing and hunting.

The only horse to beat Carl's Choice in his last season of racing was The Red One, who managed to do so on their first appearances of the season at Cottenham. This was The Red One's sole appearance in a point-to-point this season; but the nine-year-old went on to win two hunter chases before being brought down at the second in the Cheltenham Foxhunters'. Later on, he was a winner of novice chases at Stratford and Market Rasen, ridden by his 1991 Dudley Cup pilot Stephen Swiers at the former venue and by the pro. jockey Graham Bradley at Market Rasen. Sadly, in his last race of 1993, another novice chase at Stratford, where Swiers was up on him again, The Red One broke a leg and had to be put down.

Another top-class horse to run his last race in 1993 was Brunico, who never reappeared after finishing lame in his race at Bratton Down. In his magnificent career in point-to-points, which began in a quiet way in 1989, the grey son of Bruni ran in 34 races and won 25 of them, 24 of them open events, and 23 of them when he was in training with Peter Bowen. On all but one of his winning appearances he was ridden by Ron Treloggen.

The Vergettes' Perroquet, a top-class ladies' horse in the Midlands, had to be put down after breaking down badly in a point-to-point at Market Rasen on his first appearance of the season. The 13-year-old son of the Ascot Gold Cup winner Precipice Wood won 18 races from George Vergette's yard in the Cottesmore country, comprising nine point-to-points, four hunter chases, three novice chases and two handicap chases; and in all but the two handicap chases in which he was ridden by 'Tik' Saunders, he was ridden by George's daughter-in-law, Helen ("Loony") Vergette.

It was sad to see weight problems finally getting the better of Justin Farthing, who called it a day shortly after reaching his 29th birthday. But at least he had ridden 16 winners during the season and attained a grand total of 128, including four in hunter chases. He also achieved a major ambition when winning the hunt race at the Blackmore & Sparkford Vale for a trophy in memory of his father.

Paul Barber's six-year-old See More Indians, the horse Farthing won this race on, was one of the season's most exciting young horses. A newcomer to Richard Barber's yard, he was making a first appearance over fences, after winning two bumpers' races as a four-year-old and finishing second in two novice hurdles last season, when winning a Confined at Larkhill in February. The son of Seymour Hicks, bought for 21,000 guineas out of Paul Nicholls's yard, was unbeaten in his three point-to-points, with Farthing up in all of them. Following these dazzling performances, he was put away for the season prior to rejoining the Nicholls's yard, from which he was to win six chases the following season and run a good race in the Sun Alliance Chase at Cheltenham.

Two others to shine as six-year-olds were Davy Blake and Hops And Pops. Davy Blake won his first four races, including two hunter chases at Kelso, where he beat

Many A Slip in the first of them and Steele Justice in the second; while Hops And Pops won all three of her point-to-points, with Robert Alner up in the first of them and a new rider in Michael Miller ('The Jolly Miller's' son) proving an able deputy in the other two for the injured Alner.

Notwithstanding Uncle Raggy's win at the Heythrop and Ocean Day's in the Grimthorpe Cup, the staying point-to-pointer of the season has to be Roy Stevens's eight-year-old Nearly Splendid from the East Devon. A son of Nearly A Hand, he was a winner of three races over four miles, winning all three he contested, the men's opens at the Dartmoor and the Exmoor under Tom Greed and the ladies' open at the Modbury Harriers with Clare Wonnacott up; and in between he was a runner-up to Brunico in a three-mile men's open at the Dulverton West.

Teaplanter, confining himself to hunter chases, was a faller in his first at Sandown and a runner-up to Henrietta Knight's Toureen Prince at Bangor in his next; but he won his other two, trotting up from Moorcroft Boy at Huntingdon and beating The Malakarma a length at Towcester.

Mrs. Pat Rowe's Richard Hunt, a nine-year-old by Celtic Cone, was establishing quite a reputation for himself in partnership with Lisa Rowe in East Anglia. Having won three races in a row in 1992, when he lost his maiden certificate, he added four more to his score in 1993; and he was yet to run in ladies' races, the events in which he was to make his name in later years.

Donald ("Ginger") McCain's son Donald, who had ridden 20 winners under Rules, rode his first winner between the flags when scoring in the men's open at the Vale of Lune on Judy Eaton's home-bred 13-year-old Harley. A winner of five races under Rules for his owner-trainer, Harley had his second win of the season with McCain Jnr. up in the 4m 1f hunter chase at the Cheltenham evening fixture.

The veteran West Country rider George Turner, who must then, at the age of 56, be just about the oldest rider riding regularly in point-to-points, rode 13 winners during the season; and he brought his grand total of wins in point-to-points up to 49 when scoring on Persian Style in the Confined at the Spooners & West Dartmoor, where he was completing the second leg of a double, the first leg being achieved in the hunt race on one of the horses he owns and trains himself, the seven-year-old Prince Soloman, a winner of three races for him during the season.

It was a big day for the Barlow family at the South Shropshire. They won four of the seven races at Eyton-on-Severn. George Barlow's son Jeremy landed a double with two spare rides from Steven Brookshaw's yard, winning the men's open on Nodforms Dilemma and a division of the open maiden on Twelfth Man. Charles Barlow, Sir John's youngest son, won the Intermediate on Mrs. Pam Sykes's Pont De Paix; and Sir John's middle son, David, won the Confined on Vague Influence.

Mrs. Ann Blaker, in Sussex, had found a worthy successor to El Padre in another horse acquired from Joe Turner, the nine-year-old Burromariner (a son of Julio Mariner out of a mare by Aureole). Doing his best to erase the squiggle he had earned from Mackenzie & Selby, Burromariner won four races for her with Chris Gordon up, the last of them a men's open at Peper Harow. Mrs. Blaker said, "I read a description of him in Mackenzie & Selby's annual which described him as totally crooked and would do anything to avoid winning, and decided that was good enough for me."

Frank Gilman and Denis McCarthy died in August, the former at the age of 78 and McCarthy at the age of 52 after fighting cancer for three years.

A permit holder for more than 40 years, and Chairman of the Cottesmore Hunt from 1983 to 1987, Frank Gilman will forever be remembered as the owner, trainer and breeder of Grittar; and he was present at Fakenham in March when another of his horses, Neltama, a half-brother to Grittar, won a hunter chase there. A great sportsman, and a man with a tremendous sense of fun, Frank was a much-loved figure on the point-to-point courses in Leicestershire; and I have every reason to recall the occasion at Garthorpe when he and his rider, Dick Saunders, poured a bottle of champagne over me, for the purpose of my Christmas card, much to the horror of the Veuve Clicquot people, who did not appreciate their product being distributed in such a way.

Denis McCarthy, the former pro. jockey who retired from race-riding in the late 'sixties, after riding some 50 winners under Rules, subsequently established, with his wife Christine, that wonderfully successful point-to-point yard at Godstone in Surrey that Christine and their son Tim continued to maintain.

The Cheshire veterinary surgeon Ted Greenway, a noted point-to-point rider in his day, and, in later years, the vet responsible for looking after Red Rum, died the same summer at the age of 73. He was the official vet at Aintree and Haydock.

Tailpiece:
Quote from Bill Smith, the former professional jockey, after the 22-year-old Lisa Parrott had won the BFSS race for novice riders at the Vine & Craven with her first ride in a race on his 11-year-old Privateperformance: "He's an ugly duckling with no neck and bad legs. He makes a noise and I wouldn't dream of riding him myself."

1994

*In which more records are broken, the PPOA fixture moves to Barbury
Castle, a Point-to-Point Festival is introduced, a son reaches a landmark
achieved by his father, and a Welsh champion hangs up his boots.*

This was a record-breaking season, with 4,249 hunters' certificates issued,
14,148 runners (1,023 up on 1993), and the 210 fixtures scheduled including the welcome return of the Piccadilly Hunt Club's fixture which failed to
materialise last year, and the experimental appearance of a Point-to-Point Festival;
while on the hunter-chase front there was a new fixture entirely devoted to hunter
chases at Newcastle to add to those well-established hunter-chase fixtures at
Cheltenham, Leicester and Folkestone and the one that was in its first season at
Uttoxeter in 1992.

What more could one want? Well, not as many as ten point-to-points lost altogether and a further 21 postponed, on account of what the Jockey Club dryly
described as "exceptionally wet Spring weather."

The record number of runners sometimes produced overloaded cards, with a
plethora of divided races, producing as many as 12 races at the Derwent (where
the last race had to be abandoned owing to the fading light) and the Clifton-on-
Teme, where the moon was rising as the 12th race went ahead. The fixture that
produced the greatest number of runners, however, was the Cleveland with its 142
for the ten races, though there would have been 148 at the Derwent had the last
of the 12 races been run. Next to the Cleveland came the PPOA fixture at Barbury
Castle with 134 runners for ten races. The North Hereford, which more often than
not is at the top of the tree with runners, had 126 runners for its ten races, four
fewer than the Derwent and the Brecon, and five fewer than the Clifton-on-Teme
and the West Shropshire Draghounds, but the same number as the South
Midlands Area Hunt Club fixture on the Heythrop course.

There were no very significant changes to the regulations for point-to-points,
although there was a somewhat ambivalent one about prize money, stating that
"Prize money levels remain unchanged, but application may be made to the
Stewards of the Jockey Club for values higher than the stated maxima."
Presumably this stipulation was designed primarily with the object of giving some

additional incentive to the new National Point-to-Point Festival at Garthorpe which was being sponsored by Citroen.

If so, the concession was not taken up. Advantage was, however, taken of the further concession to permit travel allowances, which were not tolerated for other meetings; and there was a promise of a cast of a Philip Blacker bronze for every winning owner and rider – which must, I imagine, have cost the sponsors rather more than the peanut £100 maximum for mementoes normally allowable.

Even so, despite these concessions, and the considerable amount of hype that went on beforehand, the occasion can hardly be described as an unqualified success; if not yet quite the "dead duck" it was dubbed by Christopher Sweeting in his prophetic letter to *Horse and Hound*; and it has to be said that there were a variety of races, including races for young riders and veteran riders and one for novice horses hopefully described as a championship, as were the men's and ladies' opens. But, with few exceptions, the runners failed to come from far afield, and there were no more than 44 for the six races, with fields of five and three, respectively, for the men's and ladies' 'championships'.

Minor changes to the point-to-point regulations included a reduced safety factor of 18 for maiden races and 25 for any other race; and it was now obligatory for all meetings to have at least one paramedic in attendance; while riders were required to submit their medical record book for inspection at declaration, and to be passed fit by the medical officer if they had previously been declared unfit as the result of a fall.

And in accordance with the new N.H. guidelines concerning the use of the whip, point-to-point stewards were given implicit instructions on what was considered improper use of the whip. Fortunately, since they were amateurs, they were usually a good deal more sensible in the matter of interpreting these instructions than many of their counterparts under Rules, common sense and discretion prevailing in most cases.

In an astonishing season, even for her, and despite being out of action for the best part of a month with a broken wrist, Polly Curling, in riding 35 point-to-point winners, and winning the *Sporting Life* Cup for the second year running, achieved the highest-ever total by a lady rider in a single season, eclipsing Alison Dare's score of 26 in 1991. And when winning a mixed open on Qannaas at Badbury Rings on March 26 she sent up her century of point-to-point winners.

Polly Curling's 35 wins in point-to-points were achieved on 19 different horses, nine of which started the season as maidens; and the 14 she won on from Richard Barber's stable, including seven of the maidens, won 30 races between them. At the Wilton and the South Dorset she brought off four-timers, and on top of this she had two further wins in hunter chases, scoring at Leicester on My Mellow Man (one of the horses Jenny Litston used to ride before her accident) and at Windsor on Richard Barber's charge Brief Encounter.

It was also a record-breaking season for Richard Barber as a trainer, in more ways than one. He saddled 52 point-to-point winners and trained six of the eight winners at the South Dorset, as well as five of the winners on his home course at the Seavington and four at the Beaufort, the Wilton and the Blackmore & Sparkford Vale. One of his two winners under Rules was Quick Rapor, the winner of the Grand Military Gold Cup at Sandown, where he was ridden by his owner, Dominic Alers-Hankey.

The most exciting newcomer from the Barber yard, one ridden throughout the season by Polly Curling, was John Keighley's seven-year-old Straight Talk, who started the season as a maiden and went through the season unbeaten, winning five races without being extended in any of them. Having failed to distinguish himself over fences and hurdles in Ireland, or indeed in bumpers' races there, Straight Talk, a son of Ovac out of a mare by Golden Love, joined the Barber yard after being bought for 15,000 guineas at the Doncaster Sales in the summer of 1993. In his last race of 1994 he demolished the pretensions of Yahoo in the ladies' open at the Berkeley; and he was soon to fulfil his promise under Rules when, as an inmate of Paul Nicholls's yard, he won three novice chases and a handicap chase in the 1994-95 N.H. season, ridden on the first occasion by Richard Dunwoody and on the other three by Polly Curling.

Another of the Barber horses unbeaten in 1994 with Polly Curling up was Mrs. Susan Humphreys's Cattistock seven-year-old Rural Outfit, who won six ladies' opens, and included amongst his victims two of the best horses Alison Dare rode, Stephens Pet and Le Kingdom.

Also a winner of six races for the Barber yard was Tim Frost's home-bred seven-year-old Lewesdon Hill. A maiden at the start of the season, he won five of his races with Polly up and one with Tim Mitchell aboard. But he was not destined to do so well in later years as two of the other Barber horses who began their season as maidens, Cherrynut and What A Hand.

John Keighley's five-year-old Cherrynut (by Idiot's Delight out of a mare by Deep Run), bought for 20,000 guineas at Doncaster, was a winner for Barber at the Beaufort the first time he set foot on a course, and he won both his other races under Polly Curling; while the six-year-old What A Hand, a 3,300 guineas purchase at the Ascot Sales, and also a winner first time out, was an impressive winner of three of his four races. This one, a son of Nearly A Hand, was owned by Mrs. "Podge" Roberts, the mother of the well-known course builder "Tishy" Roberts.

But for one of the Barber stable's former stars, See More Indians, who had gone into training with Paul Nicholls and won six chases from his yard, there was a sad ending in May. He was kicked by another horse in his field and sustained so bad a break in the upper joint of his off-foreleg that he had to be put down.

Alison Dare, the runner-up to Polly Curling for the ladies' title with 17 winners, 14 of them trained by Dick Baimbridge, rode her 200th career winner when scoring on Dr. Paul Brown's 12-year-old Lover Bill in a maiden race at Badbury Rings in January, and by the end of the season she had reached a total of 198 winners in point-to-points.

Alison won five races in a row on Lover Bill, who had run in over 30 races under Rules without scoring, and was thus paying yet another tribute to Dick Baimbridge's skills as a trainer. If Lover Bill hadn't broken down in his last race at the Berkeley he would have remained unbeaten. On another of Dr. Brown's horses, Stephens Pet (a horse who needed a righthanded course to show his best form), Alison won four ladies' opens in a row; and she won three in a row on Timber Tool, her only ride from outside the Baimbridge yard. At the Ledbury in April all four of her rides from the Baimbridge yard were winners, Lover Bill, Double Handfull, Down The Mine and Di Stefano.

With Alastair Crow's bid for a second men's title coming unstuck when he broke his collar-bone in two places on March 26 at the Clifton-on-Teme, until he returned to ride the seventh of his 11 winners the best part of a month later, his mother meanwhile having saddled four of the winners at the Flint & Denbigh without his aid, the contest for the *Daily Telegraph* Cup developed into a match between the Irish-born Damien Duggan and Nigel Bloom. It wasn't resolved until the last day of the season at the Torrington Farmers.

At the start of the racing at Umberleigh that day both riders were on a total of 21, and breathing down their necks was James Tarry with 20. Duggan and Bloom began their match in the men's open, although it wasn't resolved in this race, Bloom finishing second on Melton Park to Mike Felton on Beech Grove, with Tarry third on Saybright, and Duggan fourth on Peter Bowen's charge Glen Oak. So the leading pair were still dead level, as they were after the next three races, with Duggan being without any more rides and Bloom having failed to advance his score on a spare ride in the Restricted.

Then came the last race of the day, the open maiden, in which Bloom had secured a ride on one of John Dufosee's charges, National Gypsy, thanks to a generous gesture on the part of Mike Felton. On her previous form, National Gypsy did not look much like a winner. But the firm ground was very much to her taste, and a magnificent jump at the last, combined with Bloom's strong riding on the flat, got the Blackmore & Sparkford Vale mare home by a neck from Jo Cumings's mount, the five-year-old Heather Boy. So Nigel Bloom got the 22nd winner that he needed for the title.

It was hard luck, of course, for the 24-year-old Gloucestershire-based Damien Duggan, whose skilful riding had been apparent throughout the season, never more so than when he won a division of the open maiden at the Worcestershire on Hackett's Farm, that he didn't manage to get a ride in this race. But he had a highly successful season with his 21 winners; and an exceptionally good horse to ride in The Blue Boy, a winner eight times over hurdles for Martin Pipe, seven times as a three-year-old and once as a four-year-old in 1992.

After an unsuccessful season under Rules from another yard, The Blue Boy was bought for 4,400 guineas by Peter Bowen at the Russell, Baldwin & Bright Sales at Malvern in June 1993 as a five-year-old; and in 1994 Duggan won six open races on him before the horse returned to Martin Pipe's yard in the summer and won two novice chases for him.

In winning the men's title for the first time, Nigel Bloom was following in the footsteps of his father, who won this title in 1969. And he did so in another respect when a win on a horse from outside the Bloom yard, Hugh Hodge's six-year-old Harmony Walk in an open maiden at Marks Tey on Easter Monday, gave him his 100th win in point-to-points. The Blooms were so far the only father and son to achieve either feat. By the end of the season, however, Nigel, with his 104 wins, was still a long way short of Michael's 145. But he did achieve one feat that escaped his father. In riding five of the winners at the Essex Hunt fixture at High Easter on March 26 he became the first rider to emulate Robin Greenway's similar feat at the Cheshire Forest in 1975.

One of the horses who helped Nigel Bloom achieve this feat was Jim Papworth's Melton Park, whose seven wins and six second places enabled his owner to collect the original 1970 Grand Marnier Trophy which had now replaced the *Daily Telegraph* Trophy for the most prolific winner of the season.

Melton Park can also lay claim to having put up the most spectacular performance of the season when winning a competitive men's open at the Harborough Hunt Club meeting at Dingley. His fencing there was anything but fluent and as he approached the second last he was in fourth place fully a dozen lengths behind the three leaders. Such was his acceleration, however, that, even though he was in a similar position 50 yards from the line he went by Queensway Boy and No Escort as if they were standing still and won a remarkable race by a neck from Saybright, who had looked all over a winner until he attempted to run out at the last and required all of Jimmy Tarry's strength to get over it.

The only horses to win as many races as Melton Park were the West Country mare Confused Express and Cliff Dawson's Brocklesby seven-year-old Layedback Jack, a home-bred half-brother, by True Song, to Roscoe Boy and Herman Blake. Mrs. Janita Scott's Confused Express was unbeaten in her seven races, with Ashley Farrant up on her in the first two and, after he was out of action with an injury, Philip Scholfield in the other five. Layedback Jack won six of his seven races with Jill Dawson up, including the ladies' championship at the Melton Hunt Club; and for both of them there were compensations for not winning the Grand Marnier. Confused Express was the champion mare of the season, and the seven-year-old Layedback Jack was the PPOA *Horse and Hound* young horse national champion.

Had there been an award for the rider of the most home-bred winners it would undoubtedly have gone to the South Midlands rider James Tarry, all but one of whose 20 wins were on horses bred on the Tarrys' farm at Preston Capes in the Grafton country. The exception was Lucky Christopher, who was bred by his owner, Peter Wilsdon, but sired by the Tarry stallion St.Columbus.

Although never in contention for the men's title which he had won in 1983, John Llewellyn overtook Guy Cunard's total of 268 point-to-point wins to take second place behind David Turner in the table of all-time greats when a win on Peter Bowen's charge Chibougama in the Restricted at the Carmarthenshire gave him his 269th win; and he was to have another on the same horse in the Confined at the South Pembrokeshire to take him to a grand total of 270 point-to-point wins in what proved to be his last season of race-riding at the age of 47. He made his decision to retire, after a career that had lasted for 32 years, when he broke his hip in May in an accident at home which laid him up for six months and caused the surgeons some anxiety as they had to pin and plate it. The success that gave him the most pleasure in his race-riding days was winning the Land Rover men's final at Chepstow in 1986 on Grenville Richards's Fixed Price; but the horse who gave him the best feel in point-to-points, he says, was Alan Hollingsworth's Karannsu, of whom he said. "He could always be relied upon to win even when in need of a race."

Another top rider to call it a day was Ian McKie, although not in his capacity as a Joint Master of the Bicester with Whaddon Chase. But he made his swan song as a race-rider after winning the hunt race at his home meeting on his wife's Rain Down and taking his grand total of wins in point-to-points up to 112.

It was a memorable season for several first-time winners for members of famous point-to-point families; and foremost amongst them was a 17-year-old Shropshire schoolboy, Richard Burton, a grandson of Peter Brookshaw Snr. He had his first win riding a cool race on his father's Fence Judge (a horse trained by his uncle, Steven Brookshaw) in the Confined at Sir W.W. Wynn's, where he beat Alastair Crow on Scally Muire. Young Burton won five races in a row on the 12-year-old Fence Judge, and also scored on two more of the horses trained by Steven. One of them, Mickley Secretlove, on whom he won the men's open at the North Staffordshire, where he completed a double on Fence Judge, was bred by his grandmother, Gwen Brookshaw. Richard Burton's seven wins gained him both the *Daily Telegraph* male novice rider's award and the Wilkinson Sword.

Nicky Sheppard, who had her first win in a division of the British Field Sports Society race for novice riders on Deer Fencer, a horse bought by her father for 1,400 guineas at the Russell, Baldwin & Bright Sales at Malvern the previous October, is the daughter of Roger Guilding, who rode 135 point-to-point winners and numbered amongst his successes a win in the 1969 *Horse and Hound* Cup at Stratford on his father's Touch Of Tammy.

The 19-year-old Kim Gilman had her first win in the ladies' open at the Cottesmore on Neltama, a horse bred by her grandfather, the late Frank Gilman. 25-year-old Jonathan Connell was riding his first winner when scoring in a well-filled hunt race at the Grafton on Grecian Saint, a horse owned by his father, Sir Michael Connell, a noted point-to-point rider in his day and then a High Court Judge; and the 28-year-old Angela Hinch, whose first win was on her own High Edge Grey when this 13-year-old son of Precipice Wood foiled the bid of Fort Hall to record his 30th win in a field of 18 for a club members' race at the Melton Hunt Club, is the daughter of Mrs. Pat Hinch (the first-ever winner of the *Sporting Life* Cup in 1967) and the granddaughter of Lance Newton.

The youngest of all these first-time winners was 16-year-old Joe Docker with his win on his mother's 15-year-old Raise An Argument in the Confined at the Belvoir, where he beat Johnny Greenall on Some Flash. Joe is the son of John Docker, who rode 75 winners in point-to-points and won the Players Gold Leaf men's final at Newbury in 1972 on Doctor Zhivago.

The season was also a memorable one for the husband and wife combination of Alan and Trelawney Hill as riders and trainers in bringing off trebles between them at Mollington and Kimble with horses produced from their yard at Aston Rowant. At the former venue, Alan won two of the three maiden races on the nine-year-old Arrow Valley Lad and the six-year-old AJ's Boy, and Lawney was a comfortable winner of the ladies' open on Green Archer from Angela Hinch on her High Edge Grey; and at Kimble on Easter Saturday it was the mixture as before, with Alan winning the Vale of Aylesbury hunt race on AJ's Boy and the Confined on his own horse Swooping, and Lawney taking the ladies' open on Green Archer.

Another husband and wife combination, Howard and Jeannie Brown, brought off a four-timer at the Derwent, where Jeannie won a division of the Confined on Magic Whip and the ladies' open on Duntime, and Howard won the men's open on Final Chant and one of the three confined maidens on the seven-year-old Ellerton Park, a horse trained by Jeannie.

Someone else who brought off a four-timer was Richard White, a 20-year-old pupil assistant to Tim Forster. He scored on all four of his rides at the Dulverton East, including one for his Guvnor when winning the Confined on Basilea, whose six wins during the season included three in ladies' opens, with Polly Curling up in one of them and Jane Brackenbury in the other two.

Polly Curling and Nigel Bloom were not the only riders to ride their 100th point-to-point winner this season. Simon Andrews, whose wins during the season had included one in Ireland, achieved this landmark when riding the third leg of a treble at Cottenham on Loyal Note. The veteran Peter Craggs became the first Northumbrian rider to do so when when scoring on his Generals Boy in the men's open at the Border fixture at Corbridge; and Jill Dawson joined the party with her win on Layedback Jack at the Melton Hunt Club fixture; and she made it 101 at the same meeting when scoring on Mrs. Elaine Wilson's seven-year-old Force Eight in the Marie Curie novice championship. This son of Strong Gale won five of his six races, ridden in all of them by Jill Dawson.

But for one rider, East Anglia's 29-year-old William Sporborg, the season ended in disaster. After riding five winners, he sustained severe spinal injuries in a fall on a five-year-old in a maiden race at Marks Tey on April 2 which resulted in his being confined to a wheel-chair. He still has a hand, though, in training the horses sent out from his father's yard and has since become a well-known voice on the special East Anglian point-to-point line.

The Grimthorpe Cup was the first of the three classic point-to-point races to be run this season, and there were 11 runners on the soft ground at Whitwell-on-the-Hill for this four-mile mixed open, which resulted in a popular local success for the Brotherton family. Serena Brotherton had so comfortable a ride on Across The Lake that she was able to win easing up. This was the partnership's third win of the season, and they were to have another one afterwards at the Pendle Forest & Craven. The consistently reliable 10-year-old, trained for Mrs. David Brotherton by Anthea Farrell, had now run in 25 races since he started in hunt racing in 1992, won nine of them and been out of the first three on only three occasions, twice in point-to-points and once in a hunter chase; and he had never fallen.

I do, though, just wonder what would have transpired in the Grimthorpe had Mrs. Monica Dickinson's Man's Best Friend met his engagement in it. A proven stayer, he would have been well suited by the going. The last horse bred by Tony Dickinson before he died, this seven-year-old by Mandalus out of a mare by Tarqogan was the first point-to-point runner for the Dickinson family since 1968, the year Michael Dickinson won the Grimthorpe Cup on his mother's Shandover. A winner of two chases at Hexham in the 1992/93 season when trained for Mrs. Dickinson by her son-in-law, Thomas Tate, Man's Best Friend made four appearances in point-to-points in 1994 from Anthea Farrell's yard. Ridden each time by Richard Ford, he won three point-to-points and was a runner-up in the other, a 3m 5f men's open at Corbridge, where he went under to the useful Jimmy River. His only other appearance was in a 4m 1f hunter chase at Newcastle, where the going didn't suit him and he was beaten by Four Trix, the Scottish Grand National winner at Ayr in 1990.

Another very useful horse who might well have run in the Grimthorpe was Ralph Brader's home-bred Middleton mare Magic Whip, who was retired to stud after winning six races on the trot with Jeannie Brown up.

The four-mile race for Lord Ashton of Hyde's Cup at the Heythrop took place three days after the Grimthorpe; and for this there were no more than six runners, although the going was plenty yielding enough to have attracted more. But there was a good winner, and a fitting reward for the octogenarian Ted Knight's Holland House (the horse named after his favourite tobacco and bred by him from his winning point-to-point mare Norma Can). It may be that some of the 21 entrants were frightened away by his presence.

Whatever the reason, the seven-year-old son of Chris Sweeting's successful Conduit Stud stallion Sunyboy was in no sort of danger from the moment that Charlie Vigors took him to the front three fences out, and he was being eased as he passed the post 21 lengths ahead of John Deutsch's mount Royle Speedmaster, a winner of five chases in his days under Rules.

Trained in the Vine & Craven country by Patrick Chamings, Holland House, a maiden at the start of the 1993 season, when he won four of his five races, was scoring for the eighth time; and his four wins in a row in 1994 included two over four miles, the first one in a mixed open at Larkhill.

Another fine stayer, Nearly Splendid, enhanced his reputation when crowning a successful season with his fourth win over four miles; and this one was in the 4m 1f hunter chase at the Cheltenham evening fixture. His other four wins with Tom Greed up included a hunter chase at Taunton and an amateur riders' handicap chase at Newton Abbot. He also finished third in the 4-mile National Hunt Chase for amateur riders at Cheltenham in March.

In a good field of 13 for the Lady Dudley Cup at the Worcestershire, 13-year-old Yahoo, now owned by Robert Jones and trained by his cousin the former pro. jockey Martin Jones in the Ledbury country, recorded his third win since changing hands at Malvern; and he did it in style. Ridden for the first time by 23-year-old Mark Rimell (Mercy Rimell's grandson), he sailed past the front-running Treyford four fences out and beat this seemingly perpetual runner-up in major races all ends up in a considerably faster time than Brunico had taken to do so in the 1993 race on a slower surface. When winning two previous open races Yahoo had been ridden by Julian Pritchard; but this time Pritchard picked the wrong horse in Magic Moghul, who had to be pulled up before the fourteenth. In his last two races of the season Yahoo was a runner-up, to Straight Talk in the ladies' open at the Berkeley, and to the ill-fated Connemara Dawn, who collapsed and died after beating him by a short head in a hunter chase at Worcester and giving the 18-year-old Polly Gundry her first win under Rules.

Richard Russell had a most productive season with two of the hunter chasers trained for him by Caroline Saunders, Teaplanter and Avostar. On the former he won four of his five, including one at Cheltenham in May; and in his only defeat, Teaplanter was beaten by the invincible Double Silk in the Cheltenham Foxhunters'. Avostar, a seven-year-old by Buckskin, won three of his four hunter chases and two open point-to-points with his owner up on all but one occasion;

and included amongst his successes was the final of the Land Rover men's championship at Towcester. These two horses played their part in enabling Caroline Saunders to win the Richard Russell–Johnny Greenall Trophy for the leading rider in hunter chases for the third time, though eight of her 19 winners in this field came from the horses owned and ridden by Johnny Greenall, the winner of his brother's trophy for the fifth time in six years, also with 19 wins, ten of them were on horses trained by Peter Cheesbrough in the North.

Johnny, who rode his 100th winner under Rules during the season, was the champion amateur rider of the season for the first time with his 19 winners under N.H. Rules.

With Champagne Taittinger withdrawing from sponsorship of the ladies' championship after only one season, there was no ladies' championship culminating in a final on a professional course. There was, however, a ladies' hunter chase at the new Newcastle fixture, and this was won in a field of six by Pauline Robson (the Northern Area ladies' champion for the third year running, with 15 winners) on the ever-reliable Steele Justice, a winner of three of his four races. The ten-year-old had an easy task in a weak field. Willy Manners, the horse's owner-trainer, farms a few miles from the course. Three days earlier, Pauline had ridden four winners at the Eglinton.

Nor was there any final at the Cheltenham evening fixture to the BMW Challenge Confined series. Although there was still an award for this series of point-to-points on a points basis presented at the PPOA lunch at Stratford in June, and it went to Jenny Winch, the owner of the nine-year-old Afaltoun with his three wins and two places in these races from John Porter's yard in the Vine & Craven country. Tom Lacey also won two other races on Afaltoun, a Club Moderate race at Tweseldown and a maiden hunter chase at Folkestone.

There were 15 runners for the well-named *Times* 'Rising Stars' final, which had been transferred from Towcester to Newbury. They included Cool Relation, who had won a novice hunter chase at Hereford for Denis Caro, and two good ladies' horses in Mr. Go Lightly and the Cumings' mare Flame O' Frensi. The winner, however, was Stewart Pike's home-bred Synderborough Lad. A big eight-year-old by Rymer from the East Devon, Synderborough Lad had won a hunter chase at Wincanton and been a runner-up to Avostar in his qualifying race at Lingfield. Ridden again by Mike Felton, he foiled Cool Relation's attempt to make all in no uncertain manner. Joining him four fences out, he ran on strongly to score from Linda Blackford's mount Some-Toy, who took second place off Cool Relation on the run-in. Before the season was out, Synderborough Lad had won another hunter chase at Uttoxeter.

Stewart Pike was also the owner-breeder of Proud Sun, by far the most impressive winner from far afield at the Citroen National Point-to-Point Festival at Garthorpe, where he completed a hat-trick of wins under Mike Felton. This six-year-old half-brother to Synderborough Lad by Chris Sweeting's highly successful stallion Sunyboy out of the Romany Air mare Roman Lilly was carrying on where he left off, having lost his maiden certificate on his only appearance in 1993, when he was appearing on a course for the first time; and he wasn't to disappoint on future occasions.

That exuberant character Johnny "Mad" Manners, a Wiltshire dairy farmer of inexhaustible enthusiasm, brought off a man-sized coup in the Liverpool Foxhunters' with his eight-year-old Killeshin, a horse he bought for 1,550 guineas at the Ascot Sales in March 1993. Well ridden by the 29-year-old Gary Brown, who was up on him when he won a maiden hunter chase at Leicester earlier in the season, Killeshin, whose price this time was 8-1, got to Brown Windsor on the run-in and stayed on to beat him by just over a length. It was Killeshin's third hunter-chase win in a row; and Manners said afterwards, "I was told he had all sorts of problems and that the vet lived with him."

For the second time in three years, and the third in 12, a horse from the South East won the *Horse and Hound* Cup at Stratford when Maurice Pinto's Mighty Frolic, the only mare in the race, and the youngest of the 12 runners at seven, made the running from the second under her farmer-rider Tom Hills and finished with 15 lengths in hand from Mr. Murdock. The favourite, Wild Illusion, found the trip too much for him and was a spent force by the sixth from home; and Generals Boy, who might well have given the winner plenty to do, fell at the fourteenth when well in touch.

Pinto, an American who hunted with the Chiddingfold & Leconfield, bought Mighty Frolic as an unbroken four-year-old for 6,500 guineas at Doncaster in May 1991 and sent her into training with Matt McCormack, from whose yard she won a maiden chase at Lingfield in March 1993. Soon after this she went into Stephanie Edwards's small yard at Sutton; and it was from Stephanie's yard that she won all four of her races in 1994 with Tom Hills up, the first three of them open point-to-points. The daughter of Oats came from good point-to-pointing and hunting stock. Her dam, Mighty Nice, was a half-sister to Alan Cure's dual Dudley Cup winner Mighty Red; and their dam, Mighty's Niece, won six hunter chases and an open point-to-point.

The best novice in the South East, and a very useful one, was Colonial Kelly. This six-year-old by Richard Bowers's stallion Netherkelly out of a mare by Indian Ruler, started the season as a maiden and won five of his six races from Di Grissell's East Sussex & Romney Marsh yard with Chris Gordon up.

The ladies' races in this area were dominated by Alison Hickman's little Maltby Boy, who won four on the trot for his owner-rider, including one in Suffolk at Ampton; and by the time he finished lame in his last race he had amassed a grand total of 21 wins, seven of them scored at Parham, where he was practically invincible, though he was beaten there once, when finishing third to Mountain Crash and Goodlooking Bird in 1992.

Another to dominate the scene in ladies' races was Richard Hunt in East Anglia. After an initial defeat by Alex Embiricos' owner-ridden Raglan Road on the dead ground at Higham, the ten-year-old from the Puckeridge & Thurlow won his next five ladies' opens with 22-year-old Lisa Rowe up, and the partnership was also successful in a hunter chase at Ascot. By the end of the season, Richard Hunt's grand total of wins had risen to 13, and his rider was on her way to becoming the Manager of Warwick Racecourse.

The success in January of the Point-to-Point Owners' Club fixture in its new home at Barbury Castle was by no means entirely due to the vast number of runners for it, or to its reversion to a Saturday date. Just listen to that so-often lugubrious sage Clement Freud in the *Sporting Life*: "For those who want to see us and our land at its best, a point-to-point on a winter's afternoon is the place to go. And of all the damp green fields bedecked with obstacles, portable lavatories, beer tents, tote tents, baked potato vans, mobile country clothing shops and a stewards' shed – Barbury Castle may be the finest."

Freud perhaps might also have mentioned that the quality of the racing was persistently high, with such as Sunny Mount, Wild Illusion, Starember Lad, Flame O' Frensi and Peter Greenall's promising young horse Kilfinny Cross among the winners in the well-packed fields; and that the vigilance of the stewards was reflected in no fewer than five stewards' enquiries, all of which were resolved amicably, some of them with fines.

In contrast to the happenings at Barbury Castle, there was the usual quota of bizarre occurrences at some other meetings; and they included what I think must be the first bookmakers' strike at a point-to-point, when layers at the Brecon declined to set up shop for the opening hunt race on account of what they considered to be the admission (later rescinded) of an unauthorised member of the fraternity; while a walk-over in the hunt race at the Blankney was followed by disqualification of the rider for failing to weigh in!

Most bizarre of all, though, was a ladies' race at the return of the Piccadilly Hunt Club fixture at Hereford. It turned into a fiasco when the starter's action in raising his flag to knee height in an attempt to persuade a reluctant runner to get into line was the cause of a false start resulting in the race being declared void.

The final of the Russell, Baldwin & Bright maiden-race series at Chepstow was a victim of the weather; but the Malvern auctioneers continued to operate their bonus scheme whereby the vendor and buyer of the most successful point-to-pointer emerging from their Malvern Sales were each presented with a cheque for £500; and the recipients of these awards were Jackie Retter and Peter Bowen, the vendor and purchaser of The Blue Boy.

Once again, the leading veteran rider of the season was the 57-year-old George Turner, whose 14 wins, mostly on horses he owned and trained himself, included a treble at the Lamerton. In terms of age, however, he had a rival in Yorkshire's Robin Tate, who was also 57, and rode seven winners.

The leading small owner-trainer-rider, and recipient of the *Horse and Hound* Cup at the national point-to-point dinner, was 50-year-old Chris Marriott, the Hon. Sec. of the Heythrop point-to-point. He had five wins on his home-bred Scrumpy Country.

The *Daily Telegraph* award for the leading female rider of the season was shared by 23-year-old Joanne Priest from Worcestershire and the 25-year-old Samantha Wallin from Warwickshire. Each of them rode five winners.

There were three important administrative retirements. Victor Dartnall, the man largely responsible for founding the course at Barbury Castle, gave up as clerk of the course there to form what became a highly successful livery yard in the West Country. Percy Tory, the Chairman of the Point-to-Point Owners' Association, was succeeded by Michael Bannister, a Joint Master of the Pendle Forest & Craven Harriers. And Urky Newton, for so long The Queen of Melton, relinquished her 26-

year-long position as Hon. Sec. of the Melton Hunt Club point-to-point which she had founded with Lance.

In March, full of beans to the end, Yorkshireman Harold Charlton died at the age of 90, some three months after celebrating his birthday at a splendid party in Malton which I had the privilege of attending. A great wheeler and dealer in bloodstock, Harold was a man of many parts; and I well remember the occasion when, at the age of 80, he engaged in a foot race at Garthorpe on the day of the Melton Hunt Club point-to-point. The race was run from the last fence to the winning post and Harold was beaten a whisker, though he always maintained that he had won it. He died as he would like to have done, dropping dead in a car just as he was about to set off for a meet with a life-long friend, Roland Stephenson. Like Guy Cunard, another of his friends, he has since had a hunter chase at Wetherby named after him.

In August, Donald Underwood (the father of Tim) died. The Bramley veterinary surgeon was a great producer of point-to-pointers in his day, and among the winners he trained under Rules was True Song, the winner of the County Hurdle at Cheltenham in 1974. But the horse I remember best of all is the one he saved from brachial paralysis with his inspired treatment, the late Harold Flux's point-to-pointer Peerflex, bought for £100 as a four-year-old. Two years later, Peerflex won three point-to-points on the trot; and in one of them, an open nomination race in Cowdray Park, he foiled an attempted coup by Lionel Ensten with Peeper, the horse brought from the Puckeridge country with the object of cleaning up. Roy Ware coming up from behind on Peerflex, saw that he didn't. There were two particularly sad faces afterwards; and mine was one of them.

In October, the distinguished High Court Judge Sir Bernard Caulfield died at the age of 80 after eventually succumbing to the emphysema which had plagued him for so long; though it didn't prevent him from delivering brilliantly witty speeches at two of the national point-to-point dinners at The Belfry. Sir Bernard, of course, was the man who immortalised Mary Archer with his description of her as "fragrant". He was also, as has already been mentioned, the presiding Judge at the Gay Future trial in the 'seventies involving a notorious betting coup at Cartmel. A man with a passion for horseracing, he has left behind him a legacy to the sport in one of his sons, Michael, the Secretary of the Jockeys' Association of G.B.

Tailpiece:
Huntsman Stan Luckhurst was reverently scattering the ashes of a popular member of the West Kent Hunt on the point-to-point course at Penshurst when the horse he was riding spooked and decanted him into the middle of them.

1995

In which point-to-pointing leads the way with Sunday betting, the first timber races are staged, the Sporting Life introduces its Classics Cup, the by-passing of fences is sanctioned, the PPOA becomes the PPORA, and Timeform earns a black mark.

Although the number of runners this season was down to 12,836 as against last year's 14,148, and there were as many as 19 walk-overs, including three at the Glamorgan, where the going at St. Hilary in mid-April was like concrete, once again a record number of hunters' certificates were issued, 4,311; and 203 of the record 211 fixtures scheduled were able to take place. And here's another encouraging statistic: 164 horses were the subject of random dope tests, and not one of them was found positive.

There were some welcome changes to the regulations. None more so than the long overdue one of permitting fences to be dolled off in the interest of safety. I believe Grant Cann was the first to call for this, and that was years ago. In its inaugural year, the manoeuvre was carried out successfully on 62 occasions. Another concession to common sense, in view of the great number of young horses running in point-to-points, was the decision to allow meetings to hold two maiden races, provided that they were run under different conditions.

Not quite so popular was the replacement of the old "regularly and fairly hunted" qualification by the more specific requirement of a mimimum of seven days hunting. This, said Mike Felton, a Joint Master of the Blackmore & Sparkford Vale, was "guaranteed to concentrate a number of minds and come as a rude shock to a substantial contingent." But although there were some rumblings, there was no open rebellion. Some farmers in hunting countries did, however, express concern that the new regulation might increase the number of people going hunting by 30%.

There is no doubt that the innovation of Sunday racing with betting was a success, even though the bookmakers were hardly over the moon about it. In the words of Desmond Gleeson: "Sunday point-to-pointing from a bookmaker's point of view has reduced the turnover by 50%. It has no doubt attracted a larger attendance – a family one with less emphasis on betting and more on other attractions, such as picnics, ice cream and 50p on the Tote for the kids."

"But," he added, "the point-to-point betting man is an individual who likes to bet minus the distraction of his wife and children. Saturday racing is ideal for him. His wife goes shopping and he is all alone at the races, and consequently his bets increase in volume in this self-isolation. I am also of the opinion that today's husband is the victim of tyrannical despotism and that Sunday betting is the worst sufferer."

Only two of the Sunday point-to-points managed to top the 100 mark on the score of runners, Sir W.W. Wynn's at Eaton Hall with 107 for nine races and the Middleton on the day of the Grimthorpe with 102 for the seven races at Whitwell-on-the-Hill; whereas, in the case of the Saturday meetings there were over 100 runners at 20 of them, with the Brecon at Llanfrynach producing the most, 171 for a record 13 races, the Restricted here being split four ways, the men's and ladies' opens twice and the confined maiden three times. Amazing, considering that the going was quite heavy.

Tweseldown had the privilege of staging the first of the Sunday fixtures, the Garth & South Berks on January 15, and for this there was an estimated attendance of 4,000 (more than for the usual Saturday fixture there), and 57 runners for the six races. Wild Illusion, with Polly Curling riding the 11-year-old inmate of the Pidgeon yard for the first time, was a classy winner of the mixed open in the fastest time of the day.

Proceedings at Tweseldown began quite early, with a sermon on the famous mound delivered by a vicar who advised his listeners to place their main bet on The Almighty. So presumably they got off on the right foot.

But, if figures are to be believed, by far the biggest attendance of all on a Sunday was for a race that didn't get into the official form books, either the point-to-point ones or the ones for racing under Jockey Club rules, the £20,000 final of the inaugural Marlborough Cup race over timber fences, for which the reported attendance at Barbury Castle was something between 10,000 and 12,000.

Modelled on the lines of the Maryland Hunt Cup in the United States, the Marlborough Cup was the brain-child of Count Konrad Goess-Saurau, the Austrian owner of the land; and the committee for the race included Ian Balding, Hugh Thomas (the Badminton course builder), leading event rider Virginia Elliot, Richard Pitman, and some American advisers. There were five preparatory races over a specially constructed course of timber fences at Barbury Castle on the days that the point-to-points were held there. But the final was run over over a stiffer course on the adjacent gallops, with the committee deciding which horses would run in it.

The first two preparatory races were both won by a visiting American rider who was eventually to finish a runner-up in the final, 28-year-old Michael Traurig. The leading rider over timber in America in 1992, and twice placed in the Maryland Hunt Cup, Traurig, a son of the great American pro. jockey Bernie Traurig, was riding Uriquarat, a horse he had finished second on in a point-to-point at Tweseldown; and not long afterwards he was to ride his first point-to-point winner in this country when scoring in a maiden race at the Llangibby on Lady Buchan, a six-year-old mare owned by Lee Bowles.

The final of the Marlborough Cup was described by Marcus Armytage in the

Daily Telegraph as an "unmitigated success." He should know. He rode the favourite, Reignbeau, and finished last. The winner was a horse running in the colours of Chris Leigh, Diamond Wind, who had been competing in hunter trials and won in a canter under his young rider, Millie Ball, a 17-year-old student at the Royal Agricultural College in Cirencester. Traurig was second on Uriquarat.

The result, though, might well have been different if the intention to run Mr. Frisk, the 1990 Grand National winner, had been carried out. The former point-to-pointer was to have been ridden in the race by Tracey Bailey, wife of the Lambourn trainer Kim Bailey. Public protest, however, put paid to the plans. Rather a pity, really, when one remembers that Ben Nevis, the 1980 Grand National winner with the American amateur Charlie Fenwick up, was a previous winner of the Maryland Hunt Cup.

Desmond Gleeson, who headed the team of six bookmakers present at Barbury Castle for the occasion, said that the winner of the Marlborough Cup had been backed down from 20-1 to 6-1, and that the horse's success caused "deep lacerations" to his satchel which "only time and the grace of God" helped him to overcome.

The point-to-point season began tragically when, on the opening day at Larkhill, John Dufosee's beloved wife Jane, a tower of strength in the Dorset yard, collapsed with a brain haemorrhage and died later in hospital at the age of 47.

Not long afterwards, in February, there occurred the death of the 83-year-old Hugh Gingell, who, with his wife, Betty, had been the prime mover of point-to-point racing at Cottenham, even before they bought the course from the late Jim Runciman in 1963. Something else that Hugh will be remembered for is his rare feat in 1947 when winning the first and last races of the day at the Newmarket & Thurlow point-to-point at Cottenham on his horse Cox's Orange, a prolific winner for him.

In March, Hugh was followed into the Elysian Fields by Frank Harvey, who had completed a double at the same meeting on two of his own horses, Pincushion and Corbawn Lad. Frank, who died at his Bishop's Stortford home at the age of 85, had been a familiar figure as an owner, rider and breeder in the Eastern Counties; and also as the owner of the land at Wickham Hall over which the Puckeridge held their point-to-point for many years. His luncheon parties there on the day of the races were memorable occasions.

Pincushion and Corbawn Lad were probably the two best horses Frank Harvey won on; and certainly Pincushion was the best mare he bred from, as well as the one who gave him a splendid ride in the Cheltenham Foxhunters' of 1948, landing first over the fourth from home in this four-mile race before being chopped for speed in the closing stages. It was Pincushion who produced one of Frank's best winners in later years, Two Pins, who had the distinction of beating the great Hard Frost over his favourite course at Marks Tey. Two Pins won 14 point-to-points and a hunter chase at Folkestone, ridden in 13 of these races, including the hunter chase, by Frank's son Ted.

Another good horse of Frank's was Duke Of Cinchon. Bought for 1,000 guineas, he was an even more prolific winner than Two Pins, winning 12 point-to-points with Hunter Rowe up, four with Ted Harvey aboard, and two with David

Wales in the saddle. Duke of Cinchon, too, succeeded in mastering Hard Frost on one occasion.

In April, Urky Newton died at the age of 76, and left a yawning gap at Garthorpe, where her presence had been such an inspiration for so many years, both on the scene and behind it. Her name has since joined that of Lance in the title of the men's open at the Melton Hunt Club point-to-point.

In May, the N.H. trainer John Webber died at the age of 69. A distinguished amateur rider, he rode over 70 winners in point-to-points, Open Fire and Finest Hour II, two of the horses he hunted with the Bicester & Warden Hill, coming immediately to mind. All this as well as training numerous winners under Rules from his base at Mollington. He has passed on the legacy of his skills to his two sons Anthony and Paul and his elder daughter Teresa Elwell.

It was certainly a season for innovations and record-breaking. Among the record-breakers were the two outstanding lady riders of the decade, Polly Curling and Alison Dare. Despite having her season cut drastically short in a freak accident at the Farmers' Bloodhounds fixture over the Heythrop course in March when, riding Danbury Lad in an open maiden for the Baimbridge stable, she was kicked by a faller whilst still in the saddle and broke her leg, Alison had become the first lady rider to ride 200 point-to-point winners when scoring on Stephens Pet in the ladies' open at the same meeting.

As for Polly Curling, the leading lady rider of the season for the third year in succession, she broke two records. The first of them was at the Axe Vale Harriers fixture at Stafford Cross on April 15, when, riding Richard Barber's horses, she became the first lady rider to win five races at the same meeting; and the second was on May 21 at the Bicester with Whaddon Chase fixture at Mollington, where her 38th point-to-point win of the season, achieved on Richard Barber's charge Cherrynut, the second leg of a double for her in the ladies' open, saw her smashing Philip Scholfield's 1988 record total of 37 wins in a single season.

By the end of the season the Curling score had risen to 40, and she was 18 ahead of her nearest rivals for the ladies' title, Shirley Vickery and Pip Jones, who fought out a grandstand finish for the position of runner-up on the last day of the season at the Torrington Farmers. At the start of this meeting Shirley Vickery was on a score of 21 and Pip Jones was on 20. Both of them had rides in the ladies' open, Pip on her prolific winner Handsome Harvey, and Shirley on Peter Bowen's charge Rocket Run, a winner of eight races with Damien Duggan up. Some spice was added to the contest with the presence in the field of Polly Curling on the Barber runner Cornish Cossack.

In the event, the race was virtually a cake-walk for Handsome Harvey, who extended his unbeaten sequence of nine wins to ten, drawing clear of Cornish Cossack as he approached the last and clinching the contest for the Grand Marnier Trophy in the process. Rocket Run, who had been another leading contender for this trophy, was having an off day and Shirley Vickery pulled him up before the second last.

Pip Jones was now level with Shirley Vickery, and she went one ahead when completing a double in the Confined on a chance ride, Great Gusto, whose usual rider, Linda Blackford, the horse's trainer, was on the injury list. In the last race of the season, division two of the open maiden, Shirley Vickery got one back with an easy win on Not Mistaken, a six-year-old from the Gelligaer Farmers. So there were two joint runners-up for the *Sporting Life* Cup with 22 winners apiece.

Polly Curling's 40 wins in point-to-points were achieved on 23 different horses, ten of which started the season as maidens; and all but one of her wins were accomplished on horses trained by Richard Barber, who had a record season himself, training 55 point-to-point winners and saddling three winners under Rules, one of whom, John Keighley's eight-year-old Fantus, completed a hat-trick of wins when storming home under Polly Curling in the Cheltenham Foxhunters' by 20 lengths from Holland House, the horse he had defeated in an equally convincing manner on his previous appearance in the mixed open for the Coronation Cup at Larkhill's United Services fixture in February.

Fantus was unquestionably the best horse Polly Curling rode during the season, and he was rightfully placed at the head of Mackenzie & Selby's handicap on the strength of his performances, earning a rating of 11-8. But Polly did, of course, ride some other very good ones, including Bond JNR, on whom she won a Confined at Larkhill and a ladies' open at Barbury Castle, and What A Hand, who ended his short season beating Colonial Kelly and Country Tarrogen in the final of *The Times* 'Rising Stars' series at Newbury; and with her four rides on the Somerset auctioneer Richard Williams's unbeaten seven-year-old Still In Business she also ended up winning a novice hunter chase, at Newton Abbot this time. Of the horses who started the season as maidens that Polly won on – and she was successful on ten of them from the Barber yard – none looked more promising than Richard Williams's See More Business, a five-year-old by Seymour Hicks out of a mare by Dubassoff. On this youngster, bought for 5,600 guineas at Doncaster the previous May, Polly won two races, and she was well on the way to winning a third when he crumpled up on landing over the last in a Restricted at Chaddesley Corbett on Dudley Cup Day. That was the extent of his runs in point-to-points; but, on changing hands after the season was over and joining Paul Nicholls's yard, he won three novice hurdles on the trot with Tony McCoy up.

Perhaps now is the moment to recall Lester Piggott's remark about lady riders never being able to make the grade because "their arses are the wrong size." It was quoted by Dick Saunders in his speech at what had now become the Point-to-Point Owners and Riders lunch at Stratford Racecourse. "But," added Saunders, "he didn't come up against Polly Curling, did he?"

It is worth recording, I feel, that the unbeaten Handsome Harvey never once came under the whip in any of the ten races Pip Jones won on him. This thoroughly deserving winner of the Grand Marnier Trophy, trained by Bert Lavis in Pembrokeshire, was bred by his owners, Ted and Brenda Harries, from April Airs, a mare who never saw a racecourse but whose sire, Grey Mirage, was also the sire of Desert Orchid.

A son of the local premium stallion Push On, the nine-year-old Handsome Harvey was the fourth horse hunted in Pembrokeshire to become the most prolific winner of the season in the post-war years, the others being National Clover, Timber Tool and Brunico; whilst Brigadier Mouse, who had the same distinction in 1985, was hunted with an adjacent pack, the Tivyside.

For the connections of two of Handsome Harvey's three closest challengers for the Grand Marnier, Peter Bowen's charge Rocket Run and the Tarrys' home-bred Fine Lace, there were, however, consolation prizes. The seven-year-old Rocket Run, with his eight wins, was the PPORA *Horse and Hound* champion young horse of the season; and Bunny Tarry's Fine Lace, with her eight wins under Jimmy Tarry, all of them in open events, was the champion mare of the season.

For Fine Lace, however, described by her owner-breeder as "a once in a lifetime mare," disaster was not far off. This winner of 28 point-to-points and a hunter chase in her five seasons of racing, died in August at the age of 11 following an operation for a twisted gut. A sad premature end to a great career. Even more so because she would have been invaluable at stud, where prospects had already been suffering from the death in 1993 of the Tarrys' premier stallion St. Columbus, and, more recently, from that of another of their resident stallions, Crested Lark.

The other close contestant for the Grand Marnier was another of Peter Bowen's charges, Royal Saxon, with his eight wins in open races, ridden by Damien Duggan in six of them. This was a remarkable training performance by the Welsh maestro in his last season before becoming a public trainer because this eight-year-old had shown the most dismal form in his previous point-to-point yard, though he was a winner twice over hurdles for Henrietta Knight in the 1992/93 season.

For the first three months of the season, Simon Andrews was showing them the way for the men's title, with Who's Fooling Who and Loyal Note doing him proud in East Anglia. But, as the season advanced, Shropshire's Alastair Crow was coming to the fore; and with four-timers at the Flint & Denbigh in March and the South Shropshire in mid-April and trebles in between at Sir W.W. Wynn's and the Cheshire Forest, he was well in the lead at the end of April with 21 winners to Andrews's 17. In the meantime, Jimmy Tarry was making steady progress on the family's home-bred horses; and when he had his 150th win in point-to-points on his father's Sunshine Manor in a Confined at Kingston Blount on May 13 he was riding his 23rd winner of the season, just three beind Alastair Crow. He was to ride two more, but by that time he was riding with a wired-up thumb, and this injury put paid to his title chances. So he had to rest content with being the runner-up, with 25 winners as against Alastair's 30.

In the course of winning the *Daily Telegraph* Cup for the second time in three years, Alastair Crow accomplished this feat on 12 different horses, all but two of them trained by the redoubtable Sheila. His most prolific winner was his uncle's home-bred mare Scally Muire. A winner of seven races in her nine appearances, and second on the other two occasions, Scally Muire was the runner-up to Fine Lace for the mares' championship. Alastair's next most prolific winners were two of the Irish imports trained by his mother, Korbell and Moss Castle, each with six wins, the latter's all in open events. The six-year-old Korbell, a mare by Roselier, was the leading young horse in the North Western Area. Her only defeats were on the three occasions that she failed to complete the course, falling twice and unseating Alastair on the other occasion. Moss Castle, a classy ten-year-old by Le Moss out of a mare by Deep Run, was beaten twice, the first time by a horse he got his revenge on later, and the second time, in his last race of the season, by Alan Hollingsworth's Shadow Walker, who was recording his only win of the season in the men's open at the Albrighton Woodland.

The *Daily Telegraph* leading novice riders of the season were the Midlands rider Richard Armson, who had six wins on five different horses, and Peter Easterby's 24-year-old assistant pupil Alyson Deniel, whose eight wins, five of them on the Sinnington nine-year-old Barry Owen, were all achieved on three horses who started the season as maidens. Two years later Alyson was to ride her first winner under Rules, and by that time she had ridden 15 point-to-point winners.

Nineteen-year-old Samantha Beddoes, the winner of the Wilkinson Sword for the leading rider under the age of 21 who hadn't ridden a winner before the start of the season, had five wins on her father's eight-year-old mare Squirrelsdaughter, one of the inmates of Steven Brookshaw's yard, where Samantha worked.

Peter Greenall's Cup for the leading rider in hunter chases was shared by three riders, each of whom rode six winners in this field. They were Yorkshire's Noel Wilson, Jamie Jukes from Wales and David Nicholson's 17-year-old pupil assistant Richard Johnson. All three of them were to make a name for themselves in future years.

Caroline Saunders was the winner of the Richard Russell–Johnny Greenall Trophy for the fourth successive year. The eight hunter-chase winners she trained included the massive Teaplanter, now 12 years old. But he made no more than three appearances; and his only win was on the first of them at Wetherby, where he beat Once Stung, and his bid to win the Cheltenham Foxhunters' never looked like succeeding. It ended five fences out when he unseated Richard Russell, who ended his race-riding career breaking his neck for the second time.

In the case of the three point-to-point classics, there was now something extra to play for, with the introduction by the *Sporting Life* of a Classics Cup for presentation at the national point-to-point dinner in November. Conducted on a points basis by the man who thought up the idea, the Worcestershire Hunt's Alan Cure, there were major points of 50, 40, 30 and 20 for the first four horses in any of these classics; and minor ones of 10, 7 and 5 could be collected by any of the horses running in these races who finished in the first three in other open races or hunter chases run after the first of the classic races had taken place.

It was disappointing in the circumstances that, owing to the firmness of the ground, there were no more than three runners for the first classic race of the season, the four-mile men's open for Lord Ashton of Hyde's Cup at the Heythrop, now, like the Dudley Cup, in its ninth year of sponsorship by *The Life*. But at least there was a popular local winner in Gerard Nock's 13-year-old Sevens Out, trained by his wife, Sue, at Stow-on-the-Wold.

Well ridden by Charlie Brooks's 25-year-old assistant Edward James, the old horse comprehensively outjumped another local favourite, Chris Marriott's owner-ridden Scrumpy Country, and beat him by a distance. This was the second win of the season for Sevens Out, and he was to have another before the season was out.

The Heythrop was also notable for the entry into the limelight of another young descendant of a famous point-to-pointing family, the Hutsbys of Warwickshire, when 19-year-old Rebecca Hutsby rode her first winner with her first ride in a race, scoring in the 3m5f ladies' open for the Lyon Trophy on the 13-

year-old Rymer King. The outsider in a field of four, Rymer King drew clear of the 4-1 on favourite, Katie Sunderland's mount East River, from three fences out and beat him by six lengths. This winner was trained by Rebecca for her grandfather, Geoff Hutsby, whose successes in the saddle included the 1949 Dudley Cup on his own horse Sir Isumbras.

In a highly competitive race for the Dudley Cup on the well-watered ground at Chaddesley Corbett, Richard Barber, saddling his first-ever runner in the race, was appropriately rewarded when his brother Paul's six-year-old Bond JNR, starting a narrow favourite at 2-1, and ridden this time by Tim Mitchell, completed his hat-trick of wins.

Under orders to ride a waiting race, Mitchell carried out his instructions to the letter. The moment he had been waiting for came at the second last when the South Pembrokeshire mare Final Pride, still several lengths up at the time, made a bad blunder.

Mitchell was quick to seize his opportunity, and at the line Bond JNR. had seven lengths in hand of Final Pride, who had started joint second favourite at 5-2 with the horse who finished four lengths away in third, Pont De Paix.

Richard Barber said after the race that he would not have considered running Bond JNR in it if they hadn't made such a good job of watering the course. A grandson of Deep Run on his dam's side, Bond JNR had won a bumpers' race in Ireland and a two-mile hurdle race from Paul Nicholls's yard as a four-year-old before he started his point-to-point career this season with two falls. But as the Dudley Cup was his last race of 1995 he wasn't to collect any more points for *The Life's* inaugural Classics Cup.

The best-quality Grimthorpe Cup for some years saw 14 horses going to the post on the soft ground at Whitwell-on-the-Hill in its first year of sponsorship by the *Sporting Life*. In a tight market, Nigel Tutty's mount Duright, the mare he was riding for Peter Sawney, was just favourite at 5-2, on the strength of her success in her previous race at the Bramham Moor; but there wasn't much between her and two others, Mike Sowersby's mount Speakers Corner, the winner of the men's open at the Holderness, and the promising novice Barry Owen, on whom Alyson Deniel had won three races in a row. Also well supported was Chris Coyne's mount Castlebay Lad, who had made the long journey from the Windsor Forest Bloodhounds country and had two good open-race wins behind him.

But when it came to the crunch, after Speakers Corner had cut out the running, it was the 12-year-old Duright who held all the cards. Sprinting clear of the field rounding the last bend, she won by ten lengths from Speakers Corner, with the 16-1 shot Gaelic Warrior taking third place in front of two proven stayers, the East Anglian contestant Glen Oak and last year's winner Across The Lake. Castlebay Lad was in third place when he was squeezed for room at the seventeenth and ran out through the wing.

Sadly, after finishing lame in her last race of the season, a 4m 2f hunter chase at Uttoxeter, Duright, who had been such a good servant to Peter Sawney and his trainer-daughter, Jackie, was retired permanently to stud.

Somewhat surprisingly, none of the winners of the three classics collected any further points for *The Life's* Classics Cup after their wins in these races. It was a different story, however, in the case of the Dudley Cup runner-up, Grahame Barrett's Final Pride. This nine-year-old mare, trained by Peter Bowen at Little Newcastle, near Haverfordwest, and ridden in all her races by Evan Williams, added substantially to her score.

Already a winner of two point-to-points before the day of the Heythrop, her points for the Classics Cup started to come the next day when she was the runner-up to Wild Illusion in a hunter chase at Ludlow before her Dudley Cup race. Seven days after the Dudley Cup was run, she was runner-up in another hunter chase at Worcester, and this was followed by wins at Uttoxeter and the new hunter-chase meeting at Warwick, taking her points score up to 84 and putting her well beyond reach.

So it was Grahame Barrett who collected the historic Classics Cup at The Belfry. And I do mean historic, because the trophy he received, thanks to its donor, Mrs. Felicity Macfarlane, was the one that had originally been presented to her parents by the late Sir Harold Wernher after a horse of theirs had won the adjacent hunts' farmers' race at the Fernie in 1931.

A daughter of Push On, Final Pride was bred in Pembrokeshire by Mrs. Elizabeth Thomas from an Honour Bound mare, Final Answer, who was a half-sister to the 1982 Dudley Cup winner Norman Case, a horse also hunted with the South Pembrokeshire. Mrs. Thomas received a cheque for £100 from the *Sporting Life* as the breeder of Final Pride; and, to mark the occasion of the paper's first Classics Cup, a donation of £250 was made to the Injured Jockeys' Fund.

Ten-year-old Sheer Jest, a horse with ten wins in hunter chases behind him since joining Bill Warner's Northants yard in 1990, had his biggest win of all when making it 11 in a field of 26 for the Liverpool Foxhunters'. Ridden by his regular pilot Alan Hill, he mastered Brown Windsor on the long run-in to score by a length, and behind these two were Dark Dawn and Once Stung. Mrs. Judy Wilson's good horse was beaten in his next race; but that was at Punchestown, where he came up against one of Ireland's star hunter chasers, Elegant Lord, who had finished third to Fantus and Holland House at Cheltenham and was being ridden this time by his trainer, Enda Bolger. Ten days after Sheer Jest's win at Liverpool, the Warner yard suffered a grievous blow when another of Judy Wilson's horses, the 15-year-old Good Waters, a winner of ten point-to-points since joining the yard in 1991, had a fatal fall in the hunt race at the Pytchley.

In a field of 14 for the Land Rover men's final at Towcester it was the turn of the ten-year-old Welsh Legion to shine. Vigorously ridden by Jamie Jukes, who was rewarded by the stewards for his pains with six days' suspension for "using the whip with unreasonable force and frequency" (but would he have won otherwise?), Welsh Legion was virtually presented with the race when Balda Boy broke his leg approaching the third last. This was the Carmarthenshire horse's second hard-earned win of the season.

There was no ladies' final on a N.H. course. Nor, for that matter, was there any ladies' hunter chase at all; and this lent added significance to the two ladies' championship races at Garthorpe. Both these were comfortably won, in fields of six and three, respectively, by Jill Dawson on her father-in-law's 12-year-old General Highway, five times a winner during the season. At the Citroen National Point-to-

Point Festival, which was now on its last legs, he accounted for Peajade, a winner of five ladies' opens in a row under Jill Wormall, including one at Garthorpe, where the 11-year-old son of Buckskin had beaten Layedback Jack by a neck; and in the Marie Curie at the Melton Hunt Club fixture he beat the triple winner Larry The Lamb, a horse purchased out of the Tarrys' yard (where he was still trained) and ridden by Gi Chown for her mother.

Another dual champion at these two Garthorpe meetings was Philip Newton's home-bred six-year-old Sign, who had lost his maiden certificate in an open maiden at Larkhill in February when making his second appearance over fences with Jon Trice-Rolph up. Ridden now by Alan Hill, Sign saw off several previous winners in the novice championships at Garthorpe. By the American sire Sharrood, Sign, said his owner, "was bred from a mare of Herbert Blagrave's that I paid a fortune for at the dispersal sales," and, he added, "I've got a bloody good trainer." The mare was the classy Polly Packer, by Reform; and Newton's trainer is Bill Warner.

I would say, though, that, notwithstanding the shining progress of What A Hand and the unbeaten Still In Business, the outstanding young horse of the season was Stewart Pike's home-bred seven-year-old Proud Sun. After being beaten a length by What A Hand on his first appearance of the season at Larkhill, where he needed the race, Proud Sun confined his appearances to hunter chases and won four of them, his only defeat in them coming when he came down five out as he was moving up in *The Times* 'Rising Stars' final at Newbury. His wins in these races included two in novice hunter chases at Aintree and, as the climax to his season, a convincing defeat of Cherrynut in the John Corbet Cup at Stratford.

The *Horse and Hound* Cup at Stratford was something of a let-down for the point-to-point fraternity in that neither the winner, Hermes Harvest, nor the runner-up, Honest Word, had ever run in a point-to-point, although their respective riders, Andrew Balding and Richard Ford, were well versed in the art.

Not that the race was short of runners from the point-to-point ranks. The favourite was Martin Pipe's ten-year-old Faithful Star, who had followed his successful career under Rules, firstly in Ireland and then in England, with four point-to-point wins in 1994 and a further five in 1995, plus a hunter chase at Uttoxeter. But the best he could manage this time was fourth place behind Andrelot, a winner of three hunter chases and an open point-to-point from Peter Bowen's yard; while among the others who failed to shine in the field of 16 were The Blue Boy, Fosbury, Welsh Legion and last year's winner Mighty Frolic.

And here, I feel, is the moment to award a black mark to that much-respected publication *Timeform* for its insensitivity (to put it mildly) when writing about Fantus, the winner of the Cheltenham Foxhunters', in taking an anti-hunting stance and advising the racing authorities "to put more distance between racing and hunting than has been implicit in their public statements so far." Have those at the head of *Timeform* forgotten what racing owes to hunting; and do the names of Colledge Master, The Callant, Limber Hill, Merryman II, Wyndburgh, Halloween, Oxo, Teal, The Dikler, Baulking Green, Grittar, Mr. Frisk and Norton's Coin, to name but a few, mean so little to them?

A bouquet, though, for *Talking Point*, the new point-to-point telephone information service set up by Terry Selby under the auspices of the Point-to-Point Secretaries Association. It came in for a certain amount of criticism to start with; but I can only say, having used it myself, I found it most helpful.

Paul Hacking rode his 100th point-to-point winner when scoring for the fourth time this season on Nethertara, one of Di Grissell's charges, in the Confined at the Old Surrey & Burstow at Penshurst in May. Philip Scouller had his 100th win in point-to-points with the second leg of a double on his French-bred Frere Hogan in the Confined at the Thames Valley Combined Hunts Club fixture at Tweseldown, where he was riding his 57th winner over his favourite course.

It was an especially memorable season for the 49-year-old Scouller, for more reasons than one. He was the recipient both of the Dick Woodhouse Trophy at the PPORA lunch as the leading owner-rider of the season, with his eight wins, and of the inscribed salver for special services to the sport presented at the national point-to-point dinner. The horse he had most wins on during the season was another French-bred, 12-year-old Roc De Prince, on whom he won four races. After he had bought this horse for 5,000 guineas at the Ascot Sales the previous June, his mother said to him. "What on earth do you think you are doing buying a horse Martin Pipe couldn't win with!"

But for another rider, 35-year-old Johnny Greenall, it was time for retirement. His last winning ride, in a confined maiden at the Oakley, was on a young horse making his début in his only race of the season, six-year-old Dromore Dream, Johnny's tenth winner of the season, including five in hunter chases, in which his grand total of wins had now reached 84, as against 47 in point-to-points.

At Doncaster in May all 15 of Johnny Greenall's horses came up for sale. They fetched 216,000 guineas, with the highest price of 60,000 being paid on behalf of Anne, Duchess of Westminster for the six-year-old Lord Of The West. A winner of two of his three races from Caroline Saunders's yard during the season, Lord Of The West started to get some of his purchase price back when winning a handicap hurdle at Uttoxeter the following March from Jonjo O'Neill's yard. Other high prices paid were 40,000 guineas for the nine-year-old Once Stung and 34,000 guineas for the seven-year-old Kilfinny Cross. Johnny's last winner, Dromore Dream, went for 15,000 guineas.

Sadly, Kilfinny Cross, Greenall's last winning ride under Rules, in a hunter chase at Newcastle on March 20, had a fatal fall in his new ownership when running in the Ritz National Hunt Handicap Chase at Cheltenham the following March as he was showing them the way four fences out; but before that he had won a handicap chase at Nottingham carrying his new colours in November.

The Irish-bred Coome Hill's reputation continued to grow in the West. He was unbeaten in his three races with Tim Dennis up, the last of them a novice hunter chase at Wincanton. This six-year-old was a horse who was destined to go further.

Another from the same area going through the season unbeaten was the eight-year-old Chilipour. This inmate of Victor Dartnall's yard, formerly a winner over fences and hurdles in Ireland, won five open events and a British Field Sports Society race at the Exmoor, ridden in all of them by Godfrey Maundrell. Among Chilipour's victims were two very useful horses in Mr. Murdock, beaten a length in an exciting two-horse race at Lockinge, and Ryming Cuplet, who went under to him by half a length at Williton.

Thamesdown Tootsie, the top ladies' horse in the South Midlands, was also unbeaten. Ridden each time by his owner-rider, 28-year-old Victoria Lyon, an investment banker in the City of London, this ten-year-old mare by the American sire Comedy Star never put a foot wrong in galloping the opposition into the ground in five ladies' opens, three of them well outside her own territory in the Grafton country, where she was trained by Jenny Pidgeon.

A horse who liked bottomless going, Thamesdown Tootsie was bought privately by Jenny Pidgeon from the Lambourn trainer Anthony Jones after she had failed to pass the vet, owing to temporary lameness when misbehaving herself at the Russell, Baldwin & Bright sales at Malvern the previous September. When the mare won her first race in her new ownership at Kingston Blount she was backed down from 33-1 to 10-1; but for all her other races she was an odds-on favourite.

Pat Rowe's Richard Hunt and Gurney Sheppard's Copper Thistle were the most prolific winners in East Anglia. The former won five ladies' opens with Lisa Rowe up, and a men's open with Simon Cowell riding him, and by this time the 11-year-old son of Celtic Cone had won 15 point-to-points and four hunter chases. The seven-year-old Copper Thistle was in the lead for the Grand Marnier when he had his fifth win in a row under Paul Taiano in the Confined at the Oakley on March 26. He was then three ahead of Handsome Harvey. But that was the end of his winning run; and on his final appearance of the season he finished fourth in a novice hunter chase at Fakenham.

Two up-and-coming six-year-olds in Yorkshire were John and Margaret Cooper's Fiftysevenchannels and Country Tarrogen, both trained by Tim Walford in the Middleton country and ridden by Noel Wilson. Fiftysevenchannels, who started his season winning out of his country at Cottenham and continued it with a win in a hunter chase at Hereford, ended up winning the Guy Cunard hunter chase at Wetherby; and in between he paid a visit to Ireland and finished fourth in a chase at Punchestown with Enda Bolger up. Country Tarrogen won both his point-to-points and two of his three hunter chases.

In the Northern Area, where Kevin Anderson, with his 15 wins, was the champion rider for the sixth time in nine years, and Pauline Robson, who brought off a four-timer at the Dumfriesshire, won the ladies' title for the fourth year in succession with her ten winners, Generals Boy was still going strong at the age of 13. His hat-trick of wins in open races for the 46-year-old Peter Craggs brought his grand total of wins up to 24.

Another veteran rider with a particular reason to feel pleased was the 47-year-old Tim Underwood in the Garth & South Berks country. His five wins on his tubed 12-year-old Vultoro culminated in the success he had been longing for when he won the race named in memory of his father, the mixed open at Tweseldown's Thames Valley Combined Hunts Club point-to-point.

As the most bizarre race of the season I have no hesitation in choosing the one that took the longest time to run – and I am not thinking of any of the nine that were run over four miles. The race I have in mind is the two-horse Land Rover qualifier run over three miles at the Tedworth fixture at Barbury Castle. After the odds-on favourite, Chris Bennett's owner-ridden Ufano, trained by John Porter in the Vine & Craven country, had fallen at the seventh, and the other runner, Light The Wick, had come down at the same fence on the final circuit, there was an interminable wait while Ufano, who had broken his bridle, was being caught by a huntsman; and when, eventually, he was reunited with his rider, Bennett was using a bridle borrowed from his rival, who was in no position to proceed. Ufano then completed the course in a time that must be a record one for all the wrong reasons, 14 mins. 27.9 secs., according to Mackenzie & Selby, though some watches made it longer. It is interesting to note that only one of the 4-mile point-to-points took over nine minutes to run, the 'Kent Grand National' at the West Street-Tickham meeting at Detling, and the time for that race was 9 mins. 10 secs. So perhaps Chris Bennett, who runs a data-processing company in Reading, deserved a medal for persistence, and the judge one for patience.

The coincidence of the season was surely the one that involved the Warwickshire rider Samantha Wallin. After arriving at the Cotswold evening fixture at Andoversford all set to ride a horse in the Intermediate, she discovered the hard way that she had broken her leg in a fall at another meeting earlier in the day; and she ended up in hospital at Banbury, where she found herself in the same ward that Alison Dare had been taken to with her broken leg, and being operated on by the same doctor.

The worst accident to a rider during the season, however, occurred in a hunter chase at Hereford on Easter Monday when the Anglesey rider Rebecca Hewitt (the wife of Richard) broke her back in a fall that resulted in her being confined to a wheel-chair.

The Yorkshire veteran Robin Tate rode his 100th winner in point-to-points. Cheshire's Simon Crank, with a career total of over 100 winners, announced his retirement from race-riding after riding his 97th winner in point-to-points at the age of 38; and Jeannie Brown celebrated her last season of race-riding with a training treble at the Derwent, riding two of the winners herself and leaving the other to Howard.

A few months after the season was over Jeannie became a public trainer, and she was to have her first win in that capacity when Dark Dawn, with Stephen Swiers up, won the same hunter chase at Newcastle that Jeannie had won on him in 1995.

In August, Sally Baillie died in America, where she had become one of the leading trainers after riding a string of point-to-point winners in England in the 'sixties, when she was a joint leading lady rider in 1963 and fourth to the great Pat Tollit in 1964 and 1965. She will be best remembered for her successes on those two splendid mares Orthorette and Orchid Moor. She won 16 races on the Blackmore & Sparkford Vale mare Orthorette between 1960 and 1964; and the 12 she won on the Hampshire mare Orchid Moor between 1964 and 1966 included an unbroken run of ten wins in 1965 and 1966.

October was a particularly black month. This was the month in which Bill Shand Kydd had his frightful accident and the grim reaper claimed two noted personalities in East Anglia and Tweseldown's George Dudley.

Betty Gingell, the Master of the Cambridgeshire Harriers from 1942 right up to the time of her death at the age of 80; and Hunter Rowe, the voice of point-to-point racing in East Anglia, died within a few weeks of each other.

The hounds that Betty tended so lovingly were disbanded shortly after her death on October 6. This was at her own request, made five days before she had a stroke on October 3. Some of them went to France, some to Ireland, and some to other harriers' packs in England. But the Cambridgeshire Harriers point-to-point still went ahead at Cottenham in 1996 and 1997, albeit without a hunt race. In 1998, however, it was to have a new name. By agreement with the Association of Harriers and Beagles, and with the consent of the Jockey Club, it will be known as the Cambridgeshire Harriers Hunt Club point-to-point.

The life of Hunter Rowe was cut tragically short at the age of 57 in a bizarre accident when he fell through the skylight of one of his barns at Clavering in the course of a pigeon shoot. He was attempting to retrieve a dead bird which had landed on the roof. A top-class point-to-point rider before he retired to take up commentating, Hunter rode 70 winners in point-to-points and a further 28 under Rules which included the Liverpool Foxhunters' of 1969 on Bitter Lemon, a horse owned, bred and trained by his father. As a top-class commentator at point-to-points, he was rightly described by David Turner as "a man of magic, who could make a bad race sound like a good one."

Hunter will also be remembered, by those with long enough memories, as the chief instigator of the one and only strike by point-to-point riders. It happened at the Newmarket & Thurlow point-to-point at Moulton in 1965, when six of the top riders in the area – the others were Michael Bloom, David Wales, Sam Cooper, Ted Harvey and Guy Lyster – considered the fences so dangerous that they needed re-structuring. I have every reason to remember the occasion. It was thanks to a tip-off from Hunter that I was able to mention what was about to happen in my pre-view for the *Sporting Life* on the day of the races. I was not able to be present at the meeting myself; but my correspondent there, the Royston solicitor Rex Norton, was hauled up by the stewards for what was considered to be excessive use of the pen. Good old Hunter!

George Dudley, the groundsman and fence-builder at Tweseldown, was still on active service when he died at the age of 86. George and his wife, Lillian, who looked after the needs of the ladies on the course, were affectionately known as 'Lord and Lady Tweseldown'. It was George who played a leading part in con-structing the course for the Olympic Three-Day Event at Tweseldown in 1948. For this he was awarded an Olympic bronze medal; and he had another medal for his help with the World Pentathlon Championship in 1958. But the testament he prized most of all was the one that came in 1954 from the Jockey Club inspector of courses at Tweseldown at the Garth point-to-point. "These fences," reported the Inspector, "are the best I have seen at any point-to-point, and I go to a meeting every week."

George's death was followed not long afterwards by that of Lillian, who died peacefully in Frimley Park Hospital in November 1996.

Ironically, for someone who was one of the leading point-to-point riders of his day, the 58-year-old Bill Shand Kydd was competing in the Grafton team-chasing event in Northants 17 years after his retirement from race-riding when he was paralysed from the neck down in a fall from a hunter owned by his son Caspar.

A rider of 70 point-to-point winners and some 40 under Rules, he carried the familiar yellow and white stripes with blue sleeves and cap with distinction on a wide variety of horses which became household names: No Reward, Musk Orchid, Rome Express, Matchboard, Black Baize and Golden Vale. But the best of the horses he bred himself was the one he eventually passed on to Caspar, Brown Windsor, the winner of the Whitbread Gold Cup at Sandown in 1989 and the Cathcart Cup at Cheltenham the following year. In 1995, when this 13-year-old son of Kinglet, out of the Kabale mare Cauldron, was being trained for Caspar by Caroline Saunders, he won four open point-to-points with Ben Pollock up.

Unquestionably, Bill's favourite horse was No Reward, a horse bought for 450 guineas at the Ascot Sales in May 1961 after an undistinguished career under Rules. Trained, like all the others he rode, by his stud manager, Brian Thompson, No Reward, a son of the 1943 Derby winner Straight Deal, out of a mare by Cottage, won 26 races between 1962 and 1968; and in 1963, when he was the leading point-to-point winner of the season, his eight wins included a division of the Dudley Cup.

The best race Bill won under Rules, and certainly the one that gave him most pleasure, was the 4-mile National Hunt Chase at Cheltenham that he won in 1973 on his friend Bob Dean's Foreman, trained by Harry Thomson Jones, who wanted to put "a top-class amateur" up on him, but was persuaded by Bob Dean to put up a top-class point-to-point rider instead.

Bill's last win under Rules was in a hunter chase at Folkestone in March 1975 which he won on Brown Windsor's dam, Cauldron; and his last win in a point-to-point was on his home-bred mare Rainbow's Edge (a half-sister to Gylippus, another of the horses he bred) in the hunt race at the Whaddon Chase fixture at Great Horwood in April 1978.

After his accident, Bill was taken first to the John Radcliffe Infirmary in Oxford and then to the Royal Berkshire Hospital in Reading; but the last 14 months of his hospital life were spent in Stoke Mandeville. He returned to his home in Leighton Buzzard two days before Christmas 1996 to be looked after by his wife Christina; and while he still has to have help from a machine with his breathing, he is eminently capable of conducting a conversation, and well equipped with an electric wheel-chair, which he says he drives with his chin.

Tailpiece:
"It's not the size of your whip that matters – it's the way you use it," Brod Munro-Wilson, responding to Kim Bailey's toast to the sport at the National Point-to-Point Dinner at The Belfry in November. He should know!

1996

*In which The Times withdraws its sponsorship but new sponsors arise,
Alison Dare wins another Sporting Life Cup, Jamie Jukes wins his first
Daily Telegraph Cup, an American-bred horse wins the Classics Cup,
and the Land Rover men's final transfers to Cheltenham.*

O f the 213 point-to-points scheduled for 1996, 207 actually took place, and this was the highest number so far, even though the number of runners, 13,451 (615 up on the 1995 figure), did not reach the 1994 record of 14,158. But, for the fifth successive year, there was an increase in the number of hunters' certificates issued, with the new total of 4,320, the highest numbers coming from the Blackmore & Sparkford Vale (76), the Bicester with Whaddon Chase and the Llangeinor, with 66 apiece, the Grafton (59), Middleton (58) and the Berkeley (57).

Four meetings were lost to the weather, and two more, the Citroen National Point-to-Point Festival and the Talybont were missing from the schedule. Walk-overs, however, were down to six, and four of them were in hunt members' races.

Sunday meetings were on the increase, with 56 of them scheduled and 55 taking place, as against 43 in 1995. The Jockey Club expressed themselves well satisfied, with this situation, remarking in their official report, "Point-to-Point organisers continue to be happy to hold their meetings on a Sunday and they still draw large crowds." But the Report said nothing about the extent of the betting at them, or of the bookmakers' views!

The most significant change in the point-to-point regulations was that horses which had won one Restricted were now no longer eligible to run in another. But whilst this resulted in an increase in the number of Intermediate races held, it was not exactly a popular move. The removal of an opportunity never is.

It was good, though, to see the appearance on the scene of two new Restricted race series with a final on a professional course. Especially as *The Times* had decided to drop its series of 'Rising Stars' hunter chases. Vauxhall Monterey came up with a Restricted series culminating in a £4,000 final at the hunter-chase meeting at Uttoxeter on May 8; and there was a Restricted series with qualifying races at point-to-points in East Anglia, the Midlands, South Midlands, South East and Sandhurst areas, with a £2,000 final at the evening hunter-chase meeting at

Huntingdon on April 30.

On the score of runners, the North Hereford was back at the top with 133 for its nine races at Newtown on a Saturday in February, followed by the Vale of Clettwr at Erw Lon with 127 for 12, the West Shropshire at Weston Park and the Brecon at Llanfrynach, both with 126 for ten, and the PPORA fixture at Barbury Castle with 125 for nine. The most runners for a Sunday fixture were at the Pytchley at Guilsborough in mid-April, when there were 117 runners for nine races; but the Badsworth at Wetherby in February was only just behind with 116 for ten.

Polly Curling made a good start to the season when she rode two of the four winners saddled by Richard Barber on the opening day at Larkhill. Alison Dare got off the mark a week later when, with her first ride since breaking her leg the previous March, she won the ladies' open at the PPORA on Down The Mine; but by the seventh week of the season, with one Saturday missed owing to the weather, and with no more than four wins to her credit, she was still four winners behind Polly, who had brought off two consecutive trebles on the Barber horses. But the two riders were level on Sunday, March 3, when Alison had her eighth win in nine rides in the ladies' open at the Ross Harriers on the eight-year-old Di Stefano.

As the season progressed, however, it became clear that Alison had the more powerful ammunition, none more so than Di Stefano, who was unbeaten in his seven races and, even if he wasn't the Grand Marnier winner, would have my vote as the outstanding ladies' horse of the season.

Bought out of Guy Harwood's yard for 2,500 guineas as a four-year-old at the Ascot Sales in June 1992, and now owned by a syndicate of 12 headed by Mike Gifford, a Gloucestershire farmer, Di Stefano had won 11 of his 14 races, with Alison up on him in nine of them, in the three seasons he had been racing from the Baimbridge yard.

Others who played a major part in helping Alison win the *Sporting Life* Cup for the sixth time in 11 years, with 31 winners, her highest-ever total in a single season, were Stephens Pet, who was unbeaten in his four races, Rip Van Winkle, who won four of his six, and Landsker Alfred, a winner of four of his five. To have won so many races with the ten-year-old Landsker Alfred (another son of Push On), a 1,900 guineas purchase at Ascot the previous July, was a remarkable achievement for both rider and trainer, as he had been pulled up in five of his six point-to-points in 1995 before he entered the Baimbridge yard.

Polly Curling, who finished her season with 23 wins riding 15 different horses, all but one of them trained by Richard Barber, and seven of his starting the season as maidens, never won more than three races on any one horse. The one she did win three races on was one of those who started the season as a maiden, the six-year-old Strong Tarquin, a son of the leading point-to-point sire Strong Gale. Another of the maidens she won on was the dual winner Bet With Baker, a six-year-old owned by the only point-to-point bookmaker, George Baker, who has the sartorial distinction of wearing a brown bowler. But the best of all the maidens she rode, on his future form, has to be the five-year-old Earthmover. On this Irish-bred son of an American sire, Mister Lord, she won twice and was a runner-up twice.

Behind Alison Dare and Polly Curling in the leading riders' stakes came Pip

Jones with 20 wins, Jo Cumings with 19 and Shirley Vickery with 15. Pip Jones's best rides were her 1995 Grand Marnier winner Handsome Harvey and David Brace's six-year-old Llangeinor mare African Bride. On the former she won all four of the races she rode him in, leaving three others to Jamie Jukes; and on African Bride, who started the season as a maiden, she won five races.

The most prolific winners for Joanne Cumings were two of the horses trained by her father, Khattaf, a winner of five ladies' opens and a runner-up in two others, and Flame O'Frensi, the mare who gave her four wins in point-to-points and a fifth in a 2.5-mile hunter chase at Leicester. Shirley Vickery's most productive winner was Martin Pipe's Faithful Star, who had his first success of the season with David Pipe up and won his next five races with Shirley riding him.

Welshman Jamie Jukes, the winner of the men's title for the first time at the age of 25 with 34 point-to-point winners, also won four hunter chases, including the John Corbet Cup at Stratford on the Bert Lavis-trained Handsome Harvey, who was having his first race under Rules and scored with authority in a field of 16. The runner-up, Syd Green, beaten by a comfortable three lengths, had won a novice hunter chase at Aintree on his previous appearance. Scally Muire, who finished third with Alastair Crow up, had won five open point-to-points and the North-Western Area point-to-point championship final at Bangor. Kettles, the fourth horse home, was the winner of the first of the point-to-point classics, the 4-mile race at the Heythrop; and among the also-rans were the Grimthorpe winner Highland Friend and one of the best young horses in the Northern Area, Clive Storey's seven-year-old Wudimp, a winner of three hunter chases in a row.

Before the start of the season the Middlesex bookmaker Desmond Gleeson was offering Jukes at 33-1 for the men's title; but, he says, he had no takers; though later in the season he laid two bets of £300 to £50 and £1,680 to £240, the first to that inveterate gambler Stephen Freud (the brother of Clement) and the second to the Devon bookmaker Chris Smith.

Jukes won his title riding 20 different horses, no fewer than 13 of them starting the season as maidens, and eight of them trained by Bert Lavis in Pembrokeshire. His most prolific winner was one of the Lavis horses, Mrs. Heather Gibbon's Northern Bluff, a horse who had been producing nothing over hurdles when trained by Jonjo O'Neill as a five-year-old. On this six-year-old, a maiden at the start of the season, he won four point-to-points in a row, riding a particularly brilliant race on him on a difficult course at Bassaleg, getting him up on the run-in after the horse had lost a considerable amount of ground through hanging left; and he ended up winning a hunter chase at Uttoxeter on him. Jukes was the first rider from West Wales to win the title since Fred Mathias shared it with Ted Greenway in 1956, 12 years before the *Daily Telegraph* Cup came into being; and he is only the second Welsh rider to win the trophy, the other being John Llewellyn in 1983.

Alastair Crow, the runner-up to Jamie Jukes for the title, had 27 wins on 13 horses, all of them trained at home in Shropshire; and his successes included his 100th winner in point-to-points when scoring on Korbell in the Confined at Sir W.W. Wynn's on March 2, a four-timer at the North Western Hunts Club fixture at Wolverhampton, and trebles at the Cheshire and the Meynell & South Staffs.

Alastair's best rides were the two mares Korbell and Scally Muire. The latter was the runner-up for the mares' championship for the second year running with her seven wins in point-to-points; and on Korbell Alastair won four point-to-points and was a runner-up twice.

In third place behind Jamie Jukes and Alastair Crow in the contest for the *Daily Telegraph* Cup was Scotland's Andrew Parker with 22 winners. Parker, who had been reaping the benefit of Kevin Anderson's enforced absence with a broken leg and brought off trebles at the West Percy & Milvain and the Berwickshire, was in the lead for the men's title with 18 winners as late as April 9; but after that his rides began to dry up to some extent, and the Northern Area season invariably ends too early to give Scottish riders a realistic chance of winning a major national title, although Mrs. Mabel Forrest achieved this feat when lifting the *Sporting Life* Cup in 1973; while David Mactaggart, Andrew Parker and Pat Robson have all been winners of a national novice rider's title. One promising young horse that Andrew Parker came in for the rides on in Kevin Anderson's absence was Howayman.

Anderson won three races on this horse in 1995 when he made his début as a five-year-old, and Parker won three in a row on him as a six-year-old.

The Grand Marnier winner, with ten wins in 12 appearances, was Phar Too Touchy, a nine-year-old mare from the Dulverton West; and this daugthers of Mister Lord out of a mare by Mon Fetiche was also the PPORA/*Horse and Hound* champion mare of the season; while the mare's owner, 24-year-old Rebecca Francis, who won nine races on Phar Too Touchy and a tenth on another horse trained in the same yard, was the *Daily Telegraph* female novice rider of the season. Phar Too Touchy was a first-ever winner for her when she won the Intermediate at the East Cornwall on the mare in February; and among the other races she won was the four-mile ladies' open at the Modbury Harriers in which Phar Too Touchy made all the running and came home unchallenged in the fastest time, 8 mins. 3.5 secs., since Lucky Hanassi's 8 mins. 2 secs. on firm ground in 1991.

Bred in Carmarthenshire by her former owner, Mrs. Mike Spuffard, for whom she lost her maiden certificate at the Carmarthenshire in 1995, Phar Too Touchy joined Victor Dartnall's Brayford yard prior to the 1996 season, when, apart from unseating Beccy Francis at the first fence in her first race for the yard at Barbury Castle, the mare's only defeat was in the ladies' open at the Lamerton, where she went under to Khattaf.

It was a highly successful second season for Dartnall, who trained 26 winners, including four in hunter chases. His most prolific winner after Phar Too Touchy was Nick Viney's Chilipour, who won five open point-to-points and two hunter chases with Neil Harris up and another hunter chase with Richard White riding him.

White was the leading rider in hunter chases with seven winners as against Clive Storey's six; and one of them, Gerald Tanner's home-bred 11-year-old Ryming Cuplet, trained by Mike Trickey on Exmoor, was the winner of the Land Rover men's final in its new home at Cheltenham. There were 11 starters for this championship; and, in a dramatic finish, Ryming Cuplet, a son of Rymer out of a mare by Jock Scot, got up on the run-in to beat Sheer Jest, with both horses going flat out. Among White's other winners was Wild Illusion, on whom he won three

306

hunter chases and an open point-to-point at Kingston Blount.

The leading trainer of hunter chasers, and the winner of the Richard Russell–Johnny Greenall Trophy for the fifth year running, was Caroline Saunders with seven winners, just one ahead of Northumberland's Jane Storey, who saddled Wudimp and Royal Jester to win three hunter chases apiece. The 13-year-old Teaplanter, Caroline's most prolific winner in these races, was the leading horse in hunter chases. He won four of his seven, and an open point-to-point at Barbury Castle as well, ridden in all of them by Ben Pollock.

The *Daily Telegraph* leading male novice rider of the season, and also the recipient of the Wilkinson Sword, was the 16-year-old Dorset rider Joe Tizzard, who went on to become Paul Nicholls's stable amateur. Tizzard was one of three novice riders to ride eight point-to-point winners. The others were Stuart Morris, Richard Edwards and David Nicholson's 17-year-old pupil assistant Robert Thornton; but Tizzard had the highest number of second places, six to Thornton's five. His best rides were two family horses, Qualitair Memory and The Jogger, both of them bought at the Ascot Sales, the former, an ex-selling hurdler, for 2,600 guineas, and The Jogger, an 11-year-old by Deep Run, for 3,000 guineas. On Qualitair Memory, a seven-year-old by an Irish sire, Don't Forget Me, out of a mare by the American sire Caerleon, his four wins included two in open point-to-points; and on The Jogger he won two point-to-points and two novice hunter chases.

Two of the season's point-to-point classics, the four-mile men's open for Lord Ashton of Hyde's Cup at the Heythrop and the Lady Dudley Cup at the Worcestershire, were now in their tenth year of sponsorship by the *Sporting Life* and the first of them, the Heythrop four-miler, attracted a field of ten, despite the firmness of the ground. The 9-4 favourite was Sue Woodhouse's home-bred mare Panda Shandy, who had beaten Earthmover in the Intermediate at the Wilton; but this half-sister to Hops And Pops (who was doing nicely under Rules) started to fade after a bad mistake at the eighteenth and was eventually pulled up. The winner was a 10-1 shot, Kettles, a nine-year-old mare from the Ledbury who had won a Restricted over the stayers' course at Upton-on-Severn.

Ridden for Mrs. Joanna Daniell by Alan Phillips, Kettles came up strongly from behind to pass two horses on the run-in and score by a length and a half from the well-fancied Strong Beau, who had been backed down to 4-1. Five lengths behind Strong Beau came the dead-heaters Bit Of A Clown and January Don. Last year's winner Sevens Out was outpaced and finished fifth.

Kettles, who had lost her maiden certificate over the 3-mile course at Heythrop in 1995, was trained by Mike Daniell at Upton-on-Severn. By the American sire Broadsword, she was foaled by a mare, Penny's Affair, on whom Mrs. Daniell won a ladies' open in 1982, and traces back four generations to a mare Mrs. Daniell's mother bought for very little money in 1960.

Unfortunately for Kettles, however, she wasn't able to add more than 10 points to the 50 she had collected for the *Sporting Life* Classics Cup. Although the mare ran in the Dudley Cup and earned her 10 extra points for doing so she was never able to go the pace on the good ground and finished seventh of the 15 runners after starting joint favourite with Shoon Wind, a winner of his two previous races.

The race produced its first-ever all-American-bred winner in the nine-year-old

Sharinski (by Niniski out of Upanishad, by Amber Rama). Hitting the front on the turn into the home straight with five fences to go, Sharinski ran on well under 26-year-old Mark Jackson to score by three lengths from Shoon Wind, with Better Future, the winner of the men's open at the Monmouthshire on his previous appearance, two lengths away in third.

A horse who had changed ownership several times since being bought out of Rod Juckes's N.H. yard, from which he won a novice chase as a four-year-old, Sharinski, now owned by eventing rider Mrs. Joanna Yeomans, the financial director of an electronics company in Malvern, was winning his sixth point-to-point in four seasons, ridden in the first two by Jonathan Rudge, the man who trained him in the North Ledbury country for Mrs. Yeomans, and in the other four by Mark Jackson.

There was a sad incident at Chaddesley Corbett on Dudley Cup Day when Mike Wareing's 16-year-old Treyford, the horse who had been a runner-up in the Dudley Cup on three consecutive occasions, collapsed and died in his box after running in the Worcestershire hunt race.

Thanks to a special concession from the Jockey Club, the Middleton were able to run their 12st. mixed open for the Grimthorpe Cup without penalties, a concession granted to no other race run off the 12st. mark. The race attracted a field of 19, the biggest since it became a mixed open in 1992; and, in fact, the biggest since 1977, when there was a field of 20 and the race was run over four miles 856 yards. That year the race was won by 2.5 lengths. This time it was a short head, when the judge decided that Peter Atkinson, riding Highland Friend, had held on to beat Robert Walmsley on Cot Lane – a decision that was the subject of some controversy. There was also a stewards' enquiry to debate whether interference had taken place on the run-in; but the result stood.

It can't really be described as a vintage Grimthorpe. The time of 8 mins. 47 secs. on good ground was considerably slower than Duright's on the good to firm ground in 1995. Nor was the previous form of the winner and runner-up anything to get excited about. Henry Bell's Bilsdale-hunted eight-year-old Highland Friend, trained by David Smith, had not long lost his maiden certificate at the Bramham Moor; and Cot Lane's only previous success this season was in the hunt race at the same meeting. The lightly-raced Man's Best Friend, a winner of two open events, declined his engagement.

The best Highland Friend could manage after his win in the Grimthorpe was third place in a men's open at Corbridge. So it was the Dudley Cup winner Sharinski, with his win in a men's open at Upton-on-Severn run seven days after the Heythrop, who emerged as the winner of the *Sporting Life* Classics Cup, which Mrs. Yeomans collected at the national point-to-point dinner at The Belfry in November.

Not for the first time, there was a full house for this dinner with an attendance of 280 in the new pillarless restaurant, where Ian Balding and his daughter Clare were the two principal speakers; and Sheila Crow, the mother of Alastair and Lucy, was the thoroughly deserving recipient of the dinner committee's inscribed salver for special services to the sport. The one rather sad feature was that *Horse and Hound* had dropped out of its joint sponsorship with the *Daily Telegraph*, the

Sporting Life and Grand Marnier. So there was no longer a trophy for the small owner training and riding his own horses. The 52-year-old George Cooper, who had won this trophy twice in the past was one of the riders who rode his 100th point-to-point winner during the season when scoring on his mare Busters Sister (a half-sister to the illustrious Carl's Choice) in the Restricted at the Thurlow fixture at Horseheath. Others were Julian Pritchard with the middle leg of a treble on Hacketts Farm at the Albrighton Woodland, and Mandy Hand with her win on John Weldhen's Oriental Plume in the ladies' open at the Bolventor Harriers in February. And Ron Treloggen was riding his 150th winner in point-to-points when scoring on the five-year-old Miss Ricus in an open maiden at the Dulverton East on May 25.

The final of the new Vauxhall-Montery Restricted series at Uttoxeter should by rights have been won by James Tarry on the home-bred Grecian Lark. This eight-year-old half-brother to Fine Lace was four lengths clear when he crumpled up on landing over the last and presented the race on a plate to Stephen Swiers on the American-bred Jasilu, a six-year-old mare owned by Mrs. Susan Mason and trained by Ian Mason in the Middleton country. It was Jasilu's second win of the season. Her previous one was in her qualifying race at the York & Ainsty.

In the other Restricted series with a final on a N.H. course, at Huntingdon, Candle Glow, an eight-year-old mare from the Fernie, made all the running at a furious pace under her owner-trainer, Patrick Hutchinson, and there was nothing the runner-up, Sir Michael Connell's Tarry Awhile, with Jimmy Tarry up, could do to reach this half-sister to Wild Illusion. As in the case of Jasilu, Candle Glow's only previous success during the season was in her qualifying race, the Restricted at the Essex & Suffolk over the sharp course at Higham, where she was also a runaway winner with Stuart Morris up, at a starting price of 25-1.

Although there were no longer any qualifying races for the ladies' open race for Lord Astor's Cup at the Melton Hunt Club point-to-point, it was being sponsored for the second year running by the stockbroking firm of Greig Middleton, which would be establishing a ladies' championship with a final on a N.H. course in 1997; and it was still regarded as an important race to aim at. Moreover, there was now a new generation of Newtons in charge of the meeting which Lance and Urky had founded so many years ago, with Joey Newton (a Joint Master of the Belvoir) installed as Chairman. So there was a renewed air of expectancy at Garthorpe.

The ground had been well watered for the occasion, and there were nine starters for the ladies' open, with Gi Chown's mount Larry The Lamb, a triple winner, the favourite at 6-4 on. The 11-year-old was in a challenging position when he fell at the second last, leaving the race to be fought out by Nowhiski and Heather Irving's mount Saybright, the former producing the better turn of foot to score by a length in much the fastest time of the day under his novice rider, 24-year-old Cherry Tarratt.

This was a good performance by Nowhiski, and also by his rider, who weighed no more than seven stone and was putting up a lot of dead weight. It was the partnership's third win in a row.

Jointly owned by the rider's father, Tim Tarratt (who trained him in his livery yard at Waltham-on-the-Wolds) and Christopher Morris, a London accountant who was away in Malaya but left instructions for a bet to be placed on him, the eight-year-old Nowhiski had cost his connections a mere 800 guineas when they bought him; and the former selling hurdler had been off the course for $3^1/_2$ years with leg and sinus problems before making a fresh start in point-to-points at the beginning of the season.

There were also nine runners for the Marie Curie novice championship, including two from Yorkshire, one of which, Stephen Swiers's mount Sharp To Oblige, the winner of an open maiden at the Brocklesby, started favourite but failed to live up to his name. The comfortable winner, with Julian Pritchard up on him, was Gromit, a New Zealand-bred eight-year-old from the North Cotswold, owned by Sarah Eaton and trained by Martin Brent at Badsey, near Evesham. He was winning for the third time in four appearances, twice with Pritchard up and once with Tim Stephenson riding him.

For the second time in six years, the Cheltenham Foxhunters' was won by a horse from Ireland, Elegant Lord, who earned himself the top spot in Mackenzie & Selby's handicap at 12-1. Carrying the famous green and orange colours of J.P. McManus and ridden by his trainer, Enda Bolger in Co. Limerick, the eight-year-old was a very smooth winner from the Portman eight-year-old Cool Dawn, whose owner-rider, Di Harding, was having her first ride at the Festival, having won a hunter chase at Kempton on him earlier in the season.

The 33-year-old Enda Bolger was the champion point-to-point rider in Ireland for six seasons; and in one of those years he rode 51 winners, more than any of his counterparts in Britain have ridden in a single season. By the end of the 1996 season his grand total of winners in point-to-points had risen to 346, a total exceeded only by the legendary Willie Rooney. In 1996 Enda was training 16 horses in Co. Limerick and winning with most of them. Another thing in his favour, I'm told, is that he is a Bruce Springsteen fan.

The French-bred Rolling Ball, a winner of six races on the Flat in France and of four under N.H. Rules over here for Martin Pipe, including the Sun Alliance Chase at Cheltenham in 1991 as an eight-year-old, made a remarkable comeback in 1996 as a 13-year-old when trained by Steven Brookshaw for Mrs. Hilda Clarke, whose husband, Stan, is the Chairman of Uttoxeter and Newcastle racecourses. After being hunted with the North Shropshire and beating Double Silk by a distance in a hunter chase at Warwick, he went on, under the same rider, Richard Ford, to win the Liverpool Foxhunters'.

There was a field of 26 for this 2m 6f race over the Grand National course and six of them departed at the first. Rolling Ball, however, made nearly all the running and, despite hanging right on the run-in, held off a strong challenge from Philip Fenton's mount Kerry Orchid (who had finished third in the Cheltenham Foxhunters' and won two open point-to-points and a hunter chase in Ireland) by a length and a half. Headed briefly at one stage, Rolling Ball rallied magnificently. Sadly, he was pulled up lame in his last race, the *Horse and Hound* Cup at Stratford.

Another who ended his season lame in this race was Stewart Pike's Proud Sun. But this didn't prevent the eight-year-old son of Sunyboy from winning it, as the injury occurred very late in the race, just as he was about to jump the last fence. Given a splendid ride by the 24-year-old Irish rider Jim Culloty, who ended his

1ast season as an amateur taking the amateur riders' championship with 40 winners under Rules, Proud Sun hung on gamely to score by a length and a half and four lengths from Celtic Abbey and Sheer Jest, with last year's winner, Hermes Harvest, finishing fourth. Among those who failed to finish were Faithful Star (a winner of six point-to-points in a row), What A Hand (a winner of two open point-to-points at Larkhill and a hunter chase at Windsor) and Ryming Cuplet.

The other race that Proud Sun won under Rules this year was the £5,000 *Timeform* Golden Miller Handicap Chase at Cheltenham in Aprill when he was ridden by the professional jockey Mick Fitzgerald; and he was the runner-up to Life Of A Lord in the Whitbread Gold Cup at Sandown. Mackenzie & Selby put him second in their handicap, 31b. below Elegant Lord.

But for Stewart Pike, Proud Sun's owner-breeder, there had been another misfortune. Nine days before Proud Sun finished lame at Stratford, his half-brother Synderborough Lad broke down too badly to recover in a handicap chase at Uttoxeter.

Another West Country star was the Tetcott seven-year-old Coome Hill, who began his season with an effortless win in the Dick Woodhouse hunter chase at Wincanton and finished it in the mud at Chepstow going under by a head to Holland House, before reappearing in November at Wincanton with pro. jockey Jimmy Frost up and winning a £20,000 handicap chase. This was the prelude, later the same month, to his magnificent win for his Bude permit holder Walter Dennis in the Hennessy Gold Cup at Newbury, where Jamie Osborne was deputising for the injured Jimmy Frost.

Since coming over from Ireland as a four-year-old after the 1993 season to take up residence at the Dennis dairy farm in Cornwall, the son of Riot Helmet out of a mare by Golden Love had now won all five of his point-to-points and two of his three hunter chases under Tim Dennis, in addition to his two later successes with professional jockeys up.

The day after Coome Hill won the Hennessy, another outstanding former point-to-pointer, See More Business, now in Paul Nicholls's yard, was the runner-up to the Irish star Dorans Pride in a valuable novice chase at Fairyhouse.

Moorcroft Boy, who will be well remembered for his successes in point-to-points when he was owned and trained by Graham Roach in Cornwall, made a remarkable comeback from injury when winning the Scottish Grand National at the age of 11. The former point-to-pointer broke his neck in a fall in the Becher Chase at Aintree in 1994, the same year that he finished third in the Grand National; but thanks to the skills of the veterinary team at Liverpool University, he eventually made a complete recovery and returned to David Nicholson's yard, from which, as the less fancied of Nicholson's two runners in the race, and starting at 20-1 under Mark Dwyer, he made what seemed almost a return from the dead.

The most prolific winners of ladies' races were Out The Door, who won six of his ten races under Stephanie Baxter, and Bankhead, a winner of six of his seven with Caroline Spearing up. Michael Mann's Out The Door, a seven-year-old from the Wheatland, trained by Paul Jones, was the national champion in the PPORA/*Horse and Hound* young horse awards, 15 points ahead of Bankhead (the leading young horse in the West Midlands Area) with the extra points he collected from his three placings.

Alan Brazier's Bankhead, a seven-year-old from the Croome & West Warwickshire, and a winner twice over hurdles when trained by Kim Bailey, but now trained by his 23-year-old rider (daughter of the Warwickshire trainer John Spearing), had some notable scalps to his credit, defeating horses ridden by Alison Dare on two occasions, Down The Mine at Chaddesley Corbett on Dudley Cup Day and Rip Van Winkle at the Golden Valley; and at the Ross Harriers he accounted for Khattaf.

The closest Bankhead came to defeat, apart from the time when he unseated his rider at Chaddesley Corbett in a race won by Alison Dare on Russki, was in a dramatic race at Kingston Blount when, after being headed at the last, he got up again on the line to score by a short head from Sperrin View.

The ten-year-old Sperrin View, owned and ridden by Katie Sunderland (née Mobley) and trained by her mother, Helen Mobley, in a new yard in the Bicester with Whaddon Chase country, had been stepping up considerably on her 1995 form. This mare, who had Derby winners on both sides of her pedigree, Crepello on her dam's side and Hyperion on her sire's, was a winner of four of her seven races, in two of which she had been unlucky enough to come up against the all-conquering Di Stefano.

In the South East, Burromariner, Ann Blaker's replacement for El Padre, was doing her Nutley yard proud as the most prolific winner in the area with six wins in seven appearances, four of them with Simon Cowell up and two under Adam Welsh. The 12-year-old's only lapse was at the Surrey Union, where he declined to proceed any further than the fifteenth in the men's open won by the veteran David Robinson carrying a 7lb. penalty on his Ginger Tristan, who was completing a hat-trick of wins for his owner-rider in this 12st. race and recording his fourth win of the season carrying a penalty on each occasion.

There were, of course, better horses than Burromariner and Ginger Tristan in the area, notably Peter Bonner's 13-year-old Strong Gold, who returned to form with two wins in open races under Tim McCarthy, beating Ginger Tristan in one of them.

Others to shine in the South East were three of the horses trained by Di Grissell in the East Sussex & Romney Marsh country, Colonial Kelly, Nethertara and Little Martina. Colonial Kelly, ridden by the area's leading rider, Paul Hacking (who rode 20 point-to-point winners and was fourth to Jamie Jukes in the male riders' national table), won an open point-to-point and two hunter chases, beating Still In Business in one at Newbury. Nethertara won four point-to-points in a row with Hacking up, including one out of her country at Horseheath. Little Martina completed a hat-trick of wins with three different riders up, Adam Welsh and Paul Hacking both winning point-to-points on her and Jim Culloty rounding things off in a hunter chase at Ascot, where the mare beat a much-fancied runner from Ian Balding's yard in King's Treasure, who went on to complete a hat-trick of wins in hunter chases with Andrew Balding up.

At the Crawley & Horsham, Mrs. Grissell saddled four winners with her five runners. Nethertara and Little Martina were two of them. Another was the five-year-old Croft Court, making only his second appearance on a course in the open maiden; but I feel sure the success that gave her the most pleasure must have been that of the 25-1 shot Wellington Bay, whose storming late run in the ladies' open provided her 17-year-old daughter Coral with her first winner.

The outstanding five-year-old in the South East Area was Mike Roberts's home-trained son of Strong Gale, Bitofamixup, whose two wins in point-to-points under Paul Hacking augured well for his future.

Bitofamixup wasn't the only Strong Gale five-year-old to make his mark. Another was John Keighley's Strong Chairman, produced in the Cattistock country by Richard Barber, again the leading point-to-point trainer of the season with 44 winners. Bought at Doncaster for 16,500 guineas, Strong Chairman lost his maiden certificate under Nick Mitchell at the Blackmore & Sparkford Vale.

One of the four winners saddled by Harry Wellstead at the Cattistock in his last season as a trainer was the five-year-old Aller Moor. A grandson of Shirley Heights on his dam's side, he too looked likely to progress further.

The most prolific winner in the Northern Area was Mrs. Mary Scott's seven-year-old Todcrag, ridden in all his races by Thomas Scott. A maiden at the start of the season, the Border-hunted Todcrag won six of his seven races, the last five of them in a row.

The only horse to beat Todcrag was Dennis Waggott's Sayin Nowt. This eight-year-old mare from the Dumfriesshire, trained by Kate Anderson and ridden by Andrew Parker, had lost her maiden certificate when beating Todcrag in the last of her four races in 1995 at the Buccleuch, where she was ridden by Kevin Anderson; and in 1996, when she was unbeaten in her two races with Andrew Parker up, she gave Todcrag a dose of the same medicine in a Restricted at the Cumberland Farmers. Dennis Waggott was also the owner of Howayman. This promising American-bred six-year-old, another of Kate Anderson's charges, who had lost his maiden certificate the previous season when he won three of his five races with Kevin Anderson up, won three of his four in 1996 with Andrew Parker up. In his only defeat this season he was a faller in a hunter chase at Perth.

Another promising young horse seen out in the Northern Area was Jigtime. This seven-year-old mare from the Buccleuch, who had lost her maiden certificate at the Berwickshire last season on the second of her two runs, was even more impressive on her two runs in 1996 under Mark Bradburne. Starting with a fluent win in a Restricted at her home meeting, she went on to beat Royal Jester quite comfortably in a hunter chase at Kelso. Admittedly she was receiving 131b. from the 12-year-old; but the manner of her success caused her to go into many people's notebooks, and certainly into that of the *Sporting Life* correspondent Jonathan Neesom.

Of the horses hunted in the South Midlands, the Tarrys' Lucky Christopher was the most prolific winner, with five wins in point-to-points and one in a hunter chase at Uttoxeter; and in East Anglia the most prolific winners were Richard Hunt and St. Gregory, each with five wins in ladies' races, the former's including a dead-heat with Larry The Lamb at Horseheath, where St. Gregory finished a well-beaten third. The eight-year-old St. Gregory, however, owned by Anthony and Sue Howland-Jackson and trained for them by Ruth Hayter in the Essex & Suffolk country, got his revenge on Richard Hunt later, when, with Alice Plunkett up, he beat him a length in a ladies' open at Marks Tey. St. Gregory achieved his five wins with three different riders up. Lucy Gibbon and Alice Plunkett both won two races on him and Lucy Hollis scored on him once. Richard Hunt, a runner-up to Teaplanter in a hunter chase at Towcester, was ridden in all his races by Lisa Rowe.

Fosbury was the class winner at the Torrington Farmers on the last day of the season. Well suited by the top of the ground conditions at Umberleigh, Mrs. Susan Humphreys's 11-year-old trotted up in the ladies' open to record his fourth successive win of the season, at the expense of Shirley Vickery's mount Not Mistaken, a week after he had scored over four miles at the Exmoor. He was Polly Curling's 23rd winner of the season and the 45th saddled by Richard Barber, including the one he had with What A Hand in a hunter chase at Windsor. This meeting was also notable as the 25th in the reign of the indomitable Mrs. Sally Morrish as Hon. Sec.

Jean Auvray, a 25-year-old French pupil assistant to Martin Pipe, rode his first winner when scoring on Morchard Milly in the hunt race at the Dulverton East; and the Cardiff bookmaker John Lovell made a bit of history at the Gelligaer Farmers when he introduced a portable computer to point-to-point racing. His customers were handed a print-out with the name of the horse they had backed on it and the amount of money they could expect to collect if it won.

The shock of the season, if I may call it that, was the three-year warning-off from race-riding that was handed out to a member of a distinguished point-to-point family in Kent, Peter Hickman, the eldest of the three point-to-pointing sons of maestro John Hickman, who has been the Secretary of the South East Area Point-to-Point Association ever since 1964. The horse that profited from Peter Hickman's misdemeanour concerning a lost weight cloth was Ann Blaker's good old Burromariner, whose wins went up from five to six.

The Herefordshire rider Willy Bryan had his last race before retirement riding All Greek To Me, one of the horses trained by his father, the redoubtable Bill Bryan, in the hunt race at the Golden Valley, and made it a winning one. It was his 74th winner in point-to-points; and a few months later Bill Bryan was up at Wembley riding the winner of the show hunter championship at the Horse of the Year Show, a heavyweight hunter aptly called The Showman. Bryan Snr., who last rode the winner of this championship in 1964, said afterwards, with a broad grin spreading over his face, "I've been trying to get it back ever since."

Two others to retire from race-riding this year were Brian Crawford and Mike Felton, although neither managed to go out on a winning note. The 45-year-old Brian Crawford, who rode over 50 point-to-point winners, is the clerk of the course at the Melton Hunt Club fixture.

Mike Felton, a Joint Master of the Blackmore & Sparkford Vale, is one of the few amateur-riders to have ridden over 200 winners. He rode 225 winners in point-to-points and 23 in hunter chases; and he was the champion male point-to-point rider in 1987, 1989 and 1990.

The West Midlands rider Tommy Jackson had retirement enforced on him after a very bad fall on Celtic Berry in the hunt race at the North Ledbury in March, though at least it didn't end in his being confined permanently to a wheel-chair;

and at the same meeting at Upton-on-Severn, the North Cotswold rider Sue Sadler was compelled to retire from race-riding after sustaining serious injuries when Shaker Maker was brought down in the Confined. However, she is now well enough to assist her partner Jim Collett with the training of the horses in their yard.

Chris Coyne, the tallest of all point-to-point riders at 6ft. 6in. (as against Alan Hill's 6ft. 5in. and the 6ft. 3in. Malcolm Batters), whilst continuing to ride in point-to-points, decided to stand down in 1996 as the PPORA representative in the Sandhurst Area. So perhaps this is the right moment to mention his role as an outstanding innovator. He was the first to introduce a bloodhounds fixture when the Windsor Forest Bloodhounds held their inaugural point-to-point at Tweseldown in 1993; and it was in his area that there were three other firsts. The Sandhurst Area was the first to hold a point-to-point riders' seminar, the first to have a Sunday fixture with betting, and the first to feature the legitimate dolling-off of fences on a point-to-point course.

This was also the year that the octogenarian Joe Allen, not all that far off his nineties, decided to retire from working full-time at his Horseman's Bookshop in Lower Grosvenor Place. The good news, however, is that he is to be seen there three days a week; and, thankfully, the invaluable service he created so many years ago, both as bookseller and publisher, still goes on.

Jim Papworth's 12-year-old Melton Park, the pride of East Anglia, had been running well below form in 1996, when he was battling with a navicular problem, and the decision was made to retire him after he had finished sixth of 15 in the club members' conditional race at the Melton Hunt Club fixture towards the end of May. He did, though, manage one more win during the season, and he ended his illustrious career with 21 wins, having been the most prolific point-to-point winner of the season on two occasions.

Sarah Robertson's French-bred Nenni retired at the age of 17 after winning the hunt race at the Vale of Lune on his single appearance of the season. It was his ninth successive win over the Whittington course; and his 19 wins on his 48 appearances, all but the first of them with Richard Ford up, included a hunter chase at Cartmel in 1988.

The nine-year-old Hops And Pops, whose brilliant successes as a point-to-pointer had been supplemented with nine successes under Rules, three in chases and six over hurdles including an impressive defeat of Mole Board at Cheltenham, was retired to stud in December after Robert Alner had sold the mare back to her breeder, Sue Woodhouse, who sent her to be covered by Broadsword.

A number of prominent riders had their season cut drastically short with injuries; and one of them, Trelawney Hill in the South Midlands, was put out of action with a broken leg before the season started. Another, Kevin Anderson, had no more rides after breaking his leg in a fall on Dundee Prince in the men's open at the West Percy & Milvain on the first day of the Northern Area season.

Zoe Turner was put out of action for two seasons after cracking a vertebra at the top of her neck in a fall on Ashboro in a ladies' open at Charing in February. Pauline Robson lost three weeks of her season when she broke her nose in a fall on Bridgnorth Lass in an open maiden at the Cumberland Farmers in March after she had won the ladies' open there on Minibrig. Anthea Farrell, so often the ladies' champion in Yorkshire, cracked three ribs and damaged her pelvis after the season was over when her dual point-to-point winner Choctaw collapsed and died on top of her in a rehearsal for a pageant at the Great Yorkshire Show at Harrogate in July.

Among others to have their season interrupted by injury were Malcolm Batters, who combined his point-to-pointing with his professional career as a deep-sea diver, and broke his pelvis in a first-fence fall on Mr. Sunnyside in the Restricted at the West Street–Tickham fixture at Detling in March; Philip Scholfield, with a dislocated shoulder at the Eggesford in April; Polly Curling with two nasty falls in consecutive races at the Blackmore & Sparkford Vale the same month; and, also in April, Alastair Crow with two falls at the North Staffordshire. Neither Curling nor Crow was out of action for long and both returned with a winner.

Among the star performers who became fatal casualties in 1996 were Yahoo, The Blue Boy, Generals Boy, Cool Relation, Lewesdon Hill and Starember Lad.

Having won his first race for his new owner-rider, Steven Astaire, when dead-heating with Button Your Lip in the City of London race at the Windsor Forest Bloodhounds fixture at Tweseldown on the last day of March, 15-year-old Yahoo, the horse who once had the distinction of finishing a runner-up to Desert Orchid in the Cheltenham Gold Cup, collapsed and died a month later at Tweseldown after running second to Tim Underwood's Olde Crescent in a club members' race at the Isle of Wight meeting. During a point-to-pointing career which began in 1993 with seven wins for Bernard Heffernan, Yahoo won 11 point-to-points, including a Dudley Cup.

The Blue Boy, who had returned to Peter Bowen's yard to win three hunter chases for him in 1995, was put down in November at the Bristol University Medical Centre, to which he had been sent for treatment after a bad fall at Taunton, when it was discovered that he had fractured his shoulder.

The 14-year-old Generals Boy, a winner of 13 point-to-points and two hunter chases for Peter Craggs in the Morpeth country, in addition to the six wins that Craggs had on him in handicap chases when the horse was trained for him by Jonjo O'Neill in 1990, broke his back in a fall at the Buccleuch in March.

Denis Caro's V.W.H. ten-year-old Cool Relation, a winner of six point-to-points and six hunter chases – he was unbeaten in the latter on his four appearances in 1995 and his single appearance in 1996 – died in July after bolting into a gate during a thunder-storm on his owner's farm at Oaksey.

Lewesdon Hill, one of the stars of Richard Barber's yard, collapsed and died at the age of nine after recording his 11th win in point-to-points, and his fifth of the season, in the ladies' open at the Seavington on the last Sunday in April. Twelve-year-old Starember Lad, who occupied a similar status in Keith Cumings's Devon yard, broke a pastern in the ladies' open at the PPORA fixture at Barbury Castle in January. This son of New Member was a winner of 15 races, including two hunter chases.

Sadly, the death list was not confined to horses. In January, Eric Cousins, who used to train professionally at Tarporley in Cheshire, died at the age of 74 whilst swimming in the sea off the coast of Barbados. Cousins rode over 50 winners as an amateur, many of them in point-to-points. The best horses he produced to win point-to-points were probably the two former hurdlers Dandini and Permit. Dandini, who had been racing successfully over hurdles under the name of Dame Street, and didn't start in point-to-points until he reached the age of 11, won eight open nomination races over two seasons in 1951 and 1952, after being hunted with the Vale of Lune by Cousins, who rode him in four of them. Permit, a horse bred by Cousins, and a winner of three novice hurdles for him, one as a three-year-old and the other two as a four-year-old, won three open point-to-points an a five-year-old in 1968; and after being sold into Neville Crump's yard for a substantial sum, he went on to carve out a successful career for himself as a chaser.

Another well-known trainer with a history of point-to-point racing behind him, Colin Davies, the Persian War man, died in October at the age of 68. Colin, who trained Persian War to win three consecutive Champion Hurdles at Cheltenham, was a passionately keen racing motorist before he took to point-to-pointing and went on to complete the course in the 1964 Grand National as an amateur on one of his own horses, Claymore. But the best horse he owned, rode and trained himself in the Pentyrch country, where he was the Hunt's Hon. Sec., was Master Copper, whose hat-trick of wins in 1958 included a division of the Lady Dudley Cup, in which he beat the Grimthorpe Cup winner Brown Sugar; and the four hunter chases Colin Davies won later on the son of Copernicus included the United Hunts' Cup at Cheltenham in 1960.

Capt. Willy Bulwer-Long, a Steward of the Jockey Club and Chairman of the Point-to-Point Liaison Committee from 1991 to 1993 over the same period, died in February at the age of 58. A rider of 35 point-to-point winners and two races under Rules, he twice had the distinction of getting the better of Guy Cunard in a tight finish. A steward at five racecourses, including Fakenham in his home county of Norfolk, he was described in a *Daily Telegraph* obituary as "one of the greatest countrymen of his generation and a quintessential Englishman."

In March there occurred the death of that remarkable nonagenarian Brig. C.B. ("Roscoe") Harvey, who died at the age of 95 at his home in the Heythrop country. A former Senior Stewards' Secretary, The Brig. was the most enlightened of stipendiary stewards and an utterly delightful character, with a sense of humour that was second to none. An accomplished point-to-point rider in his younger days, in later years he enjoyed many successes with the horses he had in training with David Nicholson, notably with Relkeel, a high-class hurdler that he bred himself. Another of his home-breds was his outstanding point-to-pointer Aquilo, the horse he hunted with the Meynell and won 12 races on between 1946 and 1950. There is no doubt that Aquilo would have been more than capable of winning hunter chases; but as his owner was an official of the Jockey Club he was precluded from running him under Rules. The Brig. was indeed the "Bright Shiner" that Tim Fitzgeorge-Parker christened him in the fascinating book he wrote about him; and the late Sir Gordon Richards had this to say of him: "I will always maintain that the General is the greatest man Racing has known in my lifetime."

In September, Lord Daresbury, head of the Greenall brewing family, died at the age of 67, leaving Peter Greenall, the Chairman of Aintree and a former champion amateur rider, to succeed to the title as the eldest of his three sons.

In October, the life of the Yorkshire amateur Howard Brown was cut tragically short in a motor accident at the age of 33. The husband of Jeannie, Howard was equally respected on the Yorkshire circuit. Ellerton Hill, Karakter Reference and Final Chant were just a few of the horses he won on.

In November, Alec Marsh, the Jockey Club's Senior Starter for more than 20 years, died at the age of 88. The champion amateur under N.H. Rules for three consecutive seasons, he rode 163 winners; and in the course of his distinguished career as a race-rider he won the Cheltenham Foxhunters' twice on two different horses and, in 1936, brought off the big hunt-racing double, winning the Cheltenham Foxhunters' on Herode Bridge and the Liverpool Foxhunters' over the full Grand National distance on Don Bradman.

In December, two of the best-known personalities in the South Midlands, Col. Arthur Clerke-Brown and Graham Pidgeon, died within a week of each other, The Colonel at the age of 84 and Graham losing his long and courageous battle against illness at the age of 64. At the time, they were Joint Vice-Chairmen of the South Midlands Area Point-to-Point Association, of which The Colonel had been the first Chairman, a position which this founder of the point-to-point course at Kingston Blount held for over 20 years.

Grahan Pidgeon, always an inspiring presence on a course, was a founder-member of the Point-to-Point Owners' Association, a stalwart of the Grafton Hunt, and the clerk of the course at Mollington for seven years. He owned and trained well over 100 winners, sharing ownership of some of them with The Colonel, and breeding an outstanding one in Matchplay. Most of his winners were ridden by his daughter, Jenny, the leading lady rider in point-to-points for four years running. Both Graham and The Colonel were the sort of men one never forgets.

Other familiar faces lost to the scene in 1996 were those of Westcountryman Tom Brake, who won 18 races on his Surgeon Major in pre-war days and was also well known as an international show-jumping rider; Capt. Bobby Petre, the amateur who won the 1946 Grand National on Lovely Cottage; Basil Ancil, one of the most elegant point-to-point riders in the South Midlands in his day; the retired Cambridgeshire farmer Tom Wakefield whose That Much, a horse he was intensely proud of, won 11 point-to-points and two hunter chases under Ian Loftus, never missing a season between 1959 and 1964; and the bewhiskered Robin Brereton, whose cheerful presence on the point-to-point courses in East Anglia, where he was frequently to be seen setting up his own stand, will be greatly missed by punters and bookmakers alike.

Tailpiece:

A reader of *Horse and Hound* who wrote to the Labour Party spokesman Tony Banks (the present Minister of Sport) for a clarification of the Party's views on hunting received this significant reply: "The Labour Party has always been strongly opposed to hunting with hounds and intent on achieving the highest level of animal welfare in Britain. We will allow a free vote in the House of Commons to ban it."

1997

In which the threat to hunting draws ever closer and the campaign for its preservation is stepped up, the £500 feature point-to-point races are introduced, new men's and ladies' champions emerge, a new sponsor is found for the reappearance of the ladies' championship at Chepstow, the Land Rover men's final returns to Towcester after a year at Cheltenham, and Stratford stages its first ladies' hunter chase.

I feel it is appropriate to begin this chapter with some reflections on the looming possibility of a ban on hunting, since it would have a dire effect on the point-to-point scene if it were to materialise. On May 10 there appeared in the *Sporting Life* a letter from Henry Beeby, the Director of the Doncaster Bloodstock Sales, urging the British Horseracing Board, which was dragging its feet on the subject, whilst admitting that any such ban would have an adverse effect on N.H. racing, to back foxhunting in a positive manner. Beeby's letter was followed soon afterwards by one from Michael Argyle, a former Judge of the Central Criminal Court, who had this to say:

"With some weariness and for about the tenth time in my lifetime, one repeats the unanswerable arguments in not discriminating against foxhunting." And he duly did so, pointing out in the process that, if cruelty was really the issue, it was gross hypocrisy to single out hunting in preference to fishing, in which a far greater degree of cruelty was involved. A negative argument, perhaps, but equally unanswerable.

There were, of course, plenty of other voices raised in favour of preserving hunting. Christopher Sweeting, the owner of the Conduit Stud Farm Stud in Oxfordshire, remarked in another letter that, if foxhunting were to be abolished as a result of Labour M.P. Michael Foster's proposed bill, "point-to-point racing would be replaced by low-grade flapping meetings." Does the BHB want to police that? he asked; and he was supported by Major Dick Hern, who wrote, "Surely it is now the moment for the Club and the British Horseracing Board to come out against this proposed bill."

Peter Walwyn also expressed his disappointment with the BHB, whose spokesman, Tristram Ricketts, was saying at this stage, "We are currently looking into the whole issue of a ban on hunting and will make our stance clear in the near future." This was announced in *The Life* of June 10, and later in the same paper Alastair Down ended a beautifully balanced article with these words: "All I

319

have is a voice to beseech people to look beyond kneejerk instincts and consider the possibility that hunting brings more to the world than it takes away."

Joey Newton, in his letter to the paper, asked where, if foxhunting was abolished, would retired racehorses like Young Hustler and Lumberjack find a life that would do them justice? And, for good measure, he added, "No longer would horses such as Rushing Wild, See More Indians and See More Business rise through the amateur ranks to succeed at the highest level." To these names might be added the more recent examples of Coome Hill, Harwell Lad and Moorcroft Boy.

And from Roxburghshire came the voice of the man so affectionately known as 'The Benign Bishop', Hawick trainer Ken Oliver, to recall vivid memories of the former hunter and point-to-pointer Wyndburgh, the runner-up in three of his six Grand Nationals with three different riders up. Oliver, who was no stranger to Aintree himself in his days as an amateur race-rider, dismisses the idea of drag-hunting as an alternative to foxhunting, describing it as "a nonstarter because the majority of non-hunting farmers will not stand for it. They accept the hounds and their followers on their land," he wrote, "because they are out to control the fox population which is so damaging to their property and stock."

The BHB finally came to its senses, and the right decision, when, as reported in *The Life* of June 18, it "came out solidly against the proposed private member's bill to ban hunting" and, along with the Jockey Club, which had always been less lagging with its avowed support for the sport, appealed to racing enthusiasts to join the ranks of the Countryside Rally scheduled to take place in Hyde Park on July 10. In the words of Lord Wakeham, the BHB Chairman, "The bill to ban hunting is an attack on the British countryside, and we will oppose it. A ban on hunting," he continued, "poses a serious threat to the fabric of the countryside, and to the popular country pursuit of horseracing. National Hunt and point-to-point racing are particularly vulnerable," he added.

On the great day itself, for which many thousands had marched on London from deep in the countryside of England, Scotland and Wales, and were joined by marchers from Ireland, whilst others had come in coachloads, the estimated attendance exceeded all expectations, ranging from 125,000 to 145,000. Clement Freud, writing in the *Sporting Life*, described the attendance as "greater by far than that which listened to the Pope in St. Peter's Square on Easter Sunday."

Among those who spoke from the platform were Lord Wakeham, Sir Thomas Pilkington, the Jockey Club's Senior Steward (who emphasised the point that "National Hunt racing in Britain developed out of hunting and point-to-pointing and the strong links are still there today"), Robin Hanbury-Tenison, the Chief Executive of the Countryside Alliance, Lord David Steel, the Deputy Chairman of the Alliance and former Leader of the Liberal Party, Michael Heseltine, the former Deputy Leader of the Conservative Party. And none spoke more eloquently for the cause than the Labour peeress Baroness Mallalieu, who concluded her speech with the stirring words given by Shakespeare to Henry V at the Battle of Agincourt.

Also giving voice to the occasion were Neil Greatrex, the President of the Union of Democratic Mineworkers, Roger Bennett, the Chairman of the Piccadilly Hunt Club, whose members had engaged in that historic ride of protest along Piccadilly in 1949; Newmarket trainer Sir Mark Prescott, author Frederick Forsyth, actors Jeremy Irons and Robert Hardy (who read a poem of G.K. Chesterton's), conservationists Robin Page and David Bellamy; and those irrepressible columnists Auberon Waugh and Willie Poole.

Altogether, this splendid Rally was an occasion to savour, and to reflect upon. The Point-to-Point Owners' & Riders' Association, which was celebrating its 20th birthday, had already done some reflecting. At its A.G.M. at Stratford Racecourse on May 30 the Chairman, Michael Bannister, revealed that, if the worst came to the worst and a ban on hunting were to be imposed, the Association had a contingency plan up its sleeve. He did not, however, go into any details. But one thing is for sure, whatever brilliant alternative is in the offing, the point-to-point scene as we know it today will be very different if a hunting ban does materialise; and it will not be a change for the better.

The official Jockey Club statistics show that, of the 211 point-to-point fixtures scheduled for 1997, 205 were able to take place, 60 of them on Sundays. But there was a fall in the number of hunters' certificates issued, 4,245, down by 75 on last year's record total. The Blackmore & Sparkford Vale were again in the ascendancy with 82. There was a more substantial decrease in the number of runners, 11,706, a drop of 1,745. Nevertheless, the quality was there all right.

There were some important administrative changes. Lucy Brack took over from Camilla Mason as the Jockey Club's Point-to-Point Administrator. Major Mike MacEwan was succeeded by East Anglia's Andrew Merriam as Chairman of the Point-to-Point Secretaries' Association. John Sharp, the Marketing Director of feed merchants Dodson & Horrell, the sponsors of the PPORA club races, succeeded Michael Bannister as Chairman of the Association. And it was Sharp who was presented with the special award for services to point-to-point racing at the national point-to-point dinner at The Belfry in November, when the toast was proposed by Baroness Mallalieu and replied to by the Lambourn trainer Richard Phillips.

The new season saw several significant alterations to the regulations, among them an increase in the allowance for five-year-old mares, who could now claim the 5lb. sex allowance on top of the 7lb. age allowance. Not that there were all that many of them about; and the only ones I recall entering the winner's enclosure were Krystal Haze, the winner of a maiden race at the Carmarthenshire, Magic Mole, who won a four-horse hunt race at the Wilton, Miss Madelon, the winner of an open maiden for five, six and seven-year-olds at the Cleveland, African Warrior, who scored in a maiden at the Tivyside; and the one who might well prove to have the brightest prospects, Kingussie Flower, who, on her single appearance, was a very easy winner of the faster of the two open maidens at the Gelligaer Farmers with Mark Rimell up.

Another of the new regulations now made it possible for *all* 12st. mixed opens to be run without penalties for previous winners that were still in force for men's opens run off the 12st. mark.

Most welcome of all the concessions, however, was the Jockey Club's authorisation of one £500 feature race in each of the 14 point-to-point areas wishing to take advantage of it. Not all of them did. It was good, though, to see the three point-to-point classics sponsored by the *Sporting Life* featuring amongst them, the four-mile men's open for Lord Ashton of Hyde's Cup at the Heythrop in the South Midlands Area, the four-mile 12st. mixed open for the Grimthorpe Cup in the Yorkshire Area, and the men's open for the Lady Dudley Cup at the Worcestershire in the West Midlands Area.

The other £500 feature races were the men's open at the Tiverton Staghounds fixture at Bratton Down in the Devon & Cornwall Area, the men's gold cup open at the Tedworth fixture at Barbury Castle in what had now become the Wessex Area (replacing the Taunton one), the four-mile 'Kent Grand National' men's open at the West Street–Tickham meeting at Detling in the South East Area, and the mixed open at the Isle of Wight & Thames Valley Combined Hunts Club fixture at Tweseldown in the Sandhurst Area.

The areas that did not take advantage of this concession were the Northern, North Western, South Wales & Monmouthshire, West Wales, Welsh Border Counties, East Anglia and the Midlands. Couldn't they find the extra money or didn't they consider any of their races worthy enough? It seems to me that a great opportunity was lost by the Midlands Area in not going for their Marie Curie Foundation Novice Championship as their feature race. It would have given it a well-deserved boost.

On the sponsorship front, Land Rover switched its men's final back to Towcester after one season at Cheltenham, the stockbroking firm of Greig Middleton came up with a badly-needed ladies' championship series culminating in a £5,000 final at Chepstow on May 13, Interlink Express introduced a new Restricted series with a £4,000 final at Stratford three days later, and Spillers Horse Feeds were the sponsors of the first-ever ladies' hunter chase to be staged at Stratford, a most welcome appetiser to the 38th *Horse and Hound* Cup on the last day of the same month.

There was some less welcome news from the Levy Board, whose grant of £156,750 to point-to-points was 5% lower than the 1996 one, as a result, it was said, of the increase in profits shown by point-to-points in 1995 and 1996. But surely not every point-to-point in the country was able to increase its profits in those years?

The North Hereford was again at the head of affairs in terms of runners, with 139 for its ten races. The combined Brecon & Talybont was not far behind with 136 for 12, and then came the Beaufort with 130 for nine. All these were Saturday fixtures, ten of which mustered over 100 runners. Of the 60 fixtures held on a Sunday only four topped the 100 mark. They were headed by the Farmers Bloodhounds fixture on the Heythrop course in February, with 128 runners for eight races. The other three were the Cranwell Bloodhounds meeting at Southwell, also in February, with 113 for ten, the Middleton and the Pytchley, both with 106 runners on the same day, April 13, the former with eight races and the latter with nine.

Six of the 211 fixtures scheduled were lost altogether, five of them on account of the weather making the ground impossible to race on; and one, Tweseldown's Windsor Forest Bloodhounds fixture, owing to problems with the contract.

Another meeting, the South East Hunts Club at Charing on March 8, was abandoned after Giles Hopper, a 21-year-old rider from Margate, had been killed in a fall from The Mill Height in the opening Restricted. Giles, who had ridden three winners in his four seasons of race-riding and was studying to become a black-smith, was the first rider to meet with fatal injuries in a point-to-point since another Kent rider, 25-year-old Sarah Dench, died from the injuries she received in a fall at Penshurst in 1990.

In the third week of the season five horses were fatal casualites in point-to-points, three of them at the New Forest fixture at Larkhill, where the racing was being televised by the Racing Channel. Personally, I have very mixed feelings about the televising of point-to-points. Admittedly such exposure introduces the sport to a wider audience. But, since this amateur sport inevitably produces more casualties than N.H. racing, it also renders it vulnerable to attacks from the animal rights fanatics.

The worst-hit of those fixtures which went ahead uninterrupted was the East Kent at Aldington on Easter Monday with six actual runners plus four walk-overs that included the men's and ladies' opens. This was because of the hard ground that prevailed for so much of the season and caused another of the South East fix-tures, the second of the two Southdown & Eridge meetings at Heathfield on Sunday, April 13, to be abandoned before it started. Other meetings suffering badly from a lack of runners for similar reasons were the Portman at Badbury Rings with 12 runners and a walk-over, and the Tedworth at Barbury Castle and the Puckeridge at Horseheath, each with 15 runners and a walk-over. There were 23 walk-overs during the season; and the only thing one could say in mitigation of this is that it was 10 fewer than the record number of walk-overs in 1990.

Not surprisingly, perhaps, Jonathan Neesom in his summing-up piece for the *Sporting Life*, wrote, "not, in all honesty, a vintage season for point-to-pointing"; and it is certainly true that the prolonged drought took a heavy toll. Watering, however, was successful at an increased number of fixtures; much of the racing was high-class; and there was even some increase in betting on Sundays, notably, according to Neesom, in the West Country.

There was no point-to-point racing on the first two days of the season, with the Army fixture at Larkhill on Saturday, January 11, the victim of frost, along with the Garth & South Berks at Tweseldown on the Sunday, when the other fix-ture on that day, the Cambridgeshire Harriers at Cottenham, had to be postponed to a later date. Nor was there any racing on the second Saturday, with the post-ponement of the Easton Harriers at Higham.

So the season kicked off on Sunday, January 19, with the PPORA defying thick fog to stage a first-class fixture at Barbury Castle, with an immensely satisfying 86 runners out of an original entry of 142; and with both the club members' race for novice riders and the men's open having to be run in two divisions, there were seven races on the card.

One of the human stars of this fixture was the 17-year-old Yeovil rider Joe Tizzard, now the amateur attached to Paul Nicholls's yard. By this time, the young Tizzard had five successes under N.H. Rules to his credit and had ridden a 20-1 winner on the Flat in an amateur riders' handicap at Lingfield the day before he rode a blinder to win the first division of the men's open at Barbury Castle on a 16-1 shot aptly called The Bounder, and owned by his father.

This seven-year-old from the Blackmore & Sparkford Vale lived up to his name with his magnificent fencing and won his race in much the fastest time of the day, 6 mins. 16 secs., which was ten seconds faster than Still In Business took to win the other division and four seconds faster than the time another of the Barber runners, 11-year-old Brackenfield, a winner of two amateurs flat races from Michael Hammond's yard and of six hurdle races and seven chases from Mary Reveley's yard, had taken to win the ladies' open with Polly Curling up. Prominent throughout, and with Tizzard making his move at exactly the right moment, The Bounder proved more than a match for Tim Mitchell's mount Calling Wild and the hot-pot Chilipour with Jamie Jukes up.

Although this was The Bounder's first season of point-to-point racing, he was not without his moments of distinction when trained under Rules by Oliver Sherwood. In 1994 as a four-year-old he won a N.H. flat race at Doncaster, and in 1996 he won a novices' handicap hurdle at Huntingdon. He was unbeaten in his four open point-to-points in 1997 with Tizzard up, but his season ended prematurely with a win in the Land Rover qualifier at the Quantock Staghounds in mid-March, when he was one of the winners who gave Tizzard his first four-timer. So presumably something went wrong with him. But he was certainly one of the horses punters would be hopefully looking out for in 1998, and he had earned himself a near-top rating of 11-10 in Mackenzie & Selby's handicap.

Another promising seven-year-old seen out at the first of the season's Barbury Castle fixtures was Nick Viney's King Torus, who had lost his maiden certificate in Ireland the previous season and looked every inch a budding champion when he came home under Jamie Jukes a long way clear in a 14-strong Restricted. One of the horses trained in Devon by Victor Dartnall, the Irish-bred King Torus won six of his eight races, including two hunter chases. The only horses to lower his colours were two of Polly Curling's mounts, Earthmover in the Intermediate at the East Cornwall and Bet With Baker in the Intermediate at the Bolventor Harriers.

Earthmover was unbeaten in his seven races; and Bet With Baker, the horse owned by the bowler-hatted bookmaker George Baker, was one of the unluckiest losers of the season when, in a division of the race for novice riders at Barbury Castle, he was adjudged to have gone under by a head to the 33-1 shot Paco's Boy. Almost everyone but the judge was convinced that Bet With Baker had rallied to get up on the line. This was one of those cases when Baker might have said afterwards, though he was too much of a gentleman to do so, "Some you win, some you lose, and some you was robbed of."

With five weeks of the season gone, the leading riders for the *Daily Telegraph* Cup were Tim Mitchell and Alan Hill, each with five winners; and Polly Curling, who by this time had ridden her 100th winner for Richard Barber's yard when scoring on Ray Geddes's Desert Waltz in the Dodson & Horrell PPORA club race at the New Forest fixture at Larkhill, was showing them the way for the *Sporting Life* Cup also with five winners.

But, as the season progressed, the scenario changed. The Herefordshire rider Julian Pritchard was on his way to winning his first men's title at the age of 30 and the Somerset rider Shirley Vickery, also aged 30, was in process of winning her first ladies' title.

Pritchard, who landed a four-timer at the North Ledbury on March 8, was being given most to do in the later stages of the season by Tim Mitchell, who rode seven winners over the week-end of April 26 and 27, five of them at the Berkeley on the Saturday and the other two at the Seavington the following day. Four of them were trained by Richard Barber. At this stage Mitchell was on a total of 26 and Pritchard on 25. But by Bank Holiday Monday on May 5 they were dead level with 28 point-to-point winners apiece. After that, however, Pritchard was in the ascendancy, and a treble at the Cotswold Vale Farmers on two of the nine winners (including two in hunter chases) he rode for Damien Duggan's yard, and one of the 11 he rode for Nicky Sheppard's, put him on a total of 31 winners in point-to-points, two ahead of Tim Mitchell.

Pritchard's last win was on Damien Duggan's charge Fort Gale in the Restricted at the Harborough Hunts Club meeting at Dingley in the penultimate week of the season; and it gave him a total of 37 in point-to-points, the highest for a male rider in a single season since Philip Scholfield broke the record with his 37 in 1988; and Pritchard achieved his wins riding 25 different horses, besides winning three hunter chases on two others. His most prolific winner was a horse who started the season as a maiden, Lets Twist Again, bought for 1,500 guineas at Doncaster. On this American-bred seven-year-old hunted with the Ledbury and trained by Nicky Sheppard, he won four races, the first three on the trot.

Tim Mitchell, who was riding his 100th point-to-point winner when scoring on Still In Business at the Cattistock on March 29 and finished his season with a total of 33 winners in point-to-points and two in hunter chases, all but six of them trained by Richard Barber, had his last win of the season on the last day when winning the men's open at the Torrington Farmers on John Keighley's Earl Boon, who was recording his fourth win in a row for him. He also won four races on Mrs. Susan Humphreys's Fosbury, whose successes included two races over four miles, the first in a mixed open at Larkhill and the second in a men's open at Bratton Down.

The most prolific winner of all for Mitchell, however, was another of the Barber runners, John Keighley's six-year-old Strong Chairman, who was unbeaten in his five races, three of them open events, in which his victims included one of the Tizzard stars, Qualitair Memory.

One of the 29-year-old Tim Mitchell's two winners in hunter chases for Richard Barber and owner John Keighley was the ten-year-old Fantus, the winner of the Cheltenham Foxhunters' for the second time in three years, and the third winner of the race for owner and trainer. Having missed the 1996 season and disappointed in his first two races of 1997, Fantus was allowed to start at 10-1. But he was a very different horse this time. Prominent throughout, and although nearly put out of the race by the antics of his riderless stablemate Still In Business at one stage, he ran on strongly to score by the best part of two lengths from the 4-1 favourite, Mary Reveley's charge Cab On Target; and behind these two were What A Hand (now trained by Edward O'Grady in Ireland), Celtic Abbey, Double Silk and Final Pride. Still In Business unseated Polly Curling at the first. This was the last of the three races Fantus ran in during the season.

There was no Barber runner in the Liverpool Foxhunters', and this was a triumph for the 11-year-old Blue Cheek, now trained by Jim Mahon's son Gabe and jointly owned by Jim and Mrs. Brenda Graham, the widow of the Irish bookmaker Sean Graham Senr., the first sponsor of the PPOA young horse awards. Mahon, of course, is the inventor of the air-cushioned whip, although Blue Cheek's rider, 18-year-old Robert Thornton, was not carrying it. Indeed, he had no need for a whip of any sort, as the son of Strong Gale was already looking all over the winner when the favourite, Stephen Swiers's mount Mr. Boston, came down at the second last, leaving Blue Cheek to go on and win as he liked from Highlandman, the winner of the new Arthur Clerke-Brown and Graham Pidgeon memorial hunter chase at Leicester. It was Blue Cheek's third win of the season in his four appearances, the others being in a ladies' open at Kingston Blount and a hunter chase at Ludlow.

Robert Thornton, David Nicholson's amateur, is the son of a huntsman, and he was the champion amateur rider of the 1996/97 season with 30 winners under Rules, a feat which netted him the Bollinger Trophy. Not long after the season was over he turned professional.

Up until Sunday, April 6, when she had her last win for the Barber yard on John Keighley's five-year-old False Tail in an open maiden at the Blackmore & Sparkford Vale, Polly Curling was maintaining her lead for the ladies' title with 16 wins. But there weren't to be many more winners for her after that. A week later Shirley Vickery drew level when she had her 16th win of the season on Arctic Chill in Hackwood Park; and on April 27, when Polly was still on 16, Shirley Vickery and Pip Jones were sharing the lead with 19 winners. They went on to battle it out for the title which Shirley won with 30 winners to Pip's 26.

Fifteen of Shirley's wins, including two of her four in hunter chases, were on six of the horses trained in the Blackmore & Sparkford Vale country by her mother, Rosemary Vickery, a highly accomplished race-rider in her day; and these included one of Shirley's most prolific winners, the leader in the PPORA young horse awards, seven-year-old Arctic Chill, on whom she won five ladies' opens, four of them in a row. Others were the six-year-old Passing Fair, who started the season as a maiden and won her last four point-to-points, and the seven-year-old Tinotops, whose three wins on the trot included two in hunter chases; while among the horses she excelled on from outside the family stable were the Mark Jackson-trained Grimley Gale with her four wins in ladies' opens and Stewart Pike's home-bred mare Front Cover. On this full sister to Proud Sun she won three point-to-points and two novice hunter chases.

Pip Jones's chances of making it a closer contest disappeared when she smashed her leg to pieces in a particularly bad fall on Lucky Ole Son in the ladies' open at the Harborough Hunts Club fixture at Dingley on June 1. This put her in Leicester Royal Infirmary for six days. So she had to miss the last point-to-point of the season at Umberleigh. She was still going for treatment off and on in August, and it looked as if it would be touch and go whether she would be able to resume race-riding in 1998. It was not, of course, the first serious accident this brilliant 29-year-old rider had sustained, nor the first time that her racing career had been put in doubt.

In other respects, it was a remarkably successful season for Pip. She was riding her 100th winner in point-to-points when scoring in the ladies' open at the Carmarthenshire in mid-March on Lucky Ole Son, one of the horses who helped her complete a treble there for owner-trainer David Brace; and it was on another of his horses, Carrick Lanes, that she became the first lady rider to win the 'Welsh Point-to-point Grand National' at the Pentyrch in its first year as a mixed open over a new course at Redlands Park, Bonvilston, after 16 years at Llantwit Major. It was also a season in which she achieved her highest-ever total of 26 wins without the assistance of three of the best horses she won on in 1996. Handsome Harvey was out of action throughout the season. David Brace's mare African Bride had a fatal accident in her stable; and another of the Brace horses, Goolds Gold, broke down so badly on his only appearance that he had to be put down.

Third in the table of leading lady riders with 21 winners was Alison Dare, who became the first woman to ride 250 point-to-point winners when she completed the second leg of a double in the PPORA club race at the Cotswold Vale Farmers on Down The Mine, a winner of three of his four races. But it wasn't a happy season for her nor for the man who trained all the winners she rode, Dick Baimbridge. Two of their outstanding performers over the years were fatal casualties. Dr. Paul Brown's Stephens Pet, a winner of 21 of his 27 races, two of them this season, collapsed and died after finishing a distant second to Grimley Gale in a ladies' open at Mollington on May 18; and the consistently successful Di Stefano, who had gone through the 1996 season unbeaten in his seven races, was in the process of extending this winning sequence to 11 when he crashed through the wing of the last fence in the Confined at the Clifton-on-Teme on March 29 and died, it is thought, of a heart attack. The nine-year-old was a winner of 14 of his 18 races since he started racing for the Baimbridge yard as a maiden in 1994, all but two of them with Alison up.

Any chance Alison had of winning another national title in 1997 was removed when Di Stefano and Stephens Pet had departed from the scene. But she won four races on the 13-year-old Sams Heritage, a horse Baimbridge had wrought wonders with since acquiring him from his previous yard before the start of the season, just as he had done with another of Alison's rides, the eight-year-old Dante's Pride, in getting him to lose his maiden certificate at the Harkaway Club fixture at Chaddesley Corbett in the last of his four appearances. Three more of her wins were on Dr. Brown's unbeaten Rip Van Winkle, who also won two men's opens with 23-year-old James Baimbridge (the trainer's nephew) riding him.

It wasn't the happiest of seasons for Polly Curling either, for more reasons than one. Her chances of winning a fourth national title met with a distinct setback on April 12, when a fall from a novice (not one of the Barber horses) in a maiden race at the Ludlow saw her knocked out cold for three minutes and caused her to be stood down for 21 days. But worse was to follow in the shape of a split with the Barber yard for which she had ridden 15 of the 18 winners she ended up with. The chief reason for this, it seems, was that some of the Barber owners, and perhaps Richard himself to a lesser extent, were worried by the falls she had been having and were concerned for her welfare.

So it was decided that Joe Tizzard would ride the five-year-olds and Tim Mitchell most of the older ones, as he had been doing anyway. The crunch came when Polly asked Richard Barber what she would be riding for the stable in 1998 and was informed that she could ride the horses in ladies' races. Understandably, she didn't consider this good enough and severed her commitment to the stable.

She had also been particularly unhappy at losing her ride in the Cheltenham Foxhunters' on Fantus, the horse she won the race on in 1995; and, as a result of her resignation, she lost her remaining rides on Roger Penny's exceptionally promising Earthmover, who would get my vote as the most exciting horse of the season, and on whom she had scored when he first appeared on a course as a five-year-old in 1996 and won three races on in 1997. Her replacement on Earthmover was the 21-year-old Polly Gundry, who preserved the winning sequence that Polly Curling had begun by winning two ladies' opens on him and followed this with two wins in valuable hunter chases, the Greig Middleton ladies' championship at Chepstow with a convincing defeat of Alison Dare's mount Sams Heritage, and the John Corbet champion novice hunter chase at Stratford, where he accounted for one of the star performers in the South East, the six-year-old Struggles Glory, whose veteran owner-rider, 55-year-old David Robinson, was putting up 61b. over-weight. This was Struggles Glory's sole defeat in his six appearances with his owner-up, and his five wins included two in hunter chases, at Ascot and Huntingdon.

As well as her 15 wins for the Barber yard, Polly Curling, who celebrated her 33rd birthday in August, rode three winners from other yards, He Is for Ollie Bush in a Restricted at the Quantock Staghounds, Shrewd Thought for Pauline Geering in the Restricted at the South Devon; and, most heartening of all, on the last day of the season, Ruth's Boy for Capt. Tim Forster in the Restricted at the Torrington Farmers. The Captain has always been one of her greatest admirers, and she has ridden many winners for him over the years.

Ruth's Boy was Polly's 197th winner in point-to-points; and one thing is for sure, she has every intention of reaching her double century. In fact, she says, "I shall go on as long as I still enjoy it." In the meantime, she was in course of set-ting up a new yard with Kay Rees at Sennington in the Taunton Vale country. It has all the modern facilities and there are already between ten and 15 horses there. They include a potential star in Certain Angle, a winner when in training with Philip Hobbs of a N.H. flat race, two novice hurdles and a handicap chase.

The contest for the Grand Marnier Trophy was proving a close-run one. The first horse to win five races was Simon Sporborg's mount Over The Edge when scoring by a head from Cardinal Red in a two-horse men's open on hard ground at Horseheath on April 12; and he was joined on this mark the following day by Arctic Chill, Shirley Vickery's mount in the ladies' open at the Hampshire Hunt meeting in Hackwood Park. But that was the full extent of their successes. At this stage of the season, the eventual Grand Marnier winner, Nick Viney's Butler John, an eight-year-old from the Exmoor trained by Victor Dartnall and ridden by Neil Harris, was on a total of two open-race wins in four appearances; and the horse that was to be his nearest challenger, Grimley Gale, an eight-year-old Strong Gale mare from the Clifton-on-Teme, had won three races with Adrian Wintle up and one with Alan Phillips aboard.

It wasn't until May 17 that Butler John drew level with Grimley Gale when a win in the Confined at the Dulverton West gave him his seventh win of the season, only for Grimley Gale to draw ahead again with her eighth win when beating Stephens Pet the following day at Mollington. Neither horse was beaten after that; but whereas Butler John secured three further successes, on the last occasion in the hunt race at the Exmoor with Joanne Cumings up, taking his score for the season up to ten, nine of his wins with Neil Harris up, Grimley Gale's final score was nine. It was the second year running that Victor Dartnall had trained a winner of the Grand Marnier. Butler John, a son of The Parson out of a mare by Menelek, was bought for the Dartnall stable for 13,000 guineas by bloodstock agent David Minton out of John Edwards's Herefordshire yard at the Ascot Sales in June 1995, and he had his first two wins for the Viney-Dartnall combination in 1996 with Jo Cumings up.

But there was a big consolation prize for Mr. & Mrs. Robin Phillips's Grimley Gale and her Herefordshire trainer Mark Jackson. This half-sister to Down The Mine was the winner of the PPORA national mares' championship sponsored by Weatherbys.

Both Butler John and Grimley Gale, who never met each other, were unlucky in one respect. Butler John would almost certainly have won 12 of his 13 races but for unseating Jamie Jukes at the fourteenth in the men's open at the North Cornwall on his first appearance of the season when well clear of his four opponents, and falling at the last fence in a similar race at the Modbury Harriers when Neil Harris was riding him; and Grimley Gale might have made it ten wins in ten appearances but for a fall in an Intermediate at the Beaufort on her second appearance of the season.

The most prolific winner after Butler John and Grimley Gale was the pony-sized Touch 'N' Pass. This nine-year-old from the Llangeinor, owned and trained by Robert Williams, won five ladies' opens with Pip Jones up, one with Amanda Meakins up, and a men's open with Jon Tudor up. Two horses won six point-to-points. St. Gregory, a nine-year-old by Ardross trained by Ruth Hayter in the Essex & Suffolk country, won six ladies' opens with Lucy Gibbon up, five of them on the trot. Susan Mason's Just Charlie, an eight-year-old son of Bustino hunted with the Middleton, had five of his six wins with David Easterby up. Hornblower, a ten-year-old trained by Richard & Carrie Ford in Shropshire, won six races in a row, the last of them a hunter chase at Cartmel, ridden in all of them by Carrie Ford (née Burgess).

The first of the season's £500 feature races, the four-mile men's open sponsored by the Faversham brewers Shepherd Neame Ltd. at the West Street–Tickham on March 16 at Detling, where racing was preceded by a minute of silence to reflect on the sad death of Giles Hopper earlier in the season, attracted a field of nine; and this Kent Grand National was won by a good old campaigner in The Artful Rascal, who started his point-to-point career from Richard Aston's Cheshire stable in 1992, when he lost his maiden certificate with William Barlow up. Since 1996, when he won his only race, the 13-year-old son of Scallywag has been point-to-pointing for the Suffolk-based owner-trainer Michael Kemp, for whom he remained unbeaten. Ridden at Detling by Nigel Bloom, who had been up on him when he had two of his three previous wins for the yard, he completed his hat-trick in open events unchallenged by the runner-up, Peter Bull's mount Stede Quarter, the winner of an open race at Charing on his previous appearance, and of another one there afterwards.

The next of the £500 feature races was the men's open for the Tedworth Gold Cup, run on firm ground at Barbury Castle; and for this there was a disappointingly thin field of three. But it produced a classy winner in the 13-year-old Wild Illusion, now jointly owned by the executors of the late Col. Arthur Clerke-Brown (his daughter Mrs. Angela Murray) and Graham Pidgeon (his widow Gillian). Ridden by the 20-year-old Fred Hutsby, Wild Illusion was always going too well for Royle Speedmaster.

The third of the feature races was the first of the three classics sponsored by the *Sporting Life*, the four-mile men's open for Lord Ashton of Hyde's Cup at the Heythrop, and this too was run on firm ground; but despite the sparcity of runners overall, with an unprecedented walk-over for the 3m5.5f ladies' open for the Lyon Trophy, there were seven runners for this classic, which was won for the second year running by Mrs. Joanna Daniell's Ledbury mare Kettles.

Ridden as she was before by Alan Phillips, Kettles headed John Deutsch's mount, the front-running Granville Grill, at the last and went on to beat him quite comfortably, with Scarlet Berry (a winner of her three previous races) running on well under Julian Pritchard to take third place. The only other horse to win this classic race two years running since it was first run at Stow-on-the-Wold in 1953 was Lord Fortune, the winner in 1976 and 1977.

The second of the classics, and the fourth of the feature races, the four-mile mixed open for the Grimthorpe Cup at the Middleton, was run five days later, and the going at Whitwell-on-the-Hill was good, thanks in no small measure to the sterling work put in by the clerk of the course, Tim Walford. The reward was a field of 21, one of the biggest ever for it. There was also another reward for Walford, in the shape of a local winner that he trained himself, Ask Antony, a seven-year-old grey son of Roselier owned by a party of four headed by Jim Burns.

A 5-4 on favourite, on the strength of having been a runner-up in his three previous races, two of them hunter chases, Ask Antony, confidently ridden by one of the top Yorkshire riders, Noel Wilson, was already being eased before he passed the post 20 lengths ahead of The Difference, who had made the long journey from the Belvoir country in Leicestershire after winning his hunt race. A short head behind The Difference was Fiona Needham's mount Final Hope, the winner of a hunter chase at Newcastle. Among the also-rans were the 1994 winner Across The Lake, the 1996 runner-up Cot Lane, and Thank U Jim, who was to end his season beating Final Pride in the ladies' hunter chase at Stratford with his Grimthorpe Cup rider Tina Jackson up. Thank U Jim, a nine-year-old from the Cleveland, was owned and bred by Mrs. Gillian Sunter, and trained by her on the family farm in Co. Durham.

The third of the season's classics, and the fifth of the season's feature races, the Lady Dudley Cup at the Worcestershire, was in its centenary year; and with the meeting running out of car-parking space, more money was made for the Worcestershire Hunt than ever before. The going at Chaddesley Corbett was good to firm, and the favourite for the big race in a field of seven was the Barber runner Still In Business with Tim Mitchell up; but, after holding every chance four fences from home, he failed to last out the trip and finished fourth to Reg Wilkins's Double Thriller, on whom Joe Tizzard was deputising for the injured Ron Treloggen. This seven-year-old by Dubassoff, the sire of the same owner's Double Silk, looked a vintage Dudley Cup winner, and the only serious challenge to his relentless progress on the final circuit came from the five-year-old Zambrano, who did well under the then little known Seamus Durack to finish within three lengths of him. Peanuts Pet, the third horse home, 12 lengths behind the runner-up, had won four races in Yorkshire under Robert Walmsley before coming to Chaddesley Corbett. Three of them were open events, and he was to win another one afterwards.

The Dudley Cup was the first success in an open point-to-point for Double Thriller, who had lost his maiden certificate as a five-year-old at the Cotswold Vale Farmers in 1995 with Ron Treloggen up and, after being off the course throughout 1996, won three of his four point-to-points in 1997, the Dudley Cup being the last of them; and on this historic occasion, the Countess of Dudley, well known in her younger days as the actress Maureen Swanson, was at hand to present the coveted trophy.

Reg Wilkins bought Double Thriller as an unbroken four-year-old from the Badminton farmer Anton Smith after seeing him in a field, influenced to no small extent by the fact that the horse was by Double Silk's sire; and that his jockey Ron Treloggen had won races both on Double Thriller's full brother Cape Cottage and on their mutual dam Cape Thriller, a mare bred at Badminton by the famous Tom Smith.

After the Dudley Cup it was a case of deciding which of four horses was going to be pronounced the winner of the *Sporting Life* Classics Cup, as none of the the three classic winners had collected more than the 50 points they gained from winning these races; and they were joined on this score by Granville Grill, who had added to the 40 points he derived as the runner-up to Kettles in the Heythrop four-miler a further ten for his win in a men's open at Andoversford 15 days later.

So it was up to *The Life*'s point-to-point correspondent Jonathan Neesom to make the decision, and he decided that the trophy should go to the owner of Kettles, who had gone so close to winning it in 1996 and had the additional distinction of winning one of the classic races two years running.

The other two feature races were won by the Grand Marnier victor and runner-up. Butler John made it four wins in a row when demolishing his five opponents in the men's open at the Tiverton Staghounds, and Grimley Gale, winning for the seventh time, did the same to a field of five for the mixed open at the combined Isle of Wight & Thames Valley meeting at Tweseldown.

Meanwhile the £20,000 Marlborough Cup race over timber fences, an event run outside Jockey Club rules, had been becoming increasingly professional. In 1996, when the qualifying races for it, though still being run, like the final, at Barbury Castle, had ceased to be held on point-to-point days, the race was won by the pro. jockey Graham Bradley riding one of Ian Balding's charges; and in 1997, when there was a 100,000 dollar bonus added to the first prize of £10,000 for the first winner of it who had also won the Virginia Gold Cup, a four-mile race over timber in the U.S.A., the bonus was collected by a horse flown over from America for the occasion.

Saluter, the horse in question, had won the Virginia Gold Cup on the last four occasions, and he certainly showed that he had all the right credentials for winning the Marlborough Cup under his trainer-rider Jack Fisher. Graham Bradley's ride in this year's race was the Irish-trained Fiftysevenchannels, formerly a point-to-pointer in England; and this eight-year-old, now trained by Enda Bolger, was the runner-up. In fourth place, ridden this time by Chris Stockton, was Carli's Star, a quadruple winner of the hunt race at the High Peak over stone walls when ridden by his owner, Sue Rodman; and behind him came Royle Speedmaster.

On its return to Towcester, the Land Rover men's final mustered only five runners; but at least the first two places were filled by consistent winners, Magnolia Man and Lucky Christopher. Magnolia Man was bidding for his fifth win of the season and Lucky Christopher for his fourth; and it was the 11-year-old Magnolia Man, trained in the Tiverton country by Debbie Cole, who came out on top under Neil Harris. It has to be admitted, though, that Jimmy Tarry was not seen at his best on Lucky Christopher, who was trying to give the winner 7lb.

The Interlink Express Restricted final at Stratford also produced a worthy winner in the six-year-old Aller Moor, trained by Sally Alner in the Portman country. He was recording his fourth win in a row with his third different rider up, this time Joe Tizzard, who had to work hard to get him home by half a length from another promising six-year-old, the West Somerset mare Swansea Gold.

No more than six turned out for the Marie Curie novice championship at Melton; and the race looked very much like being a match between the husband and wife combination of Kevin Needham on the seven-year-old Catchphrase and Fiona Needham on the five-year-old Last Option, until the latter made a bad mistake at the second last and Fiona was unseated. There was little between the pair at the time and the departure of Last Option left Catchphrase in complete command. But although the son of Baron Blakeney was an easy winner, and it was his third success of the season, he can hardly be considered a vintage one. It was a great day for the Needhams, however, as Fiona won the ladies' open on her father's (Robin Tate) seven-year-old Indie Rock after a spirited duel with Jill Dawson on Force Eight.

Gerald Powell's home-bred Celtic Abbey, the runner-up to Proud Sun in last year's *Horse and Hound* Cup at Stratford, went one better this time. The nine-year-old son of Celtic Cone, trained by Venetia Williams in Herefordshire, had convincingly accounted for Double Silk and Ryming Cuplet in a hunter chase at Cheltenham, and he meted out similar treatment to Bitofamixup and Mr. Boston at Stratford, where he was a 100th career winner for his regular rider Dai Jones, the agricultural correspondent of the *Western Mail*.

The leading rider in hunter chases, and the winner of Peter Greenall's Cup for the first time, was Paul Hacking with eight winners; and the runner-up to him, with seven, was Stephen Swiers, who rode his 100th winner under Rules when scoring in a hunter chase at Huntingdon on Stuart Dent's Secret Bay, an eight-year-old from the Zetland who had given him three wins in point-to-points and two in hunter chases.

Hacking's hunter-chase wins were gained on four of the horses trained by Mike Roberts in the East Sussex & Romney Marsh country. The best of them was the six-year-old Bitofamixup, who followed his win in an open point-to-point at Higham with three wins in hunter chases and had his only defeat when he was the runner-up for the *Horse and Hound* Cup. Three more of Hacking's wins in hunter chases were on Trifast Lad, and the other two were on promising seven-year-olds who started the season as maidens, Storming Lady (a daughter of Strong Gale) and Prince Buck, a son of Buckskin. Most of Hacking's nine winners in point-to-points were also trained by Mike Roberts.

But the leading trainer of hunter chasers, and recipient of the Richard Russell–Johnny Greenall Trophy, with nine winners to add to his 20 in point-to-points, was Victor Dartnall, with one more winner than Mike Roberts and two more than Caroline Saunders, who had won this trophy for the last five years.

Nick Viney's 11-year-old Slievenamon Mist, a grandson of Brigadier Gerard on his dam's side, was unbeaten in his four hunter chases for the Dartnall yard with Jamie Jukes up; and this stable also housed, among others, the 1996 Grand Marnier winner, Rebecca Francis's Phar Too Touchy, a winner in 1997 of two novice hunter chases with Neil Harris up, and a promising five-year-old by Scallywag in Peter Scott's Wicked Imp, who lost his maiden certificate at Larkhill under Jamie Jukes on his single appearance. Something else that Dartnall had going for him, on the same day that Butler John won the feature race at Bratton Down in the afternoon and Phar Too Touchy won the hunter chase at Worcester in the evening, was a first winner for his 16-year-old daughter Izzy, who won the hunt race at Bratton Down on Viney's King Torus, the horse that Jamie Jukes won five races on, including hunter chases at Newton Abbot and Uttoxeter.

Richard Barber maintained his position as the leading trainer on the point-to-point front, saddling 51 winners in this field, plus his four in hunter chases. Dick Baimbridge, despite the loss of Stephens Pet and Di Stefano, trained 30 point-to-point winners; and there were 23 for Christopher Sporborg in East Anglia, where Over The Edge was his most prolific winner with five wins in open events under Simon Sporborg.

Gerald Penfold, the West Country farrier, was the leading owner-rider of the season and the recipient of the Dick Woodhouse Memorial Trophy at the PPORA annual lunch. Six of the eight horses he won on were his own.

Pauline Robson was the leading lady rider over jumps under Rules with seven winners to add to her nine in point-to-points. One of her winners in point-to-points was Willy Manners's 13-year-old Steele Justice, whose win in the ladies' open at the Haydon was the 26th of a career in which he has never failed to complete a course. On 23 of these occasions, including the three on which he has won hunter chases, Pauline has been up on him. Now with her own livery yard at Capheaton in Northumberland, she had her first training success under Rules when Denim Blue, owned by her sister, Lesley Walby, won a novice hunter chase at Ayr ridden by Pauline, who was also up on him when he scored again in the Howard Brown Memorial novice hunter chase at Wetherby.

Scotland provided the leading novice rider of the season in the Dumfriesshire rider 21-year-old Ranald Morgan. A student at the Royal Agricultural College in

Cirencester, he had to make some long journeys to ride his ten point-to-point winners. His most prolific winner was a horse who started the season as a maiden, Bitofanatter, owned by Dundonald farmer David Caldwell, the clerk of the course at Lanark. On this nine-year-old, one of the horses who helped him bring off a treble at the Lauderdale, he won four races in a row. Morgan had his tenth win on May 17, when he won an open maiden at Corbridge on Dennis Waggott's six-year-old mare Allrite Pet, one of the ten point-to-point winners trained by Kevin Anderson, whose shoulder injury, sustained at the same time as he broke his leg in his only race of 1996, had kept him out of action as a rider throughout 1997.

Vivienne Nicholas, the daughter of Ken and Caroline Nicholas of Mantinolas fame, was the *Daily Telegraph*'s leading lady novice rider with her four wins on her parental nine-year-old Parditino, on whom she was also four times a runner-up; and the leading novice rider under the age of 21 and winner of the Wilkinson Sword was 16-year-old Anthony Honeyball, with four wins in the West Country on two of the horses owned and trained by his father, John Honeyball, who achieved fame as the man who broke in that great horse The Dikler. Three of Anthony's wins were on the home-bred Royal Turn.

It was a disappointing season for Alastair Crow, who was well down the list of leading riders this time, although he landed a four-timer at the Flint & Denbigh, as did Ashley Farrant at the Tetcott, Noel Wilson at the South Durham, Joe Tizzard at the Quantock Staghounds, and Jamie Jukes in the course of riding his 100th winner in point-to-points at the Llangeinor.

The worst blow to Alastair was the double accident that befell one of his best rides, his uncle's gallant mare Scally Muire. The first part of it happened when she broke down in front early in the season in the men's open at the West Shropshire Draghounds; the second, and most disastrous, after she had been retired to stud and sent to be covered by Roselier. She then sustained a worse injury behind; and although she was hurriedly withdrawn and despatched to an animal hospital, it was too late to save her. A winner of 25 races in her 51 appearances, she was, said the disconsolate Alastair, "a mare with a great will to win, and she never knew when she was beaten."

Another great point-to-pointer, Trevor Marks's home-bred Stanwick Lad, died peacefully in his field at the age of 20. A winner of 42 races (including two hunter chases) since he first started racing for Marks in 1983, the Grand Marnier winner of 1988 won 36 of his races with John Sharp up, one with the late Johnny Wrathall up when Sharp was injured, and his last five, in 1991, with the 16-year-old Trevor Marks Jnr. riding him. After a memorable win in the men's open at the Fitzwilliam in 1988, Stanwick Lad was described by commentator Hunter Rowe as "the most popular horse in East Anglia – poetry in motion."

Judy Wilson's Sheer Jest, one of the stars of Bill Warner's Pytchley yard, had to be put down after injuring himself badly in a hunter chase at Doncaster in March. In his eight seasons of hunt racing this 12-year-old won 19 of his 33 races, his 13 wins in hunter chases including the Liverpool Foxhunters' of 1995. In all these races he was ridden by Alan Hill, who was making 1997 the last of his 22 years as a race-rider, during which the present Joint Master of the Vale of Aylesbury rode 94 winners in point-to-points and 44 under Rules; and in all his years of race-riding, the second tallest amateur after Chris Coyne sustained no worse an injury than a broken finger.

I see with delight from Hugh Condry's report in the *Racing Post* that Alan Hill attained a long-held ambition in 1997 when winning the Confined race at the Vale of Aylesbury fixture at Kingston Blount named in memory of his grandfather, Joe Hill, doing so on one of his own horses, Run For Free, a 13-year-old son of Deep Run; and that the ladies' open at this meeting now has the name of Col. Arthur Clerke-Brown attached to it. This year's winner of it was Teresa Spearing, riding a horse owned by Alan Brazier, whose company, Vax International, had sponsored the PPORA riders' seminars.

The West Country rider Philip Scholfield, the first rider to break the men's record with his 37 point-to-point wins in 1988, had retired from race-riding before the start of the season with a grand total of 178 point-to-point winners behind him. But another rider to hang up his boots after the season was over was the 6ft. 6in. Chris Coyne, whose final race was on May 25, when he finished fifth in a Confined at the Berks & Bucks Draghounds meeting at Kingston Blount on a tubed horse appropriately called Abitmorfun, and dismissed as "useless" by Mackenzie & Selby. It was a description which Chris, who rode primarily for fun, would no doubt have endorsed, if in more polite terms.

The most emotive retirement on the equine front was that of Teaplanter, the shining star of Caroline Saunders's yard. Richard Russell's 14-year-old son of National Trust went out on a winning note with Ben Pollock scoring on him in a hunter chase at Towcester for the second time this season. In his 41 races since he started racing from the Saunders yard as a maiden six-year-old in 1989 Teaplanter won 27 races, 24 of them hunter chases. He was ridden on 18 of these occasions by his owner, seven times by Pollock and twice by Marcus Armytage. Nine of his wins were at Towcester.

Capt. Neville Crump, the former Middleham trainer whose three Grand National winners included two ex-point-to-pointers in Teal and Merryman II, died in January at the age of 86. He was a distinguished amateur rider in his day, and a contemporary of Guy Cunard. So, too, was Major Calverly Bewicke, who died in February at the age of 82. The man who trained Kerstin to win the Cheltenham Gold Cup of 1958, Verly Bewicke rode over 20 point-to-point winners between 1933 and 1938, and his wins under Rules as an amateur included one in the Territorial Army Cup at Sandown on his own horse Noble Artist. His best rides in point-to-points were on his father's Jugged Hare, a prodigious performer. Riding this horse, on whom his father won four races, he won ten more, including two Tynedale Gold Cups.

In September, George Owen, the man who saddled the former point-to-pointer Russian Hero to win the Grand National of 1949 at odds of 66-1, died at the age of 89. The Cheshire trainer, for whom Dick Francis once worked as a secretary, included amongst his numerous successes as an amateur rider a win in the Cheltenham Foxhunters' of 1930; and after turning professional a few years later he rode Brendan's Cottage to win the Cheltenham Gold Cup. Three champion jockeys started their race-riding careers from George Owen's stable as amateurs. Dick Francis was the first of them. The others were Tim Brookshaw and Stan

Mellor.

This was also the year that death claimed two of Tim Forster's patrons, both well known in the point-to-point world, Capt. Miles Gosling at the age of 69 and Gregory Phillips in Gloucestershire at the age of 79. Miles Gosling, an amateur rider before he was elected to the National Hunt Committee in 1956 and later the Chairman of Cheltenham Racecourse, was described by Richard Onslow in the *Sporting Life* as "one of racing's most able administrators of the last two decades." The courageous Gregory Phillips was the only one-armed rider I can recall riding in point-to-points. A distinction in itself, and one that was greatly admired by all who were privileged to see him in action.

And in the autumn of the year the great Australian rider Lawrence Morgan died at the age of 82. The sheep farmer from New South Wales, an individual Olympic gold medallist in the Three-Day Event at the Rome Olympics of 1960 on his own horse Salad Days, and the captain of the winning Australian team there, Laurie Morgan (as he was known in England) achieved legendary status with his exploits in the hunter-chase field on a horse he bought for 300 guineas as a five-year-old at the Ascot Sales in February 1955, the mighty Colledge Master. On this son of Grandmaster out of a mare by Columcille he won the Cheltenham Foxhunters' two years running in 1961 and 1962; and on the same horse he completed the Cheltenham and Liverpool double in 1961, having first won the Liverpool Foxhunters' on him in 1957.

It was good to see Steven Brookshaw stepping up from the hunter-chase ranks to saddle a Grand National winner in Stan Clarke's New Zealand-bred Lord Gyllene; and the Cheltenham Gold Cup being won by a horse, the Irish-bred Mr. Mulligan, who made his winning début in the maiden race at the North Tipperary point-to-point in 1994 as a six-year-old; and there was an even more welcome success for point-to-point fans when See More Business, now jointly owned by Paul Barber and John Keighley, and trained by Paul Nicholls in Somerset, beat a high-class field in the King George VI Chase at Kempton Park on Boxing Day. The seven-year-old was following in the footsteps of three other former point-to-pointers of the post-war years, Halloween in 1952 and 1954, Limber Hill in 1955 and The Dikler in 1971.

For Steven Brookshaw there was also another cause for satisfaction, with the successes of two young members of his family. His nephew, 20-year-old Richard Burton, had his best season since 1994, the year he won both the *Daily Telegraph* male novice rider's award and the Wilkinson Sword. In 1997 he rode eight point-to-point winners and five hunter-chase winners, his three wins in hunter chases on Wrexham dairy farmer Denis Nicholls's My Nominee including the Guy Cunard hunter chase at Wetherby, and his two on Ivor Johnson's Rusty Bridge embracing one over four miles and a furlong at Cheltenham.

Brookshaw's 18-year-old daughter Heidi was seen to advantage with her first ride under Rules on her father's mare Inch Maid in a hunter chase at Bangor in which Richard Burton finished third to her on My Nominee.

In the last point-to-point of the season in Ireland, the South Union two-day fixture at Kinsale, the 34-year-old Enda Bolger, making sure of his seventh national title when recording his 38th win of the season, brought his grand total of wins in point-to-points up to 384, just 17 short of the late Willie Rooney's glittering all-time record of 401. What price, they were asking, Bolger to surpass this record in 1998?

Although the 1997 point-to-point season in Ireland produced a record number of runners over there, 2,257, an increase of nearly 100 on the previous season, and there were a record 197 runners for the 12 races at the Carlow Farmers on a Sunday in January, remarkably only four lady riders managed to ride winners during the season, none of them more than one. My informant in Ireland, John Lloyd-Rogers, assures me that this was no reflection on their ability, but was caused rather by the difficulty of securing suitable rides, plus the fact that there was only a single point-to-point race confined to lady riders. What, one wonders, would the formidable Mrs. Masters, the Master of the Tipperary Hunt from 1935 to 1953, have had to say about this sorry state of affairs? In the late 'twenties and early 'thirties she rode over 100 point-to-point winners!

Tailpiece:
Quote in the *Sporting Life* from Rupert Nuttall, the 37-year-old Joint Master of the Blackmore & Sparkford Vale, after winning the Whitbread Gold Cup at Sandown on the former point-to-pointer Harwell Lad trained by Robert Alner: "I have to say that if it wasn't for foxhunting this horse would be in meat cans by now."

1998 AND BEYOND
THE MILLENNIUM

*The weather took its usual heavy toll this season, with 16 of the 209
point-to-points scheduled abandoned altogether and another one half-
way through; while new dates had to be found for a further 28. The 193
meetings that survived included 68 of the Sunday ones; but not, regret-
tably, the Middleton, with its prestigious Grimthorpe Cup race, which
was lost for the fourth time in the last 15 years; nor the Tiverton
Staghounds fixture, where Devon & Cornwall's £500 feature race was
due to be staged. But at least there was an increase in the number of
runners, 12,464, a rise of 758 on the previous season.*

Heading the field in terms of runners was the second of the two East
Cornwall fixtures, the one at Lemalla, with 165 runners for 13 races; then
came the Badsworth's Sunday fixture at Wetherby in mid-February, with
138 for 11, closely followed by the newly-formed Cambridgeshire Harriers Hunt
Club fixture at Cottenham on the opening day of the season, Sunday, January 11,
with 136 for nine. Next the North Hereford with 126 for ten, the Vale of Clettwr
with 125 for 12 and the first of the East Cornwall fixtures, at Great Trethew on
Saturday, February 14, with 120 for ten.

At the other end of the scale, there were ten walk-overs and some very poor
turnouts when the ground firmed up. Worst of all at the East Sussex & Romney
Marsh at Bexhill on Sunday, May 17, when the hard ground was responsible for
two walk-overs and 11 active runners, with no more than three in any of the seven
races on the card. The Enfield Chace at Northaw on the same Sunday in May did-
n't fare much better, with 16 runners for five of the six races and a walk-over in
the men's open.

One very welcome new rule was that meetings staging a mixed open now had
the option of being able to put on separate confined races for the two sexes should
they feel so inclined. Another significant innovation, perhaps not so wholeheart-
edly well received, was that the ranks of the amateur riders were widened to
include hunt servants, grooms and all stable staff, thus increasing the number of
riders eligible to ride in point-to-points.

Plastic wings were now mandatory on all courses in the interest of safety; and
individual stewards were now permitted to enquire into a horse's performance if
they were not satisfied with it. This regulation did not come in for unqualified
support from the *Sporting Life*'s man Jonathan Neesom. "The idea of half a dozen
bowler-hats rushing around the unsaddling area after a race whispering into various ears," he wrote, "is incredible enough, as is the thought that they would then
have to hold a major confab, to spread around the tittle-tattle they had picked up

in the process."

I don't, though, recall any instances of this new regulation raising any problems of a practical nature; and it is surely no more 'bizarre', as Neesom describes it, than the one which declares it "an offence for a rider whose horse has refused at a fence or been pulled up to wait for the field to complete a circuit before rejoining the race". This, says the Jockey Club disapprovingly, "is a form of schooling in public."

It is interesting to note, in passing, that the only new rule for point-to-pointing in Ireland was one stipulating breast-girths or similar harnessing as mandatory.

Land Rover, in the 13th year of their sponsorship, headed the field in their financial support of point-to-point racing with their £6,000 final at Towcester for their men's championship, and brought the date of it forward to April 22. This meant that five of the qualifying races at point-to-points were scheduled to be run after the closing date; but they got round this by deciding that horses who had qualified for the final the previous season would also be eligible for the 1998 one. Even so, on the day of the race at Towcester there were no more than six declared runners, although the going was described as "Soft, Good to Soft in places."

There can be no complaints, though, about the quality of the winner of this championship, the nine-year-old Cavalero, owned and trained by the exuberant Johnny Manners at his Wiltshire establishment and ridden for him by the equine sculptor Alex Charles-Jones. It was a terrific season for Cavalero, whose seven wins in his eight appearances included four in hunter chases. On the only occasion he was beaten, on his first appearance of the season, in a race for novice riders, where Charles-Jones was naturally not his pilot, he had just taken over the lead when he fell at the last fence.

One of the races won by Cavalero was the Liverpool Foxhunters', for which 30 went to the post in testing going, with Cavalero staying on strongly to beat the Irish favourite Elegant Lord by a length and repeat for Manners the triumph he had enjoyed with Killeshin in 1994. A week after winning at Towcester Cavalero was at the Cheltenham hunter-chase evening beating Double Silk in the Colin Nash Memorial hunter chase.

The top spot amongst the hunter chasers has, however, to go to Earthmover, and not only with Mackenzie & Selby, who have him heading their handicap ratings at 12-0, 21b. ahead of another of Richard Barber's charges, Fantus, who failed to win any of the three races he ran in. With Joe Tizzard up, Earthmover was as smooth a fourth winner of the Cheltenham Foxhunters' for Richard Barber as one could ever hope to see; and it was his third hunter-chase win on the trot, following an inauspicious fall in a ladies' open point-to-point at Larkhill on his first appearance of the season.

Greig Middleton, in the second year of their sponsorship of the ladies' championship series, switched their £5,000 final from Chepstow to an evening fixture at Huntingdon in May; and although they didn't have as brilliant a winner of it as they had in Earthmover last year, there was an encouraging field of eight on the firm ground, and a real turn-up for the book in the 33-1 shot Boxing Match. A winner over hurdles and fences before he started point-to-pointing, this 11-year-old was recording his first win of the season for his 19-year-old rider, Vicky Roberts, who works for the winner's trainer, *Horse and Hound* columnist Richard Phillips. Although Vicky had ridden two winners over hurdles, she has yet to ride her first point-to-point winner as Boxing Match could finish only fourth in his qualifier at the Harkaway Club. Blue Cheek, the winner of that race, unseated his rider in the final.

The final of the £4,000 Interlink Express Restricted series was again held at Stratford on a Friday evening in mid-May, clashing, as it had done before, with a novice hunter chase at Aintree; but it attracted ten runners (three more than the Aintree race) and produced another shock result, a lucky one at that, when the ten-year-old Kingsthorpe, who had failed to win any of his three previous races and was entering the winner's enclosure for the first time since he lost his maiden certificate in 1996 with the same rider, Alan Phillips, aboard, was presented with the race when one of the two joint favourites, Leslie Jefford's mount Big Bands Are Back, came down in a commanding lead at the last.

The new Intermediate series, sponsored by Bowring Countryside Insurance, with a £4,000 final at the Cheltenham hunter-chase evening in late April, produced a first winning ride under Rules at his initial attempt for Mark Wilesmith, a 21-year-old Shropshire agricultural student. Riding the family horse All Weather, he did well to get the better of a tight finish with the accomplished Fiona Needham on Last Option, who was trying to give the 12-year-old 7lb.

This was one of only two defeats for Robin Tate's six-year-old Last Option, on whom his daughter won two point-to-points and two hunter chases. The other was in the novice hunter chase at Aintree, where he went under by half a length to Cedar Square, the seven-year-old ridden by Jamie Jukes for Victor Dartnall's successful stable. In his last race of the season, the John Corbet champion novice hunter chase at Stratford, Last Option, still ridden by Fiona Needham, beat the 1997 Dudley Cup winner Double Thriller by three parts of a length receiving 4lb. from him.

Considering the rain that had been falling all over the country, causing extensive flooding in some cases, the point-to-point season had opened on a high note at Cottenham with the first-ever fixture held by the Cambridgeshire Harriers Hunt Club, which had been formed with an initial family membership of over 100 following the disbandment of the Harriers pack on the death of their much-loved Master, Mrs. Betty Gingell; with the object, said her son Michael, of keeping Cottenham at the forefront of point-to-point racing.

Four of the nine races at this meeting were open maidens, one of them split after declarations and two of them run over 2.5 miles for the first time on this course. The meeting was also notable for a treble by East Anglia's Simon Sporborg, who held the lead for the *Daily Telegraph* Cup for the first seven weeks of the season; and for the triumphant return of Pip Jones on Gunner Boon in the Greig Middleton qualifier after the fearsome fall she sustained the previous season.

And it was the 29-year-old Pip who went on to win her first national ladies' title, for which she had been the runner-up on three occasions (the first as Pip Nash in 1991). Never relinquishing her lead after taking over from the South Midlands rider Heather Irving over the Easter week-end, she finished with 30 successes on 14 different horses, seven of them trained by her brother Tim; and when she collects the trophy at the national point-to-point dinner in November she will become the first holder of what has now become the *Racing Post* Cup.

Pip's most prolific winner, Robert Williams's Llangeinor ten-year-old Touch 'N' Pass, who won six of his 12 races, must also have been her favourite one in another respect. One of the four winners she rode at the Tredegar Farmers, Touch 'N' Pass's success in the mixed open there gave her both her 148th win in point-to-points and the inscribed salver in memory of her father, Lloyd Jones, that her brother had won on two occasions before her in the days when the race was a men's open.

The runner-up to Pip Jones for the *Racing Post* Cup was last year's winner of the *Sporting Life* Cup, Shirley Vickery with 21 wins. But whilst Shirley may have been disappointed to lose her crown by such a big margin, she certainly won't be with her performances in hunter chases, which included a magnificent double at Stratford on the last Saturday in May when she won both the ladies' hunter chase sponsored by Spillers Horse Feeds on the seven-year-old Bluagale, a son of the leading point-to-point sire Strong Gale, and, even more important, the *Horse and Hound* Cup on Teeton Mill.

The 11-10 favourite for the *Horse and Hound* Cup in a field of nine was the Buccleuch mare Jigtime, who, in the course of winning three hunter chases on the trot, had been followed successfully from course to course by a man carrying wads of bank notes in a plastic bag, and who was later identified on Channel 4 television as a professional gambler called Roger Darlington. This time, however, the £30,000 handed over by the plastic bag man to bookmaker Stephen Little (whom I recall operating at point-to-points in the distant past) went straight down the drain. Jigtime barely showed with a chance and finished a distant third to Teeton Mill and Grimley Gale.

The nine-year-old Teeton Mill, who had been owned by Dick Saunders and trained by his daughter Caroline Bailey when he started his season winning three hunter chases in a row, was making his second appearance in the colours of his new owners, Winning Line Racing Ltd., and providing the Hereford trainer Venetia Williams with a repeat win in the *Horse and Hound* Cup, which she had won in 1997 with Celtic Abbey.

One rather sad aspect of the 1998 race was that it marked the retirement of Reg Wilkins's great hunter-chaser Double Silk, who finished fourth in it at the age of 14, having added one more win in hunter chases to his score at Warwick in March, taking his winning tally in these races up to 18. Wilkins, however, clearly has a useful replacement for him in Double Thriller, the only horse to beat Teeton Mill during the season when he scored at Cheltenham in April.

Congratulations would also be in order, I feel, for Heather Irving, who, in her best season ever, was third in line for the *Racing Post* Cup behind Pip Jones and Shirley Vickery with her 19 winners. It was a feat in itself to ride more winners than Alison Dare (4th in the table with 13 winners) and Polly Curling (on a score of ten). One of Heather Irving's most prolific winners, the Bicester with Whaddon Chase mare Lily The Lark, a winner of six races for her, and placed in the other two, was the champion mare of the season. But her most prolific winner of all was another of the horses she trained herself, Andronicus. On this 11-year-old by Oats she won seven races and was the runner-up in two others.

Only two horses won more races than Titus Andronicus, and they were the winner and runner-up for the Grand Marnier Trophy, St. Gregory and Shake Five. Anthony and Sue Howland-Jackson's ten-year-old St. Gregory, trained by Ruth Hayter in the Essex & Suffolk country, won nine of his 15 ladies' races with Lisa Rowe up; and the Sporborgs' seven-year-old Shake Five, trained in the Puckeridge country by Christopher Sporborg, won eight of his 12 races with Simon Sporborg up, only losing his lead for the Grand Marnier when St. Gregory went one up on him in a two-horse ladies' open at the Enfield Chace on May 17, by which time Shake Five had finished for the season. There was some compensation for Shake Five, though. This seven-year-old, owned by Mrs. Christopher Sporborg and trained by her husband, was the champion young horse of the season with his eight wins and three placings.

The first riders to move ahead of Simon Sporborg for the men's title were Jamie Jukes and Joe Tizzard, who were sharing the lead with ten winners apiece on Saturday, February 21; and Jukes was still showing them the way two months later when he was on a total of 25. But after that his mounts started to dry up to some extent; and at the beginning of May the Shropshire rider Andrew Dalton shot two ahead of Jukes when a win on The Bull Blackman, by courtesy of the horse's trainer and former rider Matthew Gingell at the Cambridge University United Hunts Club fixture in a Restricted at Cottenham on the Friday evening was followed on the Saturday by a double at the Albrighton on two horses trained by Damien Duggan, Viridian in the men's open and Woodland Cutting in a division of the open maiden, taking his score up to 27.

Dalton remained in the ascendancy until his score reached 31 with a win on Ashgan, a five-year-old trained by his wife Heather, in the Restricted at the Pentyrch on Sunday, May 17, when his nearest challenger at this time, on a score of 29, was Tim Mitchell, whose treble on the Saturday at the Dulverton West on three of the horses trained by Richard Barber, Still In Business in the mixed open, Stillmore Business in a division of the Restricted and the six-year-old Gleeming Lace in a division of the open maiden, was followed the next day by a win on High Guardian, a nine-year-old trained by Tim Jones, in the four-mile mixed open for the 'Welsh Point-to-Point Grand National' at the Pentyrch, the £500 feature race in the South Wales Area.

At this stage of the season, the contest for the *Daily Telegraph* Cup looked likely to rest between Dalton and Mitchell, though Jamie Jukes and Julian Pritchard were sharing third place with 27 winners. But by the time the Melton Hunt Club fixture came round on May 23 at Garthorpe things were beginning to look rather different. Julian Pritchard was coming into the picture. Given the ride by trainer Jayne Webber on Mrs. Vanessa Ramm's very useful front-runner Mounthenry Star, already the winner of two races with Chris Stockton up, he made full use of the opportunity in the mixed open, demolishing the pretensions of Titus Andronicus and Shake Five, and followed this with a similarly fluent success aboard a very welcome chance ride from an old schoolmate of his, the Hereford trainer Mark Jackson, in what had now become, not a moment too soon, the Midlands Area

£500 feature race, the Marie Curie Foundation Novice Championship. This was on another useful front-runner, Vic Gethin's eight-year-old Mr. Motivator.

Mr. Motivator was the 31-year-old Pritchard's 29th point-to-point winner of the season, and by Bank Holiday Monday his score had reached 31 when Mounthenry Star obliged for him again by winning the men's open at the Albrighton Woodland the day after he had won the mixed open at the Axe Vale Harriers on Dick Baimbridge's charge Far Senior. The Hereford farmer was now on level terms with the 28-year-old Shropshire farmer Andrew Dalton. But much was still to happen. On Saturday, May 30, a blank day for both Pritchard and Dalton, Tim Mitchell lifted his score to 32 with a double at the Exmoor, where he won the 4-mile men's open on the Louise Alner-trained Apatura King, who was scoring over four miles for the second time and recording his fourth win in a row, and a division of the open maiden on the John Dufosee-trained Blustery Day. The next day, however, at the Harborough Hunts Club meeting at Dingley, Pritchard and Dalton also went up to 32, the former with another unchallenged win in the men's open on Mounthenry Star, and Dalton with a win in a division of the open maiden on The Right Attitude, an eight-year-old trained by Damien Duggan.

So, with only two meetings left to complete the season, the traditional Torrington Farmers' end of term fixture at Umberleigh and the postponed Quorn fixture at Garthorpe, there was now a three-way tie for the men's title; aud, initially, the three riders concerned came to a gentlemanly agreement to share it, without seeking any further rides.

But things didn't quite work out that way. Richard Barber had a prime ride in Still In Business lined up at Umberleigh for Tim Mitchell, who also had several other rides on offer there; while Julian Pritchard and Andrew Dalton were both being offered rides at the Quorn. Mitchell was the one out of luck, when there came a bombshell announcement that the course at Umberleigh was waterlogged and there would be no racing there.

Pritchard and Dalton both had three rides at Garthorpe, and each was successful with one of them. Pritchard scored in the men's open on Far Senior; and two races later, Dalton followed suit on Damien Duggan's charge Fort Gale (another, son of Strong Gale) in the Intermediate. So, not for the first time, two riders will be sharing the *Daily Telegraph* Cup with 33 winners. The other occasion this happened was in 1980, when Ian McKie and David Turner were joint holders of the trophy with 20 winners. Justice would have been best served in 1998 if the 26-year-old Tim Mitchell had at least got a share in what would have been his first men's title.

The winner of the *Daily Telegraph* male novice rider's award (and, indeed, the champion novice rider of the season) was a 20-year-old Irishman, John Daniel Moore (son of the Irish trainer Arthur Moore), who rode 13 point-to-point winners, 11 of which, plus the two he won hunter chases on, were trained by Robert and Sally Alner's daughter Louise, who, in her first season as a trainer, was responsible for sending out 20 winners.

Another Irishman, the 17-year-old Cork-born Richie Forristal, who works in Kim Bailey's yard, won the Wilkinson Sword for the leading novice rider under the age of 21 who hadn't ridden a winner before the start of the season. All five of his winners, Hall's Mill being the most prolific with three wins on the trot, were trained by John Porter at Upper Lambourn. The *Daily Telegraph* female novice riders of the season, each with four wins on their own horses, were 26-year-old Mary Samworth from Oxfordshire with her Roly Prior and the 23-year-old Devon rider Charlotte Stucley with her American-bred Seekin Cash. The Dick Woodhouse Memorial Trophy for the owner-rider of the season, like the Wilkinson Sword presented at the PPORA annual luncheon, went to the veteran South-East rider David Robinson for the six races he won on Thats Dedication and Galaroi, two horses trained for him by Marion Robinson in the Mid Surrey Farmers country.

The leading rider in hunter chases was the 24-year-old Northants rider Ben Pollock, who is training to become a blacksmith. He had seven wins on three of the horses trained by Caroline Bailey and an eighth, at Folkestone, on one trained by Fulke Johnson-Houghton; and it was Caroline Bailey who won the Richard Russell–Johnny Greenall Trophy for the leading trainer of hunter chasers that she had won five times in the last six years as Caroline Saunders, this time with eight winners, one more than Richard Barber in this field.

Had there been a prize, though, for the leading trainer of point-to-point winners it would have gone once again to Richard Barber, who saddled 42 of them, this without having to rely on Earthmover, a winner of three hunter chases. At three meetings during the season, the East Cornwall, the Blackmore & Sparkford Vale and the Devon & Somerset Staghounds, Barber saddled four winners; and at the Mendip Farmers on March 28 he broke his own record and saddled seven of the nine. Two of the three winners ridden by Joe Tizzard for the Barber stable there, Satshoon (much the fastest of the three maiden winners) and Charlie Strong (the son of Strong Gale who won another of the maiden races), are five-year-olds and should be making a further mark for themselves next season, along with Tizzard's third winner, the six-year-old False Tail in a division of the Restricted.

Other successful stables included those of Dick Baimbridge, who saddled 20 point-to-point winners, among them all 13 of the ones ridden by Alison Dare; Victor Dartnall, who, in his last season before becoming a public trainer, saddled 19 winners in point-to-points and four in hunter chases; Nicky Sheppard, whose 15 winners included 12 of the 33 Julian Pritchard had in point-to-points and his single winner in a hunter chase, Precarium at Chepstow. Polly Curling and Kay Rees, in their first season as a training partnership, saddled 12 point-to-point winners, nine of them ridden by Polly, who had a tenth on a horse trained by Ollie Bush; while up in the North, at the Cumberland Farmers, Simon Shirley-Beavan joined the select band of trainers who have saddled four winners at the same meeting with four of the family horses hunted with the Jedforest, Better Blythe Glass and Mr. Goodbye, two of the three winners ridden by Clive Storey, and Orange Ragusa and The Alleycat, the two ridden by Pauline Robson.

Along with Pip Jones at the Tredegar Farmers, five other riders brought off four-timers during the season, Tim Mitchell at the East Devon, Jamie Jukes at the Pembrokeshire, Simon Sporborg at the Puckeridge, Alan Phillips at the Ludlow and Steve Blackwell at the Teme Valley.

One rider, Polly Curling no less, was riding her 200th winner in point-to-points when scoring on Certain Angle, one of the stars of the Curling–Rees yard with four wins to his credit, in the ladies' open at the Western meeting at Wadebridge in March. Three riders rode their 150th: Julian Pritchard when scoring on Dick Baimbridge's charge Nether Gobions in the Land Rover qualifier at the Clifton-on-Teme on March 21, Simon Andrews when winning on a horse he trains himself, The Happy Client, in a division of the open maiden at the Essex Farmers & Union at Marks Tey on April 13; and Alastair Crow had his on one of the horses his mother trains, Whatafellow in the Confined at the Wheatland at Wolverhampton on May 17. Dai Jones, Nigel Tutty and Shirley Vickery all rode their 100th point-to-point winners during the season; and there were career centuries for Andrew Sansome (87 in point-to-points), who was in the process of establishing a livery yard on the Edgcote estate near Banbury, Noel Wilson (74 in point-to-points), Pauline Robson (81 in point-to-points) and, in her retirement season, the West Country rider Linda Blackford (94 in point-to-points). Andrew Dalton was on a grand total of 95 point-to-point winners when the season ended. So was Joanne Cumings, the season's champion lady rider in the Devon & Cornwall Area. Evan Williams, on a total of 99, was very unlucky not to get his century this time. One of his three winners at the Gelligaer farmers, Storm Dai Fence in the Restricted, was demoted to second place after some slight drifting on the run-in. Philip Scouller, already with over 100 point-to-point winners behind him, improved on his record over the Tweseldown course when he scored for the 59th time over it, riding his own horse Glen Cherry in the hunt race at the Garth & South Berks.

All these feats were, however, eclipsed by the achievement in Ireland of the seven-times champion Enda Bolger. On Sunday, May 24, riding Elegant Lord for J.P. McManus in the open race at the Ormond Hunt fixture at Ballingarry in North Tipperary, he broke the late Willie Rooney's world record, riding his 402nd winner in point-to-points.

This meeting in Ireland took place on the same day as the valuable Marlborough Cup final over timber fences at Barbury Castle, otherwise Bolger would have had a ride here on another of the McManus horses. It was a race, though, which produced a shock result when two of the most fancied horses, the American horse Saluter, last year's winner, and the Irish horse Merry Gale, the latter ridden by Tony McCoy, both had crashing falls, leaving the prize in the hands of another pro. jockey, Richard Johnson, riding a horse that had finished third in a novice hunter chase last season, Symbol Of Success, owned by a Welsh syndicate and trained by Dai Williams at Great Shefford, near Hungerford.

As the best Land Rover qualifier of the season, I would have to go for the one that took place at the Army fixture at Larkhill in January. There were 11 starters for it, with three top-class point-to-pointers providing the kind of finish that one is always hoping for but gets only on rare occasions. In the dash for the line, in which all three riders were seen at their best, Seamus Durack, the champion amateur of the season with his 41 winners under Rules, got Proud Sun home by a neck and a neck from Tim Mitchell on Fantus and Michael Portman on Holland House; and there was so little to choose between second and third that some experienced observers felt a dead-heat should have been called in this instance. Unfortunately, none of these three star performers was able to contest the final at Towcester. Proud Sun broke his shoulder in a fall at Wetherby a few weeks later and had to be put down. Fantus was retired after breaking down in his bid to win the Cheltenham Foxhunters' for the second time in four years. Holland House collapsed and died after winning the 4m 1f hunter chase at the Cheltenham evening fixture in April.

A touching tribute was paid to the 12-year-old Holland House by the Oxford bookmaker Gary Wiltshire in a letter written to the *Sporting Life* afterwards. He wrote of this good old stayer, "He died directly in front of my pitch. If ever there is such a place as an equine Heaven I saw Holland House enter it at Cheltenham last Wednesday."

But another good stayer still goes on. Nearly Splendid, the East Devon 13-year-old, continues to excel in the West Country. In 1998 his six wins, five of them with Tom Greed up, included two more over four miles, the men's open at the Dartmoor which he was winning for the third time and the ladies' open at the Modbury Harriers for the second time, on this occasion with Mandy Hand up. To date, since he began his point-to-point career for Roy Stevens in 1991, Nearly Splendid has won 20 races, the seven over the longer trip including the 4m 1f hunter chase at Cheltenham.

At the Heythrop, which attracted the kind of relentless rain one has come to expect there, the going for the classic four-miler, for which there was a field of nine, put a premium on stamina and was very much in favour of the Ledbury mare Kettles, who was bidding to win the much-coveted Lord Ashton of Hyde's Cup for the third year in succession. But although she ran a most courageous race under Alan Phillips and got her head in front at the second last, she was beaten for finishing speed by Tim Stephenson's mount Better Future, who got to her on the run-in and scored by a length. The pair finished a long way ahead of the others.

The nine-year-old winner, owned by Clive Hitchings and trained by him in his well-appointed yard at Hanley Swan in Worcestershire, was completing a hat-trick of wins, and in his previous race, the men's open at the South Herefordshire, he had beaten another good horse ridden by Alan Phillips, Peanuts Pet. Better Future won one more open race afterwards; but he was found sadly lacking in the second of the season's classics, the Lady Dudley Cup at the Worcestershire.

This race, run on good to soft ground at Chaddesley Corbett, attracted a field of five out of an original entry of 24; and it may be that some of the others were frightened away by the presence of the horse who started an odds-on favourite for it, Andrew Dalton's mount, the unbeaten Solba, who at this stage was sharing the lead for the Grand Marnier Trophy with East Anglia's Shake Five, both of them having won six races. So it was not surprising to see Solba a 6-4 on favourite with the long, winding line of 30 bookmakers headed as usual by Reg Davis of Worcester.

Dalton always had the American-bred Solba in a prominent position, even though his fencing was far from fluent. It was probably one race too many for him; and, in a driving finish, he was beaten a length and a half by a horse he had beaten a mouth earlier at the North Ledbury giving him 71b., the North Hereford nine-year-old Perfect Light, who was being ridden by his trainer, Mark Jackson. This was the fourth win of the season for Perfect Light, who had been given to

Mrs. Fran Stone after breaking his knee in a novice chase at Kelso, won two point-to-points for her in 1997 when she was in partnership with Roger Lee, and was on loan in 1998 to Mr. & Mrs. Vic Gethin.

Whilst I would feel inclined to rank Perfect Light among the vintage Dudley Cup winners, and certainly as the best of the ten £500 feature-race winners, who included Solba at the North Shropshire, I see that Mackenzie & Selby have the horse who won the Sandhurst Area's feature race at the Hampshire Hunt fixture over the sharp track in Hackwood Park as the most highly rated of these winners at 11-3, the ten-year-old Moving Out, owned by Mrs. Shirley Brasher and trained by Victor Dartnall. I can hardly think that his performance in what turned out to be rather a moderate race in Hackwood Park can have had much, if anything, to do with this. Moving Out did, however, win all three of his point-to-points and looked very useful when easily accounting for Bond JNR and The Jogger in a division of the men's open at Barbury Castle in January.

The other division of this open race was just as easily won by The Bounder, who would get my vote as the big disappointment of the season. Not that this had anything to do with his performances on a racecourse, which were most impressive both times that he ran, extending his winning sequence under Joe Tizzard to six. Sadly, though, he wasn't seen out again after defeating Fantus in a three-horse hunter chase at Wincanton, where he pulled a tendon. So he had to miss taking on Earthmover in the Cheltenham Foxhunters' – which he had been all set to do. But the good news is that he is fit and well after being fired and fully expected to reappear in 1999. Whether or not this will still be in hunters' races is another matter, as the 18-year-old Joe Tizzard has now turned professional, along with champion amateur Seamus Durack and Rupert Wakley.

A strong candidate for the most bizarre incident of the season would have been the one that took place at the South Cornwall when, after landing the last leg of a treble, Neil Harris was assaulted by a spectator brandishing a pair of binoculars. It seems that his assailant (who was fined £350 by the stewards – Interesting that they had the power to do this) was labouring under the impression that Harris's winning mount in division three of the open maiden had impeded the progress of the horse he had backed by hanging left at the last.

Harris was not the only top rider involved in an incident. Shirley Vickery was fined £80 by the stewards at Larkhill after landing a double at the Royal Artillery fixture. This was her reward for complaining to the starter that he had sent them off for the Intermediate too early, resulting in her losing some 15 or 16 lengths on the horse she eventually won it on, Funny Farm; and to make matters worse, she ended her day in Yeovil Hospital when the car she was driving to another meeting became a write-off as the result of a crash. Shirley, however, was released from hospital the same night.

Another rider fined for expressing his displeasure to the starter was Yorkshireman Noel Wilson at the Bedale & West of Yore. Royal Aristocrat, his mount in the 17-strong Confined, was caught facing the wrong way round when the starter dropped his flag, and lost more ground than he could possibly have made up. It is not on record what Wilson said to the starter, but I liked his reported comment on the fine. "It was money well spent," he said.

Neither was Julian Pritchard's successful season without its controversial moment. He was accused by an indignant spectator at the Harkaway Club fixture at Chaddesley Corbett of driving Sir Gandouge, his mount in division one of the confined maiden, into the ground in order to secure his success. But, although this nine-year-old (one of the horses trained by Nicky Sheppard) was clearly exhausted after the race and had virtually to be lifted over the last fence, Pritchard had not been abusing him with the whip, and at the Jockey Club enquiry that followed the complaint no blame was attached to Pritchard's riding; besides which, Sir Gandouge was reported by his trainer the next day to be 100%.

At the Llandeilo Farmers on Sunday, May 10, history was being made at Erw Lon with the celebration of a golden jubilee; and the famous horses on parade for the occasion included Norton's Coin, Timber Tool and Yellow Jersey (the Welsh-trained winner of the 1985 Audi Grand Prix de Chasse at Sandown); while on the same Sunday at the Tetcott in Devon, three of the country's top lady riders were in action, filling the first three places in a memorable ladies' open, Shirley Vickery winning it on Tinotops from Polly Curling on Play Poker and Alison Dare on Box Of Delights. Pip Jones was missing. She was completing a double at the Llandeilo Farmers on Touch 'N' Pass in the ladies' open and Kerry Soldier Blue in the Restricted.

History of a different sort was being made on Friday May 13. This was the day that the *Sporting Life* died when it became incorporated in the *Racing Post* after a life of 139 years. A paper I was weaned on in my schooldays at Christ's Hospital, it was a loss that I found hard to bear; and I am not only thinking of its point-to-point coverage. Perhaps the last words on the subject should be given to one of the paper's brightest stars, Alastair Down. Now a feature writer for the *Racing Post*, Alastair was writing for *The Life* of March 20:

"There have been some moving moments, but if I may strike a personal note on behalf of my colleagues, the most emotional aspect of all this is that this may be the final time the *Sporting Life* will report on the Cheltenham National Hunt Festival. If that's the case, a good thing is coming to an end and, while all things must indeed pass, it does not make the fact of their passage any less sad for those who regard the old title with fond affection."

It was good to see the Hon. Dido Harding's Cool Dawn, the horse trained for her by Robert Alner at Blandford, adding his name to the list of former point-to-pointers who have gone on to win the Cheltenham Gold Cup in the capable hands of a former champion amateur who is now a professional, Andrew Thornton; but sad to see another former point-to-pointer, See More Business, the winner of the King George VI Chase at Kempton Park on Boxing Day, carried out at the seventh through no fault of his own. Who knows what would have happened but for this? Cool Dawn started at 25-1. See More Business, at 11-2, was second in the market to the Irish favourite Dorans Pride, who started at 9-4 and finished third.

It was also very pleasing to see the Countryside Alliance Rally that was organized for March 1st by the British Field Sports Society, with its retiring Chairman Robin Hanbury-Tenison at the head of affairs, assisted as usual by his indefatigable assistant Janet George, striking another highly effective blow for country sports, and attracting all kinds of personalities from both sides of the political fence in an estimated attendance of half a million; not all, of course, arriving in Hyde Park together. Speaking personally, even at my advanced age I found the march from my starting point on the Temple Embankment to the end of the Serpentine a piece of cake.

Since then, the British Field Sports Society has undergone a change of name and become the Countryside Alliance, with the Baroness Mallalieu as its President and the Yorkshire-based Edward Duke, a member of the engineering group Beauford plc., who hunts with the Bramham Moor, taking over as Chief Executive from Robin Hanbury-Tenison. He has since resigned.

Among the personalities called for by the grim reaper in February were Nat Sherwood and Raleigh Gilbert. Sherwood, the father of Oliver and Simon, was within a few days of his 74th birthday when he died. Well known as an amateur rider in his day, he rode over 50 winners in point-to-points, most of them bred on the family farm in Essex, where he was a Joint Master of the East Essex from 1953 to 1958. He was also the owner of the point-to-point course at Marks Tey, the scene of four fixtures during the season.

Walter Raleigh Gilbert, to give him his full name with its suggestion of the right connection with history, was not only a highly-respected commentator on racing under Rules but also at a few select point-to-points; and but for his sadly premature death – he was found dead in his flat in Hammersmith a few days before what would have been his 62nd birthday – his richly mellifluous voice would have been heard at the Worcestershire point-to-point on Dudley Cup Day. It seems fitting, and in keeping with his expansive personality, that Raleigh's family home was a castle in Devon. He is someone whose presence I miss very much.

Capt. Dicky Courage, who died in March at the age of 88, was described in his obituary in the *Daily Telegraph* as "probably the Royal Navy's most successful jockey of all time," though whether he was more so than Capt. Dicky Smalley, the owner-rider of Halloween, is perhaps debatable. But he was undeniably a most distinguished one in the good old days of military racing, and his successes as an amateur included the Grand Military Gold Cup at Sandown in 1935 which he won on his own horse Young Cuthbert. This was a race that another distinguished soldier rider who died in March, Major David (W.D.) Gibson, later to become a senior steward of the Jockey Club, won three years running on his own horse Klaxton in 1950, 1951 and 1952 and again in 1956 on Cottage Lace (a Dudley Cup winner in 1953, when he was owned by George Maundrell and ridden by his son David).

In May, Jack Nichols, the first post-war rider to bring off the big hunter chase double at Cheltenham and Liverpool when scoring in these races on Lucky Purchase in 1947, died at the age of 85; and in June he was followed into the Elysian Fields by the 75-year-old Lionel Ensten, who was long-reigning a two-year-old at the moment of his death.

In his days as a point-to-point rider in the Puckeridge country Lionel had a very good horse called Peeper that he won a lot of races on; and as he was a man who liked nothing better than having a tilt at the books, I persuaded him to take the horse down to Sussex for a Bank Holiday point-to-point in Cowdray Park one day in 1955, telling him that he could confidently expect to clean up there in the open race for the Pearson Cup. Unfortunately, things did not quite work out that way. In the closing stages of the race, Peeper got done by a horse from the Chiddingfold Farmers called Peerflex. I still have vivid memories of Lionel sitting in the men's dressing-tent after the race with his head in his hands. I am sure, though, that his despair didn't last for long. Peeper went on winning afterwards.

With the disbandment of the New Forest Buckhounds, Larkhill will be losing one of its point-to-points next season. But it will be gaining another at the expense of Tweseldown, with the transference of the Staff College & R.M.A. Sandhurst Draghounds fixture to Salisbury Plain. Tweseldown, in fact, is in a bit of trouble so far as point-to-pointing is concerned. Its present masters, the British Horse Society, are finding that Eventing is their big money-spinner; and there will be only two point-to-points held at Tweseldown in 1999, the Thames Valley Combined Hunts Club fixture on the first Sunday in January and the new City of London point-to-point which has replaced the Tweseldown Club fixture and will be held on a Sunday in February.

In a season which saw the revival of point-to-point racing at Buckfastleigh after a lapse of 21 years, it was also encouraging to hear that the Oakley course at Newton Bromswold which had been in grave danger of being lost to the sport had got a reprieve for at least another year.

It is anybody's guess what will happen to point-to-point racing in the Millennium; but my own would be that, despite persistent attempts by the anti-hunting brigade to destroy it and the recently-reported decision by the Labour Government to shift responsibility for the future of foxhunting onto local referenda – which would inevitably mean the loss of some point-to-point courses – this much-cherished amateur sport will continue to survive in one form or another.

I do think, though, that William Sporborg, *Horse and Hound*'s hunter-chase columnist, has got a valid argument when he says that he is "convinced that point-to-point meetings are reaching saturation point and rearranged meetings can have significant adverse impact on the fixtures of up to three contiguous meetings in the respective area." He maintains that rather than "rearranging and offering a sub-standard product to the paying public" there ought to be a 'sinking fund' for "affected Hunts, organised on an area by area basis, supplemented by self-insurance." This seems to me an idea worth thinking about.

I can't think of a better way of ending this chapter, and my book, than passing on to posterity the fruits of the views on the future of the sport that I have sought from two of the people most closely connected with it, John Sharp, the new Chairman of the Point-to-Point Owners' & Riders' Association, and Simon Claisse, the Jockey Club Point-to-Point Controller.

Sharp has told me that the only risk to the future of the sport that he sees, now that the pressure on foxhunting has been lifted to some extent, is the fear that the losses suffered by farmers to their income from beef and cereal produce will reduce their capacity to own and run point-to-pointers. And the farming industry, as we know, is the backbone of the sport. He does, however, feel that if the proposal made by his Association for the official recognition of point-to-pointers being allowed to run in group names (so long as they are not ones concerned with commercial promotion) were to be ratified by the Jockey Club it could not fail to have a beneficial effect, since it would encourage more people to take part in point-to-point ownership; and he points out that, as some horses are already being run in the name of a group without official approval in point-to-points, though legitimately under Rules, it would only be a case of regularising an existing practice. "There is no doubt," Sharp says in his summing-up, "that the sport and its contributors are in a healthy state."

And this is what Simon Claisse has to say:

"Besides the history and tradition of the sport, with its roots in hunting and the countryside, there are other ingredients that make point-to-pointing what it is today and these will see the sport continue to thrive well into the next century as a popular and unique equestrian activity. Although meetings are organised and run with more and more professionalism and the Jockey Club's standards of integrity, safety and welfare have undergone significant change in the nineteen nineties, there remains an alluring informality about point-to-pointing. Because there are no enclosures and little fencing, racegoers are free to roam the course at will and get close to the action. And participation as an owner, rider or trainer is still, within the bounds of safety and fair play, relatively unrestricted in a way that welcomes anyone wishing to have a go into an arena with as diverse a group of people as you are ever likely to meet. Taking part is for fun and not reward with the sport encompassing an amateur ethos that can still provide highly competitive racing.

"As long as those responsible for shaping the sport's future keep these qualities, which characterise the sport, at the forefront of their minds, point-to-pointing will retain its appeal and popularity well into the next century. With the threat to hunting and therefore to point-to-pointing having diminished in the short term, the future looks considerably more assured than it did following the 1997 General Election. After a faltering start, the racing industry threw its support fully behind the opposition to any prospect of a ban on hunting, something which, if it were ever to happen, would undoubtedly change the nature of the sport we know and love today."

INDEX

Horse entries are in italics